Yearbook of Islamic and Middle Eastern Law

Volume 6

1999–2000

Yearbook of Islamic and Middle Eastern Law

Volume 6

1999–2000

General Editor

Eugene Cotran, LLD
Circuit Judge, Visiting Professor of Law, SOAS
Chairman, CIMEL

Published for
the Centre of Islamic and Middle Eastern Law
at the School of Oriental and African Studies
University of London

CIMEL

SOAS

KLUWER LAW
INTERNATIONAL
THE HAGUE · LONDON · BOSTON

Published by
Kluwer Law International Ltd
241 Borough High Street
London SE1 1GB
United Kingdom

Sold and distributed
in the USA and Canada
by Kluwer Law International
101 Philip Drive
Norwell, MA 02061
USA

Kluwer Law International incorporates the
publishing programmes of
Graham & Trotman Ltd,
Kluwer Law & Taxation Publishers
and Martinus Nijhoff Publishers

In all other countries sold and distributed
by Kluwer Law International
P.O. Box 322
3300 AH Dordrecht
The Netherlands

© 2001 Kluwer Law International
First published in 2001

ISBN 90-411-1571-4

Library of Congress Cataloging-in-Publication Data is available

This publication is to be cited as *Yearbook of Islamic and Middle Eastern Law*, **Volume 6
(1999–2000)**

Printed and bound in Great Britain by MPG Books Ltd, Bodmin, Cornwall

Contents

Part III – Selected Documents and Legislation   387

Part IV – Selected Cases   463

Biographical Notes

Husain M. Al-Baharna gained a doctorate in international law from the University of Cambridge, and is a Barrister-at-Law of Lincoln's Inn and a member of the Bahrain Bar Society. He is a member of both the UN International Law Commission and the International Council for Commercial Arbitration (ICCA). He is the former Minister for Legal Affairs in the State of Bahrain, and is now an attorney and legal consultant in Bahrain. He is also a registered arbitrator.

Fares Al-Hejailan (LLB) took his degree at the School of Oriental and African Studies in 1999 and was admitted to the Bar in Saudi Arabia in the same year.

Sabah Al-Mukhtar (LLB, LLM) is a legal consultant in Iraqi, Arab and Islamic law. He is a founding member and partner of the Arab Lawyers Network, and a member of the Iraqi Bar Association, the Arab Lawyers Federation and the International Bar Association. He is also a Member of the Chartered Institute of Arbitrators, and the Arab Arbitration Association and is a registered arbitrator with the ICC. He is a fellow both of the British Institute of Management and the Institute of Petroleum. He is also a member of the Bar Human Rights Committee of England and Wales, the Royal Institute of International Affairs (Chatham House), the Muslim Council of Britain (National Legal Committee) and the National Civil Rights Movement (National Steering Committee). He is President of the Arab Lawyers Association (UK) and a member of the editorial board of *Arab Law Quarterly*.

Najeeb Bin Muhammed Al-Nauimi (LLB, PhD) is a Qatari lawyer with degrees in law gained in Egypt and the United Kingdom. He was formerly Minister of Justice for the State of Qatar and was a Professor of Public Law at Qatar University. He was the Agent and Counsel of the Government of Qatar to the International Court of Justice in the case *Qatar v. Bahrain*, Qatar's representative to the International Court of Justice on Request for advisory opinion on the legality of the threat or use of nuclear weapons, Vice-Chairman of the Working Group of Experts focusing on "liability and compensation for environmental damage from the Iraqi military activities against Kuwait" organized by the United Nations Environment Programme, National President of the World Jurist Association, former President of the Asian African Consultative Committee and Chairman of the Committee of Arab Legal Experts of the Arab League on the Law of the Sea. He has been head of Qatari delegations to various international seminars and conferences. He is a writer, author and co-editor of books, and a member of various lawyers' associations, the Cairo Regional Centre for International Commercial Arbitration and the World Commission for the Oceans. Dr Al-Nauimi has also acted as sole arbitrator in various business disputes involving major companies. He is also the Chairman of the International Trading and Investment Company involved in various investment and commercial activties.

Anis Al-Qasem (LLM, PhD), a Barrister-at-Law of Lincoln's Inn, was formerly Legal Adviser to the Government of Libya and Chairman of the Libyan Petroleum Commission during the monarchy. He is presently a practising lawyer and consultant in London in the laws of the Middle East, a licensed legal consultant in Dubai, a former visiting examiner and Associate Fellow of the Institute of Advanced Legal Studies, University of London, and Chairman of the Legal Committee of the Palestine National Council.

M. A. Ansari-Pour (LLB, LLM) was a judge in the Iranian judiciary before coming to England for further studies. He is in the final stage of his research for the University of London (School of Oriental and African Studies), a comparative study of the law of contract. He has written widely (including both articles and books) in English and Persian.

Nathalie Bernard-Maugiron is Senior Researcher at the Centre d'Etudes et de Documentation économique, juridique et sociale (CEDEJ, Cairo).

Jonathan Brown is Head of Shipping and Litigation with Clifford Chance LLP, Dubai, UAE.

Roger Clarke is a Solicitor with Trowers & Hamlins, Sultanate of Oman.

Nayla Comair-Obeid is Doctor of Laws of the Panthéon-Assas University, Paris II, Attorney at the Beirut Bar, and Professor of the Lebanese Faculty of Law. Her speciality is international commercial law, in which connection she has made comparative studies in the field of law of arbitration, particularly arbitration in Arab countries. This research has led her to make a detailed comparative study of the civil and commercial codes of the states of the Middle East. She is the author of important works in the field, notably *Les contrats en droit musulman des affaires* (Economica, Paris, 1995); *The Law of Business Contracts in the Arab Middle East* (Kluwer, 1996); and *Arbitration in Lebanese Law: A Comparative Study* (Delta, 1999).

Eugene Cotran (LLD) has been a circuit judge in England since 1992. He is a Visiting Professor of Law at the School of Oriental and African Studies,

University of London, and the Chairman of the Centre of Islamic and Middle Eastern Law within the School. He was formerly a practising Barrister-at-Law in England and the Commonwealth, a Law Commissioner and High Court judge in Kenya and an international arbitrator. He is also a Board Member of the Palestinian Independent Commission for Citizens Rights. He has numerous publications on the laws of Africa, the Commonwealth, the Middle East and international and immigration law.

Dawoud El-Alami has a *Licence en Droit* from Cairo University and a doctorate from Glasgow University. He was formerly a research fellow at the universities of Kent and Oxford and an assistant professor, Al al-Bayd University in Jordan. He has practised law in Egypt and Saudi Arabia and is now a lecturer in Islamic Studies at the University of Wales at Lampeter. He has various publications on the personal status laws of the Arab countries.

Mustafa El-Alem (LLB, LLM) is a Libyan practising lawyer and legal adviser and a member of the Libyan Bar Association. He is a member of the Board of Directors of the Arab Association for International Arbitration and the Libyan member of the Alliance of Arab Lawyers and a full Member of the Euro-Arab Arbitration Board in London.

Abdalla Ahmed Ghanem is Minister of Legal and Parliamentary Affairs in the Republic of Yemen.

Jacques el-Hakim (LLD) is *agrégé* from the French Faculties of Law and has graduated in law in Syria, Lebanon and the USA. He is a member of the Damascus Bar and is currently a Professor and Head of the Commercial Law Department, Faculty of Law of Damascus University and an Attorney-at-Law. He has produced several publications on Syrian and other laws and on economics.

Afif Gaïgi gained a degree in private law from the University of Tunis and went on to receive postgraduate diplomas in general private law and criminal science from the University of Paris. He is an attorney at the Tunis Court of Cassation, a member of the Tunis Bar and a university lecturer.

Hamzeh Haddad was educated at Cairo University, from which he graduated as a Doctor of Laws, and the University of Bristol, where he gained a doctorate. He is the author of numerous books and articles and a speaker at many regional and international conferences. He is a member of the Jordan Bar Association and of the Arbitration Board of the Arab-Swiss Chamber of Commerce, and a practising attorney and arbitrator.

Vernon Handley (BA) is an attorney with the Law Firm of Salah Al-Hejailan ("LFSH"). Since 1994 Mr Handley has been based in the Middle East and, before joining LFSH, worked for Clifford Chance, a leading London-based law firm, first on secondment to Clifford Chance's associate office in Bahrani and, latterly, on secondment to Clifford Chance's Dubai office. Vernon Handley is a British subject. He holds a BA from Durham University.

Yamina Kebir is a practising attorney at the Court and the Supreme Court of Algeria. She is a member of the Algiers Bar. She graduated in law and English literature and holds a postgraduate degree in business law from the University of Paris II. She has published several articles on Algerian law in English.

The Law Firm Kosheri, Rashed & Riad was established in 1974 by Professor Dr Ahmed El-Kosheri and Professor Dr Samia Rashed. The firm has a strong commercial and litigation practice which includes investments, international business contracts, construction, banking, mining and petroleum concessions, patents and trademarks, business litigation and transnational arbitration. The firm is composed of seventeen lawyers, including two partners who are members of the New York Bar (Tarek Riad and Hala Riad), in addition to the support staff.

Martin Lau is a Barrister and lecturer in law at the School of Oriental and African Studies, University of London, where he teaches South Asian law. He studied at the University of Heidelberg, Germany, and at the University of London. He has published extensively on South Asian law and frequently acts as an expert in proceedings for the International Chamber of Commerce and English courts.

John Wuol Makec is a Justice of the Supreme Court of the Sudan. He has an LLB, University of Khartoum (1964–1969) and an LLM, University of London (SOAS) (1978–1980). He was formerly Minister of Cooperative and Rural Development of the High Executive Council Juda – Southern Sudan and Speaker of Bahr el Ghazal Regional Assembly. He has published extensively on the Customary Laws of the Sudan, in particular of the Dinka people.

Fadi B. Nader is currently the Regional Attorney for the American Life Insurance Company (a member of the American International Group, AIG) for the Middle East, Africa and South Asia region. He qualified in 1985; was an associate 1986–1988 with Samir Saleh and Associates, London; a company secretary 1988–1992 UB (Suisse) SA, Geneva; in private banking 1992–1993 with Crédit Commercial de France, London; and a Partner since 1987 in Moghaizel Law Offices, Beirut. He is a member of the Beirut Bar Association and the International Bar Association. He was educated at College des Frères Mont La Salle, Lebanon; St Joseph University, Beirut (LLB, June 1985); Queen Mary College, London (LLM, September 1997).

Tarek Riad (SJD) has a doctorate in law form Harvard University and is a partner in the Law Firm Kosheri, Rashed & Riad. He is a special legal adviser to the speaker of the Egyptian People's Assembly.

Nageeb Shamiri (LLD) is a member of the Supreme Judicial Council of Yemen and of the Constitutional Division of the Supreme Court of Yemen. He was formerly the Chief Justice of South Yemen. He is the Chairman of the Judicial Inspection Commission, the Secretary of the Law Reform Unit at the Ministry of Legal and Parliamentary Affairs and contributed to the drafting of the Republic's main unified laws. He is a member of the National Committee regarding the Arbitration with Eritrea, and of the Joint Commission with Saudi Arabia regarding Maritime Boundaries.

Adel Omar Sherif is a Counsellor for the Supreme Constitutional Court of Egypt. He earned his LLB, Advanced Studies Diploma in Public Law, Advanced Studies Diploma in Administrative Law and PhD in Commercial Law from Cairo and Ain Shams universities. He served on the Council of the State between 1980 and 1992. He first worked at the Supreme Constitutional Court in 1992 and was assigned Acting Head of the Commissioners' Body in 1993. Judge Sherif was a visiting Fellow at the Human Rights Law Centre of the University of Essex from 1993 to 1994, the Federal Judicial Center in Washington DC in 1996, and a visiting Professor at the Faculty of Law, McGill University, from 1998 to 1999. He has served as a legal adviser in several government agencies, including the Prime Minister's Office, the Real Estate Bank of Egypt and the Cairo Regional Centre for International Commercial Arbitration. Judge Sherif often attends international conferences and seminars as a representative for Egypt. He is the Rapporteur of a series of international human rights conferences known collectively as "The Cairo Conference". He is the author of *Constitutional Adjudication in Egypt* (Cairo, Dar El-Shaab, 1988), *Judicial Independence: Requirements and Rewards* (Washington DC, The Federal Judicial Center, 1996) and many published articles on Islamic and Egyptian law. He is also co-editor of the following texts on Islamic and Egyptian law: *Human Rights and Democracy: The Role of the Supreme Constitutional Court of Egypt* (with Professor Kevin Boyle of Essex University, 1996) and *The Role of the Judiciary in the Protection of Human Rights* (with Judge Eugene Cotran, 1997) and *Democracy, the Rule of Law and Islam* (with Judge Eugene Cotran, 1999).

Saeed Hasson Sohbi is Barrister-at-Law and Advocate in Sana'a – Republic of Yemen.

David Wilson is a Partner, Trowers & Hamlins, Cairo.

Michèle Zirari-Devif is a Professor at the Faculty of Juridical, Economic and Social Sciences, University Mohammed V, Rabat, Morocco.

At the Tenth Anniversary of CIMEL

Lord Woolf (left) and Judge Eugene Cotran (right)

Preface
CIMEL: THE FIRST TEN YEARS
(1990–2000)
Judge Eugene Cotran

The year 2000 is the 10th anniversary of the establishment of the Centre of Islamic and Middle Eastern Law (CIMEL). We marked the occasion by a Reception at the School of Oriental and African Studies (SOAS) on the 4th December 2000 at which the guest of honour was Lord Woolf, the Lord Chief Justice of England and a Council Member of CIMEL. Three new publications were launched on the same occasion, namely

Democracy, the Rule of Law & Islam, edited by Judge Eugene Cotran and Judge Adel Omar Sherif, (Kluwer Law International 1999),

The Rule of Law in the Middle East and the Islamic World: Human Rights and the Judicial Process, edited by Judge Eugene Cotran and Dr Mai Yamani, (I B Tauris, 2000), and

Beyond the Code: Muslim Family Law and the Shari'a Judiciary in the Palestinian West Bank by Dr Lynn Welchman (Kluwer Law International, 2000).

Prior to the Reception, addresses were given by myself as Chairman of CIMEL, by Sir Tim Lankester, the Director of SOAS, by the guest of honour, Lord Woolf, by Dr Lynn Welchman, the Director of CIMEL and by Dr Mai Yamani, Research Fellow at CIMEL.

JUDGE EUGENE COTRAN, Chairman of CIMEL

In my address, I traced the history of the teaching and research in Islamic Law at SOAS from the establishment of the Law Department in 1947, emphasising how Professor Sir Norman Anderson and Professor Noel Coulson had made the Department the leading international centre of scholarship in Islamic law in the Western world. I continued:

"The untimely death of Noel Coulson in 1986 was a severe blow which necessitated, with the growth of the Department in the 1980s and 1990s into an undergraduate and postgraduate department, an intake of several young scholars (Ian Edge, Chibli Mallat, Martin Lau and Lynn Welchman) and of Visiting Professors and Fellows at a senior level (namely Professor William Ballantyne, Dr Doreen Hinchliffe and myself).

It is in that context of expansion that CIMEL was established in 1990, in recognition of the growing importance of law in both its Islamic and Middle Eastern dimensions. It was intended to provide both a focus and a forum for work on and with these laws, and in an increasingly interdependent world, to operate as a scholarly legal bridge for research and practice at the crossroads of Islam, the Middle East and the West. It was felt that the Law Department's academic excellence in this area could be practically promoted through the vehicle of the Centre. CIMEL's objectives are:-

(i)   the promotion of the study and understanding of Islamic law all over the world, with emphasis on modern Middle East legal systems, individually and comparatively, by encouragement of research and by means of lectures, publications, conferences, seminars, academic visits and exchanges and other related activities;

(ii)   the fostering of links between all persons involved in Islamic and Middle Eastern law, including academic specialists, judges, legal practitioners, members of the business community and of civil society, government and other interested persons, whether in the United Kingdom, the Middle East or elsewhere;

(iii)   the provision of services (academic and practical) from the resources of the Centre;

(iv)   the raising of funds, to be managed by the Centre, for the furtherance of these objects.

This is not the place to give you a detailed account of our activities in the last 10 years,[1] but I can confidently report that we are proud of what we have done. We have held countless public lectures, conferences, seminars, workshops at SOAS and elsewhere with other academic centres and institutions. We have through the structures of CIMEL – its Directors, its Executive Committee and its Council – formed a team of experts in the field from within and outside SOAS, who have in the UK, Europe, the USA, the Middle East and other Islamic countries, devoted time and energy to the activities of the Centre and contributed to its publications. We have fostered links with academic and other institutions and individuals interested in the field of Islamic law and Middle Eastern law all over the world. We have opened the horizons for the promotion and study not only (as in the past) of the history, sources and details of Islamic law, but its place in society and its modification and development by statutory and other intervention. We have looked at Islamic law not as a subject *per se* but into its codification and as part of a whole system, at problems of internal conflicts, private international law, public and international law, humanitarian law and constitutional questions involving the rule of law, human rights and the independence of the judiciary.

The publications we launch today reflect our eagerness to delve into these subjects, thus breaking new ground.

---

[1]   See for summary of major activities the Annex hereto.

A second area of major activity and concern is commercial and business law, and international arbitration. I take this opportunity of thanking Professor William Ballantyne who after a distinguished practising career in the Gulf has led the study and research into this field at SOAS. He and CIMEL generally participated and supported a one-day conference on Arab arbitration to relaunch the Euro-Arab Arbitration System in London in 1998. Lord Woolf, our guest of honour, opened a Conference on the subject in 1994 and wrote the foreword to the book on the Conference. I thank him for it and also for writing the Foreword to *Democracy, the Rule of Law and Islam*, one of the books being launched today. This book, as was the one published before it in 1997 on *The Role of the Judiciary in the Protection of Human Rights*, is the result of two Conferences held in Cairo in 1996 and 1997 on the subjects organized by the Supreme Constitutional Court of Egypt and in which CIMEL took an active part. In this context may I take this opportunity of thanking the former Chief Justice of that Court, Dr Awad el Morr, and Judge Adel Omar Sherif, my co-editor of the two books in question, for their unfailing help to CIMEL. They are of course both Council Members and have sent messages of support and regret for their inability to be with us today.

A third area in which CIMEL has been particularly active relates to the continuing legal problems associated with the Palestinian/Israeli question. We took the initiative in 1994 when we organized the first conference of its kind between Palestinian and Israeli legal scholars to discuss the *Arab-Israeli Accords and Legal Perspectives*, which was the title of our first book in the CIMEL Book Series published by Kluwer Law International. The Conference was opened by Lord Slynn of Hadley, another CIMEL Council Member who also wrote the foreword to the book.

We followed up the initiative with another Conference organized with the International Campaign for Jerusalem in 1997 on the *Palestinian Exodus 1948–1998*, the papers of which form the title to the book on the subject edited by Ghada Karmi and myself and published by Ithaca Press in 1999.

We continued our interest in Palestine when we published as the fourth book in the Kluwer Law series, Raja Shehadeh's excellent monograph *From Occupation to Interim Accords: Israel and the Palestine Territories*. We have also played a leading role in many projects associated with the laws of Palestine and the building of legal institutions there, namely the Basic Law project, the future Constitution, the Judiciary, the unification of Gaza and West Bank laws and we provided legal assistance to the Negotiation Affairs Department and participation in the Palestinian Independent Commission for Citizens' Rights (of which I am a Board Member).

May I take this opportunity of thanking my colleague and friend Dr Anis Al-Qasem, a Council Member of CIMEL, who took a leading role in these Projects and also the present Director Dr Lynn Welchman for her tireless work on human rights and the rights of women in Palestine.

Apart from our publications in the form of books by Kluwer Law

International, I. B. Tauris and Ithaca Press, I must also make special mention of our flagship publication – the _Yearbook of Islamic and Middle Eastern Law_, started in 1994 and now in its sixth volume (1999–2000). It has taken its place as the leading annual publication on the subject, covering some 20 Arab countries and other Islamic countries. May I take the opportunity of thanking the contributors – leading lawyers, judges, practitioners, government legal officials and academics – who have done wonderful work in describing and commenting on the laws of their countries whether Islamic or non-Islamic and generally on the laws in the Middle East and the world of Islam, by way of country surveys, articles, case commentaries and book reviews.

They will, I am sure, forgive me if I do not mention them all by name. However, I wish to thank specifically my former co-editor of the Yearbook, and Director of the Centre, Dr Chibli Mallat; Professor Ahmed el Kosheri and his firm Kosheri Rashed & Riad of Egypt; and Justice Nageeb el Shamiri of the Yemen for their considerable assistance and for their messages of support and regret for their inability to attend today.

I wish also to pay a special tribute to Sheikh Salah Hejailan for his continuous support – both professional and financial – which he has given to CIMEL. He too regrettably cannot be with us today, but has sent the following message which I shall read on his behalf.

MESSAGE OF SHEIKH SALAH HEJAILAN

"The historical development of Islamic law began with Mohammed (_pbuh_) sitting as judge in Madinah. At first, his decisions followed the customs of the local tribes of Madinah and, subsequently, his own personal judgment. At his death, Mohammed (_pbuh_) left behind the legislative enactments embodied in the _Qur'an_ and the memory of his legal decisions. These were collected among the traditions (_hadith_) which recorded his sayings and doings, manners and customs, and his answers to questions on religious life and faith and his decisions in legal disputes.

The first publication setting out the traditions was compiled by Malik Ibn Anas. There followed many compilations of various types, the most famous of which is that of Bukhari.

During the times of the Umayyad and the Abbasids, a divergence appears to have occurred between the day-to-day system of governance and strict adherence to Islamic principles, which may have been responsible for Islamic law having become less practical and more theoretical during this period. Indeed, in nearly all jurisdictions in the Middle East, this divergence between the day-to-day system of governance and strict adherence to Islamic principles has endured and has become more pronounced over time – even in Saudi Arabia, the courts and quasi-judicial committees apply a mixture of secular and Islamic law. In view of this divergence between the practical and theoretical, secular and theological, some may question whether Islamic law can continue to have much practical relevance outside the narrow bounds of criminal and family law in all but a few conservative countries of the Islamic world. It is, however, clear that this divergence of the practical and theoretical can be bridged by a clearer and more purposive understanding of the principles underlying Islamic law and the further endeavours of Muslim scholars, lawyers and politicians to apply those principles to the economic, political and social conditions of the modern world. The Centre of Islamic and Middle Eastern Law (CIMEL) was established in 1990, as part of the University of London's School of Oriental and African Studies, to undertake 'the promotion of the study and understanding of Islamic law and modern Middle Eastern legal systems, individually and comparatively, by encouragement and research and by means of lectures, publications, conferences, seminars, academic visits and exchanges and other related activities'. Since its establishment, CIMEL has energetically pursued this undertaking.

There may be some who question whether Western institutions such as CIMEL, being geographically so far removed from the traditional centres of Islamic scholarship, can make a proper contribution to the study of Islamic law. However, Islam is essentially a universal creed, with no geographical limitations; nor is the study of Islamic law, either itself or in comparison with other systems of law, the exclusive preserve of clergy or career academics in the Middle East. Rigorous research, sound analysis and practical experience are the hallmarks of CIMEL's work, which approach by any objective measure is accorded wide respect in the Middle East and elsewhere by lawyers, judges and scholars who are well positioned to appreciate such qualities and to utilize the knowledge gained.

One of the landmarks of CIMEL's ten years of excellence was the launching in 1994 of the *Yearbook of Islamic and Middle Eastern Law* under the joint editorial direction of Judge Eugene Cotran and Professor Chibli Mallat, but latterly under the sole direction of Judge Cotran. With such distinguished editors it is hardly surprising that the *Yearbook* has swiftly become a well-established and authoritative legal and academic periodical, attracting important contributions from many of the world's pre-eminent legal practitioners and academics in the field of Islamic and Middle Eastern law.

I believe that the *Yearbook* provides both an invaluable source of information to Islamic scholars and legal practitioners and a fresh impetus to the revitalisation of the study and application of Islamic law generally. CIMEL and the authors of the contributions to the *Yearbook* are to be congratulated on their work so far. They deserve every encouragement in carrying out this important undertaking."

* * *

I concluded my address by welcoming all the guests who have been able to be with us to mark the 10th Anniversary of CIMEL. I extended a special welcome to our guest of honour Lord Woolf. I thanked former Directors – Ian Edge; Chibli Mallat; Martin Lau; the present Director Lynn Welchman; CIMEL's Executive Committee; Council Members and Research Fellows and officers for their great help to me in the last ten years, and for ensuring

the success of CIMEL. Finally, to all our publishers, in particular Kluwer
Law International and those in charge of their Middle East Department, Mrs
Cecile Insinger and Miss Ingeborg van der Laan and to the book editor of
the *Yearbook* Ms Hilary Scannell.

SIR TIM LANKESTER, DIRECTOR OF SOAS

Also thanked and welcomed Lord Woolf on behalf of SOAS, and spoke of
Lord Woolf's work at University College, the Institute of Advanced Legal
Studies and as Pro-Chancellor of the University of London.
    He stressed the importance of CIMEL's work within the Law Department
and hoped that it will play an effective role in the planned Middle East
Institute at SOAS and thus establish stronger cross-disciplinary ties with other
Departments at the School.

LORD WOOLF

Congratulated CIMEL for its achievements in the last ten years. He stressed
the importance of CIMEL's activities in the field of the rule of law, human
rights and the independence of the judiciary. He also praised the assistance
given to other bodies and institutions in the UK and to the English Courts
by experts on Islamic law from CIMEL and for their extensive publications
in the field, thus providing information and commentaries to a wider audience
in the UK and elsewhere in the world.

DR LYNN WELCHMAN, Director of CIMEL

"I should like first of all to echo Judge Cotran's welcome to you all, and
to say especially *Ramadan mubarak*. This occasion is being held to mark
ten years of CIMEL, the Centre of Islamic and Middle Eastern Law at
the SOAS Law Department, and the launch of three new publications
associated with the Centre. You will note that we have chosen our words
carefully, feeling that at this time the word 'celebration' would be inappropriate against the background of the painful and distressing events in the
Middle East in recent months, and more particularly in Palestine and
Israel. At the same time, these and other events in the region should spur
us here at CIMEL to redouble our efforts to explore, and pursue the
critical significance of 'law' in the region – the implementation of the rule
of law, whether international law or national, and indeed the credibility
of international and national legal regimes in the eyes and lives, especially, of those vulnerable to abuse against which the law aims to protect.
The three books being launched here tonight explore different aspects of
law and society and the rule of law in different countries in the Middle
East and South Asia, and I commend them to your attention.
    The two major research projects with which CIMEL is currently

involved reflect an emphasis on what law means and the manner in which it works to support principles of justice, empowerment and protection, in different countries and communities in the Middle East and the Muslim world. The first, a global project on the application of Islamic family law directed by Professor Abdullahi An-Na'im of the Sudan and Emory University, USA, has already resulted in major research products posted on a website and generating much feedback from scholars, lawyers and researchers around the world. It includes a case study on the Islamic family law debate under the Palestinian Authority, in which I have been privileged to work with a team of scholars from the Women's Studies Centre at Birzeit University in the West Bank. The other, exploring the incidence of and strategies of response to 'crimes of honour', is carried out jointly by CIMEL and Interights, the International Centre for the Legal Protection of Human Rights, and I would like to welcome friends and colleagues from that project here tonight, particularly Sara Hossain, Emma Playfair, Vanessa Gosselin, and the CIMEL researcher Samia Bano.

Both these projects aim at 'action-oriented research' – focusing a high degree of rigour and innovative scholarship on issues of considerable domestic and international attention, with the purposes of supporting and facilitating the work of partners in the region in their efforts and their thinking. We do not, in these projects, seek to work 'on' or 'about', but rather 'with', and as with CIMEL's other activities, we are aware of our own accountability. We are in London, and we have a profile: we seek to use this to present, to English-speaking and 'Western' audiences, academic and other, the voices and perspectives of colleagues from the Arab and Muslim worlds on law and law-related matters, whether through lecture series, seminars, or research projects, as well as engaging in our own individual and cooperative research work.

We know the limits of the law, but for CIMEL, as a research forum in the SOAS Law Department, we seek to bridge the gaps between academic research and practitioners of all kinds, whether lawyers, members of the judiciary, civil society organizations, policy makers and international agencies, notably the UN. These efforts, in the two projects I have mentioned are built on the belief that those of us in academia have a role to play in what is sometimes called the 'real' world; and that we do this out of principle, in close and critical engagement with that world, and with no compromise on the values of rigour and intellectual integrity that we consider the foundational principles of our work as academics. In the words of Khalil Gibran, the Lebanese writer,

> For reason, ruling alone, is a force confining; and passion, unattended, is a flame that burns to its own destruction.
> Therefore let your soul exalt your reason to the height of passion, that it may sing;
> And let it direct your passion with reason, that your passion may live through its own daily resurrection, and like the phoenix rise above its own ashes."

DR MAI YAMANI, Research Fellow, CIMEL

"As we know the Middle East is in the midst of profound change. The economic, cultural and now political forces associated with globalization are sweeping across the region challenging existing ways of doing things and threatening the radical transformation of both states and society.

The Rule of Law in the Middle East and Islamic World highlights these processes of transformation. Each country mentioned in the books being launched today is struggling with changing attitudes to both law and demands for the application of basic human rights. Human rights violations are the starkest reminder of the failure to protect and build upon the rule of law. Every day in the majority of countries of the Middle East the most basic rights of individuals are violated by state institutions cynically rejecting the rule of law in their countries.

Violations of human rights happens in times of war and peace and in times of economic prosperity and uncertainty. What links these violations is the absence of the rule of law in the every day interactions between peoples and their governments."

Dr Yamani highlighted the nature and extent of the problems by reference to three case studies on (1) police brutality, detention without trial and the right to a fair trial, (2) the abuse of women's rights in the family, and (3) the current violent situation in Palestine/Israel.

She continued:-

"The three cases I have highlighted this evening are but a small example of the desperate need for the rule of law to be strengthened across the Middle East. The everyday lives of normal average people in the region are being blighted by the arbitrary and violent acts of state institutions who treat their populations with disregard for their basic human rights and dignity. The governments of these countries know that people's recourse to law is at best weak and at worst irrelevant.

In one of the books launched tonight, *The Rule of Law in the Middle East and Islamic World*, experts present the fundamental reasons that continue to produce the catalogues of human tragedies that I have referred to. It is a very important and long overdue book that serves both the academic and professional interest in this part of the world.

At a time of ongoing and profound change in the Middle East there is an urgent demand to come to grips with these complex issues which dominate the everyday lives of the population of the region. Laws and traditions are not static; they need to be revisited and reinterpreted in the age of globalization. One of the undeniable challenges of globalization is the demand for universal human rights. The benefits to be gained from globalization cannot be obtained without a sustained dialogue with those seeking to protect the human rights of all across the world. No one should under-estimate the profound political difficulties for governments of the Middle East involved in reforming their legal systems. But it should be stressed that the economic and technical benefits of globalization cannot be gained without political reform.

For those countries who base their constitution on the *shariʿa* the system offers flexibility and room for reinterpretation. The Middle East and the wider Islamic world is in the midst of political and economic turbulence. It is only through justice and fairness that the ruled and the rulers can live together in greater consensus, harmony and equality."

*   *   *

Eugene Cotran
December 2000

Annex

MAJOR CIMEL ACTIVITIES
(1999–2000)

I LECTURES AND LECTURE SERIES

The Noel Coulson Annual Memorial Lectures
(1990 and continuing)

The Hejailan Lectures
(1990–1994)

General Series
(1990 and continuing)

Feminism and Islam
(1993–1994) Convened by Dr Mai Yamani

Middle East Rule of Law Series
(1996–1998) Convened by Judge Eugene Cotran and Dr Mai Yamani

II MIDDLE EAST LEGAL PRACTITIONERS' FORUM
(1990–1994)

Convened jointly with the Law and Development Programme of the Institute of Advanced Legal Studies

III CONFERENCES AND WORKSHOPS

1. Constitutional Frameworks for Iraq, 1992 (in Arabic and English)

2. Water in the Middle East, 1992

3. Commercial Law in the Middle East, 1993 (opened by Lord Woolf)

4. The Arab–Israeli Peace Accords, 1994 (opened by Lord Slynn of Hadley)

5. Legal and Intellectual Frameworks for a New Middle East, 1994 (in Arabic)

6. Criminal Procedure and Evidence in Islam, 1997 (with Centre of Islamic Studies at SOAS)

7. The Palestinian Exodus (1948–1998), 1998 (with International Campaign for Jerusalem)

8. Anti-Slavery Exhibition and Seminar, 1997 (with Anti-Slavery International)

9. Conference on Middle Eastern Arbitration, 1998 (with Euro-Arab Arbitration System and Centre of Construction Law and Management at King's College, London)

10. Cairo Conference on the Role of the Judiciary in the Protection of Human Rights, 1996 (organised by the Supreme Constitutional Court of Egypt and supported by CIMEL).

11. Cairo Conference on Democracy, the Rule of Law and Islam, 1997 (organised by the Supreme Constitutional Court of Egypt and supported by CIMEL).

12. Workshop on Personal Law, Women's Rights and Uniform Debate in South Asia, 1998

13. Round Table Discussion and Conference on Honour Crimes, 2000 (in conjunction with Interrights – International Centre for the Legal Protection of Human Rights)

IV CURRENT CONTINUING RESEARCH PROGRAMMES

1. Islamic Family Law (with Emory School of Law and in conjunction – in Palestine – with the Women's Studies Centre at Birzeit University).

2. Honour Crimes against Women Project (in partnership with Interrights) and funded by Ford Foundation.

V PUBLICATIONS

Published by Graham & Trotman

1. *Islamic Law and Finance*
    ed Chibli Mallat, 1988

2. *Islamic Family Law*
    eds Jane Connors and Chibli Mallat, 1990

3. *Islam and Public Law*
    ed Chibli Mallat, 1990

4. *Commercial Law in the Middle East*
    eds Hilary Lewis-Rutley and Chibli Mallat, 1995

Published by I B Tauris

1. *Water in the Middle East: Legal, Political and Commercial Implications*
    eds Professor J A Allan and Chibli Mallat, 1994

2. *The Rule of Law in the Middle East and the Islamic World: Human Rights and the Judicial Process*
   eds Judge Eugene Cotran and Dr Mai Yamani, 2000

Published by Ithaca Press

1. *Feminism and Islamic Law*
   ed Dr Mai Yamani, 1996

2. *The Palestinian Exodus 1948–1998*
   eds Ghada Karmi and Eugene Cotran, 1999

Published by Kluwer Law International

BOOKS

Beyond the Code: Muslim Family Law and the Shari‘a Judiciary in the Palestinian West Bank
Dr Lynn Welchman, 2000

CIMEL Book Series

Series Editors
Professor HH Judge Eugene Cotran LLD
Dr Lynn Welchman
(formerly Dr Chibli Mallat)

1. *The Arab–Israeli Accords: Legal Perspectives*
   eds Eugene Cotran and Chibli Mallat, 1996

2. *Islamic Marriage and Divorce Laws of the Arab World*
   Dawoud El-Alami and Doreen Hinchcliffe, 1996

3. *Human Rights and Democracy – The Role of the Supreme Constitutional Court of Egypt*
   eds Kevin Boyle and Adel Omar Sherif, 1996

4. *From Occupation to Interim Accords: Israel and the Palestinian Territories*
   Raja Shehadeh, 1997

5. *The Role of the Judiciary in the Protection of Human Rights*
   eds Eugene Cotran and Adel Omar Sherif, 1997

6. *Democracy, the Rule of Law and Islam*
   eds Eugene Cotran and Adel Omar Sherif, 1999

Also published by CIMEL and Kluwer International:
YEARBOOK OF ISLAMIC AND MIDDLE EASTERN LAW

1. *Yearbook of Islamic and Middle Eastern Law: Volume 1 1994*
   eds Eugene Cotran and Chibli Mallat, 1995

2. *Yearbook of Islamic and Middle Eastern Law: Volume 2 1995*
   eds Eugene Cotran and Chibli Mallat, 1996

3. *Yearbook of Islamic and Middle Eastern Law: Volume 3 1996*
   eds Eugene Cotran and Chibli Mallat, 1997

4. *Yearbook of Islamic and Middle Eastern Law: Volume 4 1997–1998*
   eds Eugene Cotran and Chibli Mallat, 1998

5. *Yearbook of Islamic and Middle Eastern Law: Volume 5 1998–1999*
   ed Eugene Cotran, 1999

6. *Yearbook of Islamic and Middle Eastern Law: Volume 6 1999–2000*
   ed Eugene Cotran, 2001

At the Tenth Anniversary of CIMEL

Left to right: Dr Mai Yamani, Lord Woolf, Sir Tim Lankester, Judge Cotran
and Dr Lynn Welchman

Part I

Articles

Attacks on the Judiciary: Judicial Independence – Reality or Fallacy?

*Adel Omar Sherif**

1 JUDICIAL INDEPENDENCE

In all judicial systems, judges can hardly perform their duties properly unless they are independent and immune from either direct or indirect attacks. Attacks on the judiciary are numerous and at both personal and professional levels.[1] Any attack on the judiciary, whether it takes place by accident or on systematic basis, definitely harms judicial performance overall, detracts from litigants' fundamental rights and consequently affects judicial independence as a basic foundation for modern, democratic societies. We cannot, therefore, assume that justice exists within any given system of government in the absence of judicial independence.

When discussing judicial independence as a foundation for the notion of good administration of justice,[2] we have to be aware that the idea of judicial independence is a well-established legal doctrine that has been in force for years. It has been authorized all over the world wherever civilized government systems exist. In its essence, judicial independence is considered to be one of the fundamental human rights that have to be constitutionally guaranteed to every person in our contemporary world. When this basic guarantee is

---

* Commissioner Counsellor, The Supreme Constitutional Court of Egypt. The views expressed in this article are those of the author and do not necessarily reflect the opinion of the Supreme Constitutional Court of Egypt or its member judges.

1 The attack may be personal affecting certain judge or judges. There are other cases, however, where the attacks generally affect the whole judicial institution in a given country during a certain period of time.

2 In European jurisprudence, judicial independence is viewed as one of the elements that constitute a good administration of justice. See R. St. Macdonald, F. Matscher and H. Petzold, *The European System for the Protection of Human Rights*, MNP, 1993, p. 381.

enhanced, the need for other safeguards in the judicial process logically decreases.[3]

At the international level, we observe that many international instruments deal with judicial independence as a preliminary requirement for the judicial protection which necessitates that judges should handle their cases in an independent manner without any interference exercised either by other branches of government or by individuals themselves. A considerable number of international instruments, focusing on the protection of human rights, provide for judicial independence, as do many constitutions of different countries. International tribunals, such as the European Court of Human Rights and its Commission, as well as the concerned courts in the democratic countries, are also always keen to uphold the independence of the judiciary, either explicitly or implicitly.

For example, the Universal Declaration of Human Rights (1948)[4] provides in Article 10 that "[e]veryone is entitled in full equality to a fair and public hearing by an independent and impartial tribunal, in the determination of his rights and obligations and of any criminal charge against him". The European Convention on Human Rights (1950)[5] also provides in its Article 6 that "1 – In determination of his civil rights and obligations or of any criminal charge against him, everyone is entitled to a fair and public hearing within a reasonable time by an independent and impartial tribunal established by law".

As to national constitutions, in some of them, such as that of the United States of America (1789),[6] we find that the term "judicial independence" is not explicitly embodied in the Constitution. This independence, however, is unarguable as the Constitution itself implicitly provides for such independence throughout its structure that separates government powers and requires them to be carried out within the rule of law.

Other constitutions, such as the Constitution of France (1958),[7] explicitly provide for the guarantee of judicial independence. This Constitution states in Article 64 that "[t]he President of the Republic shall be the guarantor of the independence of the judicial authority".[8]

In more intensive terms, the Constitution of Egypt (1971),[9] ratified on

---

[3] Judge Henry Friendly noted that "as the independence of the decision-maker increases, the need for other procedural safeguards decreases". Martin H. Redish and Lawrence C. Marshall, "Adjudicatory independence and the values of procedural due process", *The Yale Law Journal*, January 1986, no. 91.

[4] Adopted and proclaimed by the General Assembly of the United Nations, Resolution No. 217 A (III) of 10 December 1948.

[5] Ratified in Rome on 4 November 1950, and entered into force on 3 September 1953.

[6] Ratified on 17 September 1787, and became effective for the ratifying states on 21 June 1788, when New Hampshire ratified it.

[7] Ratified on 28 September 1958.

[8] A law was passed on 3 June 1958 to lay down terms of reference within which the drafters of the new Constitution were to work. The fourth principle of these terms indicated that "the judicial power must remain independent in order to insure the respect of basic liberties".

[9] Ratified on 11 September 1971, and amended on 22 May 1980.

11 September 1971, ensured judicial independence in several provisions. It provides in Article 65 that "the independence and immunity of the judiciary are two basic guarantees to safeguard rights and liberties". It also provides in Article 165 that "[t]he judiciary is independent". Moreover, it provides in Article 166 that "[j]udges are independent. In their performance, they are subject to no authority but that of the law. No authority can interfere in cases or judicial affairs."

Although the existing tendency is to spell out this principle in the constitutions of democratic countries and international instruments, the degree of judicial independence varies from one country to another, and even in the same country from time to time, in the light of the many political, economic and social considerations prevailing in the country at a particular point in time.[10]

2 JUDICIAL INDEPENDENCE IN EUROPE

In Europe, for example, the fundamental basis for requiring judicial independence is derived from Article 6/1 of the European Convention on Human Rights. This article is not confined to judicial independence. Rather, it contains a variety of rights which are all related to the good administration of justice in criminal as well as in both civil and administrative matters. These rights, as noted by the European Court of Human Rights in the *Golder* judgment of 21 February 1975, are distinct but stem from the same basic idea. When they are taken together, these rights make up a single right not specifically defined in the narrower sense of the term.[11]

Judicial independence, therefore, is an element of the good administration of justice already contained in the very notion of "tribunal". In *Demicoli v. Malta*, decided on 27 August 1991, the European Court of Human Rights gave a definition of the tribunal as an organ characterized, in the substantive sense of the term, by its judicial function, that is to say determining matters within its competence on the basis of rules of law and after proceedings conducted in a prescribed manner. It must also satisfy a series of further requirements – independence, in particular from the executive; impartiality; the duration of its members' terms of office; guarantees afforded by its procedure – several of which appear in the text of Article 6/1 itself.[12] In order to establish whether a tribunal can be considered independent within the meaning of Article 6/1 of the Convention, the Court noted in the *Langborger* judgment of 22 June 1989 that regard must be had, *inter alia*,

---

[10] Further discussion of judicial independence can be found in the author's previously published article entitled "Separation of powers and judicial independence in constitutional democracies: the Egyptian and American experiences", in Eugene Cotran and Adel Omar Sherif (eds.), *Democracy. the Rule of Law and Islam*, Kluwer Law International, The Hague, 1999, p. 25.

[11] Macdonald *et al.*, *The European System for the Protection of Human Rights*, p. 381.

[12] *Ibid.*, p. 396.

to the manner of appointment of its members and their term of office, to the existence of guarantees against outside pressures, and to the question of whether the body presents an appearance of independence.[13]

3 JUDICIAL INDEPENDENCE IN THE UNITED STATES OF AMERICA

As in Europe, the notion of judicial independence plays a fundamental role in the United States of America. We find that as a result of the increasing tendency to guarantee judicial independence that describing the judiciary as the least dangerous branch of the government is nowadays no longer a prevailing theme, either in the United States of America or in any other modern democratic society. Historically, we find that more than two hundred years ago the status of the judicial branch in the United States of America was lower than it is today. When envisioning the judiciary department of the proposed government, Alexander Hamilton was much affected by Montesquieu's view on the judicial branch, where he reached a conclusion that of the three powers of the government the judiciary was next to nothing. Hamilton believed that the judiciary was, beyond any comparison, the weakest of the three departments of power, and would always be the least dangerous to the political rights of the Constitution because it had neither force nor will but mere judgment and had to depend on the executive to enforce its judgments when they were resisted.[14]

Nevertheless, the dramatic changes which have occurred in the political system of the United States of America since the adoption of the Federal Constitution in 1789 have produced some profound and favourable developments with regard to the position of the judiciary. Nowadays, the old opinion of judicial weakness is mainly viewed as merely historical, a part of the process of developing judicial power, followed by many remarkable developments which have led to judicial supremacy.

The existing culmination of judicial power, however, has left some constitutional and political experts concerned about the political role played by the judiciary in public life and its implications for the relationships between the judiciary and both the legislature and the executive. Increasing judicial interference, which reached its apex during the New Deal crisis between President Roosevelt and the Supreme Court, created a sense of judicial sovereignty. As a result, judges felt that they held a higher position than that occupied by any other power in the whole system of government. Such a superior attitude, and the assumption by the courts of a policy-making role, were not accepted by the other branches of the government.[15] Hence attacks were frequently

---

13   *Ibid.*, p. 397.
14   *The Federalist*, no. 78, *The Federalist: a Commentary on the Constitution of the United States of America*, The Modern Library, New York, 1937, p. 504.
15   It is clear, from reviewing some of Hamilton's articles on the judicial power (*The Federalist* 78) that at the time of drafting the Federal Constitution judges were seen as the same as any other public officers, that is Art. II, s. 2, of the

made on the judicial tendency led by the Supreme Court, in order to prevent the judiciary from expanding its power.[16] Judicial activism was, and sometimes is still, seen as a threat to the balance of powers which is essential to the preservation of representative government in any age.[17]

However, the judiciary has always maintained a prestigious status in the structure of the country. At the present time, the decisions of the Supreme Court of the United States on constitutional issues are not only claimed but also regarded as the supreme law of the land. This fact is supported by the idea that orderly process requires that there be finality of decision somewhere. In 1958 the Supreme Court made that claim for itself in *Cooper v. Aaron* [358 US 1, 18(1958)] when it ruled that the interpretation of a constitutional text enunciated by this Court was the supreme law of the land.[18] In addition to this, the Court's rulings on major issues of public policy, such as the abortion and flag burning issues, engage the country in a dialogue over the meaning of the Constitution by raising political conflicts to the level of

---

cont.

    Constitution provides that judges, like Cabinet officers and ambassadors, for example, are to be appointed on nomination by the President and confirmation by the Senate. However, while discussing the judicial power Hamilton considered permanence in judicial office indispensable without remarking on the difference between judges and public officers in this respect. This led to accusations that he was less than candid in his discussion of the courts. Walter Berns, "The least dangerous branch, but only if ...", in Leonard J. Theberge (ed.), *The Judiciary in a Democratic Society*, Lexington Books, 1977, p. 3.

16   The radio speech delivered on February 1937 by Homer S. Cummings, Attorney-General at the time, is an example of such attacks from the executive side. In this speech Cummings attacked the judiciary calling for new appointees as a method to infuse it. He said: "The judiciary is but a coordinate branch of Government. It is entitled to no higher position than either the legislative or the executive. If the Constitution is to remain a living document and the law is to serve the needs of a vital and growing nation, it is essential that new blood be infused into our judiciary." Cornell W. Clayton, *The Politics of Justice, the Attorney General and the Making of Legal Policy*, M. E. Sharpe, 1992, p. 125. An example that plainly shows an attack from the legislature side is the refusal of the Congress in 1964 and again in 1965 to give the Chief Justice and his associates on the Supreme Court the same US$ 7,500 pay increase granted all lower Federal Court judges. Instead, the members of the highest tribunal had to settle for only a US$ 4,500 increase. Henry J. Abraham, *The Judicial Process*, Oxford University Press, 1975, p. 169.

17   Charles E. Rice, *Judicial Supremacy and the Balance of Powers: a Blueprint for Judicial Reform*, Free Congress Research and Education Foundation, 1981, p. 17.

18   In this case the Supreme Court ruled that: "[*Marbury v. Madison*] declared the basic principle that the federal judiciary is supreme in the exposition of the law of the Constitution, and that principle has ever since been respected by this court and the country as a permanent and indispensable future of our constitutional system. It follows that the interpretation of the Fourteenth amendment enunciated by this Court in [*Brown v. Board of Education*, 349 US 294 (1954)] ... is the supreme law of the land": *ibid.*, p. 19. In fact, this claim, as noted by Rice, may lead to the conclusion that "the only remedy for those who disagree with the constitutional interpretation by the Court is a formal amendment to the Constitution": *ibid.*, p. 20.

constitutional intelligibility. Its activism has invited criticism that it has become a super legislature.[19]

Today, the courts function too broadly in reordering the economic, social and political life of the country. This was earlier perceived by the French commentator Alexis de Tocqueville when he noted in 1835 that there was hardly a political question in the United States that did not sooner or later turn into a judicial one.[20] It is noteworthy that while the judiciary assumes a more active role in the American political and legal life, the legislature [the Congress of the United States] is undergoing changes that are still taking place. Congress, for many Americans, has been gradually transformed from a representative and deliberative policy-making institution into an institution where deliberation has become little more than brokering among interested groups and individuals, and representation has become little more than responding to constituent desires and complaints. The judiciary is becoming more powerful. Not so very long ago, the debate was about the scope of judicial power. The question was whether or not judges should refrain from imposing their will over and above that of elected legislators. Today it is expected that judges will do so, and that they must.[21]

The powerful judicial structure of the United States of America, with the Supreme Court standing at its pinnacle, is bewildering and dazzling at the same time. It is perplexing because it includes separate judicial systems, one for each state, in addition to the federal judicial system. However, the federal system and the state systems together work in harmony to ensure the rule of law. The entire system receives full public respect and appreciation, which, in fact, makes the role of the judiciary an impressive one.

The elevated status now held by the American judiciary in the system of government and public life could not have been reached without the independence of the judicial function. Judicial independence is one of the main features that distinguishably characterizes the judicial function in the United States. This independence is not considered as mere privilege and immunity for individual judges. Rather, it is viewed by both the public and the government as a basic guarantee for the protection of individuals' rights and freedoms.[22]

---

19 David M. O'Brien, *Storm Center: the Supreme Court in American Politics*, 3rd edn., New York and London, W. W. Norton, p. 62.
20 The edited transcript of one of a series of AEI fora (AEI Forum 26), held on 12 December 1978, *An Imperial Judiciary: Fact or Myth?* Comment by John Charles Daly, Public Policy Research, Washington DC, p. 2.
21 Eugene W. Hickok and Gray L. McDowell, *Justice v. Law*, The Free Press, New York, 1993, pp. 196 and 203. Furthermore, the authors noted that as an institution, the Congress of the United States of America is held in a very low esteem. Most citizens feel their government is distant, inefficient, uncaring and broke: *ibid.*, p. 197.
22 In a presentation by Richard Schifter, Assistant Secretary of State for Human Rights and Humanitarian Affairs, to the international symposium of the Japan committee on the bicentennial of the French Revolution and the Asahi Shimbun which took place in Tokyo, Japan on 20 October 1989, he wrote: "In my present job as US Assistant Secretary of State for Human Rights and Humanitarian

What is also worth mentioning about the concept of judicial independence in this respect is that, as noted earlier, it exists not only in the United States of America, but also in all democratic systems that respect human rights. The experience of the United States of America provides various principles that have to be respected in order to achieve judicial independence. These principles, which are viewed as the building blocks of an independent judiciary, may be used as guides to trace how independent the judiciary is in any given country. They include, but are not limited to, the separation of powers, life tenure and adequate compensation [not subject to reduction] for judges, complete control in financial and administrative matters for the judges themselves, lawyers serving as officers of the court, judicial education and the exercise of the power of judicial review.[23]

4 SOME ATTACKS ON THE JUDICIARY IN THE UNITED STATES OF AMERICA AND EGYPT

Although there is a steady, unarguable tendency towards guaranteeing judicial independence within different legal cultures all over the world, there are still incidents and times when judicial independence is not respected. The degree of democratic progress in a given system does not change this fact; hence, we can trace violations of judicial independence in both mature and emerging democracies at the same time.

I will, therefore, demonstrate some violations of judicial independence in the United States of America and Egypt, two countries representing distinct legal systems in the developed and developing worlds.

4.1 Attacks on the judiciary in the United States of America

Despite the fact that the judiciary in the United States of America has historically been free from close outside scrutiny and has enjoyed a great deal

---

cont.
Affairs, I have become more fully aware than ever before of the importance of an independent judiciary to the cause of human rights".

[23] In an outline prepared by James G. Apple, Chief, Inter-Judicial Affairs Office at the Federal Judicial Center, he indicated eighteen elements as building blocks of an independent judiciary. These building blocks are as follows: (1) separation of powers; (2) equality of status of the judicial branch with other branches of government; (3) separation of the judicial branch from the Department (Ministry) of Justice; (4) judges appointed for life; (5) adequate remuneration for judges; (6) no reduction in judges' pay; (7) adequate staff for judges; (8) removal of judges only by impeachment; (9) the power of judicial review; (10) the disciplining of judges occurs only within the judicial branch; (11) judicial codes of conduct – prohibition against political and other kinds of public activity; (12) a conference of judges (the "Judicial Conference of the US") controls judicial administration; (13) judges prepare and submit the budget for the judicial branch; (14) judges control rules of procedure for the courts; (15) judges control the day-to-day operation of the courts; (16) judges have control over judicial education; (17) judges have control over court space and facilities; (18) lawyers serve as officers of the court.

of independence, it is now coming under the increasingly watchful eye of both the legislature and executive. Numerous attempts to circumscribe judicial independence have lately taken place, and have raised discussion on whether the judiciary is really still independent. Among these attempts were the case of the congressional questionnaire and attacks on judicial decisions.

4.1.1 The congressional questionnaire

There have been some recent attempts by Congress since 1995 to flex its muscles *vis-à-vis* the judiciary. Late in 1999, Senator John McCain, R. Ariz, introduced a proposal to establish an inspector general within the Administrative Office of the United States Courts. The proposal was viewed as an intrusion that would undermine the independence of the judiciary.[24]

But the most controversial recent incident, which has been viewed with some scepticism as to whether it really contains a threat to the independence of judges, was that concerning the congressional survey of judicial performance. This started during the 1995 budget dispute between a Republican-led Congress and a Democratic President, when Senator Charles E. Grassley, Chairman of the Senate Judiciary Subcommittee on Administrative Oversight of the Courts, announced his plan to send out to federal judges a detailed questionnaire on their judicial performance to help find ways of reducing judicial expenses. This questionnaire was mailed to all Article III judges (excluding the United States Supreme Court Justices) on 26 January 1996, containing questions quizzing them on a number of issues related to the federal judiciary, including workloads, the duties of the law clerks and the time spent on off-the-bench activities such as lecturing and writing law review articles. The announced motive for distributing this questionnaire among federal judges was to "directly communicate with, and elicit input from, the judiciary in order to better understand the needs of federal judiciary, as well as to find cost efficiencies within the federal judicial system".[25]

Nevertheless, this questionnaire was sharply criticized at the highest judicial level. Before sending out the questionnaire to federal judges, Chief Justice William Rehnquist, of the United States Supreme Court, noted in his year-end report for 1995 that "the subject matter of the questions and the details required for answering them could amount to an unwarranted and ill-considered effort to micro-manage the work of the federal judiciary". He added, however, that "there can be no doubt that answers to some form of such questions could aid Congress in making decisions about judicial salaries, permitted outside income from teaching, creating new judgeships and filling existing vacancies"; and that he hoped this coming study would give Congress the information it needed without compromising judicial independence.[26]

---

24 Kirk Victor, *Legal Affairs*, 25 May 1996, "Judgment day".
25 Report on the January 1996 Judicial Survey, Part 1, The United States Senate Judiciary Subcommittee on Administrative Oversight and the Courts, May 1996, p. i.
26 *Times Union*, Albany New York, 1 January 1996, "Rehnquist says study a threat to Federal judges".

The Chief Justice also suggested that the federal courts should not be caught in the middle of the budget dispute between the Congress and President, and that the judiciary budget, a relatively small US$ 3 billion appropriation, should be extricated from the middle of this struggle between the other two branches of government.[27]

Despite the Chief Justice's concern over the questionnaire, judges expressed mixed feelings about completing the task. While some judges felt that the questionnaire was too time consuming, and that some of the questions impinged upon the independence of the judicial branch,[28] most judges responded to it[29] as they recognized that providing law-makers with the requested information might be helpful for interbranch relations. Out of a total of 249 circuit court judges, 170 judges responded to the questionnaire: a 68.3 per cent response rate.[30] And out of a total of 902 district court judges, 529 judges responded to the questionnaire: a 58.6 per cent response rate.[31]

One of the federal judges, Judge Barrington Parker of the southern district of White Plains, commented that the concept of sending out such a survey "raised eyebrows". But after reviewing it, he decided that this survey "was not a big deal". He said that judges served public functions, and "if somebody has some reasonable questions about how the public money is being spent, I do not have any problem with that".[32] In addition, Judge Gilbert Merritt, Chairman of the Executive Committee of the United States Judiciary Conference, sent a letter to judges asking them to cooperate with the questionnaire, even though he continued to believe that more accurate information could be had from the judicial organization he headed.[33]

The findings of the questionnaire were intended to be used as the starting point for cutting the costs of the federal judiciary. Upon releasing the first part of the judicial survey on 14 May 1996, Senator Grassley declared that "from the responses received, there is no question that we can save money in the judiciary". He also said that the survey could help Congress determine when and where to fill future vacancies. "Where it is very obvious where some vacancies should not be filled or judgeships that are vacant should be eliminated, we should do that."[34]

There is no doubt that such an attempt to interfere in the judicial business represents a recent attack on the judiciary. A kind of attack that, as described by former Representative Abner J. Mikva, "has been before and it will be

---

27 The editorial of *Fort Worth Star-Telegram*, 3 January 1996 "Separate and equal"; and the *Washington Times*, 1 January 1996, "Rehnquist lobbies for court funds".
28 *Legal Times*, 5 February 1996, "Now the judges face the questions".
29 *Congressional Quarterly's News*, 15 May 1996, "Grassley says survey shows judicial costs can be cut".
30 Report on the January 1996 Judicial Survey, Part 1, p. i.
31 *Ibid.*
32 Deborah Pines and Bill Alden, "District circuit judges use Senate survey to boast gripe", *New York Law Journal*, vol. 215, no. 57, 25 March 1996.
33 Pins, Washington News Bureau, 18 February 1996, "Grassley's examination of the judiciary in full swing".
34 "Grassley says survey shows judicial costs can be cut".

again – it is a bad idea because it does compromise the independence of judges".[35]

4.1.2 Judge-bashing in the United States of America

Another example of the recent attacks on the judiciary is that committed against Judge Harold Baer Jr, federal judge in the Southern District of New York, arising from his ruling on January 1996 in the case of *United States v. Bayless*. In this case, Judge Baer granted a motion to suppress (a) the post-arrest statement of a woman charged with participation in a drug-distribution conspiracy, and (b) 80 lb of heroin and cocaine in two duffel bags that four males had placed in the trunk of a red Caprice the accused had allegedly double-parked on a street in the Washington Heights section of Manhattan.

Justifications of this ruling were founded on Judge Baer's belief that it was unsurprising that one or more of the men who had put duffel bags in the trunk of the car had run away upon seeing police officers. The neighbourhood, predominantly minority and located in the inner city, was one where flight from the police was to be expected and thus could not well support an investigative stop. The men's behaviour was not necessarily suspicious because residents of the area had reason to regard the police as corrupt, abusive and violent.[36]

The ruling was widely attacked. Frequent bipartisan criticisms and attacks were raised against Judge Baer for being too soft on defendants. In the political arena both Republicans and Democrats condemned the ruling.

Speaker Newt Gingrich (Republican) described the ruling as "the perfect reason why we are losing our civilization".[37] Senator Robert Dole, the 1996 Republican presidential candidate, said that if Judge Baer "does not resign, he ought to be impeached".[38]

On 21 March 1996, the White House press Secretary, Michael McCurry, suggested that if Judge Baer did not change his mind, the President would seek his resignation.[39] A day later, however, a contradictory statement was announced by the White House, when Jack Quinn, Counsel to the President, declared that "the President supports the independence of the Federal Judiciary, which is established by the Constitution. Although comments in the recent press reports may have led some to conclude otherwise, the President believes strongly that the issues now before Judge Baer should be resolved in the courts".[40]

---

[35] Kirk, *Legal Affairs*, "Judgment day".
[36] Louis H. Pollak, "Criticizing judges", *Judicature, The Journal of the American Judicature Society*, May/June 1996, vol. 79, no. 6, p. 299. See also *The Legal Times*, 1 April 1996, "Judges: attacks on Baer go too far", p. 12.
[37] The editorial of *Boston Globe* on 6 April 1996, "Judge Baer sees the light".
[38] Seelye, "A get-tough message at California's death row", *New York Times*, 24 March 1996, p. 29.
[39] Mitchell, "Clinton pressing judge to relent", *New York Times*, 22 March 1996, p. 1.
[40] Greenhouse, "Judges as political issues", *New York Times*, 23 March 1996, p. 11.

As a reaction to these attacks a group of judges, from the United States Court of Appeals for the Second Circuit, namely, Jon O. Newman, Edward Lumbard, Wilfred Weinberg and James Oaken, issued a statement on 28 March 1996, urging that the attacks on Judge Baer cease as they constituted a grave disservice to the principle of an independent judiciary. They indicated that such attacks, which had gone too far, threatened to weaken the constitutional structure of the nation. The framers of the Constitution gave federal judges life tenure and did not provide for resignation or impeachment whenever a judge made a decision with which elected officials disagreed. When a judge was threatened with a call for resignation or impeachment because of disagreement with a ruling, the entire process of orderly resolution of legal disputes was undermined. The judges, moreover, drew the attention to the fact that although informed comment and disagreement on judicial decisions were hallmarks of the American legal tradition, there was still an important line between legitimate criticism, which illuminates issues and sometimes points the way toward better decisions, and illegitimate criticism of judicial decisions, which risks inhibiting all judges from conscientiously endeavouring to discharge their constitutional responsibilities.[41]

Following the attacks on Judge Baer's ruling by both the executive and legislature, a reconsideration of this ruling was ordered on 1 April 1996 by Judge Baer himself. No matter how correct and accurate this new opinion is, its issuance in such circumstances created a sceptical belief that the independence of the judiciary has been reduced.

4.2 Attacks on judicial bodies in Egypt

Separation of powers in modern Egypt has always been implicitly declared within subsequent Constitutions, and announced by the rulers as a core element of the system of government. The current Constitution also guarantees judicial independence. The reading of several provisions of this Constitution ensures this understanding, both clearly and implicitly. Practice, however, produces some scepticism as to whether this principle is a real base of the system of government or just a mere theoretical concept. This confusion is attributed to the fact that throughout Egyptian political history, the executive has been the dominant branch, having the upper hand over all aspects of life in the country.

Following the Egyptian Revolution of 1952, which led to the overthrow of the monarchy and rule of Mohammed Ali's dynasty, the executive was keen to hold absolute power in order to have a commanding position over the other powers. The single-party system was therefore introduced as the basis of political participation in the political life of the country. The dominance of the executive power over this party always allowed it to control the ballots, and consequently to dominate the elected representative councils. The legislature was thus seen as an agency affiliated to, and controlled by,

---

[41] "Judges: attacks on Baer go too far", p. 12.

the executive. As an indication of executive power, it may be noted that the executive has used its constitutional authority to dissolve Parliament on many occasions, but that Parliament has never withdrawn its confidence from any member of the executive.

With such dominance of the executive the judiciary was not immune from interference in the judicial affairs. The executive has often shown its power over the judiciary; in order to establish the same level of control that it has over the legislature, the executive began to interfere in judicial business. Such interference affected the separation of judicial power, and consequently judicial independence. In addition to the powers exercised by the Minister of Justice over the judicial bodies and judges,[42] the executive has more than once campaigned to assail the integrity of the judiciary in order to bring the judicial branch under its total control.

Four incidents are worth mentioning in this respect: the first is the prepared attack on the State Council in 1954/55, the second is the judicial removal action of 1969, the third is the organized campaign attacking the Supreme Constitutional Court and the fourth is the most recent attack aiming at limiting the retroactive effect of judicial decisions on constitutional cases.

4.2.1   The first attack: the prepared attack on the State Council

The roots of this catastrophic attack go back to the period that followed the revolution in 1952. The State Council tendency under the presidency of Dr Abd El-Razzak El-Sanhoury, who was and is still regarded as the most preeminent legal figure in Egypt and the Arab world, reflected a noticeable activism toward adopting the democratic process and protecting individuals' rights. This tendency clashed with the authoritarian character of the executive power, represented in the so-called Council of Revolution Leadership at that time. A barbarous physical attack on Dr El-Sanhoury was planned by the executive authorities who incited a vulgar herd to carry out the attack in the premises of the State Council in 1954. Although the Council of Revolution Leadership condemned the attack and denied any connection with it, a few days later Dr El-Sanhoury was removed from office on a pretext of his partisan support for the abolished monarchy. The attack on the State Council did not stop at this point. Within the coming few months the executive again attacked the Council when a decree law was issued in 1955 (Decree Law No. 165 of 1955) to reorganize the Council. It provided in its Article 77 that a decree would be issued by the Cabinet, upon a suggestion of the Prime Minister and after consulting the President of the State Council, with regard to the reappointment of the Council's members. By virtue of this provision all the Council's members were removed from judicial office, and were subject to the discretionary power of the executive to be reappointed to the same posts, or to any other judicial or non-judicial post outside the

---

[42]   See the author's previously published article, "Separation of power", p. 25.

Council. Thus, twenty members were removed from the Council in an obvious breach of the rule of law and judicial independence.

4.2.2   The second attack: the judicial removal of 1969

This attack led to the removal of a great number of judges from the bench in 1969 for political reasons. After the unfortunate result of the Six Day War of 1967 an increasing judicial tendency to move towards democratization was shown. The political leadership at the time aimed to continue its domination of the judiciary and began to express a wish to have judges enrolled in the sole political party like any other group of the people. Judges claimed that this step would detract from their independence, and they therefore condemned the proposal. The reaction of the executive to this resistance was the issuance of a chain of decree laws to reorganize all judicial bodies. These decree laws, known as the Judicial Reform Laws, established the Supreme Court and the Supreme Council for Judicial Bodies. Nevertheless, they contained a reappointment policy similar to the tactics previously adopted in 1955 during the State Council crisis. This led to the removal of almost 189 members of different judicial bodies from their judicial offices.

These are the most obvious cases of executive intrusion into judicial business. They show that regardless of the constitutionally protected principles of separation of powers and judicial independence, the executive has always been ready and willing to violate these principles whenever their recognition has constituted a restriction on its power.

The question that might be raised now is whether or not the reform of the 1971 Constitution has ended the executive policy of attacking the judicial bodies. This will be explained by the following two attacks.

4.2.3   An organized campaign attacking the Supreme Constitutional Court

The establishment of the Supreme Constitutional Court in 1979 coincided with a newly announced tendency, led by the executive, to democratize the system of government and respect the rule of law. This tendency, which has been in force since then, allowed the Supreme Constitutional Court, through its power of judicial review, to impose a great number of restrictions on both the legislature and the executive in line with the proper implementation of the constitutional guarantees spelled out in the 1971 Constitution. With the culmination of the activism of the Supreme Constitutional Court in this field both executive and legislature became bothered and irritated. The worries of the executive should be understood in the light of the fact that for years the executive branch had always had a prevailing position allowing it to impose its own will over the other branches of government, and to exploit them in implementing its orders. Making it subject to judicial limitations would limit its tyranny and absolute authority, and thus it would resist such limitation. With respect to the worries of the legislature, they may be construed on the basis of its sensitivity to the principle of separation of powers, and its wish not to have its Acts reviewed or annulled by the judiciary. However, since Parliament has generally been viewed as lacking a representative and independent character, and as an institution largely managed by the executive, the legislature's worries have to be considered as a reflection of those of the executive.

Other than a number of scattered attempts by the executive to suspend some of the Court's decisions, the records have not shown direct attacks on the Court from the executive side during the last few years.[43] A memorable exception, however, was the amendment of the Court's statute by a Presidential Decree in 1998 – which will be discussed separately below. In addition, one of the recent, noticeable attacks on the Court was directed from the legislature. This was an unprecedented attack on the Court which took place in March 1996 when the Speaker of the People's Assembly[44] Dr Ahmed Fathy Sorrour led a press campaign calling for an amendment to the Court's statute that allows for the protection of what he called "legal security". In a somewhat confusing interview with *Al Mosawar* weekly magazine the Speaker, though honouring the Court with all due respect and referring to it as the stronghold of democracy in Egypt, warned of the dangers that might affect society as a result of the Court's frequent practices of declaring legislation unconstitutional; and announced that the protection of the Constitution required preventing any surprise that might arise as a result of the non-conformity of legislation to the Constitution. He also made a dramatic reference to the crisis between President Roosevelt and the Supreme Court of the United States, referring to the possibility of a similar crisis in Egypt should the Supreme Constitutional Court, like other constitutional courts worldwide, overreach itself by striking down legislation based on an understanding of the Constitution varying from that of the legislature.

Although considered to be a leading Egyptian legal figure, the Speaker paradoxically invented a strange legal theory that provided for limiting the power of judicial review in constitutional issues, and even discontinuing it, in order to maintain stability in the society. He said "when accustomed to the application of legislation for decades, declaring it unconstitutional undoubtedly would create a sort of infraction to what I call legal security". To limit judicial activism and achieve legislative stability, the Speaker called for the adoption of the method of prior review in constitutional issues such as those handled by the Constitutional Council in France. He suggested that, in addition to the power of judicial review applied by the Supreme Constitutional Court, the Court should also be invested with jurisdiction to exercise a pre-review of legislation prior to its adoption, upon a request of either the

---

[43] In an interview with the Chief Justice in *Al Mosawar* weekly magazine he declared that "what concerns the Court is clarifying the constitutional mandates; as to the issue of decisions' enforcement the Court has nothing to do with it". *Al Mosawar*, March 1996, p. 22.

[44] The Egyptian Parliament, in accordance with the 1971 Constitution as amended in 1980, consists of two Councils: the People's Assembly which handles the bulk of legislative process (Art. 86), and the *Shoura* Council which is rather a more consultative body than a legislative one (Art. 194).

President of the Republic, the Speaker or the Prime Minister. As a consequence of gaining the right of prior review, the Court would forfeit its authority to review any legislation that had earlier been subject to its prior review. Only legislation that had not previously been reviewed by the Court prior to its promulgation could be the subject of judicial review. Vesting the Court with such new authority, he said, was an expansion on the Court's jurisdiction which could be simply introduced by modifying the Court's statute without any need to amend the Constitution.

One of the confusing points in the Speaker's interview was that his eagerness to show his respect for the role played by the Court within the democratic system of Egypt and the importance of the power of judicial review was linked with his attack on the power to declare legislation unconstitutional. This attitude, however, reflected the sensitivity of the Speaker to the issue of judicial review, which he thought should be controlled by Parliament. Most Egyptian intellectuals rejected the Speaker's ideas.

Although some writers did support the Speaker's views expressed in the *Al Mosawar* interview,[45] he was much criticized in the newspapers by the legal and political community which found that the declarations of the Speaker reflected nothing but a wish to roll back the progress of the democratic process in Egypt achieved through the Court's boldness in defending human rights and protecting society. Instead of investigating the real reasons that led the Supreme Constitutional Court to strike down various laws in order to avoid legislative defects that might lead to the annulment of the legislation in the future, the Court's opponents had moved against it to limit its powers.[46] One commentator said that the vague and over-general phrases and expressions used by the Speaker, and his saying that judicial review should not become a tool for the destroying the stability of society, were a reflection of the nation's submission to a series of exceptional and emergency legislation, and an attempt to maintain non-democratic practices.[47] Another commentator noted that shifting the constitutional guarantee of judicial review into a pre-review mechanism was an extreme concept that contradicted the constitutional philosophy of maintaining the balance between the government powers. It was an attack on the Supreme Constitutional Court which, in reality, reflected an attempt to attack the Constitution itself which provided for the Court as a basic guarantee of constitutional supremacy and protection of individual rights and freedoms.[48] A third commentator noticed that establishing a new practice to interpret the legislation in a manner that always rendered it in conformity with the Constitution was a tendency that existed only within totalitarian systems of government.[49] In a sarcastic column in the *Al Akhbar* daily newspaper a popular writer suggested that, in order to conformably solve the existing problem, the People's Assembly ought to pass a law providing for the non-submission of the

---

[45] Dr Ibrahim Alam, *El Wafd*, 31 March 1996, p. 7.
[46] Mohammed Helmy Mourad, *El Shaab*, 2 April 1996, p. 5.
[47] Hassan Hafez, *El Wafd*, 23 March 1996, p. 7.
[48] Abd El-Aziz Mohammed, *El Wafd*, 4 April 1996, p. 6.
[49] Dr Mohammed Lameae El Mallah, *El Wafd*, 6 April 1996, p. 7.

legislation passed by the Assembly to the power of judicial review applied by the Supreme Constitutional Court.[50]

With the increasing public interest in following up the attack on the Court, the Chief Justice Dr Awad Mohammed El Morr himself, who rarely gives interviews or speaks directly to the media, gave an interview to *Al Mosawar* where he refuted the Speaker's argument. He explained how prior review would reduce the power of judicial review, and that vesting the Supreme Constitutional Court with such a power would require a constitutional amendment. He also explained that the supremacy of the Constitution necessitated the overruling of any legislation that contradicted it, no matter how long this legislation had been in application. The Court's rulings that invalidated existing legislation, he added, did not threaten the stability of society. Rather, they corrected legislative defects in order to ensure the proper respect for the rule of law in society, and hence they helped to secure legal stability in the light of constitutional provisions.

The Chief Justice's response to the attack on the Court refuted the arguments of those who sought to curtail the Court's powers. The Court had raised constitutional awareness among the people. It especially raised popular consciousness of the necessity of maintaining the democratic process and respecting individual rights and freedoms, and these two elements were behind the defeat of this attack on the Court.

While the furore surrounding this official attack was dying down, a new attack was launched from a private source. On 6 June 1996, a senior law professor in Alexandria University, Dr Moustafa Abu Zeid Fahmy, posed a question to his students in the final year exam for the first year in the law school that contained a disrespectful criticism of the Court.[51] While Chief

---

[50] Ahmmed Ragab, *Al Akhbar*, 23 March 1996, p. 1.
[51] In this question, Dr Moustafa Abu Zeid Fahmy, who previously had held ministerial posts during the late President Sadat's regime, asked his student to prove how the Supreme Constitutional Court breached the Constitution by determining effects to its decisions other than those specified by the Constitution and the law. In a directive manner the question went on to ask whether judicial review should be based on whim or legal grounds. And in light of the influence of the United States constitutional jurisprudence on the Court's ruling, the question further quizzed the students on which was the reference in exploring the constitutionality of legislation, the United States Constitution or the Egyptian Constitution. *Al Araby*, 17 June 1996, p. 1. Furthermore, "in an article published in *Al-Ahram* on 17 June, he persisted in his hostile position towards the court. He cited the example of a court ruling issued in 1990, declaring a 1986 parliamentary electoral law unconstitutional. The court also ruled that, from the moment its judgment is published in the official journal all subsequent acts of the People's Assembly would become legally null and void. President Hosni Mubarak responded by issuing a presidential decree dissolving the People's Assembly, elected in 1987. In this way, Abu Zeid argued in the article, the court gave a retroactive effect to its ruling. He pointed out that according to the law and the constitution, such ruling should have taken an immediate effect. In other words, the ruling should not have been applied to the standing Assembly but to the election of future assemblies. Abu Zeid concluded that the court had violated the constitution it is supposed to safeguard." *Al Ahram*, 17 July 1996, p. 1.

Justice El Morr ignored this attack, considering the issue unworthy of attention as the Court's dignity was beyond question, the professor's attitude was
condemned by the law school council on 11 June 1996.[52] Immediately after
the examinations, members of the faculty council sought to disassociate
themselves from Abu Zeid, saying in a statement that Abu Zeid's question,
put in such a manner, in no way represented the faculty's attitude to the
Court. The faculty council also sent a letter to the Chief Justice Awad El
Morr to express its appreciation of the prominent role the Court played in
upholding constitutional principles.[53] In addition, all legal circles expressed
their disagreement with the professor's attitude, which they attributed to
some political and personal motivation.[54] Moreover, they charged him with
exceeding the reasonable limits that the freedom of scientific research allows
for criticizing courts' decisions, and with violating academic traditions.[55]
Furthermore, a criminal charge of contempt the Court was filed against the
professor in the Attorney-General's office on 13 June 1996,[56] and the issue
was referred to the contempt prosecution office in Alexandria to handle the
investigation.[57] The battle the professor tried to wage against the Court had
failed before it started, and the professor's position attracted no public
support.[58] Once again, the growing public awareness of the importance of

---

[52] Moustafa Saleem, *El Shaab*, 21 June 1996. Also, Mohammed El Sadafy, *Al Ahaly*,
      19 June 1996.
[53] *Al Ahram Weekly*, 11 July 1996, p. 1.
[54] Mohammed El Sadafy, *Al Ahaly*, 19 June 1996. Also, Mohammed Saleem El
      Awa, *El Wafd*, 25 and 31 July 1996. "Legal sources attribute Abu Zeid's attack
      on the court to personal motivations. In 1988, Abu Zeid filed a lawsuit against
      Kamal Khaled, a former independent member of the People's Assembly, claiming
      that Khaled had made allegations which damaged his reputation in his book
      Nasser's and Sadat's Men. Abu Zeid claimed E£500,000 compensation. Khaled
      failed to submit evidence proving the accuracy of the facts in his book within the
      statutory five days. According to the provisions of Article 123 of the Criminal
      Procedures Law, Khaled thereby lost his right to present evidence. Khaled then
      contested the constitutionality of Article 123, and in 1993 the Constitutional
      Court ruled that the article in question was unconstitutional. It is since this date,
      the sources say, Abu Zeid began to attack the Constitutional Court after years of
      praise, describing its rulings as: 'judicial treasure'. Khaled linked Abu Zeid's latest
      attack on the Constitutional Court to the current parliamentary campaign which
      is attempting to undermine its role." *Al Ahram Weekly*, 11 July 1996, p. 1.
[55] Deya El Deen Dawod, *Al Araby*, 8 July 1996. Also, Dr Nabil Ahmmed Helmy,
      Al Ahram, 13 July 1996.
[56] The request was filled by Dr Shawky El-Sayed, lawyer and member of the *Shoura*
      Council, *Al Ahaly*, 19 June 1996. El-Sayed informed the Prosecutor-General of
      the "crime Abu Zeid has committed against the court". Prosecution
      investigations into the case began earlier that week. In reaction, Abu Zeid filed a
      lawsuit against El-Sayed, accusing him of libel and demanding E£500,000
      compensation. El-Sayed then filed a E£1 million counter lawsuit against Abu
      Zeid assuring that "Academic criticism has nothing to do with the usage of vulgar
      and indecent expressions." *Al Ahram Weekly*, 11 July 1996, p. 1.
[57] *El Akhbar*, 20 June 1996, p. 15.
[58] Nevertheless, "Merghani Khairi, professor of constitutional law at Ain Shams
      University backed Abu Zeid in his right to express his opinion. However, he had
      reservations about his approach. 'Everyone has the right to adopt whatever
      opinion he likes,' he said. 'But the problem is that Abu Zeid attempted to impose

the Court and its role in protecting human rights and freedoms and maintaining the democratic system in the country was the key factor that countered this attack on the Court. This certainly supports the Court's ongoing efforts to protect the Constitution and individuals.

4.2.4   The fourth attack: limiting the retroactive effect of the judicial decisions on constitutional cases

A very dramatic attack on the Supreme Constitutional Court was made on 12 July 1998, the date of the coming into force of the Decree Law No. 168 for the year 1998.[59] This decree law, issued right at the commencement of a parliamentary recess, introduced a fundamental amendment to Article 49/3 of the Law on the Supreme Constitutional Court, issued by Law No. 48 for the year 1979. Rulings of the Court in constitutional issues, according to the latter provision, possessed a retroactive effect, hence ensuring the highest degree of constitutional remedy when constitutional provisions were violated. This constitutional guarantee had annoyed the executive on more than one occasion, especially when the legislative provision declared unconstitutional concerned the taxation code of the country. The new amendment brought an end to the well-established concept of retroactive effect in the constitutional rulings of the Supreme Constitutional Court. As a general rule, rulings of the Court in constitutional issues, according to this amendment, do not come into force until the day after their publication date in the Official Gazette. The Court still, however, possesses the power to determine an alternative date for its ruling to be enforced. But, exceptionally, this power does not extend to cases in which legislative provisions related to tax issues are declared unconstitutional. In such cases, the Court's ruling must not apply retroactively. Restricting the retroactive effect of the Court's

---

cont.

    his opinion, using an aggressive style and improper words to defend his views.'
    According to Khairi, legal texts are flexible, and should not be interpreted word for word. 'The law said that rulings of the Supreme Constitutional Court should take "immediate effect". However, jurists agreed that the non-application of unconstitutional laws should begin from the moment those laws are issued,' said Khairi. 'In 1984, the Supreme Administrative Court decided that rulings of the Constitutional Court should be applied retroactively. These rulings, the court said, were not limited to cases that fell under the criminal law. The explanatory note attached to the law covering the Supreme Constitutional Court was of the same opinion.' Khairi believes that dissolving the People's Assembly was a logical step in view of the fact that it had been elected by means of an unconstitutional law. The Court, Khairi added, had only ruled that the parliamentary election law was unconstitutional, and the decision to dissolve the Assembly was implemented by presidential decree. The Court sustained the validity of all the laws which were passed by the People's Assembly until the date of its dissolution, and this is a point in its favor." *Al Ahram Weekly,* 11 July 1996, p. 1.

59   This decree law is published in the Official Gazette No. 28 *Mokarrar* on 11 July 1998. An explanatory memo of this decree law, as well as a correction of part of its wording, was published the following day in the Official Gazette No. 28 *Mokarrar* B on 12 July 1998.

decision here should be effected without prejudice, however, of the claimant's violated rights in the constitutional lawsuit in which the taxation legislative provision is declared invalid.

The departure from the unrestricted practice of judicial review, within which the retroactive effect of the Court's decisions prevails, to a restricted norm of judicial review, limiting this effect, is viewed by most jurists in Egypt as an undesirable detraction from judicial review and judicial independence. Judicial remedy cannot be effective in almost all cases unless the Court's ruling applies retroactively. The retroactivity principle is, in fact, a fundamental guarantee of litigants' rights. Constitutional supremacy requires that the retroactive effect of the Court's rulings in constitutional issues should always be seen as a logical consequence of revealing constitutional violations and declaring them null and void.

Limiting the Court's power, by restricting the retroactive effect of its rulings in constitutional issues, is obviously a delicate issue. Within the coming period of time, judicial activities, under this newly introduced mood of judicial review, will definitely show whether such a restriction has circumscribed the power of judicial review and reduced judicial independence or not. We therefore have to keep an eye on the judicial performance of the Supreme Constitutional Court following the 1998 amendment of the Court's statute. A developed, coherent policy of judicial activism is a must to compensate for any reduction of individuals' rights that may have occurred as a result of this amendment. It is hoped that the history of the judiciary in Egypt, and the recent promising experience of the Supreme Constitutional Court, will help to offset and limit any negative effects under this amendment.

5   CONCLUSION

Despite the fact that judicial independence is now perceived by civilized nations as a hallmark of mature democratic experience, and as an essential constitutional element to protect individual rights and freedoms, numerous unfavourable attacks have been made on the judiciary in both developed and developing democracies in recent years. The effective protection of this principle requires public powers to act within their constitutional limits and respect the rule of law and the independence of judges. It also necessitates that public opinion play an active role in this process and be alert to, and consequently defeat, any attempts to detract from this highly important constitutional guarantee.

Freedom of the Press in Egypt:
Checks and Balances

Nathalie Bernard-Maugiron *

On 20 May 2000, the Egyptian opposition paper *El Shaab* was shut down following the freezing of the activities of the Labour Party due to internal turmoil. In May 1995, a new press law nicknamed by its opponents "law on the assassination of the press (*qanun madhbahat al sahafa)*" was adopted by Parliament without prior debate. It severely limited freedom of the press by amending the Penal Code, the Code of Criminal Procedure and the Press Union Law. Following a protest campaign unleashed by the Press Syndicate, the law was finally amended a year later by the 1996 Law on the Organization of the Press. On 14 August 1999, three journalists were sentenced to two years' imprisonment for having libelled a minister.

Although freedom of the press is guaranteed by the Egyptian Constitution, and although many newspapers are issued and granted a great deal of independence, the government during the last few years seems to have tried to tighten the screw. It cannot be denied that the press under Hosni Mubarak operates more freely than before. Government controls over the press have been relaxed and restrictions on anti-government expression eased. A greater respect has been shown for the rule of law: journalists are not put into prison without trial and newspapers are not banned without a court ruling. When personally attacked in the press, public officials take legal action in the courts or respond in the press to defend themselves. Control on the press is, however, maintained by legal means: the conditions for obtaining a publishing licence may be almost impossible to fulfil; the licence may be withdrawn and journalists may be condemned to harsh penalties and jailed for press offences. More subtle extra-legal means of pressure also exist, such as denying a certain category of journalists access to information.

---

*   Senior researcher at the Centre d'Etudes et de Documentation économique, juridique et sociale (CEDEJ, Cairo).

The press plays an important role in the defence of democracy because of its power to affect the political process. Its watchdog function allows it to act in the general interest against the government. It can also be an instrument for mobilization of the public against abuses of power committed by the public authorities and can lead to the formation of an enlightened public opinion. The press in Egypt seems to encounter an ambivalent attitude which varies between recognition of its freedom and the will to silence it. It can be free as long as it behaves in a responsible way and keeps public discussion within certain bounds. It is one of the few open fora where opposition groups can challenge the ruling group. This ambivalent attitude towards the press is not new. Relations between the press and those in political power have always gone through periods of tension and appeasement. Until 1976 the ruling party was the only legal party and owned all the newspapers. Anwar el-Sadat then re-established a multiple-party system and allowed political parties to publish their own newspapers. Among the constitutional amendments of 1980 was the addition of a new chapter entitled "The Press Authority", which established the press as a "popular and independent authority" (Article 206), that "shall exercise its vocation freely and independently in the service of society through all means of expression" (Article 207) and "interpret the trend of public opinion, while contributing to its formation and orientation" (Article 207). While he was enacting these measures in favour of the freedom of the press Sadat was, however, putting limits on it and on other public liberties by issuing, among others, the Law on the Protection of Social Values from Shame (*qanun al-'ayb*) in April 1980. This law rendered journalists who published false or misleading information which could threaten national unity or social peace liable to prosecution. It also made it a criminal offence to publicize and promote views at variance with the peace treaty between Egypt and Israel.

However, resistance to restrictions exists and a number of checks and balances have appeared. Individuals may resort to the courts to recover civil rights and political liberties denied to them by the regime. In their struggle, journalists have often received support from judges who have condemned restrictions on the right of expression. If the government can rely on strong support from the legislature to pass its laws, resistance often comes from the judiciary. In many cases in the last few years, as we will see, judges have had a supportive attitude towards freedom of the press. This was especially the case with the Supreme Constitutional Court, known for having adopted a very dynamic and liberal interpretation of the Constitution and for having expanded the realm of citizens' civil rights.[1] This was also the case with the two other Supreme Courts of the country: the Court of Cassation and the

---

1 Kevin Boyle and Adel Omar Sherif (eds.), *Human Rights and Democracy: The Role of the Supreme Constitutional Court of Egypt,* The Hague, Kluwer Law International, 1996, CIMEL Book Series 3; Nathalie Bernard-Maugiron, "La Haute Cour constitutionnelle égyptienne, gardienne des libertés publiques", *Egypte-Monde arabe,* no. 2, 1999, new series, pp. 17–53 and *La Haute Cour constitutionnelle égyptienne et la protection des droits fondamentaux,* thèse, Nanterre, 1999.

State Council, which stressed the importance of due process and often set indicted journalists free.

Looking at the law alone, however, does not reveal the real dynamics of the system. Other kinds of resistance and strategies have been developed to protect the freedom of the press and resist encroachment on it. Individuals do not hesitate to exploit any legal loophole they may find to circumvent regulations without breaching them. They do not hesitate to undermine, ignore or circumvent legal norms, expressing a tendency "to exhibit the two contradictory characteristics of respect and submission to state authority, while simultaneously manifesting contempt for the government and disregard for its rules".[2]

We shall go through the main provisions regulating the press regime in Egypt and analyse the conditions for the creation and disappearance of a newspaper as well as the different forms of censorship to which it may be submitted. We shall also highlight some of the measures that have restricted the freedom of the press and the ways in which the individuals concerned have reacted to overcome those restrictions, be it through court cases or extra-legal individual behaviour. We shall then conclude with a brief analysis of the present relationships of the press to the political process.

1   FREEDOM OF THE PRESS AND THE LIFE OF A NEWSPAPER

Article 209 of the Constitution guarantees the right of political parties and private or public legal entities to publish and own newspapers. This means, *a contrario*, that private individuals do not have that right. Egypt's publications fall into four categories: state-owned, party-affiliated, independent and foreign-licensed newspapers. Except for state-run newspapers, all have to face different kinds of permanent restriction.

1.1   State-owned newspapers

According to Article 55 of Press Law No. 96 of 1996, the national press (*suhuf qawmiyya*) means papers issued by the press establishment now and in the future, and the news agencies and distribution companies privately owned by the state. The Consultative Assembly (*Majlis al-Shura*) exercises ownership over them.

The national press was nationalized by the Press Organization Law No. 156 of 1960 adopted by President Nasser. This law transferred ownership of the four private publishing houses to the National Union, later to become the Arab Socialist Union. Ownership is now exercised by the Consultative Assembly, which is the upper house of Parliament. This was created in 1980

---

2   Moheb Zaki, *Civil Society and Democratization in Egypt, 1981–1994*, Konrad Adenauer Stiftung, The Ibn Khaldoun Centre, Cairo, 1995, p. 140.

by constitutional amendment to conduct studies and present proposals. Two-thirds of its members are elected and the President of the Republic appoints the other third.

The three main national dailies (*El Ahram*, *Al Akhbar* and *Al Gumhuriyya*) are controlled by the regime, as are numerous magazines (for example *Rose al-Youssef*, *Al Musawar* and *Akhir s'a*). They represent around 95 per cent of the market. Since they are government owned, they do not face any particular problems in their production. We shall see below, however, that they may nevertheless face different kinds of pressure regarding their content.

1.2 Party-affiliated newspapers

In March 1976 Sadat tackled the one-party political system of the Arab Socialist Union by establishing three inner-party platforms. The Political Parties Law No. 40 of July 1977 authorized the creation of new political parties and Article 15 allowed them to have their own press organ to publish material supporting their political views without having to apply for a licence.[3] This principle was later confirmed by Article 209 of the Constitution, as added in 1980, and Article 45 of Press Law No. 96 of 1996: "the freedom to publish newspapers shall be guaranteed for political parties and public and private legal entities, in accordance with the law".

Legally recognized political parties only are allowed to issue their own newspapers. Article 7 of the Political Parties Law of 1977, as amended, provides that a political party must have at least fifty members, including twenty-five workers or peasants. According to Article 4, it must fulfil different conditions to be recognized. It must, among other things, show that its programme differs substantially from that of any of the parties already existing; it must not be established on an ethnic, religious, class or racial basis; it must conform with the Constitution, the principles of Islamic law, the principles of the revolutions of 1952 and 1971, of national unity, social peace and the democratic socialist system, as well as with socialist benefits. Most of these conditions are vague enough to be interpreted with latitude.

The request for party status is submitted to a special committee, called the Committee of Party Affairs (*lagna shu'un al-ahzab al-siyasiyya*). It is headed by the Speaker of the Consultative Assembly and includes the Minister of Justice, the Minister of the Interior, the Minister of State for Parliamentary Affairs and three members chosen by the President of the Republic (Article 8). All of its members are therefore expected to be close to the ruling party. The rulings of the Committee can be appealed against before the first circuit of the Supreme Administrative Court, headed by the President of the State

---

3   According to Art. 18 of that law, however, this right is limited to parties that have at least ten representatives in the People's Assembly. This provision has not been implemented so far and all recognized parties have been allowed to issue a newspaper, no matter how many parliamentary seats they have. In June 2000, however, the publication of a local paper of the opposition *Al Ahrar* Party was stopped, on the basis of this provision.

Council and formed of five councillors, joined by five "public personalities (*shakhsiyyât 'amma*)" appointed by the President.

Fifteen political parties exist in Egypt. The Committee of Party Affairs recognized four of them at the end of the 1970s and each has its own publications. *Al Ahaly*, the newspaper of the leftist National Progressive Unionist Party (*al-Tagammu'*) started publishing in February 1978; *Al Ahrar*, from the Liberals, in November 1977 and *El Shaab* was issued by the Labour Party from May 1979. The ruling National Democratic Party started issuing its weekly *Mayu* in 1978. Some of those parties issue more than one newspaper. *Al Ahrar*, for instance, owns about twenty papers, and not all of them promote the principles of the party.

Since its creation, the Committee has turned down more than forty applications, the main reason for refusal being that the proposed programmes did not differ from those of parties already existing. All but one of the other existing parties have been recognized by the judiciary and, in particular, by the Supreme Administrative Court, which has granted permissions refused by the Committee. It has interpreted the law narrowly, especially the requirement that the new party have a platform distinct from existing parties: the fact that a party shares some positions with other parties is not a sufficient ground for rejecting its application.

The New *Wafd* reappeared in 1978 after having been granted recognition by the Committee of Party Affairs. A few months later it decided to dissolve in protest against Law No. 33 of May 1978 on the Protection of the Internal Front and Social Peace (*himayat al-jabha al-dakhiliyya wa al-salam al-ijtima'i*), which prohibited those who had held high positions before the anti-monarchy revolution of 1952 from participating in present political activities or from joining present political parties. In 1982 the party attempted to come back but the Committee rejected its application. It was finally recognized in 1983 thanks to a decision of the Supreme Administrative Court. However, senior members of the *Wafd* Party were still excluded from political activities by the Law on the Protection of the Internal Front. The Supreme Constitutional Court ruled Article 4 of that law unconstitutional in 1986.[4] In its ruling, the Court stressed that this provision had deprived a certain category of citizens of the right to join political parties and to exercise political activities, which violated the Constitution. The New *Wafd* started publishing its own daily, *El Wafd*, in 1984.

When Nasserists applied for the establishment of a Nasserist Party, their application was rejected by the Committee of Party Affairs, on the grounds that some of them had signed a statement opposing the 1979 peace treaty between Egypt and Israel. According to Article 4, paragraph 7, of Law No. 40 of 1977 on Political Parties, as amended, the Committee was entitled to turn down applications submitted to it for the creation of a political party if it was proven upon sound grounds that any of its founders or leaders had

---

4   HCC, 21 June 1986, Case No. 56/6th, *SCCDC*, vol. 3, p. 353. The whole law was repealed by Law No. 221 of 1994.

advocated, encouraged, instigated or advanced principles or practices inconsistent with the peace treaty between Egypt and Israel. The Supreme Constitutional Court declared this provision unconstitutional in 1988.[5] The Court noted that freedom of expression is the core of all political rights and that all features of a democratic regime rest on it. It is a means of addressing grievances to the government and of exercising effective popular control over its activities. The Court pointed out that the provision challenged had unequivocally violated the right to form political parties to which all citizens were entitled, in contradiction of Articles 5 (multi-partyism) and 47 (freedom of expression) of the Constitution.

In spite of this ruling of the Supreme Constitutional Court, the Nasserists were nevertheless denied recognition by the Committee, on the grounds that their programme was not sufficiently different from that of the *Tagammu'*. They challenged that decision before the Supreme Administrative Court, which granted recognition to the Arab Democratic Nasserist Party in May 1992. They started publishing *Al Araby*.

On 2 March 2000 and for the first time, the Committee of Party Affairs granted a licence to a political party, the National Concord (*al-Wifaq al-Qawmi*). That new party is led by a former free officer and most of the founding members are Nasserists and renegade members of the Labour Party. It is a pan-Arab political group that wishes to unite the Arab world against the danger of Zionism and globalization. According to its platform, Egypt should possess nuclear weapons in order to maintain peace in the region and deter others from using these weapons against it. It does not as yet issue a paper. Two weeks earlier the Committee had refused recognition to another Nasserist Party (Dignity). The Muslim Brothers have not been allowed to form a political party, due to their confessional basis, as this would contravene the Law on Political Parties. They have had to join other existing parties or form alliances with them in order to be able to participate in public life. The moderate Islamist-oriented *Wasat* has been trying for years to be granted recognition, so far with no success either.

An opposition paper can exist only as long as the party to which it belongs is recognized as such. If the political party disappears, the newspaper follows. This happened on 20 May 2000, when the mouthpiece of the Labour Party, *El Shaab*, was shut down by a decision of the Committee of Party Affairs to freeze the activities of the Labour Party. A struggle had broken out over leadership of the party. Two senior party members held simultaneously and separately what they each claimed to be a party general congress. After both congresses withdrew confidence from the team in charge, each of the two dissident members approached the Committee on Party Affairs to be recognized officially as the legitimate new head of the party. Instead of recognizing one of the factions, the Committee decided to suspend the Labour Party on the basis of Article 17 of the Political Parties law,[6] until the rivals settled

---

5 HCC, 7 May 1988, Case No. 44/7th, *SCCDC*, vol. 4, p. 98.
6 Art. 17, paragraph 3, empowers the Committee to freeze party activities and suspend the publication of party newspapers in the general interest if they deviate from the conditions laid down in Arts. 3 (the political parties shall increase the

their dispute over the leadership. All the activities of the party, including the publication of *El Shaab* and all other party publications, will be frozen until the crisis is resolved. The two dissident members said they were pleased with the Committee's decision.

Both also filed charges against the President of the party, Ibrahim Shukri, and the Secretary-General, 'Adil Husayn, claiming that they had dropped the party's socialist platform and turned it into a religious group by allowing the Muslim Brotherhood to infiltrate it, thus violating the Law on Political Parties which bans the formation of parties on religious grounds. They also accused them of having changed the party's original name of "Socialist Labour Party" to simply "Labour Party". The Committee decided to refer the case to the Socialist Prosecutor's office, on the basis of Article 17, paragraph 1, of the Law on Political Parties, and charged it with investigating the claims that the party had violated Article 4 by exceeding its original mandate and platform. The report of the Socialist Prosecutor will then be submitted to the Supreme Administrative Court (formed of the same five public persons mentioned in Article 8), which will decide whether to abolish the Labour Party or not.

The object of the resentment of the public authorities was probably not the party so much as its newspaper, *El Shaab*. After launching harsh attacks against members of the government (see below), the paper had started at the end of April 2000 a campaign against the Minister of Culture for authorizing the reprinting of *A Banquet for Seaweed* (*walima li a'shâb al-bahr*), a novel by the Syrian writer Haydar Haydar, in a popular fiction series published by the Ministry of Culture. The paper printed a series of inflammatory articles, accusing the book of blasphemy and harming religious morals. The campaign triggered demonstrations of hundreds of students of *Al Azhar* university in protest against the republication of the novel. The Islamic Research Centre of *Al-Azhar* also condemned the novel for blasphemy. Liberal intellectuals from the literary and artistic scene issued statements condemning the campaign. Most newspapers, especially those that were state owned, voiced their dissatisfaction with *El Shaab*'s methods. *Rose al-Youssef*, *Al Ahram* and *Akhbar al-Yum*, for instance, accused the Labour Party of practising cultural terrorism. Several political parties implied in their papers that the campaign was motivated by the party's desire to raise its popularity before the coming parliamentary elections.

This campaign and its consequences divided the press. Government-owned papers such as *Akhbar al-Yum* and *Al Gumhuriyya* applauded the decision to suspend *El Shaab*. So did the leftist *Al Ahaly*. Other opposition party papers such as *El Wafd*, *Al Ahrar* and *Al Araby* did not, probably from fear that the same decision might apply to them some day. An open war was declared between *Al Araby* and the *Al Gumhuriyya* board chairman, Samir Ragab. The Press Syndicate expressed its solidarity with the journalists and condemned the closing of the newspaper. It decided to file a case before the

---

cont.

    economic and social development of the nation and strengthen its unity) and 4 of the law.

Supreme Administrative Court to challenge the validity of the Committee's decision. The Syndicate, however, criticized *El Shaab* and its sensationalist style, stressing the fact that an irresponsible press and attacks on the freedom of individuals and society are the main factors that may lead to the destruction of freedom of the press. Human rights groups who had previously criticized *El Shaab* for its campaign also condemned the decision of the Committee. The leaders of the Labour Party announced that they would print *El Shaab* on the internet.

1.3 Independent press

Law No. 148 of 1980 on the Authority of the Press allowed private legal entities, meaning corporations and cooperatives, to issue newspapers. It was only in the 1990s, however, that independent newspapers appeared. The procedure for obtaining a licence is so long and the conditions so difficult that only half a dozen such newspapers exist.

Newspapers may not be formed without government permission, which is frequently denied. According to Article 46 of the 1996 Press Law, anyone who wishes to publish a newspaper must present a written notification (*ikhtar*) to the Higher Press Council. The notification must include specific information required by law, regarding the publisher and the newspaper. According to Article 13 of the Publications Law No. 20 of 1936, a written notification must also be presented to the governorate or the police department under whose jurisdiction the publication falls.

The Higher Press Council is a body chaired by the Speaker of the Consultative Assembly and composed, among others, of the board chairmen of the national press establishments and chief editors of the national and party papers, the Head of the Press Syndicate, as well as senior figures such as lawyers and press professors appointed by the President of the Republic (Article 68 of the 1996 Press Law). It was set up by Sadat in March 1975 to succeed to the Arab Socialist Union to control the press. Its existence was confirmed by Article 211 of the Constitution, as amended in 1980, which also entrusted this body with consolidating freedom of the press and its independence, and licensing journalists.

The "notification" mentioned in Article 46 is actually not just a notification, since the Higher Press Council may refuse to grant the approval. According to Article 47, the Higher Press Council must issue its decision concerning the notification for issuing a newspaper within a period not exceeding forty days from the date when the notification was submitted. Decisions refusing the issue of the paper have to be substantiated. If after forty days a decision has not been issued it is considered that there is no objection to the paper being issued. If the Council refuses to grant approval the parties concerned may contest the decision before the Court of Administrative Justice in the thirty days following the decision. Until 1996 the decision was appealed against before the Court of Values, half of the members of which were "public persons" appointed by the President of the Republic.

This modification may lead to more independent newspapers being recognized, following a court decision.

According to Article 2 of the 1996 Press Law, the law applies to publications issued "periodically" (*dawriyyatan*) only. To escape its provisions and the Council's approval, some bodies started issuing publications, mainly cultural, on a irregular basis and printed them at their own expense, labelling them "non-periodicals".

In order to publish a newspaper, private legal entities must also fulfil other conditions. According to Article 52 of the 1996 Press Law, they must assume the form of a joint stock company or cooperative society. Economic restrictions have been enacted: the nominal shares must be owned by Egyptians only and the paid up capital of the company must not be less than E£1,000,000 for a daily newspaper and E£250,000 for a weekly. The capital must be deposited in full with an Egyptian bank before a paper is issued. The ownership share of one person and his family must not exceed 10 per cent of the capital.

The provisions of the Law on Companies No. 159 of 1981 regulate the procedure for setting up such a company. Article 17 of that law was amended by the People's Assembly in January 1998 and now requires that applications for establishing media joint stock companies for publication be approved by the Cabinet before they can be set up. The Press Syndicate expressed vehement opposition to this amendment. In January 2000 the State Council decided to challenge the constitutionality of this provision before the Supreme Constitutional Court, arguing that it was a breach of the principle of equality between companies, in violation of Article 40 of the Constitution.

Apart from obtaining a licence from the Higher Press Council and having the required capital, the publishers must also be informally cleared by all Egyptian major security and intelligence agencies. All this may explain why only seven independent newspapers (such as *Al Usbu'* or *Al Naba*) have been allowed so far.

An independent newspaper may lose its licence if it does not appear regularly (Article 48 of the 1996 Press Law). According to Article 51, if any change of circumstances occurs after the permission to publish has been given, the Higher Press Council must be notified in writing at least fifteen days before the change takes place, except when the change has taken place unexpectedly, in which case it must be notified within at most eight days from the date of its occurrence. The authorities normally do not adopt a strict interpretation of these provisions. However, they applied them in February 1999 to withdraw the licence given to the weekly *Sut al-Umma*. This decision was, however, struck down by the Supreme Administrative Court in December 1999.

1.4 Foreign-licensed publications

To circumvent the harsh restrictions on obtaining a local press licence, over 200 Egyptian periodicals[7] have bought permits abroad, most commonly in

---

[7]   While Egyptian regular publications comprise altogether around thirty titles.

Cyprus, Greece or Lebanon, and are distributed in Egypt as foreign publications. This is a way for many publishers to bypass government bureaucracy and circumvent licensing regulations. Those papers consist of the vast majority of English (such as *Egypt Today, Middle East Times, Cairo Times*) and many Arabic-language publications in Egypt. Most of them are magazines covering topics such as sports, culture, computers, fashion, celebrities or business. Some of them, however, also deal with political issues, like the late *Al Dustur*. They have to pass a censor before being distributed in Egypt.

Legally registered abroad, most of them are, however, owned and run by Egyptians, printed and distributed in Egypt. They may be printed abroad, but most of them prefer to avoid air flights and print in Egyptian tax-free zones where two printers have set up industries. They may also print at a lower cost but at lower quality with the public sector presses like *Al Ahram* and *Al Akhbar*. They have to obtain a licence from the Ministry of Information to be printed in Egypt, and this must be renewed periodically and can be withdrawn.

On 31 March 1998 the General Authority of Investment and Free Zones released an order banning the printing of newspapers and magazines of any kind in any language in the free trade zones in Egypt, accusing the printing houses of having violated the law. About sixty publications were forced to print outside Egypt and transport their copies, at an additional shipping cost. The printing houses, whose business was severely hurt, attacked the decree before the State Council. On 2 August 1999 the State Council ruled that the printing houses had not violated the law and that the licences that had allowed them to operate for twenty-five years were still valid. In anticipation of that ruling, the government had already partially rescinded the ban on 21 May 1999, authorizing printers to resume printing of publications of a specific technical and scientific nature.

The licence to print in Egypt may also be withdrawn, as happened with *Al Dustur*. This political and social weekly, set up in December 1995, was run by prominent political figures, mainly Wafdists and leftists. Opening up debates and taking a more independent editorial line, it quickly achieved sales of over 100,000. It was printed in the *Al Ahram* printing house in Cairo until February 1998, when its permit to print in Egypt was withdrawn by the Ministry of Information. The Ministry accused *Al Dustur* of having printed a statement allegedly received from the *Gama'a al-Islamiyya*, which carried a death threat against three leading Coptic businessmen. The *Gama'a* accused them of trying to sabotage Egypt's economy and of working for the CIA. The Minister of Information justified the sanction as necessary to control the spread of terrorist doctrine and protect the Egyptian economy. The paper protested against this measure, arguing that the issue had been submitted to the censor before printing, and that he had not objected to its publication. *Al Dustur* applied for a new printing licence, tried to print the paper in the free zone, to change its name, to publish through a party newspaper, and to take legal action against the withdrawal of its licence, but all with no success, and the paper disappeared.[8]

---

8   For an analysis of *Al Dustur*'s crisis, see Dina al-Khawaga, "Sisyphe ou les avatars

If limitation measures can be taken against the press through control of its production and distribution process in Egypt, different kinds of direct or indirect censorship measures may also be undertaken. Without legally revoking their right to publish or stopping them from appearing, the government can influence the contents of a newspaper in several ways.

2   FREEDOM OF THE PRESS AND THE CONTENTS OF THE NEWSPAPER

Censorship of domestic-licensed publications is forbidden, although this is not the case with foreign-licensed publications. In addition, different forms of indirect censorship exist and press restrictions can be exercised on both categories of newspapers. Journalists may also be charged with publication offences.

2.1   Egyptian publications

Article 48, paragraph 1, of the Egyptian Constitution of 1971 prohibits censorship: "Freedom of the press, printing, publication and mass media is guaranteed. Censorship on newspapers is forbidden as well as notifying, suspending or cancelling a newspaper by administrative means." Article 208 of the Constitution reaffirms that principle, as do Articles 4 and 5 of the 1996 Press Law. Limits to freedom of speech can, however, be defined by many factors other than censorship regulations.

Prior censorship on the press was lifted by Sadat in February 1974. Until then a resident censor, an official of the Ministry of Information, sat in each newspaper office, and all copies were submitted to him before publication. In the national papers, a responsible chief editor, who himself takes the decisions on the basis of his own judgement, has replaced the censor. Editors practise self-censorship from fear of government reprisal. This self-censorship may be worse than direct government censorship. Formal censorship may indeed be less tough than the informal variety: editors may be over-cautious and wrong in their guessing of what the government wants or does not want. As Napoli recalls: "One veteran Egyptian journalist observed that things were better when there was a real censor around to argue with. Now, she said, 'the censors are inside their heads'."[9]

In practice, however, journalists can openly express their views on a wide variety of issues without fear of retribution. The press can publish a wide range of information and criticize high official persons. Even governmental publications have managed over the years to gain independence in their operation and sometimes publish vigorous criticism of the government. Party

---

cont.

du nouveau journalisme égyptien", *Egypte-Monde arabe*, no. 3, new series, 2000 (to be published).

[9]   James Napoli "Egyptian sleight of hands", *Index on Censorship*, vol. 21, no. 2, 1992, p. 22.

newspapers frequently publish tough criticisms of government policies and attacks on government figures accused of corruption and misappropriation of public funds. The authorities have largely refrained from curtailing political expression. Journalists, however, normally follow the regime's basic policy line and avoid certain sensitive or controversial issues. In particular, they are cautious in handling domestic issues and know they have to be sensitive to the prevailing political system.

Editors-in-chief and heads of boards of directors are appointed and dismissed by the Consultative Assembly and the presidency still informally approves appointments and dismissals. Since the Consultative Council is dominated by the ruling party, it is expected that appointees will be chosen on the basis of their loyalty. Article 64 of the 1996 Press Law provides that the Consultative Council must also appoint six of the twelve other board members of each national press establishment.

The government can exercise pressure on the government-appointed editors-in-chief. In March 1998, for instance, 'Adil Hammuda, deputy editor of the government-owned weekly *Rose al-Youssef*, was transferred to a desk job at *Al Ahram*, after *Rose al-Youssef* published the story of the statement of the *Gama'a al-Islamiyya* against the Coptic businessmen. Although it is state owned, the sensationalist tone of that paper has often embarrassed the government. One month later it was the turn of the editor-in-chief of the newspaper *Mahmoud Tohami* to be replaced.

As for the party press, it has to face other kinds of influence, even though no direct censorship is allowed here either. With the exception of *El Wafd*, all party newspapers have a small circulation. The street sales and advertising revenues of those papers are low and most of them are in a permanent financial crisis. In May 2000, for instance, the Nasserist Party announced that, due to the deep financial crisis it was facing, it had to temporarily suspend publication of the daily edition of its mouthpiece, *Al Araby*. The weekly edition would, however, continue to be published. Party newspapers depend very much on the state for functioning, be it for subventions, advertisements from public sector companies, low postage rates, rescheduling of debts or delay in the payment of taxes. This allows the state to make use of their weak economic base.

Another kind of pressure can be used against party papers: they are printed in state-owned printing houses which may suddenly raise their prices, run out of paper or face unexpected printing and distribution problems. Four publishing houses share the market: *Al Ahram, Dar al-Hilal, Dar Akhbar al-Yum* and *Dar al-Gumhuriyya*. These houses were transferred in 1960 from private to public ownership. The opposition press is also very much dependent upon government institutions to circulate their newspapers.

The same kinds of pressure can also be exercised on independent newspapers since they too are printed in the state-owned printing houses and are distributed by them. Other kinds of covert censorship can also be exercised by the state, essentially through the different stages of their establishment process, as we saw above.

If censorship is forbidden by Article 49, paragraph 1, of the Constitution,

Article 49, paragraph 2, allows a limited censorship to be imposed on newspapers in a state of emergency or in time of war, in matters related to public safety or for the purposes of national security, in accordance with the law. In February 2000 the state of emergency, in force since 6 October 1981, was renewed for three more years. Article 3 of the 1958 emergency law gives the state wide powers to censor, seize, confiscate and suspend publications and to close printing houses. Even though the government has not made use of this provision, this does not mean that it will never be used in the future.

2.2   On foreign publications

Foreign-licensed publications have to pass through the Office of the Censor for Foreign Publications of the Ministry of Information before they are distributed in the country. The censor reviews each issue before allowing it to be distributed and can block it from entering the country.

Articles 9, 10, 21 and 22 of the Law on Publications No. 20 of 1936, as amended, allow the banning of foreign publications from entering the country in order to maintain public order and protect the country from corruption of morals or attacks on religion which could threaten social peace. Article 30 allows the publication to be confiscated if these provisions are violated.

Publications containing material not permitted by the censor will not be allowed circulation in Egypt. Publishers have therefore to choose between self-censorship and running the risk of losing all copies of one issue. Most papers printed in Egypt prefer to censor themselves rather than risk losing a whole issue. They submit a proof to the censor prior to its printing and remove the article, paragraph or sentence that he does not like. Some of them, like the *Middle East Times*, leave a blank space in its place, without being allowed, however, to mention in the space the reason why it is there.[10] After the ban of March 1998 on printing in free zones, publications had to be printed abroad and could only be reviewed by the censor when they entered the country.

According to the *Middle East Times*,[11] reasons for censorship may range from report on human rights abuses to criticism of the President or his family, of the military; pointing out the ill-treatment of Egyptians in "friendly" Arab countries, especially in Saudi Arabia; discussing modern, unorthodox interpretations of Islam or reporting on discrimination against Coptic Christians.

2.3   Press offences

Freedom of the press, like any other freedom, may be misused and abused and should therefore be tempered by responsibility. The Penal Code, since

---

[10]   The censored articles are, however, available on the web site of this paper, accessible even from Egypt.
[11]   See their web site.

its very inception in 1936 and reproducing provisions already included in the National Penal Code of 1883 and in the French Penal Code, contains provisions criminalizing publication offences and penalizing them by imprisonment and fines. A special chapter deals with offences committed by newspapers and other media that damage public interest (Articles 171–201). Another lists offences committed against individuals (Articles 302–310). This criminal responsibility for crimes committed through newspapers is an underlying threat that constantly menaces journalists.

Press Law No. 93 of 1995 increased jail and fine penalties for press offences. It imposed new restrictions on freedom of opinion and expression by widening the scope of incrimination and substantially increasing the penalties specified. It allowed for preventive detention of journalists accused of publication offences: prosecutors could put them into custody while they were still under investigation. It also repealed "good faith" as a basis for acquittal in defamation crimes against public officials. The law drew vehement opposition from the journalists working for national and non-national newspapers alike. A stiff protest campaign was centralized and led by the Press Syndicate, to which all journalists have to be affiliated. They protested against infringements of freedom of expression and attempts to muzzle them, expressing fear that this might lead to a reversal of the fragile democratic movement. Opposition political parties and non-governmental agencies supported them. Some of them saw a link between this measure and the then forthcoming parliamentary elections, since many newspapers had in their columns been accusing elected members of the leading party of corruption and undemocratic behaviour.

The 1995 Press Law was finally repealed by Law No. 95 of 16 June 1996, which again amended the Penal Code, and Press Law No. 96 of 18 June 1996, which replaced the 1980 Press Law as amended in 1995. This was considered a great victory for civil society against state power. The 1996 Press Law abolished (except for an attack against the President of the Republic) the provision of the 1995 law that had made preventive detention possible for journalists accused of offences involving freedom of expression. However, not all the other contested provisions of the 1995 Press Law were rescinded. The new law maintained basically the same limits but reduced fines. It also retained the imprisonment penalty for publication offences, but for shorter terms.

Prohibited offences damaging public interest include incitement to commit a felony or misdemeanour (Articles 171, 172 and 177); expressing hatred or contempt of a particular group of people (Article 176); encouraging the overthrow of the government or the Constitution (Article 174); disobeying or misrepresenting the law (Article 177); publishing false reports (Article 188); inciting soldiers to disobedience (Article 175); making offensive remarks about the President of the Republic (Article 179) or the head of a foreign country (Article 181) or any official representative of a foreign country in Egypt (Article 182); violating public morality (Article 178); influencing judges, prosecutors, witnesses or public opinion (Article 187); reporting confidential sessions or restricted court cases (Articles 189 and 193) or dishonestly reporting public sessions (Article 191); insulting Parliament, the army, the courts, the authorities or public agencies (Article 184); compromising the reputation of a judge in relation to a court case (Article 186) or libel (Article 185). Fines and/or prison sentences may be imposed in all those cases. As to offences damaging individuals, what is meant is mainly libel (Article 306), defamation (Articles 302 and 303) or invasion of privacy (Article 308).

These broad and elastic restrictions on freedom of expression give the authorities excessive powers of interpretation, which can be used to limit the exercise of this right. More and more journalists have been charged with libel and put in prison on the basis of Article 185 of the Penal Code which penalizes anyone who uses abusive language against a public official or representative. Under the current press law, libel is punishable by a maximum one-year prison sentence and/or a fine of E£5,000 to E£10,000. Defamation is defined by Article 302 of the Penal Code as the attribution to someone of actions which would, if true, incur the criminal punishment of the person to whom they were ascribed, or arouse the contempt of fellow citizens. Paragraph 2 of the same article adds that criticism of the work of a public official or representative is within the bounds of law, provided it is bona fide and does not exceed the scope of the person's professional duties. In that case, the author of the crime of defamation has the right to prove the truth of all his allegations. That latter exception permits criticism of those charged with a civic responsibility, in order to protect the public interest. Article 303 punishes defamation by a maximum one-year prison sentence and a fine ranging between E£2,500 and E£7,500. If the target of the offence is a public official, the maximum penalty is two years in jail and/or a fine of E£5,000 to E£10,000. That article offers the journalist the right to defend himself by proving the truth of the allegations. It is, however, a peculiarity of press offences that the accused journalists have to defend themselves. The basic principle of criminal law, indeed, is that an accused person is presumed innocent until proven guilty and that the onus of proof lies with the prosecution. In press offences the burden is on the journalist to exonerate himself by proving his allegations.

The fact that several journalists have been prosecuted for abuse of freedom of the press could mean that the press is freer, in practice, than it used to be: "Very few journalists during Nasser's era were arrested since the press then was tightly controlled and was not permitted to criticize the regime. In contrast, journalists now may become entangled with the law, yet the press is immeasurably freer".[12] It may also reflect the problems journalists face in

---

[12]   Zaki, *Civil Society and Democratization in Egypt*, p. 73. For an analysis of the press under Nasser and Sadat, see Sonia Dabous, "Nasser and the Egyptian press", in Charles Tripp (ed.), *Contemporary Egypt through Egyptian Eyes: Essays in Honour of P.J. Vatikiotis*, London, Routledge, 1993, pp. 100–121; Marina Stagh, *The Limits of Freedom of Speech. Prose Literature and Prose Writers in Egypt under Nasser and Sadat*, Acta Universitatis Stockholmiensis, Stockholm Oriental Studies 14, Stockholm, 1993; M.K. Nasser, *Egyptian Mass Media under Nasser and Sadat*, Journalism Monographs 124, Association for Education in Journalism and Mass Communication, 1990. For a detailed analysis until 1985, see Soliman

getting access to sources of information. If national papers benefit from their closed links with the government departments to get news, party newspapers are often denied access to official information, which may entail unreliable reporting based on rumour and speculation.

Most journalists charged with defamation work for party papers. In April 2000, the editor-in-chief and four journalists of the opposition *Al Ahrar* organ of the Liberal Party were sentenced to six months in prison following a press campaign again the chairman of Egyptair criticizing him for misman-agement and labour unrest. 'Amr Nasif, a journalist, was condemned to three months imprisonment on 28 May 1998 for publishing a libellous article against Egyptian writer and member of the Consultative Assembly, Tharwat Abaza in *Al Ahrar*.

There is a trend, however, towards journalists who go to prison not staying there for too long. In many cases the Court of Cassation sets journalists free and orders a retrial. This was the case with Gamal Fahmî Husayn, of the Nasserist daily *Al Araby*, who had been convicted of slandering the same Tharwat Abaza. In August 1998, the Court of Cassation quashed the sentence of six months' imprisonment on the grounds that the court procedures which led to the conviction were flawed and ordered a retrial by another court. The journalist had, however, already spent five months in jail.

A similar ruling was taken in the libel lawsuit initiated by the former Minister of the Interior Hasan al-Alfi against *El Shaab*. The newspaper had accused him in 1997 of corruption and misuse of power and alleged that his family was using his influence to acquire real estate illegally. While the newspaper argued that its campaign was intended to expose corruption in the interest of the Egyptian people, Alfi's lawyers accused it of having launched a campaign to sabotage the fight against terrorism. Magdi Husayn, editor-in-chief, and cartoonist Muhammad Hilal were sentenced to one-year imprisonment in February 1998 for libel. The Court of Cassation invalidated that sentence and ordered a retrial after the two had spent four months in prison. An out-of-court settlement was finally reached between Alfi and *El Shaab* in August 1998, after the former had been sacked from his post following the Luxor massacre of November 1997. Alfi and his son dropped all libel charges against the journalists.

According to Article 199 of the Penal Code, if an offence is committed through publication and the newspaper continues to publish material similar to that under investigation, the court may, following a request by the Public Prosecutor, order the suspension of the newspaper for a maximum of three issues. This provision has been applied in many cases. In September 1997, for instance, the Attorney-General obtained a court ruling to ban the publica-tion for three consecutive issues of *El Shaqb* for violating the press blackout in the Alfi case. A small note on the front page of the paper had stated that following the opening of the investigation, they would no longer publish documents, "although they had many more". The day after the court's

---

cont.

Salem, *Azmat huriyyat al-sahâfa fi misr, 1945–1985* [*The Press Crisis in Egypt, 1945–1985*], Dar al-Nashr li-l-gama'at al-masriyya, 1995.

decision, the Liberal daily *Al Ahrar* announced that it was opening its pages to its colleagues from *El Shaab*, and handed over control of a third of its front page and all page three to that newspaper in a show of solidarity. The paper even allowed *El Shaab* to print in its own colour and use its own fonts. A similar agreement was made with *Al Haqiqa*, in a clear snub to the authorities.

The Court of Cassation set journalists free in another libel lawsuit against *El Shaab*. In December 1998 the paper launched a fierce campaign against the Deputy Prime Minister, Secretary-General of the ruling National Democratic Party (NDP) and Minister of Agriculture, Yusif Wali. In issue after issue *El Shaab* levelled political and economic accusations against Wali and his policy of normalization of relations with Israel. The paper accused him of high treason and of conspiring with the "Zionists" to ruin Egypt's agricultural sector. It alleged that he was working on behalf of the "Israeli enemy" against Egypt's interests, was cooperating with the intelligence service of a foreign country to harm Egypt's economy and providing a foreign country with secret information and documents. It also claimed that Wali commissioned Israeli companies and Mossad to establish a computer network for the Agriculture Ministry and that Egypt's agricultural policy was drawn up by an American committee dominated by Jews. In addition, he encouraged Jewish settlements in Fayoum and organized a large number of visits by young members of the NDP to Israeli kibbutzim. On the economic side, he was conspiring with the "Zionists" to destroy Egypt's agricultural sector and serve Israeli interests. He was responsible for a rise in the number of cancer cases and other diseases because he imported substandard crops and contaminated seeds from Israel. On the personal side, the newspaper accused him of being of Jewish origin.

The campaign was largely ignored by other papers who did not take the allegations seriously, unlike what happened in the Alfi case, where even the national press had reported the accusations as credible and demanded that the Minister respond. The Press Syndicate, fearing that the campaign might tarnish the reputation and quality of the press, warned *El Shaab* that its campaign was violating professional ethics and code of conduct; the press should not go too far and kill democracy by abusing it. The strategy of the newspaper was clearly to have the minister testify before the courts and turn the proceeding into a political trial where the government's policy of normalization with Israel would be questioned. The journalists were calling for a "popular trial" of the government's policy through the judiciary. They were making the courts a forum for the exercise of the political rights of the people, a way for the sovereign to exercise control over its representatives.

For about four months Wali ignored the campaign and refused to confirm or deny the allegations. On 1 April 1999, he finally filed a libel complaint[13] against *El Shaab*'s editor-in-chief, Magdi Husayn, Secretary-General of the Labour Party 'Adil Husayn, journalist Salah Bedeiwi and a cartoonist, 'Isam

---

[13] According to Art. 3 of the Code of criminal procedure, only the victim of an offence committed by a newspaper can file a complaint.

Hanafi, accusing them of libel and defamation. Wali chose Numan Gum'a, deputy chairman of the opposition liberal Wafd Party, to defend his interests, probably to show that some key opposition figures were opposed to *El Shaab*'s campaign. Three other Wafdist lawyers, however, decided to join forces with *El Shaab*'s defence attorneys. The Public Prosecutor decided to prosecute the case and referred the complaint to a criminal court. The Press Syndicate provided the accused with legal support.

On 14 August 1999 the South Cairo Criminal Court claimed that the defence had failed to prove any of the accusations levelled against Wali and convicted Magdi Husayn, Salah Bedeiwi and 'Isam Hanafi of libel and defamation and sentenced them to the maximum penalty for slandering government officials: two years imprisonment and a fine of E£20,000 each for slandering Yusif Wali. 'Adil Husayn was fined E£20,000 for his participation in the campaign against Wali. The journalists had failed in their strategy of summoning Wali as a key witness.

The journalists decided to challenge the sentence. On 5 December 1999 the Court of Cassation judged that the journalists had not been given adequate opportunity to defend themselves because the criminal court had refused to summon Wali to testify as a witness.[14] The Court annulled the sentences on the grounds of this procedural error. A new trial began before another circuit of the Cairo Criminal Court. Wali agreed to testify in a closed session. On 1 April 2000, the court handed down imprisonment sentences for libelling and slandering Yusif Wali. Magdi Husayn and Salah Bedeiwi were sentenced to two years' imprisonment and fined E£20,000 each. 'Isam Hanafi was sentenced to one-year imprisonment and fined E£20,000 and 'Adil Husayn was fined to E£20,000. The three journalists were imprisoned again shortly after the sentences were handled down. They again appealed against the sentences to the Court of Cassation. At that stage, the Court of Cassation will judge on the merits of the case.[15]

Publication crimes present a procedural particularity regarding the competent court to hear the case. According to Articles 215 and 216 of the Code of Criminal Procedure, if the victim is an individual, the case will be heard by the court of misdemeanours, which is composed of a sole judge. If the offence damages the public interest, however, the case will be assigned to the criminal court, made up of a three-judge panel. This disregard for general principles of criminal law – which normally make the jurisdiction of a court depend on the kind of crime committed: felony, misdemeanour or petty offence – was probably intended to guarantee a proper hearing to the public official victim of defamation.[16] However, whereas a decision by the court of

---

[14] From the very beginning of the trial, *El Shaab*'s lawyers had submitted many requests to the criminal court to hear Wali's testimony, even walking out of the trial the last day of the hearings to protest against the court's refusal.

[15] For an analysis of this case, see Nathalie Bernard-Maugiron and Gamal Abdel Nasser Ibrahim, "Pouvoir de la censure ou censure du pouvoir? L'affaire Yusif Wali c. al-Sha'b", *Egypte-Monde arabe*, no. 3, new series, 2000 (to be published).

[16] On the origins of this competence of the criminal courts and a parallel with the French legal system, see "Presse, diffamation et justice. Le mémoire de Yahya

misdemeanours can be appealed against, there is no court of appeal for the criminal court. At the end of 1999, a criminal court authorized a litigant to challenge the constitutionality of these provisions before the Supreme Constitutional Court, which has not yet ruled on the matter.

The Supreme Constitutional Court has struck down provisions that directly or indirectly threaten freedom of the press. In 1993[17] the Court declared unconstitutional Article 123(2) of the Code of Criminal Procedure that governed the production of evidences in case of defamation against a public officer or representative, in application of Article 302 of the Penal Code. The accused was required to submit to the investigator any evidence of the facts ascribed when he was first called for questioning, or, at most, in the five days following this date. If he did not comply with the time period specified, his right to submit evidence in his defence lapsed. The Supreme Constitutional Court found this provision unconstitutional, on the grounds that it violated freedom of speech and expression and deprived the accused of the right to a defence and to be presumed innocent. The five-day deadline for submission of a statement of proof was such a severe restriction on the right to provide evidence that it effectively cancelled the exercise of that right. Whenever public officials refrain from properly fulfilling their duties and thus betray the electorate's faith in them, it is the right and duty of every citizen to hold them responsible, added the Court. The public interest requires the disclosure of any relevant information that would reveal their incompetence in conducting the responsibilities entrusted to them. The exercise of these rights enables the government to be held democratically accountable by the citizens and obliges it to be subject to popular control, however severe the criticism.

Article 15(2) of Law No. 40 of 1977 on Political Parties, as amended in 1979, provided that the president of a political party should be jointly responsible with the editor-in-chief of the party's newspaper for all material published within it. The Supreme Constitutional Court held this article unconstitutional in 1995,[18] on the basis of the violation of the presumption of innocence and of the right to defence. The Court added that this presumption of guilt would force a party president to devote his time to reviewing all published articles and thus prevent him from fulfilling his political functions.

The Supreme Constitutional Court also declared unconstitutional Article 195 of the Penal Code which attributed criminal liability to the editor-in-chief for offences committed by his newspaper, in addition to the author of the offending article. Several editors-in-chief had been sentenced to jail and/or fine on the basis of this provision. The constitutional judge pointed out that the imposition of vicarious criminal liability on individuals in the realm of publication had the potential to inhibit free expression and a free press,

---

cont.
    al-Rifa'i dans l'affaire al-Alfi contre Magdi Husayn", *Egypte-Monde arabe*, no. 34, 1998, p. 251–262.
[17] HCC, 6 February 1993, Case No. 37/11th, *SCCDC*, vol. 5, part 2, p. 203.
[18] HCC, 3 July 1995, Case No. 25/16th, *SCCDC*, vol. 7, p. 45.

two freedoms vital to democracy. The Supreme Constitutional Court found this provision unconstitutional on grounds similar to those used in the political party president case.[19]

3 CONCLUSION: THE POLITICAL ROLE OF THE THIRD AND FOURTH ESTATES

Press and courts in Egypt participate very actively in politics. They are two of the few fora where the political opposition can express its opinions, contest and mobilize. If plurality and a multi-party structure are admitted in Egypt, no alternative or sharing of power can be expected to take place through the electoral process. Political efficiency does not inhere in the channels normally set up for this purpose: political parties and electoral consultations. Since 1952 no parliamentary or presidential election has ever led to a change of majority and no party can hope to win power through elections.[20] Once elected, people's representatives have little effective power. Because of the overwhelming majority in the People's Assembly of the ruling NDP, which holds more than 94 per cent of the seats, government-proposed Bills are always passed, without amendment and without real debate on their merits or a chance for the marginalized deputies of the opposition to express their views. The opposition has no chance either to see one of its own laws passed, to question and check the executive on its policies or to bring a motion of non-confidence in the government to a vote. The NDP also dominates all the other centres of power. The opposition parties have therefore been marginalized and publishing a newspaper is often the only activity a party carries out.[21] Individuals and other social forces deprived of legal and/or political representation have looked for other arenas to express themselves.

Press debates in Egypt may be considered as a substitute for political action itself, since those debates cannot take place where they would normally: inside Parliament. If the opposition press can express itself, the government usually ignores the attacks and publishes denunciations. It very rarely replies on the merits of what is published. There is therefore no real dialogue: the opposition accuses and the majority does not reply. This attitude of marginalization is of course detrimental to the role that the press and the opposition should play in a democratic country.

The judiciary has become a site of political struggle between the power

---

[19] HCC, 1 February 1997, No. 59/18e, Official Gazette, no. 7 bis, 13 February 1997, p. 58. On those two last cases, see Adel Omar Sherif, "The Supreme Constitutional Court of Egypt and vicarious criminal liability", in Eugene Cotran and Adel Omar Sherif (eds.), *The Role of the Judiciary in the Protection of Human Rights*, The Hague, Kluwer Law International, 1997, CIMEL Book Series 5, pp. 69–76.

[20] For an analysis of the last parliamentary elections, see Sandrine Gamblin (ed.), *Contours et détours du politique en Égypte. Les élections législatives de 1995*, Paris, L'Harmattan, 1997.

[21] Alain Roussillon, *L'Egypte et l'Algérie au péril de la libéralisation*, Cairo, Dossiers du CEDEJ, 1996, p. 156.

and its opposition, whether the latter is calling upon religious values[22] or public liberties. In a state that does not allow open political debate, the courts have become a venue for political expression and play a role of arbiter between the state and various groups. As Nathan Brown pointed out:

Courts and legal systems have been the focus of intense political struggles in the Arab world, in some locations for over a century. Legal issues are, as everywhere, technical and arcane at times, but just as often they are closely connected to the definition and operation of political power and political community.[23]

The judiciary assumes a strong role in Egyptian politics. Judges have a reputation for integrity and vocational commitment to their profession and one of the main requests of opposition parties has always been that judges supervise the electoral process to guarantee its integrity.

The judicial branch has helped to defend freedom of the press and to bring checks and balances into the political system. It has on many occasions stood by the press to reverse or redress abuses imposed on it. It has also increased its own power by creating allies in the press and civil society in general. Lower courts cannot be blamed for enforcing the law and jailing journalists. But higher courts, granted more power, question the legitimacy of the law itself. Their rulings have usually been enforced, except for those given by exceptional courts such as those dealing with security and the military. This process has also legitimized the regime, by calling upon the rule of law and answering criticism through legal means.

The opposition has used two other important fields to influence the government's decision-making process: non-governmental organizations and syndicates. In these two cases as well, the judiciary has played a crucial role in the defence of public freedoms. By a ruling of 3 June 2000, the Supreme Constitutional Court declared unconstitutional, on procedural grounds, the Law on Non-Governmental Organizations that had been adopted a year before and which they had harshly contested. And the judiciary also played an active role in having the custody of the Lawyers' Syndicate released and allowing the organization of board elections on 1 July 2000. Professional syndicates have also been politicized and have become a political arena, debating and expressing political views in support or opposition of the government policy. Elections to their boards have become political events

---

22 See Baudouin Dupret and Jean-Noël Ferrié, "For intérieur et ordre public. Ou comment la problématique de l'Aufklärung peut permettre de décrire un débat égyptien", in G. Boëtsch, B. Dupret and J.-N. Ferrié (eds.), *Droits et sociétés dans le monde arabe et musulman. Perspectives socio-anthropologiques*, PUAM, 1997, pp. 193–215 and Nathalie Bernard-Maugiron, "Legal pluralism and the closure of the legal field: the *al-Muhajir* case", in Baudouin Dupret, Maurits Berger and Laila al-Zwaini (eds.), *Legal Pluralism in the Arab World*, The Hague, Kluwer Law International, 1999, pp. 173–189.
23 Nathan Brown, *The Rule of Law in the Arab World: Courts in Egypt and the Gulf*, Cambridge University Press, 1997, p. xi.

and are considered by many observers as the only elections not subject to fraud, despite allegations of informal deals. These are also a place where political groups that have been refused recognition as political parties can exercise political activities. They are also allowed to issue newspapers.

Islam and Constitutional Development in Pakistan

*Martin Lau**

1 INTRODUCTION

The purpose this article is the exploration of the Islamicization of Pakistan's legal system. The focus will, however, not be on the introduction of Islamic laws during and following Zia-ul-Haq's martial law, but the role of Islamic law in the constitutional development of Pakistan. The central hypothesis of this article is that the Islamicization of laws in Pakistan has been a primarily a judge-led process. It will be argued that the role of judges in the Islamiciza-tion of the legal system has been largely obscured by the more visible manifestations of Islamicization, namely the promulgation of the infamous Hudood Ordinances and other isolated pieces of Islamic legislation such as, for instance, the Shariat Application Act 1991.

As will be seen, the judicial appropriation of Islamic law and its integration into the vocabulary of courts was a conscious process aimed not only at the fulfilment of a general desire to indigenize and Islamicize the legal system after the end of colonial rule but was also a way of enhancing judicial power and independence. The Islamicization of law, perhaps ironically, not only preceded Zia-ul Haq's regime but was actually used to challenge him.

The judge-led Islamicization of Pakistan's legal system has continued until the present. It is no longer confined to a few discrete areas of law but has become an integral part of the legal discourse being relied on in the context of a wide range of issues from the permissibility to erect high-rise buildings in Karachi to the dismissal of a Prime Minister under Article 58(2)(b) of the 1973 Constitution or the imposition of martial law on 12 October 1999.

---

* Barrister and Lecturer in Law at the School of Oriental and African Studies, University of London.

44

2 ISLAMICIZATION OF LAWS: THE CONSTITUTIONAL FRAMEWORK

Attempts to introduce Islamic norms into a legal system can take two basic forms. There can either be a complete legal revolution, i.e. a complete removal of the old legal order and its replacement with an Islamic legal system. Examples for this type of Islamicization are rare,[1] not only because the potential chaos caused by a prolonged period of legal uncertainty makes such an endeavour too daunting a task but also because of the difficulties inherent in formulating a complete system of Islamic law that can serve as an adequate substitute for the old secular legal system. More usually, as has been the case in Pakistan, policies to Islamicize a legal system are based on the introduction of institutional and legal mechanisms which allow for a gradual and controlled introduction of Islamic law. In theory an institutionalized Islamicization provides for a gradual transformation of the legal system ensuring that political, moral and legal ideals of Islamic law can be realized within the framework of an existing secular legal system. Pakistan's experiments with Islamic law and, more specifically, with the creation of an Islamic state, have been marred by controversy since the creation of Pakistan as an independent state itself. Calls for the wholesale replacement of the inherited colonial system have been made frequently, although its proponents have never managed to muster enough support to carry out this plan.[2]

As a result of this distinct lack of commitment to radical Islamicization Pakistan's numerous constitutions have always contained provisions which would provide a mechanisms for a gradual transformation of the legal system while at the same time preserving the inherited laws of either British India, or, since independence, the legal system as it stood prior to the imposition of the various martial laws.[3] Until the creation of the Federal Shariat Court

---

[1] This appears to be the case in the areas of Afghanistan controlled and administered by the Taliban.

[2] See Afzal Iqbal, *Islamization of Laws in Pakistan*, Vanguard Publishers, Lahore, 1986.

[3] The Indian Independence Act 1947, under which Pakistan gained independence, provided in section 18(3) that "Save as otherwise expressly provided in this Act, the law of British India and of the several parts thereof existing immediately before the appointed day shall as far as applicable and with the necessary adaptations, continue as the law of each of the new Dominions and the several parts thereof until other provision is made by laws of the Legislature of the Dominion in question or by any other Legislature or other authority having power in that behalf." The contemplated adaptations were made by the Pakistan(Adaptation of Existing Laws) Order, 1947 and by The Adaptation of Central Acts and Ordinances Order, 1949. Successive constitutions contained articles providing for the continuance of existing laws. Article 224(1) of the 1956 Constitution, Article 225(1) of the 1962 Constitution and Article 280(1) of the Interim Constitution 1972 all provide for continuation of pre-existing laws in substantially the same form as Article 268 of the present 1973 Constitution. This provides that all existing laws should, subject to the Constitution, continue in force, so far as applicable and with the necessary adaptations, until altered or repealed or amended by the appropriate legislation. Continuation of existing laws also applies to periods of martial law, each of which was governed by a Laws

the locus for any introduction of Islamic law was Parliament. Earlier proposals to give the Supreme Court the jurisdiction to judicially review legislation on the basis of repugnancy were never incorporated into any of the constitutions prior to 1979, when Zia-ul-Haq created an Islamic court charged *inter alia* with the task of examining certain parts of the legal system on the basis of Islam. A contemporary critique observed with regard to the Report of the Basic Principles Committee, which had proposed giving the Supreme Court the power to strike down laws deemed to be repugnant to Islam, that "This provision gives a power to the Supreme Court which may be misused and, in any case, which the directly-elected representatives of the people could be expected to exercise without any extra-parliamentary check."[4]

The Islamic provisions of the pre-1973 constitutions shared a basic structure: there was the Objectives Resolution containing a general commitment to create an Islamic society and various constitutional provisions asking the state to promote Islam and to bring the legal system into conformity with Islam. Pakistan's first Constitution envisaged two mechanisms to introduce Islamic laws. The first took the form of a Directive Principle of State Policy which obliged the state to take steps "to enable the Muslims of Pakistan individually and collectively to order their lives in accordance with Islam".[5] However, Article 24 of the 1956 Constitution provided that the Directive Principles of State Policy were not enforceable in any court, although the state was to be guided by them in the formulation of its policies. The non-justiciability of the Directive Principles of State Policy in effect prevented any attempt to force the state to bring the legal system closer to Islam.[6]

The second mechanism centred around the creation of an advisory body which would make recommendations to Parliament as to the content and implementation of Islamic laws. Further, Article 198(1) provided in stringent terms that "no law shall be enacted which is repugnant to the Injunctions of Islam as laid down in the Holy Qur'an and Sunnah, hereinafter referred to as Injunctions of Islam, and existing law shall be brought in conformity with such Injunctions". However, the potential force of Article 198 and the advisory body on Islamic law was very carefully limited: the advisory body was to submit a report containing guidelines on Islamicization to Parliament including guidelines as to how the mandate of Islamicization contained in Article 198 could be achieved.[7] The abrogation of the 1956 Constitution following the proclamation of martial law on 6 October 1958 meant that none of the Islamic provisions had any effect on the legal system of Pakistan.

---

cont.

    (Continuance in Force) Order or similar law. Such legislation was promulgated in 1958, 1969 (see Proclamation of Martial Law) and 1977 and provided for the continuation of the main body of substantial law during the martial law period.

4   See Mazhar Ali Khan, "Minority rights", *The Pakistan Times,* 6 November 1953.

5   See Art. 25(1), The Constitution of the Islamic Republic of Pakistan, 1956.

6   It should be noted that there is one reported case where the Directive Principles of State Policy were held to be enforceable. In *Nizam Khan v. Additional District Judge,* Lyallpur PLD 1976 Lahore 930 Justice Muhammad Afzal Zullah held that these principles could be used as a source of law whenever there was a vacuum in the statute law.

7   See Art. 198 (3), *ibid.*

The Constitution Commission appointed by President Ayub Khan in 1960 to make recommendations on the structure of a new constitution for Pakistan adopted a cautious approach: the legal system should only be subject to any Islamicization if the different schools of Islamic law "could evolve unanimity with regards to the fundamentals of Islam as far as traditions are concerned".[8] The 1962 Constitution reflected Ayub Khan's secular outlook. Even the Objectives Resolution, which was retained as the preamble to the Constitution, was slightly changed in order to remove any reference to a limitation of the legislative powers of Parliament on the basis of Islam.[9] Pakistan was no longer an Islamic Republic but just the Republic of Pakistan and no legal mechanism was provided for any form of Islamicization of the legal system. Public pressure lead to an amendment of the 1962 Constitution in 1963: the amendments centred around the reintroduction of the "repugnancy formula", i.e. a constitutional provision to the effect that no laws should be repugnant to Islam and that the legal system should be brought into conformity with the Holy Qur'an and Sunnah, and the setting up of an advisory body, the Advisory Council of Islamic Ideology.[10] However, the Council of Islamic Ideology could only make recommendations regarding the conformity of laws to the injunctions of Islam to the President and the government but had no power to supervise and to enforce the implementation of its recommendations. Further, Article 8 of the Constitution provided that none of the Directive Principles of State Policy could be used to determine the *vires* of any law or any action of an organ or authority of the state.

The basic structure of non-justiciable constitutional provisions urging the state to bring all laws into conformity with Islam and a provision for the setting up of an advisory body on Islamic law was replicated in Pakistan's third Constitution. The 1973 Constitution contains a separate chapter headed "Islamic Provisions", which provides for the setting up of a Council of Islamic Ideology.[11] Again, as in previous constitutions, the Council has essentially only an advisory role and enjoys no inherent jurisdiction to ensure that its guidelines are followed by Parliament. Further, and in direct continuation of the approach taken in the previous two constitutions, no law could be challenged by way of judicial review on the ground that it had been found to be repugnant to Islam by the Council of Islamic Ideology.[12]

---

[8] See *Report of the Constititution Commission*, in Safdar Mahmood, *Constitutional Foundations of Pakistan*, Jang Publishers, Lahore, n.d., pp. 395–535, at p. 517.

[9] The preamble provided *inter alia* that "Whereas sovereignty over the entire Universe belongs to Almighty Allah alone, and the authority exercisable by the people is a sacred trust" thereby omitting to qualify the authority of the people by confining to "the limits prescribed by Him". Section 2 of the Constitution (First Amendment) Act, 1963 provided for the reintroduction of this qualification into the Constitution.

[10] See Arts. 199–206, The Constitution of the Islamic Republic of Pakistan, 1962.

[11] See Arts. 227–231, Constitution of Pakistan, 1973.

[12] See Art. 230, *ibid*. It should be noted that the setting up of the Federal Shariat Court with a power to strike down legislation on the basis of repugnancy to Islam temporarily increased the importance of the Council since it was able to provide draft legislation based on Islamic law to replace the areas of law declared to be in violation of Islamic law. An example of such draft legislation is the Criminal Law

The declaration of martial law and the introduction of a wide range of legal measures aimed at introducing the *Shariat* into the legal system in 1977 following the *coup d'état* of General Zia-ul-Haq marked the beginning of the first serious attempt by a government to Islamicize the legal system of Pakistan. The promulgation of the so-called Hudood Laws[13] reintroduced Islamic criminal law for the first time since it had been gradually displaced in favour of English criminal law during British colonial rule.[14] However, it is the setting up of an institutional mechanism to Islamicize the legal system independently from Parliament which can be identified as the main contribution of Zia-ul-Haq to the Islamicization of laws. For the first time a specialist court was created with the express purpose of judicially reviewing certain parts of the legal system so as to determine whether these parts were in accordance with Islamic law.

However, Zia-ul-Haq did not alter the essentially mixed character of Pakistan's legal system with its division between secular and Islamic spheres. The creation of the Federal Shariat Court led to a bifurcation of the legal system into an Islamic and secular wing. The Islamic Federal Shariat Court has not replaced the secular courts, but has operated parallel to them; its jurisdiction carefully separated from its secular counterpart. Similarly, the laws of the land have continued to be based to a large extent on the inherited colonial laws – the aim was not to introduce Islamic law *in toto* but to remove unIslamic elements from secular legislation. The result, as will be seen later, is a legal system which is curiously divided into secular and Islamic laws. The unique idea of creating two separate legal systems, based on different *grundnormen*, coexisting in discrete areas of the legal system has created conceptual faultlines and tensions within the legal system. The main reason for this can be located in the lack of an agreed basic legal value system which is either founded on the mainly secular values of guaranteed fundamental rights and parliamentary democracy enshrined in the Constitution or, in the alternative, based on Islam and Islamic law. An officially endorsed system of legal pluralism where both secular and religious laws are allowed to coexist, albeit in different niches of the legal system, has therefore left unanswered the question of normative hierarchy, i.e. which *grundnorm* forms the basic backbone, the philosophical and jurisprudential foundation, of Pakistan's legal system.

---

cont.
    (Amendment) Act 1997, which introduced the Islamic law of *qisas* and *diyat* into Pakistan's Penal Code, 1860.

[13] The new laws cover sexual offences, theft and the consumption of alcohol. See the Offences against Property (Enforcement of Hudood) Ordinance, 1979, Offence of *Zina* (Enforcement of Hudood) Ordinance, 1979, Offence of *Qazf* (Enforcement of Hadd) Ordinance, 1979, Prohibition (Enforcement of Hadd) Order, 1979, Baluchistan Prohibition (Enforcement of Hadd) Rules, 1980, Punjab Prohibition (Enforcement of Hadd) Rules, 1980, Sindh Prohibition Rules, 1979. Corporal punishments envisaged under these laws were further regulated by the Execution of Punishment of Whipping Ordinance 1979.

[14] See Joerg Fisch, *Cheap Lives and Dear Limbs: The British Transformation of the Bengal Criminal Law 1769–1817*, Franz Steiner Verlag, Wiesbaden, 1983 and Shadeen Malik, *The Transformation of Colonial Perceptions into Legal Norms: Legislating for Crime and Punishment in Bengal, 1790 to 1820s*, PhD Dissertation, London, 1994.

However, it is possible to see behind the coexistence of Islamic and secular laws and legal values a powerful enhancement of judicial power. It can be argued that the formal creation of a dual legal system with its own courts by Zia-ul-Haq in 1979 was preceded by a sustained period of "judicial Islamicization". A re-examination of the reported case law of Pakistani courts since independence reveals a surprising trend: since the late 1960s Pakistani courts have increasingly recognized and relied on principles of Islamic law. The most visible examples for this reliance are the celebrated *Asma Jilani* and *Nusrat Bhutto* cases of 1972 and 1977 respectively, which expressly recognized Islam as the basic structure of Pakistan's legal system.

3   THE ROLE OF ISLAM IN PAKISTAN'S CONSTITUTIONAL DEVELOPMENT: 1947 TO 1977

A study of the reported judgments of the high courts and the Supreme Court of Pakistan for the period after independence until the late 1960s indicates that the role of Islam in the judicial discourse was confined to a few discrete areas of law. Judges who tried to depart from the "Western" model were swiftly admonished by the higher judiciary, as the following example from the early days of Pakistan illustrates. In 1950, just three years after independence, a magistrate had to try six persons accused of having assaulted two landowners.[15] The defence contended that all of them were innocent. The law report is silent on the exact nature of the deliberations between the magistrate, the Attorney-General and the defence lawyers, but it appears that a deal was struck: the accused would face the large crowd of spectators assembled outside the court and would take an oath in public that they were innocent. The prosecution indicated that such an oath would be acceptable as proof of innocence and that the charges would be dropped. Two of the accused refused to take the oath but pleaded guilty instead, "stating that as they were guilty they were not prepared to take oath as they feared the wrath of God".[16] The magistrate was fully aware of the unusual nature of the trial and justified it as follows:

I am quite alive to the fact that the procedure adopted by me is wholly unwarranted. I however feel that it is high time we ceased to sit merely as Courts of law. For the sake of equity and justice we should have no hesitation in brushing aside the formal restrictions imposed by the British made law. The God law which we Pakistanis must and shall eventually follow demands vehemently that justice and equity should be our sole and only aim, and in achieving this God made law knows no procedural restrictions and formalities.[17]

The magistrate's search for an alternative to the British legacy of criminal

---

[15]   Quoted by Karam Elahee Chauhan in *B.Z. Kaikus v. President of Pakistan* PLD 1980 SC 160 at pp. 172–173.
[16]   *Ibid.*, at p. 172.
[17]   *Ibid.*

law had lead him to "God's law", i.e. Islamic law. There was no reference to any principle of Islamic law as such but there was reliance on the religious aspect of law: a Muslim would not commit perjury in the face of Allah.[18] The magistrate's justification for his actions was as simple as it was compelling, namely that his course of action was "essential for the ends of justice no matter if such a course causes infringement of prescribed procedure".[19] His statement constitutes an early precursor to Pakistan's experiments with public interest litigation since the late 1980s which have been informed by a very similar dissatisfaction with the inherited "Western" – secular – law and are based on an equally similar reference to Islamic values rather than pure Islamic law.

The conscious departure from British law and the reorientation to Islamic values constituted a direct challenge to the established legal order which was met by the Chief Justice of the Lahore High Court himself. In the Criminal Revision *Crown through Muhammad Nawaz v. Mihta and Others*, 12 May 1952, Chief Justice Munir ordered a retrial, observing that

[A]s the Magistrate does not see anything wrong in his following a "wholly unwarranted procedure" in the trial of criminal cases and feels "no hesitation in brushing aside formal restrictions" imposed by the current law, he is a complete misfit in the judicial system and a menace to the administration of criminal justice. It will be dangerous in the extreme to entrust him with any criminal case for trial under the law in force.[20]

The Chief Justice disapproved in strong terms of the magistrate's reliance on a religious oath. In his opinion most criminals would be willing to profane a religious oath in order to gain an acquittal which would not result in a public violation of an religious oath but would also mean injustice to the wronged party.

In the 1950s and 1960s judges were still able and willing to reject any express reliance on Islamic law because the areas of law occupied by Islamic law were confined to family law, which had traditionally been governed by the British system of personal laws. Any percolations of Islamic law into the secular legal system were swiftly contained, as could be seen in the Chief Justice's condemnation of the magistrate as a "complete misfit" – in practical terms Islamic law was reduced to Muslim family law and had otherwise no importance for the legal development of Pakistan.

4   ISLAM AND MARTIAL LAW

The first express attempt by the higher judiciary to break down the barrier between an essentially secular legal order and an Islamic society occurred,

---

[18]   The oath, one of the oldest institutions in legal procedure, plays a specific role in Islamic law. The oath was an integral part of legal procedure and could displace the need for witnesses. See especially Joseph Schacht, *The Origins of Muhammadan Jurisprudence*, The Clarendon Press, Oxford, 1950, pp. 187–188.

[19]   *Ibid.*

[20]   *Ibid.*

perhaps significantly, in the context of a challenge to the imposition of martial law in 1969. Pakistan's constitutional upheavals have been the subject of an extensive literature deliberating about the causes of this instability and the frequent descents of the country into martial law. From a legal perspective the attempts of the Supreme Court of Pakistan to accommodate extra-constitutional acts like the usurpation of power within an established constitutional doctrine lead to at times bizarre decisions. In the first decision on the validity of the imposition of martial law in 1958, i.e. the infamous *Dosso* decision, the Supreme Court of Pakistan yielded to the political reality and declared that the only test for the legality of the new legal order, i.e. martial law, "is the efficacy of the change".[21] Chief Justice Munir, speaking for the majority, developed a theory of constitutional law which did not distinguish between legality and legitimacy but which validated any "revolution" as long it was successful in completely replacing the old legal order.

Munir's philosophy of radical legal positivisim,[22] which could be reduced to the motto "might is right", was, however, not shared by Justice Cornelius, who in a cautious note of dissent stated that the fundamental rights which had been guaranteed by the abrogated Constitution of 1956 did not derive their entire validity "from the fact of having been formulated in words and enacted in that Constitution".[23] In his opinion the other validation of these fundamental rights was based on the fact that "a number of these rights are essential human rights which inherently belong to every citizen of a country governed in a civilized mode".[24] Cornelius' reliance on natural law enabled him to hold that human rights did not depend on a written guarantee – they

---

[21] *The State v. Dosso* PLD 1958 SC 533, at p. 538 (*per* Chief Justice Munir).

[22] It should be noted that Chief Justice Munir's willing acceptance of the abrogation of the Constitution must have come as a surprise to his contemporaries. Only a year earlier Munir had emphatically defended the fundamental right to freedom of religion guaranteed under Article 18 of the Constitution of 1956 stating that it could not be taken away by a law. Munir's reliance on the intentions of the framers of the Constitution and the notion that certain interpretations of it constitute a fraud on the people are worth quoting in full: "The very conception of a fundamental right is that it being a right guaranteed by the Constitution cannot be taken away by the law, and it is not only technically inartistic but a fraud on the citizens for the makers of the Constitution to say that a right is fundamental but may be taken away by the law. I am unable to attribute any such intent to the makers of the Constitution who in their anxiety to regulate the lives of the Muslims in Pakistan in accordance with the Holy Qur'an and Sunnah could not possibly have intended to take away from Muslims the right to profess, practise and propagate their religion and to establish, maintain and manage their religious institutions, and who in their conception of the ideal of a free, tolerant and democratic society could not have denied a similar right to the non-Muslim citizens of the State." *Jibendra Kishore Achharyya Chowdhury and 58 others v. Province of East Pakistan* PLD 1957 SC 9, at p. 41.

[23] *Ibid.*, at p. 561.

[24] Martial law was declared on 7 October 1958. Section 4 of the Laws (Continuance in Force) Order, 1958, which came into force on 10 October 1958, provided that "notwithstanding the abrogation of the late Constitution" all laws other than the 1956 Constitution and some specifically mentioned ordinances should continue to have legal force.

were elementary rights which did not disappear only because the legal instrument which had contained them was no longer in force.

Cornelius' approach had the advantage that he could continue to rely on human rights, although these had disappeared from the constitution, without having to declare martial law itself to be invalid. Certain rights did not owe their existence to any law-making act but they were inherent in every human being.

The resort to a higher legal order, or in other words, a basic legal structure which would survive the legal changes brought about by martial law was not further developed by Cornelius but his theme was taken up by the Supreme Court of Pakistan when it overruled the *Dosso* decision in the famous *Asma Jilani* case of 1972. The political backdrop of the case consisted of yet another martial law this time imposed by Yaha Khan in 1969 subsequent to his appointment as successor-in-office of Ayub Khan, who had stepped down from office on 24 October 1969. Yaha Khan used his newly acquired position to abrogate the 1962 Constitution and to declare martial law. He followed the usual pattern set by his predecessors by allowing for legal continuity by the promulgation of Continuance of Laws order on 25 October 1969, which was followed by the Provisional Constitution Order 1969, promulgated on 4 April 1969. However, the usurpation of power was not successful: elections under the Legal Framework Order promulgated by Yaha Khan saw the East Pakistani politician Sheik Mujib and his Awami League emerge with an absolute majority of National Assembly seats.

To be governed by East Pakistan appeared to unacceptable to West Pakistan's politicians and the ensuing civil war not only led to the creation of Bangladesh but also to the emergence of Zulfiqar Bhutto as the new political leader of Pakistan. Though inducted into power by yet another martial law his regime was subsequently ratified by the National Assembly, which also approved an Interim Constitution.[25] A challenge to the legality of convictions imposed by military courts set up under Yaha Khan's martial law enabled the Supreme Court of Pakistan to reconsider the *Dosso* decision.[26] Unlike Cornelius, who had resorted to Western natural law theory to distance himself from Munir's radical legal positivism and thereby from martial law, Chief Justice Hamoodur Rahman referred to the Objectives Resolution in his search for a *grundnorm* for Pakistan. Having refuted Kelson's theory of revolutionary legality Rahman held *obiter* that

In any event, if a *grundnorm* is necessary for us I do not have to look to the Western legal theorists to discover one. Our own *grundnorm* is enshrined in our own doctrine that the legal sovereignty over the entire universe belongs to Almighty Allah alone, and the authority exercisable by the people within the limits prescribed by Him a sacred trust. This is an immutable and unalterable norm which was clearly accepted in the Objectives Resolution passed by the Constituent Assembly of Pakistan on the 7th of March 1949... . This has not been abrogated by any one so far, nor has it

---

[25] See The Legal Framework Order 1970, President's Order 2 of 1970 and the Interim Constitution of the Islamic Republic of Pakistan,1972.
[26] See *Asma Jilani v. Government of Punjab* PLD 1972 SC 139.

been departed or deviated from by any regime, military or Civil. Indeed, it cannot be, for it is one of the fundamental principles enshrined in the Qur'an.[27]

Rahman developed from this a principle of sovereignty based on the idea of trusteeship, in which the body politic becomes the trustee for the discharge of sovereign functions. According to the Qur'an this trusteeship must consists of a plurality persons which "negates the possibility of absolute power being vested in a single hand".[28]

Rahman's reliance on Islamic law is significant. In spite of the fact that he began his deliberations about the *grundnorm* with an "if" he nevertheless promulgated in very uncertain terms a constitutional theory in which basic principles of Islamic law are "immutable" and "unalterable" norms. The idea of a basic structure of Pakistan's legal system based on Islam which would survive any attempts to change "the written laws", as Cornelius had called them, would impose a twofold test on the validity of a legal revolution: first, was the revolution successful, i.e. has it been accepted by the people? And secondly, is the new legal order in accordance with the norms of Islam? Rahman's definition of these norms concentrated on the plurality of political leaders which would rule in a military dictatorship, and an authority properly constituted by law, i.e. the rule of law. His approach was followed by Judge Sajjad Ahmad who also stated in emphatic terms that

the State of Pakistan was created in perpetuity based on Islamic ideology and governed on all the basic norms of that ideology, unless the body politic of Pakistan as whole, God forbid, is re-constituted on an un-Islamic pattern, which will of course, mean the destruction of its original concept. The Objectives Resolution is not just a preface. It embodies the spirit and the fundamental norms of the constitutional concept of Pakistan.[29]

Importantly, Sajjad Ahmad approved the *amicus curia*'s submission that the Supreme Court's judicial power did not flow from any legislative act of the executive but "is a trust from the Almighty Allah, is lodged in society as a whole, which, in turn, is irrevocable committed to the Courts as trustees of the society".[30]

The two other judges on the bench, Judge Yaqub Ali and Judge Salahuddin Ahmed, both chose to ignore Islam as a source of constitutional law or theory. Yaqub Ali conceded the existence of a basic structure which was according to him democracy,[31] whereas Salahuddin Ahmad was content to overrule *Dosso* on the basis that there had in fact not been a successful revolution when martial law was imposed by Iskandar Mirza in 1958.

The significant shift of the Supreme Court towards Islam in its search for stability and legal continuity in the face of frequent constitutional "breakdowns", which has not received much attention in the recent academic

---

27 *Ibid.*, at p. 182.
28 *Ibid.*, at p. 183.
29 *Ibid.*, at p. 258.
30 *Ibid.*, at p. 258.
31 *Ibid.*, at p. 237.

literature,[32] appears to be part of a broader movement within the judiciary to use religious norms as a weapon against unconstitutional impositions of martial law: the existence of an immutable basic norm was supposed to provide the touchstone by which any usurper of power could be repelled. However, the emergence of this "basic-structure" doctrine was less courageous than it might appear at first sight: at the time when the Supreme Court decided the case Yaha Khan had already been removed from office.

Nevertheless, the reliance on theology coupled with a conscious departure from Western constitutional thought signifies an important trend towards the development of a culture-specific constitutional jurisprudence. It is interesting to note that India's superior courts have so far resisted any express reliance on indigenous classical traditions of just governance. This fact has been criticized by Baxi, who argued that

The Pakistan experience certainly demonstrates that the privileging of judicial review is more appropriately and adequately achieved by reference to society's, even if it is a past (like all past) we narratively construct (though with integrity), to imbue political power with a minimum of ethic of accountability.[33]

While the Supreme Court conducted its hearings in the *Asma Jilani* case the Lahore High Court examined similar questions, namely the legality of convictions under martial laws introduced by Yaha Khan, in the case *Zia ur Rehman v. The State*.[34] Rather embarrassingly for the Supreme Court, which had condemned the Yaha Khan's martial law, these very same martial laws had not been removed from the legal system but on the contrary had been expressly saved by Zulfiqar Bhutto under Article 281 of the Interim Constitution, 1972. The rigid press laws in particular were used to silence the critical sections of the press. The petitioners, all journalists and editors of newspapers, argued that if the Yaha Khan's imposition of martial law was indeed *ultra vires*, which it was as a result of the Supreme Court's *Asma Jilani* decision, then the 1962 Constitution should be revived. In such a scenario not only the Yaha Khan's but also Zulfiqar Bhutto's martial law would be invalid. In

---

[32] Paula Newberg, for instance, does not explore the Supreme Court's recourse to Islamic law apart from one mention of Hamoodor Rahman's remark that if a *grundnorm* was necessary the Objectives Resolution would provide one. See Paula Newberg, *Judging the State: Courts and Constitutional Politics in Pakistan*, CUP, Cambridge, 1995, p. 122. A notable exception is Upendra Baxi, "Constitutional interpretation and state formative practices in Pakistan: a preliminary exploration", in Mahendra Singh (ed.), *Comparative Constitutional Law*, Eastern Book Company, Delhi, 1989, pp. 132–153. Baxi recognizes the importance of an ideological/theological discourse for the achievement of constitutionalism, calling it "unparalleled in the annals of contemporary constitutionalism" (at p. 132).
[33] See Baxi, *ibid.*, at p. 136. It might be argued in the defence of the Supreme Court of India that an express reference to the "classical traditions of good governance in the Hindu, Buddhist, Jain, Islamic, Christian, and tribal traditions" (*ibid.* at p. 136) would be more problematic since India is a secular state – in fact in *Kesvavanda Bharati* the Supreme Court of India held secularism to be part of the basic structure which could not be tampered with by constitutional amendment.
[34] PLD 1972 Lah 382.

a preliminary decision which only examined the jurisdiction of the Lahore High Court to deal with the matter and to grant interim relief, Judge Afzal Zullah, who was later to become the Chief Justice of Pakistan and the founding father of public interest litigation, advanced a position which was far more radical than anything said in the *Asma Jilani* decision handed down three days later. Zullah elevated the Objectives Resolution to a "supra constitutional instrument" which "is so fundamental and contains such mandates that it cannot at all be repealed or abrogated and is permanent for all times to come"[35] and extracted from it the following principles:

(1) the State shall exercise its powers and authority through the chosen representatives of the people;
(2) the principles of democracy, freedom, equality, tolerance and social justice as enunciated by Islam shall be fully observed;
(3) the integrity of the territories of the federation, its independence, and all its rights including sovereign rights on land, sea, and air shall be safeguarded.[36]

Zullah held that the imposition of martial law had been a violation of these principles. His reliance on Islamic law as embodied in the Objectives Resolution amounted to stating that Pakistan constitutional order had a basic structure which could not be taken away by anybody. The Supreme Court in *Asma Jilani v. The Government of Punjab*[37] seemed to endorse Zullah's view on the importance of the Objectives Resolution but did not base its condemnation of the imposition of martial law exclusively on Islamic law.

A larger bench of the Lahore High Court ruled in a substantive hearing on the legality of the convictions itself in July 1972 and could therefore rely on the *Asma Jilani* verdict.[38] An examination of the individual judgments reveals an interesting range of opinions on the role of Islam as a source of constitutional law. Judge A.R. Sheikh held that though the Objectives Resolution was indeed the *grundnorm*, it could nevertheless not be used to test the *vires* of a constitution drafted by a constituent assembly since "if, however, the Constituent Assembly fails to fulfil its obligations, the remedy will be the resistance to be offered by the people to accept the Constitution and the complexity of the problem so arising will be settled on the political forum in the country and not before the Courts".[39]

Muhammad Afzal Cheema's approach to the status of Islamic law was cautious as well: he expressly ruled out that the Objectives Resolution could be used to determine the *vires* of any law, let alone the provisions of the Constitution itself:

---

35 *Ibid.*, p. 390.
36 *Ibid.*
37 PLD 1972 SC 139.
38 *Ziaur Rehman v. The State* PLD 1986 Lahore 428. The decision was initially only reported as a headnote, see PLD 1974 Note 3 [Lahore].
39 *Ibid.*, at p. 486.

Obviously, the fundamental law of the land cannot be left to the vagaries of conflicting and changing notions leading to constantly endless litigation in Court for the resolution of theological controversies and polemics. Thus, the only sound principle of policy is to leave the matter to popular will reflected in the chosen representatives who can frame as also amend the Constitution subject, of course, to the Divine limitations.[40]

It might be added by way of comment that Cheema's doubts concerning the desirability of introducing theological arguments into the process of judicial review of legislation have a certain prophetic quality in the light of subsequent developments. Whereas Judge K.E. Chauhan did not once refer to Islamic law Judge Sajjad relied heavily on the idea that Pakistan had a *grundnorm* founded in Islam which had found its visible expression in the Objectives Resolution. However, he came to the conclusion that though the Constituent Assembly had to frame a constitution in accordance with the directions contained in the Objectives Resolution "I do not find that the National Assembly by conferring validity on the laws framed during the Martial Law regime by the usurper has offended against these directions".[41] Judge Zullah, who had already been involved in the case at the preliminary stage, repeated his heavy reliance on Islamic law pronouncing that the Objectives Resolution was a supraconstitutional document which imposed limits on the powers of any law-creating body including a constituent Assembly.

In a final analysis, however, in spite of differing interpretation of the place of Islam in the legal system all judges upheld the validity of Article 281 of the Interim Constitution, albeit with the restriction that this article did not remove the courts' power of judicial review to examine the validity of acts deemed to be *mala fide* or *coram non judice*.

The jealously guarded right of the judiciary to interpret laws was, therefore, in line with the emerging popularity of Islamic law in the legal discourse, based directly on the principles of delegation contained in the Objectives Resolution. The anchoring of the powers of judicial review in a source of law not connected to a written constitution but to a religion created boundaries which could not be over-stepped by the regime itself. In *Yusuf Ali v. West Pakistan Bar Council Tribunal*[42] the Lahore High Court held that the judiciary carried out its judicial functions as a delegate of the sovereign, who, "in the Islamic Republic of Pakistan, is God Almighty Himself exercising His will and Sovereignty through the people of this country".[43]

Nevertheless, reliance on Islam as a supraconstitutional norm was expressly rejected by the Lahore Court in a case decided only a few months after the more ambiguous judgment given in Ziar-ur-Rehman. In *Hussain Naqvi v. D.M. Lahore*[44] Justice Muhammad Iqbal held that the Objectives Resolution could be considered as a guideline for the framing of a constitution and the

---

[40] *Ibid.*, at p. 518.
[41] *Ibid.*, at p. 602.
[42] PLD 1972 Lahore 404.
[43] *Ibid.*, at p. 413, *per* Justice Mushtaq Hussain.
[44] PLD 1973 Lahore 164.

grundnorm, in my view, is a concept of Western legal theorists which has its importance only so long as the Constitution is not framed, or it operates when the country is in the occupation of an usurper, but it cannot be relied upon for challenging the provisions of a written Constitution, or to contend that a certain constitutional provision is *ultra vires* the *grundnorm*. It is only a basic ideology not actionable before the courts.[45]

The reluctance of the Lahore High Court to endorse Zullah's radical approach continued in the Supreme Court. An appeal against the Lahore High Court's decision in *Ziaur Rehman* to the Supreme Court ended – for the time being – the higher judiciary's experiments with Islamic law and its relation to the *grundnorm*: in *Zia-ur-Rahman v. State*,[46] decided by the Supreme Court after the Interim Constitution of 1972 had been passed by the National Assembly, Chief Justice Hamoodur Rahman expressly rejected Zullah's elevation of the Objectives Resolution to a "supra constitutional instrument". Having asked himself the question whether a judge could strike down any provision of the Constitution itself either because it was in conflict with the laws of God, of nature or of morality he forcefully stated that

I for my part can conceive of no situation, in which, after a formal written Constitution has been lawfully accepted by the people including the judiciary as the Constitution of the country, the judiciary can claim to declare any of its provisions *ultra vires* or void... . Therefore, in my view, however solemn or sacrosanct a document, if it is not incorporated in the Constitution or does not form part of the Constitution it cannot control the Constitution.[47]

The Supreme Court's withdrawal from its earlier endorsement of the Objectives Resolution as an expression of Pakistan's immutable *grundnorm* seemed to have ended the Supreme Court's flirtation with something which had come very close to preempting India's basic structure doctrine.[48] In effect, the Supreme Court voluntarily limited its power – it would not interfere in the traditional division of powers and would not meddle with Parliament's power to make laws or to amend the Constitution.[49] The Supreme Court's stance that any violation of principles contained in a "supra constitutional norm" like the Objectives Resolution had to be corrected by the people but

---

[45] *Ibid.*, p. 175.
[46] PLD 1973 SC 49.
[47] *Ibid.*, at p. 71. It should be noted that the Objectives Resolution was incorporated into the Constitution in 1983 in the form of a new Article 2A.
[48] See *Kesavananda Bharati v. The State of Kerala* AIR 1973 SC 1561. It should be remembered that the Indian legal discourse on the basic structure was confined to the justiciability of amendments to the constitution. The task of Pakistan's Supreme Court was therefore conceptually much wider being concerned with the creation of a new constitution or legal order.
[49] This is confirmed by *Federation of Pakistan v. Saeed Ahmad* 1974 SC 49 where the Supreme Court examined a similar ouster of jurisdiction clause, this time under the 1973 Constitution (see Article 281(1) of the Constitution 1973). The Supreme Court held that the right to review decision made *mala fides* could not be taken away but there is no reliance on any "extra-constitutional" norms to justify this result.

not by the courts is understandable in the context of the country's return to democracy in 1972. However, bearing in mind the troubled constitutional history of Pakistan, it can also be argued that the Supreme Court was unwilling to become hostage to fortune by expanding its jurisdiction to such an extent that it would never be able to condone any future "constitutional irregularity", like the imposition of martial law for a limited period, without breaching its own principles. Significant for the purposes of this thesis is, however, the refusal of the Supreme Court to recognize Islam as the immutable *grundnorm* of Pakistan – in the final analysis the Supreme Court pronounced that even a complete departure from the Islamic ideals enshrined in the Objectives Resolution would not be justiciable.

However, the Supreme Court's rejection was not an absolute one: Hamoodur Rahman conceded that the position might be different if the Objectives Resolution were incorporated into the Constitution, a course of action which was adopted by Zia-ul-Haq in 1985.

However, the idea of Islamic law as the inviolable basic norm of the Constitution was, despite the rejection of this concept by the Supreme Court in 1973, resurrected in order to challenge the flood of repressive laws introduced by Zulfiqar Bhutto. It was, perhaps ironically, Zulfiqar Bhutto himself, who, having benefited from the *Asma Jilani* decision, introduced laws which restricted both judicial independence and weakened fundamental rights. Many of these laws were challenged in the courts and judges at times relied on Islamic law to restrict this piecemeal imposition of martial law.[50] The civil unrest which followed the national assembly elections of March 1977 led the re-elected Prime Minister Zulfiqar Bhutto to call in the army to assist the overstretched police forces. This was done in reliance on Article 245 of the Constitution which allows the armed forces to act in aid of civil forces when called upon to do so. Bhutto amended the article with retrospective effect so as to prevent any judicial review of his decision to call upon the army.[51] Further, Bhutto amended the Proclamation of Emergency, which had existed since November 1971, on 21 April 1977, to the effect that the reason for the proclamation of an emergency could also be an internal disturbance rather than an external threat. In areas affected by martial law all fundamental rights were suspended. The net effect of these new laws was to make the entire population of an area in which martial law had been declared subject to the amended Pakistan Army Act 1977 and triable by military courts for a wide range of offences. In *Darwesh M. Arbey v. Federation of Pakistan*[52] the petitioners challenged this localized imposition of martial law and the setting up of martial law courts by arguing that these actions exceeded the scope of Article 245 of the Constitution, which only allowed the government to call on the army in aid of the exercise of its civil power but did not allow the army to take over the functions of the judiciary. A five-member bench of the

---

[50] For a useful account of the Bhutto years see Newberg, *Judging the State*, pp. 138–170.
[51] See Constitution (Seventh Amendment) Act 1977.
[52] PLD 1980 Lahore 206.

Lahore High Court faced the task of reconsidering the limits, if any, to constitutional amendments and yet again tackling the thorny question of the basic structure or *grundnorm* of Pakistan's legal order.

The timing of the decision is significant: the judgment was handed down on 2 June 1977 but when the judges wrote their respective judgments Zia-ul Haq had already deposed Zulfiqar Bhutto and had imposed his own martial law. Unlike the *Asma Jilani* decision, which had declared Yaha Khan's martial law to be unconstitutional after the dictator had been removed from office, *Darwesh M. Arbey* declared Zulfiqar Bhutto's martial law to be *ultra vires* while he was still very much holding on to power. However, by the time the written judgments were handed down the decision had also became a benchmark for Zia-ul-Haq's martial law itself.

Chief Justice Aslam Riaz Hussain avoided any reference to Islam or the basic structure by concentrating on the imposition of martial law itself. He found that there was no provision within the constitutional framework which would allow for the imposition of martial law. His emphasis on the absence of any reference to martial law within the Constitution seems curious at first especially since Hussain adds to this that

However, if the Constitution is abrogated, set aside or placed in a state of suspended animation or hibernation, it might be possible to impose Martial Law outside the Constitution. Such an action may or may not be justified by the doctrine of necessity.[53]

The end result is somewhat convoluted: a martial law within the Constitution is always unconstitutional, since it is not contemplated by the Constitution, whereas a martial law imposed by actually taking away the Constitution could under certain circumstances be condoned by the doctrine of necessity. The confusion is compounded by the fact that the government had in fact argued that their martial law was a "constitutional" one, whereas the previous martial law imposed by Yaha Khan had been unconstitutional. Hussain's response appears to be that only an unconstitutional martial law can ever be condoned by the doctrine of necessity. The confusion can probably be explained by the course of events which took place while the judgments were written: on 4 July 1977 General Muhammad Zia-ul-Haq staged a *coup d'état* and imposed martial law promising fresh elections within three months, i.e. on 18 October 1977. Zulfiqar Bhutto had indicated his willingness to participate in these elections and had even gone on record saying that he would not challenge the constitutional validity of that martial law. The Chief Justice of the Lahore High Court was, it appears, unwilling to declare Zia-ul Haq's martial law to be unconstitutional. Justice Hussain's judgment can therefore be regarded as a compromise: it allowed for the invalidation of Bhutto's martial law and the preservation of Zia-ul-Haq's openly unconstitutional act.

Hussain's result is highly unattractive and appears to hint at a resurrection of *Dosso*'s doctrine of revolutionary change disguised as the doctrine of necessity. Justice Karam Elahee Chauhan managed to avoid any ruling on the question of the validity of martial law itself by confining himself to a close interpretation of Article 245. As a result he found that the functions performed by the armed forces in areas subjected to martial law exceeded the scope of Article 245 and were therefore unconstitutional.

Justice Shameen Hussain Kadri, however, did not duck the issue but plunged straight into the muddied waters of the limits of constitutional amendments. It will be recalled that by virtue of the seventh amendment to the Constitution the jurisdiction of the courts to review any direction given to the armed forces to assist the civil power was ousted. Kadri decided that such an amendment was in violation of the basic structure of the Constitution and therefore *ultra vires* and invalid. The basic structure was, according to Kadri, the two nation theory and the ideology of Pakistan. Perhaps predictably Kadri located the source of the basic structure as the Objectives Resolution which in his judgment imposed fetters on the legislative powers of the national assembly. The same resolution also afforded Kadri a gateway to the resurrection of the fundamental rights which had been suspended by Zulfiqar Bhutto:

In my humble view, suspension of certain fundamental rights and in particular Fundamental Right 14(1) comes in direct conflict with the holy Qur'an. Any legislative or executive authority cannot enact a law or promulgate any Ordinance or Order in view of Article 227 of the Constitution which clearly prohibits the enactment of law which is repugnant to the Injunctions of Islam as laid down in the Holy Qur'an and Sunnah. I am conscious of the fact that Courts are not empowered to strike down such laws. But any person or authority acting contrary to the provisions of Article 227 is likely to run the risk of the consequences as envisaged in Article 6[54] of the Constitution.[55]

Islamic law also provided Kadri with the necessary ammunition to counter the submission of the Attorney-General that martial law was part of the English common law, which in turn was the law applied by a Pakistani court whenever a principle of natural justice had to be enunciated. Kadri ruled that the principles of natural justice were not based on common law but were enshrined in the Qur'an, observing also, that it was strange that the government should try to rely on English law to justify the imposition of martial law while at the same time having pursued a policy of Islamicization.[56]

The use of Islam made by Kadri did not amount to a bold assertion of "Islam as the *grundnorm*" of Pakistan but was more subtle: Islam was an additional source of law. It replaced the English principles of natural justice as contained in the common law and imposed, in a manner similar to a fundamental right, limits on the legislature. The latter can be deduced from Kadri's examination of the legal validity of extensive curfew orders made by the army in martial law areas. Kadri held these curfew orders to be invalid

---

[54] Art. 6 of the Constitution provides that anybody who abrogates or subverts the Constitution by use of force is guilty of high treason.
[55] *Ibid.*, at p. 267.
[56] Kadri mentioned the Prohibition Act, declaration of Friday as public holiday and the formation of a new Islamic Advisory Council.

because they had not allowed for a reasonable time for prayers in the mosque. This, argued Kadri, was in violation of both Article 20 of the Constitution, which provides for freedom of religion, and of Islamic law. The elevation of Islamic law to the level of fundamental rights was unprecedented but, as will be seen later, would, play an important part in the development of public interest litigation in Pakistan in the late 1980s.

Judge Zakiuddin Patel went so far as to resurrect the "basic structure" in its entirety. Relying on the Indian cases *Kesavananda v. Kerala* and *Golakh Nath*, Patel argued that the "basic structure, framework and essential features have been fully given in the preamble of the Constitution, which is an integral part thereof".[57] It is worth quoting Patel at length since his forceful formulation of a basic structure doctrine was made a time when Bhutto's martial law had just been replaced by the one imposed by Zia-ul-Haq:

According to the objectives given in the preamble, the Constitution of Pakistan would be Islamic, federal and Democratic in character... . [T]he scope of Article 238, does not allow such sweeping changes in the Constitution by way of amendment which can destroy its basic structure and essential features, otherwise such amendments would be void being beyond the scope of the relevant Articles. Any addition brought about within the broad contours of the preamble and the Constitution to carry out the objectives given in the preamble and the directive principles.

Patel gave some examples for amendments which would amount to a violation of the basic structure doctrine: the deletion of Article 2 of the Constitution, which provides that Islam shall be the state religion of Pakistan, and a declaration that Pakistan was to be a secular state would amount to the destruction of the basic structure. Further, any attempt to change the democratic and federal character of the state would be invalid for the same reason.

Patel's and Kadri's resurrection of the basic structure doctrine in a form more radical in its imposition of legislative limits than the only other precedent, namely *Asma Jilani*, is noteworthy for two reasons: first, both judges attempt to distinguish and circumvent the Supreme Court's decision in *Ziaur Rehman* which had held that the preamble, unless incorporated into the Constitution, could not control it. It can be argued that the open departure from the binding precedent set by the Supreme Court signifies a split in the judiciary between proponents and opponents of the basic structure doctrine. Second, and less obvious, is the reliance on Islamic law to oppose the imposition of martial law and the amendment of the Constitution. Especially Patel's criticism of Bhutto's opportunistic use of Islam, namely the introduction of Islamicization measures on the one hand and the reliance on English common law on the other to justify an unIslamic martial law, must have sent warning signals to Zia-ul-Haq. It is perhaps for this reason that the decision was only reported in 1980, three years after the judgment had been handed down. It is difficult to see a more determined challenge to both Zulfiqar Bhutto's and Zia-ul-Haq's experiments with martial law.

Arbey had invalidated Zulfiqar Bhutto's attempts to impose localized

---

[57] *Ibid.*, p. 297.

martial law regimes but it obviously had not in any way questioned the legality of his government as such. However, as could be seen, the Lahore High Court left little doubt that any permanent imposition of martial law would as a matter of principle be regarded as a violation of the basic structure doctrine.

The validity of Zia-ul-Haq's martial law was the central issue in the case of *Begum Nusrat Bhutto v. Chief of Army Staff*.[58] Zulfiqar Bhutto's wife moved the Supreme Court under Article 184(3) to challenge the detention of her husband[59] and ten other leaders of the Pakistan People's Party. The Supreme Court faced a by now somewhat familiar situation: a martial law dictator had established himself effectively in power and it was abundantly clear that a judgment of the Supreme Court would not remove him. Justice Qaisar Khan described the situation bluntly as follows:

The argument that a decision holding the action of the Martial Law authority immune from judicial scrutiny by Courts would encourage revolutions and coup d'etat has no substance in it as revolutions and coup d'etat cannot be prevented by judgments. Despite the judgment of this Court in *Asma Jilani*'s case a coup d'etat did take place, for whatever reason, it is immaterial. We daily see the revolutions and coups d'etat do take place despite provisions regarding treason in Constitutions of the countries. The persons who want to stage a revolution or coups d'etat do not have any regard for the judgments or the Constitutional provisions. They go forward despite these and rule if they succeed or are executed if they fail.[60]

Qaisar's rather cynical approach proceeded on the basis that Zia-ul-Haq's martial law had brought into being a new legal order which was in no way connected to the previous regime – even the 1973 Constitution, which had been partially revived by the Laws (Continuance in Force) Order 1977, was part of the new legal order, since it had been re-introduced only by the "grace" of the Chief Martial Law Administrator Zia-ul-Haq and not because it represented the legitimate basis of government. The declaration of martial law on 5 July 1977 brought the legal order based on the 1973 Constitution to a complete end. It could be revived if Zia-ul-Haq was removed and tried for treason under the revived provisions of the 1973 Constitution but until then the ultimate source of law was the Martial Law Administrator himself. Qaisar saw little point in pretending that the courts had retained any power to judicially review the actions or pledges of the martial law authorities – such powers had been taken away and any pledge made by a politician was not enforceable in any event:

The assertion that the Chief Martial Law Administrator had given statements and made pledges that he would do this and in such and such a time does not detract from the existence of the Martial Law or the powers which are exercised under it. The Courts have nothing to do with these statements as such like statements and pledges are not enforceable under any law in any Court.[61]

---

[58] PLD 1977 SC 657.
[59] Zulfiqar Bhutto was arrested on 17 September 1977.
[60] *Ibid.*, p. 747.
[61] *Ibid.*, p. 747.

But what about the idea of an Islamic *grundnorm* based on the Objectives Resolution? Qaisar did not spend much time on it. In his opinion the "total legal order" was contained in the 1973 Constitution. In any event, the extent to which this legal order was in fact Islamic was doubtful, argued Qaisar, because:

At some stage in the arguments it was suggested that the Resolution of March 1949 was the *grundnorm* in Pakistan and action should be tested keeping that as a touchstone. There is, however, no force in this contention as no body in Islam is above law but under our Constitution of 1973 the President and the Governors have been placed above law and they were not answerable to any Court or law nor could they be tried in any Court. The offence of murder is compoundable according to the Holy Qur'an but we in Courts do not accept compromise in murder cases. The resolution was the wish and ultimate aim for the realization of the Islamic order but it was not the *grundnorm* in Pakistan. It was also held so by this Court in the case of *Zia-ur-Rahman*.[62]

All judges came to the same result, namely that Zia-ul-Haq's regime was not to be declared invalid or unconstitutional. However, unlike Qaisar, who plainly stated that Zia-ul-Haq's actions amounted to *coup d'état*, the remaining judges including the Chief Justice attempted to achieve a compromise between the detrimentally opposed decisions of *Dosso*, which would have recognized the *de facto* revolutionary legal change as the beginning of a new legal order, and *Asma Jilani*, which had imposed strict limits on the imposition of martial law. It will be recalled that in the latter case the Supreme Court had argued in no uncertain terms that:

Maybe, that on account of their holding the coercive apparatus of the state, the people and the Courts are silenced temporarily, but let it be laid down firmly that the order which the usurper imposes will remain illegal and the Courts will not recognize its rule and act upon them as *de jure*. As soon as the first opportunity arises, when the coercive apparatus falls from the hand of the usurper, he should be tried for high treason and suitably punished. This alone will serve as a deterrent for would-be-adventurers.[63]

The "third way" out of the dilemma of either admitting defeat, like Justice Qaisar, or to risk ridicule by invalidating the martial law without any hope of enforcement, was to be the "doctrine of necessity" as formulated by Chief Justice Muhammed Munir in the *Reference by H.E. the Governor General*.[64] Chief Justice Munir's definition of the doctrine of necessity, namely "that subject to the condition of absoluteness, extremeness and imminence, an act which would otherwise be illegal becomes legal if it is done bona fide under the stress of necessity, the necessity being referable to an intention to preserve

---

62   *Ibid.*, p. 747.
63   *Asma Jilani* PLD 1972 SC at 242–3, *per* Hamoodur Rahman.
64   PLD 1955 FC 435. For a comprehensive discussion of the doctrine of necessity see Leslie Wolf-Phillips, *Constitutional Legitimacy: A Study of the Doctrine of Necessity*, Third World Foundation, London.

the constitution, the State or the Society and to prevent it from dissolution"[65] was an obvious solution capable of cutting the Gordian knot. A further distinct advantage of Munir's definition was the fact that he had limited the emergency legislative powers, conferred by the doctrine of necessity, to matters connected to the necessity. Any constitutional changes were, according to Munir, only permitted if referable to the emergency.[66] However, Cornelius' condemnation of the pedigree of the doctrine of necessity as undemocratic and steeped in a period of absolutism and colonialism, appears to have been noted by the Supreme Court in 1977. Chief Justice Anwarul Haq did not rule on the position of the Objectives Resolution as the *grundnorm* of Pakistan as such, but he was nevertheless at pains to find a legitimization of the doctrine of necessity not just in English common law but also in Islam. This attempt to find a new, indigenous, source of constitutional law is significant: in *Asma Jilani* it was held that the Objectives Resolution amounted to a *grundnorm* which imposed limitation on any change of the constitutional order. The negative, protective function of the Objectives Resolution was transformed by Haq into a positive, law-creating, function: whereas in the Reference, as was observed by Cornelius, the doctrine of necessity was exclusively based on English common law, *Begum Nusrat Bhutto* postulates a new, Islamic source of constitutional law.[67]

The same applies to the principle that the "Courts remain the Judges of the validity of the actions of the new regime in the light of the doctrine of necessity".[68] Chief Justice Haq effectively, if not expressly, confirmed the Islamic basic structure doctrine when he held that even if for any reason this power were to be removed from the 1973 Constitution "the fact remains

---

[65] *Ibid.*, at p. 485.
[66] *Ibid.*, at p. 486. It should be noted that Justice Cornelius disagreed with this part of the judgment, holding instead that the Governor-General could not invoke any powers except such as were available to him under the constitutional instruments in force (at p. 515). Munir's reliance on English law to legitimize the doctrine of necessity received the somewhat prophetic reply that "The record of these affairs belong to periods when, and to territories where, the power of the king was, in fact, supreme and undisputed. The record of these affairs are hardly the kind of scripture which one could reasonably expect to be quoted in a proceeding which is essentially one in the enforcement and maintenance of representative institutions. For they can bring but cold comfort to any protagonist of the autocratic principle against the now universal rule that the will of the people is sovereign. In the case of North America, the territory was eventually lost through the maintenance of just such reactionary opinions, as those which the Senior Counsel for the Federation of Pakistan has been pleased to advance for the acceptance by the Court. And in the English case, the fate of the King, and the Judges who delivered the opinion favouring absolute power in the King, stands for all time as a warning against absolutism, and as a landmark in the struggle for the freedom and eventual sovereignty of the people" (at p. 516). Justice Muhammad Sharif echoed this observation holding that "it might lead on occasion to dangerous consequences if in any real or supposed emergency of which the head of the State alone must be the judge, the constitutional structure could be tampered with" (at p. 519).
[67] *Begum Nusrat Bhutto v. Chief of Army Staff* PLD 1977 SC, at p. 708–709.
[68] *Ibid.*, at p. 717.

that the ideology of Pakistan embodying the doctrine that sovereignty belongs to Allah and is to be exercised on his behalf as a sacred trust by the chosen representatives of the people, strongly militates against placing the ruler for the time being above the law." Haq continued by stating that "[T]he Courts of Justice are an embodiment and a symbol of the conscience of the Millat (Muslim community), and provide an effective safeguard for the rights of the subjects."[69]

The Chief Justice's reliance on Islamic law was followed by the other members of the Bench.[70] Justice Muhammad Afzal Cheema observed that Islam was the ideological foundation of Pakistan and that for this reason the Kelsonian theory of revolutionary legality had no applicability at all since Islam did not recognize a legal basis divorced from morality.[71] Cheema also embarked on a detailed examination of the Islamic doctrine of necessity finding that the people were obliged to follow a ruler who had come to power under that doctrine with the objective of removing an unjust tyrant. However, this duty came to an end if the bona fide "usurper" did not himself observe the limits of Allah.[72]

Justice Muhammad Akram followed the precedent stating that:

Moreover, as observed by my Lord, the Chief Justice, ours is an ideological State of the Islamic Republic of Pakistan. Its ideology is firmly rooted in the Objectives Resolution with emphasis on Islamic laws and concept of morality. In our way of life we do not and cannot divorce morality from law.... It [i.e. the pure theory of law] has no place in our body politics and is unacceptable to the Judges charged with the administration of justice in this country.[73]

The Supreme Court's condoning of Zia-ul-Haq's martial law under the doctrine of necessity was made subject to the condition that it was to be limited in time, that the President and the courts continued to function under the Constitution of 1973 and that the courts were entitled to exercise their power of judicial review to judge the validity of any act or action of the martial law authorities notwithstanding anything contained in any martial law regulation or order, presidential order and ordinance.[74]

The fate of the *Begum Nusrat Bhutto* decision is well known. The elections promised by Zia-ul-Haq to be held in October 1977, i.e. just two months after the imposition of martial law, were postponed indefinitely while Zia-ul-Haq proceeded to rule the country under martial law until 1985. In that period he was able to introduce far-reaching changes to the legal system of Pakistan, especially in the field of Islamic law. Justice Qaisar's resigned acceptance of Zia-ul-Haq's *coup d'état* was, in retrospect, more realistic than the Chief Justice's optimistic assessment that "it would be highly unfair and

---

[69] *Ibid.*, at p. 717.
[70] Except Justice Nasim Hasan Shah, who did not refer to Islamic law once.
[71] *Ibid.*, at p. 724.
[72] *Ibid.*, at p. 727.
[73] *Ibid.*, at 733.
[74] *Ibid.*, at 715–716, *per* Chief Justice Anwarul Haq.

uncharitable to attribute any other intention to the Chief Martial Law Administrator, and to insinuate that he has not assumed power for the purposes stated by him, or that he does not intend to restore democratic institutions."[75]

To summarize: the resurrection of the basic structure doctrine in the form of Islam was a useful tool to impose limitations on the doctrine of necessity. Reliance on Islamic law also enabled judges to formulate new principles of constitutional law which were to exist independently from any written legal source, and were not based on principles of English common law. This "indigenization" of constitutional law constitutes a momentous step in the legal history of Pakistan: by 1977 it was well established that Islamic law imposed limits on the legislative powers of the government. The transcendental authority of Islamic law is, however, not necessarily based on the Objectives Resolution alone. As was made apparent in *Begum Nusrat Bhutto*, the authority of Islamic law is rooted in the genesis of Pakistan as an ideological state.

5   THE MARTIAL LAW OF 1999

The imposition of martial law by General Pervaiz Musharraf on 12 October 1999 forced Pakistan's judiciary yet again to examine the legal validity of a *de facto* regime. The judiciary was helped in its deliberations by two factors. First, the population seemed to approve of the military takeover. Second, by the standards of martial law General Musharraf's regime seems to be fairly civilized. The press has continued to report freely and to criticize openly all aspects of the General's regime. Further, all judges who had been associated closely with the former Prime Minister Nawaz Sharif's regime had been removed from their posts by virtue of the Judges (Oath of Office) Ordinance 2000.

The Supreme Court in its judgment of 30 May 2000 validated the *coup d'état* on the basis of the doctrine of necessity, holding that the country had been in so deep a crisis that General Musharraf was justified in taking over power so as to save it from otherwise certain ruin. The resurrection of the doctrine of necessity in itself does not come as a surprise. However, for the purposes of this article the interesting feature of the Supreme Court's judgment is the almost complete absence of references to Islam or Islamic jurisprudence. The Supreme Court was content to observe that even Islam recognized the doctrine of necessity and that the General's power of constitutional amendment were limited to the extent that *inter alia* he was not allowed to alter the blend of Islamic law and other constitutional provisions. There was no express recognition of a *grundnorm* or a precise delineation of the limits of constitutional amendment.

---

[75]   *Ibid.*, at 715.

6 CONCLUSION

An examination of the use of Islamic jurisprudence in the context of constitutional law reveals three surprising trends. First, that the use of Islam emerged quite independently from Zia-ul-Haq's Islamicization programme. Secondly, that the use of Islam as a source of constitutional law and principles was developed by Pakistan's judiciary consciously and independently from any political programme of Islamicization. Thirdly, that it was, without exception, used to challenge rather than to endorse martial law.

The latter is perhaps the most surprising feature of the Islamic constitutional law in Pakistan. Whenever Pakistan's higher judiciary chooses to endorse a prima facie unconstitutional act, references to Islam as a *grundnorm* are absent. This trend was repeated in the most recent decision on the validity of martial law of 30 May 2000. The use of Islam has a tool for bolstering democracy is unusual in a country like Pakistan, where many other manifestations of Islamic law are more often than not associated with a restriction of freedoms and in the case of women, with a denial of the right to equality.

The reason for the Janus-like quality of Islamic law in Pakistan is located in the political structure of Pakistan: volatile political changes and frequent abrogations of constitutions have forced the judiciary of Pakistan to derive power and jurisdiction from sources not officially capable of being abrogated. Islamic law was and is a source of law which exists independently of specific legislative acts. It is therefore available to judges who are prepared to challenge the validity of a written constitution and of military takeovers.

There is just one important reservation to be added to an otherwise inventive and constructive use of Islamic law: in virtually all cases in which martial law was declared to be invalid on the basis of Islamic law the martial law dictator had already been removed from office by the time the judgment was handed down.

State Cases in the Republic of Yemen

*Abdalla Ahmed Ghanem**

The Ministry of Legal and Parliamentary Affairs is a new phenomenon in the Republic of Yemen. It is now well known that 22 May 1990 witnessed the reunification of the two previous states of Yemen: the conservative Yemen Arab Republic and the Marxist People's Democratic Republic of Yemen. Prior to that date, and as far as state cases are concerned, the situation was as follows.

1   YEMEN ARAB REPUBLIC (OR NORTH YEMEN)

In North Yemen there was a Ministry of Justice, in charge of the administrative and financial affairs of the various levels of law courts, in addition to the execution or enforcement of final judgments against the government ministries. There was also the State Legal Office, which in 1988 became known as the Ministry of Legal Affairs, the most important functions of which were the drafting of legislation, publication of the Official Gazette, and the representation of the state in any dispute – especially before any law court or arbitration tribunal abroad – by or against any government ministry or corporation.

2   PEOPLE'S DEMOCRATIC REPUBLIC OF YEMEN (OR SOUTH YEMEN)

In South Yemen there was a Ministry of Justice, in charge of the administrative and financial matters of the courts of appeal and the magistrates' (or trial) courts, in addition to the drafting of legislation, publication of the Official

---

*   Minister of Legal and Parliamentary Affairs, Republic of Yemen.

68

Gazette, acting as the government's legal adviser and representing the government in cases filed by or against it within the country or abroad.

3   REPUBLIC OF YEMEN
(SINCE REUNIFICATION IN MAY 1990)

After reunification in May 1990, two of the ministries in the first government formed in the new Republic of Yemen were the Ministry of Legal Affairs, and the Ministry of Parliamentary Affairs. After the general elections of 27 April 1993 the two ministries were amalgamated to form the Ministry of Legal and Parliamentary Affairs. The provisions of Republican Resolution No. 46/1993, together with the Organizational Regulations of the Ministry of Legal Affairs, now govern the working of the Ministry.

The Minister of Legal and Parliamentary Affairs – as Minister of Parliamentary Affairs – is Chairman of the Political Parties and Organizations Commission, in accordance with the Political Parties and Organizations Law No. 66/1991. The Commission is composed, in addition to the Chairman, of the Ministers of Justice and the Interior, two retired judges and two practising private lawyers. The Commission is empowered to register any political party or organization which desires to operate and be active in public affairs – including the right to have a newspaper – under the provisions of the Political Parties and Organizations Law and the Executive Regulations thereof. There are at present twenty political parties and organizations registered, and – consequently – legally entitled to operate in the Republic of Yemen. During the first half of the year 2000 a conference will be held to review the experiment of the application of the law, and examine the need for any changes, especially as regards the financial provisions.

However, apart from matters connected with political parties and organizations, there are ten points which summarize the main functions of the Ministry, among which functions comes the representation – by the Ministry – of the government and its various other ministries and organs, in any dispute against or by it/them, before any court of law or arbitration tribunal – inside the Republic or abroad – a function which has come to be described as "state cases".

3.1   Legislation and legal supervision

This involves preparation and drafting, as well as revision and review, of Bills initiated by the government (in coordination with the concerned organs such as the various ministries, corporations, authorities, banks, unions, chambers of commerce and industry and private enterprise, etc.), before the said Bills are submitted to the Council of Ministers – and thereafter – to the House of Representatives (which is the Parliament in the Republic of Yemen). The Ministry also revises and reviews all the drafts of agreements and treaties to which the Republic is party. Furthermore, the Ministry lays down the systems needed for supervision as well as inspection and follow up, in order to ensure the proper application and implementation of the laws and regulations in force in the Republic of Yemen. All the legal departments, as well as the legal advisers, in the state organs come under the supervision of the Ministry of Legal and Parliamentary Affairs, as regards the performance, by the said departments or advisers, of their legal responsibilities, with special emphasis on their responsibilities affecting state cases.

3.2 Legal opinions

The Ministry gives legal opinions (sometimes called fatwas) in international, constitutional or legislative matters, or matters relating to agreements and treaties prior to execution or signing, or the Republic becoming a party to them, in addition to the other legal matters which are submitted to the Ministry – by the higher organs in the state, or any other ministry – for legal advice or opinion. The Ministry also gives reasoned legal opinions in the matters at issue among the various state ministries or authorities, the public sector, etc. Any opinions given by the Ministry of Legal and Parliamentary Affairs – in this connection – are final, and binding.

3.3 Publication and authentication

The Ministry publishes all the laws and other legislation (Presidential Resolutions, Resolutions of Parliament, Resolutions of the Council of Ministers, Resolutions of the Prime Minister, Ministerial Resolutions, Resolutions of the Supreme Judicial Council), indexing, cataloguing and surveying the same. For instance, the Ministry has – so far – published two indices and two guides to Yemeni legislation, in addition to the legislative steps as well as the results of the general elections of 27 April 1997, as under:

(a) *Guide to Yemeni Legislation* [*Al-Daleel Lil-Tashree'at Al-Yemanniyah*] for the period May 1990 to December 1994;

(b) *Guide to Yemeni Legislation* [*Al-Daleel Lil-Tashree'at Al-Yamanniyah*] for the period 1995–1998;

(c) *Index of Legislation (Laws, Regulations, Agreements) of the Republic of Yemen* [*Al-Mash Al-Tashree'y Al-'Amm: Qawaneen; Lawa'ih; Ittifaqiy-yat*] for the period 22 May 1990 to 21 May 1995;

(d) *Index of Legislation (Laws and Agreements)* of the ex-North Yemen for the period September 1962 to May 1990 and of the ex-South Yemen for the period December 1967 to May 1990;

(e) a book on the *Constitutional and Legal Steps* [*Al-Waqa'ia Al-Dostooriyah Li-Intikhabat Majlis Al-Nuwwab*] of 27 April 1997 regarding the second parliamentary elections since reunification of 27 April 1997, together with the election petitions filed against the elections results, to the Supreme Court of the Republic.

3.4 Parliamentary affairs

The Ministry of Legal and Parliamentary Affairs is the liaison between the executive (government) and the legislature (Parliament). The Ministry, including the Minister, attends and follows the sittings of Parliament and its standing committees, and calls on the concerned ministers and other public bodies to attend and submit the Bills proposed by the government and explains or clarifies the government's points of view as regards all the Bills, agreements, treaties and matters which Parliament discusses, and keeps the ministries and other public bodies informed of the results of the debates. The Ministry also keeps records of the ordinary and extraordinary sittings of Parliament and its standing committees.

3.5 Human rights

The Ministry of Legal and Parliamentary Affairs lays down policies, plans and programmes regarding protection of human rights in coordination with the public bodies concerned with dealing with human rights matters in general in accordance with the Constitution and legislation in force, and the agreements, treaties and Protocols to which the Republic of Yemen is a party or signatory. The Ministry also participates – with the public bodies concerned – in following up the implementation of this legislation and agreements or Protocols. It is worth mentioning, however, that the Minister of Legal and Parliamentary Affairs is a member of the National Supreme Commission of Human Rights in the Republic of Yemen.

3.6 The Official Gazette

The Ministry issues the Official Gazette every fortnight, in accordance with the Official Gazette Law No. 27/1992. This is done after collecting the laws, resolutions and all other matters which should – under the provisions of the Official Gazette Law – be published in the Official Gazette. The Ministry also publishes volumes of legislation, and collects and publishes treaties, agreements and Protocols to which the Republic of Yemen is a party.

3.7 Research and information

The Ministry conducts legal studies and research into the various branches and comparative studies between Arab and foreign legislation, international and regional legislation, and decisions of the international courts and arbitration tribunals. The Ministry has a legal library with up-to-date publications. The Ministry further exchanges legislation and legal publications with brotherly and friendly states, as well as regional and international organizations.

In this connection, the Ministry has – among other matters – organized, and participated in, the following seminars, workshops and conferences:

(a)   A Workshop on Law Reform took place during the period 23–25 April
      1995. The main subject of discussion was a comprehensive programme
      of law reform in the Republic of Yemen. The Workshop on Law Reform
      was organized with technical assistance from the World Bank. Many
      experts from various fields participated – lawyers, judges, businessmen,
      university professors and senior civil servants. It is worth mentioning
      that the Council of Ministers approved the Law Reform Programme
      (on 9 August 1995) and directed all government organs to implement
      the different tasks and responsibilities in this respect. Furthermore, one
      of the recommendations of the Workshop was connected with the
      establishment of a Centre for Legal Studies. The Ministry, with the
      assistance of the World Bank, gave effect to this recommendation in
      the year 1996.
(b)   A seminar was held in 1996 regarding the Bill on Local Authority – as
      it is called in the Constitution – or local government – as it is called in
      England and Wales – which is going to implement the government's
      programme on decentralization, with a view to having elected local
      councils in the provinces (called governorates) and the districts. Many
      persons – involved in the sphere of decentralization – officials, profes-
      sors, lawyers, businessmen and foreign experts from the World Bank,
      UNDP, the European Union Embassies in the Republic of Yemen, etc.
      – participated. The Bill on Local Authority (*as-Sultah al-Mahalliyyah*),
      otherwise known as the Law on Administrative and Financial Decentral-
      ization, or Local Councils Law, has recently been passed by Parliament.
(c)   A seminar was held during 1997 regarding international humanitarian
      law, attended by many interested bodies – both civilian and military –
      in addition to the International Red Cross Mission in the Republic
      of Yemen.
(d)   A Workshop on Judicial Reform in Yemen was held in December 1997,
      organized by the Ministry of Justice and the Ministry of Legal and
      Parliamentary Affairs – in coordination with the British Embassy and
      British Council in the Republic of Yemen and the World Bank – and
      financed by the British Embassy and British Council and the World
      Bank. Judges, prosecutors and lawyers from all the provinces in the
      Republic participated.

At the same time, discussions were held – and the Ministry participated in
those discussions – on the following legal topics:

(a)   the system of administrative and financial decentralization: with the
      assistance of the World Bank and United Nations Development
      Programme;
(b)   the development of legislation related to commercial litigation and
      arbitration;
(c)   the Privatization Bill, which became Law No. 45/1999 in October
      1999;
(d)   legislation regarding investment, and the legal obstacles in this respect;
(e)   the question of the Republic of Yemen becoming a party to the New

York Convention on the Enforcement of Arbitration Awards; and
(f)   the rights of the accused as well as the victim under the laws in force
in Yemen, Islamic *shari'a* principles and the international human rights
conventions in this respect.

Recently, the Ministry of Legal and Parliamentary Affairs signed – in principle
– an agreement with the World Bank, for a loan to finance a legal reform
project, as follows:

(a)   carrying out a programme to strengthen the capabilities of the Ministry
of Legal and Parliamentary Affairs in preparing, reviewing and advising
on business, financial and economic legislation, and in negotiating
international business transactions;
(b)   carrying out a diagnostic assessment of the legal framework governing
business, economic and financial activities, exclusive of the laws governing land tenure, transfer, titling and registration, such assessment to
recommend a reform programme and include an action plan to implement the recommended reform;
(c)   carrying out a diagnostic assessment of the legal framework governing
land tenure, transfer, titling and registration, with the purpose of recommending a reform programme and including an action plan to implement the recommended reform.

3.8   Legal awareness

The Ministry of Legal and Parliamentary Affairs handles any assistance that
could be rendered to help the media, within the Ministry's responsibilities,
in the form of interviews, clarifications, announcements, appropriate comments, etc., all of which help in making the people aware of topics that are
of public interest. The Ministry, too, is in the process of carrying out a
baseline study for an awareness campaign on the role of law and the judiciary
in society.

3.9   Government arbitration

The Ministry of Legal and Parliamentary Affairs settles disputes which arise
among state organs. Any dispute between two or more state organs must be
settled either by passing a legal opinion (or fatwa), which is binding upon
all the state organs which are parties to the dispute concerned, or through
the machinery of government arbitration, which is governed by provisions
to this effect in the Public Authorities, Corporations and Companies Law
No. 35/1991. But, if the dispute is between a state organ and a third party,
the dispute may be settled by legal opinion (or fatwa), which is only binding
if the third party has accepted the jurisdiction of the Ministry of Legal and
Parliamentary Affairs and – consequently – the legal opinion (or fatwa). Law

No. 35/1991, in connection with Public Corporations, Authorities and Companies, is of significance as regards the responsibilities of the Ministry of Legal and Parliamentary Affairs in relation to government arbitration. Public corporations are now governed by this law. According to its provisions (sections 106–119), disputes arising between public corporations themselves, or between them and central or local government bodies, are to be referred to tribunals for the purpose of settling them by arbitration, under the jurisdiction of the Ministry. The Awards of the Arbitration Tribunals in this respect are binding, final and not subject to appeal.

3.10   State cases

The Ministry of Legal and Parliamentary Affairs is responsible, through a department called the State Case Department, for representing the government in disputes for or against any ministry or public authority inside the Republic, or abroad before judicial courts and arbitration tribunals, in accordance with the State Cases Law No. 26/1992, as amended by Law No. 30/1996. An example is the following case.

In the matter of an Arbitration between Compagnie d'Entreprises ("CFE") SA of Belgium and the Government of the Republic of Yemen (under No. 7748/BLG/OLG of the International Court of Arbitration of the ICC) and in the matter of the International Commercial Arbitration Law 101/1987 (Application No. 35/98) – in the District Court of Nicosia – by the Government of the Republic of Yemen (through the Ministry of Legal Affairs of Yemen). The case involves a dispute that arose between the Belgium Company and the Aden Port Authority.

Another example is Constitutional Case 1/1993 in the Supreme Court of the Republic of Yemen – the Constitutional Division – where the decision was of a more direct political nature, concerning the general elections that were held in the Republic of Yemen on 27 April 1993. The Supreme Court upheld the electoral law, while restricting the explanatory resolution of the Supreme Electoral Commission (which extended the requirement of resignation of the ministers who wished to stand as candidates for Prime Minister as well).

The responsibility of the Ministry of Legal and Parliamentary Affairs as regards state cases is a very important one. The provisions of Law No. 26/1992, as amended by Law No. 30/1996 – on the subject – deal with various aspects of the subject:

(a)   the Ministry is the legal representative of the state and all its organs, before Yemeni and foreign judicial bodies and arbitration tribunals;

(b)   all legal departments of the ministries and other public organs shall be subordinate to the Ministry of Legal and Parliamentary Affairs;

(c)   the Ministry is conferred with powers to issue legal opinions as regards disputes arising among state organs, and these legal opinions shall be final and binding if the parties are state organs. But, if one of the parties to the dispute is not a state organ, the opinion is not binding on the third party unless that third party accepts the jurisdiction of the Ministry of Legal Affairs to settle the dispute, thereby accepting any legal opinion in this respect;

(d) the powers of the Ministry, as regards state cases, are the following: representing the state, or the concerned organs, in legal actions brought by – or against – them; reviewing the contracts and agreements to which the government, or one of its organs, is a party, and which impose financial obligations on the State Treasury; representing the concerned organs in legal actions related to the said contracts and agreements; settling disputes arising among the various state organs; issuing opinions in the event of ambiguity related to legal provisions in the law in force, leading to conflict of jurisdiction, or functions, responsibilities among the state organs concerned; all legal departments, and legal advisers, in the various state organs, come under the jurisdiction of the Ministry, as regards the performance, by these departments or advisers, of their legal responsibilities in this respect. It is worth mentioning, however, that the State Cases Sector at the Ministry of Legal and Parliamentary Affairs, is to be developed during the year 2000 into a public authority.

Women's Rights in Yemen Today

*Saeed Hasson Sohbi**

1 INTRODUCTION

To talk, or to write, about the rights of women in the Republic of Yemen today, means to discuss the rights of about 50.05 per cent of the population, according to the official census. It is worth mentioning, however, that reunification – in May 1990 – has brought with it better rights for Yemeni women, at least as far as legislation is concerned, although the statistics demonstrate that much more needs to be done.

2 POPULATION

The first census of the population of the Republic of Yemen since reunification on 22 May 1990 took place on 16–17 December 1994. The total number of those living within the Republic was 14,561,330, while the number of those living within the Republic and abroad was 15,804,654. However, by 1997, the total number of those living within the Republic was 16,482,000 – 8,229,000 males and 8,253,000 females – giving an average annual increase in population of 3.7 per cent.

3 THE CONSTITUTION

The Constitution of the Republic of Yemen came into force on the declaration of the new state, as a result of the reunification of the former Yemen Arab Republic (or North Yemen) and the former People's Democratic Republic of Yemen (or South Yemen) and was amended by the House of Representatives (the Yemeni Parliament) in accordance with its Resolution No. 12/

---

* Barrister-at-Law and Advocate, Sana'a – Republic of Yemen.

1994. Article 3 provides that Islamic *shari'a* shall be the source of all law. In addition, there are various articles in the Constitution which are relevant to the rights of women, and which are as follows:

(a) Article 30: the state protects motherhood and childhood.
(b) Article 31: women are sisters of men, and the rights to which they are entitled and the duties to which they are subjected are in accordance with the principles of Islamic *shari'a* and the provisions of the law.
(c) Article 40: all citizens are equal as regards public rights and rights.
(d) Article 41: every citizen has the right to participate in political, economic, social and cultural life.
(e) Article 42: all citizens have the right to vote and be elected and to give their opinion in referenda.

4   THE REPUBLIC OF YEMEN AND THE INTERNATIONAL HUMAN RIGHTS INSTRUMENTS REGARDING WOMEN

Yemen became a signatory in 1984 to the International Agreement Regarding Elimination of All Forms of Discrimination Against Women 1979, and to the International Agreement Regarding Children's Rights 1988 in 1991, as a result of Law No. 3/1991.

5   IMPORTANT WOMEN'S INSTITUTIONS SINCE REUNIFICATION

(a) The Yemeni Council for Care of Motherhood and Childhood (Republican Resolution No. 53/1991) was established in 1999 – it became the Supreme Council for Motherhood and Childhood.
(b) The National Council for the Population was established by Republican Resolution No. 113/1992.
(c) On 3 April 1999 the Prime Minister directed that Women's Departments be established in the various state ministries (Prime Minister's Circular No. P.M. – 60/2).
(d) On International Woman's Day – 8 March 2000 – women editors were appointed by the Minister of Information to take charge of women's special supplements to the state newspaper issues for that day.
(e) The Supreme Council for Women's Affairs was established by Republican Resolution No. 50/2000.
(f) Many voluntary organizations – otherwise known as non-governmental organizations (NGOs) – are involved in activities related to women's affairs socially, medically, educationally and economically.

6   NATIONALITY LAW NO. 6/1990

Section 3 of this law provides that a "Yemeni is someone of a Yemeni father; or born in Yemen of a Yemeni mother, but the father of unknown nationality

– or with both father and mother of unknown nationality". Section 10 states that "the Yemeni wife of a Muslim national keeps her nationality unless she renounces it". However, sections 9, 11 and 13 provide that "the wife of a Yemeni national by naturalization does not become a Yemeni citizen – automatically – due to marriage, but may apply for and obtain Yemeni nationality, after five years of marriage, and retains it after the termination of marriage; the children automatically become Yemeni nationals, if they reside in Yemen".

7   THE GENERAL ELECTIONS LAW NO. 41/1992, AS AMENDED IN 1996 AND 1999

Section 2 provides – *inter alia* – that the word "citizen" means every male or female enjoying the right to vote, in accordance with the provisions of the law. Section 3 provides that "every citizen who has reached the age of 18 years enjoys the right to vote". Section 5 states that the "Supreme Elections Commission shall take all measures to encourage women to exercise their electoral rights, setting up women's committees to supervise the registration process". In the 1993 parliamentary elections, 478,790 registered females cast their votes, while the figure for the 1997 parliamentary elections surged to 1,272,073. However, there are only two women Members of Parliament, out of 301 Members of the Yemeni Parliament. Not many women candidates stood in the 1993 and 1997 parliamentary elections, for most political parties pay lip-service to the issue, and talk grandly of being fully supportive of an increase in number of women MPs but when it comes to action, nothing changes – which is why there are so few women MPs. Both the women MPs belong to the ruling party, the General Popular Congress. It should be noted that there is no woman minister in the Cabinet, no woman member in the Consultative Council, in the Supreme Court or the Supreme Judicial Council, or the Supreme Elections Commission, although one woman ambassador was appointed this year to the Netherlands, and a female member of the Yemeni Lawyers Union Council was elected in February 2000.

8   POLITICAL PARTIES AND WOMEN

Political parties and organizations have within their ranks many women members. Yet almost all the parties do not have enough women occupying leading positions, for instance:

(a)   the Permanent Committee of the General Popular Congress has 35 women out of 700 members;
(b)   the Consultative Council of the Islah Party has 7 women out of 160 members;
(c)   the Central Committee of the Socialist Party has 3 women out of 109 members;
(d)   the leadership of the Ba'ath Socialist Party has 1 woman out of 45 members;

(e)   the Central Committee of the Naserite Unionist Organization has 4 women out of 74 members.

9   THE CIVIL SERVICE AND LABOUR LAWS NOS. 19/1991 AND 5/1995

Recruitment to public service – according to section 12 – is based on the principle of equal opportunities and equal rights for all citizens, without discrimination or distinction. This means – in practice – that the law has provided for equal salaries, grades, promotions, etc., for the same jobs and posts, irrespective of whether those holding them are males or females.

The Labour Law, on the other hand, provides – in section 5 – that "work is a natural right for every citizen, and is a duty for every citizen who is able to work: with terms, conditions, guarantees, opportunities and rights which are equal and without any discrimination and distinction due to sex, age, origin, colour, belief or language". Section 42 states that "equal terms and conditions should be afforded to men and women as regards works and rights – and relations thereof: without any discrimination whatsoever, in addition to affording equal opportunities as regards recruitment, promotion, salaries or wages, qualifications, training and social security". Section 46 states that "women should not be recruited to work in dangerous or hazardous jobs, or jobs dangerous to health or socially dangerous: in addition to night shifts – except during the fasting month of Ramadan – or in such jobs are as specified by the Minister of Welfare and Social Security". Section 47 makes it mandatory on employers to affix – in a clear space – the terms and conditions of work for women. The laws, too, provide for pregnancy leave, reduced working hours for pregnant women, during pregnancy as well as after delivery, and leave without pay. The details are as follows:

(a)   pregnancy leave for sixty continuous days – with full pay – in addition to twenty extra days if the delivery has been complicated, or the woman has given birth to twins;
(b)   five hours' work until the sixth month;
(c)   four hours' – maximum – work for the pregnant woman, with effect from the sixth month of pregnancy, until delivery: moreover, pregnant women should not be asked to work overtime with effect from the sixth month of pregnancy, as well as the sixth month with effect from resumption of work;
(d)   forty days' leave with pay, and an additional fifty days, without pay in the event of the death of the husband (formerly 130 days);
(e)   a woman may take leave – without pay – for one year maximum;
(f)   a woman may take a maximum of four years' leave – without pay – to accompany a husband who is leaving the country to work abroad.

10   THE SOCIAL SECURITY AND PENSION LAWS

The laws provide that the entitlement to retirement pension is due:

(a)   on completion of service due to reaching the age of sixty for men (with a minimum actual service of fifteen years) and the age of fifty-five for women (with a minimum actual service of ten years);

(b)   or thirty-five years actual service, or twenty-five years actual service in case of discharge by disciplinary action or court order;

(c)   or on completion of actual service of thirty years for men, and twenty-five years for women;

(d)   or on completion of actual service of twenty-five years as regards men, and twenty years as regards women: provided the age is fifty for men and forty-six for women;

(e)   or on disability, or death, irrespective of actual service.

The laws also mention beneficiaries, as follows:

(f)   the pension should, according to the laws in force, be distributed equally among dependants;

(g)   those entitled are the following: (i) husband, wife/wives; (ii) children: male and female; (iii) father and mother; (iv) brother and sister: all in equal shares, and provided – as regards the parents, brothers, sisters and grandchildren – they were dependants.

Finally, the laws provide that the pension should cease to be paid on the following events:

(a)   for male beneficiaries: death; reaching eighteen years for those not undergoing education; reaching twenty-one years for those in secondary education; reaching twenty-six for those at university education, the exception being those suffering from disability;

(b)   as regards female beneficiaries: death; marriage; obtaining work with constant/fixed income.

11   THE JUDICATURE LAW NO. 1/1991

Without distinction between males and females (as is the case in certain Arab and Muslim states), section 57 provides that the following principal conditions and qualifications ought to be fulfilled by those desiring to become magistrates/judges, or public prosecutors and lawyers/advocates:

(a)   they must be Yemeni citizens;

(b)   they must be at least thirty years of age;

(c)   they must be graduates (plus having taken a course at the Higher Judicial Institute);

(d)   they must not exercise any judicial responsibilities except after the two-year training course.

Furthermore, the Arbitration Law makes it possible for men and women to become arbitrators, for there are no provisions to the contrary.

There are – now – many female magistrates and judges, many female public prosecutors and legal advisors as well as lawyers and advocates. The percentage of women magistrates and judges to men magistrates and judges is 13.5 per cent for females to 86.5 per cent for males, while in the public prosecution the percentage is 6.3 per cent for females to 93.7 per cent for males; and, as far as private lawyers are concerned, the percentage is 7.5 per cent for females to 92.5 per cent for males.

12   JUVENILES LAW NO. 24/1992

The law – together with the Judicature Law – covers juvenile courts, made up of three magistrates, one of whom should be female, and the participation of the Ministry of Welfare and Social Security.

13   LAW OF CRIMINAL PROCEDURE NO. 13/1994

Section 3 of this law provides that "criminal responsibility is personal". Section 5 states that "all citizens are equal before the law", and section 324 provides that "all the parties in a criminal case should be accorded equal treatment – as regards rights and duties – including the accused". However, section 80 provides that "traditions should be respected, as regards treatment of women – when searching houses – if there are women living there"; sections 81/143 that "searching females should be done by females, and in the presence of two female witnesses"; while section 213 provides that "examination of the body of a female should be done by a female, whose name should be – as far as possible – stated in the judicial papers". However, the following points are worth remembering:

(a)   section 27: the following charges shall not be brought except upon a "complaint" to this effect: defamation; threats; personal injuries; and crimes of property between relatives, wives and husbands, and brothers and sisters;

(b)   section 484: execution of the death penalty against a convicted woman – who is pregnant – must be stayed, until delivery and custody for two years and – after that period – where there is someone to take care of the child. The convicted pregnant women should be kept in prison until it is time for execution;

(c)   section 500: a sentence of imprisonment against a female who is pregnant should be stayed until two months after delivery;

(d)   section 501: if a sentence of imprisonment is passed against husband and wife, for a term of longer than one year, there should be a stay of serving that sentence for one of them, until the other is set free, if they have a child under thirteen years of age.

14   THE LAW OF CIVIL PROCEDURE NO. 28/1992

The law provides in section 16 that "magistrates and judges should give equal rights to the parties". Section 58, however, states that "Yemeni law courts have jurisdiction as regards affiliation orders (or maintenance, or support) for mothers, wives and/or children resident in Yemen; in addition to paternity disputes, or inheritance cases, provided that the distribution of the estate has already commenced in Yemen, or the deceased was a Yemeni national, or the property of the estate is – in whole or in part – within Yemen". Furthermore, section 65 provides that the magistrates courts alone have jurisdiction as regards maintenance applications, and their decisions are not subject to appeal, provided the amount does not exceed YR 1,000 for the child, or YR 1,500 for the wife. The court within which jurisdiction the residence of the application is situated is the court enjoying jurisdiction in this respect (section 71). The Public Prosecution must intervene in cases where minors are involved, if they have no guardian (section 96). Finally, section 210/2 provides that an appeal results, automatically, in a stay of execution of the judgment appealed against, except if the judgment involves maintenance, custody, the matrimonial home and the handing over of the child to his mother.

The said law also contains provisions with regard to the enforcement of foreign judgments in the Republic of Yemen.

15   THE LAW OF EVIDENCE NO. 21/1992

Section 45 provides for four male witnesses for crimes against the person; whereas section 297 of the Penal Code provides that the evidence for theft – carrying the penalty of amputation – is as follows:

(a)   confession, or plea of guilty, in the presence of the judge or court;
(b)   testimony of two male witnesses;
(c)   testimony of one male witness and two female witnesses.

16   CIVIL OCCURRENCES AND REGISTER LAW NO. 23/1991

The law provides for the establishment of departments for the registration of births, deaths, marriages and divorces as well as granting certificates or/ and cards in this respect, in addition to issuing personal identity cards and family cardbooks. Births have to be notified within sixty days, by the fathers, adult relatives or the directors of hospitals and prisons, where the births took place. Police stations, hospitals and other institutions for receiving new-born babies are under an obligation to notify the department concerned as regards any new-born baby found or handed over to them. The director of the department should name the baby – in full – and register the baby in the register of births, but without stating that the baby is illegitimate, and without mentioning the names of the parents.

Deaths must be notified within seventy-two hours with effect from the death, accompanied by the personal identity card (if available). For military personnel and the civilians working with them, and the reserves or volunteers who die within/without the territory of the Republic, the Ministry of Defence must notify the Director General of the department concerned about such deaths.

Any notification of births or deaths more than one year after the death must be referred to a Late Registration Committee.

17   AUTHENTICATION LAW NO. 29/1992

The law provides for the appointment of notary publics to perform – *inter alia* – the execution of marriage contracts and divorce certificates (section 10/a). The fees schedule prescribes a fixed fee for the marriage contract or divorce certificate, although – in practice – most marriages still remain unregistered.

18   THE PERSONAL STATUS CODE NO. 20/1992

The Law of Personal Status is the legislation in force governing family relations and any disputes concerned with engagements, marriages, divorces, maintenance, custody, access, wills, gifts and inheritance. The law applies to Yemeni Muslims as well as those parties to a dispute where one of them is Yemeni, and those who accept being governed by the provisions of this law (sections 26 and 34, Civil Code).

The Law of Personal Status is a codification of the traditional Islamic *shari'a* principles, without any substantive deviation or radical reforms. Marriage is a relationship between two spouses, bound by legitimate bondage, according to which the woman (under Islamic *shari'a*) becomes the wife of the man. Its objective is to institute a family – the basis of which is good co-habitation (section 6).

The law stipulates that there should be a "guardian" as regards marriage of the woman, who is the father or grandfather, or one of the brothers (section 16), but that he should not unreasonably refuse (e.g. if she says yes and she is sane and adult – section 19) to allow her to be married, otherwise, the registrar (who is also empowered, if there is no guardian at all, section 17) is empowered to do the job, provided there is dowry as well as a would-be husband of equal status, which means that the condition of a would-be equal status is provided for in the law (section 18).

The husband and the guardian sign the marriage contract form in the register specified for the purpose, but not the wife (section 14).

The age of majority if fifteen, but a female who has not reached that age may get married, provided that her consent is sought on reaching the age of fifteen (section 15). Section 10 provides that any marriage contract which is concluded against the wishes of either the male or female is void. Section 23 states that the consent of the "would-be" wife is necessary: the consent of the virgin is her silence and that of the divorced/widow is her pronouncement: however, unfortunately, the age of majority has been done away with, for section 15 has been amended, thus:

The guardian of the would-be wife may enter into a marriage contract as regards her, but shall not allow consummation of the marriage until after the wife shall have reached the age of puberty, even after the age of fifteen. At the same time, a male's guardian may enter into a marriage contract, on behalf of his ward, below the age of puberty, if there is an interest in the said marriage.

The presence of two competent male adult witnesses is necessary to make a valid contract of marriage.

Polygamy, as acknowledged by traditional Islamic *shari'a*, is recognized: a man may marry four wives if he has the ability to do justice to all wives, subject to certain conditions, which ought to be fulfilled if marriage contract is concluded, as regards another wife:

(a)   permission for up to four wives, provided justice to all;
(b)   there should be legitimate interest;
(c)   the husband has the means to financially support more than one wife;
(d)   the would-be wife should be informed that the would-be husband is already married; and
(e)   the present wife should be informed that her husband desires to marry another wife.

However, unfortunately, conditions (b) and (e) have recently been abolished.

The husband is under an obligation to maintain – or support – as well as to provide clothing for his wife/wives and her/their children; to provide a home to each of his various wives (if married to more than one wife (section 42)); to do justice to all his wives (if married to more than one wife); not to harm her/them materially or morally; not to usurp her/their property (section 41). All this means good co-habitation.

The wife/wives is/are under an obligation to obey the husband: otherwise she/they may be declared disobedient (section 40). This means living with the husband at the matrimonial home provided by him; consummation; obedience; remaining at the home and not leaving except with his permission or for a good excuse.

The law provides for termination of the marriage by annulment, divorce (section 58) or death (divorce is the right of the husband: section 59). Section 71 states that the divorced wife should get "compensation" – which is a maximum of maintenance for one year – if the divorce was without any justification on the part of the husband. However – unfortunately – this provision has been repealed. Further, there are provisions regarding the different kinds of dissolution of the marriage, under Islamic *shari'a* principles (*zihar, khul', li'an*).

There are many provisions regarding dowry (sections 33, 34, 35, 36 and 37).

As regards inheritance, the principles in Islamic *shari'a* apply in this connection. The *shari'a* principles are well known and they have been in operation in this sphere for the last fourteen centuries. There is a chapter on inheritance in the Personal Status Law in force in the Republic of Yemen.

19 CIVIL CODE NO. 19/1992

"The age of majority (or capacity) is fifteen years": this means that a male or female is entitled – at that age – to enter into contracts or transactions (section 5). Furthermore, section 38 provides that "the personality of a human being commences on birth and ceases on death".

20 PENAL CODE NO. 12/1994

The law provides that "an infant – who has not reached the age of seven years – is *doli incapax*, and is thus not accountable for any (crime) or (offence)"; but if he has reached the age of seven but has not yet reached the age of fifteen, the court may impose one of the measures provided for in the Law on Juveniles; and if he has reached the age of fifteen but has not yet reached the age of eighteen, the sentence should not exceed half the maximum of the offence. If that sentence is capital punishment it shall be imprisonment for between three and ten years. The sentences of imprisonment should be served at places separate from those for adults. However, if the age of the juvenile is not ascertained, the judge shall ascertain it, with the help of experts.

Other provisions are as follows:

(a) section 42: the blood compensation for women is half that for men;
(b) section 58: an accused man should be put to death for murdering a woman;
(c) section 232: if the husband murders his wife – together with the person committing adultery with her – the husband should not be condemned to death, but may be imprisoned for a term not exceeding one year, or a fine may be imposed;
(d) sections 239 and 240: anyone who deliberately performs an abortion on a woman – without her consent – is punished by the compensation of the child – which is half that of an adult. If the woman dies, the punishment is imprisonment for a term not exceeding ten years. But if the abortion has been done with the consent of the woman, the whole compensation should be paid up. If the woman dies, only blood compensation should be paid;
(e) section 249: kidnapping of a female, or a juvenile, is punishable by imprisonment for a term not more than seven years, and if the kidnapping has been accompanied by injury or torture, for ten years;
(f) sections 251 and 252: non-return of a child to his mother – or the adjudged custodian – is punishable by imprisonment for a term not exceeding three months, or a fine. However, kidnapping of a newly born child is punishable by imprisonment for a term not exceeding five years;
(g) sections 263 and 267: adultery by a married male or female is punishable by stoning to death – or lapidation; but, if there is doubt, the punishment is 100 lashes/stripes. The latter is the punishment if the accused

is unmarried, and the court may impose imprisonment for a maximum of one year in lieu of the lashes. The punishment of stoning to death must not be carried out in case of force – or doubt – such as the existence of a promise of marriage.

21   EDUCATION AND PUBLIC HEALTH

Women are obtaining better chances, as regards education and public health services, almost on an equal basis, and according to their wishes and interests: hundreds of thousands are full-time students in the primary and secondary schools, in addition to thousands in the various faculties of the different Yemeni universities, both state and private. Similarly, many women are involved in the teaching profession as well as the public health institutions.

22   CONCLUSION

Yemeni state discourse as regards women has surfaced with reunification in May 1990 – and just recently, with the presence of many official delegations from the Arab, Islamic and other foreign countries celebrating the tenth anniversary of reunification. State discourse deals with two main issues: democracy and development. The foundation for this discourse was laid down with the referendum on the 1990 Constitution, which took place in May 1991 with both men and women taking part. In 1993 the new state conducted the first parliamentary elections, and all citizens, regardless of whether they were men or women, participated, with two women MPs being elected to Parliament. In 1995, as a result of the first judicial movement since reunification, women magistrates, judges and public prosecutors were reappointed, although they had been appointed to the judiciary in the ex-Southern sector since 1972. Moreover, in 1993, the National Preparatory Committee for the Fourth United Nations Conference on Women (Beijing 1995) was established by Republican Resolution No. 251/1993 to formulate the strategy of the Republic of Yemen on women's affairs.

In 1996, the National Committee for Women was created, with a view to formulating national strategy for women, especially as regards democracy and development – which has been demonstrated amply in the development strategies and projects which the state has endorsed within the fields of health, education, poverty alleviation, etc., with material assistance from the United Nations, the World Bank, bilateral donors and international voluntary organisations worth millions of dollars. Finally, more than one million women voters, and many women candidates, participated in the parliamentary elections of 1997, in addition to the participation of women voters in the first direct presidential elections held in September 1999. All this shows that we have to look into the future with optimism.

A New Commercial Code for Egypt

*David Wilson**

1 INTRODUCTION

A new Commercial Code was promulgated in Egypt on 17 May 1999 and came into force on 1 October 1999,[1] with the exception of Articles 472–549 dealing with cheques, which were originally scheduled to come into force on 1 October 2000.[2] The use of legislative codes has a long history in Egypt. The present Civil Code was promulgated by Law No. 131 of 1948 and came into effect on 15 October 1949, replacing both the 1875 Civil Code[3] applied by the Mixed Courts and the 1883 Civil Code[4] applied by the National Courts. The year 1883 also saw the promulgation of Egypt's first Commercial

---

* Partner, Trowers & Hamlins, Cairo. My colleagues Mohamed Nour and Karim Azmi of our associate firm, Nour Law Office, kindly gave of their time in reviewing and commenting on a draft of this article, as did my colleague in Trowers & Hamlins, Sara Hinton: thanks are also due to Amal Moussa for her research support. The usual acceptance of responsibility for any remaining errors or other defects applies.

1 Law No. 17 of 1999, Art. 1. This article has been prepared on the basis of translations prepared internally for the use of Trowers & Hamlins. The 1999 Commercial Code is referred to in this article as the new Code or the Commercial Code. Unless otherwise specified, references to articles are to articles of the new Code. For a free translation of Arts. 72–87 and 166–191 by Kosheri, Rashed & Riad see Part III, pp. 429–438.

2 Law No. 17 of 1999, Art. 3. One of the changes introduced by the new Code is to prevent the use of post-dated cheques (see section 6.3 below); implementation of the new provisions relating to cheques has been delayed in recognition of the fact that post-dated cheques are currently very widely used. At time of writing this article, it has recently been announced that the date on which the provisions relating to cheques will come into force is to be postponed for a further year to 1 October 2001.

3 Promulgated 28 June 1875.

4 Promulgated 28 October 1883.

Code,[5] being that replaced by the new Code.[6] The purpose of this article is to provide an account of the new Code and to highlight some of the changes that it has introduced: where appropriate, reference is made to other relevant legislation, particularly the 1948 Civil Code.[7]

A comprehensive comparative study is beyond the scope of this article, which is primarily descriptive in nature, but it is interesting to note the extent to which the Code is similar to the Commercial Codes that have been promulgated in Bahrain, Oman and the United Arab Emirates.[8] European, particularly French, influence on Egyptian law is often remarked on,[9] as is the further spread of that influence from Egypt into the Gulf countries. The high degree of similarity between the new Code and the three others mentioned suggests an interesting example of reverse legal borrowing or transplantation.[10]

The 1883 Code addressed a limited number of topics: split into three books, it briefly covered commercial business and book-keeping (Book 1), forms of company, brokerage and exchanges, creation of mortgages, commission agency and bills of exchange (Book 2) and bankruptcy (Book 3). Bankruptcy accounted for half of the 1883 Code's articles and bills for

---

5   Promulgated 13 November 1883. The 1883 Commercial Code is referred to in this article as the 1883 Code. During its 116-year history, the 1883 Code was subject only to minor amendments in terms of Law No. 23 of 1909, Law No. 12 of 1944 and Law No. 388 of 1953.

6   The 1883 Code has not been entirely repealed – Arts. 19–65, dealing with certain forms of company available under Egyptian law, remain in force. Those provisions are not summarized in this article as a consolidation of the Egyptian companies laws is known to be under way and it is to be expected that the remaining provisions of the 1883 Code will be repealed when the consolidating legislation is promulgated.

7   Although Egypt has long had distinct civil and commercial codes, it is the Civil Code that forms the more important codification of Egyptian civil law and which is sometimes said to enjoy a quasi-constitutional status among Egyptian lawyers. The Civil Code sets out a general foundation for the country's legal system and, therefore, deals with areas of law that are also relevant to those who are involved in some form of commercial activity. The best English translation of the Civil Code remains that produced by Mr W.R. Fanner and which was published in Egypt in 1952. As well as the Arabic text, an official French translation was also issued. The main change made to the Civil Code has been the replacement of Arts. 390–417 on Proof of Obligations with a separate Law of Evidence (Law No. 25 of 1968) but which did not introduce major changes; minor amendments to Arts. 88, 874 and 970 also need to be taken into account.

8   A commercial code was promulgated in Bahrain by Law No. 8 of 1987, covering four main areas: the nature of commercial activities and obligations, particular commercial contracts (including forms of security), banking transactions and commercial paper. The topic of bankruptcy was addressed in a separate code issued shortly after by Law No. 11 of 1987. The same five topics are covered in very similar terms by the commercial code that was promulgated in Oman by Royal Decree 55 of 1990 and by that promulgated in the UAE by Federal Law No. 18 of 1993.

9   See, for example, Michael H. Davies, *Business Law in Egypt*, Kluwer, Deventer/ Netherlands, 1984, pp. 26–29.

10 This is particularly true in relation to those provisions of the new Code dealing with banking transactions, commercial paper and bankruptcy.

another quarter, leaving the remaining topics to be dealt with relatively briefly in its first 104 articles.[11] The new Code is greatly expanded as compared with the 1883 Code, both in terms of subject matter and length;[12] as a general comment, the material in the 1883 Code finds an updated counterpart in the new Code.[13]

2   COMMERCIAL ACTIVITIES IN GENERAL

2.1   Application of the Commercial Code

The new Code applies to all merchants and to all commercial activities;[14] as to what is a commercial activity, a large number of specific commercial acts are set out by way of examples,[15] covering most trading and professional activities, but they are not intended to be definitive and analogous activities are also treated as commercial in nature.[16] Farming is expressly not a commercial activity[17] and small craftsmen on a subsistence income are also excluded from application of the Commercial Code.[18]

Subject to proof to the contrary, any activity of a merchant is to be treated as connected with his trading activity and, therefore, commercial in nature, attracting application of the Commercial Code.[19] It is possible for one party's obligations under a contract to be treated as commercial but for the other party's obligations under that same contract to be treated as civil (i.e. non-commercial) and, therefore, not subject to the Commercial Code or to commercial practice.[20] Exceptions arise with Articles 300–377 of the new Code, addressing the relationship between banker and customer, which apply even if the customer is not engaged in commerce or the particular transaction

---

[11]   The 1883 Code comprised a total of 419 articles.

[12]   The new Code extends to 772 articles – a full contents listing is appended to this article.

[13]   Thus Arts. 1–43 replace 1–18 of the 1883 Code on commercial obligations and books; Arts. 44–46 and 192–207 replace 66–75 of the 1883 Code on brokers and stock exchanges; Arts. 119–129 replace 76–80 of the 1883 Code on possessory pledges; Arts. 148–176 replace 81–104 of the 1883 Code on commission agency; Arts. 378–549 replace 105–194 of the 1883 Code on bills of exchange and Arts. 195–419 of the 1883 Code (which cover bankruptcy) find their counterparts in Arts. 550–772 of the new Code. As mentioned (see note 6 above), Arts. 19–65 of the 1883 Code remain in force. A brief comparison of the contents listing of the 1883 Code and of the new Code shows that there is a wide range of topics on which the new Code legislates for the first time.

[14]   Art. 1.

[15]   Arts. 4–6.

[16]   Art. 7.

[17]   Art. 9.

[18]   Art. 16.

[19]   Art. 8.

[20]   Art. 3; for example, the granting of a guarantee need not, in itself, be a commercial act, unless the guarantor is a merchant or has granted the guarantee for a commercial purpose. This particular example is expressly recognized in Art. 48(1).

is not commercial in nature from the customer's point of view,[21] and with Articles 378–549, dealing with commercial paper, which apply irrespective of the nature or qualities of those creating an instrument.[22]

Any person who enjoys legal capacity and who engages in commercial activity is considered a merchant.[23] Any corporation is considered a merchant, regardless of its legal objects.[24] The government and state bodies are expressly not commercial in nature but the Commercial Code does apply to any commercial activities carried on by the government, unless otherwise stated in legislation of specific application.[25]

2.2 Legal capacity

Legal capacity is dependent upon a person reaching eighteen years of age and being subject to no other legal impediment,[26] although a minor may carry on business under court order.[27] The capacity of a woman engaged in commerce is subject to the law of her country of nationality.[28] There are certain restrictions governing the funds of a minor invested in business whereby, for example, the court may order such funds liquidated or withdrawn from the business if the court considers this to be in the minor's interests.[29]

2.3 Commercial books and data

A merchant who maintains an entry in the commercial register is required to indicate its trade name, together with details of the commercial registry office where the entry is maintained and the registration number, prominently at the place of business and on correspondence and printed material relating to the business.[30]

Merchants whose capital exceeds E£20,000[31] are required to maintain commercial books, including a day journal and inventory,[32] and must retain

---

[21] Art. 300.
[22] Art. 378.
[23] Arts. 10(1) and 11.
[24] Art. 10(2).
[25] Art. 20.
[26] Art. 11(1)(b); reduced from twenty-one years under Art. 4 of the 1883 Code. Note, however, that Art. 11(1)(a) applies the age of majority provided by a non-Egyptian's domiciliary law, provided that it is not more than twenty-one years.
[27] Art. 12(2).
[28] Art. 14(1). Under the 1883 Code (Art. 5), women of any nationality were subject in Egypt to limitations imposed by Egyptian law.
[29] Art. 13.
[30] Art. 31.
[31] At the time of writing, the Egyptian pound (*livre égyptien*) has an approximate value of US$ 3.45, on which basis E£20,000 equals US$ 5,800.
[32] Art. 21.

copies of all correspondence despatched and received.[33] A copy of the annual balance sheet and profit and loss accounts should be included in the inventory.[34] At the close of each financial year, commercial books must be submitted to the commercial registry for official endorsement.[35]

Commercial books, correspondence and other documents must be kept for at least five years after they have been closed.[36] Commercial books may be produced in court and constitute evidence for or against the merchant whose books they are.[37]

3   COMMERCIAL OBLIGATIONS IN GENERAL

3.1   Evidence of obligations

In determining legal obligations, priority is given (subject to public order requirements)[38] to the terms of any agreement between the parties and, thereafter, to the rules set out in the Commercial Code.[39] Any means of proof may be used to establish the existence of a commercial contract unless the law expressly stipulates otherwise.[40] The new Code contains no general requirement that commercial obligations be evidenced in writing but there are particular cases where this is required.[41]

3.2   Consideration

Under Egyptian law, a contract is void where an obligation is assumed without consideration or for a consideration contrary to public policy or morality.[42] It is to be assumed that goods and services provided on a commercial basis are provided in return for a consideration, although evidence may be accepted to the contrary (i.e. that they are given by way of gift); if not expressly addressed in the contract, consideration is assumed to be present and will be assessed according to commercial custom and practice.[43]

3.3   Prescription and limitation

The general rule is that rights of action arising from commercial obligations prescribe after the lapse of seven years from the time when the obligation

---

[33]   Art. 24.
[34]   Art. 23(2).
[35]   Art. 25(3).
[36]   Art. 26; but note Art. 68 of the new Code, which establishes the general rule that commercial obligations prescribe seven years from their due date.
[37]   Art. 70.
[38]   Art. 2(2).
[39]   Art. 2(1).
[40]   Art. 69.
[41]   E.g. sale of a business – Art. 37(1).
[42]   Civil Code, Art. 136.
[43]   Art. 49. The same rule appears in Art. 137 of the Civil Code.

should have been fulfilled. A final court ruling on an obligation lapses after ten years.[44]

3.4 Joint liability

A number of persons who are liable in respect of a commercial debt are jointly liable unless otherwise provided by law or agreement;[45] this rule applies also to multiple guarantors.[46]

3.5 Notices

The Commercial Code requires that debtors be advised of commercial matters by registered post with a record of receipt or, in case of urgency, by cable, telex, fax or equivalent.[47]

3.6 Means of payment

Where an amount due exceeds E£ 100,000, the creditor may request payment by cheque.[48]

3.7 Interest

Where a merchant's business requires him to make payments on account of clients, he may claim interest from the date of disbursement until the date of reimbursement. In the absence of agreement, the applicable rate of interest is the rate at which the Central Bank of Egypt deals.[49]

---

[44] Art. 68. The new Code contains a number of other limitation periods of more specific application: see, for example, Art. 67(5) (product liability), Arts. 101(2) and (4) and 102(6) (sale contracts), Arts. 143 and 146 (pledges), Art. 190 (contract agency), Art. 254 (carriage of goods), Art. 272 (carriage of persons), Art. 296 (air transport), Arts. 304 and 376 (correction of bank statements) and Arts. 437, 465, 504, 511, 531 and 546 (claims arising from bills and other commercial paper).

[45] Art. 47(1); i.e. each person liable is liable for the full amount of the debt. More generally, see Civil Code, Arts. 279–302, on plurality of parties to an obligation.

[46] Art. 47(2).

[47] Art. 58.

[48] Art. 62.

[49] Art. 50(2). Interest rates continue to be regulated in that persons other than those licensed to conduct banking business are unable to enforce interest provisions to the extent that the rate stipulated exceeds 7 per cent per annum (Civil Code, Art. 227). The ability to charge interest is set out in Art. 542 of the Civil Code: the analysis adopted is that interest represents the required consideration in terms of the relevant loan agreement.

3.8 Application of inheritance rules

Obligations entered into by a merchant will generally bind his estate following his death unless the heirs discontinue the business, in which case compensation may be payable to creditors.[50]

4 RULES RELATING TO SPECIFIC CONTRACTS

4.1 Sale of a business

A commercial concern or business is defined as a group of movable assets (tangible and intangible), including goods, furniture, machinery, clients, trade names, leasing rights, trademarks and other forms of intellectual property.[51] Central to this definition is the concept of a business as a bundle of obligations, as distinct from the person who is the common party to those obligations. Title to the land or premises from which the business is carried on does not form part of the assets comprising a business but a business sale may, by agreement, be dependent upon a concurrent transfer of any relevant title.[52]

Sale or lease of any interest in a business requires a written contract, which must be entered in the Commercial Register and published in the relevant gazette.[53] The seller or lessor of a business is prohibited from engaging in a similar activity in such a way as to harm the sold or leased business for a period of ten years from the date of registration of the transfer, unless a shorter period is agreed.[54]

4.2 Other sale contracts

Articles 88–103 of the Commercial Code set out provisions of general application to sale contracts in which the consideration is payable partly or all in cash. These provisions are subject to any obligations arising in terms of international treaties or conventions to which Egypt has acceded.[55] As a general comment, the rules set out in the new Code relate to matters such as determining price,[56] specifications[57] and delivery times[58] in cases where

---

[50] Art. 50(3).
[51] Art. 51.
[52] Under Egyptian law, leases do not give rise to any interest in land or other real right – Civil Code, Art. 558 *et seq.*; lessees do, however, enjoy various statutory protections – see, for example, Arts. 558–609 of the Civil Code and Law No. 4 of 1996 extending the application of those articles.
[53] Art. 38(1).
[54] Art. 42(2).
[55] Art. 88(2). Relevant treaties include the Vienna Convention for the International Sale of Goods.
[56] Art. 89.
[57] Art. 92.
[58] Art. 93.

the relevant agreement does not deal with these issues: the new Code also sets out available remedies or bases of claim where one party does not perform.[59]

4.3   Sale by instalments and retention of title

Where payment in terms of a sale contract is by instalments, a claim for rescission of the sale based on the purchaser's failure to pay an agreed instalment will not be accepted where the purchaser has already paid three-quarters or more of the purchase price; in such a case, the seller's claim is for compensation only.[60]

If the seller retains title against payment of instalments, the purchaser acquires title only upon payment of the final instalment but is responsible for any damage to the item sold as from the date of its delivery.[61] A retained title will only defeat the claim of a third party if recorded in a document evidencing a date before the date on which the rights of such third party arose or prior to actions being taken by creditors against the property being sold.[62]

Disposal by the purchaser prior to payment of the final instalment is subject to the seller's written agreement and any other attempted disposal is invalid as against the seller if it is established that the party receiving the property being sold was aware that payment had not been made in full.[63] Contravention of this requirement is a criminal offence;[64] in addition, the seller may require immediate payment by the purchaser of all remaining instalments.[65]

4.4   Sale by liquidation or public auction

Articles 108–114 of the Commercial Code apply to seasonal sales, stock liquidations and public auctions. Auctions must be conducted through a registered valuer.[66]

4.5   Supply contracts

Articles 115–118 of the Commercial Code address contracts for the supply of goods on an ongoing basis; in this case, a one-off failure to perform does

---

[59]   Art. 96–103.
[60]   Art. 105(1).
[61]   Art. 106(1).
[62]   Art. 106(2). Date certainty must be established in accordance with the requirements of Art. 395 of the Civil Code.
[63]   Art. 107(1).
[64]   Art. 107(3).
[65]   Art. 107(2).
[66]   Art. 110(1).

not allow the other party to rescind the contract unless gross damage has been caused or the failure indicates a general inability to perform in the future.[67] Attempts by suppliers to restrict customer sourcing are subject to the limitation that a customer may be contractually required not to use other sources for a maximum period of five years.[68]

4.6 Pledge

The nature of a pledge under Egyptian law has not undergone any radical change. Most of the law relating to pledge is actually to be found in Articles 1096–1129 of the Civil Code, which are now joined by Articles 119–129 of the new Code,[69] which apply where the secured debt is commercial in nature as regards the debtor.[70]

To summarize, creation of a commercial pledge depends upon transfer of possession of the pledged asset, either to the creditor or to a third party custodian.[71] A written pledge agreement is not required but there should be some form of receipt.[72] Enforcement of the pledge is by application for a court order permitting the sale by public auction of some or all of the pledged assets.[73] The debt to the creditor may be satisfied in whole or in part by transfer of ownership of the pledged asset to the creditor but any contractual term in a pledge agreement allowing the creditor to require such a transfer will be invalid; thus, any agreement to transfer may only be entered into after the secured debt has become due.[74]

4.7 Transfer of technology

The Commercial Code regulates technology transfer contracts.[75] A technology transfer contract is defined as an agreement whereby a supplier of technology undertakes to transfer, against payment, technical know-how for the development of a specific commodity, for the installation or operation

---

[67] Art. 117.
[68] Art. 118.
[69] Replacing Arts. 76–80 of the 1883 Code.
[70] Art. 119. Other forms of security, such as mortgage, lien (including landlord's lien) and guarantee, are also dealt with in the Civil Code. The Civil Code also makes provision for a form of judicial security over immovable property, similar to inhibition in Scots law.
[71] Art. 120(1).
[72] Art. 122(1).
[73] Art. 126.
[74] Art. 129.
[75] The relevant provisions take up a whole section of the new Code – Part 2, section 1, comprising Arts. 72–87. This section of the new Code finds no counterpart in the other Gulf codes mentioned above (see note 9 above) and is therefore covered here in slightly greater detail than some other parts of the new Code.

of machinery or other equipment, or for the provision of services.[76] The mere sale, purchase, lease or rental of commodities is not considered a transfer of technology, nor is the sale or licensing of trademarks or commercial titles, unless set forth in a technology transfer contract or otherwise forming part of a technology transfer arrangement.[77] The technology transfer provisions of the Commercial Code apply regardless of whether the relevant contract has an international element or is purely domestic.[78]

A technology transfer contract must be in writing[79] and should comprise a statement or description of the know-how to be transferred and of anything "ancillary" to the basic know-how.[80] The purpose here seems to be to try and avoid situations where the supplier of technology only makes available limited applications and the transferee is prevented from realizing the full benefit of the relevant technology. This approach is evident in the requirement that any term of a technology transfer contract that might restrict the freedom of the transferee to use, develop, understand or publicise the relevant product or service are voidable; this applies, in particular, to terms restricting the transferee as follows:

(a) requiring the transferee to accept and pay for improvements to the technology;

(b) prohibiting the introduction of improvements or modifications to suit local conditions or the conditions of the transferee's establishment;

(c) requiring the use of specific trademarks to distinguish products produced using the technology;

(d) limiting the volume of production, pricing or methods of distribution or export;

(e) involvement of the supplier in the running of the transferee's business, including selection of employees;

(f) requiring the transferee to purchase raw materials, equipment or spare parts from the supplier alone or from establishments exclusively specified by the supplier; or

(g) restricting the sale of production exclusively to the supplier or its nominee.

The provisions outlined above are clearly protectionist in tone and apply

---

[76] Art. 73. The reference to both products and services is interesting as raising the possibility of application to, for example, fast food franchises – a specified product delivered in a specified manner in specified surroundings. For a free translation of Arts. 72–82 by Kosheri, Rashed & Riad, see Part III, pp. 429–431.

[77] Art. 72.

[78] *Ibid*. Although the provisions of this section are stated to apply irrespective of the nationality of the parties, some articles (e.g. 75, 76 and 80–85) refer to the transferee as the "importer". The section appears to be a reaction to the ongoing need to make use of foreign technology, coupled with an ongoing wariness of the terms on which it is made available.

[79] Art. 74(1).

[80] Art. 74(2).

unless disapplied in the relevant contract in order to protect the consumer or to safeguard "a serious and legitimate interest" of the supplier.[81]

Positive obligations on the supplier include a requirement to disclose risks involved in using the technology and the measures that can be taken to limit their consequences, any legal rights or current proceedings that might limit the transferee's ability legitimately to use the technology and, where the supplier is foreign, any relevant provisions of the supplier's local law concerning requirements for export of the technology.[82] During the period of the relevant technology transfer contract, the supplier is also required to provide, on an ongoing basis, relevant technical information, including as to training,[83] improvements[84] and spare parts (or information as to their availability from other sources).[85]

Although there is a clear protectionist approach to the technology transfer provisions of the new Code, certain requirements are imposed on the transferee: these include a restriction on assignment without the consent of the supplier,[86] a confidentiality obligation which applies during as well as after contract negotiations,[87] a requirement that exclusivity be limited both as to geographical area and as to time.[88]

In the event that harm is caused to third parties, the supplier and transferee are separately, not jointly, liable.[89] Technology transfer contracts are subject to five-yearly renewals.[90] The application of Egyptian law to technology transfer contracts is mandatory.[91] The jurisdiction of the Egyptian courts may not be excluded save to the extent that agreement may be made to settle disputes by arbitration held in Egypt under Egyptian law.[92]

4.8 Commercial agency

The provisions of the Commercial Code which deal with commercial agency must be read in conjunction with the provisions of the Commercial Agency Law[93] and the provisions of the Civil Code dealing with agency in general.[94]

Prior to the new Code, Egyptian law allowed a principal to terminate a fixed-term commercial agency agreement upon the expiry of its term, although successful claims for compensation were known if the non-renewal

---

[81]   Art. 75.
[82]   Art. 76.
[83]   Art. 77(1).
[84]   Art. 77(2).
[85]   Art. 78.
[86]   Art. 81.
[87]   Art. 83.
[88]   Art. 84.
[89]   Art. 85(2).
[90]   Art. 86.
[91]   Art. 87(2).
[92]   Art. 87(1).
[93]   Law No. 120 of 1982. For a free translation by Kosheri, Rashed & Riad of Arts. 166–191, which deal with commercial agency, see Part III, pp. 435–438.
[94]   Civil Code, Arts. 699–717.

was clearly unjustified. The onus has been changed as the Commercial Code now expressly provides that an agent has the right to compensation if a fixed-term contract is not renewed, unless there is a serious and justifiable reason for the termination.[95] Similarly, in respect of a commercial agency agreement of indefinite duration, it was previously the case that either party was free to implement an agreed termination clause, whereas the agent now has the right to claim compensation if the agreement is terminated without prior notice or at an unsuitable time.[96]

A commercial agent is liable for failure to follow express instructions.[97] An exception arises where a commercial agent realizes that to follow a principal's instructions will result in excessive damage to the principal's interests, in which case the agent must consult the principal before carrying out the instructions.[98] Despite the requirement to take instructions, a third party dealing with the agent will not be bound by any restrictions on the authority of the agent unless aware of them at the time.[99] Anyone dealing with the agent has the right, but no duty, to request information, including copy documentation, as to the scope of the agent's authority.[100]

A commercial agent has a right of lien over goods in his possession until paid what is due to him[101] and that right transfers to any proceeds of sale in the event that the goods are sold.[102]

Where a principal has no domicile in that of the commercial agent, the domicile of the agent is deemed also to be that of the principal and proceedings may be initiated against the principal in that jurisdiction.[103]

The Commercial Code distinguishes between the relationship of contract agent and that of commission agent. The essential difference between the two is that a contract agent introduces business to the principal, whereas a commission agent does business in his own name on his principal's account,[104] although a contract agent may also be his principal's attorney for signature purposes.[105] Commission and contract agencies are simply specific forms of commercial agency; the general provisions described above apply equally.[106]

4.8.1 Commission agency

As mentioned, a commission agent does business in his own name on his principal's account; however, a commission agent may disclose a principal's

---

[95] Art. 163.
[96] *Ibid.*
[97] Art. 151(1).
[98] Art. 151(2).
[99] Art. 157.
[100] *Ibid.*
[101] Art. 159.
[102] Art. 160.
[103] Art. 164. Obviously the practical effect is to allow an Egyptian agent to sue a foreign principal without going abroad.
[104] Arts. 166 and 177.
[105] Art. 177.
[106] Art. 166.

name to purchasers and must disclose to the principal the names of his purchasers, failing which the agent is deemed a guarantor for the purchase price.[107] Where a commission agent concludes a contract on terms which are more favourable than those agreed between agent and principal, the agent must account to the principal for the difference.[108]

A commission agent should obtain his principal's consent to any sale by instalments or deferred payment, failing which the principal may request the agent to pay the price in full forthwith subject to the agent then retaining any profit accruing as a result of such payment by instalments or deferred payment;[109] an exception to this rule is allowed in favour of local trade practices but is still subject to the express instructions of the principal.[110]

A commission agent is directly liable to third parties with whom he deals. A principal and any such third party have no direct claim against each other, save where specific legislative provision is made,[111] but, should a commission agent be declared bankrupt before receiving payment from a third party, the principal may request the third party to make payment directly.[112]

4.8.2 *Contract agency*

In appointing a contract agent, the principal has a duty to provide such information and facilities as are required in order to enable the agent to carry out his commission.[113] A principal may not appoint more than one contract agent in the same geographical area for the same purpose unless expressly agreed, similarly, an agent may act for more than one principal unless expressly agreed.[114] The agent is under a duty to protect the principal's rights, in particular any trade secrets, even after the agency has ended.[115]

If the duration of a contract agency is unlimited, the principal may only terminate for fault on the part of the agent, failing which compensation will be payable in respect of any loss caused. An agent may terminate but is also liable for losses caused by a termination made without justifiable cause and at an inappropriate time.[116]

In relation to fixed-term contracts, termination ahead of time will always give the agent a right to compensation even if there is an agreement to the contrary.[117] In order for compensation to be payable, the agent should not be at fault and his activities should have led to evident success in developing

---

[107] Art. 173(2).
[108] Art. 169.
[109] Art. 170(1).
[110] Art. 170(2).
[111] Art. 174.
[112] Art. 175(1).
[113] Art. 185.
[114] Art. 179.
[115] Art. 187.
[116] Art. 188.
[117] Art. 189(1).

the principal's business.[118] A claim on this ground must be made within ninety days of the termination[119] – an exception to the general two-year limitation period in relation to agency disputes.[120]

4.9   Brokerage

Brokerage is understood as a particular form of agency, in terms of which a broker undertakes to search for another party with whom the principal may conclude a specific contract and to act as intermediary in concluding that contract.[121] Unless specifically agreed, a broker is not a guarantor for the creditworthiness of a client and is not responsible for the performance of a contract concluded on behalf of a client.[122]

Where a broker's commission is not determined by law or agreement, it is determined according to commercial custom or, failing that, is assessed by the court.[123] A broker is not entitled to remuneration unless his mediation leads to the conclusion of a contract and, where such remuneration is conditional, he is not entitled to payment until the condition is satisfied.[124] A broker is not entitled to recover expenses unless there is agreement to that effect, in which case they are payable even if no contract is concluded.[125]

A broker is subject to a general obligation of good faith, requiring him to inform his client of all conditions affecting a proposed contract.[126] A broker may not be party to a contract which he is mediating unless specifically authorized to do so, in which case he is not entitled to any remuneration.[127]

The 1883 Code contained a general requirement that transactions carried out on a formal exchange had to be conducted through a broker registered with that exchange.[128] The new Code applies this requirement only to the Stock Exchange.[129] The provisions of the new Code apply to brokers registered with the Stock Exchange.[130]

---

[118]   Art. 189(2).
[119]   Art. 190(1).
[120]   Art. 190(2).
[121]   Art. 192. Under the 1883 Commercial Code, a broker who did not disclose the name of his principal was specifically a commission agent (see Art. 66 thereof); under the new Code, the agency aspect of the role is left implicit.
[122]   Art. 203. Under Art. 67 of the 1883 Code, a broker through whom a negotiable bond was sold was responsible for the genuineness of the seller's signature. This rule has not been carried forward into the new Code.
[123]   Art. 193.
[124]   Art. 194.
[125]   Art. 199.
[126]   Art. 200.
[127]   Art. 201.
[128]   1883 Commercial Code, Art. 74.
[129]   Art. 45(1). The reference is to the Cairo and Alexandria Stock Exchanges.
[130]   Art. 207.

4.10 Carriage

A contract of carriage is defined as an agreement whereby a carrier undertakes to transport an item or a person from one place to another in return for payment.[131] The new Code clarifies such matters as the nature of a carrier's liability and the extent to which it may be excluded; carriers are expressly not permitted to exclude vicarious liability for the acts or omissions of employees.[132] Unless otherwise specified, the Commercial Code does not apply to maritime transport.[133]

4.10.1 Carriage of goods

A contract of carriage does not need to be in writing but, where a bill of carriage (consignment note) is prepared, the new Code lays down minimum requirements as to the information contained in the bill.[134] In the absence of a bill of carriage, the carrier must, upon request, deliver a receipt to the consignor in respect of the relevant goods; the receipt should be dated and should include sufficient information to identify the relevant goods and freight charges.[135] The carrier's unconditional receipt is *prima facie* evidence that the goods have been received in good condition in accordance with the terms of the bill.[136]

A bill of carriage may be drawn in the name of a specific person (in which case it is transferable according to the usual rules on transfer of debt),[137] to the order of a specific person (in which case the bill is negotiable by endorsement) or to bearer (in which case the bill is negotiable by delivery).[138] While an item is in the possession of the carrier, the consignor may order it to be returned to him or sent to a person other than the consignee against appropriate payment, save in circumstances where the consignor cannot present a bill of carriage or where the item has arrived and the consignee has requested delivery to him.[139] Once the consignee holds a bill, any right to order return of the item or its delivery to another destination is transferred to the consignee.[140]

Any contractual provision exempting a carrier from responsibility for total or partial destruction of goods being transported, or for their deterioration, is void.[141]

---

[131] Art. 208.
[132] Art. 213(3).
[133] Art. 209(1). Maritime transport is covered by the Maritime Law, Law No. 8 of 1990.
[134] Art. 218.
[135] Art. 219.
[136] Art. 226.
[137] I.e. those set out in the Civil Code, namely Arts. 315–322.
[138] Art. 220.
[139] Art. 232(1) and (3).
[140] Art. 232(2).
[141] Art. 245(1).

4.10.2   *Carriage of persons*

Payment due in terms of a contract for carriage of persons must be made, even if the passenger chooses not to appear, unless due notice is given prior to commencement of the journey; the minimum period of notice that may be given is one day but can be less in cases of necessity.[142] A carrier has a right of lien over passengers' luggage as security for the fare due, subject to the usual rules on enforcement of pledges;[143] a carrier also has the right to inspect luggage to ensure compliance with applicable transport regulations.[144]

A carrier is not liable to pay compensation if an event of *force majeure* prevents him from performing the contract;[145] if failure to perform is the fault of the carrier, the passenger may make other arrangements and claim reimbursement, or make the journey at a later time with the same carrier and claim compensation.[146] A carrier is responsible for the prompt and safe arrival of passengers, any agreement to the contrary notwithstanding;[147] this liability may only be removed by an applicable event of *force majeure* or passenger fault.[148] Any attempt to require passengers to insure against risks for which the carrier is responsible is treated as an attempt to avoid liability.[149]

4.10.3   *Air transport*

The provisions summarized in sections 4.10.1–2 apply to air transport but the Commercial Code also sets out additional provisions of specific application but without prejudice to the terms of international treaties or conventions to which Egypt has acceded.[150]

The nature of an air carrier's liability extends to (a) any death, injury or other physical damage to a passenger occurring on board the aircraft or during embarkation or disembarkation,[151] (b) destruction, loss or damage of or to luggage or goods occurring during carriage, including all periods during which such luggage or goods are in the custody of the carrier,[152] and (c) damage arising from a delay in the arrival of a passenger, luggage or goods.[153]

The financial extent of an air carrier's liability is limited to (a) compensation of E£150,000 per person,[154] and (b) E£50 per kilogram in respect of

---

[142] Art. 257(1).
[143] Art. 262.
[144] Art. 263(2).
[145] Art. 256(1).
[146] Art. 259.
[147] Art. 267(1).
[148] Art. 266.
[149] Art. 267(2).
[150] Art. 285. The Warsaw and Chicago Conventions are specifically referred to in the Aviation Law, Law No. 28 of 1981.
[151] Art. 287.
[152] Art. 288(1).
[153] Art. 289(1).
[154] Art. 292(1).

transport of luggage or goods,[155] unless a higher value has been declared by the consignor and accepted by the carrier. No limitation on liability applies where damage arose from an act or omission of the carrier or its employees (acting in the course of their duties) either with intent to cause damage or by way of lack of care in avoiding foreseeable consequences.[156]

Claims in respect of air transportation of goods generally prescribe after one year;[157] claims arising from the death or injury of a passenger prescribe after two years.[158]

5 BANKING TRANSACTIONS

Articles 300–377 of the Commercial Code set out provisions addressing the relationship between bank and customer. As mentioned, these provisions apply even if the relevant customer is not a merchant or if the particular transaction is not commercial in nature from the customer's perspective.[159]

5.1 Deposit of cash

Deposit accounts are a contract between bank and customer whereby the bank is authorized to possess and to dispose of cash deposited, subject to its obligation to refund the equivalent amount to the depositor.[160] The bank must open an account for each depositor to reflect transactions concluded between bank and customer or with third parties on account of the customer.[161] If a customer is permitted to withdraw sums in excess of those deposited, the bank is expected to give the customer prompt notification to regularize his account.[162]

Cash deposits are repayable to the customer upon request, unless otherwise agreed.[163] Statements of account must be sent to depositors at least annually unless otherwise agreed or established by custom.[164] If a passbook is issued, all transactions must be recorded in it and all entries signed by a bank officer, that signature constituting those entries as evidence of the position.[165]

All deposits and withdrawals must be made at the branch where the account is held, unless otherwise agreed.[166] Where a depositor has more than

---

[155] Art. 292(2).
[156] Art. 292(4).
[157] Arts. 296(1) & (3).
[158] Art. 296(2).
[159] Art. 300.
[160] Art. 301.
[161] Art. 302.
[162] Art. 303(2).
[163] Art. 305(1).
[164] Art. 304(1).
[165] Art. 309(1).
[166] Art. 306.

one account, each account is treated independently,[167] although the right to combine or offset accounts will generally be available.[168]

Joint accounts may be established for two or more persons to operate.[169] Unless otherwise agreed, these are operated on the following basis:[170]

(a) all holders have equal rights to operate the account;
(b) drawings must be made by all holders;
(c) any attachment against one or more of the holders relates only to their share of funds at credit of the account and any remaining holder may continue to operate the account in respect of his share;
(d) if one of the holders notifies the bank in writing of any dispute between the holders, the bank must freeze the account pending settlement by agreement or by judicial decision;
(e) where a holder dies or is judged incompetent, the remaining account holders must notify the bank within ten days whether they wish to continue to operate the account. The bank is under an obligation to stop withdrawals pending determination of successors or appointment of a guardian.

As can be seen, the result of these rules is that, although an account may be set up so as to be operated by any one holder in respect of the full amount at credit, any difficulty or dispute results in that amount being treated as made up of distinct shares, rather than passing to the continuing or surviving account holders.

5.2   Deposit of securities

A bank is under a duty to safeguard any securities deposited by a customer and may not use such securities or exercise any rights arising from them save in the interests of the depositor, unless otherwise agreed;[171] any agreement seeking to exempt the bank from this duty of care is invalid.[172]

Any sums received by the bank by way of interest or other return, or as a result of disposal of deposited securities, must be placed to the credit of the depositor.[173] The bank is under a duty to notify the depositor of any matters requiring his decision; in the absence of express instructions from the depositor, any right must be exercised in the manner beneficial to the depositor but at his cost.[174]

---

[167] Art. 307.
[168] Civil Code, Arts. 362–9.
[169] Art. 308(1).
[170] Art. 308(2)–(5).
[171] Art. 310.
[172] Art. 311.
[173] Art. 312(1).
[174] Art. 313.

The bank must return any deposited securities upon request of the customer, subject only to the time required for their preparation;[175] even where the instrument indicates a third party interest, the bank's obligation to redeliver is owed to the depositor.[176]

5.3 Pledge of securities

The general rules of pledge, outlined in section 4.6 above, apply. Where the pledge is of partly paid securities, the depositor is required to deposit cash to meet further calls on the securities at least two days before payment is due; failing such payment, the pledgee may apply for a judicial sale of the securities in the usual way.[177]

5.4 Documentary credits

A documentary credit is defined as an agreement whereby a bank opens a credit at the request of a customer in favour of another person (the beneficiary) using as security documents representing movable goods[178] or goods under carriage.[179] A documentary credit is a commercial paper which gives rise to obligations independent of the underlying transaction.[180] ICC rules on documentary credits, as issued from time to time, apply, save where inconsistent with the Commercial Code.[181] A bank is not liable where the documents conform on their face with instructions received from the customer opening the credit.[182]

A bank has a lien over goods that are the subject of a documentary credit and may, at any time after expiry of six months from notifying arrival of the documents, apply to the court for an order to sell the goods; application is made in accordance with the procedures followed in enforcing pledges.[183]

5.5 Discounting

A discount is understood as an agreement whereby a bank, in consideration of the transfer to it of a negotiable instrument, advances to its transferor the value of the instrument less the bank's commission, which may be expressed

---

[175] Art. 314(1).
[176] Art. 315(1).
[177] Art. 327.
[178] E.g. a warehouse receipt.
[179] Art. 341(1).
[180] Art. 341(2).
[181] Art. 341(3).
[182] Art. 342.
[183] Art. 350.

as a percentage.[184] The transferor is under an obligation to pay the full value of the instrument to the bank if it is dishonoured.[185]

5.6 Letters of undertaking

Often referred to as bank guarantees or letters of guarantee, these instruments are not guarantees but bonds or undertakings which create independent obligations as between bank and beneficiary. The Commercial Code defines such instruments as an undertaking issued by a bank for payment of a specific or determinable sum within a stipulated period and for a specific purpose; international commercial custom applies, save where the Commercial Code provides otherwise.[186] A letter of undertaking expires in accordance with its terms and no payment obligation survives beyond its validity period save where agreement is reached to extend that period.[187]

A bank may request security against payment under a letter of undertaking, which security may take the form of an assignment of rights or the more usual counter-indemnity.[188] A paying bank has a statutory right of subrogation against its customer.[189] The beneficiary under a letter of undertaking may not assign that benefit to third parties without the consent of both the issuing bank and its customer.[190]

5.7 Current accounts

A current account is defined as an agreement between two persons whereby they agree to make entries in an account by means of reciprocal and overlapping payments arising from transactions concluded between them.[191] It is clear from this definition that, although the rules on current accounts are placed in the section of the new Code dealing with banking transactions, they are not limited in application to a current account opened with a bank:[192] indeed, a current account opened with a bank appears not to fit the definition in full, to the extent that payments to and from the account will not necessarily relate to business conducted by the customer with the bank (and in most cases will not do so, save where the bank debits its own charges to the account). Although the definition is clearly intended to apply to a current account opened with a bank, it more accurately describes a running account

---

[184] Art. 351. Art. 351(2) refers to both a percentage fee and a commission; thus a bank may charge a minimum commission in addition to an agreed percentage of the value of the instrument.
[185] Art. 353.
[186] Art. 355.
[187] Art. 359(1).
[188] Art. 356.
[189] Art. 360.
[190] Art. 357.
[191] Art. 361(1).
[192] Art. 361(3).

between merchants. The rules on joint deposit accounts[193] apply also to joint current accounts.[194]

Sums at credit of a current account do not bear interest unless agreed[195] and compound interest may not be agreed upon unless one of the parties is a bank.[196]

Where a current account is opened with a bank, the bank may not reveal information relating to the account other than to its customer, his nominees or heirs or otherwise in accordance with Law No. 205 of 1990, which deals with bank confidentiality.[197]

6 COMMERCIAL PAPER

Articles 378–549 of the Commercial Code deal with commercial paper, mainly in the form of bills of exchange, promissory notes and cheques. Cheques and notes are separately defined and cheques are dealt with in some detail but the provisions of the Commercial Code dealing with bills of exchange apply also to promissory notes and cheques save where they differ from provisions applying specifically to those instruments.[198] The 1883 Code dealt with bills, including those payable to order or to bearer but did not deal with promissory notes or cheques as distinct instruments.[199] The nature of these instruments has not changed significantly but the relevant provisions have been expanded.

6.1 Bills of exchange

To constitute a bill of exchange, an instrument must comprise the following:

(a) an unconditional order to pay a specific amount of money;
(b) the date and place of creation of the bill;
(c) the name of the drawee;
(d) the name of the person to whom or to whose order payment is to be made;
(e) the date of maturity;
(f) the place of payment;
(g) the term "bill of exchange" expressed in the body of the bill; and
(h) the signature of the drawer legibly written.[200]

---

[193] See section 5.1 above.
[194] Art. 361(4).
[195] Art. 366(1).
[196] Art. 366(2).
[197] Art. 377.
[198] Arts. 378, 470 and 472.
[199] 1883 Code, Arts. 105–194.
[200] Art. 379.

If an instrument lacks one of the above characteristics, it will not constitute a bill save in the following cases:

(a)   a bill with no stated date of maturity is payable at sight;
(b)   if no place of settlement is stated, it shall be made at the drawee's address as stated on the bill; and
(c)   if no place of issue is stated, the bill is deemed to have been issued at the drawee's address as stated on the bill.[201]

If interest is stipulated, the rate must be specified in the bill and will run from the date of the bill, unless otherwise stated.[202] A bill may be negotiated by endorsement even if not expressly drawn to order.[203] Negotiability is protected by the rule that parties liable on a bill may only use those defences available to them against their immediate predecessor as holder (if any).[204] An endorsement following maturity effects negotiation in the usual way but endorsement following protest for dishonour is effective only to transfer such right as the endorser has on the bill.[205]

A bill may be presented to the drawee for acceptance at any time prior to maturity.[206] A bill payable at a fixed period after sight must be presented for acceptance within one year of its date; the drawer may extend or reduce this period and endorsers may reduce it.[207] Payment of the whole or part of the amount of a bill of exchange may be guaranteed by a precautionary (or alternative) guarantor; such a guarantor may be a signatory to the bill or any third party.[208] A bill may mature at sight, upon expiry of a fixed period after sight, upon expiry of a fixed period from the date stated on the bill, or on another fixed date; bills containing other maturity dates are null and void.[209]

Dishonour for non-acceptance or non-payment must be proved by protest;[210] protest for non-acceptance dispenses with presentation for payment and protest for non-payment.[211] A holder of a bill may proceed against those liable on it jointly or severally in no particular order; this right accrues to any signatory who has paid its value.[212] A holder of a bill for which protest for non-payment has been made may apply for a precautionary attachment on the assets of those liable on the bill.[213]

---

[201]   Art. 380.
[202]   Art. 383.
[203]   Art. 391(1).
[204]   Art. 397.
[205]   Art. 400.
[206]   Art. 409.
[207]   Art. 411.
[208]   Art. 418.
[209]   Art. 421.
[210]   Art. 434(1).
[211]   Art. 439(4).
[212]   Art. 442.
[213]   Art. 449.

6.2 Promissory notes

The Commercial Code provisions applicable to bills apply equally to promissory notes, amended only so far as is required to take account of the fact that a note is payable by the writer.[214]

6.3 Cheques

The provisions of the Commercial Code relating to cheques come into force on 1 October 2000.[215] The requirements for creation of a cheque are as for a bill save that a cheque must be described as such on its face, is drawn on a bank and may not be post-dated.[216] If an instrument lacks one of the required characteristics, it will not constitute a cheque except in the following cases:

(a)   if no place of payment is stated, it shall be made at the head office of the drawee bank; and
(b)   if no place of issue is stated, the bill is deemed to have been issued in the domicile of the drawer.[217]

A cheque cannot be accepted in the same way as a bill[218] but the drawee bank may be requested to certify on the face of a cheque that it will honour it, meaning that sufficient consideration was held as at the date of certification.[219] A drawee bank may not refuse certification if funds are available;[220] upon certification, the amount for which the cheque is drawn is frozen pending collection.[221] Any stipulation of interest on a cheque is void.[222]

A cheque payable to a named person, whether or not expressed payable to order, may be negotiated by endorsement.[223] In order to be valid, an endorsement must (a) be unconditional,[224] (b) not be partial,[225] and (c) made on the reverse of the cheque.[226] An endorser guarantees payment unless there is a contrary stipulation;[227] an endorser may forbid further endorsement, in which case he gives no guarantee to endorsees subsequent to his immediate

---

[214]   Art. 470.
[215]   Law No. 17 of 1999, Arts. 1 and 3.
[216]   Arts. 473 and 503(1).
[217]   Art. 474.
[218]   Art. 482(1); a cheque draws on the drawer's own funds.
[219]   Art. 482(2).
[220]   Art. 482(3).
[221]   Art. 482(4).
[222]   Art. 483.
[223]   Art. 486(2).
[224]   Art. 487(1).
[225]   Art. 487(2).
[226]   Art. 488.
[227]   Art. 490(1).

endorsee.[228] An endorsement after protest, or after expiry of time for pre-sentment, merely transfers the endorser's right on the cheque.[229] A cheque expressly not payable to order may be transferred in accordance with the usual rules on assignment.[230]

Value must be available to meet cheques issued;[231] if full value is not available, the holder of a cheque is entitled to any available partial value but may choose whether to accept partial payment and lodge a protest for the balance or to refuse partial payment and lodge a protest for the full value of the cheque.[232] Deliberately issuing a cheque for which value is not available, or subsequently taking steps to prevent payment, renders the drawer liable to imprisonment and a fine of up to E£50,000;[233] these penalties also apply to one who endorses while aware that value is unavailable.[234] The right to countermand a cheque is generally not available, save where a bearer cheque is lost or damaged.[235] A payee is entitled to lodge a civil claim in criminal proceedings for an order for payment of the outstanding debt.[236]

A cheque is payable at sight; any attempt to provide otherwise is void, save on cheques effecting payment of government salaries and pensions.[237] A cheque drawn and payable in Egypt must be presented within three months of its date, foreign cheques within four months.[238] Presentation to a clearing house is deemed presentation for payment.[239] Despite these time limits, the drawee bank may not refuse payment on a cheque drawn and payable in Egypt even after expiry of the three-month time limit if funds are available.[240]

The Commercial Code makes provision for general and special crossings in accordance with normal banking practice.[241] The drawee bank may only pay on a generally crossed cheque to one of its customers or to another bank.[242] Payment on a cheque with a special crossing may only be made to the bank named, although that bank may entrust another bank with collection.[243]

---

[228] Art. 490(2).
[229] Art. 496.
[230] Art. 486(3).
[231] Art. 497. To issue a cheque for which value is not available is presently a criminal offence under the Penal Code; from 1 October 2000, the relevant offences and penalties will be those set out in Arts. 533–539 of the Commercial Code.
[232] Art. 499.
[233] Art. 534(1); no maximum period of imprisonment is specified.
[234] Art. 534(2).
[235] Art. 512.
[236] Art. 539.
[237] Art. 503.
[238] Art. 504(1) and (2).
[239] Art. 504(4).
[240] Art. 506.
[241] Art. 515.
[242] Art. 516(1).
[243] Art. 516(2).

6.4 Procedures for protest

Protest of a commercial instrument is made in accordance with the requirements of the Civil and Commercial Procedure Law[244] or its equivalent in the
actual or last known domicile of an obligor.[245] In relation to cheques, failure
to pay may be proved, in lieu of protest, either by (a) a statement by the
drawee, giving the date of presentment, or (b) a statement by the clearing
house through which the cheque was presented stating that the cheque was
presented in time but dishonoured; in each case, the statement must be made
on the cheque itself and dated.[246]

6.5 Signatures

A signature on an instrument must be legible or accompanied by the name
of the signatory legibly written.[247] A personal seal or fingerprint may stand
for a signature[248] and, if witnessed by two witnesses, will bar any claim of
ignorance as to the content of the instrument.[249]

6.6 Substitution of debts

Acceptance by a creditor of a commercial instrument in settlement of a debt
does not continue or renew that debt unless it is clear that this is intended.[250]

7   BANKRUPTCY AND COMPOSITION

Bankruptcy is dealt with in Part V of the Commercial Code[251] and is almost
identical to the equivalent legislation in Bahrain, Oman and the United Arab
Emirates.[252] That said, the 1883 Commercial Code rules on bankruptcy *per se*
have not undergone radical amendment, having formed one of the sources
of the Arabian Gulf legislation; instead, the main change has been the
introduction of composition arrangements (including preventive composition) and specific rules relating to corporate bankruptcies.

7.1   Filing for bankruptcy

Any merchant, being a natural person or company required under the code
to maintain commercial books and an entry in the commercial register, who

---

[244] Law No. 13 of 1968.
[245] Art. 540.
[246] Art. 541.
[247] Art. 548(2).
[248] Art. 548(1).
[249] Art. 548(3).
[250] Art. 549.
[251] Arts. 550–772.
[252] See note 9 above.

ceases to pay his commercial debts, is considered to be in a state of bankruptcy,[253] subject to a court order being issued to that effect. A creditor in a civil (i.e. non-commercial) debt may seek a declaration of bankruptcy of his debtor if he can show that his debtor has ceased to honour his commercial debts as well as his civil ones.[254] A bankruptcy application may also be made in respect of a foreign business with a branch or agency in Egypt, even in the absence of any similar proceedings abroad.[255] A state of bankruptcy exists in law only when a judgment has been passed to that effect.[256]

A merchant may be declared bankrupt on his application, that of one or more of his creditors, that of the Public Prosecutor or by the court on its own initiative.[257] Where application is made by a creditor, it must be in respect of a debt which is due and not in dispute or, if in respect of a debt not yet due, the application must be made on the basis that the debtor has fled or carried out other acts to the prejudice of his creditors.[258] This is in addition to the underlying requirement that payment of commercial debts generally must have ceased. In certain circumstances, application for bankruptcy of a natural person may be made after his death.[259]

Non-payment of taxes or criminal fines does not give a basis for a bankruptcy application, emphasizing the point that bankruptcy is a civil process.[260] Although the Public Prosecutor may initiate a bankruptcy application, and is notified of any application by another party,[261] this is to ensure that the requirements of public order generally are satisfied. Where the Public Prosecutor initiates an application, the same supporting evidence must be provided as in any other application.[262]

In making a bankruptcy declaration, the court must make an initial determination of the date on which payment of commercial debts ceased.[263] This date is important because certain transactions entered into after that date, such as gifts or transfers at undervalue (including the granting of rights in security), can be unwound by the trustee in bankruptcy.[264] This is an important point for banks and other creditors to be aware of when taking security, particularly when taking security for existing debts (which could be analysed as a separate transaction for which the debtor's estate receives no value). The date on which payment of debts ceased cannot be set more than two years prior to the date on which the court makes its declaration of bankruptcy.[265]

The court will appoint a trustee in bankruptcy[266] and will also designate

---

[253] Art. 550(1).
[254] Art. 554(1).
[255] Art. 559(2).
[256] Art. 550(2).
[257] Art. 552.
[258] Art. 554.
[259] Art. 551(1).
[260] Art. 555.
[261] Art. 561(3).
[262] Art. 553.
[263] Art. 561(1).
[264] Art. 598.
[265] Art. 563(2).
[266] Art. 571(1).

a judge to oversee the bankruptcy, to whom the trustee will report.[267] The court may appoint up to three joint trustees in bankruptcy.[268] The court will normally have power to take the bankrupt into custody, if appropriate.[269]

The trustee in bankruptcy will then proceed to register the declaration of bankruptcy in the commercial register[270] and to publish an announcement in a daily newspaper of the court's choosing; the newspaper announcement must be made within ten days of the trustee in bankruptcy being notified of the court's ruling.[271] Any interested party, other than the parties to the initial bankruptcy application, may contest the declaration within thirty days of its publication; where the initial declaration is appealed, any contestation is made to the court hearing the appeal.[272]

7.2 Effects of bankruptcy on the bankrupt

The court generally has power to order the detention of the bankrupt or to prevent him from travelling;[273] a bankrupt may not change his domicile without the bankruptcy judge's permission and may not absent himself from his existing domicile without permission from the trustee in bankruptcy.[274]

A bankrupt must resign from any public offices or directorships, may not engage in certain commercial activities[275] and has no right to dispose of or deal with any of his remaining property.[276] One exception to this is that, if the bankrupt holds commercial paper, its value may be settled to him unless the trustee in bankruptcy objects or unless the drawee was aware that the bankrupt had ceased payment of debts.[277]

In addition, bankruptcy does not affect the following:

(a) property which cannot be legally attached, including any allowance assessed for the bankrupt;
(b) property held but not owned by the bankrupt;
(c) rights connected with the person of the bankrupt or which are an incident of his personal status; and
(d) payments made under insurance policies concluded prior to the declaration of bankruptcy, subject to the beneficiary reimbursing the bankrupt's estate with premiums paid after the date set by the court as being when payment of debts ceased.[278]

---

[267] Art. 561(1).
[268] Art. 571(2).
[269] Art. 561(2).
[270] Art. 564(2).
[271] Art. 564(3).
[272] Art. 565(1).
[273] Arts. 561(2) and 586.
[274] Art. 587.
[275] Art. 588(1).
[276] Art. 589(1).
[277] Art. 590(2).
[278] Art. 592.

7.3 Effects of bankruptcy on creditors generally

The main consequence of a bankruptcy ruling is that individual actions against the bankrupt and his property are no longer possible; any existing actions will generally be swept into the bankruptcy.[279] Enforcement proceedings can be allowed to continue subject to proceeds of sale being remitted to the trustee in bankruptcy for the benefit of creditors generally.[280] Actions by secured creditors may proceed but against the trustee in substitution for the bankrupt.[281]

7.4 Effects of bankruptcy on secured creditors

Secured creditors are, to some extent, left to look after their own position. The trustee in bankruptcy will generally be expected to give priority to enhancing the position of unsecured creditors,[282] even to the extent of being able to require a secured creditor to proceed with enforcement, with any excess coming into the estate and any shortfall being claimed on an unsecured basis.[283]

The importance to secured creditors of the date on which payment of debts ceased has already been mentioned: the main consequence is that transactions prejudicial to the body of creditors generally are at risk of being unwound.[284] Where a transaction is unwound, the party benefiting is required to refund the bankrupt's estate with the value of the benefit received, with interest, and thereafter claim as an ordinary creditor for a dividend in the bankruptcy.[285]

It is also specifically provided that the court may refuse enforcement of security rights registered after that date if, when registered, it was also more than thirty days after creation of those security rights.[286]

Interest on secured debts can only be claimed from any proceeds of enforcement against the secured assets. Interest on unsecured debts can be claimed but payment out of claims is prioritized between creditors as follows:

(a) payment of capital claims;
(b) payment of interest accruing prior to the bankruptcy declaration; and
(c) payment of interest accruing after the bankruptcy declaration.[287]

Where there is a pledge or lien over moveable assets forming part of the bankrupt's estate, the trustee in bankruptcy has the option of paying out

---

[279] Art. 605(1).
[280] Art. 605(2).
[281] Art. 605(3).
[282] Arts. 613 and 615(1).
[283] Art. 615(2).
[284] See notes 266 and 267 above.
[285] Art. 602.
[286] Art. 601(1).
[287] Art. 607.

that creditor and bringing those assets into the estate for the benefit of unsecured creditors.[288] This can be useful, for example, in trying to sell a business as a whole or as a going concern in order to enhance the value realized.

As to payments out of the estate, priority is given to the costs of the bankruptcy and outstanding salaries due to employees of the bankrupt.[289]

The Code recognizes a lien in favour of the bankrupt's lessor where the business has been carried on from leased premises. This lien covers rental due in respect of the year prior to declaration of bankruptcy and the year in which it is made. A landlord's lien also extends to moveable property on the leased premises at the time of the declaration, even if that property is subsequently sold or removed from the premises.[290]

The government also enjoys a lien for taxes due in respect of the two-year period prior to the declaration of bankruptcy.[291]

7.5   Effects of bankruptcy on existing contracts

A declaration of bankruptcy does not generally invalidate any existing contracts. An exception to this would be where there has been a reason specific to the person of the bankrupt which has led another party to enter into a contract with him: for example, if the bankrupt has been retained as a consultant because of his personal skill and experience, it is inappropriate to expect the trustee in bankruptcy to continue to perform that contract.[292]

Inevitably, the process of winding up a business will result in non-performance of ongoing contracts: recognizing that those contracts are nevertheless valid, the Code allows claims in the bankruptcy for losses arising from non-performance.[293] Such a claim may also be made for the remaining period of a lease[294] or of a fixed-term contract of employment.[295]

7.6   Restitution

A person may recover from the bankruptcy anything to which he proves his right of ownership,[296] including:

(a)   goods deposited for sale or delivery on account of the owner;[297]
(b)   the price of goods sold but not accounted for (which may be settled

---

[288] Art. 614.
[289] Art. 616.
[290] Art. 617.
[291] Art. 618.
[292] Art. 623(1); essentially the concept of *delectus personae*.
[293] Art. 623(2).
[294] Art. 624.
[295] Art. 625(3).
[296] Art. 626(1).
[297] Art. 627(1).

in cash, by commercial paper or by reconciliation in a current account);[298] and

(c)   commercial paper delivered for collection.[299]

Cash may not be recovered unless particular notes can be identified,[300] a point which is relevant to the use of custodians in Egypt.[301]

7.7   Corporate bankruptcy

The Code contains a number of provisions designed to take account of the particular characteristics of bankruptcy of a corporation rather than of a natural person; subject to the specific rules set out, the general regime is the same for both.[302]

A corporation can initiate its own bankruptcy but only upon a decision of the members.[303] A corporation in the process of liquidation may be declared bankrupt if there are insufficient funds to repay creditors and shareholders.[304] The court may, on its own initiative or on request of the corporation, postpone a decision on the issue of bankruptcy for up to three months if this is in the interests of the national economy or if there are grounds to believe that the corporation will be able to trade through its difficulties.[305]

If the members of a corporation do not enjoy limited liability for its debts, a declaration of bankruptcy of the corporation also constitutes a declaration of bankruptcy of each of the members, including any who ceased to be members after the company ceased payment of its debts (unless their departure was more than one year prior to the declaration of bankruptcy, in which case no liability attaches).[306]

If the assets of the corporation are insufficient to settle at least 20 per cent of its debts, the court may order payment of contributions from its board members unless they can establish that, in running the company's affairs, they attended to their responsibilities in an attentive and careful manner.[307]

A trustee in bankruptcy may make additional calls on partly paid stock. Loan stock issued by a bankrupt corporation is not subject to the verification procedures applicable to ordinary creditors generally, but is automatically admitted in bankruptcy at its nominal value less any redemptions made.[308]

---

[298] *Ibid.*
[299] Art. 628(1).
[300] Art. 628(2).
[301] Particularly by US institutions seeking to comply with SEC rule 14f-5.
[302] Art. 698. Egyptian commercial partnerships are juristic persons: Civil Code, Art. 506.
[303] Art. 700(1).
[304] Art. 699(2).
[305] Art. 702.
[306] Art. 703(1).
[307] Art. 704(2).
[308] Art. 706.

7.8   Termination of bankruptcy and rehabilitation

Bankruptcy can terminate in the following ways:

(a)   payment of creditors in full;[309]
(b)   entering into a composition (rescheduling) with creditors;[310]
(c)   distribution of dividends;[311] or
(d)   appointment of a receiver, who may be given power to continue the bankrupt's business, on behalf of creditors.[312]

A bankrupt may be rehabilitated after three years[313] or within two years if creditors are fully paid out.[314] Extended rehabilitation periods apply to bankrupts whose actions have given rise to criminal proceedings.[315]

7.9   Preventive composition

A merchant whose financial situation is such as to give grounds for a declaration of bankruptcy may instead petition for preventive composition (essentially a court-sanctioned rescheduling);[316] approval of the members is required for such an application by a corporation.[317]

An application for preventive composition may not be made in respect of an applicant which has not been in business for less than two years[318] and may not be made in respect of a corporation which is already in liquidation.[319] In the event of competing applications for bankruptcy and preventive composition, a decision as to preventive composition must be made first.[320] The court is bound to refuse an application for preventive composition if the required supporting financial information is not submitted, if the applicant is no longer in business or has absconded, or if the applicant has existing criminal convictions (convictions arising from a previous bankruptcy are disregarded if the applicant has been formally discharged in respect of that bankruptcy).[321]

If an application for preventive composition is approved, the procedure that follows is similar to bankruptcy, and involves appointment of a trustee in composition and a judge with responsibility for the composition, to whom

---

[309]   Art. 660.
[310]   Arts. 662 *et seq.*
[311]   Art. 683.
[312]   Arts. 684 *et seq.*
[313]   Art. 712.
[314]   Art. 713.
[315]   Art. 716.
[316]   Art. 725(1).
[317]   Art. 726(2).
[318]   Art. 726(1).
[319]   Art. 725(3).
[320]   Art. 729.
[321]   Art. 733.

the trustee reports.[322] The trustee undertakes an appraisal of the applicant's business,[323] leaving the applicant in charge of the business but under the trustee's supervision and subject to the limitation that, in the absence of approval from the composition judge, he may only make disposals in the ordinary course of business and for value.[324] Third party proceedings against the applicant remain valid, subject to the trustee being introduced as a party to the proceedings.[325]

Creditors are required to submit details of their claims within ten days of publication of the court's decision to initiate composition proceedings[326] (thirty days for creditors resident abroad);[327] failure to submit claim details prevents a creditor from participating in the composition.[328]

A copy of the trustee's report, incorporating details of claims admitted, and the debtor's proposals for rescheduling, is made available to all participating creditors prior to a creditors' meeting;[329] the purpose of the meeting is to vote on whether or not to accept the debtor's proposals.[330] The meeting is quorate if attended by creditors representing two thirds of the value of claims admitted; resolutions are valid if passed by a majority (by value) of creditors attending and creditors who fail, or are not entitled, to attend are bound by resolutions passed at the meeting.[331] If the meeting is not quorate, or fails to make a valid decision, further meetings are held at ten-day intervals.[332]

If the composition is approved at the creditors' meeting, the matter is referred back to the court; objections from creditors may be received at this stage and will be taken into account by the court in deciding whether or not to ratify the proposed composition.[333] Judicial ratification of a composition is registered in the commercial register in the same way as an adjudication of bankruptcy.[334] Once a composition arrangement comes into effect, all existing creditors are bound by its terms.[335]

8   CONCLUSION

Certain provisions of the new Code have given rise to some adverse criticism. The provisions on transfer of technology are clearly protectionist in aim and

---

[322] Art. 735.
[323] Art. 739(2).
[324] Art. 740.
[325] Art. 741(1).
[326] Art. 744(1).
[327] Art. 744(2).
[328] Art. 750.
[329] Art. 752(1).
[330] Art. 751.
[331] Art. 754(1).
[332] Art. 756(2).
[333] Art. 757(3).
[334] Art. 763(3).
[335] Art. 761.

may have the effect of discouraging foreign licensors; certainly, such provisions seem at odds with Egypt's current trade negotiations with the European Union and its negotiations on membership of bodies such as the World Intellectual Property Organization and the World Trade Organization. Similarly, the protectionist tone of the commercial agency provisions dealing with termination stands out at a time when countries such as Bahrain and Oman are in the process of relaxing their commercial agency laws as part of their ongoing programmes to encourage foreign investment.

Another aspect that has attracted attention is the decision not to allow the continued use of post-dated cheques: at present they are widely used in Egypt and the GCC countries. Certainly, there are justified regulatory concerns about the extent of the future commitments covered by post-dated cheques but, in my opinion, the traditional reliance on such instruments derives at least partly from the practice of making it a criminal offence to draw a cheque without funds being available – an approach which continues under the new Code. The wisdom of banning a useful instrument must, in some degree, be questionable: it becomes even more so when there is the alternative of allowing dishonoured cheques only to give rise to a civil action – an approach which, at the very least, has the merit of forcing creditors to be more inquiring as to the creditworthiness of their debtors. At time of writing this article, it has recently been announced that the date from which the prohibition on post-dated cheques will apply has been postponed for a further year to 1 October 2001.[336]

Taken in context, such criticisms are minor and should not be allowed to overshadow the extent to which promulgation of a new commercial code for Egypt is to be welcomed. The 1883 Code had become outdated and the new Code more clearly meets contemporary commercial requirements. The new Code has also been drafted with the commercial codes of some of the GCC countries in mind;[337] indeed, the similarities are such that it appears partly to have been drafted on the basis of those codes. This approach does much to assist both those doing business across the Middle East and their advisors, for which we are indebted to the draftsmen involved.

9 APPENDIX

9.1 Commercial Code contents

Part and Chapter	Title	Articles
Part 1	*Commercial Activities in General*	*1–46*
	General Provisions	1–3
Chapter 1	Commercial Activities	4–9
Chapter 2	The Merchant	10–20

---

[336] Actually a postponement of the provisions relating to cheques generally – see note 2 above.
[337] See note 9 above.

Strict Liability in the Law of the Sudan

*John Wuol Makec**

1 INTRODUCTION

Towards the end of 1898, the Anglo-Egyptian government, known as the "Condominium" government was set up in the Sudan. The government was faced with the problem of which laws to apply. *Shari'a* and customary laws largely governed personal matters only. The first Civil Justice Ordinance 1900 was adopted from India and modified to suit conditions in Sudan. Section 9 of this Ordinance permitted the importation of principles of any foreign law to be applied on the ground of "justice, equity and good conscience". As the judges were British, principles of English common law, which they knew better, were imported and applied, after it had been properly ascertained that they were compatible with local conditions in Sudan. Local conditions in Sudan included *shari'a* law. For example, a rule was imported by the Court of Appeal in the case of *Ahmed Wagenlla v. El Hag Ahmed Mod* (1964) SLJR 221, after it was confirmed by the Grand Kadi that it was compatible with *shari'a* law. Justice Babiker Awaddalla was not sure whether *shari'a* law recognized recovery of damages for "pain and suffering". He submitted a written request to Grand Kadi who replied that the Court was entitled to award damages provided that death resulted from the pain and suffering.

The Sudanese judges consistently held that these imported principles become part of Sudanese common law after their application. The first case in which this view was expressed by Owen J. is the case of *Heirs of Ibrahim Khalil v. Ahmed Hassan Abdel Moneim & others* – App – 42. 1926.

A rule of English law was not applied when it was found to be incompatible with local conditions. Hence in the case of *Bakhitta Ibrahim v. Hamed Mahgoub*, Ac – Rev. 8 (1957); or 1957 SLJR 25, Chief Justice M.A. Abu Rennat, refused to apply a rule of English land law on ground of its incompatibility with land law in Sudan.

---

* LLB; LLM; Justice of the Supreme Court of Sudan.

123

Although the imported principles of English law properly regulated the legal system in Sudan for several decades, pan-Arabists were not satisfied with the application of alien rules. This group achieved its objective in 1983. The introduction of *shari'a* law in 1983 brought a new revolutionary concept which is antipathetic to principles of alien origin even though they are compatible with local conditions in the Sudan. New legislation consists of imported laws from Arab countries to substitute for principles of English origin which, in fact, were believed to conform with *shari'a* law. One of these new laws is the Civil Transactions Act, 1984, which deals with liability in tort. Section 138 of this Act prescribes the basis of liability in tort cases. The theme of this article is the examination of the scope of the application of section 138 of Civil Transactions Act 1983 which provides "strict liability" as the basis of liability in the whole law of tort in Sudan. This is deemed to be a return to the roots of Islam and Arabism.

2 PROVISIONS OF SECTIONS 138 AND 148 OF THE CIVIL TRANSACTIONS ACT 1984

The provisions of sections 138 and 158 of the Civil Transactions Act 1984 purport or are deemed by others to be the sole basis of liability in the whole range of the law of tort in Sudan. While section 138 establishes strict liability, the provisions of section 148 seem to establish absolute liability. Hence the liability in Sudan law of tort, beginning from 1984, is either strict or absolute. But this general presumption seems to be contradicted by the existence of liability on the ground of negligence in other laws, such as the Traffic Act, 1991 or other provisions of Civil Transactions Act itself, such as section 145(1). Under sections 23, 25 and 49 of the Traffic Act, negligence is the basis for determination of drivers' liability. Under section 145(1) of CTA 1984, the liability of a guardian for the act of a minor (under his control) is rebutted when he proves that he had performed all his duties as a guardian with due care. In other words he did not perform his duties negligently and in this way he cannot be held liable.

2.1 Liability under section 138

2.1.1 *Content and exceptions*

The provisions of section 138 state: "Every act whether committed by an adult or minor which causes injury to another binds him to pay compensation." A number of exceptions to this general rule are set out in the succeeding sections and these are:

(a) where the act may be described as an act of God or *force majeure*; or where it has been done by a third party or where the act has been caused by the victim himself;[1]

---

[1]   CTA 1984, section 141.

(b)   where the act has been done in exercise of right of private defence of body, honour or property of the defendant or of another person;[2]

(c)   where the act has been done under necessity;[3]

(d)   where a person is confronted by two evils he is entitled to choose the lesser evil. He is entitled to avert a greater evil by doing a lesser evil. In the latter case the plaintiff is entitled to recover reduced amount of damages from the defendant.[4] In other words he is not completely exempted from liability. The provisions of this clause do not really constitute exceptions. But the provisions merely mitigate damages;

(e)   where the act has been committed by a public servant in obedience to the order of his superior, provided that he is legally bound or he believes to be legally bound to obey his senior orders.[5]

Under the provisions of section 138, the defendant's liability arises from injuries caused by his own acts. But there are also instances where he is liable for the acts of other persons. These are:

(a)   the liability of a guardian for the act of his/her ward or minor. The guardian is liable for the act of a minor unless he/she can prove that he/she had performed his/her duties as a guardian with "due care".[6] The use of phrase "due care" implies that liability is determined on the basis of "fault" or "negligence". It is wondered why this single instance escaped the application of strict liability under section 138. This seems to arise from the haste with which the provisions of the Act, which embodies nearly the whole civil law, with almost one thousand sections, was prepared and enacted;

(b)   liability of the master for the act of his servant who was acting in the course of his employment.[7]

2.1.2   Interpretation of the provisions of section 138

This section provokes a discussion in this article because of its apparent ambitious or implicit claim that it is the basis of the whole liability in the law of tort where a defendant's act causes injury to another. The provisions of this article were imported from Jordanian law (originally from *Magalla El Hakaam*) without its background, interpretations and explanations (if any) made on it by the courts of the country of origin. The application of such a dry legal provision in a country which has been applying a completely different legal system is bound to create difficulties.

The following issues pose themselves for discussion:

---

2   *Ibid.*, section 142(1).
3   *Ibid.*, section 142(2).
4   *Ibid.*, section 143(1).
5   *Ibid.*, section 144(1).
6   *Ibid.*, section 145(1).
7   *Ibid.*, section 146(1).

(a)   whether or not the words "act" and "injury" under section 138 mean only "physical act" and "physical injury" respectively;
(b)   the immateriality of defendant's conduct in determining his liability;
(c)   whether the defendant is liable for all the consequences of his act; or only for direct physical consequences of his act.

2.1.2.1   The meaning of the words "act and injury" – the meaning of the word "act" also determines the meaning of "injury"

There are a number of reasons which support the submission that the meaning of the word "act" under section 138 only covers a physical act.

The first reason is the inclusion of the act of a minor under the section. Under the provisions of section 145(2) of the Civil Transactions Act 1984, a minor is a person who has not yet attained the age of fifteen years and who needs supervision by an adult (guardian) person because he has no legal capacity to be responsible for his own affairs. What this means is that his mental capacity has not yet developed and consequently adult persons or companies cannot rely on statements he makes in legal, economic and public or serious matters. But while he is incapable of making statements on serious matters, he is capable of inflicting physical injury on other people or their property. It follows from this explanation that reference to a minor's act under section 138 is a reference only to his physical acts and does not include statements or non-physical acts. Further, since reference to the act of a minor covers only his physical acts, it equally follows that reference to the act of an adult person is confined to his physical act. The word "act" under the section cannot mean "physical and non-physical acts" in the case of an adult person and only "physical" acts in the case of a minor. There must be consistency in the meaning. More will be said later in the discussion of liability for statements (under the English case of *Hedley Byrne*).

The second reason is the separation of liability for defamatory statement from section 138. Liability for publication of a defamatory statement is provided under section 153 of the Civil Transactions Act 1984. This separation of defamatory statement is indicative of the fact that section 138 does not envisage liability for statements in particular or in general. Thirdly, the Act separates liability for omission (section 140) from section 138. This means again that section 138 does not cover liability for an omission or non-physical act. Fourthly, the provisions of section 138 (originally derived from *Magalla El Hakaam*) represent a very old, rudimentary concept of the law of tort. The extension of the meaning of the word "act" to cover non-physical acts is more or less a phenomenon of the modern development. Under the system represented by the provisions of section 138 most claims are settled by criminal courts through criminal orders or sometimes in form of liquidated damages such as *dia* (compensation). Hence the development of the law of tort is bound to be very limited since most claims of compensation are settled during criminal proceedings. Since 1984, there have been hardly any reported cases of tort in Sudan and none at all under section 138. It follows from the scarcity of the litigation in the law of tort (under *shari'a* law), that its scope of development is very limited and, consequently, words such as "act" retain their ordinary meanings.

2.1.2.2 The immateriality of the defendant's conduct

The provisions of section 138 establish strict liability, as stated above, and so the defendant's conduct at the time of the act is immaterial. The use of the phrase "every act" plus the inclusion of the "act" of a minor confirm that the section establishes strict liability. It follows that the defendant is liable to pay damages for all the consequences of his act. Causation is the determination of liability.

Under the general principles two provisions of section 5(t) and (u) of the CTA 1984 are relevant here. Section 5(t) says: "He who does an act directly is liable for it even if he did it unintentionally." This means that a person is liable for all the direct consequences of his act. His conduct at the time of the direct act is immaterial, this provision supports the provision of section 138 to the extent of establishment of strict liability. On the other hand, the provision under section 5(u) constitutes an exception to the strict liability expressed under section 5(t). It states: "He who causes an act indirectly is not liable for it unless it is done intentionally". This section introduces a mental element, "defendant's conduct" as a basis for liability. Mental element or conduct is not envisaged under section 138 and so there is a conflict between the provisions of the two sections. The second difference is the use of the words *directly* and *indirectly* in section 5(t) and (u). The words "directly or indirectly", are immaterial under section 138.

2.1.2.3 Whether the provisions of section 138 cover the whole range of tort

There may be two divergent views of Sudanese judges[8] on whether or not the provisions of section 138 cover the whole range of the law of tort. It has already been stated that the "act" means physical "act". It follows also that "injury" means physical injury, and it follows further that the provisions of section 138 cover only cases where there is a physical relation or linkage between the act and the result. It is very doubtful indeed if its provisions extend to cases where there is no physical relation or where connection between the act and the result is non-physical or where the act is done by anything under defendant's control.

2.1.3 *Cases where provisions of section 138 may not apply*

It is doubtful whether the provisions of section 138 apply to the following case: *Heirs of Ramatalla Ahmed Medani v. Sudan and Light Power Co. Ltd* (1964) SLJR 75. This is one of the cases where injury was caused by something under defendant's control.

---

8   According to the background of their legal training, political and ideological orientation.

In this case the applicant's deceased father was an employee of the defendants in their factory. While the deceased was walking over the checker plates above an unguarded boiler in the factory yard, the plates opened and deceased fell into the boiler and was scalded to death by the boiling water. The defendants were held liable in negligence. But if the defendants were tried under the provisions of section 138 it is doubtful it they could also be held liable because the injury was caused by a thing under their control (the boiler). It is true that the defendant installed the boiler. That is all. They did not push the deceased into the boiling water. He chose to walk over the boiler and he fell down. The second example of the category of cases where section 138 may not apply consists of cases where the plaintiff or victim suffers nervous shock from what she sees or hears. These cases include: *Dulieu v. White* (1901) 2 KB 669; and *Bourhill v. Young* (1953) 1 QB 444; and *King v. Phillips* (1953) 1 QB 429.

In each of these cases a woman who stood outside the area of physical danger suffered nervous shock resulting from seeing a traffic accident taking place in front of her. In each case there was no physical connection between the act and the nervous shock. The defendants (drivers) were all held liable on the principle of negligence. But it is very doubtful if they could have been held liable if the courts were to apply the provisions of section 138 because there was no physical connection between the acts and the results.

The third example of the category of cases where the provisions of section 138 may not apply consists of cases of negligent misstatements or statements in general. This has been discussed above but the discussion may now be illustrated with cases. The first is the Sudanese case of the *Nile Import & Export Co. v. Mohd. Nuri Osman* (1967) SLJR 184. In this case the applicants in a contract signed with the respondents for the import of goods, stated the country of origin (of the goods) to be Belgium when in fact it was France. The respondents incurred economic loss as a result of the misstatement. They sued the applicants in negligence. The former Court of Appeal allowed the appeal – it relied on the principle established in *Hedley Byrne & Co. v. Heller & Partners Co.* (1964) AC 465. It was held that a plaintiff cannot recover damages in an action for negligence for loss caused to him by a negligent misstatement unless he can prove that the maker of the statement was under a special duty to him to be careful and the maker has failed to exercise such a duty. In this case there was no duty of care owed to the plaintiff by the defendant and so there was no negligence on the latter. On the other hand in the case of *Hedley Byrne*, the defendants, who made a negligent misstatement which resulted in the plaintiff's economic loss, were held liable in negligence.

The defendants had given information that a certain Eassipower Co. was economically viable. The plaintiffs incurred economic loss when they acted in reliance on the defendants' information and made an investment. The defendants were held liable for making a negligent misstatement in circumstances where they knew plaintiffs would rely on it and act to their detriment.

In each of these cases there was no physical act done by the defendant and the result was economic loss and not a physical injury. Further, as stated above, a minor cannot be expected to provide an information involved in each case on economic matters and even if he were to make such a statement it would not be relied upon by the adult plaintiffs, because he has no legal capacity to make such statements or give information. It may therefore be concluded that, as stated above, the provisions of section 138 do not or may not extend to liability for statements. If the section was intended to cover liability for statements, it would include liability for statements of a minor who has no legal capacity to provide business or scientific or legal, etc., information.

The fourth example of the category of cases where section 138 cannot or may not apply consists of cases of omission (as stated earlier). It cannot or may not apply to the case of *Groom v. G. W. Railways (1892)* 8 TLR 253 where the defendant was held liable in negligence for failure to comply with modern inventions or modern standard of development. This invention was used by other railway companies except the defendant company.

Before these examples are concluded it may be stated it is doubtful if section 138 covers all cases, for example, of nuisance or trespass or assault and so on, where no physical injury or damage is involved.

2.2   Liability under the provisions of section 148

While the provisions of section 138 of CTA 1984 purport to establish liability in generality, section 148 establishes liability in particular. The section establishes absolute liability for things under the defendant's control. Section 148(1) states: "whoever is keeping something shall be liable for injury caused by that thing to another person, whether such thing is an animal or matter, movable or immovable".

The following observations have been made over the provisions of this section:

(a)   A person keeps everything at his risk. Liability on him is imperative if the thing he keeps causes injury to other or his property.

(b)   The defendant is liable even if the injury is caused by the thing in his premises. He must be liable to suits of trespassers since the section is silent about where the injury was caused or the "escape" of thing when it caused injury.

(c)   Since liability does not depend on non-natural use of the land the defendant is liable for injury caused by thing which is very essential to his livelihood.

(d)   The section 148 (1) is silent about the distinction between things which are inherently dangerous and those which are not; or between *mensuetae naturae* and *ferae naturae*.

The provisions of section 148 (2), on the other hand, state: "In assessing liability or responsibility (*masulia*) in case of animals regard shall be had to the type of animal and the degree of control exercised over it at the time it caused the injury."

Clause (2) of section 148, of course, draws the attention of the court to the distinction between the type of animals involved (in causing injury) when determining the keeper's liability or responsibility. The second remark is to note the meaning of the Arabic word *masulia* (or *masul*) which appears under the two clauses. The word *masul* in clause (1) of the section corresponds with the word "liable" in English. It may also mean "responsible" for the act of animal or thing under control.

But the use of the word *masulia* in clause (2) seems to be wrong as it still corresponds with the word "liability" or "responsibility" or the degree of "control" over the animal. This implies that the defendant's liability may exist or cease to exist according to a particular class of animal and the degree of control exercised over it.

Precisely the court must regard or consider:

(a)   the type or kind of animal involved; this means whether, the animal belongs to the class of *mansuetac naturae* or of the *ferae naturae*, and,

(b)   the degree of control (*masulia*) exercised over it at the time of injury; whether it was of high standard or low. Of course, the degree of control must be very high in case of *mansuetac naturae* and ordinary in case of *ferae naturae*. But the big question is what purpose is served by drawing the court's attention to the distinction between (i) the category or type of animal and (ii) the degree of control over the animal when determining liability. This attention serves no purpose because section 148(1) has already imposed absolute liability on the keeper, irrespective of the kind of animal and the degree of control exercised over it. Such a distinction and degree of control under section 148(2) will not change or affect the liability already imposed under section 148(1).

If a sensible meaning is to be made out of section 148(2) the use of the word *masulia* is to be omitted and the word "compensation" (or damages) put in its place. Hence the section would read this way: "In assessing compensation (damages) in case of animals, regard shall be made to the kind or type of animal and the degree of control exercised over it at the time it caused the injury" provided this was the intention of the law-makers.

This would mean that damages or compensation might be aggravated or mitigated according to the type of animal involved and the standard or degree of control exercised over it. Probably, the makers might have intended this reconstructed form.

2.2.1   *Whether the provisions of section 148 cover all acts caused by things*

Although section 148 purports to cover all cases where things under control cause injuries to others, there are in practice many cases in which it cannot apply.

A typical example of these cases is the case of *Donoghue v. Stevenson* (1932) AC 562. In this case manufacturers (defendants) sold goods (bottles of cold drinks) they manufactured to a retailer who sold one bottle to the ultimate consumer. The consumer found the remains of a decomposed snail at the bottom of the bottle when he was drinking its content. He vomited and became ill. He sued the manufacturers on the basis of negligence and he succeeded in recovering damages.

If the manufacturer were sued by the consumer under section 148, he would not succeed in view of the definition of the meaning of "keeper or controller" of thing, under section 149 of CTA, 1984. Clause (1) of the section says the keeper of thing is: "One who has actual authority to supervise or dispose of thing whether by himself or through another, is guarding that thing even if it is a minor." Section 149 (2) provides: "The owner is presumed to be guarding his own property unless he proves that control over it vests in another person."

Hence it must be proved by the plaintiff that the defendant: (a) has actual authority to dispose of the thing and/or (b) that he is the owner of the thing and he has not vested the control of the thing on another person. But in the case of *Donoghue v. Stevenson* the defendants (manufacturers) no longer had the actual authority to supervise or dispose of the bottles after they had sold and delivered them to the retailer. They had also lost the ownership over such goods after the sale. They became the property of the retailer after the purchase. Hence the provisions of section 148 cannot apply to this case.

Further, it is even very doubtful, for the same reasons stated above, if the retailer who sold the bottle to the plaintiff could also be held liable. By the time the plaintiff was drinking the content of the bottle, he was the owner of the thing because he had bought it. The retailer after the sale no longer had actual authority to supervise or dispose of the bottle, nor was he the owner.

The other important thing to be noted in the decision of the House of Lords in the case of *Donoghue v. Stevenson* was the extension of the duty of care for the first time to a manufacturer where the ultimate consumer of goods (who bought them from a retailer) suffered injury as a result of using the goods. Prior to the decision in this case the manufacturer was not liable at the consumer's action in absence of contractual relation between them.

But under the provisions of section 148 of CTA 1984 it is very doubtful if the court would be able to extend the principle of absolute liability, which is static and inelastic, to the manufacturer in absence of the conditions provided under section 149 of CTA, 1984. The flexibility of the principle of negligence cannot be found in strict or absolute liability.

The same could be said about the extension of the duty of care to the defendant who makes a negligent misstatement resulting to economic loss in absence of contractual relationship between the plaintiff and the defendant.[9] This was done on the application of the principle of negligence. But the rigid and inflexible principle of strict or absolute liability cannot be used as a basis of extension of responsibility or liability in tort to an area where such responsibility or liability did not exist before. Lack of extension of the liability or responsibility (i.e. duty of care) to new areas because the inelasticity

---

9   See the cases of *Hedley Byrne* and *Nile Import & Export Co. Ltd* (*supra*).

of the principle is one of the great defects in strict liability under section 138 or absolute liability under section 148.

3   THE NEGATIVE EFFECTS OF STRICT LIABILITY

It must at the outset be stated that strict or absolute liability is not a peculiar phenomenon of the Sudanese law of tort. It is embodied in nearly every system in the world. But in all other legal systems, strict or absolute liability cannot be the exclusive basis of the law of tort. Strict or absolute liability is incorporated where the public policy or opinion requires the maintenance of certain standards for the safety of the people or employees of certain works which involve great hazards, such as radiation in nuclear plants, or where it is necessary to protect the reputation of people, for example, against defamatory statements. Of course, publication of a falsehood which hurts the reputation of others is not a necessary aspect of the likelihood of the maker and so such publications must be absolutely or strictly punished or prohibited.

But it is inconceivable when the strict or absolute liability is made the basis of whole liability in the law of tort in this century. Apart from its inelasticity and the static feature, it is a principle which has a high degree of likelihood of impeding (unless it is limited to few areas) all social, economic, scientific and technological development. It tends to discourage private or public companies from carrying out hazardous or risky works or jobs; and these works or jobs are so essential to life and human development that they should not be abandoned for fear of liability. Strict liability may discourage factories, nuclear plants, the driving of motor vehicles, or bicycles and so on, because they involve widespread injuries or death. If the liability is absolute, the owners of companies or municipal councils who render public services are compelled to close down if a large number of their employees or numbers of the public are likely to be endangered. They may be held liable, if their employees suffer injuries, to pay out all their money. The daily activity of an individual or business owner(s) involves risks to the lives of others. If he cannot undertake these risky jobs for fear of absolute liability, he cannot live, nor can services or development be carried out.

Despite the fear of strict or absolute liability which is highlighted above, it is observed that in Sudan the factories are normally working, municipal councils normally render their public services, motor vehicles are being driven and the public is going about its normal daily life business. A conclusion from this general observation shows that the application of strict or absolute liability in generality and in particular does not hinder development in the Sudan.

But what is the answer to this contradiction? The answer is very simple. The answer lies in the contradiction itself. While section 138 purports to be the basis of liability in the law of tort, there are other laws such as the Traffic Act 1991 or even the provisions of CTA 1983 which apply the principle of negligence in the determination of defendant's liability. If the law makers intended that strict liability under section 138 and absolute liability in other sections like section 148 should be the only basis of liability in tort in Sudan, other laws which use fault as the basis of liability ought to have been repealed.

Consequently, the courts continue to determine liability using *fault* or *negligence*. Further even the proponents or advocates of the contents of section 138, when they are dealing with liability in a case, use the parameters or ingredients of the principle of negligence without stating that they are applying the principle of negligence (but section 138). In this way it is really the principle of negligence which they are applying in disguise.

In conclusion the answer to the question posed above lies in this contradiction.

Remedy or Device? The System of *Khul'* and the Effects of its Incorporation into Egyptian Personal Status Law

*Dawoud el-Alami**

The aim of Law No. 1 of 2000, Regulating Certain Circumstances and Procedures in Personal Status Litigation is, according to a prominent commentator, "the attainment of a balance between the legislative requirements necessitated by considerations of facilitation of judicial procedure and the expedition of justice, and the social requirements for the stability of the family and avoidance by its members, and consequently society, of tension, turbulence, ruin and deviation".[1] Although ostensibly a law designed to rationalize and consolidate judicial procedure in personal status cases in a single law, where heretofore procedure had been scattered across a range of piecemeal laws, this law has arguably had the more impact on family law, particularly divorce law, in Egypt and caused more controversy than any law since the discredited and annulled Law No. 44 of 1979. This is due to the fact that it sets out explicit procedures for the implementation and facilitation of the *shari'a* principle of *khul'*, by which a woman may effectively buy her release from an unsustainable marriage.

Of the various ways in which the marriage contract may be terminated under Islamic law, the most common is *talaq* or unilateral divorce by the husband. No formality is required to conclude this type of divorce beyond the verbal formula uttered by the husband. The husband is entitled to revoke the divorce simply by resuming married life at any time within the three-month waiting period, upon the termination of which the marriage may only be reinstated by a new contract. Divorce may be revoked twice; a third divorce is irrevocable. This form of divorce can be delegated to the wife by

---

*   Lecturer in Islamic studies, University of Wales at Lampeter.
1   Commentary on Law 1 of 2000, Muawwad Abd al-Tawab (President of the Court of Appeal). p. 25.

the husband at the time of the contract subject to terms agreed between the spouses, but this is a relatively rare occurrence.

It is not easy to assess in any realistic manner statistics with regard to the circumstances of the breakdown of marriages in Egyptian society. The many cases in which spouses part by mutual agreement are not recorded as such but as unilateral divorce effected by the husband.

The options for a woman unilaterally to instigate divorce, however, have always been limited, and access to them is difficult. There are provisions that allow a woman to seek divorce if she has suffered harm. The concept of harm may include physical or psychological abuse, failure of the husband to provide maintenance, impotence (and certain other physical defects subject to specific conditions and delays) and in some cases and at the discretion of the court the taking of a second wife.[2] It may, however, be difficult to substantiate a claim of harm, and the bureaucratic court system and sheer volume of cases mean that this type of divorce may often take three, four, five or more years to resolve. In such circumstances women in desperation often make huge financial and personal sacrifices in order to negotiate a release from an unhappy marriage. They may give up money, property or even child custody rights in an out of court settlement in exchange for a divorce which will be registered as a unilateral divorce by the husband.

The establishment of *khul'* as a simply regulated procedure that allows a woman to seek divorce on the grounds that she does not wish to remain married to her husband is, therefore, nothing short of revolutionary and needless to say it has caused great controversy in Egyptian society. It is perhaps to some extent a recognition by the Egyptian legislature of a woman's equal right of choice, a response to an irresistible sense that in this day and age it is unacceptable for a woman to be held in a marriage against her will.

Article 20 of the law reads as follows:

The two spouses may agree between themselves upon *khul'*, but if they do not agree mutually and the wife files a claim requesting [*khul'*] and ransoms herself and releases herself by *khul'* from her husband by forfeiting all of her lawful financial rights and returns to him the dowry that he gave her [upon marriage], the court shall grant her a divorce from him.

The court shall only grant a divorce by *khul'* after there has been an attempt at reconciling the two spouses and it has appointed two arbitrators to undertake the endeavour to reconcile them within a period not exceeding three months and in the manner stipulated in paragraph 2 of Article 18 and paragraphs 1 and 2 of Article 19 of this law,[3] and after the wife declares explicitly that she detests life with her husband

---

2   Law No. 25 of 1929, as amended by Law 100 of 1985, Arts. 6 and 11 bis. See D. El-Alami and D. Hinchliffe, *Islamic Marriage and Divorce Laws of the Arab World*, Kluwer Law International, London, pp. 56, 58.

3   Art. 18, para. 2: "In cases of divorce and judicial divorce, ruling shall not be made for these until the Court has made an effort to reconcile the parties and failed therein. If the spouses have a child, the court is obliged to propose reconciliation at least twice, there being an interval between these [proposals] of not less than thrity days and not more than sixty days." Art. 19, paras. 1 and 2: "In petitions for judicial divorce in which the law requires the appointment of

and that continuation of married life between them is impossible and that she fears that she will not maintain the "limits of God" due to this detestation. The consideration for *khul'* may not be the forfeiting of custody of minors, or their maintenance or any of their rights.

In all cases *khul'* shall take the form of irrevocable divorce.

The ruling, in all cases, shall not be subject to contestation by any of the means of contestation.

As we can see, under the new law a woman may apply to the court for divorce without having to show grounds as such other than her declaration that she is unable to tolerate marriage to her husband. The requirement of an attempt at arbitration and reconciliation is a wholly Islamic principle established in the *shari'a* and stipulated explicitly in the Qur'an.[4]

Looking at the origins of *khul'*, linguistically the verb *khala'a* from which the word *khul'* is derived, means to take off, detach or uproot. In legal terms it is a system that was known before Islam. Smith notes that "under the Khol system, the marriage contract was absolutely cancelled because the material consideration paid by the husband in order to acquire marital rights was returned to him".[5]

The principle of *khul'* in the *shari'a* is not in itself an innovation.[6] It has its origins in the Qur'an and *hadith* and is described in the divorce sections of all the major works of jurisprudence. The jurists derived the system of *khul'* from the sources of the *shari'a* as a means by which a woman might be released from a doomed relationship by returning to the man that which he had given her in return for his divorcing her.

The textual foundation for the system of *khul'* can be found in Surat al-Baqara:[7]

Divorce must be pronounced twice and then [a woman] must be retained in honour or released in kindness, and it is not lawful for you that you take from them anything of which you have given them except in the case where both fear that they may not be able to keep within the limits imposed by Allah. And if you fear that they may not be able to keep the limits of Allah, in that case it is no sin for either of them if the woman ransom herself. These are the limits imposed by Allah.

The verse does not mention the term *khul'*, but the concept may be inferred

cont.

two arbitrators, the Court must instruct each of the spouses to nominate an arbitrator from his/her family, insofar as this is possible, no later than at the next session. If either of them fails to appoint his/her arbitrator, or fails to attend this meeting, the court shall appoint an arbitrator on his behalf. The two arbitrators must appear before the court at the session immediately following their appointment to report what conclusions they have reached. If they disagree, or either of them fails to appear, the Court shall hear their statements or the statement of the one who is present following the swearing of an oath.".

4   Sura 4, v.35.
5   Robertson Smith, *Kinship and Marriage in Early Arabia*, pp. 112, 113.
6   El-Alami and Hinchliffe, *Islamic Marriage and Divorce Laws of the Arab World*, pp. 27, 28.
7   Sura 2, v. 229.

from the statement that a woman may ransom herself in the case where the marriage cannot be sustained.

An example of a woman ransoming herself in the case of an insupportable marriage is reported in most of the major *hadith* collections and is cited as the first incidence of *khul'* in Islam. A woman named Habiba bint Sahl told the Prophet that she was the wife of Thabit b Qays and that she could not tolerate to live with her husband. The Prophet asked her what he had given her [as *mahr*], to which she replied that he had given her a garden. The Prophet told her to return this to him in return for her divorce.

The Muslim jurists in general are in agreement on the system of *khul'* but there are certain differences of opinion with regard to the circumstances in which it is permissible, and the nature of the divorce that it entails. With only minor exception, the majority of the schools consider it permissible on the basis that the *shari'a* gives men the right to divorce their wives while providing corresponding recourse for women in the form of *khul'*.[8]

The second point of disagreement is with regard to the nature of the divorce resulting from *khul'*. The jurists are divided between two main opinions. The Shafii's and Hanbalis consider *khul'* to be annulment (*faskh*), which is irrevocable, on the basis of the opinion of the companion Ibn Abbas, who held that the first part of the verse 229 above is concerned with divorce, the middle with ransoming, and the end with divorce.[9]

The Hanafis and Malikis, however, consider *khul'* to be a lesser irrevocable divorce. The *Hedaya* says: "And where the compensation is thus offered and accepted a single divorce irreversible takes place in virtue of *khoola*."[10]

Khul' is considered to be an oath on the part of the husband, that is a divorce suspended upon acceptance of the consideration (money). If it is the husband who proposes *khul'* he may not withdraw his offer before the wife has either accepted or rejected it. If, however, the offer was uttered by the wife, the husband should, if he accepts, divorce the wife immediately, where-upon the return of the dowry is confirmed. If the husband makes no response but at a later date divorces his wife, he is not entitled to any compensation. According to Malik this is due to the financial nature of the *khul'*. The wife may retract her offer of *khul'* before the husband's response. Moreover she has an option to change her mind within three days. Most important is that the wife should be fully aware of all the financial considerations and make her decision on that basis, contrary to the divorce which is a termination of the contract over which she has no control.

There is no strict formula for *khul'*. It may be concluded using any form of words indicating divorce including references to buying, release, or any form of material consideration. If no material consideration is stipulated then

---

8   One of the successors, al-Hasan Ibn Yasir Abu Said al-Basri 642–728, rejects this opinion saying that *khul'* is only permitted in the case where the wife has committed adultery and the husband has witnessed the act.

9   Chapters on Marriage and Divorce, Responses of Ibn Hanbal and Ibn Rahwayh. Translated by Susan Spectorsky, p. 51.

10 *The Hedaya*, translated by Charles Hamilton, 2nd edn., 1870, Book IV, "Of *Talak* or Divorce", Chapter VIII, "Of *Khoola*".

the divorce will be just that, a straightforward *talaq*. If, however, the husband offers to release his wife on the basis of *khul'* but later denies that he intended to divorce his wife, the *khul'* will be valid on the basis that intention was expressed.

The jurists maintain that the consideration for *khul'* may be anything that has a lawful monetary value. They differ, however, with regard to the amount. Malik and al-Shafi'i say that there are no limits to the amount, which may be greater than the amount of the dowry paid by the husband. This is due to the fact that it is a financial transaction like any other and is based on the mutual consent of the parties. The Hanafis, however, base their opinion on the *hadith* mentioned above and argue that *khul'* should not exceed the amount of the dowry.

The requirements for *khul'* are the same as for any other type of contract. The parties should be of legal age, and the *khul'* may not take place under duress or coercion. If the wife is a minor she may be represented by her guardian, but in this case the guardian must make the payment from his own resources as he is not permitted to dispose of the property of his ward. He may, however, reclaim the amount he has paid when the ward comes of age. If the wife is of legal age and on her behalf her father agrees on *khul'* with the husband the wife will be liable to pay.

Those Arab states that have fully codified their personal status laws almost without exception have provisions with regard to *khul'*. Although it would be virtually impossible to assess to what extent it has been used, the possibility of *khul'* has always existed in Egyptian law. Prior to the new law, however, there was no specific provision describing or defining the process of *khul'*. The only reference to be found is contained in a procedural law, No. 78 of 1931, Article 6 of which stipulates that the *shari'a* First Instance Court will have jurisdiction in cases of divorce, *khul'* and *mubara*. Article 24 of the same law indicates that a case may be raised before the court appropriate to the domicile of the wife [or female custodian] whether she is claimant or respondent in the case of divorce *khul'* or *mubara*.[11] There are Appeal Court and Cassation rulings dealing with cases of *khul'*. In a principle established by the Court of Cassation, *khul'* and divorce in return for financial compensation were considered matters of personal status, not financial transactions, and it was therefore the *shari'a* that applied rather than the Civil Code.[12] As such, in accordance with Article 280 of Law 78 of 1931, in the absence of specific textual provision it is the most appropriate opinion of Abu Hanifa that is applicable, and as noted above Hanafi opinion supports the principle of *khul'*.

To what extent, then, does this law provide a real remedy or recourse for ordinary Egyptian women? For a woman who has the means and who wishes

---

[11] *Mubara'* is similar to *khul'* but is usually referred to as "mutual discharge" inasmuch as it is a mutual agreement, whereas *khul'* is at the instigation of the wife. El-Alami and Hinchcliffe, *The Islamic Marriage and Divorce Laws of the Arab World*, p. 27.

[12] Ahmad Nasr Mabadi' Al-Jindi, *al-Qada' fi'l-Ahwal ash-Shakhsiyya*, Khul' Principle 2, pp. 508–509.

to divorce for no other reason than that she does not wish to be married to her husband it provides a simple solution. For a woman at the point of desperation in an abusive or exploitative relationship, however, it is little more than a "quick-fix", an almost immediate release, but at the cost of her legitimate rights. The fact is that it is those who are most desperate and most vulnerable who are likely to resort to this device, in the knowledge that to pursue proper redress will be a painful and protracted process with no guarantee of success. Even if we accept that this may be a pragmatic solution in some cases, how many women are actually in a position to return their dowry to the husband? The pressures of the cost of living mean that the dowry will most probably already have been spent on household items, the education of children or generally have been absorbed into the family budget.

The new provision regulating *khul'* represents progress inasmuch as it is a recognition of a woman's right of choice, but it does little to rectify the injustice of a system that denies women access to real remedies and just settlements.

The Legal Relationship of a Father with his Illegitimate Child under Islamic and Iranian Law

M.A. Ansari-Pour*

The legal relationship between a father and his children involves certain rights and obligations. For example, under Article 1199 of the Civil Code of Iran (hereinafter cited as the CC), the maintenance of the child including food, housing and clothing, must primarily be provided by the father if he is financially capable and if the child is in need.[1] The father is the natural guardian of the child.[2] Generally speaking, the father is the legal custodian of the child after a certain age[3] if the child has a mother, otherwise he would be the sole custodian.[4] This is also the case where the mother of the child during the period of custody marries another man or becomes insane.[5]

Inheritance is another instance of legal relationship between a father and his child. A father and his child inherit from each other, according to whoever dies sooner in line with the criteria stated in the CC and the relevant laws.[6]

It should be noted, however, that this legal relationship exists between a father and his legitimate child.[7] A child is only legitimate if his or her parents

---

[*] Chairman of the Iranian Law Institute. I would like to thank Dr Menski in the SOAS law department and Judge Pearl for reading the first draft of this article.
[1] See also Arts. 1167–1168 and 1204 of the CC.
[2] Art. 1180 of the CC, *inter alia*, states: "A minor is under the natural guardianship of his father and paternal grandfather".
[3] Art. 1169 of the CC provides that a "mother has priority for the custody of her child up to two years from the date of child's birth. After the expiry of this period, the custody is with father except for daughters whose custody is with the mother up to the age of seven.".
[4] Art. 1171 of the CC.
[5] Art. 1170 of the CC.
[6] See Arts. 862 and 906–915 of the CC.
[7] H. Imami, *Huquq-i Madani*, vol. 5, 6th edn., Tehran, 1357, p. 172; H. Safa'i and A. Imami, *Huquq-i Khanawadih*, vol. 2, 2nd edn., Tehran, 1997, p. 117. See also in Arabic, B.A. Badran, *Ahkam al-Ziwaj wa al-Talaq fi al-Islam*, 2nd edn., 1961, p. 309; Z. Sha'ban, *Al-Ahkam al-Shar'iyyah lil-Ahwal al-Shakhsiyyah*, 3rd

were legally married when he or she was conceived.[8] It is useful to note that the formality of marriage under Islamic-Shiite and Iranian law is quite simple. The only thing that the competent couple[9] must do is to make the marriage contract. The marriage contract, under Article 1062 of the CC, is concluded by the offer and acceptance in words which explicitly convey the intention to marry[10] whether these words are uttered by the couple themselves or by somebody else on their behalf.[11] Under Iranian law every marriage must be registered[12] but non-registration of marriage does not affect its validity.[13] Issues like dower (*mahr*) and its amount must be fixed[14] but their omission does not make the contract void.[15] It can be fixed later by the subsequent agreement of the parties and in certain cases it must be fixed according to the criteria provided by law.[16] If the couple intend to make a fixed-term marriage (*mut'ah*),[17] then the term of the marriage must be definitely

---

cont.

    edn., Beirut, 1973, p. 533; B. Bilani, *Qawanin al-Ahwal al-Shakhsiyyah*, Beirut, 1971, pp. 144–151.

[8] Imami, *Huquq-i Madani*, pp. 151, 154; Safa'i *et al.*, *Huquq-i Khanawadih*, pp. 42–144; S. Ameer Ali, *Mahommedan Law*, vol. 2, 7th edn., Lahore, 1979, pp. 178–179. Under Sunni law also the legitimacy of a child is based on its conception during a lawful wedlock. See M. Al-Dijwi, *Al-Ahwal al-Shakhsiyyah lil-Misriyyin al-Muslimin*, Cairo, 1969, p. 319; M. Abd al-Tawwab, *Al-Mustahdath fi Qada' al-Ahwal al-Shakhsiyyah*, Iskandariyyah, 1991, pp. 173–174; T. Mahmood, *Statutes of Personal Law in Islamic Countries*, 2nd edn., New Delhi, 1995, p. 266; K.N. Ahmed, *The Muslim Law of Divorce*, Islamabad, 1972, p. 880. See also *Hamida Begum v. Murad Begum* in [1975] 27 The All-Pakistan Legal Decisions (PLD), Supreme Court, 624.

[9] The couple must be of age, sane and have the intention to marry. If the potential wife is a virgin, then her father, if she has one, must give his permission. If the suitor is a match for and equal (*kufu'*) to the girl concerned then she, following the court's permission, can marry him without the permission of her father. See Arts. 1041, 1043–1044 and 1064 of the CC.

[10] Art. 1062 does not specify whether the offer and acceptance should be in Arabic or it could be concluded in other languages as well. But in Shiite jurisprudence, which is the main source of the CC, conclusion of marriage in other languages has been permitted. For example, one jurist states that marriage should be concluded in Arabic. However, if the parties or their representatives cannot pronounce Arabic terms correctly they can conclude the marriage in any language provided that the words which they use signify the offer and acceptance for marriage. R.H. Khomeini, *Risali-yi Tawdih al-Masa'il*, Tehran, 1985, Problem 2370; R.M. Khomeini, *Tahrir al-Wasilah*, vol. 2, 3rd edn., Beirut, 1981, p. 246.

[11] Art. 1063 of the CC.

[12] See Art. 993 of the CC and Arts. 31–33 of the Registration of Personal Status Act 1976 as amended in 1985.

[13] H. Safa'i and A. Imami, *Huquq-i Khanawadih*, vol. 1, 6th edn., Tehran, 1998, pp. 48–49.

[14] Art. 1079 of the CC.

[15] Art. 1087 of the CC.

[16] See generally Arts. 1087–1094 and 1100 of the CC.

[17] There are many materials in English regarding this kind of marriage but unfortunately the majority of them are poor and misleading. There are few writings which, to some extent, have examined the issue well. For example, see M.H. Tabataba'i, *Shi'a* (translated by S.H. Nasr), Qom (Iran), 1989, pp. 227–230; M. Mutahhari, *The Rights of Women in Islam*, Tehran, 1353 (1974), (translated from Persian into English in 1981), pp. 25–57; A. Gourgi,

fixed,[18] otherwise the marriage, according to the majority of Shiite jurists, would be regarded as a permanent marriage.[19] The couple can make the marriage quite privately.[20] There is no need for any witness[21] as required in Sunni jurisprudence.[22]

If a couple are married or claim that they were married when the child was conceived, then their child will be legitimate provided that the following conditions are met:

(a)   An act of sexual intercourse must have taken place between the parents.[23] Article 1158 of the CC refers to this requirement by stating that the gestation period starts from the date of coitus.[24]

(b)   The child must be born between the shortest gestation period and the longest one from the date of coitus. The shortest gestation period, under Shiite law, is six months. But with respect to the longest period there are three opinions: nine months, ten months and one year. The

---

cont.

    Temporary Marriage (Mut'ah) in Islamic Law (translated by S. Murata), Qom (Iran), 1991.

18   Arts. 1075–1076 of the CC. In addition, in the fixed-term marriage the dower must be fixed, otherwise the marriage would be void (Art. 1095 of the CC).

19   Shahid II (Z. Al-Juba'i al-'Amili), *Al-Rawdat al-Bahiyyah fi Sharh al-Lum'at al-Dimashqiyyah*, vol. 5, Beirut, n.d., pp. 286–287; S.A. Ha'iri, *Sharh-i Qanun-i Madani*, vol. 2, new edn, Tehran, 1376, p. 936.

20   In practice, however, few marriages are made privately and in the absence of other people.

21   Although the conclusion of marriage before witnesses has been recommended in Shiite law, it is not a necessary condition for the validity of the marriage. See Shahid II, *Al-Rawdat al-Bahiyyah*, p. 112; Shahid II (Z. Al-Juba'i al-'Amili), *Masalik al-Afham*, vol. 1, Qom, n.d., p. 431.

22   For the position of Sunni jurisprudence on this issue, see (in Arabic), A.A. Ibn Qudamah, *Al-Mughni*, vol. 6, 3rd edn. (edited by Sayyid Muhammad Rashid Rida), Cairo, 1367 lunar (1947), pp. 448–453; Al-Dijwi, *Al-Ahwal al-Shakhsiyyah*, pp. 18–20; M. Al-Siba'i, *Sharh Qanun al-Ahwal al-Shakhsiyyah*, 2nd edn, Damascus, 1958, pp. 61–65; A. Al-Hasri, *Al-Nikah*, Cairo, 1967, pp. 183–202, and (in English), see D. Pearl and W. Menski, *Muslim Family Law*, 3rd edn, London, 1998, p. 41; J.J. Nasir, *The Islamic Law of Personal Status*, 2nd edn., London, 1990, pp. 54–55.

23   This is also the position of Shiite law. See A.N.J. Al-Hilli, *Sharayi' al-Islam*, vol. 2, Najaf, 1969, p. 340; M.H. Najafi, *Jawahir al-Kalam*, vol. 31, 7th edn., Beirut, 1981, pp. 222–224. There are also many cases in which sexual intercourse has been regarded as a necessary condition for the establishment of paternity. See Supreme Court (chamber 33), Judgment 2995–14.1.1372; Judgment 5321–4.12.1373; Judgment 4521–18.4.1373.

24   Sunni jurisprudence differs from Shiite law in this respect. According to the Hanafi school, the starting point for gestation period is the date of marriage, even if the marriage has not been consummated. But under three other schools of Sunni jurisprudence it is from the date of marriage with the possibility of sexual intercourse. For details, see Al-Dijwi, *Al-Ahwal al-Shakhsiyyah*, pp. 320–322; Al-Siba'i, *Sharh Qanun*, pp. 196–197; M.H. Hanafi, *Al-Ahwal al-Shakhsiyyah*, 4th edn., Cairo, 1965, pp. 14, 34–38; Nasir, *The Islamic Law*, pp. 158–159; J.J. Nasir, *The Status of Women Under Islamic Law and Under Modern Islamic Legislation*, 2nd edn., London, 1994, pp. 117–118; M. Abu Zahra, "Family law", in M. Khadduri and H.J. Liebesny (eds.), *Law in the Middle East*, Washington, 1955, p. 151.

last view, however, is now obsolete and the first one is the majority view in Shiite law.[25] The CC has adopted the ten-month period of gestation. Article 1158 states that "a child born during the marriage belongs to the husband provided that the interval between the date of coitus and the birth of the child is not less than six months and not more than ten months". If the child is born after the termination of marriage, he or she, under Article 1159 of the CC, belongs to the husband provided that "the mother has not yet married again and that no more than ten months have passed from the date of dissolution of marriage, unless it is proved that the interval between the date of coitus and the birth of child is less than six months or more than ten months".[26]

If the above conditions are met the child will be legitimate, unless the child is denied by the father according to the rules and procedures provided in the CC and Islamic law.[27]

Paternity can also be established by express or implied acknowledgement of the father. Article 1161 of the CC refers to this principle by stating, *inter alia*, that "if the husband has expressly or impliedly acknowledged his own paternity, his subsequent denial of paternity will not be admitted".

In addition, there are some other children who are treated as legitimate.

(a)   The first group consists of children who are conceived as a result of

---

[25]   For a detailed discussion about gestation periods in Shiite law, see Al-Hilli, *Sharayi'*, vol. 2, p. 340; Najafi, *Jawahir-al-Kalam*, vol. 31, pp. 222–230. See also Safa'i *et al.*, *Huquq-i Khanawadih*, vol. 2, pp. 49–51; Ameer Ali, *Mahommedan Law*, pp. 185–186. The shortest gestation period in Sunni law is also six months but with respect to the longest one there are several opinions. They consist of nine lunar months, one lunar year, two years, four years, five years and even seven years. See A.A. Ibn Qudamah, *Al-Mughni*, vol. 7, 3rd edn. (ed. Sayyid Muhammad Rashid Rida), Cairo, 1367 lunar (1947), pp. 477–478; W. Al-Zuhayli, *Al-Fiqh al-Islami wa Adillatuh*, vol. 7, Damascus, 1984, pp. 676–678; Al-Siba'i, *Sharh Qanun al-Ahwal al-Shakhsiyyah*, pp. 193–195. See also Ameer Ali, *Mahommedan Law*, pp. 169–173. Nasir argues that the minimum term of six months for pregnancy is approved by all modern Arab personal status laws which are almost unanimous on a maximum term of one year, with the exception of Algeria, where this term is reduced to ten months (Arts. 42–43). However, the Syrian Art. 128 specifies a solar year, while the Jordanian Art. 185 stresses that the year is a lunar one. Kuwaiti Art. 166 defines the minimum and maximum term of pregnancy as six lunar months and 365 days respectively. Moroccan Art. 84 makes the two terms subject to the provisions of Art. 67 which deals with cases of suspicion which should be referred by the court to medical experts to decide thereon. Nasir, *The Islamic Law*, p. 157–158; Nasir, *The Status of Women*, p. 117.

[26]   For other relevant provisions, see Arts. 1160–1164 of the CC.

[27]   There are certain rules for the denial of a child which are dealt with under Arts. 1162–1163 of the CC. In Islamic law, the denial of a child is discussed under the title of *li'an* (imprecation). See Najifi, *Jawahir al-Kalam*, vol. 31, pp. 232–237; M.H. Najafi, *Jawahir al-Kalam*, vol. 34, 7th edn., Beirut, 1981, pp. 2–85; Shahid II (Z. Al-Juba'i al-'Amili), *Al-Rawdat al-Bahiyyah fi Sharh al-Lum'at al-Dimashqiyyah*, vol. 6, Beirut, n.d., pp. 181–218.

sexual intercourse by mistake.[28] The error or mistake (*shubhah*) may be *de facto* or *de jure*. Many examples have been given of such errors. For instance, a man or a woman may have sex with a woman or a man respectively supposing that the other party is his or her own partner. Or a man may marry his foster sister believing that such a marriage is lawful. If both man and woman have sex by mistake then their child has the same legal relationship with the parents as a legitimate child. If one of them has sex by mistake but not the other, the child has a legal relationship with the mistaken party only.[29]

(b)   Where the marriage because of a legal impediment is void and the parents did not know the impediment when they married, the child is to be regarded as legitimate. If one of the parents, but not the other, was aware of the impediment, the child has no legal relationship with him or her.[30]

(c)   The child conceived as a result of sex by a sleeper (such as a sleepwalker), a lunatic and a drunkard (if he has not made himself drunk intentionally) will have full legal relationship with the above people if conception did take place when they were asleep, insane and drunk respectively.[31]

(d)   Moreover, where a man or woman, under duress and coercion, is forced to have sex, then the child will have full legal relationship with the forced party but not with the other.[32]

The only child who is treated differently from a legitimate offspring by law is an illegitimate child, i.e. a child who is conceived as a result of adultery or fornication and these unlawful relationships are established in court.[33] The

---

28   Art. 1165 of the CC states: "A child born as a result of sexual intercourse by mistake belongs to the party who made the mistake and in case both parties made the mistake the child belongs to both of them". Such a child, under Art. 884 of the CC, like a legitimate child, inherits from his father, his mother and their relatives and vice versa. See also Khomeini, *Tahrir al-Wasilah*, pp. 264–265; Imami, *Huquq-i Madani*, vol. 5, pp. 173–178 especially p. 178.

29   For details, see Ha'iri, *Sharh-i Qanun-i Madani*, pp. 1027–1028; Safa'i *et al.*, *Huquq-i Khanawadih*, vol. 2, pp. 90–91. See also M.H. Najafi, *Jawahir al-Kalam*, vol. 29, 7th edn., Beirut, 1981 pp. 244–256 especially pp. 244–247; Khomeini, *Tahrir al-Wasilah*, pp. 264–265; Imami, *Huquq-i Madani*, pp. 173–174; Ameer Ali, *Mahommedan Law*, pp. 186–188.

30   Art. 1166 of the CC.

31   Khomeini, *Tahrir al-Wasilah*, p. 265. See also Imami, *Huquq-i Madani*, p. 174; Safa'i *et al.*, *Huquq-i Khanawadih*, vol. 2, pp. 91–92.

32   Art. 884 of the CC after providing that an illegitimate child does not inherit from his father, his mother and their relatives, states that if the unlawfulness of the relationship, from which the child is conceived, is established with respect to one of the parents but not the other because of duress or mistake, the child will inherit only from the latter parent and his/her relatives and vice versa. See also Imami, *Huquq-i Madani*, pp. 179–180; H. Imami, *Huquq-i Madani*, vol. 3, 2nd edn., Tehran, 1362 (1983), pp. 212–215; Ha'iri, *Sharh-i Qanun-i Madani*, p. 799.

33   Fornication or adultery is proved either through confession or testimony of witnesses according to the criteria provided in the Islamic Penal Code (Arts. 68–81).

question is whether or not a legal relationship exists between a biological father and his illegitimate child. This issue is very important since the institutions of legitimation[34] and adoption[35] have not been recognized in Islamic law.

This article examines the Plenary Assembly of the Supreme Court (hereinafter cited as PASC) judgment on the legal relationship of a biological father with his illegitimate child, in particular the parental responsibilities of the father, under Islamic and Iranian law. In order to highlight the importance of the judgment and its contribution to the development of Islamic and Iranian law on illegitimacy, the position of Islamic law and Iranian family law on the question is examined in brief first.

1   ISLAMIC LAW: SUNNI SCHOOLS

It should be noted at the outset that, under Sunni law, the legal relationship of an illegitimate child with his/her mother is similar to a legitimate one.[36] But this is not the case with respect to the father.

According to the Maliki and Shafi'i schools there is no legal relationship between a father and his illegitimate child whatsoever. They even reject the blood relationship between a father and his illegitimate children. According to them, a father can marry his illegitimate daughter and a brother marry his illegitimate sister. This rule is applicable to other paternal relatives like uncles and aunts as well.[37] With such a position, it is natural for them to say that the father has no responsibility to provide maintenance for his illegitimate child.[38]

On the other hand, the Hanafi and Hanbali schools make a distinction between natural lineage (i.e. blood relationship) of an illegitimate child with

---

34   It is a well established rule of Islamic law that if the child is conceived as a result of fornication or adultery and later the natural parents get married, even if the child born during the marriage, the child will not belong to the father. See Al-Hilli, *Sharayi' al-Islam*, vol. 2, p. 341; Najafi, *Jawahir al-Kalam*, vol. 31, pp. 236–237. See also A.A.A. Fyzee, *Outlines of Muhammadan Law*, 4th edn., Delhi, 1974, pp. 189–190, 193–194; Abd al-Tawwab, *Al-Mustahdath*, p. 173.

35   Almost all writers who deal with the issue of legitimacy and paternity stipulate that adoption existed in pre-Islamic Arabia, but it was abolished by Islam. In addition, adoption has been ruled out expressly by the law of many Islamic countries. For example, see B. Al-'Arabi, *Abhath wa Mudhakkarat fi al-Qanun wa al-Fiqh al-Islami*, Algeria, 1996, pp. 632–633; Al-Siba'i, *Sharh Qanun*, p. 192; Al-Dijwi, *Al-Ahwal Al-Shakhsiyyah*, pp. 330–331; Hanafi, *Al-Ahwal al-Shakhsiyyah*, pp. 21, 66, 68, 94–95; Abd al-Tawwab, *ibid*, pp. 164, 178–179; Bilani, *Qawanin*, p. 158; Nasir, *The Status of Women*, pp. 115–116, 124–125; Nasir, *The Islamic Law*, p. 157; Pearl *et al.*, *Muslim Family Law*, p. 408.

36   Nasir, *The Islamic Law*, p. 157; Nasir, *The Status of Women*, p. 116; Al-Zuhayli, *Al-Fiqh al-Islami*, p. 675; Al-Siba'i, *Sharh Qanun*, p. 192; Bilani, *Qawanin*, p. 153; Hanafi, *Al-Ahwal al-ShakhsiyyahI*, pp. 19–21, 66–69.

37   Ibn Qudamah, *Al-Mughni*, vol. 6, p. 578.

38   *Ibid.*

his father and other relationships, such as inheritance.[39] Thus they prohibit a marriage between a father and his illegitimate daughter, or between a boy and his illegitimate sister.[40] But they deny all other legal relationships, such as inheritance, guardianship, custody and the obligation to provide maintenance for the illegitimate child, since, according to them, there is no lineal kinship or paternity (*nasab*) between an illegitimate child and his father.[41]

It has been generally argued that the legal relationship of a father with his child depends on the legitimacy of the child. The entitlement of a child to maintenance and inheritance from the father and the right of the father to custody, guardianship, inheritance and the like all depend on legitimacy.[42] In other words, no legal relationship is recognized between a father and his illegitimate child because no paternity is established for such a child.

The principle that the legal relationship between a father and his child depends on legitimacy and paternity and that there is no legal relationship between an illegitimate child and his father has been adopted expressly or impliedly by statute and by courts in a number of Arab countries.

For example, under Moroccan law no paternity can be established for the illegitimate offspring. Article 83 of the Personal Status Code provides that "illegitimate filiation is utterly void for the father, and shall have no effect whatsoever, but for the mother it shall be the same as the legitimate, because it is her child".[43] The Tunisian Personal Status Code[44] also does not recognize paternity for an illegitimate child and, under Article 72, the absence of paternity excludes the child from the kindred and deprives him of the right to claim maintenance and inheritance.

Under Article 40 of the Algerian Family Act, paternity is established through several means, including a valid marriage. It impliedly rejects the establishment of paternity by fornication or adultery. The Algerian Supreme Court has also ruled in 1984 that the status of legitimacy cannot be granted to an illegitimate child conceived from relationships before marriage or during

[39] M.J. Mughniyyah, *Al-Fiqh ala-al-Madhahib al-Khamsah*, 5th edn., Beirut, 1960, p. 369.

[40] See Ibn Qudamah, *Al-Mughni*, vol. 6, pp. 578–579; A.A.S. Al-Mardawi, *Al-Insaf*, vol. 7, Beirut, 1957, p. 113.

[41] Ibn Qudamah, *Al-Mughni*, vol. 6, p. 266; Ibn Rushd (Muhammad Ibn Rushd al-Qurtubi), *Bidayat al-Mujtahid wa Nihayat al-Muqtasid*, vol. 2, Qom, 1966, p. 355; Al-Zuhayli, *Al-Fiqh al-Islami*, pp. 675, 688–689; Fyzee, *Outlines*, pp. 201, 215, 396. Ibn Qudamah, when discussing the issue of maintenance, also argues that one of the conditions for the provision of maintenance is the "inheritance relationship" between the provider and the beneficiary. Therefore an illegitimate child who cannot inherit from his father has no right to claim maintenance. See Ibn Qudamah, *Al-Mughni*, vol. 7, p. 584.

[42] K. Hodkinson, *Muslim Family Law: A Sourcebook*, London, 1984, p. 307. See also Nasir, *The Islamic Law*, pp. 156–157; Nasir, *The Status of Women*, p. 125; Al-Zuhayli, *Al-Fiqh al-Islami*, p. 689; Hanafi, *Al-Ahwal al-Shakhsiyyah*, pp. 21, 66, 68, 94–95; Abd al-Tawwab, *Al-Mustahdath*, pp. 151, 161; Al-Siba'i, *Sharh Qanun*, p. 199.

[43] A. Al-Khamlishi, *Wejhat Nazar*, vol. 2, Rabat, 1998, pp. 89–90; Nasir, *The Islamic Law*, p. 157.

[44] For example, see Arts. 68–69 and 71.

the stage of betrothal and engagement. Paternity cannot be established for a child unless there is a marriage contract concluded according to law.[45]

Under the Syrian Personal Status Act, the establishment of parentage for an illegitimate child has been impliedly ruled out.[46] Moreover, Article 133(2) provides that when paternity is established, all the consequences resulting from such a relationship, such as maintenance and inheritance, will follow. It implies that where the paternity is not established no legal relationship can be established.

Egyptian courts, following Islamic law, recognize no paternity for an illegitimate child and as a result no legal relationship.[47]

2   ISLAMIC LAW: SHIITE SCHOOL

It should be noted that, unlike Sunni law, Shiite law does not draw a distinction between the legal relationship of an illegitimate child with his father on one hand, and the legal relationship of the child with his mother on the other.[48] There is no difference in this regard between a father and a mother.

The issue of illegitimacy and the legal relationship of a father with his illegitimate child are discussed under different headings and topics in the classical texts of Shiite law.

One of those topics is inheritance. Some Islamic jurists, without listing illegitimacy as one of the legal impediments to inheritance, state that an illegitimate child does not inherit from his father and vice versa.[49] But some others, when discussing the legal impediments to inheritance, enumerate illegitimacy as one of those impediments. Illegitimacy eliminates the inheritance relationship between the father and mother on the one hand and the child on the other.[50]

Marriage is another place where illegitimacy is discussed. One of the legal impediments to marriage is lineal kinship (*nasab*). A man or a woman cannot marry his or her lineal kindred. Here Islamic jurists deal with the ways according to which a lineal kinship is established. But it is stipulated that lineal kinship cannot be established through fornication or adultery.[51]

---

45 See Al-'Arabi, *Abhath wa Mudhakkarat*, pp. 621–633, especially pp. 621–624.
46 For example, see Arts. 129–133.
47 For some of these cases see Al-Dijwi, *Al-Ahwal al-Shakhsiyyah*, pp. 328, 341, 344, 348, 358; Abd al-Tawwab, *Al-Mustahdath*, pp. 163, 173; A. Kharufah, *Sharh Qanun al-Ahwal al-Shakhsiyyah*, vol. 2, Baghdad, 1963, p. 186.
48 It has been argued that in Shiite law an illegitimate child does not inherit from his mother as well, since the impediment to the inheritance is adultery or fornication which has been committed by both parents. Therefore the rule must apply to both. Mughniyyah, *Al-Fiqh ala al-Madhahib al-Khamsah*, p. 530. See also Ameer Ali, *Mahommedan Law*, p. 212.
49 A.N.J. Al-Hilli, *Sharayi' al-Islam*, vol. 4, Najaf, 1969, p. 44; M.H. Najafi, *Jawahir al-Kalam*, vol. 39, 7th edn., Beirut, 1981, pp. 274–275; M. 'Allamat al-Hilli, *Idah al-Fawa'id*, vol. 4, Qom (Iran), 1389 lunar, pp. 247–248.
50 For example, see Khomeini, *Tahrir al-Wasilah*, p. 369.
51 Al-Hilli, *Sharayi' al-Islam*, vol. 2, p. 281; Najafi, *Jawahir al-Kalam*, vol. 29, pp. 256–259.

Another place where the issue of illegitimacy is addressed is lineage and paternity (*nasab*). It is here that the classical Shiite jurists (with the exception of blood relationship) categorically reject any lineal kinship, and consequently any legal relationship between a father and his illegitimate child.[52]

One contemporary jurist, however, recognizes a kind of lineal kinship and paternity between an illegitimate child and his/her biological father. In one of his earliest writings, he divides lineal kinship into the lawful and unlawful. He argues that lineage is either lawful, where it results from a lawful cause such as marriage, or unlawful, where it results from adultery or fornication. Although certain legal relationships resulting from lineage, such as inheritance, are peculiar to lawful lineage, the rules relating to marriage are general and they apply to unlawful lineage as well. Consequently, an illegitimate boy cannot marry a blood relative such as an aunt and a girl cannot marry her uncle.[53]

It can be concluded that the classical Shiite jurists recognized no legal relationship between a father and his illegitimate child. It is argued that, under Shiite law, an illegitimate child is *filius nullius* or *filius populi*.[54] No legal relationship is recognized with the mother or father or with any other relatives.[55] Hence, the child has no right to inherit from his or her parents, or to receive maintenance and other benefits deriving from parentage.

3   IRANIAN FAMILY LAW

The main body of Iranian family law has been enshrined in the CC. The issue of illegitimacy in the CC, as in Shiite law, is dealt with under different headings. First, Article 884 of the CC, which has been incorporated in the section dealing with the conditions for and impediments to inheritance, *inter alia*, provides that an illegitimate child does not inherit from his parents and their relatives or vice versa.

Secondly, Article 1045 of the CC, which has been enshrined in the section dealing with the impediments to marriage, states that marriage with the following blood relations is forbidden, even if the relationship is the result of mistake or fornication and adultery; (a) marriage with father and grandfathers, and with mother or grandmothers howsoever high; (b) marriage with children, howsoever low; (c) marriage with brothers or sisters and their children howsoever low; and (d) marriage with one's own paternal and maternal aunts and those of one's father, mother, grandfathers and grandmothers.

---

[52]   Al-Hilli, *Sharayi' al-Islam*, vol. 2, p. 341; Najafi, *Jawahir al-Kalam*, vol. 31, pp. 232–237.
[53]   Khomeini, *Tahrir al-Wasilah*, p. 265.
[54]   Professors Cretney and Masson argue that "at common law a child was only legitimate if his parents were married when he was born or conceived. A child born to unmarried parents was a *filius nullius* or *filius populi*". S.M. Cretney and J.M. Masson, *Principles of Family Law*, 6th edn, London, 1997, pp. 602–603.
[55]   Ameer Ali, *Mahommedan Law*, pp. 85, 188; Fyzee, *Outlines*, p. 463.

Thirdly, Article 1167, which has been placed in the section dealing with lineage (*nasab*), generally states that: "An illegitimate child does not belong to the fornicator (or adulterer)".[56] The absence of a filial relationship between a father and his illegitimate child, as stressed by this article, indicates that there exists no legal relationship between them. For example, the parents have no legal right to ask for the custody of their child and they have no duty to take the child into their custody as well. The child has no right to claim maintenance and the parents also are under no obligation to provide it. This is the interpretation which has been adopted by the most well-known commentators of the CC.[57]

If no legal relationship exists between an illegitimate child and his/her parents who will be responsible for taking care of the child, taking him or her into custody and maintaining him or her? It should be noted that there is no legal barrier to the biological parents of an illegitimate child fulfilling their parental responsibilities, by taking the child into their custody. If the biological parents, however, do not take the child into their custody and do not maintain the child, who will be responsible? Can a court compel the biological parents to fulfil these responsibilities?

One commentator on the CC, without any further detail, has argued that the guardianship of an illegitimate child rests with the state.[58] Another writer has proposed two arguments in this regard. First, he argues that if the fornication or adultery has been on the part of the father only but not the mother (for example, where the father deceives the mother into believing, contrary to the fact, that their relationship is lawful), the father, in this case, has to provide maintenance for the child on the basis of the rule of causation (*tasbib*).[59] Secondly, he argues that the provision of maintenance for illegitimate children may be a community obligation (*wajib-i kifa'i*). In other words, it is the duty of those who are financially able to provide maintenance for such children. He then adds that the parents who have produced these children have prime responsibility in this regard. In the end, he suggests that the parents should be responsible for the maintenance on the basis of causation (*tasbib*). An almost similar argument has also been put forward by the same writer concerning the custody of illegitimate children.[60]

It is also argued that the society is responsible for the upbringing and custody of an illegitimate child. The Public Prosecutor, as the representative of the society, must propose to the court a person as the guardian of the child. Although the custody of an illegitimate child is not the right of his

---

[56] The CC employs the Arabic term *zani*, which literally means a male fornicator or an adulterer but not a female fornicator or an adulteress. For this reason, a trial court has ruled that an illegitimate child belongs to his/her mother and the Supreme Court did not consider the validity or invalidity of this argument. It was noted above that, under Shiite jurisprudence, such a child does not belong to the mother as well. See Supreme Court (chamber 33), Judgment 1406–19.10.1370.

[57] Imami, *Huquq-i Madani*, vol. 5, pp. 181–184; Ha'iri, *Sharh-i Qanun-i Madani*, p. 1029; Safa'i et al., *Huquq-i Khanawadih*, vol. 2, pp. 106–107, 110–113.

[58] Ha'iri, *Sharh-i Qanun-i Madani*, p. 1029.

[59] Imami, *Huquq-i Madani*, vol. 5, p. 183.

[60] *Ibid*, pp. 182–183.

parents the court can, if appropriate and following the proposal of the Public Prosecutor, give the custody of the child to the parents. It seems, it is added, that the court can also, on the basis of civil liability and causation, compel the parents to take care of their child and to pay maintenance for him/her.[61]

The courts also had different approaches towards the issue of illegitimacy both in the pre-revolution and post-revolution era until this problem was resolved by the binding judgment of the PASC in 1997.

In one case, decided in the pre-revolution era, the father of two illegitimate children (according to an agreement reached between him and the mother of the children) had promised to obtain an identity certificate (IC) for his illegitimate children and to provide for their maintenance, but he later reneged on doing so. The mother took legal action and the court held that the father had to fulfil his obligation. The father appealed and the Appeal Court upheld the judgment. Then the father appealed to the Supreme Court (SC). At this stage, the mother argued that they were married but the appellant denied any marital relationship. The SC held that a decision about lineage and paternity was dependent on the existence of marriage and since the lower courts, before examining the dispute concerning marriage, could not adjudicate the case, quashed the judgment. The case was sent back to the Appeal Court. In this court the father argued that the agreement with the mother was void. He gave a couple of reasons for the invalidity of the agreement, one of which was that it was in contravention of Article 1167 of the CC which rules out any kind of legal relationship between a father and his illegitimate child and that the content of the agreement was against public order. The court decided against the father and he appealed.

The case was referred to the PASC under Article 576 of the Civil Procedure Code.[62] The PASC, *inter alia*, held that the agreement was valid and it was not contrary to public order. The court added that since the respondent had only asked the appellant to obtain the IC for the children, and the illegitimacy of the children (the subject matter of Article 1167 of the CC) was not an issue to be decided by the court, the appellant's protest in this respect was also dismissed.[63] The PASC did not address the question, apart from the agreement, of whether or not it was the duty of the father to obtain the IC and to maintain the children.

The post-revolution cases indicate that some courts, following the ruling of Article 1167 of the CC, did not recognize any legal relationship between a father and his illegitimate child.[64] Other courts, however, made the biological father responsible on the ground that, under custom, an illegitimate child

---

[61]   Safa'i *et al.*, *Huquq-i Khanawadih*, vol. 2, pp. 113–114.
[62]   Art. 576, *inter alia*, provides that: "If a judgment is quashed in the Supreme Court and the judgment of the court to which the case is referred after the quash is based on the same grounds and reasons as of the quashed judgment, and one of the parties appeals against such judgment, then the appeal will be examined by the plenary assembly of the civil chambers of the Supreme Court.".
[63]   See PASC, Judgment 1383–27.4.1346, in (1968) 20 [*Majalli-hi*] *Kanun-i Wukala*, pp. 137–140.
[64]   For example, see Supreme Court (chamber 33), Judgment 753–27.10.1369.

is considered to be the child of the biological father, and therefore the biological father has all the responsibilities which a father has towards his legitimate children, except for the issue of inheritance.[65] In addition, some courts on the basis of the rule of causation ruled that the biological father was responsible for the maintenance, upbringing and custody of the child, even though such a child, legally speaking, did not belong to him.[66]

4 THE PLENARY ASSEMBLY OF THE SUPREME COURT JUDGMENT

The parental responsibilities of a biological father towards his illegitimate child was considered by the PASC in 1997.[67] The judgment of the PASC was delivered following two conflicting judgments given by two chambers of the SC.[68] The main question in the above two judgments was whether or not a biological father was responsible for registering the birth of his illegitimate child and obtaining an IC from the Department for the Registration of Personal Status (registry office) for him or her.[69]

Article 16 of the Registration of Personal Status Act 1355 (1976)[70] lists a number of people who can register the birth of a child and sign the relevant documents. The first and the second of those people are relevant to this discussion. The first is father or paternal grandfather. The second is mother in the absence of the father. The last paragraph of the article states that if

---

[65] For example, see Supreme Court (chamber 33), Judgment 3332–20.4.1372.

[66] A lower court had ruled for the responsibility of a father towards his illegitimate child regarding the payment of maintenance and other expenses on the basis of causation, but the Supreme Court quashed the judgment on a number of grounds one of which was that there was no proof of causation since the defendant had denied any sexual relationship with the mother of the child. See Supreme Court (chamber 33), Judgment 3024–25.1.1372.

[67] The Supreme Court is the highest court under the Iranian legal system. The main body of lower courts, at present, are "general courts" and "appeal court". According to the information provided by the publications of the Supreme Court, it consists of thirty-five chambers. It is mainly based in Tehran. In most chambers there are three judges and the judgments are passed by the majority. See *Mudhakarat wa Ara'-i Hay'at-i 'Umumi-yi Diwan-i 'Ali-yi Kishwar* (1374), Tehran, 1376 (1997), *Mudhakarat wa Ara'-i Hay'at-i 'Umumi-yi Diwan-i 'Ali-yi Kishwar* (1375), Tehran, 1377 (1998).

[68] See PASC, judgment 617–3.4.1376, in *Ruznami-yi Rasmi*, 10.6.1376, No. 15293; *Majmu'ah Qawanin*, 1376, pp. 476–479.

[69] Generally speaking, when the birth of a child is registered by the parents, an IC is issued for the child in which the names and other particulars of the parents are recorded. In addition, the name and other particulars of the child are written in the ICs of the parents. See generally Arts. 12–14 of the Registration of Personal Status Act 1976. It is useful to be noted that the IC is the most important personal document in Iran. It is the proof of Iranian nationality. For getting a passport or a driving licence, for employment in the public sector, for participation in the general elections, for signing an official document, for studying at the schools and universities and for many other issues the presentation of the IC is necessary.

[70] *Ruznami-yi Rasmi*, 23.5.1355, No. 9212.

the marriage of the parents has not been registered the parents must jointly register the birth of the child and sign the relevant documents. If the registration of birth jointly is not possible, then the IC will be issued following the request of one parent for registration and the first name (but not family name) of the other parent is recorded in the IC. Finally, if the mother alone registers the birth, the family name of the mother will be given to the child.

As is clear, the last part of the above provision deals only with the registration of the birth of a child born to a couple whose marriage has not been registered. It does not provide for the registration of the birth of an illegitimate child. In fact, the Registration of Personal Status Act has no express provision with respect to the registration of the birth of illegitimate children. This issue which had been considered by two trial courts was subsequently examined by two chambers of the SC but since they had given conflicting judgments, it was referred to the PASC.

4.1   The first case

In the first case the mother of an illegitimate child filed a petition against the biological father asking the court to rule on the lineage (*nasab*) between the child and the defendant and to oblige the latter to obtain an IC for their child. The court, after acknowledging that the parties to the dispute had had an unlawful relationship, and the fact that genetic tests had not rejected the lineage between the father and the child, by referring to a legal opinion of Imam Khomeini and a judgment of chamber 30 of the SC (Judgment 438–29.61374 (1995)), and the fact that illegitimate children in respect of obtaining the IC and relevant responsibilities, under custom, are regarded as the children of their fathers, ruled in favour of the plaintiff and held that, under custom, there is a lineage between the defendant and the child. Therefore the defendant had to get an IC for his child. The only exception, which the court mentioned in its judgment with respect to an illegitimate child, was inheritance. The defendant appealed against this judgment and chamber 22 of the SC, *inter alia*, held:

The judgment appealed against is objectionable since the provisions of the Registration of Personal Status Act relate to legitimate children and to the issuance of identity certificate for them. They do not apply to illegitimate children. Therefore the judgment is not compatible with legal principles and is quashed.

4.2   The second case

In the second case, the mother of an illegitimate child took legal action against the child's biological father, asking the court to confirm the lineage between the defendant and the child and to order him to obtain an IC for the child. The court found that the parties to the dispute had been convicted earlier of fornication (through their confession) and by referring to a certificate issued by the Forensic Medicine (or Legal Medicine) Department[71]

---

[71]   This department is part of the judiciary.

rejected the allegation of the mother that their child was legitimate and as a result the action was dismissed.

The mother made an appeal against this decision and the case was referred to chamber 30 of the SC. This court ratified one part of the judgment of the trial court and quashed the other part. First, it stated that although the appellant claimed that the child was legitimate, i.e. the parents had a lawful relationship, this claim was not acceptable. As the relevant criminal file and the judgment of the criminal court in that case indicated, they had no marital relationship when the child was conceived. Consequently, the appeal of the plaintiff in this respect was dismissed. The court then went on to object to the other part of the judgment and, *inter alia*, held that:

but from the point of view of obtaining the identity certificate and other relevant responsibilities, in view of the legal opinion [fatwa] of Imam Khomeini as stated in Problems 3 and 47 of *Mawazin-i Qada'i* [a book containing some legal opinions of Imam Khomeini], these children [illegitimate children], under custom, are regarded as the children of the *zani* [adulterer or fornicator] and he, under custom, is considered to be the father and he must fulfil his paternal responsibilities including the payment of maintenance, custody and obtaining the identity certificate. It is only the issue of inheritance that under Islamic precepts and articles of law has been rejected. Therefore the judgment appealed against is objectionable on this point and is quashed.

As is clear, there was a conflict between the judgment of chamber 22 and that of chamber 30 of the SC. Chamber 22 held that the provisions of the Registration of Personal Status Act on the registration of birth and the issuance of the IC do not apply to illegitimate children while chamber 30 stated that, under custom, illegitimate children are the children of their biological fathers and the fathers must fulfil their paternal responsibilities, which include the registration of birth and obtaining the IC, towards these children. In accordance with the Uniformity of Judicial Decisions Act 1328 (1949),[72] which provided that when, with respect to a certain legal issue, conflicting judgments were given by different chambers of the SC, the issue had to be decided by the PASC, the case was referred to the PASC.[73]

---

72 This Act can also be translated as the "Law Relating to the Uniformity of Judicial Decisions". It provided that "when different judgments have been given by [two or more] chambers of the Supreme Court with respect to similar cases ... the Plenary Assembly of the Supreme Court, which consists, at least, of three-quarters of the presiding judges of the Supreme Court and their counsellors, is convened and considers the controversial issue and makes a decision in that respect. In this case, the majority view of the Assembly is to be followed by all chambers of the Supreme Court and [all other] courts in similar cases and [it] cannot be changed unless by a [subsequent] decision of the Assembly or by statute". The provisions of the above Act were reintroduced in Arts. 270–271 of the Procedure of General and Revolution Courts Act 1999 (which was adopted on an experimental basis for three years). However, this Act differs in some respects from the old one. For example, the PASC now cannot overrule its own judgments while it could do so earlier. Under the new law, the judgments of the PASC can be overruled only by statute.

73 For a brief introduction to the function of the PASC and the structure of courts, see M.A. Ansari-Pour, "Iran", in this *Yearbook*, vol. 1 (1994), pp. 387, 392–395.

Before dealing with the PASC judgment it is useful to look primarily at the two legal opinions given by the late Imam Khomeini regarding the maintenance and custody of an illegitimate child. In the first case, the questioner asked that: if an illegitimate child does not belong to his biological father who must pay maintenance for him or her? The answer was that it must be paid by the father. In the second case, the questioner by referring to a legal opinion of the Imam (stated earlier in section 2 of this article), asked him whether it was his opinion that paying maintenance for an illegitimate child and also for the child's custody and upbringing were not the responsibilities of the adulterer (or fornicator)? He replied that an illegitimate child in respect of maintenance and custody is similar to other children.

A large part of the PASC debate relates to the issue of the IC. With respect to the issue of parental responsibilities of a biological father, the judges of the PASC were divided into two groups and the arguments presented were conflicting. Some judges rejected any relationship and paternity. On the other hand, other judges by considering an illegitimate child to be the child of his biological father under custom and by referring to the aforementioned legal opinions of Imam Khomeini stated that the biological father (adulterer or fornicator) must fulfil the parental responsibilities which a father has towards his legitimate child, with respect to his illegitimate child.[74]

In the end, the PASC by a majority of 54 out of 73 judges, *inter alia*, held that:

According to Paragraph A of Article 1 of the Registration of Personal Status Act 1355 [1976] one of the responsibilities of the Department for the Registration of Personal Status is the registration of birth and the issuance of the identity certificate. The legislature has made no difference in this regard between legitimate and illegitimate children. The note [or sub-article] of Article 16 and Article 17 of the above Act have regulated the [status of the registration of births in] cases where the marriage of parents has not been registered and there is no joint request by the parents concerning the registration of the birth [of their child] for the issuance of the identity certificate or where the parents are unknown. But in cases where the child is illegitimate and the *zani* [fornicator or adulterer] does not [register the birth of the child to] get the identity certificate [the law is silent]. In accordance with the generalities and purport of the above articles and Problems 3 and 47 of *Mawazin-i Qada'i* ... the *zani*, under custom, is considered to be the father of the child and consequently all responsibilities of a father including the obtaining of the identity certificate, are to be fulfilled by him. And under Article 884 of the CC it is only the issue of inheritance between them which is excluded.

The PASC, in effect, approved the judgment of chamber 30 of the SC, which had not differentiated between a legitimate and an illegitimate child in any respect except for the issue of inheritance, as being given in accordance with Islamic and legal precepts.

---

[74] For the full text of the proceedings, see *Mudhakarat was Ara'-i Hay'at-i 'Umumi-yi Diwan-i 'Ali-yi Kishwar*, vol. 3, Tehran, 1378, pp. 205–222.

5   CONCLUSION

The judgment of the PASC constitutes the present law on the legal relationship of a father with his illegitimate child. It is interesting to note that the PASC, because it takes into account the interests of illegitimate children and refers to a legal opinion of Imam Khomeini, qualified (if not overruled) Article 1167 of the CC. Consequently, a father has all responsibilities which he has towards his legitimate child, in respect of his illegitimate child as well. The only thing which an illegitimate child does not enjoy, and which has been excluded expressly by the CC, Islamic law and the PASC judgment, is inheritance.

Although this judgment deals with the legal relationship of a biological father with his illegitimate child and more specifically with the parental responsibilities of the father towards his illegitimate child it would be applicable to the legal relationship of a mother with her illegitimate child as well. It should be noted, however, that since, under Islamic and Iranian law, a father has more responsibilities with respect to his children than a mother, the legal relationship of a father with his children is of prime importance. For example, maintenance primarily must be provided by the father; the birth primarily must be registered by the father; the natural guardian is the father, and so on. In addition, the above judgment implies that an illegitimate child also has to bear certain responsibilities towards his/her biological father. For example, where the father is in need the child, if he/she is financially able, must provide maintenance for him.

This judgment removes many problems which may arise concerning maintenance, custody and upbringing of an illegitimate child. Certainly such a ruling is in favour of the child, who has done nothing to be punished for, especially if we take into account the position of such a child in Islamic society. In addition, this judgment protects the community against the financial consequences which care of illegitimate children might impose on it. Although it might create an additional burden for the father, he must bear the consequences of his acts.

The Status of Children and their Protection in Algerian Law (Part II)

*Yamina Kebir**

1 THE PROTECTION OF THE CHILD BY THE STATE

The state of Algeria ensures the protection of the child by means of legislation at all stages of the child's life until he or she reaches the age of majority determined by the Civil Code at the age of nineteen.

Not only are the child's rights recognized and guaranteed but they are highly protected by specific laws and regulations which take account of the child's interest. Such rights include the child's rights to an identity, to education, to welfare and health. The child is also protected from all forms of exploitation, and benefits from the care of the state for social security and can be placed in judicial care should his or her life be endangered; the philosophy behind these laws is the interest of the child.

The law takes a twofold approach to the protection of the child. First, it guarantees children's rights and ensures their protection, and in particular that of abandoned or maltreated children, or those in physical or moral danger by means of administrative, social and educational measures. Second, it punishes all kinds of offences committed against minors.

2 THE GUARANTEE OF CHILDREN'S RIGHTS

2.1 The right to life

As soon as he or she is conceived the child is entitled to some rights. And his right to live starts at that point, based on Islamic law which considers the

---

* Attorney-at-law, Algiers Bar, admitted to appear before the Supreme Court of Algeria. Part I of this article appeared in vol. 5 (1998–1999) of this *Yearbook* at pp. 162–170.

unborn as a human being from the time of his conception; abortion can only be regarded as a crime. This is the position of Algerian law, which punishes abortion at any stage of pregnancy.

The criminal law punishes a woman who commits abortion and the same applies to anyone who helps her. Abortion is punished by imprisonment and a fine (Articles 304 to 314, Criminal Law). However, these provisions do not apply to therapeutic abortion, which is a "necessary measure to preserve the life of the mother" and in the case where the mother was raped. The Public Health Law forbids the sale of "abortive devices and drugs" (Article 349).

However, the use and sale of contraceptives is authorized (Article 350). While abortion is not contemplated as a device for curbing the extremely high rate of demographic increase, contraception is admitted and organized, especially at centres for the protection of the mother and child. A fatwa issued in 1968 by the Supreme Islamic Council gives an account of the legislative approach to this matter. This fatwa, which was based on "the legal provisions of the Islamic religion" admitted that contraception was licit and made a number of recommendations which have been incorporated into the Public Health Law.

2.2 The right to an identity

The child has the right to a name and he is automatically given the name of his father. This right has been reinforced in Algerian legislation by Decree No. 92–24 of 19 January 1992 on the *kafala*, called Decree Ghozali,[1] Article 64 of the Civil Code. The Civil Code provides that the right of the child to his name and nationality are recognized and protected under Algerian laws.

2.3 The right to a nationality

This right is ensured by the Nationality Law. At his birth the child automatically assumes the nationality of his father. But if the child is born to an unknown father or a father deprived of nationality, the child is given the nationality of his mother.

2.4 The right of education

This right is strongly protected under Algerian laws; according to Article 53 of the Constitution education is a right guaranteed by the state and is compulsory during the years of primary school.

In addition, education is entirely free of charge from primary school to university. As noted before, under the Constitution there is no discrimination

---

[1]   From the name of the Prime Minister who initiated this decree.

between girls and boys, who are equally entitled to the same rights of education. Decree No. 76–70 of 16 April 1976 extends this regime to preparatory schools, which are schools preparing children to read and write.

2.5 The right of health

With education, the right to health is a subject of great concern and is highly protected not only under the law but by a whole series of social measures. The right to health is guaranteed by the state under Article 54 of the Constitution which provides that all citizens enjoy the right of health and of prevention against epidemic and endemic diseases.

Specific measures relating to children are provided by Law No. 85–05 relating to the Protection and the Promotion of Health called Public Health Law as amended and supplemented by Law No. 90–17 of 31st July 1990. The law provides as well that prevention against diseases and medical monitoring constitute a right of the child at all stages of his development.

The state assumes important responsibilities with regard to health care which is available to all citizens, with special emphasis on the protection of the mother and child.

It is to be noted that access to medical services is free of charge in public hospitals and that all children and youths are entitled to social security. Vaccination of children is compulsory with respect to a number of diseases and is carried out in health centres in every city and village and in maternal and child health centres throughout the country. These centres provide family planning facilities, maternity care during pregnancy and child care. They also provide, for children, early detection and treatment of numerous diseases including dental care and prevention.

The Public Health Law provides also for measures ensuring the protection of children against drug consumption.

3   THE PROTECTION OF CHILDREN AGAINST OFFENCES AND MALTREATMENT

3.1 Offences against children

Specific punishment is provided by the Criminal Law for individuals who commit offences against the life of children and their physical and moral integrity; child murder is punished with solitary confinement (Article 261). Article 320 punishes any sale or dealings in foundlings and children born or about to be born and the abandonment of children for profit.

Hardship inflicted on a minor or the leaving of a child without food and care resulting in illness are punished with imprisonment and fines. The abuse of the right of visitation is punished with imprisonment and the kidnapping of a minor and removing or her him from the parent who has custody is also punishable with imprisonment and a fine.

The violation by parents of their parental obligations is sanctioned by the

Criminal law Articles 330 to 332 of the Criminal Law, which provide that if one of the parents abandons his or her family or if the father does not pay the alimony due to his children after a divorce procedure, he is liable to imprisonment.

3.2 The protection of the child's morality

Article 335 of the Criminal Law punishes with solitary confinement "any outrage on decency" and the penalty is higher if committed on a minor. But, with more specific protection of minors, Article 342 represses the incitement of minors to debauchery and prostitution.

3.3 The protection of children without a family

Article 246 of the Public Health Law determines all the categories of children who are under the tutelage of the state. These are foundlings, whose parents are unknown, and abandoned children, even when their parents are known, and poor orphans.

3.3.1 Foundlings and abandoned children

The deep socio-economic changes affecting Algerian society, and their outcome – the breaking up of the traditional family – have fostered new and sometimes dramatic problems such as the problem of abandoned children, which is steadily increasing.

In modern society children are the most vulnerable members. We saw earlier how by the institution of civil status the Islamic legal principle according to which parental filiation cannot but be legitimate regained its strength. The maternal filiation applies whatever the circumstances, and the mother gives her name to the child. But the child is definitively stained with his illegitimacy, the maternal filiation being the evidence of illicit sexual intercourse.

All the burden is borne by the mother alone. This burden is heavy to bear in a society where the person who violates the moral, social and familial rules is excluded from it and the single mother is totally rejected by her family. This is the reason why so many infants are abandoned and sometimes even killed.

Faced with this completely new and dramatic problem, the state tried to bring about a solution by enacting some specific legislation. The Public Health Law regulates the situation of children without a family by a twofold approach. First, it aims to prevent mothers in distress from abandoning their new-born infants, and secondly it sets the framework for the protection of abandoned children.

3.3.2   *The prevention of the abandonment of children*

This consists in giving single mothers material and moral support. In this respect the law provides for the organization of mothers' homes; these homes welcome pregnant women in their seventh month and mothers with their new-born infants (Article 243). In cities where there is no mothers' home, the hospitals are open to such women on the same conditions. The stay in these homes is limited to three months during which the social workers try to find a job to the mother.

The mother does not have to comply with any formality on her admission to the home or hospital, which remains secret. An office remains open day and night where mothers can leave their new-born infants.

Financial assistance is then proposed to the mother in order to help her and to incite her to keep the child. If she decides to do so, she will receive a monthly allowance for supporting the child until the latter reaches the age when he or she is no longer obliged to go to school (Article 247). If the mother still wants to abandon her child, the latter is then placed in guardian-ship. But she can reverse her decision and the child may be returned to her within six months.

3.3.3   *The protection of abandoned children*

The abandoned child then become a ward of the state and is settled in one of the children's homes for children without a family; the foundlings, poor orphans and minors under the age of twenty-one whose physical and moral health is threatened. They remain there further to a court order.

Orphanages are far from offering the best emotional and educational conditions for these deeply wounded children. This is the reason why law provides that this form of settlement should be exceptional and that, when-ever possible, the child should be reared by a family (Article 258).

In fact the homes, considering the scope of the problem, are quite insuffi-cient and do not offer the best conditions for the normal psychological and social development of these children.

In addition, during their whole life these children will suffer from an identity problem, which is aggravated by the fact that their name reveals their situation. In application of the Civil Status Law, foundlings are given two first names by the register, the second one serving as family name.

3.4   **The protection of handicapped children and of children in physical or moral danger**

State action is twofold:

(a)   The Public Law provides for special treatment and measures in favour of handicapped children, in particular for their education and rehabilita-tion. Important facilities have been assigned to them: under Article 268 of the Public Health Law they are taken care of by specialized institutions and the state provides for their "treatment, their re-education, their education and their social readaption". Decree No. 80–59 of 8 March 1980 set up educational and medical centres as well as educational and vocational centres for handicapped children.

(b) Various laws and regulations such as tax laws, custom laws and social security laws contain specific provisions. Under such laws, handicapped children are granted a number of exemptions, allowances and they benefit from social security.

The protection of the morality of children and young people is ensured by Ordinance relating to the Protection of Childhood and Youth. The scope of this law includes minors and youths under twenty-one years of age whose health, security, morality and education are imperilled. The court can decide to remove the child from its parents or guardian and settle it in a home or in a family.

3.5 Specific provisions of the Criminal Law with regard to juvenile offenders

Under Article 49 of the Criminal Code, children under the age of thirteen can never be condemned to penalties but only to a measure of protection and re-education. From the age of thitreen to sixteen, they receive the same treatment or can be condemned to mitigated punishment.

Under the age of thirteen, they cannot be put in a house of detention; from the age of thirteen to the age of eighteen, they can be imprisoned if necessary, but in such a case, they must be isolated in special quarters.

Juvenile offenders are settled in the homes of the poor-law administration or in training centres.

Various specialist centres have been set up in order to ensure the protection and the re-education of children deprived of their liberty. These are centres for re-education, centres for protection and multidisciplinary centres to safeguard youth.

3.6 Protection against economic exploitation

This protection is ensured by Article 15 of Law No. 90–10 of 21 April 1990 which is the Labour Law.

In order to protect the child's health and to ensure that his or her education is not hindered, no child under the age of sixteen can be employed unless he is in an apprenticeship contract.

A youth under the age of nineteen can be employed only upon a written authorization of his legal tutor, in most cases, his father.

In addition, under the Labour Law, working children from sixteen to nineteen are protected by specific provisions and cannot work in dangerous jobs or under unhealthy conditions.

The legislation relating to children is consistent with the proclaimed principles to ensure security for individuals and especially protection for children.

It results from this overview of the Algerian laws relating to children that *de jure* the state guarantees and is highly protective of children's rights. In this respect this legislation is in total compliance with the International Convention on the Rights of Children; in fact in some instances Algerian legislation goes further than the Convention in protecting such rights.

However, this protection could be better ensured by the passing of a progressive Family Code which would provide for the equal share of mother and father in the care and education of children and in authority over the children.

During the troubled period which the country has undergone, children were the most vulnerable and affected; and considering the percentage of children and youth in the country, the biggest challenge with which the state is now faced is to cater for the enormous social, psychological and material needs which result from the effects of terrorism. All the efforts made and the existing facilities throughout the country are insufficient to meet these needs.

Part II

Country Surveys

Egypt

*Tarek Riad**

*Kosheri, Rashed & Riad**

The survey this year deals with constitutional cases and arbitration in civil and commercial matters.[1]

1 CONSTITUTIONAL CASES

1.1 Judgment dated 2 January 1999 in Case No. 15 of the 18th judicial year: *Mrs Jamila Gad Elhak Said Ahmed and others v. the President of the Republic, the Prime Minister and the Minister of the Interior*

Article 74 of the Egyptian Constitution provides that:

If any danger threatens the national unity or the safety of the motherland or obstructs the constitutional role of the State Institutions, the President of the Republic shall take urgent measures to face this danger, direct a statement to the people and conduct a referendum on those measures within sixty days of their adoption.

And Article 147 of the Constitution provides that:

If it becomes necessary during the absence of the People's Assembly, to take measures which cannot suffer delay, the President of the Republic shall issue decisions in this respect which have the force of law.

---

* Legal Consultants & Attorneys at Law, Cairo. Tarek Riad is a Partner and Special legal counsel to the speaker of The Egyptian People's Assembly.

[1] See article by David Wilson on "A New Commercial Code for Egypt", pp. 87–122, and translation of Arts. 72 to 87 (Transfer of Technology, Chapter 1, Part II) and Arts. 166 to 191 (Commercial Agency, Chapter 5, Part II) by Kosheri, Rashed & Riad in Part III, pp. 429–432 and pp. 435–438.

Such decisions must be submitted to the People's Assembly, within fifteen days from the date of issuance if the Assembly is standing or at its first meeting in case of the dissolution or recess of the Assembly. If they are not submitted, their force of law disappears with retroactive effect without a decision being taken to this effect. If they are submitted to the Assembly and are not ratified, their force of law disappears with retroactive effect, unless the Assembly has ratified their validity in the previous period or settled their effects in another way.

The President of the Republic issued the Decree having force of Law No. 154 of 1981 in accordance to Article 147 of the Constitution, amending Law No. 95 of 1980 and provided in this decision for a change in the court that has the competence to decide upon the recourse against measures taken in accordance to Article 74 of the Constitution.

The Plaintiff in his legal action before the Supreme Constitutional Court claimed that the President's Decision having force of Law No. 154 of 198, was issued at a time when there was no case of necessity which empowered the President to take decisions which had the force of law in accordance with Article 147 of the Constitution.

The Court mentioned in this case that all the Egyptian Constitutions have adopted the theory of necessity which allows the executive authority to take special measures – which cannot be postponed – in the absence of legislative authority.

Nevertheless, the Constitution provided for conditions and limitation on the use of those special measures in the field of exercise of the legislative function, in order to guarantee that it would not be transformed into an exercise by the executive authority of the totality of the legislative authority's function as provided in the Constitution.

The Court added that these special measures that might be exercised by the executive authority were mentioned in detail in the Constitution and should be strictly adhered to, because they were an exception to the principle of the division of powers adhered to by the present Constitution in accordance to the democratic values that are applied in civilized states.

The Court then stated that legislation is the task of the legislative authority, but that in spite of this principle, the necessity to preserve the basis of the state and the urgent need for intervention of the state through a legislative act in the absence of the legislative authority allow the executive authority to exercise this exceptional task. The Court recalled that the urgent measures taken by the executive authority in the above-mentioned cases of necessity were linked to their existence, that the executive authority is not free to decide upon the existence of a case of necessity, but is subject in this respect to the control exercised by the Supreme Constitutional Court, which ascertains the existence of a case of necessity within the limits provided for by the Constitution, so as to guarantee that this exceptional legislative right is not transformed into a full unlimited legislative authority, exercised by the executive authority.

The Court thereafter mentioned that the government – in the case under review – stated that the reason for promulgation of the President's decree, was to allow for recourse against decisions taken in accordance to Article 74 of the Constitution. And the Court added that this might be a reason for approval of a law by the normal legislative authority, but that was not an acceptable reason for exercise by the executive authority of this exceptional right without the existence of a specific condition that could be considered a case of necessity allowing for exercise of this right.

The Court also recalled that the President of the Republic was responsible for respecting the Constitution and the rule of law, that his right to issue decrees having force of law was subject to the limitations provided for in the Constitution, including *inter alia* its Article 147.

And the Court then concluded that the stated reason for issue of the Presidential Decree having the force of law subject of the recourse did not constitute a state of necessity allowing the President to issue such a decree, and therefore that this decree having force of law was unconstitutional even if the People's Assembly approved it after its issue, because such approval did not remove its constitutional defect on the date of its issue, and did not therefore transform the decree into a normal law whose procedures in relation to its proposal, approval and promulgation had been respected in order to ensure its constitutionality.

And the Court ruled that the above-mentioned Decree having the force of Law No. 154 of 1981 was unconstitutional.

1.2 Judgment dated 2 May 1999 in Case No. 182 of the 19th judicial year: *Mr Tawfik Said Mohamed Basaraa v. the President of the Republic, the Prime Minister and Others*

Article 13 of Law No. 117 of 1983 concerning the protection of antiquities provides that registration of the immovable antiquity and notifying the owner thereof, results in the following:

(a) prohibition from demolishing the immovable antiquity;
(b) prohibition from expropriating it;
(c) prohibition from imposing any servitude rights on it in favour of third parties;
(d) prohibition from renovating or altering it without the permission of the Head of the Antiquities Authority and under its supervision;
(e) the necessity to obtain the written permission of the Antiquities Authority concerning any and all transactions relating to it;
(f) the right of the Antiquities Authority to do whatever it deems necessary to maintain the immovable antiquity, at its own cost.

The plaintiff in his recourse to the Supreme Constitutional Court alleged that this article imposed such restrictions on the right of ownership as to render it of no substance, without allocation of just damages to the owner, and that it was therefore contrary to Article 34 of the Constitution which protects private ownership, its Article 35 which provides that nationalization may only be for public interest and against compensation, and its Article 36 which prohibits general confiscation and also prohibits private confiscation except by a judicial decision.

The Court in this case stated that the Constitution imposed on society and the state a national obligation to preserve the historical heritage of the people.

It also recalled that the Constitution accorded full protection to the right of private ownership – national and foreign – and only allowed infringements of this right in exceptional cases and within the limits necessitated by the organization of this right.

The protection accorded by the Constitution to the right of private ownership necessitates that the limitations drawn on this right by the legislation – within the scope of the social function of ownership – should not negate the basis of this right, or hinder its enjoyment to the extent that renders the existence of this right valueless. Any interference of legislation that limited the right of private ownership through the imposition of stringent restrictions was a negation of this right.

The rule is that ownership should remain with the owner, and that he should not be deprived of it except in the cases and by the means decided by law and against a just compensation.

This rule is mentioned in different Constitutions and limits the rights of the legislative and the administrative authorities to expropriate without reason or without compensation or outside the rules stated by law.

The Court added that the legislator's interference that retains the owner's ownership of a certain property and at the same time reduces to a large extent its economic value, even under the pretence to the social function of ownership, or the need to preserve the national heritage, is a diminution of the right of ownership whose legality – constitution-wise – is conditional upon just compensation.

The Court then mentioned that it appeared from review of the article subject of the recourse that it imposed restrictions on private ownership that obliterated its basis, without according damages compensating for those restrictions, and that it negated the right of the owner to use his property economically for the purposes for which it was intended.

Therefore, the article subject of the recourse was contrary to Articles 38 and 34 of the Constitution that protect private ownership and to Article 36 which prevents private confiscation except by a judicial decision.

The court therefore ruled that Article 13 of Law No. 117 of 1983 concerning the protection of antiquities was unconstitutional in its application to private property and in not providing for any compensation for the owner of antiquities.

2   ARBITRATION IN CIVIL AND COMMERCIAL MATTERS

Egypt modernized its Arbitration Law in 1994 by adopting the UNCITRAL Model Law with very limited modifications. The new Law No. 27 of 1994 as amended applies to all arbitrations conducted within the country or any international commercial arbitration conducted abroad where the parties agree to abide by the provisions of this law, with the possibility of obtaining assistance from the judicial courts to implement the arbitration agreement, to secure the proper functioning of the procedures, as well as for the enforcements of the awards rendered thereunder. Awards made abroad are enforceable under the New York Convention of 1958 to which Egypt adhered in 1958.

In this respect it is important to note that the setting aside of a foreign award is subject only to the grounds provided for under Article 5 of the New York Convention, but an award rendered in Egypt under the new legislation can be set aside for an additional ground, which is the failure of the arbitral tribunal to apply the law chosen by the parties to govern their contract. Equally, the request for enforcement becomes admissible only after the expiration of the period required for lodging an annulment plea, i.e. the requesting party has to wait ninety days before submitting the request for enforcement before the competent court, which is in principle the Cairo Court of Appeal.

2.1 Recent development in arbitration

It is natural that a certain duration of time would pass before any judgments were pronounced in the Commercial Courts relating to the application of the new Arbitration Law No. 27 for 1994 as amended ("the Arbitration Law"); we are therefore only able to mention here a few judgments that are linked to Articles 52 and 53 of the Arbitration Law which provide for the rules concerning the action for nullity of the arbitration as the only way of challenging arbitral awards.

The following judgments are relevant in this respect.

2.1.1 *The Cairo Court of Appeal's Decision on 11 August 1996 in Commercial Case No. 61 of the 113th judicial year*

The Court judged in this case that an arbitrator's non-signature of the arbitral award did not mean that deliberation of the arbitral panel had not take place, but only that the arbitrator concerned had not approved the award after deliberations in the case under review. The Court also indicated that the arbitral award was not obliged to mention the reasons for the refusal by an arbitrator to sign it if he did not mention those reasons himself.

Finally, the judgment added that the dispositive part of the arbitral award did not have to indicate the source of an obligation that it imposed on one of the parties, if the basis for such imposition was contained in the reasoning of the award.

2.1.2 *The Cairo Court of Appeal's Decision on 19 March 1997 in Commercial Case No. 64 of the 113th judicial year*

The Court of Appeal rendered a very important judgment in this case concerning the legality of arbitration in disputes relating to Egyptian administrative contracts, and indicated that the agreement to refer disputes relating to administrative contracts to arbitration was perfectly legal for the following reasons.

Article 1 of the Arbitration Law provides that it applies to "all arbitrations between Public Law or Private Law persons whatever the nature of the legal relationship around which the dispute revolves" and this text thus clearly allows for an agreement to arbitrate, even when one of the parties is a governmental entity and whatever the nature of the dispute. Therefore, there is no basis for the claim of nullity of arbitration clauses in administrative contracts.

The Court added here that this is also confirmed by review of the explanatory note of the Arbitration Law, the report of the committee of the Egyptian People's Assembly concerned, and by the discussions relating to the Arbitration Law, all of which confirm that arbitration in administrative contracts is legal under Egyptian law.

The objection that Article 10 of the Council of State's Law No. 47 of 1977 provides that only the courts of the Council of State are competent to judge the disputes relating to administrative contracts does not stand because this provision aims to regulate the division of competencies between the Council of State and the normal courts and not at prevention of arbitration in disputes relating to administrative contracts.

This is specially so if we take into consideration that Article 58 of the Council of State's Law provides for the obligation of all ministries, public authorities and public departments to obtain the opinion of the competent advice department of the Council of State before concluding an arbitration agreement or the enforcement of an arbitral award valued at more than E£ 5,000.

Article 3 of the law promulgating the Arbitration Law provides that "any provision contrary to the provision of this law is repealed", and this would include Article 10 of the Council of State's Law No. 47 of 1977. There is no basis for relying on Article 172 of the Egyptian Constitution to ascertain that arbitration is not allowed for in administrative contracts, because this article refers to the Council of State in its capacity as part of the judicial authority and it aims at dividing power between the Council of State and the civil courts as aforesaid. In addition, nobody can claim that providing for the competence of the courts in general to review certain disputes means that arbitration concerning those disputes is prohibited.

The Court of Appeal also recalled that unlike French civil law (Article 2060), Egyptian civil law does not contain any article prohibiting arbitration in relation to governmental entities. The Court of Appeal noted that even French law allows for international arbitration in administrative contract disputes.

The Court of Appeal reiterated that the governmental authority's claim that the arbitration clause in an administrative contract was null and void despite being signed by this same governmental authority, was not only illegal, but was also contrary to the principle of the necessity to execute obligations in good faith whether in civil or in administrative contracts.

Finally, the Court of Appeal added that such a claim was also contrary to the agreed upon rules relating to international commercial arbitration, that the state or governmental authority cannot refrain from applying an arbitration clause contained in its own contracts by relying on local legislative constraints and that adoption of the opposite view would also affect the confidence that must prevail in the state's dealings with other parties and also negatively affect needed foreign investments.

2.2 The Cairo Court of Appeal's Decision on 2 October 1997 in Case No. 41 of the 114th judicial year

One of the reasons for the appeal in this case was that the judgment subject of the appeal was null and void because it allowed for interest over the maximum allowed for by law – which maximum is of public order in accordance to Egyptian Law.

The Court of Appeal mentioned in this case that Article 39(4) of the Arbitration Law provides that:

The Arbitral Panel may, if it has been expressly empowered to act as an *"amiable compositeur"* by agreement between the two parties to the arbitration, adjudicate the merits of the dispute according to the Rules of Justice and Equity without being bound by the provisions of Law.

And the Court of Appeal added that in view of the above there is no contradiction with public order – in this case – if the arbitral panel decides that the interest rate mentioned in its judgment is consistent with the rules of justice and equity, even if this interest rate is over the maximum allowed for by law, because this judgment is based upon the agreement of the parties to apply the rules of justice and equity and not the provisions of the law.

2.3 The Cairo Court of Appeal's Decision on 31 December 1997 in Case No. 62 of the 113th judicial year

The Court of Appeal rendered a judgment which indicated – *inter alia* – that Article 23 of the Arbitration Law provided that "the Arbitral Clause is deemed to be an agreement that is independent from the other conditions of the contracts and that nullity, rescission or termination of the contract shall not affect the arbitral clause therein provided such clause is valid *per se*" and the Court decided therefore in the case under review that nullity, rescission or termination of the Contract does not have any effect on the Arbitral Clause under consideration.

2.4 The Cairo Court of Appeal's Decision on 25 November 1998 in the Case No. 42 of the 115th Judicial Year

The judgment in this case stated that Article 16/3 of the Arbitration Law, provides that "the arbitrator when accepting the mission entrusted to him", must disclose any circumstances "which cast doubt on his independence or neutrality", and that Article 53 of the law provides that "an action for the nullity of the Arbitral Award is admissible" if the arbitral panel was constituted or the arbitrators were appointed contrary to law or the agreement between the two parties.

The judgment mentioned that in the case under review, the arbitrator – appointed by one of the parties – accepted his position without disclosing that he was a partner in the law firm defending this same party. The Court added that this fact was only discovered after the arbitral award had been pronounced, and the Court decided that the arbitral award was null and void by reason of its contravention of the Arbitration Law.

2.5 The issue of the judicial control of the constitutionality of laws and regulations is exclusively entrusted in Egypt to its Supreme Constitutional Court

This Court passed a judgement on 6 November 1999 in Case No. 84 of the 19th judicial year, which directly bears on the subject of the constitutionality of Article 19 of the Arbitration Law which provides in its subclause 1 that the arbitral panel decides on the request for its own challenge.

The plaintiff in this case had previously requested the challenge of an arbitral panel which was determining a dispute in which the plaintiff was a party and the arbitral panel has rejected his request. The plaintiff then brought the case before the Supreme Constitutional Court and alleged that allowing the arbitral panel to decide upon challenge of its members contravened the necessity of neutrality that is guaranteed by the Constitution for those engaged in judicial activity. It was therefore contrary to the basic principle of equality before the law provided in the Constitution.

The Supreme Constitutional Court in this case mentioned the judicial nature of arbitration that is based upon a voluntary agreement between its parties and which results in negation of the right of the judiciary to review the disputes subject to arbitration.

The Supreme Constitutional Court reminded that the right to challenge the arbitrator is linked to the basic rights of litigation that are necessary for all judicial action and is also closely linked to the right to litigate provided in the Constitution, which necessitates independence and impartiality in the authority that dispenses justice.

The Supreme Constitutional Court then stressed that Article 69 of the Constitution guarantees the right of defence as a cornerstone of the rule of law and that subjection of the state to the law means that its legislation may not encroach upon the rights and guarantees which are considered in democratic states as the basis for the existence of the rule of law.

The Supreme Constitutional Court finally stated that the article subject of the recourse allowed the arbitral panel the right to decide upon its own challenge, that this was contrary to the values of justice and to the principle of impartiality of the judicial act in favour of one category of litigants and to the detriment of another and was therefore unconstitutional by reason of contravening Articles 40, 65, 67, 68 and 79 of the Constitution which guarantee equality before the law, subjection of the state to the law, the right of defence and the right of litigation.

2.6 Judgment dated 3 July 1999 in Case No. 104 of the 2nd judicial year: *Mr Sadek Kamal Kotb in his capacity as the representative of Kotb Co. for Industry and Trade v. the President of the Republic, the Prime Minister and others*

Articles 57 and 58 of the Customs Law No. 66 of 1963 provide that disputes between the Customs Authority and the importer concerning the type, origin or value of the imported goods are to be decided by two arbitrators, one of whom is appointed by the Customs Authority and the other by the owner of the imported goods, and that in the case of dissenting opinions of those two arbitrators the disputes shall be decided by a higher arbitral panel composed of three arbitrators, one of whom is appointed by the Minister of Finance, another appointed by the Department of Customs and a third representing the trade syndicate appointed by its chairman, and that this panel's decision is executable.

The plaintiff in his recourse alleged that those two articles rendered arbitration obligatory, contrary to its voluntary nature, and that they prevented the decisions of the above-mentioned arbitral panel from being subject to the control of the judiciary.

The Supreme Constitutional Court acknowledged that the legislator had created in the case under review a system of obligatory arbitration in order to decide upon disputes relating to the type, origin and value of the goods instead of presenting those disputes to the judiciary.

The Court then stated that arbitration was by its very nature a voluntary system for solving disputes, based upon the agreement of its parties which formed the sole basis of the authority of the arbitrators. And the Court added that the obligatory system of arbitration created by the above-mentioned articles negated the most important base of arbitration, which is the free will agreement of the parties to solve their disputes by arbitration and that it prevented the judiciary from reviewing those disputes.

The Court then recalled that Article 68 of the Constitution guaranteed the right of every citizen to refer to his natural judge in order to decide upon his case, and that the legislator may not impose restrictions on the right to litigate that prevents enjoyment of this right.

The Court added that the articles subject of the recourse also gave executory force to the decisions rendered by the obligatory arbitral panel and that this was contrary to the voluntary nature of arbitration and prevented litigants from presenting their cases to their natural judges, which are the normal courts.

And the Court judged that Articles 57 and 58 of the Customs Law No. 66 of 1963 were unconstitutional.

Syria

*Jacques el-Hakim**

1 CONSTITUTIONAL LAW

Following the death of President Hafez Assad, who has been President of the Syrian Arab Republic since 1970, the People's Assembly has amended Article 83 of the Syrian Constitution so that the minimum age of the President was reduced to thirty-four years, which is the age of the new President Dr Bashar Assad. The new President was elected by plebiscite for seven years and his election confirmed by the People's Assembly on 11 July 2000.

2 ADMINISTRATIVE LAW

2.1 Military service

Many Syrian citizens residing abroad failed to carry out their military service (two and a half years) and could not therefore come back to Syria if they wished to avoid the penalties provided for in LD No. 115 of 5 October 1953. On 29 July 2000, LD No. 11 authorized them to pay the following amounts in foreign currency to be exempted from that service on the following basis:

(a) US$15,000 if they had resided abroad for fifteen years or were over forty years of age;
(b) US$10,000 if they had resided abroad for ten years and held a scientific degree (medical doctors, engineers, etc. ...) or wanted to invest money in Syria;
(c) US$5,000 if they were born abroad and resided there until the age of

---

* Professor of Law, Damascus University; Attorney at Law.

eighteen or if they emigrated at the age of twelve and resided abroad for fifteen years.

Thanks to this legislative decree, many Syrians will be able to come back to their home country, resume their work or residence there and be united with their families.

2.2 State employee's salaries

Although the cost of living in Syria is quite low, the salaries of state employees are much lower than their counterparts in the private sector (the highest salary is about US$140 per month). For several years, such employees have been requesting a reasonable increase of their salaries enabling them to live decently with their families and to overcome the temptations of growing corruption. A partial solution was achieved, on 26 August 2000, by LD No. 36 providing for a salary increase of 25 per cent, and LD No. 37 providing for a 20 per cent increase in redundancy pensions. This has been welcomed by the state employees and retired state officers and will certainly enable them to improve their standard of living. However, a fundamental solution will only consist in reducing the huge number of state employees (through privatisation, rehabilitation of existing employees, restructuring of existing state agencies and organizations) in order to reach a reasonable number of efficient employees who will then receive a decent salary.

3   CRIMINAL LAW

3.1   Smuggling

On 15 February 1974, LD No. 13 increased the penalties for smuggling and referred it to the Economic Security Court (a special jurisdiction acting as a criminal court, created by LD No. 37 of 6 May 1966 and composed of three magistrates of which only one is empowered to judge serious criminal offences against the state). The increased penalties do not seem to have reduced criminal behaviour and on 22 April 2000, LD No. 5 restricted the jurisdiction of the above-mentioned court to offences where the value does not exceed S£ 300,000 (US$6,000) and, in case of amicable settlement with the Customs, reduced imprisonment to one-third of the legal period, except for drugs offences. Two other decrees were also issued on the same date: LD No. 4 excluded the enforcement of LD No. 37 on all offences resulting in damage which does not exceed S£ 100,000 (US$2,000) for cases of deliberate offence and S£ 200,000 (US$4,000) in case of negligence. LD No. 6 authorized the possession of precious metals, foreign banknotes or other means of payment and reduced the penalty punishing their export or use in domestic dealings without the Central Bank (Exchange Bureau)'s approval. On 14 May 2000, LD No. 8 authorized the release on bail of the defendants in all cases before the a/m court, contrary to the previous legislation.

4   COMMERCIAL LAW

4.1   Amendment of the Law on Investments No. 10 of 4 May 1991

This law provided for several incentives (customs and income tax exemptions, the investor's right to operate a cheque account in foreign currency to repatriate the investor's profits and equity after five years), in projects approved by the Higher Council of Investments (HCI) headed by the Prime Minister, particularly in the fields of agriculture, industry, tourism and transport. A legislative decree (LD) No. 7 dated 13 May 2000 has amended Law No. 10 increasing these incentives, and has incorporated other amendments to company and tax law.

4.2   Ownership or exploitation of real estate

Under Syrian law, non-Arab foreigners cannot own agricultural land and can only own real estate in urban areas with the approval of the Minister of Interior. Arab citizens (i.e. citizens from Arab League countries – now twenty-five in number) need the same approval to own real estate in rural areas. When foreigners incorporate a Syrian company owning real estate, the Finance Ministry tends to ignore the fact that the land is owned by a Syrian corporate body and contends that the company can only own the land with the Ministry's approval since one of the shareholders is a foreigner. LD No. 7 (Article 1) overcame that obstacle and authorized foreign investors to own or rent real estate used to carry out a project governed by Law No. 10 provided the ownership is transferred to a Syrian citizen (or to a company also authorized under Law No. 10) at the end of the project. Article 6-f of Law No. 10 was therefore amended accordingly.

4.3   Period of implementation of the incentives

Article 13 of Law No. 10 extended the tax and duties exemption to five years from the beginning of the exploitation of the project if the owner was an individual or a private entity (seven years if the state was a shareholder). LD No. 7 (Article 2) extended the tax exemption provided for in Law No. 10 to sea transport and agricultural projects for any period (thereby amending Article 13-c of Law No. 10).

   LD No. 7 (Article 3) also amended Article 14 of Law no. 10 so that if the start-up of the project requires more than three years, only the extended period will be deducted from the tax exemption period, unless the HCI authorizes that exemption for an additional period of two years. The HCI may also grant such an exemption for two additional years after start up (thus amending Article 15 of Law No. 10).

   The following additional incentives were also introduced in Article 16 of Law No 10:

(a)   increase by the HCI of the hard currency exporters are authorized to keep under the exchange regulations in force (Article 5-c of LD No. 7);
(b)   opening with the HCI's approval of foreign bank accounts to finance its activities up to an amount of 50 per cent of the investment in foreign currency (Article 5-d of LD No. 7);
(c)   use of the investor's deposits in a foreign currency with the HCI's approval to finance its local expenditure at the rate of exchange in force in the free exchange market in " neighbouring countries" (e.g. Lebanon or Jordan).

Special advantages were granted by Article 6-b (amending Article 19 of Law No. 10) in projects with state participation of at least 25 per cent in a joint stock company (*société anonyme* – SA) or a limited liability company (SARL), provided such derogation is authorized by the Prime Minister after the HCI's approval:

(a)   derogation from the provisions of the Commerce Code regarding the nationality or number of directors (who could be below three or over seven in number – Article 178/1 of the Commercial Code (Co. C.)) or represent a majority of foreigners or a percentage thereof exceeding their share of the capital – Article 179 of the Co. C.), their age (which could exceed sixty without need to the approval of the President of the Republic, even if the director holds less that 10 per cent of the shares – Article 184/3 Co.C.), their remuneration (which may exceed the maximum set by Article 200 Co. C., i.e. S£3,000 to 6,000, US$ 60 to 120), or their appointment (some shareholders might be entitled to specific number of seats in the board of directors without being elected, contrary to Article 219/1-d Co.C.).
(b)   stipulation of a capital and shares calculated and payable in a foreign currency.
(c)   the same advantages can be extended by the HCI to the same companies without state participation (Article 6/c).

Article 7 of LD No. 7 (amending Article 22 of Law No. 10) also exempted companies with state participation from the stamp duty (1 per cent of the issued shares in joint stock companies and 1.5 per cent in the other companies – Law No. 15 of 5 July 1993) and joint stock or holding companies with only private stock from only 50 per cent of that duty.

Article 8 (amending Article 24/a of Law No. 10) authorized foreign investors to repatriate the net value of their investment in foreign currency after five years from the exploitation of the project (that provision originally only authorized repatriation of the amount actually invested in foreign currency).

Article 9 granted investments relative immunity from confiscation, expropriation or seizure and provided for the settlement of disputes between investors and state entities by court litigation or recourse to the Arab Investment Court (1980 agreement) or under the agreements concluded by Syria on guarantees and protection of foreign investments.

Article 10 (amending Articles 31 and 34 of Law No. 10) also authorized the HCI to extend the benefits of that law (except tax exemptions) to the already existing projects or to the future projects not licensed under that law.

4.4 Holding companies

The draft amendment of the Commerce Code, which had been approved in 2000 by the last Council of Ministers, contained comprehensive provisions on holding companies. Instead of inserting those provisions in the Commerce Code, the authorities managed to insert in LD No. 7 one article (numbered 2) extending to those companies the advantages granted by Law No. 10 to joint stock companies falling under its provisions (paragraph a). The same advantages were extended by paragraph b of that article to the projects executed by holding companies under the provisions of Law No. 10 with a participation of a least 51 per cent. The incorporation of those companies must be authorized by the Prime Minister (paragraph c) and the profits derived from the companies in which it participates are exempted from income tax (paragraph d).

4.5 Enforcement of the new provisions

The new provisions issued by LD No. 7 apply even to previous investment projects in the fields of agriculture, industry and sea transport governed by Law No. 10. Other projects licensed after the implementation of LD No. 7 can also benefit from Articles 4 (extension of the period of implementation of incentives) and 7 (exemption from stamp duty).

4.6 Income tax on joint stock companies (SA)

Article 4 of LD No. 7 reduced the rate of income tax applicable to all joint stock companies (SA), whether or not they are governed by Law No. 10, to a single fixed rate of 25 per cent (the previous rates were escalating and had reached a global rate varying between 42.88 per cent (for industrial companies) and 53.6 per cent for non industrial companies), for range of profits exceeding S£1 million (US$20,000) per year.

It is strange to include such an amendment in a law regarding investment incentives when it should have been provided for a law on income tax. But it seems that the authorities wished to take advantage of the mood aiming at encouraging investments to amend the tax on joint stock companies as was unanimously requested in Syria.

The above-mentioned legislation has been welcomed by all classes of the Syrian people. It was, however, very limited and should have been inserted in much wider legislation providing for a comprehensive amendment of commercial law.

4.7 Opening of private banks in the free zones

Banking activities in Syria have been a state monopoly as from 1965, when the existing banks were nationalized and a single bank established in each sector of the banking activities: commercial, industrial, agricultural, real estate and popular. Most of the credits granted by the Commercial Bank of Syria (CBS) benefit the public sector, the private sector relying mainly on foreign credit. In 1971, free zones were established in some Syrian cities (Damascus, Aleppo, Tartous, Latakia) where goods could be freely imported, re-exported and manufactured as if those activities were taking place outside the Syrian territory. The CBS's branches opened in those free zones could not obviously satisfy the needs of the enterprises operating, which is why the Ministry of Economy and Foreign Trade issued on 22 May 2000 under No. 793 a decree authorizing foreign banks to operate in the free zones provided their activities were restricted to enterprises located there. The Board of Directors of the free zones issued on 27 June 2999 under No. 20 the regulations governing the registration and operation of the CBS bank under the control of the Central Bank but the coming months will prove how those banks will be able to operate and will establish with the Central Bank the procedure enabling them to satisfy their clients' needs.

It seems that this first step will be followed by a more comprehensive decision which may authorize private banks to operate in Syria without limiting their activity to the free zones.

4.8 Car imports

Up to now, cars (which have never been manufactured or assembled in Syria) could not be imported there except in very limited cases and through a state-owned organization (Sayyarat) for Syrian expatriates in the Gulf countries, invalid soldiers, newly elected representatives at the People's Assembly, etc. In addition to the high customs duties (250 per cent of the car value) those restrictions resulted in a considerable increase of the car prices.

A recent decree from the Council of Ministers No. 3412 of 4 July 2000 partially resolved that problem by authorizing import of cars with the foreign exchange purchased from exporters (at a rate higher than the official rate) and after payment of Sayyarat's commission. The customs duties were also reduced to half their value and the registration duty to 75 per cent of the present amount. Despite those reductions, the import of cars was not increased substantially because circulating Syrian currency is very scarce and duties are still very high. Cars prices nevertheless fell by about 20–30 per cent.

Iraq

*Sabah Al-Mukhtar**

1 CONSTITUTIONAL AND ADMINISTRATIVE LAW

1.1 Defence of the realm

The division of the country into three military zones in anticipation of the US/UK bombing of Iraq (Desert Fox) in February 1999,[1] was revoked. Presidential Decree No. 45 of 2000 was published in the Official Gazette and came on 3 July 2000. The decree expressed the gratitude of the nation to the commanders of the three military zones for their work.

1.2 Local People's Council

Law No. 25 of 1995[2] was amended by Law No. 26 of 1999. The amendment calls for the election of Local People Councils to be carried out in one day instead of two.

1.3 National Assembly Election

Presidential Decree No. 31 of 2000, ordered that Monday 27 March, 2000 be the day on which the national elections of the National Assembly are held However, RCC Resolution No. 18 of 2000 was gazetted on 7 February 2000 providing that election of the National Assembly in the Autonomous Region of Kurdistan was to be postponed until a "Return to normal circumstances". This is obviously a reference to the insurrection in the north of Iraq which is backed by the USA in what it terms as a "No fly zone/safe

---

*   Legal consultant in Iraqi, Arab and Islamic law.
1   See Sabah Al-Mukhtar, "Iraq", in this *Yearbook*, vol. 5 (1998–1999), p. 201.
2   See Sabah Al-Mukhtar, "Iraq", in this *Yearbook*, vol. 3 (1996), p. 190.

haven". Law No. 38 of 2000 amended the provisions of the National Assembly Law No. 26 of 1995, providing that the legislative year is made up of two terms. One begins on the first Monday of April and ends on the last working day of May and the other begins on the first Monday of October and ends on the last working day in December.

1.4 National Assembly Procedures

The National Assembly has approved new procedures which were gazetted on 7 February 2000 to replace the earlier ones adopted under the National Assembly Law No. 55 of 1980. The rules and procedures are set out in 154 clauses, divided into six parts and divided into a number of chapters. The first part deals with speaker of the Assembly, his election, duties and powers. The second part deals with the election of members of the Assembly, their rights, privileges and duties, and disciplinary measures. It also establishes and details rights and duties of various permanent committees (legal, ways and means, foreign affairs, environment, human rights, oil, education, finance) as well as temporary ones. Part 4 deals with procedures and rules dealing with the Assembly in session, rules of conduct, voting, proceedings, minutes and the like. Part 5 deals with the Assembly's legislative powers, setting out the process and procedures to be followed in respect of drafting and debating draft legislation. It also details the powers to question ministers and officials, to summon and investigate persons and matters. The last part details the management, finance, security and protection of the Assembly and its members.

1.5 War veterans

In the last year Iran has released a large number of prisoners of war who have been detained in Iran since the first Gulf War of 1979. Some have been detained by Iran for almost twenty years but all, despite being war prisoners, have still been detained for well over ten years. RCC Resolution No. 125 of 1999 has given all returning prisoners the right to accept civilian posts instead of retiring. Those decorated for bravery may stay in active military service if they so wish. In all instances the period of detention as well as service as a civilian if chosen is to be taken into account for the purpose of pension.

Families of martyrs, those lost in action or those still prisoners of war, are given the right to exceptionally terminate a lease of a residential property which the family has leased to others and apply for eviction of the tenants. RCC Resolution No. 99 of 2000 which so provided was published on 5 July 1999.

The Minister of Finance issued Instructions No. 8 of 1999 which were gazetted on 2 August 1999 The Instructions provide that veterans of the war who become handicapped are granted a lump sum amount of ID 500,000 to enable them to get married. The Instructions set out details of the procedure to be followed.

Returning prisoners of war are afforded certain privileges by RCC Resolution No. 145 of 1999. Among these privileges are that if the family home is owned by a government agency then the prisoner of war and his family are entitled to stay in the house for at least five years from his return notwithstanding any claim that any party may have on the property. If the house is to be sold then the ex-prisoner is entitled to a preemptive right to buy and he is entitled to purchase the property at 50 per cent of the price if the owner is a state entity. The ex-prisoner is entitled to a tax holiday for five years and all demands for payment or interest are suspended for that period.

1.6   Cabinet reshuffle

By Presidential Decree No. 152 of 1999, Mr Hikmat Mizban Al-Azawi, the Minister of Finance is additionally appointed as Deputy Prime Minister.

1.7   Iraqi passports

New Passport Law No. 32 of 1999 was promulgated and was gazetted on 25 October 1999. The new law repeals its predecessor (No. 55 of 1959) and its many amendments. The new law defines certain terms including three types of document: passports, travel documents and transit passes. It contains the normal provisions providing that travel is illegal without the proper documents. It contains the description and contents of passports and the other documents. It sets out the certain provisions relating to fees and formalities for obtaining and renewing documents both within Iraq and by embassies outside Iraq, all of which are to be detailed by statutory regulations to be issued. It provides that the Presidential Office may order the withdrawal of the passport of a national who while abroad commits an act which is against the national interest and refuses to return to be tried, or if his whereabouts are not known. However, if at any time he is willing to return the relevant Iraqi embassy must issue him with the necessary document to enable him to do so. The security services may prohibit any citizen from leaving the country in the national interest; however, such a person is entitled to apply to the court for an injunction. Iraqi embassies are charged with renewing expired Iraqi passports regardless of the reason why the holder is outside Iraq. The *raison d'être* of the law states that the reason for the new law is that the old law contained too many details which are better left to delegated legislation and that it had acquired too many amendments over its forty-year life.

1.8   Expatriate Iraqis

RCC Resolution No. 110 of 1999, has granted an amnesty to all Iraqis living outside Iraq who left the country illegally. This includes violation to immigration rules as well as such crimes needed to leave the country such as forging documents, desertion, or failure to return after a term of duty outside Iraq, secondment and other circumstances.

1.9 Immigration and visas

RCC Resolution No. 102 of 2000 imposed new fees to be paid by Arab nationals and foreigners for obtaining residency certificates, extensions and renewals. Various other forms and compliance with residency and immigration legal requirements attract fees as detailed in the Resolution.

1.10 The oil industry[3]

Under the Companies Law No. 21 of 1997 and Law of Public Sector Companies No. 22 of 1997 which were gazetted in September 1977[4] the "Constitution" of many public sector companies were published in the official gazettes during the second half of 1999. These companies were established with the approval of the Council of Ministers, registered with the Registrar of Companies and their capital is paid by the Treasury. Among them are the fourteen oil sector companies; each has replaced the existing "state owned entity" which was dissolved accordingly and its assets, rights and obligations transferred by law.

Each of these companies has an independent juridical personality and paid up capital in millions of Iraqi dinars as follows:[5]

North Oil Company	2,189
South Oil Company	3,003
Northern Refining Company	694
Central Refining Company	248
Southern Refining Company	994
Oil Drilling Company	396
Oil Projects Company	395
Oil Pipelines Company	209
Oil Tankers Company	839
Oil Products Distribution Company	1,478
Oil Exploration Company	207
Northern Gas Company	787
Southern Gas Company	258
Gas Distribution Company	293

1.11 Electricity sector

Among the main problems that Iraq faces is loss of electricity-generating ability. The bombing of Iraq during the Gulf War resulted in the destruction

---

3 See Al-Mukhtar, "Iraq", in this *Yearbook*, vol. 5, p. 205.
4 See *ibid.*, p. 269.
5 For guidance it is safe to assume that the capital of these companies is in thousands of US dollars.

of almost the entire Iraqi capability of production of electricity. The Agha Khan Report in 1991 estimated that the allied bombing has destroyed 96 per cent of Iraqi production capability, which puts into question the legality of such a massive destruction of civilian infrastructure, especially as the Geneva Convention prohibits the destruction of infrastructure needed by the civilian population, and in any event the destruction had no relation to the liberation of Kuwait.

Over the last ten years Iraq, despite the blockade, has rebuilt a very large part of its capability. UNSCR 986 (Oil for Food) was adopted to enable Iraq to alleviate the suffering of the civilian population; however, the US and UK representatives on the sanctions committee continually veto contracts for desperately needed material for the electricity sector. It is believed that depriving Iraqi civilians of the use of electricity will increase their discontent against the regime. To overcome this Iraq has established a state owned company with a capital of half a billion Iraqi dinars to manufacture electricity generating systems. The new company is to use and develop national resources and capabilities, to cooperate with the private sector and to use all available means to achieve its objectives.

Because of the importance of this sector and its crucial effect on every aspect of life in Iraq, the government is continually reorganizing and frantically trying new approaches including power cuts and rationing distribution in terms of time and supply. On the structural level, the electricity sector has been moved from the Ministry of Industry to a new Electricity Commission attached directly to the Council of Ministers, where President Saddam Hussain is also the Prime Minister. RCC Resolutions Nos. 94–96 of 1999, which were gazetted on 5 July 1999, detailed this reorganization. The Electricity Commission divided Iraq into three generating zones (north, centre and south) and four distribution zones, with Baghdad as a zone on its own.

The Electricity Commission on 30 August 1999 gazetted detailed and extensive Instructions dealing with the supply of electricity. The Instructions set out the terms and conditions under which electricity is supplied to consumers. It detailed the rights and obligations of property owners, the liability of the Commission, and types of power supplied, and penalties, billing, charges and consumption measurements.

1.12   Water and Sewerage Commission

The Law establishing the Water and Sewerage Establishment was repealed and replaced by Law No. 27 of 1999. The new Commission has an independent juridical personality and is attached to the Ministry of the Interior. The Commission is charged with providing drinking water throughout Iraq outside the capital Baghdad. It has the statutory duty to dispose of sewage and rainwater. Statutory Instructions No. 37 of 1999 were gazetted on 21 February 2000, in accordance with Article 15, to implement the provisions of the law.

1.13 Local and village elders (*mukhtars*)

Statutory Regulations No. 1 of 1999 was approved by the Council of Ministers and gazetted on 7 June 1999. It is a delegated legislation under the Governorates Law No. 159 of 1969. The Regulations provide that each district within a city and each village shall have a *mukhtar*. He will be nominated by head of the local administration (*qaimmaqam* or *mudeer al-nahiya*), approved by the local council and appointed by the governor in whose governorate the village or district is situated. The Regulations set out the qualifications that a person must have to be so appointed. The *mukhtar* has a number of semi-judicial functions, including matters relating to the civil structure of the community, bailiff service, public funding, public health matters and some functions under the Criminal Procedures Law, such as being an independent witness in cases concerning warrants, property searches and arrests of suspects. They receive an honorarium, as they are expected to be persons of means or are willing to serve without expecting to be paid. In accordance with the provisions of Article 8 of the said Regulations, the Minister of the Interior issued Instructions No. 24 of 1999 to implement the Regulations as of 1 November 1999.

1.14 Local Baath Party

The secretariat and leadership of the Baath Party (ruling party) in certain governorates were granted some executive powers over the civil servants in their governorate. These powers, such as transferring civil servants from one department to another, reprimand and penalties, were reserved for ministers of state. This includes the Bable Governorate (RCC Resolution 111 of 1999) and Wasit (171 of 1999).

1.15 Ministerial status

The Iraqi Nuclear Authority, Military Industrialization and National Planning Authority,[6] which are not ministries, have by RCC Resolution No. 117 of 1999 been granted the status and powers of ministries of state.

2 JUDICIARY AND JUDICIAL SYSTEM AND PROCEDURE

2.1 Criminal Procedures Code

Article 3 of the Criminal Procedures Code No. 23 of 1971 was amended by Law No. 20 of 1999. The amendment enables the Public Prosecutor to commence proceedings in cases of libel, defamation, threats and assault even

---

6   See Al-Mukhtar, "Iraq", in this *Yearbook*, vol. 5, pp. 206 and 207.

if the victim does not report it or file a complaint. Previously, aside from crimes against public officials, the Public Prosecutor had to receive a complaint before it can act.

2.2   Civil Procedures Code

RCC Resolution No. 167 of 1999 imposed addition legal fees on litigants, where 70 per cent of the proceeds is earmarked to be distributed amongst members of the judiciary and court staff. These are 2 per cent of the value when commencing a case in the first instance, 3 per cent in appeal, ID 5,000 in appeal to the Court of Cassation, ID 1,000 to transfer cases to another court.

2.3   Appeal circuits

Presidential Decree No. 167 of 1999 was gazetted on 13 September 1999. It provides for dividing the Baghdad Appeal Circuit into two appeal circuits, Risafah (east of the Tigris) and Karkh (west of the Tigris). A new appeal circuit was created for the governorate of Salah Eldin. Thereby Iraq is now divided into nine appeal circuits instead of seven.

2.4   Public Prosecution Service

The Public Prosecution Service Law No. 159 of 1979 was amended by Law No. 7 of 2000. The amendment is to enable the PPS to appeal against decisions relating to juveniles even if the appeal period has passed without an appeal by the child. Obviously the appeal is only possible where there is a violation of the law by either the courts or the administration to the detriment of the child. Appeals must be lodged within fourteen days of the service of the judgment; under the amending law the PPS are given the right to appeal within three years of the final judgment. The appeal must be lodged with the Court of Cassation of Iraq, which must consider the case by the full Bench. Law No. 19 of 2000 was gazetted on 3 April 2000, empowering the Council of Justice (the regulatory body of judges) the ultimate power of recommending the removal of a member of the PPS if found to be unsuitable to hold his post.

2.5   The Judiciary Regulating Law

Law No. 9 of 2000 was gazetted to amend the Judiciary Regulating Law No. 160 of 1979. The amendment provides that senior judges such as the President of the Appeal Court is to have ministerial status and be appointed by a Presidential Decree. It further provides that judges are to be seated on official occasions, as a matter of protocol in such a manner that is consistent with the high office they occupy. This is to be determined by delegated legislation to be promulgated for this purpose. Law No. 18 of 2000 was gazetted on 3 April 2000, giving the Council of Justice (the regulatory body of judges) the ultimate power of recommending the removal of one of its members if found to be unsuitable as a member of the bench and transferring him to a non-judicial post. This will then be confirmed by a Presidential Decree.

2.6 Law of Establishing Societies

New Law No. 13 of 2000 was gazetted on 14 February 2000 to replace Law No. 1 of 1960. The Law prescribes the process for the setting up of societies in Iraq. The main reason for the new law is to update the provisions of the 30-year old law. Another important change is that it no longer includes political parties, which were regulated by the same law whereas now they are regulated by Law No. 30 of 1991. The new law enables every ten or more people to apply to the Ministry of the Interior for a licence to establish a society. It sets out the membership requirements, rights and obligations of the societies and its membership. The objectives must not be against the public or national interest, must not be sectarian, racist or promote any form of discrimination nor have secret objectives.

2.7 Official papers

The Minister of Justice issued Statutory Instructions No. 2 of 199 amending those of 1989 setting out the length of time that official documents must be archived. These Instructions which came into effect on 21 June 1999 are issued in accordance with the provisions of Law on Preserving Official Papers and Archives No. 70 of 1980. Under the law all official papers and documents have to be retained for a minimum and a maximum period. They are classified according to their importance. For instance, in criminal cases the judgment must be kept for a period no less than fifteen years and no more than twenty. Papers relating to marriage (not the marriage certificates) are to be kept for three to five years. These Instructions set out the various documents held by the courts and registry offices.

3 FAMILY LAW AND CIVIL LIABILITY

3.1 Personal status

Article 24 of the Law of Personal Status No. 188 of 1959 was amended by Law No. 19 of 1999. It reduced the limitation period relating to maintenance that is due to the wife to one year from the date of failure of the husband to pay. Originally there was no specified limitation period, hence the general principles applied then. The other article amended was No. 26 regulating the sharing of the matrimonial home with others. The amendment prohibits the husband from forcing his wife to live with his second wife. It obliges the wife to accept that her stepson living at home until he is eighteen years of age. It also obliges the wife to accept her parents in law living at home.

A further amendment to Article 26 was effected by Law No. 22 of 1999 obliging a wife to accept that not only her parents-in-law live at home but also all those persons whom her husband has a legal duty to care for.

3.2   Inflation-linked dowry

During the Iraq–Iran war, the Iraqi currency value dropped dramatically, hence some married women began to have their dowry specified in their marriage contract to be revised upwards. To stem the trend at the time a tax was imposed by RCC Resolution No. 352 of 1987 on couples who vary their marriage contracts by an amount equal to 50 per cent of the increase in dowry. This Resolution has now been repealed by RCC Resolution No. 105 of 1999 to take account of the collapse of the Iraqi currency, which has been devalued to 6000 times less than its former value.

A further RCC Resolution No. 127 of 1999, dealing with this matter, was gazetted. It provides that a divorcee who is entitled to her dowry shall have such dowry valued by the price of gold at the time of marriage.

3.3   Liability of civil servants

RCC Resolution No. 100 of 1999 repealed RCC Resolutions No. 137 of 1994 and No. 140 of 1996. The Resolution provides that civil servants are liable to the Treasury for all damages resulting from their negligence or violation of laws. If the damage was caused by a wilful act then the penalty would be twice the value of the harm. The civil servant ordered to pay the damages must do so within the specified period, otherwise he will be liable to be detained and his assets distrained. No release from detention is possible until full payment is made. The most important element of this Resolution is that these measures are extra-legal and administratively applied by the minister concerned. Inquiry and investigation is to be carried out by a ministerial commission headed by the legal department of the ministry. More important is that the minister's decisions are not appealable and the ordinary courts are prohibited from considering such cases.

4   COMMERCIAL LAW

4.1   Registrar of Companies

RCC Resolution No. 82 of 2000 empowered the Registrar of Companies to levy fees for many of the services it renders. This includes, for example, the levy of ID 50,000 for verification of the documents required by law for foreign companies to register in Iraq. This levy is in addition to the legal fees set out in the Companies Law. Verification and approval of most company documents (national or foreign) such as accounts, change of shareholders, applications for liquidation, constitutions, attending meetings, companies' head offices, AGMs and the like all attract additional fees. These fees range between ID 5,000 and 30,000. Half the revenue received is distributed to the employees and the other is to be paid the Treasury.

4.2   Chambers of commerce

The Law of Chambers of Commerce No.43 of 1989 provides for the establishment of a chamber of commerce in the centre of each of the eighteen governorates of Iraq. The law has a number of annexes, one of which sets out the fees to be paid by the members, which are mandatory for most trades and commercial activities. The fees payable depend on the size and importance of the entity or the member, of which there are five grades. Since the Iraqi dinar been devalued, the Council of Ministers issued a Declaration (No. 60) dated 2 May 1999 increasing the fees and charges made by the chambers of commerce to their members and others to reflect the collapse of the currency (Official Gazette 3777).

4.3   Printing Houses Law

Printing Houses Law No. 189 of 1969 was repealed by Law No. 5 of 1999. The new law regulates the licensing of establishing printing houses, which are divided into three categories depending on their size and equipment. In each case a fee is to be paid upon licensing and also an annual renewal fee. The law provides for a variety of obligations relating to change of ownership, the name of the house, management, safety, censorship requirement and record keeping. There are a number of instances where the licence will be revoked in the public interest, which include publishing material deemed immoral, discriminatory, blasphemous, supporting Zionism, imperialism and the like. Violations of the provisions of the law carry penalties including closure of the printing house as well as both monetary and prison sentences up to one year.

4.4   Rafidain Bank

New internal regulations for Rafidain Bank were gazetted on 28 June 1999, as required by the Public Companies Act No. 22 of 1997. The regulations set out the Bank's objectives: it is a state-owned entity, with independent juridical personality, with full powers to undertake banking operations and services. The operations and services are set out in detail and include all high street banking services as well as all investment banking operations. The Bank is managed by a board of directors made up of nine including the managing director. Every three years four directors are nominated by the Minister of Finance from the heads of department of the Bank, two are senior bank officials elected by the employees of the bank and two are independent members from outside the Bank who are known for their banking expertise. The regulations set out the structure of the Bank and show it as having twelve divisions, each divided into a number of departments. It is to be noted that the Commercial Court in London has for the last ten years classed the Rafidain Bank as being in "provisional liquidation". The English court order is supposed to apply not only to the English branch in London but to the bank in Iraq and elsewhere.

4.5 Foreign currency

RCC Resolution No. 98 of 1999 was gazetted on 5 July 1999 providing for exemption from the Central Bank Law No. 64 of 1976 and foreign exchange regulations. It permits foreigners to hold and use foreign currency in Iraq as well as opening interest bearing bank accounts in the said currencies. Iraqi nationals also are now allowed to hold bank accounts in foreign currencies to settle debts which they have within Iraq. Expatriate Iraqis are permitted to re-export any foreign currency which they have formally brought into Iraq along with accrued interest. Thereafter, the Central Bank of Iraq issued Statutory Instructions enabling banks to pay in foreign currency (OG 3785).

4.6 Income Tax Law

To reduce the tax burden on those resident in Iraq (nationals as well as foreigners) a major change in the Income Tax Law No 113 of 1982 was effected by Law No. 25 of 1999. The change increased the level of income below which residents are exempt from income tax to ID 50,000 annually. This becomes ID 70,000 for widows or divorcees and ID 90,000 for those over sixty-five years of age. These levels are increased by a child allowance of ID 15,000 for each child. This level is thought to be above that which more than half the population would earn, thereby at most only half the population pays tax. Further, the law has reduced the rate of tax to 10 per cent on income of up to ID 250,000, 20 per cent up to one million, 30 per cent up to two million and 40 per cent above that. Since the Income Tax Law also covers corporation tax, this was also reduced 15 per cent on the first 1.5 million dinars, and then increased to 25 and 35 per cent.

4.7 Stamp duty

Law No. 31 of 1999 was gazetted on 11 October 1999, amending the Stamp Duty Law No. 16 of 1974. The amendment enables the contracting ministry to collect the stamp duty payable on its contracts in instalments if a project is executed in stages.

4.8   Internet services

Despite the blockade imposed on Iraq, it managed in 1999 to establish internet connection with the outside world. The service is available to all the ministries as well as most of the important state-owned entities and universities. The service is open to the public only through central "internet cafes". This is a major breakthrough for the country which still lacks the simpler forms of contact with the outside world. Iraq is being denied the ability to rebuild its telephone system, and there is no normal airmail postal service with the rest of the world as all post has to go by road from Jordan to Iraq. There is no courier service to Iraq and the UK Royal Mail still refuses to accept parcels, registered mail or relatively thick letters, insisting on a DTI export licence!

This service is provided by a state-owned company, The National Company Internet and Information, with a capital of 400 million Iraqi dinars, whose constitution was gazetted on 7 February 2000. The homepage is http:\\www.uruklink.net.

4.9   Non-governmental consultants

Law No. 16 of 2000 was gazetted on 13 March 2000 to regulate the opening and operating of consultancy partnerships that are not owned by the state. The law provides that the professional bodies (lawyers, doctors, accountants and economists) are the bodies to which applications should be made in the first instance. Once these professional bodies have certified the competence of the partner then licence is granted accordingly. Licences are issued to the natural persons who are the partners carrying the liability of the Bureau. This law has become necessary because the current legislation does not cover this aspect of work. It is also aimed at encouraging qualified Iraqis to participate in the revival of the economy and encouraging more participation by those who otherwise are not.

4.10   Mining regulations

In accordance with the provisions of the Law Regulating Mineral Mining No. 91 of 1988 the Director General of the Mining and Geological Survey Company gazetted (11 October 1999) Statutory Instructions No. 1 of 1999. The Instructions deals with the extraction and mining of most minerals such as iron, chrome, manganese, copper, lead, phosphate, sulphur, zircon, asphalt, salts and industrial muds such as pentolite, flint, etc. They detail the licensing system, contractual relationship, regulatory powers, inspection and penalties.

4.11   Public sector companies

The Registrar of Companies continued to gazette the constitution of state-owned companies. These include:

Company Name	Capital Mil. ID	Sector	Official Gazette
Electricity Generating Systems	500	Manufacturing	3781
Al-Mansour Electric & Solar	121	Manufacturing	3778
Al-Obour Manufacturing	2,674	Manufacturing	3778
Al-Zawraa Electrical	91	Manufacturing	3781
Al-Hudda Tourism	200	Religious tours	3782
Al-Shaheed Copper	484	Manufacturing	3782
Saad Consultancy	167	Manufacturing	3782
Saddam Manufacturing	812	Manufacturing	3784
General Produce	200	Agriculture	3787
Oil Exploration Company	207	Oil	3792
Oil Projects Company	395	Oil	3792
Southern Gas	259	Oil	3794
Gas Distribution	294	Oil	3794
Oil Pipeline	310	Oil	3796
Northern Gas	787	Oil	3797
Oil Products Distribution	1,488	Oil	3798
Oil Tankers	840	Oil	3798
Central Electricity	1,164	Electricity	3793
Northern Electricity	581	Electricity	3793
Southern Electricity	630	Electricity	3794
Electricity Generating System	5,000	Electricity	3794
Internet	400	Communications	3812
Anfal Constructions	Internal Rules	Construction	3783
Ashour Constructions	Internal Rules	Construction	3793
Ramadhan Constructions	Internal Rules	Construction	3793
Industrial Construction	1,311	Construction	3807
Iraqi Cement	1,523	Manufacturing	3807
Northern Cement	957	Manufacturing	3807

4.12   Arab horses

The 1979 Equestrian Law No. 167 was replaced by Law No. 43 of 1999. It establishes the Equestrian Club whose objectives, *inter alia*, are to improve the breeding of Arab horses and to protect their lineage. Working with the Ministry of Agriculture it handles the blood register of the pure Arab horses in Iraq. It is to be managed by an elected board and charged with establishing equestrian schools and training courses.

4.13   Auditors and chartered accountants

New Statutory Regulations No. 3 of 1999 were gazetted on 3 January 2000 to replace No. 7 of 1984 regulating the practice of the profession. The

Regulations establish a professional body made up of fifteen members of the Iraq Auditors Association, and also to represent various bodies (the university, National Audit Office, ministries of higher education, finance, President of the Auditors Association) as well as other elected members. The Regulations establish the licensing requirements, rules of conduct, liability, discipline and penalties. Those licensed must be Iraqi nationals, living and working in Iraq, with the academic and professional qualifications set out in the Regulations.

5 INTELLECTUAL PROPERTY

Certain provisions of the Patent Law No. 65 of 1970 were amended by Law No. 28 of 1999. The changes became necessary to reflect the change in the authority charged with registering the patents from the Commercial Registrar to the Quality and Standardization Authority. It also empowered the administrative court to deal with certain aspects of patents, and provided for the giving of awards to inventors as an incentive. The amendment provides that new patents are protected for twenty years generally, and for ten years for medical and pharmaceutical products, extendable for further five-year terms on certain conditions.

6 LABOUR LAW

The provisions of the Labour Law No. 71 of 1987 were amended by the second amendement Law No. 17 of 2000. The amendments are aimed at bringing the Law into line with Iraq's obligations under the Arab and international labour treaties to which Iraq has acceded. It deals with rights of nationals of other Arab countries, payment of wages in cases of *force majeure*, collective bargaining of workers, inspection of the workplace and such matters.

7 LAW OF PROPERTY

7.1 National road network

Law No. 12 of 1999 amended Law No. 55 of 1985 Regulating the Use of National Roads Network. The law amended a number of provisions giving the Roads and Bridges Commission established by Law No. 62 of 1987 (new name), the power to remove violations. The law calls for the issuing of notices for the removal of any unauthorized or illegal incursion on the perimeter of main roads. Failure to do so within the notice period entitles the authorities to effect the removal at the cost of the owner. State-owned production entities and projects are exempted from the removal notice; however, once they cease to be a production centre then they must immediately be removed.

7.2   Property of expatriate Iraqis

For many years expatriate Iraqis have been prohibited from selling their property in Iraq as long as they were abroad. The reason has been to use this as a means of illegally transferring money outside Iraq and to prevent property from passing to non-nationals. However, RCC Resolution No. 165 of 1999 has now permitted expatriates who are lawfully resident outside Iraq to sell their property to third parties.

7.3   Rice plantations

Since the planting of rice requires flooding of agricultural land, planting of rice is regulated by Law No. 135 of 1968. Under the present blockade of Iraq and the resulting economic circumstances, the government pays hand-somely to farmers to encourage agriculture and production of food. This has led many people to plant crops disregarding environmental, regulatory or legal restrictions. Flooding agricultural land in the south of Iraq (rice growing area) normally leads to high salinity making the land infertile. Law No. 42 of 1999 has amended Law No. 135 of 1968 by imposing a penalty of ID 25,000 per *dounam* of land that is illegally planted with rice.

8   CRIMINAL LAW

8.1   Street beggars

Due to the increase in the number of people who are unemployed (almost 40 per cent of the population) and destitute many have resorted to street begging. In certain instances this is thought to be by organized gangs who are faking deformities and wounds to look like handicapped persons. To stem the tide the Iraqi Penal Code No. 111 of 1969 was amended by Law No. 16 of 1999 to provide for imprisonment of up to three months for adults who are found begging in the streets. The sentence is increased to one year if the begging is associated with faking illness or handicap or the use of other means of deception. Article 392 is amended to provide for the imprisonment for no more than three years for those encouraging, enticing or forcing others to beg.

8.2   Interference with justice

Articles 233 and 234 of the Penal Code No. 111 of 1969 were amended to increase the penalty imposed on any court official or civil servant attempting to influence judges or interfere with the due process for the benefit of a litigant or to cause harm to the standing of another. Such persons are now liable for six to twelve months' imprisonment and the judge so influenced to a prison sentence of no more than six years.

8.3   Guns Law

Law No. 13 of 1992 Regulating the Possession of Weapons, was amended by Law No. 15 of 2000. The amending law is aimed at encouraging the citizens who hold licences to own weapons to sell their weapons. It is also aimed at improving the regulation of the sale and purchase of licensed weapons retailers and shops. The Minister of the Interior has issued Statutory Instructions No. 15 of 1998 but these were only gazetted on 6 March 2000. The main provisions are the penalties that may be imposed on those who fire in the air in certain occasions. The penalty includes fines and the confiscation of the weapon.

8.4   Release of prisoners

Prisoners who have served at least half of their sentence may apply for their prison sentence to be substituted for payment of money in lieu. RCC Resolution No. 20 of 2000 provides that the tariff payable is set at ID 2,500 per day of remaining term (almost US$ 500 per year). The Resolution details the process to be followed to release the prisoner, which involves a number of committee reports and hearings before a reasoned decision is announced. These applications do not apply to cases involving premeditated crimes, those involving treason, drugs, murder, rape and other serious crimes. The provisions of the Resolution has are valid for only one year from 12 February 2000 to 12 February 2001.

8.5   Traffic fines

RCC Resolution No. 83 of 1999 repealed the provisions of RCC Resolution No. 104 of 1969. The Resolution confers upon traffic police officers the power of magistrates to issue on the spot fines for a number of traffic offences. It lists the offences and the fine to be imposed. The fines are final and not subject to appeal.

8.6   No detention for women

RCC Resolution No. 101 of 1999, prohibits the detention of females at any stage until a prison sentence is handed down by a court of law. Therefore, except in cases of premeditated crimes a female suspect may not be detained while she is being questioned or being tried. A female is automatically released on bail even in cases of unintentional killing until sentencing. This Resolution extends this special treatment to all offences while RCC Resolution 47 of 1999[7] related to particular offences only.

---

[7]   *Ibid.*, p. 211.

9   INTERNATIONAL LAW

9.1   Arab Free Trade Zone

The regional treaty creating the Arab Free Trade Zone called on the member states to gradually reduce custom and excise duty on goods produced within the region to be able to benefit from the two treaties. For this purpose the Council of Ministers reduced the customs and excise duty imposed on goods whose origin is an Arab state signatory to the Arab Free Trade Zone by 20 per cent (Decision 61 of 31 May 1999 gazetted 14 June 1999).

9.2   International Convention on Carriage by Rail

Law No. 14 of 1999 (gazetted on 14 June 1999) is the enabling Act to ratify the 1990 Protocol of the International Convention to Facilitate the Crossing of Frontiers for Passengers and Baggage Carried by Rail signed in Bern Switzerland in December 1990.

9.3   UNESCO Technical and Vocational Training Treaty

Law No. 15 of 1999 (gazetted on 14 June 1999) is the enabling act to ratify the 1989 Agreement on Technical and Vocational Training adopted by UNESCO in Paris on 10 November 1989.

9.4   International Treaty on Training of Seamen

Iraq has ratified the International Treaty on the Training, Monitoring and Licensing of Seamen which was adopted in 1987 (effective 28 April 1984) and its amendments of 1991, 4 and 5. The enabling Act Law No 44 of 1999 was gazetted on 10 January 2000.

9.5   International Civil Aviation Protocol

The Protocol amending the International Civil Aviation Treaty signed in Montreal on 29 May 1995 adopting Arabic as the official text of the treaty was ratified. The enabling Act Law No. 2 of 2000 was gazetted on 24 January 2000.

9.6   The Rights of the Child Treaty

The amendment to Article 43 of the Treaty was adopted on 12 December 1995 increasing the number of the Commission from ten to eighteen. As Iraq has already acceded to the Treaty by Law No. 3 of 1994, it has now ratified the amendment by Law No. 3 of 2000.

9.7   Islamic Educational, Scientific and Cultural Organization IESCO

The treaty on the recognition of studies, qualifications and degrees under the IESCO was ratified by Law No. 4 of 2000.

9.8   International Civil Aviation Treaty

The Additional Protocols Nos. (1 and 2) amending the Warsaw Treaty on the Uniformity of Civil Aviation Treaty, which were signed in Montreal on 25 September 1975, was ratified by Law No. 11 of 2000.

9.9   Unified Arab TRIPTICK Treaty

The pan-Arab treaty on the use of unified Arab vehicle travel document, adopted by the League of Arab States in Cairo on 15 September 1994, was ratified by Law No. 12 of 2000.

9.10   Law of Treaties

The provisions of the Law of Treaties No. 111 of 1979 was amended by Law No. 31 of 2000. The amending Law is aimed at simplifying the ratification of certain treaties and agreements where the minister concerned is empowered to do so. It also empowers the President to authorize ministers to act in his name.

9.11   Iraq–UN relationship

Under the US hegemony of the Security Council backed by the UK, Iraq has more than its share of the resolutions adopted yearly. There were six resolutions in 1999 and three in the first six months of 2000,[8] one every other month! Iraq is being treated as a UN mandate territory (not a UN founding member state), and UN agencies are now charged with tasks that have never been or should not be entrusted to it. The UN is charged with distributing food to 25 million people, deciding what they need, how much, when, even the number of loaves and how many aspirin tablets they can each have or whether children should wear shoes that are made in Egypt or China, or at all!

What seems to be the pride and joy of the ethical foreign policy of the UK in UNSCR 1284 boils down to renaming the discredited UNSCOM (United Nations Special Commission) as UNMOVIC (United Nations Monitoring, Verification and Inspection Commission). For ten years Iraq

---

[8]   See Part III, pp. 404–413 for the text of UNSCRs 1280, 1281 and 1284.

was ridiculed for complaining that UNSCOM was abusing its international privileges by spying for Iraq's enemies (USA and Israel). In the early part of 1999 senior members of UNSCOM admitted spying for the US and a number of revelations were made including at least one book.[9] The objection which Iraq has to Resolution 1284 may be summed up as follows:

(a) Paragraph 22 of UNSCR 687 of 1991[10] calls for the lifting of the embargo on Iraq once its weapons of mass destruction have been eliminated. It provides

    22. Decides also that upon the approval by the Security Council of ... the prohibitions against the import of commodities and products originating in Iraq ... contained in resolution 661 (1990) shall have no further force or effect;

(b) Instead of deciding that the ten-year blockade "have no further force or effect" the new UNSCR 1284 instead calls for keeping it indefinitely and only suspending it if the USA agrees. Paragraph 31 provides:

    31. Notes that in the event of the Council ... to suspend the prohibitions referred to ... including suspension of provisions of resolution 986 (1995) and related resolutions;

(c) Additionally to this disadvantageous position that Iraq is being pushed into (which Iraq says is a non-compliance by the Security Council with its own obligation under paragraph 22 of UNSCR 687), Iraq has to readmit the inspectors whose predecessors admitted to being spies.

Therefore, Iraq views the new UNSCR 1284 as a choice between "blockade with spies" or "blockade alone", and hence has refused to admit the inspectors or to cooperate with the UN regarding this Resolution.

9.12 Memorandum of Understanding (MOU)[11]

This is the document regulating the relationship between the UN and Iraq in respect of the implementation of the UNSCR 986 (oil for food). This document was drawn up by the Secretariat of the UN and Iraq 20 May 1996 on the implementation of UNSCR 986. Under the MOU parties wishing to trade under and avail themselves of the Resolution, have to obtain the approval of both the UN and the Iraqi government. The UN charges all of its costs to Iraq by withdrawing money directly from the Iraqi funds in the UN escrow account. RCC Resolution No. 256 of 1999 was

---

9 See Al-Mukhtar, "Iraq", in this *Yearbook*, vol. 5, p. 223. See also Scott Ritter, *Endgame*, Simon & Schuster, April 1999, ISBN 0684864851.
10 See Part III, pp. 389–395, for the text of UNCR 687 of 1991.
11 See Part III, pp. 396–404, for the text of the MOU (S/1996/356).

gazetted on 3 January 2000 to impose a fee of ID 150,000 every six months on Iraqi companies and persons requiring the approval of the Iraqi Ministry of Foreign Affairs.

10   EDUCATION

10.1   Higher Education Fund

The Minister of Higher Education has issued Regulations No. 122 of 1999, which were gazetted on 9 August 1999. The Regulation establishes independent funds in the academic and higher education institutions of Iraq with independent juridical personality. Each is to be managed by the head of the institution, his deputy and a number of heads of departments and the head of finance of the institution. The fund is financed by a certain percentage of the income from the national budget, college fees, donations and other income. The major part of the income (50–70 per cent) into the fund is earmarked to be paid to the teaching and other staff. The reminder is to be spent on the servicing the needs of the institution.

10.2   Working after graduation

To ensure that graduates of engineering colleges serve in the government, RCC Resolution No. 169 of 1999 provides that each graduate must serve a minimum period of five years after graduation. Should the graduate be in breach then he must pay twice the cost of his studies. The Ministry of Higher Education must set aside a percentage of places for women engineers. There is also a carrot, namely that engineers who work for the public sector are given a monthly allowance of ID 10,000.

10.3   Diyallah University

A new state university has been established in Iraq thereby bringing the number of state universities to fourteen in addition to a further eleven private universities. RCC Resolution No. 173 of 1999 established the university. The Resolution decreed that it should be added to those universities listed in Article 8 of the Law of the Ministry of Higher Education No. 40 of 1988.

11   HEALTH

11.1   Centre for Heart Disease

The Minister of Health issued Ministerial Instructions No. 6 of 1999, in accordance with the powers conferred upon him by RCC Resolution No. 747 of 1988. The Instructions established the Centre for Heart Diseases as a specialized medical centre attached indirectly to the Ministry of Health. The Instructions set out the procedure for referral to the Centre for Heart Surgery and treatment of other heart conditions.

11.2 Pesticides

The Ministry of Agriculture was empowered by RCC Resolution No. 115 of 1999 to charge farmers and owners of agricultural land for the cost of treating their fields. The revenues are used to acquire the pesticides and to apply them. Twenty-five per cent of the net revenues are thereafter distributed to the pilots undertaking the spraying flights.

11.3 Privatization of health care

Iraq has finally been pushed to take the dramatic step of partly privatizing its health care. After seven decades of providing totally free health care service, Iraq under sanctions is no longer able to do so. RCC Resolution 132 of 1999 has empowered the Minister of Health to turn within one year 50 per cent of all hospital beds in state hospitals into private rooms and wings. These hospitals are to be run as fund holders and self-financed centres. The policy introduced in 1997[12] has now been developed into what seems to be a strategy looking into the future. It is evident from the way the revenues are distributed that a major aim is to keep Iraqi doctors from fleeing the country. Most are doing so to avoid watching helplessly so many unnecessary deaths due to lack of medicine and equipment under the embargo imposed in the name of the UN. The Resolution provides that 60 per cent of the treatment and operating fees goes to the doctors and surgeons doing the work and 30 per cent of all income is distributed to the medical staff at the hospitals.

11.4 AIDS

All Iraqis, Arabs and foreigners entering Iraq must be checked for AIDS (HIV). RCC Resolution No. 159 of 1999 replaced (RCC Resolution No. 6 of 1995)[13] which was triggered by an absence of three months for Iraqis. The Minister of Health accordingly issued Instructions No. 1 of 2000 which were gazetted on 3 April 2000 and detailed the process and penalties. RCC Resolution No. 97 of 2000 has however, exempted members of the RCC, Council of Ministers, Members of Parliament and other holders of high office from having to take the test.

---

12   See Sabah Al-Mukhtar, "Iraq", in this *Yearbook*, vol. 4 (1997–1998), p. 283.
13   See Sabah Al-Mukhtar, "Iraq", in this *Yearbook*, vol. 2 (1995), p. 142.

11.5 Iraq Specialist Medical Authority

The Minister of Higher Education and Scientific Research gazetted Statutory Instructions No. 124 of 1999 on 18 October 1999 to replace No. 52 of 1992. The Instructions establish the specialist council made up of the deans of the medical and dentistry colleges of all the Iraqi universities, senior specialist physicians and representatives of the relevant ministries. The council is charged with regulating the practice of the profession, setting out the educational and professional programs for the various medical disciplines, recognizing qualifications, promoting academics and other medical matters.

11.6 Health and Medical Professional Qualifications

The various medical and health professions are regulated by a number of pieces of legislation, including Law No. 99 of 1970 (Medical Professional Promotion,) No. 44 of 1973 (Medical Occupation) and No. 15 of 1982 (Pharmacists). This legislation regulates academic and professional qualifications, apprenticeships and training. It sets out the promotional scales, work to be undertaken to qualify for professional promotion, research, teaching and the type of institutions (teaching hospitals and academia). However, to bring into line the various medical and health professionals, Law No. 6 of 2000 was gazetted on 31 January 2000. This deals with physicians, dentists, pharmacists and other medical and health-related services.

Jordan

*Hamzeh Haddad**

1 JUDICIAL AND LEGAL SYSTEM

No major legislative changes have occurred under this title.

2 CONSTITUTIONAL AND ADMINISTRATIVE LAW

No major legislative changes have occurred, but reference may be made to the following cases of interest.

2.1 High Court of Justice, Decision No. 464/97[1]

The court concludes that whenever a dispute relates to a contract to which the (public) administration is a party, the jurisdiction lies in civil courts not in this Court.

2.2 High Court of Justice, Decision No. 256/98[2]

According to this decision, the possibility of challenging administrative decisions is confined to situations mentioned in the law of this Court No. 12/1992, and a challenge to the election of political parties does not fall within this law. Therefore, the Court has no competence over such a challenge.

---

[*] Professor of Law; Attorney at Law; main owner and managing partner of the Law and Arbitration Centre (LAC) in Jordan.
[1] Bar Association Journal (BAJ), 2000, p. 155.
[2] *Ibid.*, p. 150.

3   CIVIL LAW

No legislative changes have occurred under this title, but an interesting case is reported in BAJ relating to this subject.

3.1   Civil Court of Cassation, Decision No. 153/99[3]

A joint venture is regarded as a legal entity separate from the parties composing it.

4   CIVIL PROCEDURE AND EVIDENCE

No legislative changes have occurred under this title, but some interesting cases are reported in BAJ relating to evidence.

4.1   Civil Court of Cassation, Decision No. 1776/98[4]

A party's admission that a message via facsimile was issued by him leads to the fact that the message would be considered as good evidence against that party though such a message may not be regarded as evidence in writing according to traditional thought.

4.2   Civil Court of Cassation, Decision No. 2553/98[5]

It is permissible by law to raise a civil case against the government of Jordan in a jurisdiction other than this country (Jordan). Therefore, if a dispute to which the government is a party relates to real estate located in the West Bank, Jordanian courts have no jurisdiction over such a dispute but only the courts of the West Bank. This is due to the general principles of jurisdiction in Jordan whereby the competent court at the place at which real estate is located has jurisdiction in disputes relating to such real estate.

5   COMMERCIAL LAW

No legislative changes have occurred to the Commercial Code No. 12/66.

5.1   Arbitration

5.1.1   *Civil Court of Cassation, Decision No. 948/98[6]*

A clause in an arbitration agreement that the award will be final and definitive in the sense that it will not be subject to be challenged, is null and void though the arbitration agreement in itself remains valid and operative.

---

3   *Ibid.*, p. 382.
4   *Ibid.*, p. 312.
5   *Ibid.*, p. 358.
6   BAJ, 1999, p. 1880.

5.1.2   Civil Court of Cassation, Decision No. 1980/98[7]

An arbitrator is like a judge in the sense that he may not be brought before the court for examination in respect of the arbitral award rendered by him/her.

5.1.3   Civil Court of Cassation, Decision No. 2285/98[8]

According to Article 20 of the Agents and Mediators Act No. 44/1985, Jordanian courts have exclusive jurisdiction over a dispute between a Jordanian agent and his principal abroad in spite of any agreement to the contrary. However, the application of this provision is limited to a commercial agency relationship. Therefore, while an arbitration agreement concerning such relationship is null and void, it is considered valid when the matter relates to a distribution contract, which is different from an agency one.

5.2   Banking

5.2.1   Civil Court of Cassation, Decision No. 1776/98[9]

A bank guarantee (a bond) is an undertaking issued by a bank to the beneficiary upon an order given to it by its client. Such a bond is separate and independent from any legal relationship between that client and beneficiary. Therefore, a bank is bound to pay the amount of bond to the beneficiary without reference to any matter falling outside the scope of the terms and provisions of the bond.

5.3   Insurance

The Insurance Works Control Act (the Act) abolishing Law No. 30/84 has been issued under No. 33/99. Some of the main provisions under the Act are referred to in the following paragraphs.

Insurance policies are divided into life insurance and general insurances.

The Act has created a new official entity called the Corporation for Organization of the Insurance Sector; its purpose is to supervise and control the insurance works, including the protection of insured people and their beneficiaries, as well as the improvement of the performance of the insurance companies.

It is not permitted to obtain a policy from outside Jordan covering the liability of a third party in Jordan, or to cover any assets in Jordan.

While an insurance company operating in Jordan is not permitted to have

---

[7]   *Ibid.*, p. 2323.
[8]   *Ibid.*, p. 3119.
[9]   BAJ, 2000, p. 312.

reinsurance policy outside Jordan, to cover its labourers, such a company may reinsure any other matter abroad.

6   LABOUR LAW

No legislative changes or developments have occurred under this title.

7   PROPERTY LAW

No legislative changes or developments have occurred under this title.

8   INTELLECTUAL PROPERTY

The following legislative changes have occurred under this title.

Jordan has adhered to the Berne Convention for the Protection of Literary and Artistic Works of 1971 as was amended in 1979.[10] The Law of Copyright Protection No. 29 amending the Law No. 22/92 was enacted in 1999. The Law of Patents No. 32/99 was enacted in 1999. The Law of Trade-Marks No. 34/99 amending the law No. 33/52 was enacted in 1999. The Law of Layout – Designs of Integrated Circuits No. 10/2000, was enacted in 2000. The Law of Industrial Designs and Models No. 14/2000, was enacted in 2000. The Law of Unfair Competition and Trade Secrets No. 15/2000 was enacted in 2000.

9   FAMILY LAW AND SUCCESSION

No legislative changes or developments have taken place under this title.

10   CRIMINAL LAW AND PROCEDURE

No legislative changes or judicial decisions of particular interest have taken place under this title.

11   PUBLIC INTERNATIONAL LAW

The government of Jordan signed in 1999 and 2000 several bilateral conventions with other governments relating, *inter alia*, to transport by air (Iran), tourism (Algeria and Yemen), encouragement of investments (Romania),

---

[10]   Official Gazette, 1999, p. 1585.

judicial assistance (Tunisia and the United Arab Emirates) and double taxa-tion (India and Canada). In addition, as has been mentioned under the heading of intellectual property, the government of Jordan has adhered to the Berne Convention. One of the most important events relating to this title is the adherence of Jordan to the World Trade Organization Treaty, by Law No. 4/2000.

12   PRIVATE INTERNATIONAL LAW

No changes or developments have occurred under this title (see, however, Civil Court of Cassation, Decision No. 2553/98, above in section 4, and Decision No. 2285/98, above in section 5).

13   TAXATION

A new law amending the Sales Tax Law No. 6/94 has been issued under No. 24/99. The most important provision under the new law is the increase of the general tax percentage from 10 per cent to 13 per cent on all local and imported products as well as on services.

14   PRINTING AND PUBLICATIONS

A new law on printing and publications amending the Law No. 8/98 has been promulgated under Law No. 30/99. The new law has made some amendments to the original law, two of which are of particular interest.

A journalist has the right to obtain the necessary information from any governmental body, and all official entities are bound to facilitate his mission. A publication may publish the minutes of courts and cover the hearings unless the relevant court decides otherwise.

Palestine

*Anis Al-Qasem**

1 CONSTITUTIONAL LAW

The draft Basic Law for the Interim Period, which was passed by the Legislative Council on 2 October 1997, has not yet been promulgated by the President, and the constitutional status has remained unchanged.

The Central Council of the PLO, which met on 27 April 1999, had already decided to ask for the help of the Secretary General of the Arab League in drafting a constitution in anticipation of a possible declaration of the state of Palestine by mid-September 2000 (the date on which the final status talks between the Palestinians and Israelis are scheduled to end).[1] A Palestinian constitutional committee was established under the chairmanship of Dr Nabil Shaath, the Minister for International Development. Dr Shaath reported to the Central Council at its meeting of August 1999, and the Council repeated its request for the finalization of the draft constitution.

At the meeting of the Central Council held on 2–5 July 2000 Dr Shaath presented a first draft for a Constitution for Palestine drafted by the Committee. He reported to the Central Council that it would be subject to wide consultation in the West Bank, Gaza and the Palestinian diaspora.

The following laws have been passed by the Legislative Council and promulgated by the President:

(a)   Law No. 12 of 1998 on Public Meetings;
(b)   Law No. 1 of 1999 on Natural Resources;
(c)   Law No. 2 of 1999 on Civil Status;

---

*   Barrister, Consultant on the Laws of the Middle East (London), former Chairman of the Legal Committee of the Palestinian National Council (PNC).
[1]   The Central Council of the PLO has now postponed the Declaration of a state at least until 15 November 2000 pending intensive negotiations with Israel. This followed failure of the Washington talks under the mediation of President Clinton early in August.

(d)   Law No. 3 of 1999 on Organization of the Legal Profession;
(e)   Law No. 4 of 1999 on the Rights of the Disabled;
(f)   Law No. 7 on the Environment;
(g)   Law No. 8 on Government Tenders for Public Works;
(h)   Law No. 3 (sic) Amending the Legal Profession Law;
(i)   Law No. 1 of 2000 on Non-Governmental Organizations;
(j)   Law No. 2 of 2000 on the Organization of the Activities of Commercial Agent.

Of special interest is Law No. 12 of 1999 on Public Meetings. This law provides that citizens shall have the right freely to hold public meetings and demonstrations, which may not be subject to any restrictions other than those set out in the law (Article 1). The organizers of the meeting or demonstration are required by Articles 3 and 4 to give notice of the meeting or demonstration to the district governor or head of the police at least forty-eight hours before the meeting or demonstration. The notice should specify the date, place and object of the meeting or demonstration. Without prejudice to the right of assembly, the district governor or head of police may, "for the purpose of organizing traffic", determine criteria for the duration and route of the assembly, provided the organizers are informed in writing within twenty-four hours from the time of receipt of the notice. If no reply is received, the assembly may take place in the manner set out in the notice. Under Article 5, the appropriate authorities, at the request of the organizations, should take such measures as may be necessary for the protection of the assembly, provided that such measures shall not interfere with the freedom of participants or the progress of the assembly.

This is encouraging legislation. No permission or authorization is required. The role of the police is limited to routeing in order to organize flow of traffic and the provision of protection, at the request of the organizers.

The second law of interest to those engaged in human rights activities is the Law on Non-Governmental Organizations. Under Article 1 of this law, "Palestinians shall have the right freely to carry out social, cultural, professional and scientific activities, including the formation of non-governmental bodies and societies in accordance with the provisions of this Law." The establishment of non-governmental organizations is made subject to a registration, not licensing or authorization, system. Application for registration is made to the Ministry of the Interior. The Ministry has two months to study the application and determine whether it meets registration requirements as set out in the law. If no decision is notified to the founders within the period of two months, the organization will be deemed registered by force of law. If the application is rejected, the reasons for rejection should be stated, and the founders may challenge this decision before a court of law within thirty days of notification of the rejection.

The organization must keep accurate financial records and the Ministry may follow the activities of these organizations to ensure that funds are spent for the purposes of the organization in accordance with the law and founding documents of the organization.

Non-Palestinian NGOs may apply to establish branches in Palestine.

These two laws are steps in the right direction in the exercise of the right of assembly and civic responsibility.

The process of unification and modernization of basic legislation has been started. Under a project financed by the British Department of International Development (DFID), four commissions have been established to prepare a civil code, a penal code, a commercial code and specialized legislation. To assist the commissions in their work, DFID has provided two international consultants, this author and Judge Eugene Cotran, to review the drafts while the work is in progress. The civil and penal codes commissions are approaching finalization of their work, while the commercial code commission has just started.

A Code of Civil Procedure and another on Penal Procedure have already been completed in draft form and are before the Legislative Council.

An Arbitration Law has been passed but is awaiting promulgation.

In conclusion, one must say that the legislative process is advancing. However, apparently a legislative policy is lacking and the priorities are not always in their proper place. This is to be expected. Nevertheless, one notes greater maturity of approach and a lessening of tension in the legislative process between the Legislative Council and the Executive.

2 THE JUDICIARY

The Judicial Authority Law, which was passed by the Legislative Council, was returned by the President for reconsideration of one provision. The draft, as passed by the Council, required approval of the Council for the appointment to the office of Attorney General. The President objected, and the Council reconsidered the matter and approved the necessary amendment. However, to date the President has not promulgated this law.

The Legislative Council is now debating a draft law on the formation of courts, which seems to have been a condition for the promulgation of the Judiciary Authority Law. Normally, this type of legislation is subsidiary to and dependent upon the judicial authority law. However, very few things are normal in the Palestinian situation.

Another anomaly is that the President has appointed a Higher Judicial Council under the new Judicial Authority Law, which has not been promulgated!
The judiciary is still struggling to assert its full independence in running its own affairs.

3 PUBLICATIONS

In addition to the Official Gazette, the Ministry of Justice (*Diwan Al Fatwa Wa al Tashri*) has published an experimental Issue No. 0 April 2000 of its *Journal of Law & Judiciary*. This experimental issue has five articles, one document, one law, two court judgments, legal news and a short biography of a former chief justice of Gaza.

The five articles deal with (a) domicile in Palestine, (b) the rules on search in Palestine, (c) Israeli settlement and deportation policy, (d) the art of setting up the grounds for and drafting of judgments, and (e) values and traditions of the judiciary.

The document published in this issue is the Basic Agreement between the PLO and the Vatican of 15 February 2000. The law published is Law No. 1 of 2000 on Non-Governmental Organizations.

The two judgments are one by the High Court of Ramallah and the second in a civil action by the Court of Appeal. The judgment of the High Court is of particular interest because of the parties involved and the grounds of the decision. The action was brought by a headmistress against the Council of Ministers and the Minister of Education. The claimant was placed on pension by decision of the Council of Ministers in pursuance of the Civil Pensions Law of 1953 which gave the Council the power to place on pension any official who had completed fifteen years of pensionable service. The claimant had completed the fifteen years, but alleged that the challenged decision gave no reasons for taking it, was an abuse of power by the Council of Ministers and that it had violated the rights of the claimant and the public interest.

The Court held that although the law did not specifically require the Council of Ministers to give reasons, this requirement was essential in order to determine whether the decision had been taken in the public interest or was for other motives. The discretionary power given to the Council of Ministers had to be exercised for the purpose of serving both public interest and the interest of the official. The exercise of discretionary powers was subject to the rule of legality and must fall within the bounds of legality and the reasons for which the power was given. The Court annulled the challenged decision.

Lebanon

*Nayla Comair-Obeid**

For Lebanon, 1999–2000 was a year when political developments followed each other at an ever-increasing pace, both on the internal and the regional scenes. The Israeli air attacks, which three times destroyed electric power installations and so held up economic recovery, finally ended with the withdrawal on 24 May 2000 of the Israeli Army, the Tsahal, whose departure had originally been anticipated in July. However, as far as Lebanon is concerned, a definitive peace can be reached only within the framework of a global regional settlement. Economic recession has made itself felt in the form of a slowing down of investment in vital sectors in the country, particularly industry, construction, hotel bookings and tourism. However, thanks to the prudent policy of the Bank of Lebanon, the Lebanese pound has remained steady; the dollar continuing to be exchanged at L£1,500, as in 1998 and 1999.

The fight against corruption has followed its course with a healthier administration as a consequence; ministers, Members of Parliament and high officials have been called to account, sanctioned for their bad management and ill-gotten gains, and charged before the courts. On the initiative of the President of the Republic, Parliament has adopted a law against illicit profit-making, with some amendments.

Other important laws have been passed, in particular one modifying the electoral law applicable to the parliamentary election of July 2000. Others making modifications to the Code of Penal Procedure, the Lebanese Code of Commerce and the Labour Code are still under consideration. We shall give details below of the laws promulgated and published in the Official Gazette, as well as of the decrees of principle concerning the civil, commercial and administrative domains. We shall also present three decisions of principle handed down by the Constitutional Council.

---

*   Doctor of Laws, Professor of Law at the Lebanese University and Attorney, Beirut Bar.

1 CONSTITUTIONAL AND ADMINISTRATIVE LAW

1.1 Parliamentary elections

A law amending the law on the election of Members of Parliament was promulgated.

The new law redrew the boundaries of the constituencies as follows:

(a) three constituencies in the city of Beirut, each including a certain number of quarters;

(b) four constituencies in the Mount Lebanon Mohafazat, each of them including one or more *cazas*: the first constituency includes the two *cazas* of Jbeil and Kesrouan, the second constituency the *caza* of Metn, the third the two *cazas* of Aley and Ba'abda and the fourth the *caza* of the Shouf;

(c) two constituencies in the north, including several *cazas* and localities as follows: Bsharri, the first constituency, includes Akkar and Denniyeh and the second constituency includes Tripoli, Al-Menieh and Zgharta;

(d) two constituencies in the south, with the first including the *cazas* and localities of the cities of Saida, Zahrani, Tyre and Bint Jbeil, and the second including the *cazas* of Marjeyoun, Hasbaya, Nabatiyeh and Jezzine;

(e) three constituencies in the Bekaa, the first including the *cazas* of Baalbek and Hermel, the second the *caza* of Zahleh and the third including the *cazas* of West Bekaa and Rashaya.

The number of seats in each constituency is fixed according to a table annexed to the law, as well as the number of deputies of each religious community in each region or *caza* within each constituency. Candidature for parliamentary seats is determined according to the table annexed to the law.

All voters within a constituency, of whatever religion, must vote for the candidates of that constituency.

No modification has been made to the conditions required for the right to stand for election or to vote, in particular to the age requirements for voting (twenty-one years of age) and for candidature (twenty-five years of age), to the method of voting (which must be general, secret and direct), or to the procedure of the elections.

1.2 Administrative law

A law was promulgated with the intention of modifying some articles of the Council of State statutes and notably creating regional administrative courts beside the Council of State as a Supreme Court.

The new law created regional administrative courts headed by a Supreme Court, the Council of State, located in Beirut, whereas the previous law regulating the Council of State statutes vested the sole Council of State with the attributions of the administrative judiciary power (Article 1).

The Council of State is composed of a president, commissioner of the government, and of Court Chambers presidents, counsel and assistant counsel, while administrative courts are composed of presidents and counsel, at first instance, whose judgments are rendered by a president and two members for each court.

The jurisdiction of the regional administrative court was initially fixed by the law according to nine rules, ranging from the petitioner's domicile, the location of immovables or movables, the place of contract enforcement, the place of conclusion of the contract, the location of the prejudicial action, the location of the board of directors of public and private establishments, concluding with the seat of the authority which undertook the administrative action. The choice of the above rules will depend on the nature of the dispute before these courts.

The new law classified the recently created courts as common courts for administrative issues, while it rendered the Council of the State the competent appeal authority to look into all the judgments rendered by the administrative courts, and as competent appeal and cassation authority to settle administrative cases for which the law fixed a special court, and as a first and last resort court for certain cases (Article 60).

Litigation that the Council of State settles at first and last instance was exclusively fixed by the law as follows:

(a)   petitions in annulment of executive and individual decrees and regulatory actions emanating from ministers, for misuse of power;
(b)   cases of employees appointed by decrees;
(c)   reviews regarding administrative decrees whose implementation lies outside the district jurisdiction of an administrative court;
(d)   claims for information or for the assessment of the validity of an administrative decision.

For the present, we are waiting to see when the first instance courts begin their functions, following the Minister of Justice's decree after the approval of the Council of State board, fixing the time when these courts will come into existence, their number, their location and the number of judges in each chamber (Article 34).

1.3   Constitutional Council

The Sheikh Akl, supreme religious authority of the Druze community, filed a case before the Constitutional Council to invalidate the law relating to the constitution of a board of trustees for the *waqfs* of the Druze community for its violation of the Constitution, claiming that this law removes the community's *waqfs* from the control of the religious authority and substitutes for it a non-religious authority, breaching provisions of Article 9 of the Constitution and Article 2 of the law establishing the Religious Council of the Druze religious community published on 13 July 1962. Both articles nominate the Druze religious chief as a complete independent supervisor and administrator of this community's charity *waqfs* independently of the political authority.

On the basis of the above pleadings, the Constitutional Council rendered its judgment stipulating that Article 9 of the Constitution implies the state's neutral position towards religions and recognizes their autonomy over the administration of their religious affairs and interests. When the legislator enacts a law regulating fundamental rights and liberties, he cannot modify or abrogate the statutes in force guaranteeing these liberties without substituting for them more advantageous or at least equal status in terms of efficiency and guarantee.

The contested law had created a board of trustees for the *waqfs* of the Druze community and entrusted this board with the administration of these *waqfs* within a regulatory framework, showing the extent and the limits of these attributions and submitting this board, its members and its activities, to very strict control from the Religious Council, and its decisions to a prior approval of the Council (Article 122 of Law No. 127(99), thus constituting real guarantees for the autonomous administration by the Druze community of its own affairs, especially those relating to the *waqfs*.

Nevertheless, the Constitutional Council pointed out that Article 11 of the contested law (produced within the interim provisions) exceptionally transgressed the principle of the election of the Board of Trustees (Article 3 of the contested law), by stipulating the designation of the first board of trustees by the Council of Ministers for a period of five years (for a mandate equivalent to that of the regular board of Trustees). By so stipulating Article 11 of the contested law deprived this article of its interim and temporary quality, by adopting the designation of the first Council for a period of five years, thus breaching the principle of the autonomy of the Druze community, guaranteed by the Constitution.

The Constitutional Council ruled equally that Article 12 of the contested law (within the interim provision), by granting a choice – the possibility of either designation or elections of the Religious Council for the Druze community – breached the principle of election laid down by the law dated 13 July 1962, prime guarantee of the autonomy of the Druze community consecrated by the Constitution (Article 9).

The Constitutional Council ended its decision as follows:

(a)   consider the following words "for a five year period" mentioned in Article 11 of Law No. 127/99 as unconstitutional, and consequently null and void;
(b)   consider the word "designation" mentioned in Article 12 of Law 127/99 as unconstitutional and therefore null and void;
(c)   consider Law 127/99 as constitutional except for the above-mentioned words.

2 COMPANY AND COMMERCIAL LAW

2.1 Promulgation of the law bearing on the constitution of a joint stock company named "The Arab Corporation for Financial Compensation"

The above-mentioned company will undertake the operation of compensation and regularization of stocks between Arab financial markets or between these and the international financial markets. Its head office will be in Beirut. The corporation will act as an Arab Central Chamber of Compensation dedicated to undertaking the following tasks and operations:

(a) compensation operations between Arab markets and other financial markets;
(b) operations of financial transfer and monetary regularization;
(c) opening of accounts for the purpose of investing in deeds and various other financial securities;
(d) accepting the deposit of deeds and various financial securities negotiated in Arab markets;
(e) supporting the constitution of chambers of compensation in the Arab markets and developing those already existing;
(f) organizing the issue of financial deeds and various financial securities, their promotion, and subscription thereto;
(g) representation of Arab compensation organizations in their dealings with international compensation organizations;
(h) coordination between the Arab compensation organizations to assist them in performing their tasks locally and abroad;
(i) assisting in the introduction of issues between the Arab financial markets, the administration of operations resulting from these issues and the participation in any company or enterprise performing similar tasks;
(j) operations of deeds and financial securities lending;
(k) fiduciary operations in the capacity of fiduciary acting to the benefit of the company's shareholders, in conformity with the grounds and rules of the laws in force;
(l) acting as a deposit centre for GDR issues.

The corporation may carry out any kind of operation complementary to its object specified above.

Members of the Arab Stock Exchange Union will enjoy priority for participating in and subscribing to the company's capital.

Notwithstanding the provisions of Article 144 of the Code of Commerce, the majority of the members of the company's board of directors may be of non-Lebanese nationality.

The following entities, enumerated for information but not restrictively, will act as the founders of the company:

(a) the Beirut Stock Exchange;
(b) Midclear SAL;

(c)   the Stock Exchange Union and organizations of the Arab Financial Markets;
(d)   the Kuwaiti Market for Transferable Stocks;
(e)   the Company of Egypt for Central Compensation, Regularization and Guardianship;
(f)   the Kuwaiti Company for Compensation.

The corporation shall be exempt from constitution duties and registration taxes in the Companies' Commercial Register and from all kinds of taxes and duties whatsoever for a period of ten years as from the date of its establishment.

The corporation is bound by the provisions of this law, by those of the Lebanese Code of Commerce that do not conflict with it, and by the law on banking secrecy as well as by all other texts of Lebanese legislation.

2.2   Licence to import oil

The Council of State rendered a judgment invalidating a decree of the Minister of Petroleum by virtue of which he refused to deliver a licence to a private company to import fuel oil and restricted the importation of fuel to the Ministry exclusively.

The Council of State considered in its judgment that state fuel policy, in accordance with Article 27 of Decree No. 6821 dated 28 December 1973, is established on an immutable basis linked to the public order, that is to say the national economic interest, public security and safety, national defence requirements and international commitments.

European legislation clearly rejects the idea of a monopoly that leads to the realization of a mere commercial bargain. Article 27 provides that the state fuel policy consists in a regulatory function performed to meet various considerations, conflicting situations and fluctuating elements, because fixing the sale price of liquid fuel oil is linked to what is called "the market mechanism". The various kinds of hydrocarbons include without distinction their importation, stocking and distribution according to the standards and specifications set forth by multinational organizations. The core objects of state fuel policy thus have a threefold basis: first, the strategic and economic importance of oil, second, the investment of funds and third, the measures and standards adopted for the trade of fuel (importation, stocking, distribution).

Considering the facts pertaining to this case, the Council of State ascertained that the contested decree was issued for motives having no relation whatsoever to the public interest and not matching the core objectives of the state's fuel policy as described above.

In any case, even if the contested decree had been issued in the public interest, its preamble reveals that it went beyond the framework fixed by the law, which lacked provisions restricting the importation of liquid fuel into the state, thus making the import licences granted to private companies alone useless.

The general principles of law allow an administrative judge to stop an administrative action in the economic field when it is misused and arbitrary.

The Council of State concluded by considering that the contested decree violated the law and the general principles as an abuse of administrative action, and should therefore be annulled.

Although this judgment could be seen as part of the continuing and stable string of judgments dealing with established principles, it diverges from that line with regard to the control of the Council of State on the legality of an administrative action relating to one of the most important economic sectors in the country, i.e. the fuel sector. No monopoly can be granted except by virtue of a law and for a limited period of time; the judgment considers that should exclusivity exist and the monopoly be allowed, that import licences granted to private companies by virtue of the law would be valueless.

3   LABOUR AND SOCIAL SECURITY

3.1   Promulgation of the law stipulating the grant of food assistance and work clothing allowances to employees and wage-earners affiliated to social security

By virtue of this law, employers are bound to assist employees and wage-earners affiliated to social security by granting them, in kind, food assistance and work clothing allowances within the limits of specified amounts (food assistance or a meal ticket at a restaurant or a grocer's to a value of L£ 5,000 for each wage-earner per effective working day and an annual work clothing allowance of a value equal to the official minimum monthly wage). These benefits in kind are not subject to income tax, and should not be considered as revenue items liable to be included in payments to the National Social Security Fund.

Nevertheless, these provisions will be annulled if the meal ticket, food assistance and work clothing allowances are replaced by a monetary allowance, which will necessarily lead to these allowances being considered as supplements to wages, subject to income tax, and thus taken into account in calculating Social Security Fund contributions.

3.2   Illicit Enrichment Law

A law on illicit enrichment applicable to any employee, official of a public service, judge or any of their accomplices in enrichment was promulgated. This law defines three types of illicit enrichment:

(a)   enrichment by an employee, civil servant, judge, any accomplice to them in enrichment, or any persons who shall lend their name, by accepting bribes, exploiting the influence, position or work they are entrusted with (Articles 351–66 of the Penal Code), or any illicit means, even when these means do not constitute a penal offence;

(b) enrichment by an employee, a civil servant, a judge or any other moral or physical person, whether by appropriation or by obtaining an export–import licence, or any other profit of whatever kind, if obtained in breach of the law;

(c) obtaining or abusing contracting terms, privileges and licences granted by a civil servant with a view to realizing an illegal profit.

This law also specifies, for the application of its provisions, what is meant by the word "employee": that is to say, any civil servant, contractual dealer, servant or wage-earner, permanent or temporary, in whatever cadre or corps, of any grade or degree, in ministries or public services or departments of the Ministry of Defence or in public institutions, including chairmen of the boards in autonomous services, municipalities or municipal unions, as well as any officer or person in the military, security or customs services.

The following are considered as performing a public service: the President of the Republic, the Speaker of Parliament, the President of the Council of Ministers, Members of Parliament, heads and members of municipal councils, municipal unions, *mukhtars* (officials locally elected as official witnesses), public notaries, members of administrative committees whose work has financial consequences, representatives of the state in mixed economy companies, and executives of public services or companies serving the public interest.

Members of the Constitutional Council, the judiciary, administrative and financial judges, and the members of any judicial panel considered as part of the state organizations are all considered as judges.

The law does not stipulate that the illicit enrichment should occur directly or immediately but it may also result from the profit intended to be derived from future projects.

The law imposes on the employees covered by its provisions the duty to declare the their wealth (movable and real estate) as well as their spouse's and minor children's belongings, within one month of their assuming office, and within three months if the employee was in office before the entry into force of the present law.

The legislator did not include the teaching staff of the Lebanese University and of public schools.

Although these declarations are confidential and kept, upon their deposition before the competent authorities, at the Bank of Lebanon, the competent judicial authority may refer to these declarations in the event of a prosecution. The penalty for non-declaration of assets, pursuant to the regulations set down in this law, is for the civil servant, the judge, the employee or the member of the board to be considered as having resigned. The declaration of assets by the President of the Republic, the Speaker of the Parliament, the Prime Minister and ministers is one of the conditions laid down for their appointment to public office.

Finally, the law lays down rules for prosecution and investigation in cases of illicit enrichment according to which any prejudiced party has the right to present a written and signed complaint either to the Public Prosecutor or directly to the investigating judge of first instance in Beirut and to pay the banking warranty indicated. If it is decided to stay the introduction of proceedings or to abandon the prosecution of the accused, the competent authority may decide to fine the ill-intentioned accuser a sum of L£200 million at least and sentence him to between three-months and one-year imprisonment, with payment of damages to the prejudiced person if the latter so demands. The law empowers the Beirut Penal Courts of Appeal, acting as first degree of jurisdiction, to decide on cases of illicit enrichment, with the proviso that their judgments may be appealed against before the Court of Cassation.

4 COMMUNICATIONS

4.1 Law No. 140/99

The Constitutional Council rendered a judgment invalidating three articles of the Law No. 140/99 on the preservation of the right of secrecy of communications operated by any means of communication. It is to be noted that the law regulates wiretapping or the interception of communications operated on any wired or wireless means and fixes the conditions for allowing tapping and interception in cases on the basis of a judicial or administrative decision.

Following a petition filed by ten Members of Parliament to suspend the law, and declare the total or partial invalidation of Articles 15 and 16 of Law No. 140/99 due to their violation of the Constitution, especially the principle of equality before the law, and the principle of separation of powers, the Constitutional Council rendered its judgment allowing the petition in its form and on its merits; it also decided, on its own initiative, to invalidate Article 8 of the same law, for being unconstitutional by application of the Council's jurisprudence, deciding that the Council has full competence to exercise its control on all and every text of law by the mere fact that a petition has been regularly filed before the Council without this latter being in any way bound by the petitioner's submissions.

The Council based its judgment on the following grounds.

Article 15 of the contested law forbids the interception of communications made by presidents, Members of Parliament, or ministers, whether operated either on the grounds of a judgment, or on the grounds of an administrative decision. The Constitutional Council, first, distinguished between the interception of communications operated by virtue of a judgment or by virtue of an administrative decision. The Council then distinguished between the President of the Republic and the other presidents, ministers or Members of Parliament, and considered in its judgment that the principle of equality before the law is one of the general principles having its roots in the Constitution itself (the preamble and Article 7), which should result in an equal application of the law to everybody, whether the law protects or imposes restrictions. However, this principle is not absolute, and the legislator may allow an exception and discriminate between citizens if this discrimination proceeds from the Constitution, or if citizens are in a different legal situation, or if the public interest so requires, as long as this discrimination is in accordance with the aim of the law.

The Constitutional Council ruled that, if the interception was operated by virtue of a judgment, the discrimination between the Speaker of Parliament, the Prime Minister, Members of the Parliament, or the ministers, on the one hand, and citizens on the other hand, was not justified either by a public interest or by a constitutional disposition, such as that included in Articles 39 and 40 related to parliamentary immunity.

The situation is different regarding the President of the Republic, this latter person being expressly included in Article 60 of the Constitution, whereby the President can only be indicted by Parliament, and then prosecuted before the Higher Council for Presidential Impeachment, and cannot thus be criminally prosecuted by the Public Prosecutor or by an investigating judge; his communications cannot therefore be submitted, in any way, to interception or wiretapping.

However, if tapping is effected by virtue of a judgment, confirmed guarantees for the preservation of public liberties, whether of citizens or officials, are satisfied, due to the fact that tapping has been entrusted to a judicial power, guardian of the constitutional rights. But it is to be practised only in the case of extreme emergency and it is therefore not permitted in this case to discriminate between citizens and officials, the President of the Republic excepted.

The situation is different if tapping is allowed by an administrative decision emanating from an administrative authority, because there is no guarantee against an abuse of power, and because entrusting to a minister, who is an administrative authority, the attribution to control another similar or higher administrative authority, is not feasible.

It follows that discrimination between citizens, on one hand, Parliament, the President, the Prime Minister, Members of Parliament and the ministers on the other hand, is justified if based on an administrative decision.

The Constitutional Council ended by invalidating the whole Article 15 of Law No. 140/99, since it was worded in absolute terms and did not distinguish between wiretapping by virtue of a judgment and wiretapping allowed by an administrative decision.

4.2 Article 16

According to Article 16 of the contested law Members of Parliament participated in the constitution of an independent board to which was entrusted the verification of the legality of the measures related to the interception of communication and taken in conformity with an administrative decision. The Constitutional Council decreed that the disposition of the Constitution preamble paragraph H, which is an integral part of the Constitution and has a constitutional authority equivalent to that of Constitution clauses, corroborates the principle of separation of powers, the balance of powers and their cooperation in such a way that each power should have jurisdiction within the field reserved by the Constitution and not trespass on the jurisdiction of other powers.

However, the participation of Members of Parliament in the constitution of the independent board entrusted with the task of verification of the legality of the measures connected to the interception of communications taken in conformity with an administrative decision, constituted a trespass by the deputies on the field of action of the executive power, and took Members of Parliament out of the sphere of the powers and functions fixed by the Constitution.

Although Parliament is entrusted with the functions of general control over the government's performance, it is not permitted to exercise these powers except within the frame and the limits fixed by the Constitution and the status of Parliament.

On these grounds, the Constitutional Council decreed the invalidation of all the dispositions of Article 16 of the Law No. 140/99, for breaching the Constitution and general principles having a constitutional authority, especially the principle of separation of powers.

4.3 Article 8

Article 8 of the contested law permits the interception of communications of barristers under two conditions: the first is that the President of the Bar should be informed, the second is to certify that the barrister committed, or was an accomplice in a tort or in a crime.

Concerning the first condition (informing the President of the Bar prior to the interception decision), the Constitutional Council decreed that this article discriminates between lawyers and other persons without any motive deriving from the Constitution or from public interest or from barristers being in situations and legal positions different from other citizens.

Moreover, this law discriminates between barristers and persons of other professions regulated by a law whose charter granted the same immunities and guarantees enjoyed by lawyers by virtue of Charter No. 8/70, which cannot be taken as an argument to justify this discrimination, since it is not based on a law of exception in the Constitution, especially since wiretapping does not relate to barristers' personality as lawyers but their quality as citizens.

The Constitutional Council decreed, with regards to the second condition (ascertaining that the concerned lawyer committed, or was an accomplice in, a tort or a crime prior to the interception decision) that the text of the law fails in its purpose since the aim of the wiretapping is to ascertain the occurrence of the criminal act. There will be no reason for wiretapping if this has been ascertained prior to the interception decision.

In conclusion, the Council of the State ruled the total invalidity of Article 8 of Law No. 140/99 for being unconstitutional, and especially breaching the principle of equality before the law.

5 CIVIL LAW

The Fifth Chamber of the Lebanese Court of Cassation rendered a judgment partially confirming the judgment of the Appeal Court of Beirut 17 February

1997 and stipulating that the Court was not competent to adjudicate the case. The Supreme Court ruling was founded on Article 102 of the Civil Proceedings Code that gave the suitor an option, in disputes arising from a tort or offence, of bringing an action before the Court having jurisdiction at the appellant's place of residence, or of suing the tortfeasor in damages before the Court having jurisdiction at the place where the prejudicial action arose, or the Court where the prejudice liable for damages arose.

The Court of Cassation considered that this option, based on Article 102 above, was practically limited to two competences:

(a) the first was the competence of the court of the appellant's place of residence, which is the application of the general rule provided for in Article 97 of the Civil Proceedings Code;
(b) the second is the competence of the court having jurisdiction at the place where the prejudicial action occurred, as stipulated in Article 102.

The Court of Cassation established its analysis on the ground of the impossibility of separating the prejudicial action and the place where the action occurred, except in very rare cases.

Consequently, the Court of Cassation restricted the competence relating to the criminal act and offence to the court within whose jurisdiction the action arose, because the competence of the court of the place of residence of the appellant does not need a special mention, given the text of Article 97.

What makes this judgment interesting is that it enjoined the court which is competent to examine the cases of tort and offence with the law that applies to the merits of the conflict, which is the law of torts, because the law is applicable in the place where the prejudicial action arose.

This judgment of the Court of Cassation has three positive aspects:

(a) The first one is that the place of occurrence of the prejudicial action is the only objective and neutral element within the legal relation. There could be a discrepancy between the tortfeasor's nationality and the prejudiced person's and between the place of residence and the place of the prejudicial occurrence. Giving competence to the court in the place where the prejudicial action arose avoids giving preference to either party in the legal relation, because the place where the prejudicial action arose is an objective element not related to the nationality of the tortfeasor or that of the prejudiced person, or to the place of residence or to the means which caused the damage. Moreover, the place of the occurrence of the prejudicial action is fixed and connected to a determined place, which is easy to prove, making the proof easier.
(b) The second positive aspect is that, by setting down the prior determination of the law that the parties should observe, it reconciles their various interests.
(c) The third positive aspect is that it balances the parties' rights in their legal relationship.

6 INTERNATIONAL PRIVATE LAW

The Eighth Chamber of the Court of Cassation rendered a judgment, dated 28 May 1998, stipulating that juridical logic requires the enforcement of the principle of referral in inheritance and will issues, except that the principle should be enforced without breaching the fundamentals of foreign law, and especially respect for the mutual sovereignty and public order of the foreign country.

In the above judgment "the Court of Cassation considered that the foreign rule of conflict, by adopting referral to the law of the location of real estate (namely Lebanese law), implied that public law was applicable to all citizens and not the law applicable to a particular religion". In the Lebanon this implies the principle of referral in principle and its rejection in practice, due to the impossibility of selecting a Lebanese law governing inheritance and will issues among the numerous confessional laws, that is to say because of the non-existence of a unified law applicable to all religious communities.

The Court of Cassation had rendered a recent judgment whereby the Court totally failed to bring a rule to the conflict disputed in the case concerning the validity of a will made in Lebanon, the testator being an American national.

The Court of Cassation decided to confirm the outcome of the contested first instance judgment, i.e. the submission of the will drawn up according to Lebanese law, without having to refer to the principle of the referral, without even using this principle, which was one of the principal grounds for cassation, since the contestor did not report the objective, mandatory rules in the US laws which were violated, or at least did not show causes of forfeiture of the will as provided in foreign law. The appellant failed to clarify the causes of forfeiture or annulment; consequently the Court of Cassation considered in this judgment that it was necessary to enforce the New York state law whose application was requested, and to consider the will as valid and regular as to its object, making it thus necessary to confirm the first instance judgment, which gave this solution though by adopting different reasoning with no need to discuss the applicable law, since the ground of the judgment (the enforcement of the US law) which the Court was not entitled to modify or change, was unproductive.

In view of the fact that the opposing party did not invoke any foreign rule limiting the freedom to make a will, or preventing a person from so doing, the reasoning of the first instance judgment which rejected this ground, even if for another reason – the non-violation of the applicable Lebanese law stipulations – was inappropriate. So the Court of Cassation enforced Lebanese law on the ground of the existence of a prior presumption saying that the national law (the law of the judge deciding on the case) was the law applicable, due to the analogy between the applicable Lebanese and foreign law, and whoever invoked the contrary, had to prove it.

The position of the Supreme Court is the continuation of a judicial and doctrinal trend inherent in this issue, founded on the presumption of analogy between national and foreign law. The rule requires that the judge enforces this law, and whoever argues the contrary has to prove his allegations. The

Lebanese Court of Cassation had followed this trend in the past, but the question remains: has the Court of Cassation totally abandoned the principle of referral when its enforcement proves to be impossible and inconvenient in legal systems founded on religious factors in issues like inheritance and personal status, making this theory regress continuously or even vanish, as certain people would wish?

In order to form an opinion of this subject, other judgments are needed giving consistent rulings on this in the Lebanese judicial system. In this judgment the Court did not examine the principle of referral but ignored it. We cannot make a hasty deduction that keeps the above judgment dated 28 May1998, as the guide, agreeing the principle of referral but ignoring it when enforcement is not convenient.

7 ARBITRATION

A recent judgment rendered by the Civil Court of Appeal in Beirut, deciding on arbitration cases, rescinded the judgment of the Beirut Court of the First Instance, which refused to ratify the arbitration decision issued by Sheikh Mohammed Hassan Fadlallah, on the grounds that the contested arbitral award did not contain a summing up, and subsequently did not resolve the conflict, thus infringing the provisions of Article 790 of the Civil Procedure Code. The Appeal Court ruled that it is for the arbitrator to resolve the dispute he is examining and that his decision becomes executory when the legal conditions are met; although the law requires that the arbitral award should contain a pronouncement sentence, it does not fix a special form for that sentence or require that it be similar, in form and the way it appears in the decision, to a sentence pronouncing judgment, because the formulation and the style adopted by long-practised judges in the drafting of judgments cannot be developed by arbitrators, especially if they are not practising lawyers with wide experience and acquainted with the classical form of judgments.

The Court of Appeal considered that what should be emphasized in the pronouncement sentence was its content, which should be clear and executable, and not the way it is written or the expressions and words used by the arbitrator when drafting the judgment. It is neither important nor necessary for the arbitrator to use expressions such as "we decide" or "we rule"; it is sufficient to use any other expression that indicates his clear and steadfast decision, as consideration is given to intentions.

Further, it was clear when Sheikh Fadlallah accepted the arbitration task entrusted to him by the parties and started to fulfil it, he rendered a decision settling the dispute and not mere advice with no effect; the fact that he used the expression "in our opinion" had no incidence in the case, since we know that the decision of a judge or an arbitrator is his opinion, albeit an opinion whose basic factors are constant and steadfastness.

The judgment concluded by considering the contested arbitral decision as an arbitral award possessing all the required elements and conditions and ruled the reversal of the decision apealed against and readjudication to grant the decision the executory formula.

This judgment was bold and daring as it gave a wide interpretation to Article 790 of the Civil Procedure Code which lays down the essential conditions that an arbitral decision should fulfil; among these conditions, is the incorporation of a pronouncement sentence under liability of refusing to attribute the executive formula to the arbitral decision. The judgment considered that the most important element was the content of the pronouncement sentence and not its form or its being reported separately at the end of the judgment.

8   INTELLECTUAL AND ARTISTIC PROPERTY PROTECTION

The first judgment rendered in Lebanon in application of the Law on Intellectual and Artistic Property Protection is that of the third Civil Chamber of the Court of Appeal, which rescinded the appealed first instance judgment and passed a new judgment, in virtue of the authority entrusted to the judge of summary procedure to grant any creditor an interim advance on account of his due entitlements (when the existence of the debt was not contested), binding the appellee (the publisher) to pay to the appellant (the author) an interim advance on account of his lawful remedy for the moral prejudice he suffered as a consequence of the breach of the intellectual property rights secured by the law on the protection of literary and artistic property, recently enacted, and in application of the contract concluded between the two parties.

The facts may be summed up as follows. The appellant (the author) had concluded an agreement with the appellee (the publisher) to publish his book, *A Syntactical Dictionary of Expressions of the Holy Koran*. The contract contained an indication that the appellant was the author and that a formula would be later agreed upon in order to mention his name in the book.

Not only was the dictionary published without any mention of the author's identity, but the publisher had proceeded to publish the name of another as author, which led the appellant to request the judge of summary procedure to compel the publisher to pay him an advance on account of the remedy due to him by the publisher on the grounds of the moral prejudice he incurred due to the publisher's infringement of the law on artistic and literary rights and of the contract concluded between the two parties. The judge, in the first instance prosecution, dismissed the author's claim on the ground of non-fulfilment of the conditions provided for in Article 579 clause III of the Code of Civil Procedure, allowing the judge of summary procedure to grant an interim advance to the creditor whose debt was due and mature.

The appeal judgment stipulates that the omission of the author's name, as per the agreement, does not mean, in any way, that the publisher may freely proceed to the marketing of the book, through advertising publications or price lists or general catalogues under another person's name having no relation whatsoever with the author, as did the appellee; this was liable to cause an incontestably serious moral prejudice to the real author and thereby breach the appellant's copyrights, especially his moral rights. This was corroborated by Article 14 of Law No. 75/1999 recently enacted (the Law on the Protection of Artistic and Literary Copyright) stipulating that any copyright holder enjoys material and moral rights, and by Article 21 of the same law that set forth these rights in detail and Article 22 that elaborated the manner of assigning these rights. Subsequently, the Court of Appeal rescinded the appealed judgment which did not meet that disposition, and passed a new judgment ruling the obligation for the appellee to pay to the appellant an interim advance on account of his right to receive a due remedy for the moral prejudice he incurred, as detailed above.

The peculiarity of this judgment is that:

(a)   It has been rendered by the Court of Summary Procedure, which does not usually examine the merits of the case; its judgments are considered intermediary and do not enjoy the status of *res judicata*.

(b)   It involves a case of remedy to be paid to an author for moral prejudice he incurred when the tort was not contested, in application of Article 14 of Law No. 75/99.

Libya

*Mustafa El-Alem**

1 CONSTITUTIONAL AND ADMINISTRATIVE LAW

1.1 Reorganization of the Secretariat of the General People's Committee (GPC)

According to Resolution No. 3/1430 issued by the General People's Congress on 1 March 2000, the members of the Secretariat of the GPC[1] are reduced to eight as follows:

(a) Secretary of the GPC;
(b) Assistant Secretary for Services Affairs;
(c) Assistant Secretary for Production Affairs;
(d) Secretary of the GPC for Foreign Affairs and International Cooperation;
(e) Secretary of the GPC for Justice and Public Security;
(f) Secretary of the GPC for Information, Culture and Tourism;
(g) Secretary of the GPC of Finance;
(h) Secretary of the GPC for African Unity.

The Assistant Secretary for Services Affairs will supervise the works of the institutions, authorities and departments undertaking service activities, including the services of education, health, economy, trade and other services which fall within the competence of the GPC.

The Assistant Secretary for Production Affairs will supervise and coordinate the works of the institutions, authorities and companies carrying out production activities.

Each Assistant Secretary shall have the powers and authorities vested by

---

* Attorney at Law before the Libyan Supreme Court.
[1] The GPC is the highest administrative unit and is equivalent to the Council of Ministers.

law in the Secretary of the GPC and the Secretary originally in charge as regards the functions and units operating under his supervision.

1.2   Consulting firms

The Administrative Contracts Regulation (ACR)[2] was issued in 1994, laying down the legal rules governing the formation, performance and termination of administrative or state contracts. Chapter 4 of this regulation contained special provisions concerning contracts concluded with consulting firms.

On 28 November 1999 the GPC issued Resolution No. 454/1429 promulgating the Regulation relating to Employment of Consulting Firms. Article I of this regulation provided that only the provisions contained therein shall be applicable to the employment of consulting firms. According to Article II administrative units are not allowed to deal with any consulting firm unless duly registered in accordance with the provisions of this regulation. Registration may be effected upon request of the firm. This request must be made on a special standard form, and submitted to the Head of the Consulting Firms Committee with the Secretariat of Planning. Registration is to be made in special registers classified according to the different specializations and experiences.

In order to be registered, a consultative firm, whether national or foreigner, must satisfy the following conditions:

(a)   The manager of the firm must hold a university degree.
(b)   The firm must possess at least five years of the experience relating to performance of the consultative works for which registration is requested.
(c)   The firm must be officially recognized and registered in its own country.
(d)   The experts and technicians employed by the firm must be solely engaged in the activity of the firm. They should not be engaged in any other commercial activity.

According to Article 14, contracting with a consultative firm may be limited to one or more than one stage of the consultative services as follows:

(a)   first stage: primary technical and economic feasibility study;
(b)   second stage: detailed technical and economical feasibility study;
(c)   third stage: supervision of performance.

The contract concluded with a consulting firm must be drafted on the standard form prepared for this purpose. Amendments or alterations to the provisions of the said draft may be allowed by permission of the GPC for Planning if the nature or the circumstances of the contact so require.

Contracting with a consulting firm must be effected directly with the firm.

---

[2]   The ACR was surveyed in this *Yearbook*, vol. 2 (1995), p. 185.

It is not permitted to contract with a foreign firm through its agent or representative in Libya.

1.3 Official mourning day

In implementation of the Resolutions made by the People's Basic Conferences regarding the substantial damage suffered by the Libyan people under Italian occupation, the GPC issued Resolution No. 385/1999 on 23 November 1999, under which 26 November each year is declared an official mourning day in the Great Socialist People's Libyan Arab Jamahiriya.

Accordingly, all citizens are required to wear black dress throughout this day. If this is not available, a black label may be visibly attached to the dress. Black labels may also be attached to public means of transport.

Flights of the Libyan Arab Airlines are to be suspended on this day. All land and maritime trips inside or outside the country, which are carried out by Libyan public companies or establishments, must be suspended as from the dawn of this day until 6 pm. All postal, telegraphic and telephone communications shall be suspended during the same period of time. Libyan citizens are not allowed to travel to Italy on the mourning day.

The GPC for Information and Culture is requested to produce intensive programmes on this occasion through different mass media so as to explain the concepts and motives of the mourning day, with emphasis on the claims made by the Libyan people against Italy for fair compensation, clarification of the destiny of extradited Libyans, removal of the mines which were buried in the Libyan land, and handing over of the maps indicating the locations of those mines.[3]

1.4 Social Care Fund

Act No. 20/1428 established the Social Care Fund. This is an independent institution charged with the organization of matters relating to social security pensions and social care services.[4]

The Executive Regulations of this Act have been issued by virtue of Resolution No. 318/1428 made by the GPC on 20 November 1999.

2 ISLAMIC LAW

2.1 Alms Law (*ganun azzakat*)

In continuation of its legislative policy aiming at the codification of the rules and principles of Islamic Law *shari'a*, the Libyan legislature promulgated

---

[3] The mourning day as decided by the Resolution No. 222/1424 was surveyed in this *Yearbook*, vol. 2 (1995), p. 184.

[4] Act No. 20/1428 was surveyed in this *Yearbook*, vol. 5 (1998–1999), p. 292.

Alms Law No. 13/1427, which codified the Islamic rules relating to *azzakat* (Islamic taxation), which is considered one of the five Islamic religious duties.

According to this law the Alms General organization is to be established by resolution of the General People's Congress. This resolution has been issued and came into effect on 15 April 1999. Accordingly, the Organization is situated in the city of Sirt, and operates under the auspices of the GPC. It is charged with the collection of the alms funds from the citizens according to the provisions of the Alms Law and its Executive Regulations, which has also come into effect on 15 April 1999.

3 TRADE LAW

3.1 General Organization for Free Trade Zones

On 3 February 1999 the General People's Committee issued Resolution No. 20/1429 establishing the General Organization for Free Trade Zones. This is an independent legal body operating under the auspices of the Secretariat of Economy and Trade.

The main office of this organization will be in the city of Misurata; branch offices may be established elsewhere in the country. The organization will undertake the management of the free trade zones to be established by resolution of the Secretary of the GPC for Economy and Trade according to the Provisions of Act No. 10/1959 relating to free zones. The General Manager of the Customs Department shall, upon suggestion of the General Manager of the Organization, grant licences for establishing industrial, commercial and financial projects, and also for carrying out services and activities inside the free trade zones. Goods and commodities imported to or exported from the free zones shall not be subject to any restrictions in respect of the period of their stay in the free zone. Such goods and commodities shall also not be subject either to the customs taxes and duties or to the rules relating to import and export. The enterprises established in the free zones shall be allowed to export their products without any restrictions, and without registration in the Exporters Register.

All equipment, stationery, materials, furniture and means of transport to be used by the establishments licensed to operate in the free trade zones shall be exempted from customs duties and other taxes. Industrial and commercial investment enterprises in the free zones shall enjoy exemptions and prerogatives prescribed by the Foreign Capital Investment Act.[5]

Free trade zone projects may only be nationalized, confiscated or expropriated through an Act or court judgment, and in consideration of an immediate and fair compensation the value of which may be transferred abroad within a period not exceeding one year at the exchange rates prevailing at the time of transfer. The capital invested in the free zone and its profits may be

---

5   This Act was surveyed in this *Yearbook*, vol. 4 (1997–1998), p. 305.

transferred abroad according to Article 12 of the Foreign Capital Investment Act.

The Free Trade Zones Organization shall start its activity by administrating a free zone adjacent to Misurata Harbour.

The Organization may agree with the investors to settle disputes by way of commercial arbitration.

3.2 Import and distribution of commodities

On 17 July 1999 the GPC issued Resolution No. 242/1429 which contained some rules regarding importation and distribution of commodities to be carried out according to the provision of Act No. 4/1426 regulating the import and distribution of commodities.[6] The resolution classified commodities for the purpose of imports into four categories as indicated in four tables attached to the resolution.

There are some different rules governing the procedures to be followed for import and distribution of the commodities of each category.

3.3 Encouragement of exports

On 19 April 2000 the GPC issued the Resolution No. 226/1430 deciding some provisions for the encouragement of exports. Accordingly, public and private joint stock companies are allowed to export all local commodities and products without the need to obtain an export licence or any other restrictions.

The exported commodities and products must conform to standard specifications and technical conditions approved by the competent authorities. The exporter must supply the value of the exported commodity in foreign currency within three months as from the date of shipment.

4   PUBLIC INTERNATIONAL LAW

4.1   International Convention against Taking Hostages

By virtue of Resolution No. 412/1429 issued by the GPC on 30 October 1999, Libya has ratified the International Convention Against Taking Hostages which was approved by the General Assembly of the United Nations on 17 December 1979.

---

6   This Act was surveyed in this *Yearbook*, vol. 4 (1997–1998), p. 304.

Sudan

*John Wuol Makec**

1 INTRODUCTION

The survey of the laws of the Sudan for the *Yearbook* has always concentrated on the review of the constitutional or public law. The reason is simple. Sudan has never had a permanent Constitution since it obtained its independence on 1 January 1956. As already mentioned in the previous surveys in the *Yearbook*, the Transitional Constitution, which was promulgated in 1956, has always been annulled by military governments and re-emerged after the overthrow of those governments. Democratic governments have always restored its operation pending the making of a permanent Constitution through the consensus of all political parties. But that political consensus has never been forthcoming, even after the passage of forty-four years.

As a consequence of this political instability, public and other laws are subject to frequent changes. In other words there is a great deal of legal instability. The period from 1989 to the time of writing this survey has experienced the greatest legal instability. For example, the Press Law of 1996 has been repealed; the *Qanun El Tawaally El Siaasia* of 1998, which regulated political associations (parties) was repealed in the year 2000 after the emergence of the power struggle between the President Omer El Bashir and Dr Hassan Abdalla El Turabi, the great Islamic ideologist.

The future of the Constitution of 1998 is now uncertain. This constitution was promulgated when the leadership of the current Salvation Government was united. However, it has always been publicly criticized on the grounds that it was put forward by one political party, the National Islamic Front, and therefore it does not represent the popular will of all the Sudanese people. But Sudanese political parties or people fear abrogation of what has been labelled as Islamic. This explains the survival of Islamic laws passed in September 1983. Those who demanded their repeal slyly described them as

---

* LLB.; LLM; Justice of the Supreme Court of Sudan.

September laws, instead of Islamic laws. A demand for the repeal of Islamic laws is viewed as sacrilege. This fear may lead to the continued survival of the present Islamic Constitution despite the mounting opposition from the major political parties which are actually formed on religious basis.[1]

After the leadership crisis,[2] Dr Hassan Abdalla El Turabi, at present, appears to have suffered a major political setback. However, there is also doubt whether the president, Omer Hassan El Bashir, can manage to run a government alone without the help of another dynamic political leader to fill the vacuum left by Dr Turabi.

The Umma Party, led by former Prime Minister Saddig El Mahdi, declared its return to the country in March 2000. But it seems, according to its demands, that the Umma Party may make an alliance with Omer El Bashir either at the expense of or after the amendment of the Constitution of 1998, and some other major laws which were enacted by the Salvation Government on the initiative of Dr Abdalla El Turabi.

In this year's survey I shall deal in detail with the Constitutional Court Act 1998, the General Elections Act 1998 and finally with the leadership crisis culminating in the decision of the Constitutional Court.

2   THE CONSTITUTIONAL COURT ACT 1998

The Constitution of 1998 created the Constitutional Court for the first time in the Sudan as a distinct judicial institution. Jurisdiction to determine constitutional cases, which has now been vested in the Constitutional Court had, prior to 1998, been vested in the Supreme Court which was the custodian of the Constitution and the law. Reasons for the creation of this Court have not been given. If the objective was claimed to be the creation of a specialized Court, this may not be genuine because the Constitutional Panel in the Supreme Court used to consist of judges of high calibre, many of whom are now members of this new court.

But of course, the creation of the Constitutional Court came at the time when the judiciary was being divested of most of its important powers. For example, the power to try most important administrative cases has been removed and vested in tribunals which fall under executive control. The decisions of those tribunals are final and cannot be questioned by courts through judicial review.

The second example is that the pre-trial process in criminal cases, which used to be exercised by the judiciary, was divested and conferred on the attorneys in the Ministry of Justice, which is an executive organ. Besides the public order courts staffed by soldiers or by lay people, the police and the army also have their own distinct courts. Hence the judiciary is left with only residual powers to exercise.

---

1   Or at least major amendments may be introduced into the Constitution.
2   See below under section 4.

2.1   The Formation of the Constitutional Court

In 1998 the Constitutional Act was enacted in order to implement the
Constitution of 1998.

The composition of the Court comprises the President, Deputy President
and five ordinary members. The President, his deputy and the five members
are appointed by the President of the Republic in exercise of his discretionary
power. These appointments have to be confirmed by the National Assembly.[3]
The judges' tenure of office is a period of five years and it is subject to
renewal at the expiry of such tenure.[4]

The quorum of the Court when it is sitting for a case before it consists
of five judges.[5] The President of the Court chairs the sittings. But in his
absence, the Deputy chairs the sittings. However, if both the President and
his Deputy are absent, the member whose name appears first before others
in the list of appointments chairs the sittings.[6]

Section 5 of the Act prescribes the qualifications of a person to be
appointed in the Constitutional Court. In the first place, he must be a
Sudanese citizen; secondly, he must be a person of good conduct, thirdly he
must have obtained a high degree in *shari'a*[7] (which is in fact a law that
essentially regulates personal affairs of Moslems) or law in a university recognized in the Sudan. Experience in any one of the judicial organs or in a
teaching career is a very important condition for appointment to this Court.
The teaching of law subjects must be in a recognized university or law school.
The period of experience in law must not be less than twenty years.

After the appointment of the judges of this Court they are required to
take the oath before they exercise their judicial functions. They take the oath
before the President of the Republic and in the presence of the Speaker of
National Assembly. It is not clear who would take the place of the Speaker
if the National Assembly had been dissolved.

They swear to defend the Constitution of the Sudan.[8]

The role of a judge of this Court is limited in public life. A judge is
prohibited[9] from carrying out any work or activity which is incompatible
with his official duties and the "independence of the Court". It is remarkable
here to note that although the "independence" of this Court is casually
mentioned, there is no section of the Act which substantially provides for
the independence of judges or the Constitutional Court. Further, there is
no procedure laid down for removal of judges besides the provision which
prescribes that judges may be removed from office by the President of the

---

3   Section 3(11) of the Constitutional Act 1998.
4   *Ibid.*, section 3(3).
5   *Ibid.*, section 7.
6   *Ibid.*, section 4.
7   Since the Constitution is Islamic its provisions will be interpreted in the spirit of
    shari'a law. Hence, knowledge of *shari'a* law is relevant.
8   Section 8 of the Constitutional Court Act 1998.
9   *Ibid.*, section 9.

Republic on grounds of health or where they have been convicted for commission of an offence affecting their honour.[10]

Of course, if these are the only grounds for the removal of the judges, it may be submitted that their tenure of office is well secured. But the time since the enactment of the Constitutional Act is too short for anyone to conclude that judges may not be removed on other grounds which are not mentioned by the Act. Removal of a judge of this Court on a ground which has not been mentioned under the Act will be regarded as unconstitutional or null and void. But what if the President of the Republic removes a judge or all the members when acting under the emergency powers? Of course, the President of the Republic has already (on 12 December 1999) taken decisions under the emergency powers in areas where he had no express constitutional power.

Judges of the Constitutional Court have a temporary immunity in relation to criminal proceedings. They cannot be arrested or investigated, nor can they be charged with criminal offences. But they can be subject to arrest or investigation on criminal charge where the President of the Republic has given a sanction or permission.[11]

It is not clear if the stated arrest or investigation or criminal charge may arise out of what the judge had done in exercise of his official functions.

2.2 Jurisdiction of the Court (Section 11)

The jurisdiction of the Constitutional Court consists of:

(a) interpretation of the Constitution and the laws submitted to it by the President of the Republic, or National Assembly or half of the number of state governors or half of the number of state assemblies;

(b) entertainment of a suit raised by an individual who claims that his freedom has been infringed or that he has been deprived of a constitutional right. But many such cases do not successfully pass through procedural hurdles;

(c) jurisdictional dispute between central or state government units;

(d) the instituting of criminal proceedings against the President of the Republic or Council of Ministers or central minister or state governor in accordance with the law. It is very unlikely that such a criminal suit will ever be entertained by the Constitutional Court, especially against the President of the Republic. This provision is bound to remain theoretical, however, in the prevailing circumstances;

(e) where an individual claims that an act of the President of the Republic or Council of Ministers, or central minister or state governor or minister in a state has injured him it may again be submitted that this section if

---

10 *Ibid.*, section 6.
11 *Ibid.*, section 10.

bound to remain theoretical, especially when the act has been committed by the President. An individual of course would not dare take the risk of direct or indirect reprisals;

(f)   revision of the proceedings or judicial decisions to ascertain that they are in conformity with the constitution. It follows from this provision that the Constitutional Court is entitled to revise the decisions of any judicial authority including the decisions of the Supreme Court. It may further be submitted that the Supreme Court is not the final judicial authority in the land.

2.3   Powers of the Constitutional Court (section 12)

The Act confers wide judicial powers on the Constitutional Court under the provisions of section 12. These powers are summarized below. The section states:

1.   Acting according to its jurisdiction which is provided under section 11 [of the Act]; the Court shall exercise all the decision-making powers to revise any law or act which violates the Constitution and to restore the right of or compensate the aggrieved person.
2.   Notwithstanding the provisions of section 12 (1) above, the Court shall exercise the following powers:
     (a)   to order anybody, in respect to a matter before him or it, to send papers to the Court for revision in order to ascertain the constitutionality of any act or decision.
     (b)   to order anybody to bring any person arrested or detained before the Court in order to ascertain the constitutionality of such arrest or detention.

The word "anybody" in clause 2 includes the Supreme Court.

The provisions of this clause imply that the Constitutional Court has power to order the State Security, at any time and in relation to any other matter, to bring any person arrested or detained before it. However, it is uncertain whether the Constitutional Court in practice can exercise this power in every case.

     (c)   The Constitutional Court is vested with criminal powers where a criminal charge has been raised against the President of the Republic or State Governor.

As indicated above, it is highly doubtful whether any citizen or state institution will ever attempt to raise any criminal proceedings against the President of the Republic or state governor for reasons already mentioned. Hence, it is again likely that the contents of this clause will remain a theoretical possibility.

3.   The Constitutional Court, when requested by means of a petition presented by an aggrieved person or plaintiff, may order stay of execution of the decision or act, subject of the constitutional suit, pending the final deciding of that suit.

But the provisions of this clause (section 12(3)) emphatically state that the raising of any constitutional suit does not automatically or imperatively imply the stay of execution. It follows therefore that the Constitutional Court has a discretionary power, when it is requested to grant an order to stay execution. It may reject the petition requesting the stay of execution whenever it deems it reasonable to do so.

Clause 4 of section 12 is not really a power of the Constitutional Court and it ought to have been made a separate section. It imposes criminal responsibility on violators of court orders. The clause provides that: "Any person who violates any order made in accordance with the powers of the Court shall personally be held responsible for making such violation." But the whole section falls short of stating any penalty that may be imposed on the violators and the authority that has the power to punish, if any, the violators.

2.4 Procedure for the requesting of constitutional interpretation

Section 13 of the Act provides a procedure to be followed whenever a request for the interpretation of the Constitution and the law is made.

In the first place the section[12] indicates the persons who are entitled to make the request for interpretation. These are:

(a)   the President of the Republic;
(b)   the Speaker of the National Assembly;
(c)   half of the number of state governors;
(d)   half of the number of state assemblies; and
(e)   the Minister of Justice.

Clause 13(2) provides that the petition made in accordance with the provisions of section 13(1) shall include:

(a)   the name of the petitioner or applicant;
(b)   a statement in respect to the provision for which interpretation is requested and the reasons for its interpretation;
(c)   any information that may assist the Court in the interpretation.

Where the petition fails to conform with legal procedure, the Court may reject it outright or request the petitioner to amend it within a time fixed by it (i.e. the Court).[13]

2.5 Procedure for raising a suit for constitutionality of a law or act (section 15)

A suit for the constitutionality of any law or legal provision or act in accordance with provisions of section 11 is raised by means of a petition addressed to the Constitutional Court. The suit plaint must contain:

---

[12]   *Ibid.*, section 13(1) a–e.
[13]   *Ibid.*, section 14.

(a)   the plaintiff;
(b)   the interest which has been affected; and
(c)   the law or act which is subject of the suit or constitutional violation.

The Court is entitled to settle the suit on the contents of the documents submitted before it. But it may hear the evidence from the parties to the suit if it deems it necessary.

2.6   Dismissal of the suit summarily (section 16)

A constitutional suit, like an administrative suit, is attended by numerous hurdles or procedural obstacles. Many suits may always be dismissed for failing to comply with procedural requirements.

The procedural requirements are stated as follows:

(a)   the plaintiff or petitioner must have a direct right or interest in the suit he raises;
(b)   the petition or plaint must contain a justiciable issue;
(c)   the petition must state the nature of the right or deprivation of right guaranteed by the constitution which has been violated;
(d)   where the plaintiff has exhausted other remedies available to him.

A petition or application which fails to fulfil the above requirements is bound to be dismissed summarily by the Court.

But if an act of the President of the Republic or Council of Ministers, or state government or central minister or governor or minister in a state caused the injury which has given rise to the constitutional suit, the question is what other remedies are available besides the remedy that may be provided by the Constitutional Court? It is usually possible, of course, that the act of a subordinate authority may be questioned or overturned by a superior author-ity. But the situation may be different when matters regulated by a statute or law are concerned. In such matters, a superior must question the decisions on his subordinate where the law confers on him the power to question those decisions. Hence, where an aggrieved party immediately raises his suit to the Constitutional Court, it may not legally be stated that the petitioner should have appealed to the superior administrative authority before he proceeds to the Court unless it can be established that there is a legal provision which provides that decisions of a specific subordinate authority are appealable to a specific authority or his direct superior. In the absence of such a legal provision, specifying the authority to which an appeal must lie, it cannot be legally held that the aggrieved party has failed to exhaust available remedies (before coming to the Court). The fact that there is superior authority does not imply that this is an appellate authority in relation to the legal decisions of subordinates because the right of appeal exists only where it has been created by law.

Further, if we take the President, who is the highest authority in the land, or an act of the Council of Ministers, which is presided over by the President of the Republic, can a petitioner be expected to exhaust remedies available to him when there is no other (besides the Constitutional Court) authority which can provide a remedy? Can an aggrieved party in this case be expected by way of exhausting remedies, to submit his constitutional suit to the Supreme Court?

It has been provided under section 3 of The Constitutional Administrative Cases Act 1996 that a person aggrieved by the constitutional act of any of the authorities mentioned above must resort to the Constitutional Circuit in the Supreme Court. But this Act was enacted before the Act establishing the Constitutional Court in 1998. However, when the latter (Act) was enacted, the constitutional jurisdiction was removed from the Supreme Court and vested in the Constitutional Court. This is the only institution which has original jurisdiction in constitutional cases or disputes.

2.7 Admission of the suit (section 17)

Where an aggrieved party has exhausted available remedies before resorting to the Court, or where the highest authority to which the complaint (or appeal) has been presented, fails to make a decision within thirty days from the date the complaint was submitted to him, the Court is entitled to allow the suit or take any action it deems fit.[14]

Where the petition has fulfilled the requisite legal form, the Court orders the admission of the suit and payment of Court fees unless the petitioner is exempted from payment of the fees by the Court.[15]

2.8 Procedure for raising specific suits

Sections 18, 19 and 20 of the Act deal with procedure in cases of

(a) jurisdictional dispute;[16]
(b) violation of freedoms, rights and privacy right[17] and procedure where criminal proceedings are raised against the President of the Republic or state governor.[18]

2.8.1 *Jurisdictional dispute*

A suit about a jurisdictional dispute raised by any federal or state organ must be submitted by the Minister of Justice (in the case of a federal organ), or the Federal Government Chambers (in case of a state organ). The suit must

---

14   *Ibid.*, section 17(1).
15   *Ibid.*, section 17(2).
16   *Ibid.*, section 19.
17   *Ibid.*
18   *Ibid.*, section 20.

state the subject of dispute and the reason for the claim of the jurisdiction. Documents supporting such claim must be attached. The Court may, if it deems fit, hear the two parties to the suit before it makes the judgment or order.

2.8.2   *Violation of freedom to privacy and rights*

A suit raised under this section[19] must contain the following:

(a)   the name of petitioner, his address and occupation;
(b)   the defendant's name and his job;
(c)   the relief claimed by the plaintiff.

The Court may decide the suit on the contents of the documents submitted to it by the parties. But the Court may if it deems it necessary for ascertainment of justice hear the parties to the suit.

2.8.3   *Criminal proceedings against the President or governor*

Under this section,[20] no criminal proceedings can be raised against the President of the Republic, or a governor, unless a written sanction has been obtained from the National Assembly, in case of the President, and the state assembly, in the case of the state governor.
   But the question is whether under the present constitutional arrangement any assembly can give the sanction required. Where the Court has obtained such a sanction it must, therefore, follow the procedure below:

(a)   assign or delegate one of its members to investigate the President or governor; this member will not sit in the Court during the trial later;
(b)   after the completion of the investigation, the investigator submits the results of his work to the Court;
(c)   where the Court has either convicted or acquitted the President of the Republic or the state governor, it has to submit its decision to the National Assembly, in the case of the President, or state assembly, in the case of the governor.

2.9   Court decisions (section 21)

Decisions of the Court may be passed unanimously or by majority.[21] Where the judgment has been passed by majority, dissenting judgment(s) must be

---

19   *Ibid.*, section 19.
20   *Ibid.*, section 20(1).
21   *Ibid.*, section 21(1).

made.[22] The Court must make a decision on all the issues raised.[23] The judgments and decisions of the Constitutional Court are final and are not subject to any objection (or appeal) to any other authority.[24] Judgments and decisions of the Constitutional Court must be published in the Official Gazette.

Decisions and judgements of this Court bind all the state institutions as soon as they are made,[25] and they must enforce them.

Where the Court has decided on the unconstitutionality of a legal provision, then the President of the Court must notify the Minister of Justice or the Chief Justice as the case may be, so that he may thereafter initiate the necessary legal procedure. But a decision on the unconstitutionality of the procedure has no retrospective effect.[26]

Before the close of this paragraph, it may be remarked that the Constitutional Court is the first and the last High Court for constitutional matters. It has first jurisdiction, but there is no appellate judicial authority above it to entertain appeals against its judgments, which are final.

The finality of its decisions in cases of first instance seems to be an affront to the traditional conception developed in people's minds that there must be an appellate authority to settle appeals from the decisions of a court of first instance. There was a mixed people's reaction when the Court passed its first important constitutional judgment in the case which arose out of the crisis between the president and the Speaker of National Assembly (or the leadership crisis).[27]

After the advent of the leadership crisis, the Constitutional Court dismissed the suit which was raised by the supporters of Dr Turabi. Some, including prominent makers of the Constitution of 1998, wondered why there was no appellate authority to try the appeal. But many neutral lawyers who looked at the judgment of the Court objectively concluded that it was a qualitative standard that matched the calibre of the judges who made it, and that an appellate authority (if there were one) would confirm it.

3   THE GENERAL ELECTIONS ACT 1998 (ACT NO. 15)

3.1   General Election Commission

All elections in the country are run by an organ called the General Elections Commission. Its functions and the general election procedure are regulated by the General Elections Act 1998 (Act No. 15). Section 4 of the Act creates the General Elections Commission, which has a distinct corporate personality. According to the provisions of section 4(1), it is an "independent" body.

---

[22]   *Ibid.*, section 21(2).
[23]   *Ibid.*, section 21(3).
[24]   *Ibid.*, section 21(4).
[25]   *Ibid.*, section 22(1).
[26]   *Ibid.*, section 21(3).
[27]   See below under section 4.

The General Elections Commission consists of a Chairman and two members who are appointed by the President of the Republic with the approval of the National Assembly.[28] They are supposed, according to the legal provision, to be men of high integrity. Their emoluments are fixed by the President of the Republic.

Despite the prescribed independence of the General Elections Commission, it is directly responsible to the President of the Republic and the National Assembly[29] for its performance. Its real independence remains to be tested by time and events.

3.2 Jurisdiction of the General Elections Commission (section 5)

The General Elections Commission has jurisdiction and powers to:

(a) prepare a general election register, publish it, keep it revising it annually and authenticate it;
(b) prepare election registers for indirect elections;[30]
(c) run the election for the Presidency of the Republic or state governors, members of the national and state assemblies and the local councils;
(d) conduct referenda as prescribed under the constitution and ultimately announce the results;
(e) establish the geographical constituencies for direct elections;
(f) arrange a fair presentation of candidates to the voters or the public; prepare symbols for each candidate to be exhibited to the public or voters and arrange agents for candidates;
(g) arrange election manifestos, timetables (election schedules), local polling stations and polling procedures;
(h) ensure discipline, freedom and fairness of elections at the polling centres. The results of election are finally announced publicly after the counting of the votes;
(i) postpone elections or referenda on grounds of *force majeure*, or cancel the election results when there is sufficient evidence showing rampant corruption during the polling in any station or constituency;
(j) settle any problems or disputes or undertake any procedure or any necessary action for registration or elections or referenda.

In order to run the elections or referenda more effectively in the country, the General Elections Commission sets up various committees in all the regions or states. In each state there must be a High Election Committee for the purpose of reviewing the registration or the elections or referendum procedures or carrying out any functions under its jurisdiction.[31]

---

[28] *Ibid.*, section 4(2).
[29] *Ibid.*, section 4(3) of the General Elections Act 1998.
[30] "Indirect election" refers to election of candidates through certain colleges. Most of or all the elected candidates support the government.
[31] Section 6 of the General Elections Act 1998.

3.3 Jurisdiction of the High Election Committee and its powers (section 7)

The high election committees are autonomous bodies in the sense that they lay down their own rules with regards to the election procedure in the field. They exercise the following jurisdiction and powers:

(a) to promulgate orders or directives or guidelines for the purpose of conduct of registration or election or referendum in accordance with the provisions of this Act and the regulations issued by the General Election Commission;
(b) to issue the necessary guidelines for voting or polling and the general presentation of candidates to voters; arrangement and publication of electoral lists and public scrutiny of the candidates;
(c) to provide the necessary guidelines for voting and polling;
(d) to submit election results or any recommendations to the General Election Commission;
(e) to exercise any other powers conferred on it by the General Election Commission.

The High Election Committee, in addition to the powers mentioned above, has power to appoint branch committees in the constituencies to conduct the elections (or referenda) directly.[32] The General Election Commission appoints permanent officers for the preparation and maintenance of the general election registers and temporarily appoints officers to revise registers in the geographical constituencies, or at the office of the branch committee concerned.[33] Further, the High Election Committee has power to appoint temporary election or referendum officers for the headquarters of any branch committee in any constituency or any centre for indirect elections.[34] Again the General Elections Commission may appoint officers temporarily for any purpose or investigation or revision of any matter related to elections or referenda.

3.4 Qualification of voters (section 10)

Section 10 of the Act defines the qualifications of voters during the general elections or referenda. The voters must be Sudanese nationals who have attained the age of seventeen. They must be mentally sound.

A voter in the referendum or direct general elections must have resided in the constituency for at least three months prior to the date of registration of voters.[35] Those voters residing in countries abroad must have residence

---

[32] *Ibid.*, section 8.
[33] *Ibid.*, section 9(1).
[34] *Ibid.*, section 9(2).
[35] *Ibid.*, section 10(2).

permits in those countries before they are entitled to vote for the election of
the President or in a referendum.

A voter for a technical sector must have graduated with a certified educational certificate at the level of 60 per cent or above from a secondary school.
On the other hand voters of a professional organization must be members
of the national union of that profession.[36]

Sections 14 and 16 of the Act deal with nomination of candidates,[37] their
qualifications[38] and their obligations.[39] A person must be nominated for the
National Assembly by no fewer than twenty people provided that they are
all of sound mind.[40] A candidate is required to pay a surety fee. The qualifications of candidates are as prescribed under section 68 of the Constitution.
But the nomination of a candidate cannot be completed without the
following:

(a)   the making of a declaration that he is bound by the Constitution, which
      is Islamic. Non-Moslems are expected to declare their support for the
      Constitution if they are contesting elections;
(b)   presentation of a certificate of resignation if he has been a public servant,
      provided that the non-production of a certificate does not lead to the
      disqualification of a worker;
(c)   announcement that the candidate is independent or is a member of a
      political organization which has been registered under the *Qanun
      Tawaally el Siaasia* 1998.[41]

The law provides that the candidates of one constituency may reach a compromise allowing one candidate to go forward unopposed. This is done through
a committee called an agreement committee, which is temporarily set up by
the General Elections Commission in each national or state or council consti-
uency.[42] This committee contacts and discusses with each candidate after the
period of administrative and legal objections is over. The aim of such contacts
and discussion is to convince one candidate to withdraw his candidature in
favour of another.[43] Of course, the objective of this provision cannot work
under a multi-party political system. The makers of this Act contemplated a
one party political system when they incorporated this provision. The Elections Act, in fact, followed the Political Parties Act 1998, (i.e. *Qanun
Tawaally el Siaasia*).

3.5   Election of the President of the Republic (section 20)

The election of the President of the Republic requires that a number of
persons, no fewer than one hundred in every state and in no less than half

---

36   *Ibid.*, section 10(5).
37   *Ibid.*, section 14.
38   *Ibid.*, section 15.
39   *Ibid.*, section 16.
40   *Ibid.*, section 14(2).
41   *Ibid.*, section 16.
42   *Ibid.*, section 18.
43   *Ibid.*, section 20(2).

of all the states in the Sudan, who are qualified voters in their constituencies, are entitled to nominate any person who satisfies the qualifications for presidency of the Republic to be the President of the Republic.[44]

In the application for the nomination of the candidate for presidency, the name of the candidate, his address, qualifications, the names of persons who made the nomination, their addresses and qualifications must be mentioned.[45] Their agreement or consent to the nomination must be attached.

Nomination of a candidate for the presidency of the Republic or for state governor requires the presentation of the following:[46]

(a) a declaration that he will be bound by the Constitution, even though he may be a believer in a religion other than Islam;
(b) a certificate of acceptance of resignation, if he has been a public servant; and
(c) a declaration that he is an independent candidate or that he is a member of a registered organizaton in accordance with organization of the *Tawaally el Siaasia* Act 1998.

The General Elections Commission which conducts elections for the presidency of the Republic has a duty to prepare regulations and schedules for nominations and objections to be made against candidates, appeals against decisions made on the objections and the time for deciding on those objections and appeals.[47]

Further, it is the duty of the General Elections Commission to fix the polling stations which are near to the places of voters' residence. The Commission must ensure that the polling stations are free from any visible evidence of corruption.[48] Polling is regulated by rules (or regulations) made by the Commission. The candidates' agents are admitted to the polling stations to observe the voting and later the counting of the votes.[49]

Judges, lawyers and other responsible persons are appointed by the Commission to evaluate the election procedure or voting and ultimately submit certificates showing either the fairness of the election or its rigging.[50]

When the polling is over, the entire membership of the High Election Committee issues a certificate of election result as follows:[51] (a) that all candidates withdrew their nominations except the one who passed unopposed; or (b) that one of the candidates has succeeded in obtaining the highest majority after the counting of the votes.

The results are despatched to the Commission. In accordance with regulations, complaints or objections of aggrieved candidates are raised to the

---

44 *Ibid.*, section 19.
45 *Ibid.*, section 20(2).
46 *Ibid.*, section 21.
47 *Ibid.*, section 22(1).
48 *Ibid.*, section 23(1).
49 *Ibid.*, section 23(3).
50 *Ibid.*, section 24.
51 *Ibid.*, section 25.

Commission. The Commission may order a second counting (where it deems it reasonable) and thereafter it must certify, as soon as possible, the results finally as correct or null and void. After the Commission has announced the final results there is no longer any right for a candidate to raise a legal or administrative objection. The Commission then makes a public announcement of the result.[52]

Section 26 of the Act deals with a referendum. The General Election Commission carries out a referendum where its reference has been made by the President of the Republic or by the consensus or majority of at least half of the number of the members of the National Assembly. The subject of referendum must be a matter of high value or national desire (or will) or public interest.

The Commission must put the subject of the referendum to the people to consider, consult among themselves, and to form their general opinion upon it. Those who are qualified as voters in elections are qualified to vote in a referendum. Voting must take place within a period that does not exceed sixty days from the date when the subject of referendum was referred to the Commission. The Commission collects the people's opinion (by counting the votes) and announces the results. Where the subject matter of the referendum is supported by at least half the number of the votes counted, it is deemed to enjoy the confidence of the people. Every decision which wins the confidence of the people through a referendum is deemed to be above the law and it cannot be overturned except in accordance with provisions of the Constitution.[53]

3.6 Membership of national and state assemblies

Sections 28 and 29 of the Act deal with numbers of members of the national and state assemblies respectively.

Under section 28, the National Assembly consists of 360 members elected as follows:

(a) 270 members who are directly elected from the geographical constituencies;
(b) 90 members are specifically and indirectly elected as follows:
    (i) 35 (women) members are specially elected by (women) voters. Every state is represented by one woman member, except in the three densely populated states where each state is represented by three (women) members and in the next most dense states, each is represented by two (women) members;
    (ii) 26 members are specially elected from the states by voters of technical sectors (technicians) in accordance with provisions of Section 10 (4) (of this Act) who are registered in every state, and each state is represented by one member;

[52] *Ibid.*, section 25(2–4).
[53] *Ibid.*, section 27(1–6).

(iii) 29 members are specially elected by professional voters as follows: first, 11 members are elected by the members of the General Congress of National Union of Workers of all Sudan, secondly, 10 members are elected by the members of the General National Union of Farmers of all Sudan, thirdly, 3 members are elected by the members of the General Congress of the National Union of Business Owners of all Sudan; fourthly (and finally) 5 members are elected by the members of the General Congress for the National Union of Pastoralists of all Sudan.

Section 29 deals with the number of members of each state Council which is fixed according to the population of the state. For example, where the state population does not exceed 1 million, the number of Council members is 48 or 60 when the population exceeds 1 million but does not exceed 2 million; 72 where the population exceeds 2 million but does not exceed 3 million.

The representation of all those organizations under section 28 constitutes their recognition. But since each member of these organizations is also entitled to vote for a candidate of a geographical constituency he enjoys a double right *vis-à-vis* the ordinary voter who does not belong to any of these organizations. This is unfair.

3.7 Emergency powers of the General Election Commission

The provisions of section 34 of this Act confer emergency powers on the General Elections Commission where there is an extreme necessity to conduct, with the approval of the President of the Republic, an election for the presidency of the Republic or state governorship, or to carry out a referendum in coordination with the state organ concerned.

The extreme necessity may be the result of doubt whether the President of the Republic or state governor, before the expiry of his tenure of office, still enjoys the confidence of the people or not, or where the safety or existence of the state is seriously and extremely threatened by a struggle for power which involves the President of the Republic or the state governor.

Further, extreme necessity which demands the conduct of a referendum may arise where an event of great public interest becomes the subject of general debate, or where a very important decision of the President of the Republic or National Assembly or state governor requires the support or will of the people in the country or state, as the case may be.

But it is not clear whether in practice the General Elections Commission on its own volition and without an indirect instruction from a political authority, such as the President or the National Assembly, can decide to conduct an election or referendum. The conduct of an election or referendum as a result of an indirect instruction from one of the stated political authorities seems to be the truth because the alleged independence of the General Elections Commission is doubtful.

4   THE LEADERSHIP CRISIS

4.1   The conflict

The battle for leadership (in the Sudan) between Dr Hassan el Turabi and President Omer Bashir which had existed in an underground form for a number of years after the military coup of 30 June 1989, ultimately exploded on the night of 12 December 1999 when Omer Bashir declared a state of emergency in the whole country and dissolved the National Assembly. Bashir also suspended some specific articles of the Constitution. With the dissolution of the National Assembly, Turabi was deprived of the use of a very important forum for staging the struggle for power. The National Congress remained the only forum where Turabi continued to wage his political struggle against Omer Bashir. But afterwards he was even deprived of the use of this forum when the National Congress and his political functions were frozen on 6 May 2000 by Omer Bashir.

President Omer Bashir justified the declaration of state of emergency on 12 December 1999 on the ground that he was saving the country from collapse, partly as a result of external forces and partly as a result of his struggle with Turabi which had almost totally paralysed the public administration and the political institutions.

It is in fact true that the conflict between the top leaders and their supporters almost crippled the political and government institutions. Bashir lost effective influence over the political institutions. He was also losing effective control over the executive institutions. State governors, who nearly all supported Turabi, on many occasions silently and sometimes openly defied the decisions or orders of the President of the Republic. The public was virtually led to believe that there were two independent governments in one state, namely the government of Omer Bashir in the Republican palace and the government of Turabi in Minshia (Turabi's residential area).

4.2   The mechanisms of the power struggle

In order to stage a political struggle one must have a forum to use. Secondly, there must be some reason to justify the struggle. The cause may be realistic or unrealistic.[54] Turabi alternately used the National Assembly and the National Congress as the forum in which he staged his political struggle against Omer Bashir. He used democracy as the cause of his political struggle: for example, when he talked to the editor in chief (Ahmed Bilal) of *Akhbar el Yom* newspaper after the dismissal of the constitutional case by Court he said:

you should refrain in your newspaper from painting the present crisis as if it were a

---

[54]   Turabi's justification for the struggle he makes is the protection of democracy and fundamental freedoms. It has to be noted, of course, that he is trying to undo the system he has made in order to achieve his ultimate political objective.

conflict between personalities … I am not searching for power but I am working to affirm public freedoms and if you lose these public freedoms you will even lose your present newspaper.

On the basis of this argument, Turabi bitterly and openly condemned the decision of the Constitutional Court on the case. He fell short of concluding that the Court was under the influence of the undemocratic government of Omer Bashir.

4.3 The struggle for the use and control of the National Congress

Turabi understood that the person who was able to use and control the National Congress as a political institution could take over the leadership of the state. Hence he had to make sure that he enjoyed the overwhelming support in this institution, and in fact he did. He had the majority of the party members. Turabi began his political struggle using the National Congress as his forum. But Omer Bashir blocked his route here. Turabi had to shift the battle to the floor of the National Assembly where it was practically difficult for Omer Bashir to directly obstruct his political manoeuvres.

4.4 The introduction of constitutional amendments in the National Assembly

Turabi observed that it was difficult to remove Omer Bashir through political process alone. Using the National Assembly he devised another mechanism of struggle. Executive power is vested in the Council of Ministers and the ministers are appointed by the President of the state (see Article 47(1)). It is also the President who presides over the meetings of the Council of Ministers (see Article 43(b)). Strictly speaking the Constitution provides a presidential executive. Turabi's supporters submitted proposals for the amendments[55] to specific articles of the Constitution in order to dismantle presidentialism and create a pure parliamentary system where Omer Bashir would remain a nominal head of the state. Under the amended Constitution ministers would be appointed by the Prime Minister who would preside over the meetings of the Council of Ministers. The ministers would be responsible to the Council of Ministers, Prime Minister and the National Assembly. The state governors[56] would be directly elected by the people and they would be responsible to the Council of Ministers and the National Assembly. Turabi was sure to bring his supporters to staff these institutions, through elections conducted under the present established system. He was also sure to become the Prime Minister and wield political and executive power.

---

[55] In Arts. 43, 47 and 56.
[56] At present the system of indirect election of state governors under Art. 56 gives the President of the state power to determine that the candidate to be elected is the choice of the President.

Omer Bashir requested Turabi to postpone the discussion on the amendments so that the executive would be able to discuss them (within forty-eight hours) and offer their opinion, but Turabi refused. He excluded from the discussion the Executive Organ and the President, who was also part of the legislature. What disappointed Omer Bashir and his supporters the more was the contemptuous manner in which Turabi handled and commented on the President's letter before the members of the Assembly. Omer and his supporters regarded this attitude as a disgrace to the seat of the nation.

Two days before the voting on the proposed amendments could take place, Omer Bashir went on air in the night of the 12 December 1999 to declare a state of emergency, the suspension of the operation of certain articles of the Constitution and the dissolution of the National Assembly. Many party persons who held key positions, both in the political institutions and the executive organs, owed more allegiance to Turabi than to the President. In fact much of this allegiance had been induced by fear and the belief that Turabi was the more powerful and formidable and nobody was prepared to risk his job by standing in his way. Omer was sincerely convinced that the system would collapse unless he acted swiftly.

4.5   Constitutional case

The Constitutional Court was used as the third forum for the power struggle. A legal challenge to the Presidential Decrees of 12 December 1999 was made when Turabi's supporters and members of the dissolved National Assembly submitted a petition to the Constitutional Court on 18 December 1999. The petition alleged that the Presidential Decree which dissolved the National Assembly violated the provisions of Article 72 of the Constitution which prescribes a tenure of four years for the life of the National Assembly beginning from the day of its first sitting after the elections. The first sitting of the dissolved National Assembly was 12 February 1996 and the tenure of four years was to expire on 12 February 2000.

The second charge in the petition was that the President of the state exceeded his constitutional powers under Article 43. This article, the petition states, does not permit the President to dissolve the National Assembly and that there is no other article in the Constitution which confers power on him to take that action. In fact the article does not expressly confer or preclude the President's power to dissolve the National Assembly. It is simply silent. The third charge is that the declaration of state of emergency violates the provisions of Article 131(2), which prescribe that such a declaration must (if made) be placed before the National Assembly within fifteen days when the Assembly is in session.

The declaration of state of emergency is based on the existence of certain conditions. These are "the occurrence or approach of any emergent danger, whether it is war, invasion, blockade, disaster or epidemics, as may threaten the country or any part thereof or the safety or economy of the same". The petition states that these conditions did not exist when the presidential decrees were made.

Omer Bashir supported his declarations by stating that external and internal dangers were threatening the country. Implicitly he proclaimed that he was acting under necessity to save the country from collapse.

The hearing of the case was completed in the third week of February 2000 but the judgment was suspended to be declared at a future date.

On 9 March 2000, the Constitutional Court delivered its judgment in which it dismissed the constitutional case. The Court in its judgment made wide reference to the decisions of courts in constitutional cases in various countries, including Pakistan. Reference was also made to various English constitutional authorities, including Ivory Jennings and Glanville Williams. The Court justified the decision of the President for the dissolution of the National Assembly on the doctrine of necessity. It said that the country was almost torn to pieces by the conflict between the President and Turabi, the then Speaker of the National Assembly. The Court acknowledged the fact that there was no express provision in the Constitution which conferred power on the President to dissolve the National Assembly. But the safety of the state and its stability are vested in the first place in the President of the state. If these are imminently threatened with collapse, the President must act under necessity to save the country. The Court deplored the act of the Speaker of the National Assembly in denying the President his right of participation in the proposed amendments while he was part of the legislature.

Before concluding this section it is essential to mention that Dr Hassan el Turabi's response to the judgment of the Constitutional Court is not only negative, but hostile and he appealed to the people to defend the system and their "civilization"[57] (i.e. the Islamic *shari'a*). His comments on the Court's judgment are tantamount to questioning the independence of the judiciary (the Constitutional Court in this particular case). Many observers, however, asked this question: "But who destroyed the independence of the judiciary?"

One of these observers, Ahmed Bilal, the editor in chief of *Akhbar el Yom* newspaper,[58] wondered why Turabi then complained since he prides himself that he drafted the Constitution and passed it (when he was the Speaker) in the National Assembly; he created the Constitutional Court (and made its decisions final) and participated in the appointment of its President and members. In his own words he said to Turabi:[59]

So you participated in the creation of this Court and you made its decisions final; that you consented (as Speaker) to the appointment of its members (when their names were submitted to the National Assembly by the President of the Republic).. you should now accept its judgments[60] upon which there is no appeal, except to God.[61]

---

[57] *Akhbar el Yom*, vol. 1926, 11 March 2000.
[58] *Ibid.*
[59] *Ibid.*
[60] *Ibid.*
[61] "Implicitly you wanted to create a Court which will always make judgments in favour of the government if you hold the power. But you are now against its judgment when you are out of power and a victim of its judgment.".

Turabi replied: "But there could be a resort to the people because they are the Supreme Custodians of the Constitution, after God."

It must however be finally stated that the people, referred to above, in a referendum confirmed the Constitution in the form in which it was presented to them and so they may also be expected to accept the judgment of the Constitutional Court.

Kuwait

*Fadi Nader**

During most of 1999 Kuwait was affected by low oil prices and uncertain revenue earnings, leading to worries about long-term economic performance. However with the beginning of the new millennium, stability and rising oil prices have led to recovery and measurable growth in various areas. This positive environment provided the backdrop for a legal reform programme that the country is pursuing.

It is within the framework of this programme that the Kuwaiti Parliament has ratified a number of pieces of legislation that could contribute to the recovery of Kuwait's ailing stock exchange and in attracting foreign investments to the country. Moreover, a new health insurance scheme was introduced in an attempt to relieve the government of the burden of providing free medical care to the country's foreign work force.

1 DISCLOSURE OF INTEREST IN SHARES OF LISTED COMPANIES

By virtue of the Law No. 2/1999, any shareholder of a listed joint stock company in Kuwait must disclose to the Kuwait Stock Exchange (KSE) any direct or indirect interest he might have in the company if his ownership is equal or greater than 5 per cent of the company's capital.

Pursuant to the new law, natural and legal persons are obliged to notify the KSE and the exchange-listed company if their voting rights reach or exceed the threshold of 5 per cent. In its turn, the joint stock company should notify the KSE of the names of its shareholders whose ownership reaches or exceeds, at any time, the 5 per cent level. Such notification must be made on the dates announced by the KSE from time to time.

---

* LLB, LLM, Regional Attorney, Middle East, Africa and South Asia American Life Insurance Company.

The notification and publication requirements relate to voting rights and shares in the capital of joint stock companies whose shares are admitted to official trading on the Kuwait Stock Exchange.

As a rule, shareholding in a Kuwaiti joint stock company represents voting rights in such a company, i.e. the same voting right is attached to each share.

However, investors are not only interested in obtaining information on the shareholdings which are directly held but also on how it is possible to have an indirect influence on the voting rights of third persons. This is the reason why voting rights are counted additionally so as to provide the public with a true picture of the real voting right structures. Thus the law has provided for certain mechanisms aimed at preventing non-compliance with the reporting requirements.

In addition to the notifying party's own direct shareholding, he or the company (if such information becomes available to it) should declare any shares that:

(a)   are held by a third party for him or for a company controlled by him;
(b)   are held by a company controlled by him;
(c)   are held together with those of other persons in a pool through which voting rights are jointly exercised;
(d)   he has assigned as security to a third party by retaining the possibility to exercise voting rights;
(e)   in which a usufruct is created in his favour;
(f)   in respect of which he or a company controlled by him may demand a transfer of title;
(g)   are entrusted to him for safekeeping in so far as he may exercise the voting rights at his own discretion.

KSE has the discretion to independently investigate any notification received and has the power to impose penalties in the event the reporting requirements are not complied with or if the notifications are not accurate. Accordingly, the KSE might suspend the voting right arising from the share for up to two years but will maintain the right to receive dividend payments and to transfer the share with the voting restrictions imposed until the end of the sanction period.

2   INCENTIVES FOR KUWAITIS TO JOIN THE PRIVATE SECTOR

The Kuwaiti Parliament approved a bill that will encourage Kuwaitis to work in the private sector. In the second and final reading, fifty-one law-makers and Cabinet members voted for the legislation, while nine members abstained.

According to the Bill, the government and private companies will set up a fund to pay Kuwaitis that work for private companies the monthly benefits they are entitled to in civil service jobs. The benefits include a monthly allowance of 50 dinars ($163) per child for up to five children (civil servants get the allowance for an unlimited number of children) and the payment of unemployment benefits.

The Fund's finances will come from the government as well as a 2.5 per cent tax on all local private companies, but law-makers decided to limit the tax to listed firms. Companies will also be required to pay higher fees for licences and work permits especially for non-Kuwaiti labour.

3   FOREIGNERS TO OWN AND TRADE LISTED STOCKS

Kuwaiti MPs have approved a Bill allowing foreigners to own stocks and trade in its bourse.

The indirect foreign investment law was passed by a margin of thirty-six to five. The new Bill is expected to be given the final approval of the Council of Ministers as all Cabinet ministers present in Parliament voted to accept it in principle.

The law will allow foreign investors to own up to 100 per cent stock of Kuwaiti companies listed on the KSE, based on regulations to be issued by the government.

Ownership of Kuwaiti shares is currently limited to citizens and other Gulf nationals, but foreigners can take part through mutual funds.

Some MPs objected to the law, warning that it would allow foreigners to control sensitive companies in Kuwait and could have a devastating impact on the local economy.

4   A NEW HEALTH INSURANCE SCHEME

A new Law No. 1/1999 – compelling expatriate workers and their families in Kuwait to have medical insurance – entered into effect on 10 April 2000. The promulgation of the new law was followed by the issuance of an immigration requirement that requires expatriates seeking to renew their residency permits in Kuwait to submit evidence of medical insurance coverage.

Although the 1999 law gives the expatriates the choice of either enrolling themselves under the government insurance scheme or purchasing private insurance cover, two Ministerial Decisions (Nos. 126/2000 and 127/2000) have announced the application of the government insurance scheme and have regulated its annual premiums for the insured and his dependants.

Subsequently, the Ministry of Health announced that a private insurance cover is acceptable provided that the insurance provider is a licensed insurance company in Kuwait and that the medical coverage extends to the duration of the residency permit of the insured expatriate.

Saudi Arabia

*Vernon Handley and Fares Al-Hejailan**

1 INTRODUCTION

In light of Saudi Arabia's wish to join the WTO a number of significant legal developments have recently taken place in Saudi Arabia. The long awaited new Foreign Capital Investment law, which replaces the old Foreign Capital Investment law enacted by Royal Decree No. M/4 dated 2/2/1399 AH that had been in effect for over twenty years, was approved by the Council of Ministers on 10 April 2000 upon the recommendation of the newly established Supreme Economic Council (SEC). In addition, a new governmental agency was also formed in order to complement the new law. The General Investment Authority (GIA) is responsible for the implementation of the new regulations and the review and approval of foreign investment applications. The GIA effectively replaces the Foreign Capital Investment Committee (FCIC).

Furthermore, other developments have also been witnessed in the areas of property law and enforcement of foreign judgments in Saudi Arabia.

2 SUPREME ECONOMIC COUNCIL

The Supreme Economic Council (SEC) has been established by Royal Decree No.A/111 of 17/5/1420AH (corresponding to 28 August 1999) in order to update the organization and the administrative structure of the Kingdom's economic institutions, and formulate a sound economic policy through coordination of the efforts of the various government agencies, including the Council of Ministers (see Article 2), whose activities are directly related to the national economy, in order to achieve coherence and integration of these efforts.

---

*   Advocates of the Law Firm of Salah Al-Hejailan, Riyadh, Saudi Arabia.

The Supreme Economic Council law consists of ten articles. Article 5 sets out its powers as follows:

(1) finalization of economic policy and formulation of what are referred to as "appropriate substitutes";
(2) coordination with the government authorities whose business is directly connected to the national economy, in order to achieve and take all measures needed for cementing interrelations and integration of their responsibilities;
(3) following up, and taking all the measures that are needed for implementation of economic policy and the resolutions of the Council of Ministers regarding economic matters; and submitting a periodic report to the same to the Council of Ministers;
(4) to study the following:
   (i) the general framework of the development plan prepared by the Ministry of Planning, the draft plan, the follow-up reports and the economic report;
   (ii) financial policy, the bases for preparing the draft budget and the disbursements that are anticipated by the Ministry of Finance and National Economy, in the light of which the Ministry prepares the State Budget;
   (iii) drafts of the State Budget, and the budgets of the legal public institutions that are prepared by the Ministry of Finance and National Economy;
   (iv) international and local commercial policies, the rules that regulate the labour and stock market and protect consumer interests, as well those that establish the appropriate climate for competition, investment and the industrial and agricultural policies prepared by the authorities concerned;
   (v) reports and other matters referred by the committees and governmental authorities to the Council of Ministers, that are related to economic affairs and matters, including those which relate to the levels of the prevailing prices, dues, taxes, different kinds of tariff, state revenues, investments, disbursements, expenditures, the situation of the public debt, loans and privileges, as well as those which are passed by the Ministerial Committee for allocation, the Economic Control Committee and the Ministerial Committee formed in pursuance of Royal Decree No. 154/8, dated 27/1/1404 AH (2 November 1983); business carried out by the mixed committees in the economic field; the state's final account; and the final accounts of the public agencies;
   (vi) Bills of laws and regulations pertaining to economic affairs and matters, the drafts of economic and commercial agreements and environmental protection laws, all of which will be effected in cooperation with authorities concerned; and
   (vii) matters which are passed by the Council of Ministers and the High Position;
(5) to take such action as may be necessary for the preparation of studies,

reports and researches concerning economy-related subjects, by assigning these to the government authorities concerned or entering into contracts with professional bodies, or seeking assistance from experts, as may be deemed appropriate; the Supreme Economic Council will review the information, reports and cash policies submitted by the governor of the Saudi Arabian Monetary Agency;

(6) to prepare a periodic report regarding the national economy based on that which has been prepared by the authorities concerned; and

(7) to exercise the powers that may be assigned to it.

3 THE GENERAL INVESTMENT AUTHORITY (GIA)

3.1 Regulatory provisions of the GIA

Article 2 of the Regulatory Provisions of the GIA provides as follows:

Pursuant to these regulations, there shall be established a general authority and be named "the General Investment Authority" that shall enjoy legal identity and be linked to the President of the Supreme Economic Council with headquarters in the city of Riyadh.

The above shows that the GIA will have a separate legal identity and, as such, be competent to acquire rights and assume obligations. It will also have a separate budget to be issued in accordance with the rules governing the issuance of the government Budget. The above provisions have also determined the name and headquarters of the GIA and the administrative agency that will have administrative control over the GIA's activities. The administrative agency is represented by the President of the Supreme Economic Council (SEC).

The nature of the GIA can be determined by reference to its objectives and the activities that it is to perform. These are provided for under Article 3 of its regulatory provisions. Based on these objectives and activities, the GIA can be viewed as one of the general economic institutions which enjoys legal independence.

3.2 Objectives of the GIA

Article 3 of the regulatory provisions provides that the main objective of the GIA is to look after investment affairs in the Kingdom, including foreign investment. The activities provided for under Article 3 are given only by way of example in order to permit the addition of other activities, should these be deemed necessary. Accordingly, paragraph 8 of Article 3 provides for the possibility of adding to these activities. It appears from the provisions of paragraphs 1 to 7 that the activities of the GIA include enhancement of domestic and foreign investment, coordination between the competent authorities, implementation of regular programmes for the promotion of investment, preparation of studies on investment opportunities, organizing, holding and participating in conferences, symposia, local and external exhibitions and other fora relating to investment.

The Comprehensive Service Centre provided for under Article 9 of these regulatory provisions will assist in simplification of the procedures and in defining the competent agency for ease of reference. The Centre will include offices for the relevant government agencies and will provide its services to all investors. These services include receiving investment applications, deciding on such applications, prompt conclusion of the formalities and the issuance of the necessary licences.

3.3 Administrative structure of the GIA

3.3.1 *The board of directors*

Articles 4–6 of the regulatory provisions provide for the composition of the board of directors, its powers, meetings and voting rights.

Article 4 provides as follows:

The Board of Directors of the Authority shall be set up as follows:

1. the governor (chairman);
2. a representative of the Ministry of Interior (member);
3. a representative of the Ministry of Foreign Affairs (member);
4. a representative of the Ministry of Commerce (member);
5. a representative of the Ministry of Agriculture and Water (member);
6. a representative of the Ministry of Petroleum and Mineral Resources (member);
7. a representative of the Ministry of Industry and Electricity (member);
8. a representative of the Ministry of Finance and National Economy (member);
9. a representative of the Ministry of Planning (member);
10. a representative of the Ministry of Labour and Social Affairs (member);
11. a representative of the Saudi Arabian Monetary Agency (member).

The rank of a government agency's representative in the Board of Directors shall not be less than the fourteenth grade. The term of membership of the Board shall be three years only.

3.3.2 *Powers of the board*

Pursuant to Article 5 of the regulatory provisions, the board of directors of the GIA is deemed to be the supreme authority that controls its management and takes the decisions necessary to carry out its objectives. These powers have been detailed and include deciding and rejecting investment applications, proposing a list of the types of activity which are exempted from foreign investment and filing this list with the Supreme Economic Council, as well as proposing amendments to the regulatory provisions and any other regulations dealing with investment (for more detail on the powers of the GIA refer to the text of Article 5).

3.3.3 *Meetings and decisions of the board*

Under Article 6 of the regulatory provisions, the board of directors must hold its meetings at least once a month, pursuant to an invitation to be extended by the governor, who may also invite the board for extraordinary meetings whenever that is deemed necessary, or upon a request by at least 50 per cent of its members. The invitation for such meetings must specify the agenda. Decisions of the board must be passed by majority vote of the members attending any meeting, and when the votes are equal the chairman will cast a deciding vote.

3.3.4 *The governor*

Under Article 7 of the regulatory provisions, the GIA shall have a governor with the rank of a minister and the governor will be appointed by a Royal Decree pursuant to a recommendation by the President of the Supreme Economic Council. The governor will be the executive officer of the GIA and shall be responsible for the discharge of its activities.

The powers of the governor have been enumerated under Article 8 of the regulatory provisions and include supervising and preparing for meetings of the board of directors, following up on the implementation of resolutions passed by the board, as well as representing the GIA before government agencies and third parties.

3.4 The Comprehensive Service Centre

Article 9 of the regulatory provisions provides for the establishment of a Comprehensive Service Centre to render administrative services to enable foreign investors to obtain the necessary licences. That Centre will include liaison offices for all the relevant government agencies, such as some sectors of the Ministry of the Interior (Passports and Recruitment Offices), the Ministry of Foreign Affairs, the Ministry of Commerce, the Ministry of Industry and Electricity, the Ministry of Finance and National Economy (represented by *Zakat* and the Income Tax Department), the Ministry of Agriculture and Water, the Ministry of Labour and Social Affairs (represented by the Labour Office), the Ministry of Petroleum and Mineral Resources and the Saudi Industrial Development Fund.

The Centre will operate under the supervision of the governor and must provide its services to investors in such a manner as to facilitate the reception of, and decisions on, investment applications, conclusion of transactions, issuance of licences, approvals, and such visas and stay permits as may be necessary for the carrying out of its activities.

Because of the vital role to be played by the Centre with regard to investment services, it is hoped that it will acquire a sophisticated image and add more flexibility with respect to the conclusion of transactions and will render its services in a manner satisfactory to investors.

3.5 Supervision of the GIA

The GIA is subject to dual control, the first of which is administrative control over its employees and activities, and the second of which is financial control over its funds and financial statements. Although the GIA is, in principle, a legal entity capable of enjoying financial and administrative independence, it is nevertheless subject to these controls. As such, the regulatory provisions have vested the powers of administrative control over the affairs of the GIA in the Supreme Economic Council to which it is closely related (for more details on supervision over the GIA and the financial structure of the GIA see Articles 10–14).

4 FOREIGN CAPITAL INVESTMENT LAW

The new Foreign Capital Investment Law includes eighteen articles that deal with the privileges to be enjoyed by the foreign investor, the prerequisites for enjoying such privileges, the guarantees for foreign investments, the means of settling of investment disputes to which a foreign investor is a party and the acquired rights relating to foreign investments that had been lawfully established prior to the implementation of this law. Additionally, the law includes provisions relating to its promulgation and the date on which it will be implemented. Furthermore, Article 1 includes definitions of the important terms and phrases used in the law such as "foreign investor", "foreign investment" and "foreign capital". These constitute principal definitions under this law.

Under paragraph (e) of Article 1, a "foreign investor" is a natural person who is not a holder of Saudi nationality or a legal person in which the shareholders are not all holders of Saudi nationality. Under paragraph (f) of the same article the term "foreign investment" denotes investment of foreign capital in an activity in respect of which a licence has been issued pursuant to this law. Under paragraph (g), the term "foreign capital" has been defined to include, by way of example, the under-mentioned property and rights whenever title to these is enjoyed by a foreign investor:

(a) bank notes, financial papers and commercial paper;
(b) profits realized from foreign investment if used in the increase of capital, the expansion of existing projects or the establishment of new projects;
(c) machinery, equipment, instruments, spare parts, means of transport and other implements related to investment and necessary for production.
(d) intangible rights such as licences, intellectual property rights, technical knowhow, administrative skills and ways and means of production.

The most important feature of the Foreign Capital Investment Law is perhaps that it has struck a balance between the protection and guarantees available to the foreign investor, and the substantial role that may be played by foreign investment in the Kingdom's economic development.

4.1   Scope for the privileges to be enjoyed by the foreign investor

The correlation between the volume of foreign investments in any country and the scope of protection available to these investments under the laws of that country is unquestionable. A foreign investor normally seeks the environment that is most suitable for investment of its capital. Most probably, foreign investors would look for the environment that satisfies several considerations including, *inter alia*, free entry and departure, residence and movement for foreign recruits within the host country. A foreign investor would also consider the range of economic sectors available for foreign investment. Furthermore, it may consider the tax policies that can have a great impact on the investment of foreign capital.

4.1.1   *Rules governing the foreign investor's entry and residence in the Kingdom*

The Foreign Capital Investment Law does not include special rules on entry, residence and departure of foreign investors. It appears that the legislature has left such matters to be regulated by the law now in force and if the need arises, upon implementation of the New Foreign Capital Investment Law, the appropriate regulations will then have to be enacted to remedy the situation in a manner compatible with the prevailing circumstances and regional autonomy. It is to be noted that the Kingdom will be dealing with the situation in the manner that would serve its interest. In this connection, Article 9 of the Foreign Capital Investment Law (FCIL) provides that sponsorship of the foreign investor and its non-Saudi employees shall be vested in the licensed facility. In effect, this adds more flexibility to the sponsorship regulations.

4.1.2   *Economic sectors open for foreign investment*

The Foreign Capital Investment Law is very flexible in specifying the economic sectors that are open for foreign investment. A foreign investor is now able to invest in all economic sectors except those that are excluded by a special resolution of the Supreme Economic Council. As such, the new law has departed from the trend of the old law which limited the investment of foreign capital to certain economic fields.

The old law issued by Royal Decree No. M/4, dated 2/2/1399H, defined the projects that could be treated as "development projects" pursuant to a recommendation by the Foreign Capital Investment Committee (FCIC). Under Ministerial Resolutions No. 925, dated 4/11/1400H, and No. 11/K/W, dated 17/7/1401H, development projects included the following:

(a)   industrial development projects;
(b)   agricultural development projects;
(c)   health care projects;

(d)   service projects;
(e)   construction projects.

Articles 2–6 of these Ministerial Resolutions defined the term "economic sectors" and listed the projects that come under each sector.

Unlike the old law, the new law does not include a definition of the sectors that allow foreign investment. The new Law is more liberal with regard to the definition of "economic sectors" and, as such, permits a foreign investor to invest in all economic sectors except those excluded by a special resolution of the Supreme Economic Council, pursuant to a resolution by its board of directors (Article 5-2 of the regulatory provisions).

This is what may be understood from the plain language of Articles 2 and 3 of the new law. Article 2 provides as follows: "Without prejudice to the Provisions of the Relevant Regulations and Agreements, the Authority shall issue a temporary or permanent license in respect of any foreign investment in the Kingdom". This means that foreign investment is permitted in any economic activity except the activities which will be excluded from the scope of the new law pursuant to Article 3 thereof.

In addition to the right of a foreign investor to invest in any permissible field as provided for under Article 2, a foreign investor is also granted another privilege under Article 8, namely the right to own land or any other real estate within the Kingdom. Article 8 provides as follows: "A foreign facility holding a licence pursuant to these regulations shall be entitled to own real estate as may be necessary for the conduct of the licensed activity or for housing of all or any of its staff members, subject to the rules governing ownership of real estate by non-Saudis."

4.1.3   Tax regulation governing foreign investments

Article 14 of the new law provides as follows: "All foreign investments that are licensed pursuant to this law shall be subject to the provisions of tax regulations in force in Saudi Arabia as may be amended from time to time."

Article 14 as above quoted makes it clear that foreign investments in Saudi Arabia shall be subject to tax regulations. It is to be noted that the Council of Ministers has issued resolutions that will enable foreign investors to deduct the losses that might accrue on commencement of the relevant project from the profits that may be realized in the future, a feature that did not exist previously. It may also be noted that the tax payable by a foreign facility whose profits exceed SR 1 million has been reduced from 45 per cent to 30 per cent. This is one of the important measures approved by the Council of Ministers with a view to attracting foreign capital.

The 15 per cent tax reduction now available to the foreign investor in addition to the possibility of carrying the losses forward for an indefinite period of time represent incentives to foreign investors, who can make use of the reduced taxes on the one hand, and also benefit from the possibility of deferring payment of the due tax until their businesses prosper, on the other.

4.2 Prerequisites for qualifying to the privileges under the Investment Law

Article 2 of the new Investment Law makes it a condition that a foreign investor should first obtain the necessary licence before commencing activities. This has been designed to ensure effective control over such activities in a manner that will best serve the country's interest.

Article 2 provides as follows: "Without prejudice to the provisions of the relevant regulations and agreements, the GIA shall issue a temporary or a permanent license in respect of any foreign investment in the Kingdom". As may readily be seen, Article 2 permits a preliminary government control over foreign investments. It entitles the GIA to study the applications submitted by foreign investors, whether they be for the execution of a new investment project, or the expansion of an already existing project. Before approving any such activity, the GIA must ensure that all the prerequisites under the rules for implementation of these regulations have been satisfied.

The preliminary control referred to above is intended to ensure that the foreign capital to be invested in the Kingdom is capable of contributing to the economic development of the country. Therefore, the GIA has been vested with powers to enable it to ascertain that the applicant has satisfied all the prerequisites. The non-fulfilment of the prerequisites entitles the GIA to dismiss the application.

Article 2 also provides for the procedure for obtaining the necessary licence. It states as follows:

The GIA shall decide on the investment application within thirty days from the date of filing the documentation provided for; if the Authority rejects the application within the above-mentioned period, the reasons for such rejection shall be stated. The person whose application has been rejected shall be entitled to appeal from such rejection pursuant to the provisions of the applicable regulations.

This shows that a foreign investor should first file its application with the GIA giving details of the capital to be invested, type of investment and any other information as may be required by the implementing rules of the new law. A decision on the application has to be made within thirty days, failing which the required licence must be issued to the investor. It is noticeable that only thirty days are available under the law for deciding on the relevant application. This is a relatively short period and was intended to encourage the GIA to issue its decision as promptly as possible. If the decision is withheld beyond that period, the application is deemed to have been accepted. This is likely to reassure foreign investors that their applications will be considered without unnecessary delay.

Under Article 4 of the new law a foreign investor may apply for more than one licence for various activities. Such an incentive may help boost foreign investment in important sectors of the Saudi economy and this will have a positive impact on the country's economic development.

The above reflects keenness on the part of the legislature to make it easy for foreign investors to invest in the Kingdom. Apart from government control over the foreign entity provided for under Article 2 of the law, it may be noted that Article 12 provides for a continuing government control following the issue of the licence and commencement of the activities of the relevant venture. This has been intended to ensure that foreign investors will continue to respect the terms and conditions pursuant to which the relevant licence will be issued.

Article 12 provides as follows:

12/1 Should the provisions of these regulations and those for implementing rules thereof be violated, the Authority shall serve a written notice on the foreign investor in order to remedy such violation within a period to be specified by the Authority as may be appropriate for correction of that violation.

12/2 Without prejudice to a more severe penalty, a foreign investor shall, where the violation continues, be subject to any of the following penalties:

Withholding of all or part of the incentives and privileges as may be available to the foreign investor.

A pecuniary penalty not exceeding SR500,000 (five hundred thousand Saudi Riyals).

Cancellation of the foreign investment license.

12/3 The penalties provided for under paragraph 2 above shall be inflicted pursuant to a resolution of the Board of Directors.

12/4 Appeal from any such penalty shall lie with the Board of Grievances in accordance with the procedure set forth in the regulations of the Board.

The above provisions show that the board of directors of the GIA is empowered to impose certain penalties on a foreign investor in case of any violation of its duties.

4.3 The guarantees available to foreign investors under the new law

Apart from the protection bestowed on foreign investors under the new law, including *inter alia*, easy access and residence in the Kingdom, expansion of the relevant investment project and the application of flexible tax rules, the law also provides the foreign investor with additional protection against non-commercial risks, such as confiscation or expropriation. Such risks are normally taken into consideration before a foreign investor decides to invest in any country. The protection available to foreign investors under the new law against so-called "non-commercial risks" is compatible with the Kingdom's policy of attracting foreign capital.

The risks to which foreign investors may be subject could either be expropriation, or any similar hazard. A foreign investor may be ready to accept commercial losses, but no foreign investor is ready to accept losses resulting from non-commercial risks. Being fully cognizant of these concerns, the legislature was keen to prescribe rules that would protect foreign investors against such risks, which is an added advantage to a prospective foreign investor.

In this connection Article 11 of the new law provides as follows:

Investments by a foreign investor shall not be confiscated in whole or in part except pursuant to a judicial decision. Similarly, such investments shall not be subject to expropriation, in whole or in part, except for public interest, and against the payment of just compensation, in accordance with the applicable laws and regulations.

Naturally, a competent judicial tribunal would not issue a writ for confiscation of the property of a foreign investor except for good cause. Additionally, the judicial system in the Kingdom is known to be unbiased, and this also constitutes a further guarantee to foreign investors.

Expropriation of foreign investment can be effected only if the conditions provided for under Article 11 have been satisfied. These are as follows:

(a) The said expropriation, whether it be in whole or in part, must be for the public interest.
(b) Expropriation must be effected in accordance with the relevant regulations. This has been intended to counter arbitrary processes and misuse of power.
(c) There should be no discrimination in effecting expropriation.
(d) Expropriation can only be effected against just compensation. Such compensation must represent the actual value of the expropriated property. It must be paid promptly and there should not be any restrictions with respect to the transfer thereof.

The above conditions constitute an obligation to pay fair compensation if the property of a foreign investor has been expropriated in the public interest. Promptness of payment of the said compensation is an indication that the compensation was fair and has been properly assessed.

4.4   Means of settlement of investment disputes to which a foreign investor is a party

We have previously dealt with the rules relating to the protection bestowed by the Foreign Investment Law on foreign investments in the Kingdom. It remains to discuss the procedure for settlement of investment disputes to which a foreign investor is a party. This issue has received special treatment under the law that provides for the amicable settlement of any such dispute in way that is compatible with protecting the interest of both parties.

In that connection, Article 13 of the Investment Law provides as follows:

Without prejudice to the Agreements to which the Kingdom of Saudi Arabia is a party:

Disputes that may arise between the Government and a foreign investor in relation to investments licensed pursuant to these regulations shall, as far as possible, be settled amicably, failing which the dispute shall be resolved in accordance with the relevant regulations.

Disputes that may arise between a foreign investor and its Saudi partners in relation to the foreign investments that are licensed pursuant to these regulations shall, as far as possible, be settled amicably, failing which the dispute shall be resolved in accordance with the relevant regulations.

The above provisions refer to two types of investment dispute that may arise between a foreign investor and the government on the one hand, or between a foreign investor and its Saudi partners, on the other. The implementation of the relevant principles and rules may give rise to many disputes whether they be *vis-à-vis* the government (in relation to investments wholly owned by a foreign investor), or the Saudi partners (in relation to joint investments). Such disputes normally arise upon the interpretation of certain terms and conditions of any relevant agreement. The legislature has been keen that good relations be maintained between a foreign investor and the host country through effective procedure for resolution of any such dispute.

The law has provided for the following procedure.

4.4.1   Amicable settlement

Under Article 13 of the Investment Law, the parties should first seek amicable settlement of their disputes. It is to be pointed out in this respect that an amicable settlement is deemed to be the most effective means for the resolution of any dispute. It saves time and cost, reconciles the varying viewpoints and ultimately achieves a settlement that is normally based on the joint interest of both parties. This also provides an additional assurance to foreign investors that their disputes can ultimately be resolved without any bias.

4.4.2   Judicial process

If no such amicable settlement is possible, the parties may then seek judicial process in accordance with the provisions of the relevant Saudi regulations. The judicial process under the Saudi law provides an additional assurance to a foreign investor that the relevant case would be decided by a competent authority and in accordance with the relevant regulations and the merits of the case.

The new law has repeatedly referred to the possibility of resorting to any such means in order to ensure a foreign investor that its investment is properly protected.

In that connection, under Article 2 of the new law a foreign investor whose application for a licence has been rejected by the GIA within the prescribed period of thirty days as from the date of such application is entitled to appeal against the decision pursuant to the regulations.

Similarly, under Article 11 of the new law, a foreign investor is entitled to appeal before the Board of Grievances against a decision imposing on the foreign investor any of the penalties prescribed by that article. The regulations of Article 11 have been discussed above at length.

Lastly, where any dispute to which a foreign investor is a party cannot be resolved amicably, the dispute may be resolved pursuant to the applicable regulations, i.e. through the judicial process.

4.4.3   Settlement under international bilateral or multilateral agreements

Settlement of disputes under international agreements to which the Kingdom is a party is deemed to be an effective means of settlement that is satisfactory to foreign investors. It is understood that, in case of any contradiction between the regulations of an international agreement and the domestic law, the provisions of the international agreement would prevail. It is also understood that the implementation of the terms and conditions of an international agreement relating to dispute resolution contributes to the achievement of a common understanding with respect to such disputes and to the development and unification of the standards that govern the relation between the country of origin of a foreign investor and the Kingdom.

Articles 2 and 13 of the new law have therefore confirmed the principle that international agreements to which the Kingdom is a party must be honoured. At the same time, Article 15 of the new law imposes an obligation on foreign investors to abide by all laws and regulations in force in Saudi Arabia and by the international agreements to which Saudi Arabia is a party.

The Kingdom of Saudi Arabia has concluded several bilateral and multilateral agreements that are intended to protect foreign investments. One of the most important guarantees provided for in these agreements is the possibility of settlement of disputes arising out of foreign investments through arbitration that may be conducted outside the jurisdiction of the courts of the host country. Since arbitration is characterized by features that make it more appropriate for settlement of disputes involving foreign investment, practice has shown that foreign investors tend to prefer that method of settlement of disputes to other methods.

The Kingdom of Saudi Arabia has adopted a flexible approach with regard to arbitration as may be envisaged in the several agreements concluded by the Kingdom, and in the Kingdom's resort to that means for the settlement of the various disputes involving a foreign element.

The Kingdom has acceded to the International Convention for Settlement of Investment Disputes (ICSID) of 1965. Accordingly, it has become possible to settle disputes arising in Saudi Arabia involving foreign investments through institutional arbitration. It may also be possible to settle such disputes through regional arbitration centres, such as the Commercial Arbitration Centre of the GCC states in Bahrain. The role of arbitration, as an important procedural guarantee for a foreign investor, is also enhanced by the Kingdom's accession on 4/7/1414 AH (17 December 1993) to the New York Convention on Recognition and Implementation of Foreign Arbitral Awards of 1958, pursuant to which the state parties to that Convention are bound to implement foreign arbitration awards. Furthermore, foreign investment disputes may also be resolved through arbitration to be conducted in Saudi Arabia, pursuant to the Saudi Arabian Arbitration Regulations, issued in the year 1403AH (1982).

5   ENFORCING FOREIGN JUDGMENTS

In the context of judicial reforms necessitated by Saudi Arabia's application to join the WTO, there has been a recent expansion of the jurisdiction of the Board of Grievance to include enforcement within Saudi Arabia of a foreign court order placing a preventative attachment on money and other property.

After reviewing the proposal submitted by the Minister of Justice, and after considering the Shoura Council decision No. 27/33/18 dated 13/9/1418 AH (11 January 1998) the Council of Ministers decided to approve the addition of a paragraph to Article 8(1) of the Board of Grievances Regulations issued by Royal Decree No. M/51 dated 17/7/1402 AH (10 May 1982) stating as follows: "I: Request of foreign courts to place preventative attachment on properties or funds within the Kingdom." A proposed Royal Decree to that effect is being prepared by the Council of Ministers.

It has not yet been clarified whether the exact meaning of "preventative" is in the classic sense attachment *before* there has been a full judgment on the merits in the foreign court, or a full judgment on the merits in the foreign court, possibly pending appeal, but while the Saudi court is considering rather whether to enforce the foreign judgment.

The change may also be read more broadly as possibly referring to authorizing a Saudi court's implementing specific enforcement action as ordered abroad, rather than its simply upholding a foreign judgment in principle. Stated otherwise, it is not clear, in the absence of legislative history or practical experience, whether some change may also be meant to apply in the actual enforcement of final foreign judgments, in which case the word "preventative" would apply in the sense of preventing a judgment debtor (not a mere defendant) from hiding or misapplying his assets, without the use of the word "preventative" itself being intended to refer to any particular, especially preliminary, phase of the foreign or Saudi judicial process. It is also not clear whether "attachment" extends to seizure as well as some lesser form of provisional restraint on disposition, and whether by "attachment" is meant only court process of the specific type set forth under that name in the Saudi Commercial Court Regulation, Chapter 12, even if the foreign court has ordered preventative action of a different nature, or on different bases.

6 PROPERTY LAW

The new Regulations for Real Estate Ownership and Investment by Non-Saudis have recently been announced. The legislation includes eight articles covering the ownership of real estate properties by foreigners for the purpose of carrying out properly licensed professional, vocational or economic activity or for the purpose of private residence and the residence of their workers as well as rules for the issue of real estate licences. These Regulations replace the non-Saudi real estate regulation in the Kingdom of Saudi Arabia which was issued by Royal Decree No. M/22 dated 12/7/1390 AH (13 September 1970).

Subject to the new regulations, a minimum of SR 30 million is required as capital and as total project cost for real estate investment either by selling or renting.

The regulations authorize the Interior Ministry to grant licences for foreigners to own real estate properties for the purpose of their private residence.
Article 1 states that

(a)   Non-Saudi investors, whether natural or legal persons, who are licensed to
       practise any professional, vocational or economic activity may own real estate
       necessary for the practice of such activity. This includes the real property
       necessary for residence and the residence of employees after obtaining the
       approval of the licensing authority. The said real property may be rented, taking
       into consideration the provisions of Article 5 of this Regulation;
(b)   If the said licence includes the purchase of buildings or lands for the erection
       of buildings thereon and investment thereof by selling or renting, the total
       project cost, as to land and building, shall not be less than SR30 million. The
       Council of Ministers may change this amount. It is also provided that such real
       estate property must be invested within five years of ownership.

An important aspect of this regulation is that pursuant to Article 5, non-
Saudis may not acquire the right of ownership, easement or usufruct on a
real estate property within the boundaries of the holy cities of Makkah or
Medina by any means other than succession. Acquiring the ownership right
is excluded if in conjunction with the endowment of the real property to a
particular Saudi body over which the Supreme Endowment Council has the
supervision right. Muslim non-Saudis may rent real estate within the boundaries of the two holy cities of Makkah and Medina for not more than two
years renewable for similar term or terms.

Finally, it should be noted that the new law is intended as per Article 7,
to work together with other existing property laws and regulations of the
Kingdom. Application of the provisions of the regulation may not prejudice
the following: (a) ownership rights acquired by non-Saudis as per the previous
regulations; (b) the privileges included in the rules regulating real estate
ownership for GCC citizens; (c) acquiring the ownership right or any other
original real estate right on real property by way of inheritance; and (d) the
regulations, Council of Ministers decisions and the Royal directives banning
ownership in some locations.

United Arab Emirates

*Jonathan Brown**

1 SOURCES OF LAW: JUDICIAL AND LEGAL SYSTEM

1.1 Conciliation and Compromise Committees at the UAE federal courts

In November 1999 a new federal law (Federal Law No. 26 of 1999) was published in the Official Gazette with effect three months after the date of its publication. The new law provides for a compulsory submission (under Article 3) of any action relating to a civil or commercial dispute before a conciliation and compromise committee comprising a judge and two individuals from the judicial body or other appointed persons of sufficient experience, impartiality and integrity (Article 1). It is important to note that according to the new law, no civil or *shari'a* court will be able to consider any action relating to civil or commercial dispute unless this action has been first submitted before the Conciliation and Compromise Committee.

Up to now, although in force, the law has not been applied by the UAE courts. This is presumably because there are a number of complications that will arise if the law is applied in its current form. The law does not clarify, in a situation where an action is submitted before the civil court shortly before the underlying claim is time barred under UAE law, whether such submission would stop the time from running. It is not clear whether only submission before the Conciliation and Compromise Committee would achieve this. It is possible that a claim is submitted before the civil courts a few days before it is time barred. Thereafter the plaintiff will be redirected to the Conciliation and Compromise Committee. If any attempt to conciliate and amicably settle the dispute fails before the Committee, it is possible that when the matter is subsequently resubmitted before the civil courts the relevant time limit would have expired.

---

*   Head of Shipping and Litigation, Clifford Chance LLP, Dubai, UAE.

271

One further point relates to urgent attachment applications. If the court action cannot be accepted by the civil courts unless the Conciliation and Compromise Committee route has been exhausted first, the plaintiff runs the risk of remaining unsecured because any assets that may be readily available for attachment may have dissipated after the Compromise and Conciliation procedure is complete.

Provided a degree of fine tuning is effected in the drafting of the law to address issues similar to those raised above, this is a welcome step by the UAE judicial system. It sets up an organized committee to consider whether disputes can be amicably settled, thus relieving the UAE courts from what has up to now been a very substantial case load. This has so far resulted in delays in issuing court judgments or in rushed decisions that have not considered in detail the merits of the dispute.

2   CONSTITUTIONAL AND ADMINISTRATIVE LAW

There have been no significant developments in the relevant period.

3   CIVIL LAW

There have been no significant developments in the relevant period.

4   COMMERCIAL LAW

4.1   Federal law on Securities and Commodities Market Authority

A new federal law on the establishment of the Emirates Securities and Commodities Market Authority has recently been enacted. The federal law anticipates the creation of an authority which is to have financial and administrative independence and the power to promulgate rules and safeguards in its licensing of the UAE Securities and Commodities Market.

The federal law anticipates trading in the Securities and Commodities Market. Securities are defined to include stocks, shares and financial notes issued by joint stock companies, bonds, treasury notes issued by the UAE federal or individual emirate governments, public authorities and institutions in the UAE and any other local or foreign financial instruments that are acceptable. Commodities are defined as any agricultural products and any natural resources extracted from the ground and seas following the processing and preparation of such products and resources for natural use. Although it is not expressly stated in the draft law, it is understood that this definition may include futures.

The Authority will be responsible for the formulation of its administration structure and the licensing and monitoring of the financial market as well as the listing, cancellation and suspension of trading of any securities or commodity. The law requires the Authority to work in close consultation and coordination with the licensed markets in the country. The Authority will also regulate membership and transparency of the market as well as the arbitration of disputes resulting from trading.

4.2   Establishment of Dubai Financial Market

The Dubai Financial Market ("DAM") has recently been established and is the UAE's first official trading floor. While the DAM has been established pursuant to a decree of the Ruler of Dubai and subsequently ratified by Federal Law No. 4 of 2000 (concerning the UAE Stock Exchange and Commodities Market and Authority), it has not yet published official regulations relating to its set up, conduct and operation. Ten locally owned companies have already been listed on the DAM and it is expected that in due course it will be open to foreign investors. The DAM has a compliance division to ensure that traders observe the rules. Based on the information currently available it is understood that the DAM has the following features.

The DAM will require that brokers satisfy a minimum capital requirement of 5 million dirhams, provide a bank guarantee for 10 million dirhams and pay an annual fee of 250,000 dirhams. Brokerage fees are currently set at the equivalent of half a percent of the transaction value.

In order to obtain a listing, companies must complete a listing application form and provide the usual details in relation to incorporation together with details of shareholdings and corporate structure. The company's share register is to be submitted on disk format. All applications are treated in confidence and there are strict controls in place to ensure that only certain DAM personnel can view the share register. This is achieved by designating access to certain DAM users. Records of all share registers are to be kept for five years.

In order to trade through the market an investor has to deposit its share certificates with the market and its interest is recognized through a book entry system. The UAE Central Bank has issued a circular disallowing the trading of DAM listed shares outside the DAM, which effectively prohibits trading of such shares in the OTC market.

Where a security is taken over shares this will be marked on the registrar's records and transfers of the shares will be blocked.

It remains uncertain how the new market will relate to the offshore market currently anticipated in the Abu Dhabi Free Zone in Saadiyat. The draft rules of the Abu Dhabi Free Zone Authority have been drawn up to international standards and will clearly provide formidable competition. It is hoped the new markets in Dubai and Abu Dhabi follow the same route.

4.3   Establishment of Dubai Internet City

The Dubai Technology, Electronic Commerce and Media Free Zone, more commonly referred to as Dubai Internet City (the "DIC") came into being by virtue of a decree of the Ruler of Dubai concerning the Dubai Technology,

Electronic Commerce and Media Free Zone Law. The new law is an enabling Act which merely provides for a framework for the establishment of the DIC. This approach follows a similar pattern to previously enacted legislation to create other free zones in Dubai such as Jebel Ali Free Zone and the Dubai Airport Free Zone.

Unlike other established free zones in Dubai, the DIC is industry specific. The law provides that the business and activities carried on in the DIC shall include the design, development, use and maintenance of everything relevant to information technology. Additionally, the DIC will include the business of electronic commerce (e-commerce; telecommunications and media services; integrated marketing and public relation services). The law also envisages the provision of services through the internet to include banking, financial services, insurance, education, call centres and marketing operations. In pursuance of any internet-related marketing activities, businesses will be permitted to assemble and package products manufactured within or outside the DIC; import, export and store products; develop and manufacture products; warehouse and organize distribution and redistribution services.

The law also takes advantage of Federal Law No. 15 of 1998 which exempts free zones from certain of the provisions of the UAE Federal Law No. 8 of 1984 concerning Commercial Companies (the "CCL"). These provisions enable free zones to establish their own regulations on the types of entity that may be incorporated within a given free zone. Accordingly, in the DIC, the law specifically provides for the incorporation of companies with limited liability which may have one or more shareholders.

Interestingly, the law provides for a discretion on the Ruler of Dubai to establish a court and/or arbitration tribunal with the jurisdiction of hearing claims and suits arising out of or in connection with activities carried out by business entities established in the DIC. The jurisdiction would include claims and suits between such establishments and any other parties outside the DIC.

As an added incentive to foreign investors, the law provides for a guaranteed fifty-year tax holiday, including income tax, for all establishments in the DIC. This initial period may be renewed for similar periods by a resolution of the chairman of the DIC. Similarly, the DIC authority may grant leases of plots and buildings within the DIC for periods of up to fifty years.

4.4 Carriage of goods by sea: contradictory rulings from the Court of Cassation in relation to sea carrier's fire defence

In two cases arising out of the same set of facts, contradictory rulings were issued by the Dubai Court of Cassation.[1] The claims were for damages to similar types of cargo carried from Hong Kong to Dubai via Singapore. During the carriage, a chemical fire broke out in one of the containers and

---

[1]   Case No. 261/1997.

this released sulphur dioxide gas. The gas then penetrated and contaminated nearby containers. On arrival at the port in Dubai the nearby containers were opened and the contents were found to be badly damaged and no longer suitable for their intended purpose.

In both actions, each brought by a different plaintiff against the same defendant, the latter raised the defence under Article 275(1)(c) of the UAE Marine Commercial Code (which broadly incorporates Hague-Visby rules) that the carrier is not liable if damage was caused by fire unless the fire arose as a result of the carrier's fault.

In the first case, the court of first instance dismissed the case on the ground that the plaintiff had failed to prove that the fire was caused by the act or mistake of the defendant. The judgment was subsequently overruled by the Court of Appeal and the Court of Cassation on the basis of the court expert's report. The report indicated that the damage occurred when the defendant carrier's agents opened the containers to ventilate them. This action allowed sulphur dioxide to escape from the container on fire and enter the nearby ventilated containers. Accordingly, the defendant had failed to take the necessary precautions to protect the transported goods and, in consequence, was unable to raise a successful defence.

In the second case, the court of first instance, relying on the expert's report, found that the carrier had not taken the necessary safety precautions when stowing and arranging the containers as they had been placed alongside other containers stuffed with dangerous/inflammable materials. The decision was upheld by the Court of Appeal and the Court of Cassation.

The contradictory approach of the Court of Cassation to the defendant carrier's fire defence might be explained on the basis that the damaged goods were not burnt, i.e. directly affected by the fire. Nevertheless, such contradictory rulings by the Court of Cassation make it increasingly unclear as to which course of action would be appropriate for a defendant carrier to take in order to resist liability arising out of a fire incident.

4.5 Commercial agency

An agent may claim compensation from a principal even if the agency was not registered in accordance with the UAE Commercial Agencies Law 1981 (revised 1988). An action was filed by an Abu Dhabi company against an international principal where the agent claimed compensation and damages for termination of an unregistered agency.

The Abu Dhabi Federal Supreme Court[2] overruled the judgment delivered by the lower courts which had ordered the action to be dismissed on the grounds that the company had an unregistered agency and, in accordance with the UAE Commercial Agency Law, the courts had no jurisdiction to hear the case.

The Abu Dhabi Federal Supreme Court held that even if the agency

---

2   Case No. 484/1999.

was not registered under the Commercial Agencies Law, this fact did not preclude the agent from obtaining relief under general principles of UAE law for compensation and commission for his agency when it was terminated by the principal. Accordingly, the case was referred back to the to the Court of Appeal to appoint an expert to calculate the damages and losses suffered by the agent as a result of the termination of the unregistered agency. The case is currently waiting to be reheard by the Court of Appeal.

4.6   Company Law

A manager of a limited liability company who drew a dishonoured cheque in the company's name was personally liable for the issuance of the cheque and was liable to pay to the drawee the amount that exceeded the funds in the company's bank account. The Dubai Court of Cassation[3] held that the drawer of a cheque has the burden of proving that there were sufficient funds in the limited liability company's bank account at the time of its issue. Where the drawer of the cheque fails to discharge his burden of proof he will be personally responsible for honouring the cheque. The decision represents a significant departure from previously accepted practice in relation to the supremacy of the corporate veil and directors' liability.

The plaintiff lodged an application for a precautionary attachment order on the stock and other assets owned by the defendant who was a sole proprietor and general manager of a limited liability company. The defendant had issued a cheque to the plaintiff as payment for goods supplied by the plaintiff to the defendant. The cheque was returned unpaid on account of the lack of funds in the limited liability company's bank account.

At the court of first instance, the application for an attachment order was dismissed. Similarly, the Court of Appeal dismissed the claimant's appeal and upheld the decision of the lower court. The claimant further appealed against the judgment before the Court of Cassation.

Before the Court of Cassation, the claimant argued that the judgment of the Court of Appeal was erroneous both in interpretation and application of the law under Article 252(3) of the UAE Civil Procedure Law and Article 599(3) of the UAE Commercial Transactions Law.

The Court of Cassation dismissed the judgment of the Court of Appeal and found that the claimant was in possession of the cheque which is a formal deed of debt due for payment without conditions. Accordingly, pursuant to Article 252(3) of the UAE Civil Procedure Law, the application for attachment could be granted. Further, the Court of Cassation held that under Article 599(3) of the UAE Commercial Transactions Law, the defendant had the burden of proving that there were sufficient funds for honouring the cheque at the time of its issue, failing which, he was under a duty to secure the payment of the cheque. As the defendant had failed to discharge his burden of proof, he was personally liable to honour the cheque.

---

[3]   Case No. 348/2000.

4.7 Arbitrators have the power to order the liquidation of a limited liability company formed by a UAE national and a foreign partner

The Abu Dhabi Supreme Court[4] has held that arbitrators have the power to appoint a liquidator to liquidate a limited liability company where requested to do so by the foreign partner. The decision of the Abu Dhabi Supreme Court is particularly noteworthy since it is a significant departure from previously accepted practice.

A limited liability company was set up by a UAE national and a foreign partner to carry out contracting work in Abu Dhabi. It was agreed the foreign partner would manage the business technically and financially. The foreign partner decided to leave the UAE without notifying his UAE partner. An action was filed by a national partner of an Abu Dhabi limited liability company against his foreign partner requesting the courts to order the foreign partner to return to the UAE and resume his duties as manager of the company.

The Federal Supreme Court upheld the parties' agreement to refer any dispute to arbitration and further to grant the arbitrator the right to appoint a liquidator to liquidate the company where requested to do so by one of the parties.

5   EMPLOYMENT AND LABOUR LAW

5.1   Proposed amendments to Federal Labour Law No. 8 of 1980

According to reports, the Ministry of Labour and Social Affairs is undertaking a study to consider a draft of proposed amendments to Federal Labour Law No. 8 of 1980. In its present form, the draft proposes a significant number of amendments to the statutory provisions of the Federal Labour Law No. 8 of 1980. If enacted, employees in the private sector will lose a number of privileges, particularly covering annual leave and end of service benefits or gratuity payment. It has been emphasized that the draft is likely to be changed further by input from chambers of commerce and lawyers' associations before it is submitted in its final form to the UAE Cabinet for approval.

In respect of the end of service benefits an employee completing one year or more of service will be entitled to a gratuity payment equivalent to nine days of salary, instead of twenty-one days, for each year of service during the first five years of service, and thirty days for the following years under the current law. Additionally, the suggested amendment stipulates that the amount of gratuity will not exceed six months' basic salary while the upper limit in the present law is two years' salary.

Another proposed amendment will reduce the annual leave from thirty days a year to twenty-one days per year. The reduction will be based on the fact that an employee with a service of more than six months and less than

---

4   Judgment No. 193 of 1999.

one year would be entitled to one day's leave every month instead of two days under the current provision on annual leave. Private sector employees would also lose their entitlement to two out of ten public holidays on account of religious occasions.

Muslim employees wishing to exercise their right to pilgrimage leave once during their employment would only be entitled to a maximum of fifteen days' leave instead of the current thirty days. Similarly, working hours during Ramadan will be changed so that all workers, whether Muslim or non-Muslim, will be required to work a normal day instead of the current six hours.

The proposed amendments also include measures aimed at giving the Ministry of Labour and Social Affairs more time to settle labour disputes before they are referred to the courts. Under the present law, the Ministry has two weeks to settle a labour dispute. If the proposed amendment is adopted, the period for settling a dispute will be extended to four weeks.

Other proposals are aimed specifically at the large foreign work force in the UAE which is made up of a multiplicity of nationalities. The amendments would introduce stricter measures to prevent expatriate workers from working for anyone other than their original sponsor when the employee is on annual leave or sick leave. Similarly those employees who absent themselves from work without just cause will be subject to an employment ban in the UAE of two years instead of the present ban of one year's duration. Where employees leave their employment to work for a competing employer, the employee would be subject to an employment ban of three years. Employers will also find it much easier to cancel an employee's employment visa since it is proposed to extend the current provisions which lay down the circumstances in which an employer may terminate a contract of employment.

Commentators from the UAE Jurists Association have stated that if the proposed amendments are adopted in their present form it is likely that the UAE federal government's policy of encouraging more UAE nationals to seek employment in the private sector under its "emiratization" plan will be severely impeded. The suggested amendments to the present law, if adopted in their present form, will widen the gap even further between the prevailing employment conditions in the public and private sectors.

6   SOCIAL SECURITY LAW

There have been no further significant statutory developments in the relevant period.

7   PROPERTY LAW

There have been no further significant statutory developments in the relevant period.

8   INTELLECTUAL PROPERTY (TRADEMARKS)

There have been no significant statutory developments in the relevant period. There have, however, been other matters of interest.

8.1   UAE removed from United States Trade Representative (USTR) 301 Watch List

The UAE has been removed from the US Special 301 Watch List of countries monitored for violation of intellectual property rights, following written commitments made recently by the UAE government to take specific measures to ensure adequate and effective protection of patented products. The measures include specific commitments on the implementation of the agreement on Trade-Related Aspects of Intellectual Property (TRIPS), data protection and the withholding of marketing approval for unauthorized copies of patented products.

Pursuant to the UAE government undertaking, the Ministry of Health issued a decree banning the registration of any unauthorized copies of patented medicinal or pharmaceutical products as required by the TRIPS agreement. In April 2000 the Pharmaceutical Research and Manufacturers of America (PhRMA) requested that the UAE be removed from the Special Watch List.

The UAE has been actively promoting the protection of intellectual property rights so as to promote confidence among foreign investors. The UAE joined the World Intellectual Property Organization (WIPO) in 1975. In 1992 the UAE issued Federal Law No. 44 for the Regulation and Protection of Industrial Property, Patents and Industrial Designs. On 20 March 1996, the UAE became a member of the Paris Convention for the Protection of Industrial Property and the following year, the UAE joined the World Trade Organization.

8.2   Fine for selling counterfeit goods in the UAE

The Dubai Court of Cassation[5] has held that the minimum fine to be applied in cases where the defendant has sold counterfeit goods should be in accordance with the statutory provision in the UAE Trade Mark Law No. 37 of 1992 and not a lesser amount based on the discretion of the presiding judge.

The case was brought by the Dubai Prosecutor's Office against two defendants accused of selling counterfeit "Pioneer" brand goods. The Prosecutor requested the court to find the accused guilty of violating the UAE Trade Mark Law. Police had raided the accused defendants' shop in Dubai where they found the counterfeit goods. Following the Prosecutor's

---

5   Case No. 97/1999.

investigation a case was filed before the court for judgement in accordance with the UAE Trade Mark Law No. 37 of 1992.

The court of first instance delivered a judgment ordering the two defendants each to pay a fine of 3,000 dirhams. No order was made in respect of the confiscation of the counterfeit goods. The Prosecutor's Office appealed against the judgment to the Dubai Court of Appeal.

The Court of Appeal upheld the fine imposed on the defendants but amended the judgment to include confiscation of the counterfeit goods attached by the Dubai Police Department. The Prosecutor's Office appealed against the judgment to the Dubai Court of Cassation.

The Court of Cassation held that when the Prosecutor's Office appealed against the judgment of the court of first instance, the Court of Appeal had erred in not considering the whole subject matter of the case, including the facts and evidence and the relevant article of the law relied upon as this was in the public interest. In consequence, the Court of Appeal had omitted to give consideration to the fact that the fine imposed by the court of first instance was not made in accordance with the UAE Trademark Law. The article relied upon by the Prosecutor provides that where a person is found guilty of counterfeiting a registered trademark or imitating it so as to mislead the public, he shall be liable to imprisonment and/or a fine of at least 5,000 dirhams.

9   FAMILY LAW AND SUCCESSION

9.1   Draft law on child protection

According to reports, a draft of the first UAE law on the protection of children has recently been completed. The draft has been sent to various government and private organizations for review. The new law was prepared by a committee established by the Supreme Council of Childhood which also included representatives from the Ministry of Labour and Social Affairs, the UAE University, the University of Sharjah and the UAE Lawyers Association.

The draft law comprises ten chapters including one which is devoted to specific provisions on the role of the Supreme Council of Childhood. The new law covers a diversity of subjects affecting children, including their public rights, health and social care, education and cultural needs. There are also provisions on the rights of working mothers and how their needs impact on children. Provisions have been included on the care and rehabilitation of children with special needs. Additionally, the draft law proposes measures to deal with the problem of juvenile delinquency.

10   CIVIL PROCEDURE AND EVIDENCE (ENFORCEMENT OF FOREIGN JUDGMENTS)

There have been no significant statutory developments in the relevant period. There have, however, been a number of Abu Dhabi and Dubai Court of Cassation cases of interest.

10.1 Dubai Court of Cassation overrules lower courts and declines jurisdiction

The Dubai Court of Cassation[6] reversed the judgments of the court of first instance and the Court of Appeal and held that, in circumstances where a contract is executed in Sharjah, delivery of the cargo is to take place in Sharjah and a carrier's agent has his place of business in Sharjah, the Dubai courts cannot accept jurisdiction in accordance with the provisions of Article 41 of the Civil Procedure Law.

The claim involved the deterioration of cargo stuffed in a container on a voyage from Denmark to Jebel Ali. The insurers settled the claim with the consignees and were subrogated to their rights. The Court of Cassation upheld the general principal that, in accordance with marine practice, the domicile of an agent appointed on behalf of an owner or carrier will have the effect of giving the court jurisdiction to hear the case. However, it overturned the decision of the lower courts on the grounds that the actual location of the agent was in Sharjah and not Dubai.

The decisions of the lower courts failed to appreciate the importance of the fact that the agent in question was not actually domiciled in Dubai. Decisions like these often render it necessary to proceed to appeals before higher courts, even in cases where the monetary value of the claim does not warrant this.

10.2 Jurisdiction to hear a dispute over payment of a letter of credit

The Dubai Court of Cassation[7] held that, in accordance with the UAE Law of Civil Procedure, the Dubai courts had jurisdiction to hear an action filed before the Dubai courts by the beneficiary of a letter of credit against an Islamic bank despite the fact that the letter of credit was opened in Sudan and the bank was domiciled in Sudan because the documents required for the letter of credit transaction were submitted through a correspondent bank in Dubai.

The plaintiff was a local investment company which filed an action against an international Islamic bank based in Sudan. The plaintiff requested the court to order the bank to pay the letter of credit because the defendant bank had issued an irrevocable letter of credit for an amount on behalf of the plaintiff. The plaintiff had complied with the terms of the letter of credit to complete a commercial transaction and present the relevant documents to the correspondent bank in Dubai.

---

[6]   Case No. 353/1998.
[7]   Case No. 39/99.

11 CRIMINAL LAW AND PROCEDURE

There have been no significant developments in the relevant period.

12 PUBLIC INTERNATIONAL LAW

There have been no significant developments in the relevant period.

13 PRIVATE INTERNATIONAL LAW

There have been no significant developments in the relevant period.

14 ENVIRONMENTAL LAW

14.1 Federal Environmental Law

Federal Law No. 24 of 1999 concerning the protection of the environment came into effect on 1 February 2000. The new law includes 101 articles divided into nine chapters and covers, *inter alia*, development and its impact on the environment, emergency measures to be taken in the event of environmental catastrophes, protection of marine environment, protection of drinking water and underground water sources and measures to prevent pollution and/or contamination of land and air. However, not all articles will be implemented immediately since these are dependent on the issue of further regulations.

The law includes a number of regulations on environmental protection and development in addition to penalties against persons and/or entities causing damage to the sea and land. In particular, there are penalties for the pollution of the marine environment caused through oil spillage. All vessels passing through UAE waters must provide a list of the cargo or items they are transporting (Article 33). Additionally operators of maritime vessels must report to the UAE Coast Guard in case of any unintentional oil spillage. Where maritime operators are found guilty of discharging waste into UAE waters, they will face fines ranging from 150,000 dirhams up to an upper limit of one million dirhams (Article 73).

Similarly, oil and gas exploration companies will also face fines ranging from 200,000 to 500,000 dirhams under Article 73 if they are found guilty of discharging or dumping any dangerous waste or material which subsequently causes damage to the environment in contravention of Article 18.

There are particularly harsh sanctions aimed at preventing the importation, storage or dumping of nuclear waste in the UAE's territory. Offenders who are found guilty of violating the ban on the importation of nuclear waste knowingly under Article 62 may face the death sentence or fines ranging from 1 milion to ten million dirhams (Article 73). Additionally, offenders will be obliged to return the nuclear waste to its original location at their own expense. The passage of nuclear materials and waste in UAE territory is to be strictly controlled and will require the written permission of the Federal Environment Agency in accordance with Article 62 of the Act.

Bahrain

*Husain M. Al Baharna**

Bahrain promulgated the following legislation between June and December 1999, and January and June 2000.

1 DECREES RATIFYING INTERNATIONAL AGREEMENTS AND CONVENTIONS

1.1 Labour

1.1.1 *Law by Decree No. 11 for 2000 Ratifying the International Labour Agreement No. 111 for 1958 Concerning Discrimination in Employment and Profession*

In accordance with Article 1 of this decree, the International Labour Agreement on Discrimination in Employment and Profession No. 111 of 1958, was ratified and attached to the said Decree, dated 18 April 2000.[1]

---

*   PhD in International Law (Cambridge); Barrister-at-Law of Lincoln's Inn; Council Member of ICCA; Member of the UN International Law Commission (ILC); Attorney, Legal Consultant and Arbitrator, Bahrain; Former Minister for Legal Affairs, Bahrain.
[1]   Official Gazette No. 2421, 19 April 1991.

1.2   Human rights

1.2.1   Law by Decree No. 34 for 1999, Amending Certain Provisions of Law by Decree No. 4 for 1998 Concerning Accession by Bahrain to the Agreement on the Prohibition of Torture and other similar Forms of Severe Inhuman or Degrading Punishments, Adopted by the United Nations General Assembly on 10 December 1948

By this amending law, it is provided that the provision of the first article of the Law No. 4 for 1998 concerning the accession of the state of Bahrain to the said Agreement should be amended as follows:

Article 1:

The accession of the State of Bahrain to the Agreement on torture and other similar forms of treatment or severe or inhuman or degrading punishments, adopted by the United Nations General Assembly on 10 December 1984, has been approved, subject to reservation to article 30, paragraph 1 of this Agreement in the following term: (The government of Bahrain does not consider itself bound by Article 30, paragraph 1 of this Agreement.) The Law was issued by the Amir of Bahrain on 17 August 1999.[2]

1.2.2   Decree No. 6 for 2000 Ratifying the Amendment to Article 8 of the International Agreement Concerning the Eradication of all Forms of Racial Discrimination of 1965 to which Bahrain Acceded by Decree No. 8 for 1990.

According to Article 1 of this Decree, Bahrain has ratified the Resolution of the United Nations General Assembly No. 47/111 approving the amendment of paragraph 6 of Article 8 and the addition of a new paragraph to it under No. 7 of the International Agreement on the Eradication of all forms of Racial Discrimination of 1965. The Amiri Decree ratifying the said General Assembly resolution was issued on 12 March 2000.[3]

1.2.3   Law by Decree No. 8 for 2000 Ratifying the Amendment to paragraph 2 of Article 43 of the United Nations Agreement Concerning the Rights of the Child, approved by the General Assembly in November 1989.

According to Article 1 of this Law, the Resolution of the United Nations General Assembly No. 155/50 of 21 December 1995, approving the amendment to paragraph 2 of Article 43 of the United Nations Agreement on the Rights of the Child, has hereby been ratified by this law, issued by the Amir of Bahrain on 7 May 2000. The amendment to paragraph 2 of

---

[2]   Official Gazette No. 2386, 18 August 1999.
[3]   Official Gazette No. 2416, 15 March 2000.

Article 43 of the Agreement concerns the substitution of the phrase of "eighteen experts" for "ten experts".[4]

1.3   Housing projects

1.3.1   Law by Decree No. 27 for 1999 Approving the Loan Agreement for Providing the Funds (BD 20 million) for Housing Projects in Bahrain.

This was signed between the government of Bahrain and the Arab Fund for Economic and Social Development on 18 May 1999. The law takes effect from the date of its publication in the Official Gazette.[5]

1.4   Investment

1.4.1   Law by Decree No. 31 for 1999 Concerning the Ratification of the Agreement on the Encouragement and Protection of Investments between the government of Bahrain and the government of Malaysia

The ratified agreement was signed by the two governments in Kuala Lumpur on 14 June 1999. The agreement appended to this law was ratified by the Amir of Bahrain on 2 August 1999.[6]

1.4.2   Law by Decree No. 29 for 1999 Concerning the Ratification of the Agreement Regarding the Protection of Mutual Investments between the government of Bahrain and the government of the Chinese People's Socialist Republic

This was signed in Beijing on 17 June 1996, and attached to this law. The agreement takes effect from the date of its publication in the Official Gazette.[7]

1.4.3   Law by Decree No. 37 for 1999 Ratifying the Agreement on Encouragement of Investment and Providing Mutual Protection thereto between the government of Bahrain and the government of the United States of America, signed in Washington, DC on 29 September 1999

The agreement appended to this law was ratified by the Amir of Bahrain on 13 November 1999.[8]

---

4   Official Gazette No. 2424, 10 May 2000.
5   Official Gazette No. 2375, 2 June 1999.
6   Official Gazette No. 2384, 4 August 1999.
7   Official Gazette No. 2381, 14 July 1999.
8   Official Gazette No. 2399, dated 17 November 1999.

1.4.4 Law by Decree No. 1 for 2000 Ratifying the Agreement on Encouragement and Protection of Investment between the government of Bahrain and the government of Jordan

This agreement, signed on 8 February 2000, was ratified by the Amir of Bahrain on 12 February 2000. The agreement is attached to the said law.[9]

1.5 Taxation

1.5.1 Law by Decree No. 30 for 1999 Concerning Ratification of the Dual Taxation Exemption Agreement Regarding Return Arising from the Operation of Air Navigation between the government of Bahrain and the government of the Chinese People's Socialist Republic

This was signed in Beijing on 17 June 1996, and attached to this law. The law takes effect from the date of its publication in the Official Gazette.[10]

1.5.2 Law by Decree No. 2 for 2000 Ratifying the Agreement on Avoiding the Dual Taxation and the Prohibition of Escaping Taxes in Relation to Taxes on Income and Capital between the government of Bahrain and the government of Jordan

This agreement signed on 8 February 2000, was ratified by the Amir of Bahrain on 12 February 2000. The agreement is attached to the said law.[11]

1.6 Aviation

1.6.1 Decree No. 10 for 1999 Ratifying the Protocol, signed in Montreal on 1 October 1999 Concerning the Amendment of the Final Provision of the International Civil Aviation Agreement, signed in Chicago on 7 December 1944.

The Protocol provides for the adoption of the Chinese language as one of the official languages in the Final Provision of the said Agreement. The decree takes effect from the date of its publication in the Official Gazette.[12]

1.6.2 Law by Decree No. 33 for 1999 Ratifying the Addition of two New Articles to the Agreement on Aviation Services between the government of Bahrain and the government of Thailand, dated 14 July 1980 and Ratified by Law by Decree No. 9 for 1981

The two new articles added to the said agreement are Article 16 concerning aviation security and Article 17 concerning airports fees for the use of airports and other aviation facilities.

---

[9]   Official Gazette No. 2412, 16 February 2000.
[10] Official Gazette No. 2381, 14 July 1999.
[11] Official Gazette No. 2412, 16 February 2000.
[12] Official Gazette No. 2328, 23 June 1999.

*1.6.3   Law by Decree No. 3 for 2000 Ratifying the Agreement on Aviation
        Services between the government of Bahrain and the Islamic Republic
        of Iran*

This agreement, signed by the two governments on 8 February 2000, was
ratified by the Amir of Bahrain on 20 February 2000. The agreement is
attached to the said law.[13]

*1.6.4   Law by Decree No. 4 for 2000 Ratifying the Agreement Concerning
        Aviation Services between the government of Bahrain and the
        government of Jordan*

This agreement, signed in Amman on 24 March 2000, was ratified on 10
April 2000. It is attached to the said law.[14]

*1.6.5   Law by Decree No. 7 for 2000 Ratifying the Agreement Concerning
        Aviation Services between the government of Bahrain and the
        government of India*

In accordance with Article 1 of this law, the agreement Concerning Aviation
Services, signed on 5 April 2000, was ratified and attached to this law. The
Amir of Bahrain ratified the agreement on 25 April 2000.[15]

*1.6.6   Law by Decree No. 25 for 1999 Ratifying Air Navigation Agreement
        between the government of Bahrain and the government of the
        Vietnam Socialist Republic*

This law was signed in Bahrain on 4 May 1999. The law takes effect from
the date of its publication in the Official Gazette.[16]

2   PETROLEUM LAW

2.1   Law by Decree No. 42 for 1999 Establishing the Bahrain
         Petroleum Company

This law provides for merging both the Bahrain Petroleum Company
(Closed) established by its Articles of Association dated 1 April 1998, and
the Bahrain National Oil Company, established by Law by Decree No. 9 for
1976, as amended by Law No. 3 for 1981, into one new company known
as the New Bahrain Petroleum Company (Closed).

---

[13]   Official Gazette No. 2413, 23 February 2000.
[14]   Official Gazette No. 2420, 12 April 2000.
[15]   Official Gazette No. 2422, 26 April 2000.
[16]   Official Gazette No. 2375, 2 June 1999.

According to this Law No. 42 for 1999, the new Bahrain Petroleum Company, established under this law, shall have personal shares fully owned by the state, in accordance with its Basic Regulations, attached to this law (Article 1). According to Article 2 of this law, the two merged companies, namely, the Bahrain Petroleum Company and the Bahrain companies, namely, the Bahrain Petroleum Company and the Bahrain National Oil Company, shall be dissolved and liquidated, in accordance with their respective Basic Regulations. According to Article 3 of the law, the Law by Decree No. 9 for 1976, establishing the Bahrain National Oil Company, has been terminated together with any other provision contrary to this Law. The law was issued by the Amir of Bahrain on 29 December 1999.[17]

3 ARBITRATION

3.1 Law by Decree No. 6 for 2000 Approving the Regulations of the Centre for Commercial Arbitration of the States of the Gulf Co-operation Council (GCC)

According to Article 1 of this law, the Regulations of the GCC Centre for Commercial Arbitration, approved by the Resolution of GCC Summit, dated 22 December 1993, was approved and attached to this law. The law was approved by the Amir of Bahrain on 25 April 2000.[18]

4 IGC COOPERATION

4.1 Decree No. 12 for 2000 Approving the Establishment of a High Joint Committee for Cooperation between Bahrain and Qatar

According to Article 1 of this decree, the Agreement Establishing a High Joint Committee between Bahrain and Qatar, signed on 20 February 2000, was approved by the said decree, issued by the Amir of Bahrain on 22 April 2000, and attached to the said decree.[19]

5 PASSPORTS AND IDENTITY CARDS

5.1 Law by Decree No. 9 for 2000 Amending Certain Provisions of Law No. 11 for 1975, Concerning Travel Passports

Article 1 of this law states that Article 1 of Law No. 11 for 1975, Concerning Travel Passports shall be substituted by the following provision:

---

[17] Official Gazette No. 2405, 29 December 1999.
[18] Official Gazette No. 2422, 26 April 2000.
[19] Official Gazette No. 2422, 26 April 2000.

Article 1:

A Bahraini national shall not leave Bahrain and return to it without holding a passport, in accordance with the provisions of this law. The passport may be substituted by any other form of a travel document in such cases are as specified in an edict issued by the Minister of Interior. This passport may also be substituted by the travel document issued by the Ministry of Interior to Ship Captains and Ship Crews and to Captains (*Nokhadhas*) of the group of aircraft personnel. However, Bahrainis may leave Bahrain and return to it during their travel to and from one of the Gulf Cooperation Council's countries by their own identity cards, in accordance with the edict issued by the Minister of Interior which specifies such countries.

Article 2 of the law provides that a third paragraph (paragraph 3) shall be added to Article 5 of the Law No. 11 for 1975 concerning travel passports as follows:

Article 5, paragraph 3:

As an exception from paragraph 1 of this Article, Bahrainis may leave Bahrain and return to it, to or from any of the countries of the Gulf Cooperation Council specified by an edict issued by the Minister of Interior, by virtue of their identity cards or passports, without any requirement for these documents to be stamped at the point of entry or departure.[20]

5.2   Law by Decree No. 10 for 2000 Amending Certain Provisions of the Law No. 2 for 1975, Concerning Identity Cards

Article 1 of this law states that the two articles, 3 (last paragraph) and 11, of the Law No. 2 for 1975 concerning identity cards shall be substituted by the following:

Article 3 (last paragraph):

Any person of 16 years old may obtain an identity card by an application made on his behalf by his custodian.

Article 11:

The Minister of Interior shall, after the approval of the Council of Ministers, issue an edict providing for the fees to be paid for the issuance or renewal of the identity cards, as well as for changing the information, data contained in them or for replacing them by original copies. Article 2 of the Law states that any Bahraini national who has not obtained an identity card at the age of 16, shall do so within the period of two years from the enforcement of this law.

This period may be renewed for similar periods by an edict issued by the Minister of Interior.[21]

---

[20]   Official Gazette No. 2427, 31 May 2000.
[21]   Official Gazette No. 2427, 31 May 2000.

6 ISLAMIC ESTABLISHMENT FOR THE DEVELOPMENT OF THE PRIVATE SECTOR

6.1 Law by Decree No. 11 for 2000 Ratifying the Agreement Forming the Islamic Establishment for the Development of the Private Sector

In accordance with Article 1 of this law, the Agreement Forming the Islamic Establishment for the Development of the Private Sector, signed by Bahrain in Jiddah (Saudi Arabia) on 3 November 1999, was ratified by the Amir of Bahrain on 28 May 2000. The Agreement is attached to the law.[22]

---

[22] Official Gazette No. 2427, 31 May 2000.

Qatar

*Najeeb Bin Muhammed Al-Nauimi**

1 CONSTITUTIONAL AND ADMINISTRATIVE LAW

1.1 Amiri Decree No. 11 for the year 1999 (formation of the Constitution Committee)

This decree was enacted as a second genuine step to enter a new era of establishing the state of constitutional organizations after the formation of the Municipal Central Council through the process of free elections in the year 1998.

Section 1 of this decree formed the "permanent Constitution Committee" of thirty well-qualified and notable Qatari national members.

1.1.1 Sections 3–6

These sections laid down the objectives and procedures for the committee. The main objective of the committee is to prepare a permanent Constitution draft for the country. This is to be completed within a period not exceeding three years from the date of the issuing of the decree.

The committee is to raise a report showing the progress of work to his Highness the Amir every six months – also by the end of the prescribed period the committee is to handle the draft of the permanent Constitution annexed to the committee's recommendations.

1.2 Law No. 12 for the year 1998 regulating the Central Municipal Council

This law was enacted after a long study and research by the political and governmental bodies. The law was followed by a procedural law (Amiri Decree) which regulates the elections for the Central Municipal Council.

---

* LLB; PhD; Attorney at Law, Qatar; Former Minister of Justice, Qatar.

This piece of legislation has drawn the attention of the outside world to Qatar as giving an example of democracy, establishing the Municipal Council through free elections in the Gulf area, and has started a genuine step towards the constitutional organization of the state of Qatar.

This law lays down the basis and rules that govern the jurisdictions and functions of the Council and regulates the relationship between the Ministry of Municipal and Agricultural Affairs and the Central Municipal Council in many fields and aspects.

Article 2 provides that the Council shall comprise twenty-nine members representing the towns, villages and areas of Qatar; they are freely elected according to the rules of a decree which will be issued later.

Article 5 lays down the conditions to be satisfied by a Qatari national for this council membership, i.e. he should be a national of Qatar, of age not exceeding twenty-five years, educated with a good manner and qualifications, with no criminal record and not be working in the army or police force.

Article 6 specifies the duration of the membership to be four years.

Article 8 is the kernel of this law where the jurisdiction, powers and responsibilities of the Council are laid down to achieve its objectives, i.e. to act through the available means for the development of the country in the municipal affairs. The most important powers are:

(1) to supervise the execution of the laws, decisions and rules connected with the powers and jurisdiction of both the Ministry of Agricultural and Municipal Affairs and the Municipal Council including the laws and decisions concerned with building regulation, land planning, roads, commercial and industrial enterprises;
(2) to supervise planning systems, programming, economic, social, financial and administrative aspects of agricultural and municipal affairs;
(3) any other jurisdiction, powers and responsibilities attached by the law to the Council.

The Council must express its views in terms of recommendations and decisions to be addressed to the Minister of Agricultural and Municipal Affairs.

Article 10 provides that the Council may issue local regulations in matters which are not regulated by valid legislation, although these regulations will come into force unless approved by the Minister of Agricultural and Municipal Affairs.

Articles 12–30 lay down the rules and systems of the internal management of the Council.

Article 31 provides for the process of the dissolution of the Council, i.e. by Amiri Decree for the sake of the public interest upon the initiation of the Minister or of the Council's members. The decree will nominate a committee to take over the Council's powers until the process of constituting a new Council takes place.

Article 32 lays down rules for the automatic dissolution of the council if the numbers fall to less than half, and in such a case an Amiri Decree will be issued to satisfy the dissolution requirements.

2   ECONOMIC AND INVESTMENT LAW

2.1   Decision No. 1 for the year 1995 establishing the system for representation of foreign banks in the state of Qatar

This enactment was mainly made to facilitate foreign financial establishments and banks having a representative office in Qatar to offer services to banks or customers. This decision was issued by the Central Bank governor in the year 1995 and is still valid.

Article 3 lays down the means of obtaining the Central Bank's approval through an application form with certain annexes that prove the presence of the main bank in the foreign country with at least five years of continuous operations plus a copy of the accredited annual budget for the previous three years. There should also be an approval from the authorities concerned in the bank's own country, and the last requirement is that the representative office should observe the laws, rules and regulations of the state of Qatar, particularly those issued by the Central Bank, and should be subject to the supervision of the Central Bank with respect to records and documents.

Article 6 provides for the activities to be carried out by the representative offices as follows:

(a)   representing the bank or the financial establishment to deal inside Qatar and make contacts with the bodies concerned;
(b)   giving advisory services to customers;
(c)   any other works allowed by the law or regulations.

Article 7 lays down the following restrictions upon the representing offices:

(a)   the representative office is not allowed to accept savings;
(b)   it is not to carry out banking activities;
(c)   it is not to deal in security bills, trade in valuable metals or open accounts for correspondents;
(d)   it is not to carry out any other works having to do with exchange offices or financial and investment corporations.

Article 8 provides that the Central Bank will cancel the office's licence in the following cases:

(a)   if the office does not commence work within six months from the date of licensing;
(b)   if the office suspends work for three consecutive months;
(c)   if the office carries out activities that are not permitted;
(d)   if the office violates the provisions of the laws, rules or systems issued by the Central Bank;
(e)   if the main office goes bankrupt or ceases to trade;
(f)   upon the initiation of the main office the licence may be cancelled.

2.2 Law No. 1 for the year 1998 concerning the public debt

This law was enacted in the year 1998 to enable the government to receive a loan by means of issuing loan public bills or through the direct loan procedures of the Central Bank. This process should be set in motion by a Cabinet decision after taking the Central Bank's opinion.

The law heralds a new era of investment for both national and foreigners to own and exchange public debt bills allotted through banks and investment companies in the country. This law is concise and brief with clear provisions, and it will be of benefit if we set out its most important provisions.

Article 2 is the kernel of the law which provides that the government is licensed to receive loans in Qatari or any other currency through the issuance of public debt or direct loans and to specify the amount by a Cabinet decision after taking the advice of the Central Bank.

Article 3 indicates that a decision from the Ministry of Economy, Finance and Trade will specify the nominal value of each issue of the public debt, the mode of its issuance, its duration, the public debt bills for coverage, the mode of its allotment to creditors or allotters inside and outside Qatar and the purposes stipulated for its funding.

Articles 4 and 5 state that the Central Bank will on behalf of the government issue public debt in Qatar – by bills or Treasury permits.

Article 6 states that the period between the date of issuance and the date of performance should not exceed fifteen years for bills and one year for Treasury permits.

Under Article 7 public debt bills will be allotted by the banks and investment companies for both Qatari nationals and foreigners. The Central Bank will regulate the system for issuance and allotment.

Under Article 8 public debt bills will be kept in a register at the Central Bank, and the ownership of the bills will not be transferred unless registered in such a way.

The remaining Articles 9–13 are procedural and give the powers and jurisdiction of both the Ministry of Economy, Finance and Trade and the Central Bank in relation to the public debt and the mode of coordination between the two governing bodies.

Article 14 states that public debt bills may be exchanged on the Doha Security Market or other markets.

Article 15 states that the public debt bill should be exempted from taxes.

2.3 Decision No. 15 for the year 1997 concerning the supervisory rules for investment companies

This decision was again issued by the governor of the Central Bank laying down the types of investment activities to be practised by such companies and the supervisory powers to be exercised by the Central Bank to guarantee the correct application of the banking rules.

Article 2 of the rules laid down the investment activities to be taken by the investment companies in Qatar, of which the main works are as follows:

(a)   investment for others, i.e. opening investment accounts, management of investment treasuries, and establishment of investment funds for others;

(b)   financial mediation, i.e. dealing with bills of exchange through buying, selling, transferring ownership and registration in the local or international security markets on an agency basis;

(c)   underwriting, i.e. arrangement and marketing of shares, bills or otherwise for companies and others;

(d)   corporate finance, i.e. arranging finance for corporations finance and the sale and buying of investment companies;

(e)   finance and participation in capital, i.e. financing of companies and different projects by capital participation;

(f)   investment advice, i.e. giving investors the appropriate advice and economic analysis of projects;

(g)   custody services, i.e. holding bills of exchange for local and foreign investors;

(h)   other investment activities to be defined and approved by the Central Bank;

(i)   works of investment companies shall be on a traditional or Islamic basis as allowed by Qatari commercial laws and approved by the Central Bank;

(j)   companies are not allowed to receive savings;

(k)   investment companies are prohibited from dealing with the financing of companies, exchange dealings and banking except to provide loans and investment;

(l)   companies are allowed to receive loans from the banks and the security markets within the prescribed limit acknowledged by the Bank;

(m) companies are allowed to invest on their own account.

Article 3 regulates the capital of the investment company and its reserves by making a precondition for licensing that the capital should not be less than QR 20 million. There should be a capital reserve of not less than 20 per cent annual percentage from the paid up capital.

Article 6 lays down the rules that govern the constitution of the board of directors of investment companies.

Article 7 is the most striking article of this law, as it lays down the supervisory rules to be exercised by the Central Bank upon the investment companies, as follows:

(1)   The Bank may issue the conditions and requirements as contained in the Bank instructions especially in the following contexts:

   (a)   the interest, commissions and profits which companies are allowed to retain that seem reasonable according to lending market competition in the state of Qatar;

   (b)   according to the licence the Bank will fix the types and duration of loans and the trust facilities permissible for the investment companies to deal with;

   (c)   the maximum limit that the company may give to the person (natural or legal) as ownership rights;

(d)   the cash percentage and the mode of its accounting.

(e)   any other percentages as seem necessary by the Bank to maintain its cash policy and to protect investors' money and the resources of borrowed money and accounts.

(2)   The instructions issued as mentioned in Article 7(1) shall be valid and executable by all companies after thirty days' written notice.

(3)   Each company is obliged to have the Bank's prior consent for any amendment as to its legal status or to its Articles or Memorandum of Association.

(4)   Each company will be be subject to a daily fine of QR 5,000 if it contravenes Article 7(1).

(5)   The company must periodically give notice to the Bank of the list of the banks or financial corporations with which it deals in depositing or investing part of its assets.

(6)   Instructions made by the company to foreign banks and financial corporations are not executable unless accredited by its chief executive or an authorized staff member – the Bank should be notified of the names of the authorized signatories within forty-eight hours from the time of its issuance.

(7)   The Bank may require at any time from the depositing foreign company any particulars about the deposit.

(8)   Any contravention of Article 7(4–6) will be subject to a fine of not less than QR 10,000.

(9)   No company is allowed to open a branch or place without the prioir consent of the Bank.

(10)   No company is permitted to merge with any financial corporation or bank or exchange or any commercial corporation without the same prior consent of the Bank.

(11)   Companies may fix their working hours upon the consent of the Bank.

(12)   Any contravention of Article 7 (10) will be subject to a fine not exceeding QR 5,000.

(13)   Each company must provide the Bank with any particulars or information that seem necessary to enable it to do its work.

(14)   The company may partially or wholly publish such information on condition that the publication will not lead to disclosure of customers' financial affairs.

(15)   The company must comply with international accounting requirements.

(16)   The Bank will inspect any company whenever it seems necessary to ensure proper financial probity and the correct application of the Bank's regulations.

(17)   Every company must allow the Bank's representative to have access to all accounting books, and documents concerning its works in and outside Qatar.

(18)   The Bank may require the company to provide a copy of the reports raised by the accounts' auditor.

(19)   If it appears to the Bank that the company is managed in an illegal

way or that its cash situation is dangerously unstable in a way that might harm the rights of investors or creditors or that it is repeatedly contravening Bank regulations, the Bank may require the company to take urgent measures to rectify the situation and the Bank may also take any of the following measures:

(a) to prohibit the company from dealing in particular operations or to place restrictions on the company's works;

(b) to remove any members of its board of directors or any of or any of its main managers;

(c) to appoint one inspector or more to take the necessary measures to maintain the proper management of the company;

(d) to take over the management for a specified period, after which the Bank may decide either that the company may resumes its own management or recommend the cancellation of the permit and the liquidation of the company.

Article 8 provides that each company must have legal auditor registered in Qatar, to give a report to the partners on the budget, and the annual profit and loss accounts.

Article 9 stipulates that the fiscal year shall start on the 1 January and end by the 31 December every year.

Articles 10–12 lay down a group of guiding and regulative provisions as follows:

(1) The Bank may give unsecured loans to the company wherever it is necessary to prevent the company's bankruptcy or in cases of failure to repay loans.

(2) It is not permitted during the Bank management period to attach or give preferential right upon the company's assets or properties.

(3) The Company's board of directors, staff officer and advisers are prohibited from disclosing any information relating to any customer unless (a) by the written consent of the customer or (b) in accordance with a legal provision or (c) in accordance with a judicial order or judgment, and this prohibition is enforced by punishment, i.e. imprisonment for one year and a fine of QR 10,000 or both.

(4) Each company is to publish in a local daily newspaper its annual budget and the profit and the loss account agreed by its auditor within four months after the end of the fiscal year.

(5) The company is not allowed to own real estate except with the Bank's consent.

(6) Foreign investors may participate in investment companies in accordance with the commercial and investment laws in Qatar.

(7) The company has to establish the legal form for temporary and permanent relationships with its customers in such a way as to avoid risk.

(8) The company is obliged to disclose its interests and secure the approval of its customers for the case of handling investment operations whenever there is conflict of interest between them.

Oman

*Roger Clarke**

1 SOURCES OF LAW, JUDICIAL AND LEGAL SYSTEM

At the end of 1999, four new Royal Decrees were issued which introduced significant changes to the court system in the Sultanate of Oman. Until comparatively recently courts established for different purposes (e.g. tenancy disputes, employment disputes, etc.) fell under different administrative authorities. Two years ago, in line with 1996 Basic Law of the State, responsibility for all courts was transferred to one authority, the Ministry of Justice. The new Royal Decrees go towards achieving harmonization of courts and defining their hierarchy and jurisdiction.

1.1 Royal Decree No. 90/99 issuing the Judicial Authority Law

This new law, which was due to come into force in June 2000 (but its effective date has been extended), sets out the different levels of courts in Oman as follows:

(a)   the Supreme Court;
(b)   the appellate courts;
(c)   the preliminary courts;
(d)   the courts of summary jurisdiction.

These courts will be competent to hear commercial matters (including labour, tax, tenancy disputes, etc.) in addition to applications for arbitration. Personal matters will continue to be heard at the *shari'a* court.

    Royal Decree No. 90/99 contains transitional provisions to ensure that current actions will be referred, without additional court fees, to the relevant court in the new structure.

---

*   Solicitor, Trowers & Hamlins, Sultanate of Oman.

A code of conduct for judges has been developed. For example, a judge is not permitted to carry out commercial activities or any work which is inconsistent with the independence of the judiciary. The courts are not permitted to express political opinions. Judges may not engage in any political activity.

The decree includes provisions providing for the publication of judgments and a system for the automatic review, by the Supreme Court, of any judgment which contradicts an earlier decision. It is unclear whether this is intended to create a system of precedent more akin to that found in common law jurisdictions. Currently, no formal system of precedent exists.

1.2 Royal Decree 91/99 setting up the Administrative Court and issuing its law

The Administrative Court will be an independent judicial body which will have the exclusive power to review decisions issued by government bodies and matters relating to administrative disputes. The review process contemplated will take into account such matters as lack of competence, erroneous perception, violation of laws or regulations and misapplication, misinterpretation or misuse of authority when deciding whether a particular administrative decision is appropriate. Article 8 provides that the Administrative Court shall not have jurisdiction over sovereign matters or Royal Decrees or Orders. Administration of the Administrative Court will fall under the Minister for the Diwan of the Royal Court.

This law marks a significant step towards ensuring accountability of administrative decision-makers.

1.3 Royal Decree No. 92/99 setting up the Public Prosecution Authority and issuing its law

The Public Prosecution Authority is to be set up as an independent body under the supervision of the Inspector General of Police and Customs. It is not clear if this law is an interim measure towards the total separation of the Public Prosecution from the Royal Oman Police.

The Public Prosecution Authority's functions include acting in criminal cases on behalf of the public, monitoring the enforcement of penal laws, surveillance of culprits and enforcement of judgments.

1.4 Royal Decree No. 93/99 setting up the Supreme Judicial Council

The decree sets up and details the membership of a Supreme Judicial Council. The objectives of the Council are to formulate the general policy of the judiciary and to ensure its independence and continued development.

2 CONSTITUTIONAL AND ADMINISTRATIVE LAW

Royal Decree 10/2000 effected an administrative reshuffle of the Ministries of Communications, Housing and Posts, Telegraphs and Telephones. The duties of these three Ministries are now undertaken by the newly organized Ministry of Transport and Housing and the Ministry of Telecommunications.

Royal Decree 66/99 ordered the creation of a Civil Register, in which all births, deaths, marriages and divorces are recorded. The registry also deals with the issuing of identity cards for Omani citizens, and residence cards for expatriates.

Ministerial Decision 52/99, issued by the Ministry of National Economy, sets out the Regulations for Control of Government Revenue and Expenditure. The regulations require the Ministry of Finance, *inter alia*, to ensure that contracts entered into by the government do not contain provisions which have the effect of shifting the burden of any tax on to the government. It would appear that Ministerial Decision 52/99 is an internal regulation and as such should not affect the enforceability of a contract signed by the government.

3 CIVIL LAW (CONTRACT AND OBLIGATIONS)

There have been no developments under this title.

4 CIVIL PROCEDURE AND EVIDENCE

There have been no developments under this title.

5 COMMERCIAL LAW

5.1 Foreign commercial representative office

Ministerial Decision 22/2000 allows foreign entities to establish a representative office. This is a fairly significant development.

The scope of activities that may be undertaken by a representative office are set out in Articles 3 and 4 of this decision. In summary, representative offices may be used for the purpose of liaising with clients in the public and private sector with the aim of introducing a company's products and expanding the market for such products.

Representative offices may not import goods (with the exception of commercial samples), sell products in Oman or promote products or services other than those originating from the represented company.

Representative offices, once established, may employ staff in accordance with the general rules and regulations that apply to Omani commercial companies.

A company wishing to set up a representative office must have been registered for a continuous period of ten years and needs to have three foreign branch offices to be eligible for the establishment of a representative office in Oman.

5.2   Issues of shares: private placements

Royal Decree 85/99 has added a new paragraph to Article 82 of the Commercial Companies Law, which allows a company, on a resolution of an extraordinary general meeting, to allot shares to a third party non-shareholder.

This would appear to have the effect of allowing a company to make private placements of shares, on an increase in issued share capital, by resolution of the extraordinary general meeting and without having to go through the strict pre-emption right procedure set out in Article 83.

5.3   United Nations Customs Organization

Royal Decree 21/2000 ratified Oman's affiliation to the United Nations Customs Organization.

5.4   Double taxation treaties

Oman has ratified double taxation treaties with Algeria (Royal Decree 43/2000), Egypt (Royal Decree 52/2000) and Pakistan (Royal Decree 58/99).

6   EMPLOYMENT AND LABOUR LAW

Ministerial Decision No. 40/2000, issued by the Royal Oman Police (ROP), details amendments to the Executive Regulations of the Expatriate Residence Law. Among the more interesting amendments made pursuant to this new Decision are the following.

6.1   Transit visa

The transit visa is now for a duration of seventy-two hours, rather than twenty-four hours.

6.2   Business visit visa

Previously, the business visit visa could only be extended for a period of one month. Extensions shall now be for such periods of time as the ROP shall, in its discretion, decide.

6.3   Tourist visa

The tourist visa has been divided into two categories, with the addition of a group tourist visa. Both the individual tourist visa and the group tourist visa will enable the holder to stay in Oman for three weeks, renewable for such period as the ROP, at its discretion, shall decide.

6.3.1   Individual tourist visa

This is to be stamped in the foreigner's passport within six months of its issue. There is no restriction as to the length of time within which the visa must be used.

6.3.2.   Group visa

This will be granted by the competent authority at the request of and under the responsibility of a local sponsor.

7   PROPERTY AND LAND LAW

Royal Decree 20/2000 promulgates the regulations governing real estate ownership, in Oman, by citizens of the states of the Arab Gulf Cooperation Council ("GCC"). The regulations allow citizens of GCC member states to own up to 3,000 square metres of real estate in residential areas of the Sultanate. Ownership shall, in general, be for the purpose of residence of the owner and his family.

The owner may not dispose of the real estate within the first four years of becoming the registered owner unless prior permission from the concerned authorities is obtained.

8   INTELLECTUAL PROPERTY

There has been a spate of legislation in the field of intellectual property. The most significant of these new laws are Royal Decrees 37/2000 and 38/2000.

8.1   Royal Decree 37/2000 – Copyright Law

Royal Decree 37/2000 deals with the protection of author's copyright and related rights. It details the nature of work and the "authors" who can enjoy the protections afforded by the law, what rights are enjoyed and penalties for non-compliance.

In essence, the protection is afforded to the registered authors of original literary, scientific, technical and cultural works in general (irrespective of the value of these works). The protection provided by the law shall also be enjoyed by a person who translates a work into another language, who summarizes or adapts or changes the work such as to make it appear in a new form.

The rights which are enjoyed shall include the author's right to have his work ascribed to him or published under a pen name. Also, no omission, change, addition to or other alteration shall be made to the author's work without his prior approval. These rights shall not be subject to waiver or disposal and nor shall they end with the passing of time.

Financial rights are also enjoyed. The author shall have the right to receive royalties for any copying, translation, adaptation, public performance or other material exploitation of his or her work.

Royal Decree 37/2000 makes exceptions as to when uses of an author's work shall be legitimate, though not accompanied by the author's approval, provided the source and name of the author is specified clearly. These shall include quoting the work by way of illustration or explanation, and using the work for educational purposes.

The protection of the author's financial rights shall continue during his life and for the fifty years of the Gregorian calendar commencing from the first year following his death.

Article 23 of Royal Decree 37/2000 sets out the penalty for infringement of the literary or financial rights of the author. This shall be imprisonment for up to two years and/or a fine of no more than RO 2,000.

8.2   Royal Decree 38/2000 – Law on Trademarks, Data, Trade Secrets and Protection against Illegal Competition

Royal Decree 38/2000 lists in some detail which trademarks may or may not be registered as such. Marks which do not conform with the requirements of decency, marks of a purely religious nature, marks incorporating false information or marks bearing a resemblance to an already established trademark or trade name will not be registered.

Royal Decree 38/2000 also sets out various provisions as to the registration of trademarks. In due course, the Minister concerned will issue regulations specifying the exact procedures for registration. Until such time as those regulations are issued, the current regulations established under the existing law will subsist.

The law states that the protection arising from registration of the marks will continue for ten years, after which time the registration may be renewed.

Articles 23 to 26 of Royal Decree 38/2000 set out the rules governing the licensing of the use of products and services in respect of which the mark is registered. Such a licence may not exceed the period specified for protection of the mark.

Article 33 is concerned with protection against illegal competition. It is illegal to engage in competitive business which violates good trade practice. The decree gives some guidance as to what will be considered a breach of good trade practice, but this is somewhat limited.

Article 34 criminalizes the disclosure of trade secrets. Again, the decree only gives limited guidance as to what will be classed as a trade secret, but it seems safe to assume that matters will be considered confidential if, *inter alia*, their trade value is derived from their secrecy or if reasonable provision has been made to safeguard their secrecy. How the Court will interpret Articles 33 and 34 remains to be seen.

8.3 Other intellectual property legislation

In addition to the above, other Royal Decrees have been promulgated, dealing with illegal use of geographical descriptions, protection of topography and integrated circuit design, and protection of trade/industrial drawings.

9 FAMILY LAW AND SUCCESSION

There have been no developments under this title.

10 CRIMINAL LAW AND PROCEDURES

10.1 Royal Decree 4/2000 – Extradition Law

The provisions of the Extradition Law set out in this Royal Decree are without prejudice to any specific agreements entered into by the Sultanate with other states.

Criminals shall be surrendered to the requesting country in the following circumstances:

(a) The offence was committed in the territory of the requesting country.
(b) The criminal to be surrendered is a national of the country in question.
(c) The offence, though committed outside the lands of the requesting country, affects that country's security, financial position, or the conclusiveness of its official seals.

In each of the above situations, the offence committed, and in relation to which the surrender is requested, must be punishable under the laws of Oman by not less than one year's imprisonment. If the person to be surrendered has been found guilty already, the sentence awarded must have been at least six months' imprisonment.

Criminals shall *not* be surrendered in the following circumstances:

(a) The person to be surrendered is an Omani national.
(b) The offence was committed in Oman.
(c) The subject individual is immune from legal proceedings in Oman.
(d) The subject individual has been granted political asylum in Oman.

(e) The crime committed was of a political nature, or the extradition is
      requested for a political reason.
(f) The subject individual is being pursued, investigated or tried for the
      same offence in Oman.
(g) Or if the trial of the offence is time-barred according to the laws of
      either Oman, the requesting country or the country in which the offence
      was committed.

If there are requests for the same individual from more than one country,
the magistrate's court of appeal shall decide to which country the individual
in question should be surrendered.

11   PUBLIC INTERNATIONAL LAW

There have been no developments under this title.

12   PRIVATE INTERNATIONAL LAW (CONFLICTS)

There have been no developments under this title.

Yemen

*Nageeb Shamiri**

1 CONSTITUTIONAL, ADMINISTRATIVE AND INTERNATIONAL LAW

1.1 The First Direct Presidential Elections (23 September 1999)

President Ali Abdalla Saleh, the President of the Republic and also the leader of the main ruling party, the General Congress Party, was the official candidate of that party as well as of two other political parties: the Yemeni Congregation for Reform (which is the second largest party in Parliament and a religious and tribal alliance) and the Baath Party (which is a Pan-Arab nationalistic party). He was one of the two candidates for the first presidential elections based on direct and free competitive elections by universal suffrage in the history of modern Yemen, held on 23 September 1999. He was declared the President of the Republic of Yemen for a new term of five years. The result was declared on 25 September 1999 by the Supreme Elections Commission. The candidate Ali Abdalla Saleh won a landslide victory, receiving 96.3 per cent of the votes cast in the elections, after gaining 3,577,960 votes. The other candidate, Mr Nageeb Qahtan Al-Sha'bi – from the same political party as the other candidate, but standing as an independent candidate – is a Member of Parliament and the eldest son of the first President of ex-South Yemen after it was granted its independence from British rule on 30 November 1967. He received 3.7 per cent of the votes cast, or 132,352 votes. It is worthwhile mentioning, however, that the turnout of the voters was 66 per cent of the 5,619,000 eligible voters, or exactly 3,600,000. The two candidates carried out extensive election campaigning, which started officially on 9 September 1999, taking the form of public rallies, drawing masses of people throughout the Republic.

The results of the elections were declared by the Supreme Elections

---

*   Judge of the Supreme Court, Yemen.

Commission, in a press conference, on 25 September 1999, in accordance with section 71 of the General Elections Law No. 27/1999. This provides as follows.

The Supreme Elections Commission shall receive the results of the Elections and shall declare the same. The final results shall be declared within a period not later than seventy-two hours, with effect from the closure of the voting process.

In connection with the presidential elections, and in order to make it more convenient for the registered voters to cast their votes anywhere in the country – irrespective of the electoral constituency where they were registered – the President of the Republic promulgated Law No. 41/1999, amending the General Elections Law No. 27/1999, which provided that, for the purposes of the presidential elections and referenda, the whole Republic should be considered a single constituency. Any registered voter would be entitled to cast his or her vote, on polling day, anywhere outside the elections centre where he or she was registered, in accordance with the arrangements made by the Supreme Elections Commission.

1.2   Information on the elections

Republican Resolution No. 20/1999 was issued on 23 August 1999, according to the provisions of the General Elections Law No. 27/1996 and amendments thereto, calling on citizens registered in the General Election Registers in all of the electoral constituencies to cast their votes in the presidential elections on 23 September 1999.

Parliament approved the spending of 50 million Yemeni riyals (YR) for the two candidates for the presidential elections held on that date. Seventeen thousand cabins were used for voting, in 4,359 ballot stations all over the Republic, and 13,077 persons, males and females, were involved in staffing the ballot stations.

Over 50,000 military persons were involved in keeping law and order in the said ballot stations, together with 2,075 military vehicles and 2,075 pieces of telephone equipment, which had been assigned to take charge of protection of the stations, for the sake of the smooth running of the elections.

Observers from Indonesia, Korea, India, Finland, the Czech Republic, the International Association for the Electoral Systems in Washington, the Centre for the Reform of the Electoral Systems in Britain, in addition to 300 local observers, attended the elections.

Seventy foreign journalists, representing news agencies, newspapers and space television channels participated in the coverage of the elections. The Supreme Elections Commission established, for the purpose, an information centre, rendering all possible information services to the representatives of the press, and local, Arab and foreign journalists.

Voters to the number of 5,600,119 were registered for the presidential elections, with 301 elections units and 2,083 election centres. Male registered voters were 3,891,966 with 11,048 male election committees and the female registered voters 1,690,426 with 6,135 female election committees. The number of registered voters represented 71 per cent of those who were entitled to register, numbering in total 7,774,800.

1.3 International Arbitration: Yemen/Eritrea (17 December 1999)

The award in the second stage of the International Arbitration between the Republic of Yemen and the State of Eritrea, concerning their dispute over certain southern Red Sea islands, on the Delimitation of the Maritime Boundaries between them, was announced by the International Arbitration Tribunal, under the President, Sir Robert Jennings, in the Foreign and Commonwealth Office in London, on 17 December 1999.

The Yemen–Eritrean Arbitration is now drawing to a close. A Communication of the President of the Arbitration Tribunal to the Parties, dated 25 February 2000, the Hague/the Netherlands, states the following:

> The Registry encloses a Communication from the President on behalf of the Tribunal in response to your letters. The historic Eritrea/Yemen arbitration conducted under the Arbitration Agreement of October 1996 draws to a close. The Parties will soon receive a final accounting from the Registry. Copies of the final submissions of the Parties and the Awards will be maintained in the Registry archives. It has been an honour and privilege to work with the representatives of both governments who have presented to the international community an inspiring example of peaceful dispute resolution.

Moreover – and in connection with the application and implementation of the Award in the Second Stage – the President of the Republic issued Presidential Resolution No. 6/2000, as regards the Formation of a Committee for the Follow-up of the Application and Implementation of the Awards of the International Arbitration Tribunal between the Republic of Yemen and the State of Eritrea, on the Questions of Territorial Sovereignty over the southern Red Sea Islands and the Delimitation of Maritime Boundaries. It is worthwhile remembering, however, that the Award as regards the First Stage of the Arbitration, on the Questions of Territorial Sovereignty as well as the Scope of the Dispute, was communicated – by the International Arbitration Tribunal – to the Parties, on 7 October 1998.[1]

1.4 Jeddah Treaty of Delimitation of the International Land and Maritime Boundaries: Yemen/Saudi Arabia (12 June 2000)

The Cabinet in the Republic of Yemen, in its weekly meeting, presided over by President Ali Abdalla Saleh, unanimously approved the treaty on 20 June

---

[1] In this connection, the President of the Republic issued Republican Resolution No. 6/2000, Regarding the Formation of a Committee for Follow-up, Application and Implementation of the Awards of the International Arbitration Tribunal, between Yemen and Eritrea. See this *Yearbook*, vol. 5 (1998–99), p. 513. The award of the International Arbitration Tribunal, in the Second Stage of the

2000, and referred it to the House of Representatives – the Parliament in the Republic of Yemen – for approval in accordance with Article 91 of the Yemeni Constitution. Parliament commenced debating the treaty on 21 June 2000 and approved it unanimously on 24 June 2000. Furthermore, the Consultative Council – which is an advisory body to the President of the Republic, in accordance with Article 125 of the Constitution – held an Extraordinary Session, and greeted with satisfaction the signing of the Treaty, congratulating the President for his historic and courageous stance, which will put an end to negotiations on the sixty-year dispute on 22 June 2000. On 26 June 2000 the President of the Republic promulgated Law No. 16/2000, giving effect to the treaty.

On 18 June 2000, the Advisory Council in Saudi Arabia approved the Jeddah Treaty. In addition, the Cabinet approved the treaty, at its weekly meeting, held in Jeddah presided over by King Fahd b. Abdul-Aziz 19 June 2000.

In the last decade – which is the first ten years since reunification, and the declaration of the new Yemeni state of the Republic of Yemen in May 1990 – the disputes regarding its boundaries with the Sultanate of Muscat and Oman, the state of Eritrea and the Kingdom of Saudi Arabia have all been settled, once and for all.

As regards Yemen and Oman, this dispute was amicably settled in 1992 by Law No. 44/1992, in connection with Approval to the Delimitation of the International Boundaries Between the Republic of Yemen and the Sultanate of Oman, was promulgated on 31 October 1992.

As regards Yemen and Eritrea, this matter has been settled peacefully through international arbitration and the awards were given in October 1998 and December 1999 on the question of territorial sovereignty and the question of maritime boundaries respectively.

As regards Yemen and Saudi Arabia: this dispute was settled amicably in June 2000 by Law No. 16/2000, dated 26 June 2000.[2]

1.5   The first Yemeni woman ambassador appointed

An ambassador has been appointed to the Netherlands and – for the first time in the history of Yemen – a woman has been chosen. Republican Resolution No. 80/2000 was issued, in this respect, by the President of the Republic.

1.6   The Supreme Elections Commission

Four by-elections had taken place in four parliamentary constituencies in the country, as a result of the death of the Members elected to Parliament in the

---

cont.
     Arbitration Proceedings on Maritime Delimitation, is in Part IV of this volume, pp. 465–500.
[2]   An English translation of the Treaty is at Part III of this volume, pp. 415–418.

general elections held on 27 April 1997, during the period November 1999 to May 2000. The four constituencies are in the governorates (provinces) of Abyan, Al-Hudaidah, Dhamar and Sana'a. The Supreme Elections Commission will play an important role as regards the preparations for the expected – and first – local council elections for the governorates and districts since reunification in May 1990.

Section 153 of the new Local Authority Law No. 4/2000 is connected with the tasks, responsibilities and duties to be accomplished by the Supreme Elections Commission. The Supreme Elections Commission has to prepare and supervise the local council elections in all the administrative units – governorates and districts – as well as compiling registers of voters and an elections' guide for local councils, showing the wards, the procedures for nomination of candidates, the organization of the election campaigns, the declaration of the results of the elections, the appeal petitions against the results, and the competent law courts with jurisdiction to hear and determine such appeal petitions according to the provisions of the law.

1.7 Institutionalizing the legislative process

During the period 10–12 November 1999 a parliamentary seminar was held in Sana'a, arranged by the Yemeni Parliament, under the coordination of the International Parliamentary Union, with the title "Institutionalizing the Legislative Process and Strengthening the Supervisory Role of the House of Representatives with a view to increasingly Organizing the Lives of the People on the Basis of the Legislative and Legal Process". The relationship between Parliament and the government leads to better relations and reciprocal effects, with a view to strengthening the role of Parliament to ensure effective supervision and improve the efficient performance of the government. Several Members of Parliament, as well as government ministers – together with officials and experts from the International Parliamentary Union – participated in the seminar.

1.8 Establishment of the Supreme Civil Defence Council

The President of the Republic issued Republican Resolution No. 389/1999, regarding the Establishment of the Supreme Council for Civil Defence, under the Civil Defence Law No. 24/1997[3] and the Executive Regulations thereof.

1.9 Promulgation of Local Authority Law No. 4/2000

The Local Authority Law No. 4/2000 was promulgated on 9 February 2000. It is one of the most important laws, for it concerns administrative and

---

3   See Yemen survey in this *Yearbook*, vol. 4 (1997–1998).

financial decentralization. It is made up of 174 sections, under nine chapters. It aims at establishing elected local councils in the provinces (called governorates in Yemen, of which there are twenty, forming the administrative divisions of the Republic of Yemen) and districts all over the country.

The main contents of the Local Authority Law are as follows:

(a) the principles;
(b) the composition of the local authorities in the governorates and districts, and their executive apparatus;
(c) the joint powers of the local councils;
(d) the financial powers of the local authorities;
(e) their planning, budget and financial affairs;
(f) the system of inspection or control over the work of the local authorities;
(g) the dissolution of local councils;
(h) transitional and general provisions.

A Ministerial Committee with the Prime Minister as its Chairman was appointed by Republican Resolution No. 75/2000, issued on 27 April 2000, to prepare the Republic for the application and implementation of the provisions of the Local Authority Law No. 4/2000.

2   THE JUDICIAL SYSTEM, COURTS AND THE POLICE

2.1   The Supreme Judicial Council – October 1999 session

The Supreme Judicial Council held a session on 30 October 1999, presided over by the President Ali Abdalla Saleh, President of the Republic and Chairman of the Supreme Judicial Council.

The Council discussed topics connected with the reform, modernization, development and progress of the judiciary, in the interest of justice, and as a part of the building of the Yemeni modern states and the state of law and order. A number of resolutions were taken, as follows:

(a) appointment of a number of divisions in various courts of appeal;
(b) approving appointments and transfers of a number of judges and public prosecutors, all over the country;
(c) setting up a specialized first instance criminal court in the capital, Sana'a, to hear and determine cases of kidnapping, sabotage, terrorist activities against oil pipelines and installations, criminal activities against public order, security and stability, bombings and explosives, and attacks against judges and public prosecutors, wherever the said crimes have been committed;
(d) setting up a specialized criminal appeal division, as part of the Court of Appeal in the capital, Sana'a, to look into appeals lodged against the judgments and decisions of the specialized first instance criminal court;
(e) the establishment of juvenile courts in the capital, Sana'a, Taiz, Hadhramawt, and Al-Hudaidah, as there is already a juvenile court in Aden, established since June 1995;

(f) the appointment of judges for administrative matters and cases, in five provinces: the capital, Sana'a, Aden, Taiz, Hadhramawt and Al-Hudaidah;

(g) the reorganization of the commercial courts in the Republic.[4]

2.2 Establishment of specialized criminal trial court and specialized criminal appeal division in Sana'a

A Republican Resolution No. 391/1999 was passed, in connection with the establishment of a specialized first instance (or trial) criminal court, and a specialized criminal appeal division, both in the capital, Sana'a, with jurisdiction – alone, and to the exclusion of other courts – to hear and determine certain types of crimes according to the laws in the Republic of Yemen.

The main provisions of the said Resolution are as follows:

(a) A specialized first instance criminal court, as well as a specialized criminal appeal division – as part of the Court of Appeal – shall be established, based in the capital, Sana'a, and shall come under the court of appeal of the capital, Sana'a.

(b) The specialized first instance criminal court shall consist of a president and a number of judges, with cases being heard and determined by a single judge; and with the president of the court performing the administrative supervision of the court, in addition to the judicial duties.

(c) The jurisdiction of the specialized first instance criminal court shall be confined – or limited – to hearing and determining, as a trial court, the following crimes: armed robbery; kidnapping of foreigners, and sea and air piracy; causing damage, arson and explosion to the oil pipelines, the oil and economic installations, institutions and enterprises which are of public utility; theft against public and private transport services and means, committed by armed or organized gangs, or by one or more individuals by force; participation in a gang trespassing on the lands and property of the state and the citizens; attacks on judges and public prosecutors, as well as kidnapping thereof or the families thereof.

(d) The territorial jurisdiction of the specialized first instance criminal court shall be the whole territory of the Republic of Yemen, its territorial waters and air space.

(e) The specialized first instance criminal court shall hold its sittings in the capital, Sana'a, or at any other suitable place in the Republic. The court shall abide by the provisions related to summary trials provided for in the Criminal Procedure Law and the laws in force as regards the crimes specified in paragraph 3(c) above.

---

4 The Republican Resolutions regarding the establishment of the specialized first instance criminal court as well as the specialized criminal appeal division in the capital, Sana'a, and the reorganization of the Commercial Courts in the Republic, are explained below.

(f)   The specialized criminal appeal division shall have jurisdiction to hear and determine the appeals filed against the judgments and decisions passed by the specialized first instance criminal court below, according to the law.

(g)   Appeals against the judgments and decisions of the specialized criminal appeal division will be investigated by the Criminal Chamber of the Supreme Court of the Republic.

(h)   The specialized first instance criminal court and the specialized criminal appeal division will have independent financial estimates, sufficient to meet their needs and requirements, within the courts and the judiciary budget.

(i)   A specialized first instance public prosecution, as well as a specialized appeal public prosecution, will be established to perform the functions of public prosecution as regards the crimes specified in paragraph 3(c) above, according to law. A ministerial resolution will be issued by the Minister of Justice, acting on a proposal submitted by the Attorney-General.[5]

2.3   Reorganization of the commercial courts in the Republic of Yemen

Republican Resolution No. 378/1999, regarding the reorganization of the commercial courts in the Republic, was issued, to replace a similar Resolution No. 22/1996. The main provisions of the new resolution are as follows:

(a)   Specialized commercial first instance courts shall be established in the capital, Sana'a, and in Aden, Taiz, Hadhramawt and Al-Hudaidah, at the rate of one or more courts – according to need, and in order to dispose of cases speedily – to hear and determine the commercial cases and disputes.

(b)   Cases in each court will be heard and determined by a single judge, and it is possible – when there is a sufficient number of judges – that cases be heard and determined by a panel of three judges.

(c)   The commercial courts shall have jurisdiction – alone and to the exclusion of all other courts – to hear and determine cases and disputes which have commercial nature, in accordance with the Commercial Law and the other laws connected therewith, the exceptions being as follows: the ordinary courts in the centre of the governorates which are first instance courts in the districts – shall have jurisdiction to hear and determine cases and disputes of commercial nature, provided that the claims do not exceed YR 2,000,000, which is equivalent to US$ 13,000, and the said claims are not connected with cases and disputes regarding commercial paper, insolvency, banks, trade marks, foreign companies, and where one of the parties is a foreigner.

---

[5]   The laws in force, in this respect, are as under: the Judicature Law No. 1/1991; the Penal Law No. 12/1994; the Criminal Procedure Law No. 13/1994; the Struggle Against Kidnapping Law No. 24/1998. See this *Yearbook.*, vol. 5 (1998–99).

(d) A commercial appeal division will be established, as part of the Court of Appeal, in the government concerned, namely, the capital, Sana'a, Aden, Taiz, Hadhramawt and Al-Hudaidah. The jurisdiction of such a commercial appeal division will be to hear and determine – alone and to the exclusion of any other Appeal Division – appeals lodged against the judgments and decisions passed by the commercial first instance courts below. Each appeal division shall consist of a panel of three judges.

(e) The Commercial Chamber of the Supreme Court of the Republic – which is the highest law court in the land – shall have jurisdiction – alone and to the exclusion of any other chamber in that court – to look into the appeals, on points of law, lodged against the judgments and decisions of the commercial appeal divisions below, in addition to determining the admissibility or otherwise of the said appeals – a task carried out normally, in other appeals, by the Appeals Scrutiny Chamber of the Supreme Court. Moreover, more than one panel, of five Supreme Court judges – and within the commercial chamber – may be formed.

(f) The judges of the commercial first instance courts, the commercial appeal divisions in the courts of appeal, and the Commercial Chamber of the Supreme Court of the Republic shall be appointed according to the provisions of the Judicature Law No. 1/1991. In addition to the terms and conditions provided for in section 57 of the Judicature Law, the following conditions, too, shall have to be fulfilled by anyone to be appointed as judge in the commercial courts: he shall be experienced in commercial litigation and laws connected with the various commercial activities. Furthermore, priority will be given to those specialized (in commercial law) from among the commercial law personnel in the Yemeni universities, as well as from among private lawyers with experience in litigation before the commercial courts.

(g) The jurisdiction of the commercial first instance courts and the commercial appeal divisions (specified in paragraphs (a) and (b) shall be as follows:

   (i) the court and division in the capital, Sana'a: their jurisdiction covers the capital, Sana'a and the governorates of Sanaa, Imran, Saadah, Dhamar, Al-Baidha, Marib and Al-Jawf;

   (ii) the court and division in Aden covers the governorates of Aden, Lahej and Abyan;

   (iii) the court and division in Taiz covers the governorates of Taiz, Ibb and Al-Dhala;

   (iv) the court and division in Hadhramawt covers the governorates of Hadhramawt, Shabwah and Al-Mahharah;

   (v) the court and division in Al-Hudaidah covers the governorates of Al-Hudaidah, Hajjah and al-Mahweet.

(h) The commercial first instance courts and the commercial appeal divisions shall have independent financial estimates, sufficient for their needs – as part of the courts and the judiciary budget. The presidents of the commercial appeal divisions shall have responsibility as regards the administrative and financial affairs over the commercial first instance courts.

(i) A general department for the commercial courts shall be established, under the supervision of the Minister of Justice, with responsibility relating to their affairs. The Minister of Justice shall issue a Ministerial Resolution regarding the establishment of the said general department as well as duties and responsibilities thereof.

2.4 The Convention on the Settlement of Investment Disputes between States and Nationals of Other States (ICSID)

The President of the Republic promulgated Law No. 49/1999, approving Yemen becoming a party to the Convention on the Settlement of Investment Disputes between States and Nationals of other States (the ICSID Convention) – the Washington Agreement 1965 – signed by the Republic of Yemen on 28 October 1997.

2.5 Agreement with the World Bank for a legal and judicial reform project in the Republic of Yemen

The President of the Republic promulgated Law No. 58/1999, approving an agreement with the World Bank, for a loan of US$2.5 million, for a project for legal and judicial reform. The main components of the project are as follows:

(a) judicial reform;
(b) legal reform;
(c) awareness campaign.

The government is raising the salaries of judges and public prosecutors, to improve their living conditions. The new salaries will take effect in July 2000.

2.6 Promulgation of the Police Organization Law No. 15/2000

The President of the Republic – on 25 June 2000 – promulgated the Police Organization Law No. 15/2000, which replaces – as regards the Police – Law No. 67/1991, in connection with the armed forces and security forces. The principal provisions of the Police Organization Law are as follows:

(a) title and definitions;
(b) establishment of police organization, and their duties and responsibilities;
(c) Supreme Police Council;
(d) appointments, ranks, registers and reports;

(e)   vacations;
(f)   transfers and secondments;
(g)   scholarships and courses;
(h)   medical services;
(i)   honours, medals and certificates;
(j)   duties of the officers and forbidden activities;
(k)   salaries, allowances and bonuses;
(l)   termination of service;
(m) recruitment to the organization;
(n)   personnel; and
(o)   general provisions.

The new law replaces, as regards the police, Law No. 67/1991, which was enacted shortly after reunification. The new law takes into consideration the changes that are taking place in the world, in this respect, especially, modern techniques, equipment and technology. This is the first law to govern the police.

3   COMMERCIAL LAW AND TRADE

3.1 Promulgation of Privatization Law No. 45/1999

Privatization Law No. 45/1999 13 was promulgated.[6]

3.2   Establishment of the Higher Privatization Committee

In this connection, the President of the Republic issued Republican Resolution No. 399/1999, regarding the establishment of the Higher Privatization Committee, in accordance with section 6 of the Privatization Law No. 45/1999, under the chairmanship of the Prime Minister.

The Committee has prepared – with technical assistance rendered by the International Development Organization – a Privatization Rules and Procedures Guide.[7]

3.3   Promulgation of Tourism Law No. 40/1999

The law was promulgated to replace Law No. 22/1994, in connection with the same subject. The main provisions of the Law No. 40/2000 are as follow.
The aims and objectives to be realized are:

---

6   See Part III of this *Yearbook*, pp. 419–427.
7   The responsibilities and powers of the Higher Privatization Committee, set up on 11 December 1999, by Republican Resolution No. 399/1999, under section 6 of the Privatization Law No. 45/1999, are enumerated in the provisions of Law No. 45/1999 itself – and, in particular, sections 6–9.

(a) organizing, regulating and encouraging tourism, in addition to developing and utilizing tourism resources with a view to setting up a developed tourism industry, participating in supporting comprehensive economic and social development;

(b) preserving tourism and environment areas and sites, and the care thereof, in addition to an awareness campaign regarding the archaeological and natural heritage and preparation thereof for tourism;

(c) encouraging the local and foreign tourism investment;

(d) preserving the traditional craft industry, in addition to encouraging the development thereof;

(e) activating internal, regional and international tourism, in addition to training of tourism guides.

There shall be established a Supreme Council for Tourism, under the Prime Minister as Chairman, with the Minister of Culture and Tourism as Vice Chairman.

The duties and responsibilities of the Supreme Council for Tourism are as follows:

(a) laying down the policies and plans essential for building tourism in Yemen;

(b) studying and approving the proposals and plans essential for the tourism sector, in addition to defining the tourist areas, sites, natural protectorates and preservation thereof;

(c) coordinating the ministries and various organs concerned, with a view to application and implementation of the tourism development plans, in order to activate tourism;

(d) declaring an area/site – where the conditions for tourism attraction are available – as a tourism area/site to be utilized solely for tourism investment and activities; in addition to encouraging investment in the islands, and in building tourism towns and villages.

The organization of the tourism installations shall be based on the following rules and regulations:

(a) an obligation to be licensed;

(b) the Corporation will oversee hotel installations, tourism installations, travel agencies, tourism agencies;

(c) rates for accommodation and services, in addition to reservation regulations;

(d) supervision regarding compliance with the rules and regulations in force, in this respect;

(e) provision for the cancellation of licences;

(f) making known to foreign tourists that they should respect the beliefs and traditions of Yemenis, in addition to public morals.

The tour guides should be Yemeni nationals, but not civil servants, licensed from the corporation, healthy, honest, graduates and experienced in tourism duties/work, knowledgeable in history and civilization. Tourism and travel agencies should not take tourists to tourism and archaeological sites unless they are accompanied by tourism guides.

The penalties for violations of the provisions of the law and regulations thereof are fines, imprisonment, closure of hotels/etc., and stoppage of tourism guides.[8]

3.4   The World Trade Organization and Yemen

The National Committee for the Preparation – and Negotiations – with the World Trade Organization, established pursuant to the Resolution of the Prime Minister No. 239/1998,[9] under the chairmanship of the Minister of Supply and Trade, has been enlarged – by the Resolutions of the Prime Minister Nos. 558/1999 and 589/1999.

It is worth mentioning, however, that the Cabinet issued a Resolution on 21 March 2000, as follows:

(a)   authorizing the Minister of Supply and Trade to submit an application regarding our country becoming a Member of the World Trade Organization;
(b)   setting up the negotiating team, in this respect, under the Minister of Supply and Trade;
(c)   setting up a Committee, for laying down the general policies for the negotiations with the World Trade Organization, comprising the Prime Minister, the Minister of Legal and Parliamentary Affairs, the Minister of Finance, the Minister of Planning and Development, the Minister of Industry, and the Minister of Supply and Trade.[10]

3.5   Promulgation of the Central Bank Law No. 14/2000

The President of the Republic – on 25 June 2000 – promulgated Law No. 14/2000, in connection with the Central Bank of Yemen. The main provisions of the Central Bank Law concerning the bank are as follows:

(a)   the title and definitions;
(b)   its aims, objectives, duties and responsibilities;
(c)   its capital, profits and reserves;

---

[8]   The law provides for the Establishment of a Tourism Procurement Fund, the responsibilities of which shall be defined by the law.
[9]   See this *Yearbook*, vol. 5 (1998–1999).
[10]   A notification, by Yemen, of its desire to join the WTO, was submitted, in April 2000. It is expected that an application for membership – involving the policies, according to which the negotiations with the WTO will take place – will be submitted within one year, approximately during the first half of the year 2001. It is estimated that the negotiations are likely to be completed within three to four years.

(d) its management;
(e) its currency;
(f) its relations with the government and other institutions;
(g) its foreign reserves and foreign currency transactions;
(h) its responsibilities and other activities;
(i) the accounts; and
(j) the general provisions.

The Central Bank Law confers wide power on the Central Bank, in line with the monetary policies and programmes of the government, emanating from the economic, administrative and financial reforms currently being implemented in the Republic of Yemen, which began in 1995.

3.6   Laws in connection with avoidance of double taxation

The following laws have been promulgated, approving agreements between the Republic of Yemen and certain Arab States, as follows:

(a) Law No. 46/1999, with Jordan;
(b) Law No. 47/1999, with Tunisia;
(c) Law No. 48/1999, with Egypt.

4   SOCIAL, COMMUNITY CARE AND EDUCATIONAL LAW

4.1   Promulgation of Law No. 36/1999, in connection with Amendments to the Fund for Youth and Sports Law No. 10/1996

Section 11 provides that the resources of the Fund shall consist of the following:

(a) the grant of the government, within the general budget of the Ministry of Youth and Sports, to support the Fund;
(b) legitimate grants and donations given to the Fund, from individuals and local as well as foreign organizations;
(c) a proportion of the proceeds of the advertisements at the stadia and playing fields, to be fixed by a ministerial resolution to be issued by the Minister of Youth and Sports;
(d) a fee of YR5 on cigarettes locally manufactured or imported;
(e) 5 per cent additional tax on *qat*;
(f) a fee of YR5 on every 59 kg of cement;
(g) the proceeds of investing the property of the Fund.

The amendment provides for more resources to enable the Ministry of Youth and Sports to construct more institutions, stadia, playing-fields, etc., for the benefit of the younger generation and sports generally.

4.2 Promulgation of Law No. 47/1999, in connection with Amendments to the Yemeni State Universities Law No. 18/1995

The main provisions of the law are as follows.

Section 7(1) shall be amended, thus:

A Supreme Council for the Universities, based in Sana'a, shall be established as under:

(1) the Minister of Education;
(2) the Minister of Planning and Development;
(3) the Minister of Finance;
(4) the Minister of Civil Service;
(5) the Minister of Labour and Vocational Training;
(6) the Rectors of the State Universities;
(7) a Faculty Dean for every State University, appointed by its Faculty annually;
(8) three academic cadres chosen by the Supreme Council of the Universities.

The Council is under the chairmanship of the Prime Minister; the Minister of Labour and Vocational Training, in addition to three distinguished academic, or educational, persons have been included to the membership of the Council. All these matters represent recognition of the question of vocational and technological training, as well as the role to be played by well-known persons in this respect and not just officials.

4.3 Promulgation of Law No. 38/1999, in connection with Amendments to the Social Development Fund Care Law No. 10/1997

The main amendments are concerned with sections 7 and 15: Section 7 concerns the management of the Fund by a board of directors, which is established as follows:

(a) the Prime Minister (chairman);
(b) the Minister of Welfare and Social Security (deputy chairman);
(c) the Minister of Planning and Development (member);
(d) the Minister of Finance (member);
(e) the Minister of Local Administration (member);
(f) the Minister of Education (member);
(g) the Minister of Labour and Vocational Training (member);
(h) two representatives of the non-governmental organizations (NGOs), (members);
(i) two representatives of the private sector (members);
(j) two specialists recommended by the Prime Minister (members);
(k) a representative of the financial and banking sector (member);

(l)   the Executive Director of the Fund (member and secretary of the board of directors).

Section 15 states that the Chairman of the Board of Directors (who is the Prime Minister) shall appoint the Executive Director of the Fund – who should be the most qualified applicant – upon a recommendation to this effect from the Minister of Welfare and Social Security, after an advertisement for the post by the Ministry of Welfare and Social Security.

The amendments are intended to increase the involvement of the NGOs, as well as the private sector, in the social development process.

4.4   Promulgation of the Public Sanitation Law No. 39/1999

The aims and objectives of the law are as follows:

(a)   protection of the environment and the health of the community;
(b)   getting rid of the garbage in the towns and villages, in accordance with proper means, etc.;
(c)   realizing the principle of decentralization, as regards the question of cleaning, and regulating – as well as simplifying – the rules and procedures for the implementation thereof.

The responsibilities of the governors and/or the directors of the districts are the collection, transport and disposal of refuse and waste; the transport of the liquid waste and its disposal; disposal sites for refuse and waste; the terms and conditions regarding contracting with cleaning labourers.

The Minister of Constructions, Housing and Urban Planning – and governors or district directors – are conferred with powers to apply and implement the provisions of the law. Some provisions in the law concern privatized services.

Section 15 provides that the governor, or the director of the district, may execute an agreement with a contractor, to transfer dirty water from the buildings and installations. Sections 23–29 regulate the conditions regarding the contracts with the private sector, for cleaning purposes, in the towns. Section 40 permits entering into contracts with sanitary overseers, who are authorized to prosecute those violating the provisions of the law, to supervise cleaning activities and collect fines.

4.5   Promulgation of the Private Medical and Health Institutions Law No. 60/1999

The main provisions of this law are as follows:

(a)   aims and objectives;
(b)   establishment of the committees concerned with the private medical and health institutions;

(c) the conditions/prerequisites for the establishment and operation of the private institutions;

(d) the technical conditions/prerequisites for the private institutions; and

(e) inspection.

The new legislation gives the opportunity for the private sector – whether national or foreign – to invest in the public health sector.

4.6 Promulgation of the Care and Rehabilitation of the Handicapped Law No. 61/1999

This law covers care and rehabilitation, recruitment, penalties and general provisions.

4.7 Promulgation of Law No. 1/2000, in connection with Amendments to the Social Security and Pensions Law No. 25/1991

The main amendments are related to the basic wage as well as minimum wage, and are as follows. The definition of the basic wage has been amended to mean the complete wage, which means basic salary plus allowances, which is the amount on which contributions are due from the employee/labourer/civil servant; but incentives and overtime do not come within the complete wage. Previously, the definition provided that the basic wage was the amount received, but excluding allowances.

Section 26 has been amended so that if the service of the worker comes to an end because of natural death or complete incapacity – but not of the kind which is considered a work accident of the said employee – he is entitled to a pension calculated in accordance with the actual period of service, provided that that pension should not be less than YR 7,000, which is equivalent to US$ 45, or half of the last complete wage, whichever is greater.

Previously, the employee/servant was entitled to the minimum wage, or half of the basic wage – whichever was greater – though, legally, there was no minimum wage and the basic wage excluded all the allowances. Section 27 has been amended to provide that the pension shall not, under any circumstances, be less than YR 7,000. The pension was formerly the minimum wage, but legally there was no minimum wage.

An additional new provision provides that pensioners, or the families of those who are dead, shall be granted 50 per cent of any increase in salaries or subsistence allowances, granted to the civil service, state workers in the public and mixed sectors.

The amended provisions shall take effect as regards new cases which arise after the coming into force of these amendments.

The definition of basic wage wherever it is mentioned in Law 25/1991, means the basic salary plus allowances.

4.8 Yemen becomes party to the International Convention Regarding the Worst Forms of the Employment of Children

The Republic of Yemen became a party to the International Convention No. 182/1999, regarding the Worst Forms of the Children's Employment and the Immediate Steps to Eliminate Them. Republican Resolution No. 432/1999 was issued in this connection.

4.9 Prime Minister's Resolution No. 68/2000, Regarding the Establishment of the Supreme Council for Women's Affairs

The Cabinet approved the establishment of the Supreme Council for Women's Affairs, under the Prime Minister, and it enjoys administrative and financial independence.

The duties and responsibilities of the Council are the following:

(a) endorsing the policies, strategies, plans and programmes essential for realization of the aims and objectives of the Council;
(b) discussing and approving the annual budget and audit report;
(c) defining the principles regarding the regulation of the relations and coordination, with the national government and non-government bodies, as well as the regional and international organizations working in women's affairs;
(d) supervising and directing the Council's organs, as well as following up the level of implementation of the duties and responsibilities thereof;
(e) reviewing the legislation related to women's affairs, and endeavouring to develop that legislation further to take into consideration the developments taking place in society;
(f) representing the Council in participation in activities, seminars, conferences related to women's affairs, locally, pan-Arab and internationally.

The National Committee for Women performs the following duties and responsibilities:

(a) suggesting the policies, strategies, plans and programmes connected with women's affairs;
(b) reviewing the proposed annual budget and audit report;
(c) periodically reviewing the prevailing conditions of the executive organ and submitting the proposals for the further development thereof;
(d) submitting the proposals essential for improving the performance of the Council and the Secretariat.

5 HUMAN RIGHTS

5.1 Establishment of the National Commission on the International Humanitarian Law

Republican Resolution No. 408/1999 was issued, regarding the Establishment of the National Commission on International Humanitarian Law, pursuance of Law No. 43/1999.

The responsibilities of the National Commission are:

(a)   revision of the legislation in force in this respect, in order to determine the consistency thereof with the provisions of the international humanitarian law;
(b)   submission of proposals with a view to improving the legislation in force to make it consistent with developments in international humanitarian law;
(c)   supervision of the implementation of the provisions of Law No. 43/1999, in connection with Regulating the Signs of the Red Crescent and Red Cross, and Prohibition of the Misuse thereof;
(d)   defining mechanisms, steps and procedures which ensure the application and implementation of the principles as well as the provisions of the international humanitarian law;
(e)   affirming plans and programmes which ensure the publication of the international humanitarian law, in order to create public awareness in this respect;
(f)   coordination between the government and international efforts in the field of the international humanitarian law;
(g)   any other responsibilities relating to the subject.

5.2   United Nations Human Rights Commission and Yemen

The Working Group related to the United Nations Commission for Human Rights on the Human Rights Situation in the Republic of Yemen (established by Resolution 1990/41 of the Economic and Social Council of the United Nations) welcoming, and noting with satisfaction, the progress achieved by the Yemeni government as regards its record in the field of human rights, decided on 31 March 2000 to discontinue consideration of the human rights situation in the Republic of Yemen.

5.3   Prime Minister's Resolution No. 621/1999, Regarding Naming the Members of the Advisory Bureau of the Supreme National Human Rights Commission

The Prime Minister issued this Resolution, in which the following persons and bodies have been named to constitute the Advisory Bureau of the Supreme National Human Rights Commission:

(a)   eight persons (equivalent to Justices of the Peace – JPs – in the UK);
(b)   six women;
(c)   five academics, representing the universities;
(d)   three persons representing the NGOs active in the sphere of human rights;
(e)   the professional syndicates: lawyers, journalists, trade unions, teachers, doctors, women, the Red Crescent and agricultural cooperatives.

5.4   National Centre for Human Rights and Development of Democracy

The National Centre for Human Rights and Development of Democracy in Yemen was inaugurated on 13 September 1999, in accordance with Ministerial Resolution No. 130/1999, issued by the Ministry of Culture. The main objectives of the Centre are connected with an awareness campaign regarding the importance of democracy and human rights in many fields – political, economic and social – and the impact thereof on the comprehensive development process.

5.5   Memorandum of Intent: Yemen and United Nations Human Rights Commission

The government of the Republic of Yemen – represented by the Deputy Prime Minister and Foreign Minister, Chairman of the Supreme National Commission for Human Rights/Abdul-Kader Abdul-Rehman Ba-Gammal – and the United Nations Office of the High Commission for Human Rights – represented by the Commissioner, Mary Robinson – signed a Memorandum of Intent, in Sana'a, on 4 February 2000 on the Mutual Agreement to Cooperate in the Development and Implementation of Comprehensive Programmes for the Promotion and Protection of Human Rights in Yemen.

Iran

M.A. Ansari-Pour*

Many legal developments occurred in Iran during the period covered by this survey. In addition, two political developments took place which may have considerable impact on the direction of future legal developments. First, in 1999 the Head of the Judiciary was replaced. The present Head of the Judiciary[1] taught Islamic law (*fiqh* and *usul al-fiqh*) in Qom before his appointment. Although he had no working experience in the judiciary, in terms of legal learning he was regarded as one of the top jurists. Secondly, following the recent parliamentary election in February 2000, the Sixth Period of Parliament (since the revolution) with a new formation is now in session.

This survey deals with the most significant legal developments which occurred during February 1999 to February 2000.[2]

1 CONSTITUTIONAL LAW

1.1 Parliamentary elections

The legal framework for parliamentary elections until 1999 was the Islamic Consultative Assembly Elections Act 1362 (1984).[3] Although it had been

---

*   Former Iranian judge. I would like to thank the staff of the International Institute of Islamic Studies in Tehran and of the Iranian Law Institute for providing the primary sources of this survey.

1   I.e. Ayatollah S.M. Hosseini Shahrudi.
2   I.e. from 16.11.1377 to 5.12.1378 according to the Iranian calendar.
3   *Ruznami-yi Rasmi*, 23.12.1362, No. 11377; *Majmu'a[h] Qawanin*, 1362, pp. 497–515. *Ruznami-yi Rasmi* (hereinafter cited as RR) is the Official Gazette of the Islamic Republic of Iran which is published by the Judiciary, and *Majmu'a[h] Qawanin* (hereinafter referred to as MQ) is the Collection of Laws which is published yearly by the same organization.

subject to some minor amendments since its adoption,[4] the structure had remained intact. This Act consisted of eighty-nine articles divided into ten chapters. It was replaced with a new statute under the same title, i.e. the Islamic Consultative Assembly Elections Act in 1378 (1999).[5]

The new statute consists of ninety-four articles divided into ten chapters dealing with general provisions (Articles 1–6), manner of elections (Articles 7–26), qualifications of electorate and candidates (Articles 27–30), executive bodies for elections in constituencies (Articles 31–44), candidacy and examining the competence of candidates (Article 45–55), election campaigns (Articles 56–65), election offences and violations (Articles 66–67), complaints and the procedure for dealing with them (Articles 68–74), punishments for the election offences (Articles 75–88) and finally preparation of preliminaries, convening and opening of Parliament (Articles 89–94). The executive regulation of this Act was also adopted by the Council of Ministers on 21.9.1378.[6]

1.2   Increase of number of Members of Parliament

Article 64 of the Constitution provides that there are to be 270 representatives or deputies in Parliament. This article also states that after every ten years period from 1368 (1989) onwards, taking into account the population, political, geographic and other factors, twenty deputies, at the maximum, can be added to the Members of Parliament. Finally, it provides that the limits of constituencies and the number of deputies are to be fixed by law.

On the basis of the above provision the boundaries of some constituencies were changed and the number of deputies were increased from 270 to 290 by parliamentary legislation in 1378 (1999).[7] As a result of this legislation, there are 290 representatives or deputies in the present Parliament.

2   LEGAL SYSTEM

The Court of Administrative Justice, which deals mainly with complaints lodged against government measures, decisions and regulations, was established by the Court of Administrative Justice Act 1982 (hereinafter cited as CAJA)[8] following the ruling of Article 173 of the Constitution.[9] The CAJA

---

[4]   For example, see RR, 28.12.1362, No. 11381, MQ, 1362, p. 516; RR, 25.2.1363, No. 11421, MQ, 1362, pp. 575–576; RR, 6.5.1363, No. 11479, MQ, 1363, pp. 102–103; RR, 20.12.1366, No. 12541, MQ, 1366, pp. 963–964; RR. 26.11.1370, No. 13674, MQ, 1370, pp. 808–810.
[5]   RR, 18.9.1378, No. 15960; MQ, 1378, pp. 496–518.
[6]   RR, 30.9.1378, No. 15970; MQ, 1378, pp. 536–559.
[7]   RR, 9.9.1378, No. 15952; MQ, 1378, pp. 475–480.
[8]   RR, 18.12.1360, No. 10790; MQ, 1360, pp. 170–175.
[9]   Art. 173, *inter alia*, provides that "In order to investigate the complaints, grievances, and objections of the people with respect to government officials or organs or regulations … a court to be known as the Court of Administrative Justice will be established under the supervision of the Head of the Judiciary".

consists of twenty-five articles. Some of these provisions (i.e. Articles 1 and 18–21) were amended by Parliament in 1999 and a new article, Article 26, was added.[10] According to the parliamentary proceedings, the CAJA had a number of shortcomings but three of them, which the amendment aimed to rectify, were of paramount importance.[11]

2.1 Structure of the Court

Article 1 of the CAJA stipulated that the court would consist of two judges: a presiding judge (or his alternate) and a counsellor, unless the dispute related to the cases mentioned in paragraph A of Article 11 (which is referred to below) in which case two counsellors were needed. The authority to decide was vested in the presiding judge (or his alternate).

Under the new law, each court consists of a presiding judge or an alternate member. If the presiding judge or the alternate member needs a counsellor he can ask the president of the court (i.e. the Chief Justice) to appoint a counsellor. The presiding judge will give his judgment following the written opinion of the counsellor.[12]

2.2 Right of appeal

Under Article 18 before its amendments, the judgments of court given against government departments, stipulated in paragraph A of Article 11 (1) of the CAJA,[13] could be appealed against.[14] The case then could be reconsidered in terms of law not fact. In other cases, the judgments were final and

---

[10] RR, 26.2.1378, No. 15790; MQ, 1378, pp. 48–50.

[11] See *Mashruh-i Mudhakarat-i Majlis-i Shura-yi Islami*, 5th period, 3rd session, 6.8.1377. *Mashruh-i Mudhakarat-i Majlis-i Shura-yi Islami* (hereinafter cited as MMMSI) is the proceedings and minutes of the Islamic Consultative Assembly (i.e. Parliament) which is published along with the Official Gazette.

[12] Art. 1 also had other provisions which were affected by the amendment. For example, under the former law, the court could be established in the capital and other cities (though it was established only in Tehran) but under the new law it will be established in Tehran only. Secondly, under the former law, in the absence of the president of the court the presiding judge of the second chamber acted as his deputy. Under the present law, the president of the court can, to the extent necessary, have deputies and counsellors. The number of deputies and counsellors will be determined following the proposal of the president of the court and the approval of the Head of the Judiciary. In addition, the president of the court can delegate some of his authorities to his deputies.

[13] Art. 11 divides the cases where the court has jurisdiction into three categories. The first category consists of dealing with complaints, grievances and objections of natural and legal persons against (a) decisions and measures taken by government departments including ministries, government organizations, institutions and companies, municipalities, revolutionary establishments and institutions and affiliated institutions. There are also two other sub-categories (b) and (c).

[14] The time limit for appeal under the former text of Art. 19 was ten days from the date of the notification of the judgment.

could not be reconsidered. In other words, no right of appeal had been provided for claimants against the judgment of court, although government departments enjoyed such a right. This system was in conflict with the system followed by the mainstream courts in which the right of appeal exists for both parties to a dispute.

Under the new text of Article 18, the judgments of the first instance court can be appealed against by one of the parties to the dispute. In other words, the claimants and defendants have both been given the right of appeal. The time limit for lodging an appeal is twenty days, but for those living abroad it is two months from the date of the notification of judgment.

2.3   Court of Appeal

Under the former law, there was no separate appeal court. The body which dealt with government appeals, according to Article 19, consisted of the president of the court or his deputy and six judges from the presiding judges of the court on a rotating basis. The decision was made by majority.

The new law provides for the establishment of a separate appeal court. Under the new text of Article 19, for hearing the appeals against the judgments of the first instance court five appeal chambers, each of which consists of one presiding judge and two counsellors, are to be established. The appeal chambers can be increased following the proposal of the president of the court and the approval of the Head of the Judiciary. The president of the court is also the presiding judge of the first chamber of the appeal court.

Article 19 also has two notes. Under note 1, the judges of the appeal court are selected from the judges of the first instance court who have a working experience of at least two years in the court. Under note 2, each chamber of the appeal court can start proceedings by the presence of, at least, two judges. The judgment is passed by majority.

In addition to the above changes, a number of other provisions of the CAJA also were affected by the amendment.

(a)   According to the former text of Article 20, when in similar cases conflicting judgments were delivered by one or several chambers of the court, the president of the court had to raise the issue in the Plenary Assembly of the court. To convene the Assembly the presence of at least three-quarters of the presiding judges of the court was necessary. The majority decision of the Assembly was binding on all chambers of the court and other relevant authorities. Under the new text of Article 20, when in similar cases conflicting judgments are delivered by the first instance chambers or by the appeal chambers of the court, the president of the court must raise the issue in the Plenary Assembly of the court. To convene the Assembly the presence of at least three-quarters of the presiding judges of the first instance court and presiding judges and counsellors of the appeal court is necessary. The judgment of the Assembly has no effect with respect to cases already decided, but with respect to other similar cases it must be followed by all chambers of the court and other relevant authorities.

(b) Article 21 formerly provided that the relevant government departments had to execute the judgments of the court. Otherwise, the officials in the above departments, following the judgment of the court, would be banned from working in government departments. Under the new version of Article 21, the officials concerned will be banned by the judgment of the president of the court from working in government departments for a period of one to five years.

(c) Article 26 was added to the CAJA by the amendment and states, *inter alia*, that cases where a judge can be rejected by the parties to a dispute are those that have been provided in the Civil Procedure Code.[15]

3   CIVIL LAW

3.1   Family law

One of the conjugal duties of a husband towards his wife, under Article 1106 of the Civil Code (hereinafter cited as the CC), is the provision of maintenance.[16] This duty is lifted when the wife refuses to fulfil her conjugal duties.[17] The refusal of any spouse (including the wife) to fulfil his/her conjugal duties is referred to, under Islamic law, as *nushuz* (literally meaning disobedience and recalcitrance).[18]

Article 1085 of the CC provides that a woman can, as long as the dower (*mahr*) has not been paid to her, refrain from fulfilling her conjugal duties towards her husband, provided that the dower is payable.[19] This refusal does not affect the right of the wife to maintenance. Under Article 642 of the Islamic Penal Code (hereinafter cited as IPC) a husband can be punished for not providing maintenance for his wife if the wife obeys him, i.e. she is ready to fulfil her conjugal duties.

With respect to the interpretation of the above two articles (Article 1085 of the CC and Article 642 of the IPC) two courts had given conflicting judgments. Before examining these judgments it is useful to note that, under Article 1086 of the CC, if the wife, before receiving her dower, voluntarily fulfils her conjugal duties, she cannot benefit from the ruling of Article 1085. None the less, her right to demand her dower remains intact. In the following

---

15 See Arts. 208–217 of the CPC.
16 Art. 1107 of the CC defines maintenance by stating that "maintenance consists of dwelling, raiment, food and household property which is, under custom, in proportion to the status of the wife, and servant in case the wife is accustomed to having a servant or if she needs one because of illness or disability".
17 Art. 1108 of the CC.
18 For details, see Shahid II (Z. Al-Juba'i al-'Amili), *Al-Rawdat al-Bahiyyah fi Sharh al-Lum'at al-Dimashqiyyah*, vol. 5, Beirut, n.d., pp. 427–429; M.H. Najafi, *Jawahir al-Kalam*, vol. 31, 7th edn., Beirut, 1981, pp. 200–209.
19 Under Art. 1083 of the CC, a time limit can be fixed for the payment of dower or part of it. In addition, it can be paid in instalments.

cases, the legal action was taken by the wife before fulfilling her conjugal duties.

In the first case a woman after her marriage demanded her dower from her husband and, on the basis of the permission given by Article 1085 of the CC, refused to fulfil her conjugal duties. The husband not only did not pay the dower, but also refrained from paying maintenance. The wife took legal action, and referring to Article 642 of the IPC asked for the punishment of her husband because of non-payment of maintenance. The court, *inter alia*, argued that the husband could be punished because of non-payment of maintenance only if the wife fulfilled her conjugal duties. In the present case, she had refused to fulfil those duties, and such a refusal was based on law (i.e. Article 1085 of the CC). However, the court, by referring to the Islamic principle of *bara'at* (presumption of innocence), and Article 37 of the Constitution,[20] acquitted the defendant with respect to the criminal aspect of the case.

In the second case, a woman lodged a complaint against her husband asking for his prosecution because of non-payment of maintenance. She also argued that she did not consent to the consummation of the marriage until her husband paid her dower first. The husband argued that he was not able to pay the dower and accepted that he had not paid maintenance to his wife. The court by referring to the fact that the wife was ready to fulfil her conjugal duties and that she was entitled to ask for her dower before fulfilling those duties, and by referring to Article 1085 of the CC and the acknowledgement of the husband in that he had not paid maintenance to his wife, *inter alia*, held that the husband was guilty and under Article 642 of the IPC sentenced him to three months and one day in prison.

Since the above two judgments were contradictory, the case was referred to the Plenary Assembly of the Supreme Court (hereinafter cited as PASC). The PASC, *inter alia*, held that

although under Article 1085 of the Civil Code, as long as the dower has not been paid to the wife, if the dower is payable, the wife can refuse to fulfil her conjugal duties and this refusal does not deprive her of the right to maintenance. However, the provisions of this article merely deal with the legal relationship of the wife and her entitlement to ask for maintenance. From the criminal point of view, by taking into account the purport of Article 642 of the Islamic Penal Code ... according to which the punishment of husband because of non-payment of maintenance has been made dependant on the obedience [*tamkin*] of the wife, and the refusal of the wife to fulfil her conjugal duties, even based on invoking the authority given by the provisions of Article 1085 of the Civil Code, the husband will not be sentenced to any punishment.[21]

---

[20]   Art. 37 of the Constitution states: "Innocence is to be presumed, and no one is to be regarded as guilty, unless his guilt has been established by a competent court".

[21]   Plenary Assembly of the Supreme Court, Judgment 633–14.2.1378, in RR, 17.4.1378, No. 15832; MQ, 1378, pp. 147–150.

3.2   Rate of inflation as damages

The Law of Cheques has been mainly incorporated into the Issue of Cheque Act 1355 (1976). Some provisions of this Act were amended by Parliament in 1993[22] and one note (*tabsirah*) was added to Article 2 of the Act in 1997.[23] This note, *inter alia*, provides that the holder of the cheque can ask the drawer to pay all damages and expenses sustained for the recovery of his claim from the drawer.

The following question was put forward to the Council for Determining the Expediency of the State (hereinafter cited as CDES)[24] with respect to the phrase "all damages and expenses" in 1997.[25] The question was whether the above phrase stated in the above note, includes all damages and expenses, such as legal costs, lawyers' fees, liability resulting from causation, damages for delay in paying a debt and the like. If it did include the above items, was the basis for the assessment of damages the banking regulations or custom? If the latter the court could, by referring to the view of experts or other means, assess the damages.

The CDES stated that:

The meaning of the phrase "all damages and expenses caused" mentioned in the note ... consists of: damages for late payment [of debt] on the basis of the rate of inflation, from the date of the cheque until its clearance, which has been announced by the Central Bank of the Islamic Republic of Iran, and legal costs and lawyers' fees based on the tariffs fixed by law.[26]

Under the above statement, the rate of inflation can be demanded from the debtor if he delays in paying his debt.

4   CRIMINAL LAW

Article 36 of the Constitution provides that "the passing and execution of a sentence must be only by a competent court and in accordance with law". This principle was illustrated by the PASC in a criminal case. One crime which, depending on the circumstances concerned, has different punishments is theft. One punishment of theft, if all conditions are met (which may

---

[22]   RR. 1.9.1372, No. 14189; MQ, 1372, pp. 535–538.
[23]   RR. 16.4.1376. No. 15242; MQ, 1376, pp. 289–290.
[24]   This council was established to decide *inter alia*, in cases of difference between Parliament and the Council of Guardians. If the Council of Guardians rejects a parliamentary bill on the basis that it is either inconsistent with Islamic law or the Constitution, Parliament, where it considers the enforcement of the bill to be necessary, can send the bill to the CDES. The CDES may approve the bill either on the basis of necessity for a specified period or on the basis of a different interpretation from Islamic principles. See also Art. 112 of the Constitution.
[25]   The reason that the question put forward to the CDES was that this note was presented to the CG for ratification but the CG rejected it. Then it was ratified by the CDES.
[26]   RR, 17.11.1377, No. 15716; MQ, 1377, pp. 605–606.

happen quite rarely),[27] is *hadd*.[28] If the conditions are not met then other punishments, such as imprisonment, may apply to theft (Articles 651–667 of the IPC). For the attempt of certain thefts which have been stipulated in Articles 651–654 of the IPC (and to which the punishment of *hadd* does not apply) a punishment has been fixed (i.e. inchoate theft) in Article 655. But with respect to the attempt of a theft other than those mentioned in Articles 651–654 no punishment has been fixed by the IPC. The question was whether or not such an attempt should be punished. Three conflicting judgments had been given by three courts in this regard.

In the first case, a neighbour had broken into the home of the plaintiff in order to steal, and he was arrested there. The accused pleaded guilty. The court by referring to Article 109 of the IPC (*Ta'zirat*)[29] and Article 16 of the IPC[30] and the fact that such an act, under Islamic law, is illegal[31] provided a punishment for him.

In the second case, the plaintiff argued that for a moment he put his bag on the ground and it was stolen by the accused. The accused pleaded guilty. The court held that the attempt to commit one of the thefts stipulated in Articles 651–654 of the IPC was regarded as a crime for which a punishment had been fixed by Article 655 of the IPC. But the stealing of the bag did not accord with one of the cases of theft mentioned in the above articles. In other words, the attempt committed here (i.e. the attempt to steal the bag) was not governed by the provisions of Article 655. The court then stated that an attempt to commit a theft, other than of a kind mentioned in these articles, was not regarded as punishable; and that Article 109 of the IPC (*Ta'zirat*), because of the expiry of the period of experimental implementation, also could not be applied.[32] Moreover, Article 41 of the PCC[33] impliedly

---

27 There are many conditions for the administration of *hadd* punishment to a theft. Art. 198 of the IPC lists sixteen conditions expressly and two conditions impliedly for a theft to which the *hadd* may apply. In addition, Art. 200 lists five conditions for the administration of *hadd*.

28 *Hadd*, under Art. 13 of the IPC, consists of a punishment the type, quantity and quality of which have been fixed under Islamic law.

29 Art. 109 of the IPC (*Ta'zirat*) provided that "The punishment for attempt to steal is flogging up to 74 lashes." The IPC (*Ta'zirat*), which was adopted in 1362 (1983), was replaced by book 5 of the IPC which was adopted in 1996 by Parliament itself. See also note 32 below.

30 Article 16 defines the punishment of *ta'zir* as a punishment the type and amount of which have not been fixed in Islamic law and they have been vested with court, such as imprisonment, pecuniary punishment and flogging.

31 Generally speaking, if a person knowingly commits an unlawful act, for which no specific punishment has been fixed under Islamic law, he will be sentenced to a *ta'zir* punishment. R.M. Khomeini, *Tahrir al-Wasilah*, vol. 2, 3rd edn, Beirut, 1981, p. 481.

32 This judgment had been given before the adoption of book 5 of the IPC by Parliament, which incorporates the *ta'zirat* punishments. Before May 1996 the IPC (*Ta'zirat*) was a separate statute which had been adopted by the Judicial and Legal Affairs Committee of Parliament in 1983, under Art. 85 of the Constitution, on an experimental basis. See RR, 4.4.1375, No. 14943; MQ, 1375, pp. 161–197. See also my survey in vol. 3 of this *Yearbook* (1996), pp. 342–351.

33 Art. 41, *inter alia*, provides that he who intends to commit a crime and attempt

provides that the attempt to commit a crime is not punishable; and in view of the fact that the present law is more lenient than the old law and provides no punishment for such an attempt, and by invoking Article 11 of the IPC[34] and Article 37 of the Constitution, the court ruled for the acquittal of the accused.

In the third case, the accused while trying to break into a car to steal had been arrested. The accused pleaded guilty. The court by referring to Article 109 of the IPC (*Ta'zirat*) provided a punishment for the attempt.

The issue as a result was referred to the PASC. The PASC, *inter alia*, held that:

according to the express wording of Article 41 of the Islamic Penal Code, an attempt is considered to be a crime and punishable if it is expressly provided by law. In the section dealing with theft and robbery of others' property only the attempt to commit thefts, the subject matter of Articles 651–654, have been regarded as a crime. Attempts to commit thefts other than those mentioned under the above articles, including Article 656 of the Code, because of the absence of an express provision in law, are not crimes and are not punishable, unless the act itself [i.e. the attempt] is a crime in which case it will be punished by its own punishment only.[35]

In other words, the PASC upheld the judgment of the second court which had acquitted the accused and maintained that as long as the law does not provide a punishment for an act, that act cannot be punished, even though that act was punishable under Islamic law.

5 CRIMINAL PROCEDURE

One of the first and oldest statutes under the Iranian legal system, which was formally repealed in 1999, was the Criminal Procedure Code 1911 (hereinafter cited as CPC). It originally consisted of 506 articles. It had received many minor amendments since its adoption but the structure remained intact.

The CPC was replaced with a new criminal procedure in 1999.[36] It was

---

cont.

    to execute it but the crime does not take place, if the measures taken are regarded as a crime the culprit will be sentenced to the punishment of that crime.

[34] Art. 11, *inter alia*, provides that every punishment must be given according to the law adopted before the commission of the crime. No action or omission can be punished as a crime by a subsequent law. There is, however, one exception. If a law, which is adopted after the commission of a crime, reduces the punishment or provides no punishment at all or from other aspects is more favourable to the culprit, it will have retrospective effect with regard to crimes committed before its adoption.

[35] Plenary Assembly of the Supreme Court, Judgment 635–8.4.1378, in RR, 22.6.1378, No. 15889; MQ, 1378, pp. 275–278.

[36] Art. 1 of the CPC defined "criminal procedure" as "arrangements and rules which have been adopted for the detection and investigation of crimes and determining the responsibility of the criminals according to provisions of law". Art. 1 of the new procedure defines a criminal procedure as "a body of principles and laws which have been adopted for the detection and investigation of crimes,

discussed in Parliament that, after the changes made to the judicial system by the Establishment of General and Revolution Courts Act 1994 (hereinafter cited as the EGRCA), a coherent procedure to be applied by courts was lacking.[37] A new procedure divided into two parts or two books was adopted by Parliament and by the Judicial and Legal Affairs Committee of Parliament in 1999. This can be translated as the Procedure of General and Revolution Courts Code (hereinafter cited as PGRC). The first book, which is on civil procedure, was adopted by Parliament itself,[38] but it did not come into force during the period covered by this survey. The second book, which is on criminal procedure, was adopted by the Judicial and Legal Affairs Committee of Parliament[39] under Article 85 of the Constitution,[40] for three years on an experimental basis.[41]

There are many differences between the CPC and PGRC which relate almost to all aspects of criminal procedure. But some of these differences are prominent. For example, a large part of the CPC (mainly Articles 33–180) dealt with the authorities and responsibilities of the *parquet* (i.e. the Public Prosecutor's department) and the judges working in this department. The *parquet* was abolished by the EGRCA in 1994 and consequently there is no provision in the PGRC in this regard. Article 3 of the CPC stated that the institution of legal proceedings against and prosecution of a criminal or an accused from the public rights aspect rested with the department of Public Prosecutor. Under Article 3 of the PGRC the prosecution of the accused and criminal with respect to divine aspect of crime and protection of public rights and Islamic *hudud* has been vested with the president (or Chief Justice) of each jurisdiction.

Another example is that the CPC had been mainly borrowed from French law[42] and consequently many of its concepts were French concepts. These concepts were replaced with mainly Islamic ones. One of the provisions

---

cont.

   prosecution of criminals, trial procedure, passing of judgment, judicial review, execution of judgments and determining the duties and powers of the judicial authorities".
[37]   MMMSI, 5th period, 3rd session, 22.1.1378. See also MMMSI, 5th period, 3rd session, 11.9.1377; MMMSI, 5th period, 3rd session, 22.9.1377.
[38]   For details and parliamentary proceedings, see MMMSI, 5th period, 3rd session, 14.2.1378l; MMMSI, 5th period, 3rd session, 15.2.1378; MMMSI, 5th period, 3rd session, 19.2.1378; MMMSI, 5th Period, 3rd session, 21.2.1378; MMMSI, 5th period, 3rd session, 22.2.1378; MMMSI, 5th period, 3rd session, 26.2.1378; MMMSI, 5th period, 3rd session, 28.2.1378; MMMSI, 5th period, 3rd session, 29.2.1378; MMMSI, 5th period, 4th session, 9.3.1378.
[39]   For the text of the PGRC, see RR 18.7.1378, No. 15911; MQ, 1378, pp. 340–389.
[40]   Art. 85 of the Constitution, *inter alia*, provides that "The Assembly [Parliament] cannot delegate the power of legislation to an individual or to a committee. But whenever necessary, it can delegate the power of legislating certain laws to its own committees, in accordance with Article 72. In such a case, the laws will be implemented on an experimental basis for a period specified by the Assembly, and their final approval rests with the Assembly".
[41]   MMMSI, 5th period, 3rd session, 22.1.1378.
[42]   It has been reported that even some French lawyers took part in preparing the draft of the CPC.

which highlights this difference is Article 2 of both statutes. Article 2 of the CPC stated that a crime had two aspects: a public aspect because it infringed public rights and order, and a private aspect because it caused an injury to a person or persons or a certain group. Then it was stated that a crime had two aspects that could result in two claims:

(a)   a public claim to protect public rights, and
(b)   a private claim demanding compensation for injury and loss suffered by private individuals.

Article 2 of the PGRC reiterates a general principle of Islamic law that all crimes have a divine aspect and are divided into three categories: (i) crimes for which a punishment has been provided in Islamic law, such as the cases of *hudud*[43] and *ta'zirat*;[44] (ii) crimes which are in violation of public rights or against public order; and (iii) crimes which are in violation of the rights of certain natural or legal person or persons. According to note 2 of this provision, a crime which has two aspects can give rise to two claims:

(a)   a public claim to protect divine laws (*hudud*) and public rights and order, and
(b)   a private claim demanding a right, such as *talion* and *qadhf*[45] or damages for loss and injury suffered by natural or legal persons.

The PGRC consists of 308 articles divided into general provisions[46] and six parts. It is beyond the scope of this survey to refer to all the provisions of this statute. Here the headings of the relevant sections are highlighted.

5.1   Part I: detection of crime and preliminary investigations

This part is divided into six chapters. Chapter 1 deals with the law enforcement officers (e.g. the police) and their responsibilities (Articles 15–25). Chapter 2 deals with the authorities of an examining or investigative judge. Issues such as the start of criminal proceedings and detention orders, rejection[47] of judges and examining judges,[48] the jurisdiction of the court, referring

---

43   *Hudud* is plural of *hadd*. See note 28 above for the definition of *hadd*.
44   Note 1 of Art. 2 of the PGRC defines *ta'zir* as a punishment which has been provided for the commission of an unlawful act or omission of a duty without fixing the type or the amount of the punishment. See also Art. 16 of the IPC for the definition of a *ta'zir* punishment, referred to in note 30 above.
45   Art. 139 defines *qadhf* as the imputation of adultery or fornication and sodomy to another person. Under Islamic law and the IPC (Art. 140) the victim can ask for the punishment of the offender.
46   Arts. 1–14.
47   Under Art. 46 of the PGRC, a judge must refrain from considering certain cases brought before him and the parties to the dispute can also reject him on a number of bases, such as where the judge has kinship with one of the parties to the dispute or where there is a conflict of interest.
48   Investigative judges work under the supervision of the presiding judge of the

a case to another court (*ihalah*), the start and manner of investigation and finally the examination of locality as well as local investigations are included in this chapter (Articles 26–95). Chapter 3 deals with the inspection of dwellings and places and detection of means and instruments of crime (Articles 96–111). Chapter 4 deals with summoning and questioning the accused and various court measures and procedures to secure the attendance of the accused at court (Articles 112–147). Chapter 5 is on witnesses, testimony and summoning a witness to court as well as the procedures according to which a witness is discredited or the reliability of a witness is proved (148–172). Chapter 6 relates to limitation of action with respect to deterrent punishments (Articles 173–176).

5.2 Part II: trial procedure

This part is divided into five chapters. Chapter 1 deals with the measures taken by a judge following the completion of investigations (Articles 177–184). Chapter 2 is on attorneyship and representation in courts (Articles 185–187). Chapter 3 concerns the trial process and passing of judgment (Articles 188–216). Chapter 4 relates to the judgments given against the accused *in absentia* (Articles 217–218). Chapter 5 deals with the procedure of trying crimes committed by children (Articles 219–231).

5.3 Part III: judicial review

This part is on judicial review of a judgment and is divided into three chapters. Chapter 1 includes the general provisions (Articles 232–250). Chapter 2 deals with the procedure in the provincial appeal courts (Articles 251–260).[49] Chapter 3 is on the Supreme Court and the Plenary Assembly of the Supreme Court (Articles 261–271).

5.4 Part IV: retrial

This part deals with cases where a retrial can be ordered by the Supreme Court (Articles 272–277). According to Article 272, under seven circumstances a retrial can be ordered. Retrial can be demanded from the Supreme Court by (a) the convict or his legal representative, and where he has died or is absent by his spouse, his heirs and his executor, (b) prosecutor general, and (c) the president (i.e. Chief Justice) of the jurisdiction concerned.

---

cont.
    court. See Arts. 14 (1) and 15 of the EGRCA. See also my survey in vol. 1 of this *Yearbook* (1994), p. 394.
[49] According to Art. 233, the appeal court for judgments given by the general and revolution courts of each jurisdiction is the appeal court of the province concerned, except for four cases for which the appeal court is the Supreme Court. In other words, the appeal court has been established in the capital city of each province not other cities.

5.5 Part V: execution of judgments

This part, which is on the execution of judgments, is divided into two chapters. Chapter 1 defines the judgments that can be enforced (Articles 278–280). Chapter 2 deals with the procedure for executing the judgments (Articles 281–300).

5.6 Part VI: Legal expenses

This part deals with legal costs of criminal proceedings, who should pay and the assessment of those costs (Articles 301–307). Article 308, which has been enshrined in this part but relates to the statute as a whole, provides that from the date when the PGRC comes into force, the General and Revolution courts must act exclusively according to this Act and the Criminal Procedure Code of 1290 (1911) and its subsequent amendments and all other laws and regulations which are inconsistent with the PGRC (with respect to the General and Revolution courts) are to be abrogated. In other words, the former laws are still applicable to certain special courts, such as military courts.

6 FOREIGN INVESTMENT

The first legislation regarding foreign investment, which was adopted in 1334 (1955) and which is still the main legal framework for foreign investment in Iran, is the Attraction and Protection of Foreign Investment Act (hereinafter cited as APFIA).[50] The Council of Ministers on 28.7.1378, on the basis of Article 138 of the Constitution,[51] passed a decree entitled the "Rules for the Acceptance of Foreign Investment" (hereinafter cited as RAFI) as provided by the APFIA.[52]

Before examining the RAFI, it is useful to explain briefly here the procedure and institutions which are responsible for the approval and acceptance of foreign investments. According to the information provided by the Organization for Investment, Economic and Technical Assistance of Iran (hereinafter cited as the Organization)[53] the application for participation in the execution of the sanctioned project along with the relevant documents (after

---

[50] RR, No, 3187; MQ, 1334, p. 466. For an introduction to this Act, see J.A. Westberg, "Foreign Investment in Iran", 24 *The Business Lawyer* (1969), pp. 1263–1273.

[51] The above article, *inter alia*, states: "In addition to the cases in which the Council of Ministers or a single minister is instructed to adopt executive regulation [for the implementation] of laws, the Council of Ministers has the right to pass a decree (*taswib-namah*) and regulation for doing its administrative duties, ensuring the implementation of laws and setting up administrative bodies".

[52] RR, 30.8.1378, No. 15945; MQ, 1378, pp. 467–469.

[53] The above Organization is part of the Ministry of Economic Affairs and Finance.

finding an Iranian partner and obtaining the "Agreement in Principle" from the relevant Ministry) are to be submitted, in the first place, to the Organization. The Organization then prepares a report regarding the application. The application then is referred to a committee, the subject matter of Article 2 of the APFIA, known as the Supervisory Board, for examination.[54] If the board agrees with the project it will announce its view to the Council of Ministers. At this stage, if the Council of Ministers approves the project it will issue a decree according to which the foreign investor has permission to start its operations and will enjoy all the rights and protection provided by the APFIA for foreign investors.

RAFI consists of five articles the most important of which are as follows.

Article 1 provides that the proposals for foreign investment within the framework of the provisions of RAFI, which have been approved by the Supervisory Board, following the approval of the Supreme Council for Investment, the subject matter of Article 7 of the articles of association of Organization, will be covered by the APFIA. There is a note to Article 1. This states that the criterion for the approval of a proposal mentioned above is the agreement of the majority of the cabinet ministers of the Supreme Council for Investment's members, and that after the approval of the President it will be implemented. It seems that the RAFI replaces the Council of Ministers with the Supreme Council for Investment.

Article 2 states that foreign investment projects must, in addition to the creation of job opportunities, secure at least one of the following objectives:

(a)   increasing non-oil exports;
(b)   increasing the number of productive enterprises;
(c)   the discovery and exploitation of natural resources and manufacturing;
(d)   enhancing the competitive market, improving the quality of products and services, and lowering prices within Iranian territory.

Under Article 3, the repatriation and transfer of profits and other foreign currency transfers are possible only through the foreign currency earnings or revocation of foreign currency obligations relating to the export of goods and services of the unit in which the foreign investment has been made. If the export of goods or services of the unit has been prohibited or may be prohibited in the future by the government, the foreign currency needed for the repatriation will be supplied from a special foreign currency credit which, to this end, has been given to the Organization.

According to Article 4, the transfer of different ratios of shares to foreign investors in companies which are registered in Iran for the implementation

---

[54]   Art. 2 of the APFIA, *inter alia*, provides that for the examination and assessment of proposals received regarding the import of foreign capital, a committee headed by the Minister of Economic Affairs (or the Vice Minister) and consisting of the deputy of Ministry of Economic Affairs, the deputy of the director of the Organization of Plan and Budget, the deputy of the Central Bank and the president of Chamber of Commerce or one of his deputies will be established at the Ministry of Economic Affairs.

of the projects of foreign investment, or in the existing registered companies in which foreign investment is made in order to improve production and capacity, as follows, is permissible. The fixed percentage of the foreign investor's shares in each of the following cases will be determined on the basis of mutual agreement of the parties:

(a) In projects with the objective of increasing non-oil exports and building productive units and manufacturing plant, improving the competitive market, improving the quality of goods and services and lowering of prices, up to 80 per cent of the equity of a joint company is transferable to foreign investors.

(b) In projects with the objective of discovery and exploitation of natural resources and mines, up to a maximum of 49 per cent of the equity of a joint company is transferable to foreign investors.

According to Article 4 (note 1), the volume of the shares of foreign investors in special projects can be increased following the proposal of the Supervisory Board and the approval of the Council of Ministers.

Under Article 4 (note 2), projects which are financed through counter sale, build-own-operate (BOO), build-own-operate-transfer (BOOT), and other modes of project financing by foreign investors and are implemented under the APFIA, are not subject to restrictions on the transfer of different ratios of shares to foreign investors.

7   JURISDICTION AGAINST FOREIGN GOVERNMENTS

A very important piece of legislation was adopted in 1999 by Parliament which provides for the jurisdiction of Iranian courts in civil cases brought by Iranian nationals against foreign governments.[55] This legislation, according to the parliamentary proceedings, was mainly adopted in response to several American laws adopted against Iran,[56] in particular the Iran and Libya Sanctions Act signed by Clinton on 5 August 1996 (known as the D'Amato Act),[57] by which the American government imposes its domestic law on other countries, especially foreign companies investing in Iran. In addition, it was added that the American government, by breaching the judicial and political immunity of Iran and its official authorities, was prosecuting the

---

[55]   RR, 7.9.1378, No. 15950; MQ, 1378, pp. 473–474.
[56]   MMMSI, 5th period, 4th session, 17.8.1378; MMMSI, 5th period, 4th session, 18.8.1378.
[57]   For a brief introduction to this Act which was initiated by Alfonse D'Amato (Republican Senator) and the American Israel Public Affairs Committee (AIPAC), see V. Petrossian, "Europe, US lock horns over Iran and Libya", *Middle East Economic Digest*, 9 August 1996, p. 9; V. Petrossian, "Iran: US signals sanctions war", *Middle East Economic Digest*, 16 August 1996, p. 23; V. Petrossian, "US escalates war of words against Iran", *Middle East Economic Digest*, 30 August 1996, pp. 2–3.

Iranian government and its officials in its domestic courts. This legislation is, in fact, a countermeasure against the above American actions.[58]

The legislation consists of a single article with three notes (*tabsirah*). It provides that according to this Act Iranian nationals can, in the following cases, take legal action against the measures of foreign government which have violated the judicial immunity resulting from the diplomatic immunity of the Islamic Republic of Iran or its official authorities, in the justice administration of Tehran. The court must, as a countermeasure, examine the suit and deliver its judgment according to law. The list of governments which are subject to the countermeasure will be prepared by the Ministry of Foreign Affairs and will be announced to the judiciary.

Then the cases where Iranian nationals can take legal action are listed:

(a) losses caused by any action or measures of foreign governments which are inconsistent with international law, including interfering in the internal affairs of Iran and which result in death, physical and mental injuries or damage and loss to the property of people;

(b) losses resulting from any action or measures of individuals or terrorist groups, who are supported by the foreign government, or where the foreign government has given such people leave to live or to make regular visits or to carry out activities within its territory, and these actions or measures result in death or physical and mental injuries or financial losses to Iranian nationals.

Under note 1, this Act has retrospective effect and it applies to all cases which occurred before the adoption of the Act. Consequently, Iranian nationals who suffered losses and injuries before the adoption of this Act can now take legal action against the foreign government concerned.

Note 2 states that if any other government coooperates in the execution of laws (e.g. laws adopted by the US government) which violate the immunity of the Islamic Republic of Iran or its official authorities, it will be subject to the provisions of this Act.[59]

8 INTERNATIONAL LAW

During the period covered by this survey, the Iranian government entered into a number of bilateral and multilateral treaties, the most important of which are dealt with below.

8.1 Bilateral treaties

The Iranian government entered into three important agreements with the government of Azerbaijan regarding transfer of prisoners, extradition of criminals and judicial cooperation:

---

[58] MMMSI, 5th period, 4th session, 17.8.1378; MMMSI, 5th period, 4th session, 18.8.1378.

[59] Note 3 provides that the executive regulation of this Act will be prepared within

(a) The agreement on the transfer of prisoners consists of one preamble and twenty-one articles.[60] Under Article 20 of the agreement it comes into force thirty days after the exchange of documents. According to Article 21, the disputes resulting from the interpretation and implementation of the agreement will be settled through direct negotiation and/or through political channels. In accordance with Article 22, the agreement was concluded for an unlimited period. If one of the parties decides to annul the agreement it must announce its intention through political channels to the other party with six months' notice of its intention.

(b) The extradition agreement consists of one preamble and nineteen articles.[61] The provisions of Articles 20–22 of the first agreement have been provided in Articles 17–19 of this agreement.

(c) The third agreement, i.e. the agreement on judicial cooperation,[62] consists of forty-five articles divided into three parts.[63] The first part includes general provisions (Articles 1–18); the second part is on special provisions (Articles 19–42); and the third part deals with the coming into force of the agreement (Articles 43–45). These last three articles repeat the provisions of Articles 20–22 of the first agreement.

8.2 Multilateral treaties

On 17.5.1378 Parliament ratified the amendment to the INMARSAT Convention which had been adopted in 1998 by the Assembly of the International Mobile Satellite Organization.[64] It was added that referring the disputes resulting from this Convention to arbitration must be approved by the competent authorities under law.[65]

9 PUBLICATIONS

Generally speaking, the judgments of courts, even those of the appeal courts and the Supreme Court, are not published, except for those judgments given in the absence of defendants, which are published in the Official Gazette.

---

cont.

three months by the Ministry of Justice and Ministry of Foreign Affairs and will be approved by the Council of Ministers.

[60] RR, 26.2.1378, No. 15790; MQ, 1378, pp. 50–55.

[61] RR, 26.2.1378, No. 15790; MQ, 1378, pp. 57–61.

[62] According to the parliamentary proceedings, under the agreement the Iranians, who travel to Azerbaijan, enjoy the same legal protection as the nationals of that country and vice versa. MMMSI, 5th period, 3rd session, 25.1.1378.

[63] RR, 13.11.1378, No. 16003; MQ, 1378, pp. 647–656.

[64] For a brief introduction to the INMARSAT Convention and the amendment, see D. Sagar, "Recent Developments at the International Mobile Satellite Organization (INMARSAT)", 23 *Annals of Air and Space Law* (1998–9), pp. 343–347.

[65] RR, 3.7.1378, No. 15790; MQ, 1378, pp. 295–304.

Sometimes, however, some judgments, especially those of the Supreme court are published by private individuals or by judges themselves. The only exception is the judgments of the PASC and the judgments of the Plenary Assembly of the Court of Administrative Justice.

A summary of the judgments of the PASC, when it sits in full, are published in the Official Gazette (*Ruznami-ni Rasmi* (RR)) and in the yearly publication of all laws, i.e. Collection of Laws (*Majmu'a[h] Qawanin* (MQ)). The judgments of the PASC: Civil Division and the PASC: Criminal Division, however, are not published in the above sources. The Organization of the Official Gazette published some of these judgments in separate volumes. In 1374 (1995–1996) the Supreme Court itself began to publish all the judgments of the PASC, which also include the full minutes of the Court. The third volume of this series, which covers the year 1376 (1997–1998), was published in the year 2000.[66]

10   CONCLUSION

The most important development during the period covered by this survey was the adoption of a new criminal procedure. Although it has been adopted for three years, on an experimental basis, the experience concerning book 5 of the IPC and the amendment of the CC shows that few changes may be made with respect to this statute when it is approved by Parliament as a whole. It should be noted, however, that since the *parquet* system has constituted part of the legal system and legal culture for a very long time its abolition has created a lot of problems both for the judges and people. At present there is a call for the revival of the *parquet* system; if its revived criminal procedure will face major changes.

---

[66]   See *Mudhakarat and Ara'-i Hay'at-i 'Umumi-yi Diwan-i 'Ali-yi Kishwar: 1376*, Tehran, Supreme Court, 1378.

Algeria

*Yamina Kebir**

The major legislative changes during the year 1998 were in the field of commercial and intellectual property law. Important laws were adopted in order to complete the reform of the economic system and to prepare for the accession of Algeria to the World Trade Organization.

With the change in the presidency and the election of the new President the emphasis in 1999 was on legislation aimed at restoring peace in the country.

For the first semester 2000 the major law which was voted in by Parliament was the Telecommunications Law.

1 ADMINISTRATIVE LAW

In connection with the reform of the judiciary, Law No. 98-05 of 3 June 1998 was passed, relating to the competence, organization and functioning of the Court of Conflicts. This law came into force only after a statement was issued by the Constitutional Council on 24 May 1998 declaring its conformity to the Constitution. A number of amendments were proposed by the Constitutional Council in order to make the law comply with the Constitution.

The judicial system of Algeria consists of two types of courts: civil courts and administrative courts. The Court of Conflicts has been established to arbitrate conflicts over competence between the two orders of courts and it is entitled to intervene in order to settle such conflicts only.

Executive Decree No. 98-381 of 1 December 1998 set out conditions and modalities of administration, management and protection of *wakfs*. This

---

*   Attorney-at-law, Algiers Bar – admitted to appear before the Supreme Court of Algiers. This survey covers the years 1998, 1999 and the first half of 2000.

345

decree is an implementation decree of Law No. 91-10 of 27 April 1991 relating to *wakfs*.

It applies to what the law determine as *wakfs*:

(a) public *wakfs*;
(b) private *wakfs*;
(c) *wakfs* made in favour of an association;
(d) cemeteries and shrines;
(e) assets of religion associations.

Executive Decree No. 99-47 of 13 February 1999 relating to the indemnification of individuals injured or having suffered material losses as a consequence of acts of terrorism or in the context of anti-terrorism actions.

All victims of the violence in Algeria, whether they are victims of a terrorist act or were injured during an action of the security forces, are eligible for indemnification. The rightful claimants on behalf of persons killed during such acts – wives, children and parents – are eligible to receive various allowances, in the form of capital or monthly allowances to be paid by the employer in the case of civil servants or by a special fund in the case of victims who were employed in the economic sector, private sector or unemployed.

President Zeroual resigned before the term of his mandate and the elections resulted in the accession of Mr Bouteflika to the presidency on 20 April 1999. After his election the President made the restoration of security his top priority.

Presidential Decree No. 99-234 of 19 October 1999 established the National Committee for Reform of Justice. The reform of the judiciary is considered a priority for the government. In order to pave the way to this reform a committee has been set up with the task of analysing and evaluating the functioning of the judiciary and of proposing any necessary measures or recommendations.

2   COMMERCIAL LAW

2.1   The year 1998

The amendments brought about by Law No. 98-05 of 25 June 1998 modifying Ordinance No. 76-80 of 23 October 1978 relating to the Maritime Code aimed at setting out the framework for opening the sector to private investment. Maritime transport is no longer a monopoly of the state.

A ship can have Algerian nationality only if she is fully owned by Algerian individuals or legal entities. The other significant changes brought by the law consist in widening the range of penalties for breaches of the Maritime Law.

In particular, offences to the security of maritime navigation are considered crimes and punishable by fines and imprisonment. It is to be noted that new offences have been added to the list of punishable acts, in particular those affecting the environment.

In line with the international treaties signed by Algeria, pollution of the sea caused by hydrocarbons is heavily punishable. Offences against the environment are considered crimes and the sanctions have been aggravated.

Law No. 98-06 of 27 June 1998 setting out general rules on civil aviation is a totally new law in this field. The aim of the law is to set out the framework for the development of air transport and to lay down rules for the use of the national air space within the ambit of international treaties on international civil aviation. Algeria is a signatory to the international treaties on civil aviation and in particular the Chicago convention and all subsequent conventions.

It is to be noted that until the passing of the law, air transport was a state monopoly which was exercised by the National Airline Company only.

The law reasserts the principle that air transport is a public property; as such it is under the control of the state.

The law suppresses the state monopoly on air transport since all activities of air transport and related services are now open to competition. In this context the building and operation of airports can be the responsibility of Algerian private companies. Aviation services are clearly included within this principle.

The most significant innovation of the law is that public transport services, whether internal or international, can be provided by private companies. But only Algerian private companies as defined by the law are entitled to operate in the field of public transport.

Law No. 98-10 of 22 August 1998 modifies and completes Law No. 79-07 of 21 July setting out the Customs Law. This law introduces many changes in order to prepare for the accession of Algeria to the World Trade Organization. Its aim is also to modernize customs and to contribute to the elimination of some discrepancies and pernickety procedures; by means of this law customs are intended to be the engine of the development of economy, of the fight against corruption and of respect for industrial property rights.

The rules of customs are thus made consistent with the Code of Commerce, the Maritime Law and other laws and regulations in their revised versions.

All monopolies and discriminatory measures and procedures between public and private sector, national and foreign operators have been abolished. All customs users are now treated on an equal footing, whatever their status. They are likewise given guarantees as the respective rights and obligations of the custom authorities and the users are laid down.

All procedures have been simplified.

Another important point is that a new mode of dispute settlements is laid down by the law: disputes can now be settled amicably with the Customs authorities. Penalties have been reduced except for smuggling and introduction of counterfeited products in Algeria.

2.2 The year 1999

A number of laws were passed in 1999 to complete the process of economic reform, in particular in the field of tourism.

(a)   Law No. 99-01 of 6 January 1996 sets out rules relating to hotels.
(b)   Law No. 99-06 of 4 April 1999 sets out the rules governing the activity of travel and tourism agents.
(c)   Law No. 99-09 of 28 July 1999 relates to the control of energy.

2.3 The year 2000

Law No. 2000-03 of 5 August 2000 sets out general rules on Post and Telecommunications. The law sets out the general framework for the services of post and telecommunications, which will be split. It also dismantles the state monopoly in this sector.

3   INTELLECTUAL PROPERTY

3.1 The year 1998

Executive Decree No. 98-366 of 21 November 1998 sets out the status of the National Office for Copyright and related rights. The status of the copyright office has been completely modified in the light of the new Copyright Law, which is Ordinance No. 10 of 6 March 1997 relating to Copyright and Related Rights. The office which is empowered with the protection of the author's rights under this law has now become the National Office for Copyright and Related Rights (ONDA) in order to include the protection of related rights in conformity with the law. The Office is a public organization with an industrial and commercial purpose.

It is placed under the aegis of the Ministry of Culture; the mission assigned to the Office is wide: it is aimed essentially at the protection and defence of the moral and material interests of authors and owners of copyright and related rights and to ensure the protection of works of the national cultural heritage.

3.2 The year 2000

It is to be noted that Algeria is a signatory to the Patent Cooperation Treaty, which is applicable as from the date of 8 March 2000.

4   CRIMINAL LAW

Law No. 99-08 of 13 July 1999 relates to the restoration of civil peace. The aim of the law is to restore civil peace and to rehabilitate individuals involved in acts of terrorism. The individuals concerned who expressly declare that they will cease terrorist activity will benefit from the following measures:

(a) exemption of prosecution;
(b) a probation period;
(c) reduction in penalties.

Consequently individuals who belonged to any of the organizations referred to by Article 87 *bis* 3 of the Criminal Code (i.e. terrorist organizations) and who have not committed an offence or crime which has resulted in death or rape or who have not used explosives in public premises will not be prosecuted. Exemption from prosecution is extended to any person who unlawfully carried arms and ammunitions. The law also provided that in any case these persons would be deprived of their civil rights for a period of ten years (Article 5).

Individuals who "did not participate in collective massacres or use explosives in public premises", benefit from a reduction in the imprisonment penalty. This penalty is reduced to twelve years when the maximum was the death penalty and to seven years when the maximum sanction was a ten-year penalty.

This law was further modified in an even more favourable manner in what was called the "Free Pardon and Amnesty Law". Article 5 of Law No. 99-04 was cancelled in order to restore full civil rights to all beneficiaries of the law.

It is to be noted that in order to benefit from the provisions of the law members of terrorist organizations as defined by the criminal law are only required to declare that they will cease their participation in terrorist activities and to give up their arms. This is sufficient to grant them amnesty. No prior judgment establishing their responsibility for terrorist activities or their repentance is required.

5   PUBLIC INTERNATIONAL LAW

The following agreements and treaties signed by the Government of Algeria were ratified.

5.1   The year 1998

(a) Presidential Decree No. 98-03 dated 12 January 1998 setting out ratification of the Convention on Temporary Admission signed at Istanbul on 26 June 1990;
(b) Presidential Decree No. 98-110 of 4 April 1998 setting out ratification of the Cooperation Agreement in the field of information between the Government of the People's Democratic Republic of Algeria and the Government of Mauritania signed at Nouakchott on 23 April 1996;
(c) Presidential Decree No. 98-123 dated 18 April 1998 setting out ratification of the Protocol of 1992, amending the international convention

of 1969 on civil liability for damages due to pollution caused by hydrocarbons;

(d) Presidential Decree No. 98-124 dated 18 April 1998 ratifying the Protocol of 1992, amending the international convention of 1971 setting up an international fund for the compensation of damage due to pollution caused by hydrocarbons;

(e) Presidential Decree No. 98-125 dated 18 April 1998 setting out the accession of the People's Democratic Republic of Algeria to the convention of 18 April 1951 for the establishment of the European and Mediterranean Organization for the Protection of Plant Life amended by the Council on 27 April 1955, 9 May 1962, 18 September 1968, 19 September 1973, 23 September 1982 and 21 September 1988;

(f) Presidential Decree No. 98-129 dated 25 April 1998 setting out ratification of the agreement for the protection of plant life between the government of the People's Democratic Republic of Algeria and the Government of Mauritania signed at Nouakchott on 6 July 1996;

(g) Presidential Decree No. 98-130 dated 25 April 1998 Agreement between the government of the People's Democratic Republic of Algeria and the government of Mauritania on cooperation in the cultural, scientific and technical fields signed at Nouakchott on 23 April 1996;

(h) Presidential Decree No. 98-158 dated 16 May 1998 setting out accession, with reservations, of the People's Democratic Republic of Algeria to the Basle Convention on the control of movements across borders of hazardous wastes and their disposal;

(i) Presidential Decree No. 98-159 dated 16 May 1998 setting out ratification of the agreement between the government of the People's Democratic Republic of Algeria and the government of the Islamic Republic of Mauritania in the veterinary field, signed at Nouakchott on 6 July 1996;

(j) Presidential Decree No. 98-160 dated 16 March 1998, ratifying the agreement between the government of the People's Democratic Republic of Algeria and the Arab Republic of Egypt in the field of information, signed at Cairo on 29 March 1997;

(k) Presidential Decree No. 98-224 dated 11 July 1998 setting out ratification of the agreement between the government of the People's Democratic Republic of Algeria and the government of Hungary in the fields of plant life and sanitation quarantine signed at Algiers on 29 July 1997;

(l) Presidential Decree No. 98-225 dated 11 July 1998 setting out ratification, with reservations, of the Constitutive instrument of the African Organization of Cartography and Remote Detection signed at Kinshasa on 14 March 1998;

(m) Presidential Decree No. 98-251 dated 8 August 1998, approving the agreement, signed in Beirut on 6 May 1998 between the public corporation SONELGAZ and the Arab Economic and Social Development Fund (FADES), for a supplementary loan for the complementary financing of the Hassi Messaoud power station project and also the related guarantee agreement, signed in Beirut on 6 May 1998, between the government of the People's Democratic Republic of Algeria and the Arab Economic and Social Development Fund (FADES);

(n) Presidential Decree No. 98-252, dated 8 August 1998, ratifying the agreement between the government of the People's Democratic Republic of Algeria and the government of the Hashemite Kingdom of Jordan on a commercial cooperation, signed in Algiers on 19 May 1997;

(o) Presidential Decree No. 98-320, dated 11 October 1998, ratifying the agreement between the government of the People's Democratic Republic of Algeria and the Arab Republic of Egypt on reciprocal encouragement and protection of investments, signed in Cairo on 29 March 1997;

(p) Presidential Decree No. 98-321, dated 11 October 1998, ratifying the agreement between the government Republic of Algeria and the government of the State of Qatar on commercial exchange and technical cooperation, signed in Doha on 24 October 1996;

(q) Presidential Decree No. 98-340, dated 4 November 1998, ratifying the agreement between the government of the People's Democratic Republic of Algeria and the government of the Hashemite Kingdom of Jordan for mutual administrative assistance in the correct application of legislation and to prevent, seek out and suppress Customs offences, signed in Amman on 16 September 1997;

(r) Presidential Decree No. 98-357, dated 15 November 1998, ratifying the People's Democratic Republic of Algeria and the Hashemite Kingdom of Jordan on international road haulage, signed in Algiers on 20 May 1997;

(s) Presidential Decree No. 98-413, dated 7 December 1998, ratifying the Arab Convention on the fight against terrorism, signed in Cairo on 22 April 1998;

(t) Presidential Decree No. 98-430 of 27 December 1998 ratifying the agreement between the government of the People's Democratic Republic of Algeria and the government of the Syrian Arab Republic on reciprocal encouragement and protection of investments signed at Damascus on 14 September 1997;

(u) Presidential Decree No. 98-431 of 27 December 1998 ratifying the agreement between the government of the People's Democratic Republic of Algeria and the government of the Republic of Mali on reciprocal encouragement and protection of investments signed at Bamako on 11 July 1996;

(v) Presidential Decree No. 98-433, dated 27 December 1998, authorizing the participation of the People's Democratic Republic of Algeria in the increase of the shares of the member states of the IMF under the eleventh general revision;

(w) Presidential Decree No. 98-434, dated 27 December 1998, announcing the acceptance by the People's Democratic Republic of Algeria of the fourth amendment to the statutes of the International Monetary Fund;

(x) rider to Presidential Decree No. 92-354 of 23 September 1992 setting out accession of the Vienna Convention for the protection of the ozone layer signed in Vienna on 22 March 1995, published in the Official

Gazette of the People's Democratic Republic of Algeria (no. 69 of 27 September 1992);

(y)   rider to Presidential Decree No. 92-355 of 23 September 1992 setting out accession to the Montreal Protocol of the 16 September 1987 and to its amendments (London 27/29 June) published in the Official Gazette of the government of the People's Democratic Republic of Algeria (no. 69 of 27 September 1992).

5.2   The year 1999

(a)   Presidential Decree No. 99-92 of 15 April 1999, Algeria ratified with reservations the PCT of Washington 19 June 1970, modified 28 September 1979 and 3 February 1984 and its execution;

(b)   Presidential Decree No. 99-101 of 15 May 1998 ratifying the agreement on military and technical cooperation between the government of the People's Democratic Republic of Algeria and the government of the Russian Federation signed at Algiers on 1 April 1998;

(c)   Presidential Decree No. 99-115 of 14 June 1999 setting out ratification of the amendment to the Montreal Protocol adapted by the fourth meeting of the parties at Copenhagen on 23–25 November 1992.

5.3   The year 2000

(a)   Presidential Decree No. 2000-56 of 13 March 2000 setting out ratification of the agreement on reciprocal collaboration at administrative level, aimed at preventing, investigating and suppressing Customs offences between the People's Democratic Republic of Algeria and the Syrian Arab Republic signed at Damascus on 14 September 1997;

(b)   Presidential Decree No. 2000-57 of 13 March 2000 setting out ratification of the sanitation quarantine and life plant between the People's Democratic Republic of Algeria and the Republic of Iraq, signed at Algiers on 23 July 1996;

(c)   Presidential Decree No. 2000-57 of 13 March 2000 setting out ratification of the memorandum of agreement on the control of ships by the state of the harbour in the Mediterranean region signed at Malta on 11 July 1997;

(d)   Presidential Decree No. 2000-58 of 13 March 2000 setting out ratification of the Protocol on the amendment of convention relating to international civil aviation (Article 3*bis*) signed at Montreal on 10 May 1984;

(e)   Presidential Decree No. 2000-91 of 4 May 2000 setting out ratification of the agreement between the government of the People's Democratic Republic of Algeria and the government of the Republic of South Africa for the establishment of a joint cooperation committee signed at Algiers on 26 April 1998;

(f)   Presidential Decree No. 2000-92 of 4 May 2000 setting out ratification of the cooperation agreement in the fields of science and technology between the government of the People's Democratic Republic of Algeria and the government of the Republic of South Africa signed at Algiers on 28 April 1998;

(g) Presidential Decree No. 2000-93 of 4 May 2000 setting out ratification of the cooperation agreement between the government of the People's Democratic Republic of Algeria and the government of the Republic of South Africa in the fields of tourism, signed at Algiers on 28 April 1998;

(h) Presidential Decree No. 2000-94 of 4 May 1998 setting out ratification of the cooperation agreement between the government of the People's Democratic Republic of Algeria and the government of the Republic of South Africa in the fields of sports and leisure, signed at Algeria on 28 April 1998;

(i) Presidential Decree No. 2000-95 setting out ratification of the agreement between the government of the People's Democratic Republic of Algeria and the government of the Republic of South Africa aimed at avoiding double taxation and laying down rules for reciprocal aid in the fields of income tax and wealth tax signed at Algiers on 28 April 1998.

Morocco

Michèle Zirari-Devif*

Cette chronique présente les principaux textes parus du 1 juillet 1999 au 30 mai 2000. Au mois de juin 2000 ont été publié au Bulletin officiel une série de textes réformant totalement l'enseignement. Ils seront présentés dans la chronique 2000–2001.

1 DROIT PÉNAL

Le 16 septembre 1999 est publiée une loi n° 23–98 relative à l'organisation et au fonctionnement des établissements pénitentiaires.[1]

La nécessité d'une loi organisant le régime pénitentiaire se faisait sentir avec acuité et depuis des années. En effet, jusqu'à présent, le fonctionnement des prisons et le régime pénitentiaire étaient organisés par deux dahirs de 1915 et 1930[2] particulièrement désuets et ne répondant pas aux normes actuellement admises en matière de respect des droits des détenus. A titre d'exemple on peut citer l'article 1er du dahir de 1915 prévoyant que "les Européens devront toujours être séparés des indigènes" ou l'article 20 prévoyant à titre de sanction la privation de tout aliment autre que le pain et l'eau pendant une durée de un à huit jours.

La nouvelle loi comporte 141 articles répartis en neuf chapitres.

L'article premier pose une distinction entre les détenus préventifs, c'est à

---

*   Professeur à la faculté des sciences juridiques, économiques et sociales de Rabat-Agdal.

[1]   Loi n° 23-98 relative à l'organisation et au fonctionnement des établissements pénitentiaires, promulguée par dahir n° 1-99-200 du 25 août 1999, Bulletin officiel n° 4726 du 16 septembre 1999, p. 715.

[2]   Il s'agit du dahir du 11 avril 1915 réglementant le régime des prisons, Bulletin officiel du 12 avril 1915, p. 187 et du dahir du 26 juin 1930 portant règlement du service et du régime des prisons affectées à l'emprisonnement en commun, Bulletin officiel du 8 août 1930, p. 917.

dire les personnes non encore définitivement condamnées mais privées de liberté pour les nécessités de l'instruction, les condamnés c'est à dire les détenus ayant fait l'objet d'une condamnation irrévocable à une peine privative de liberté et les contraignables c'est à dire les personnes faisant l'objet d'une contrainte par corps.

Le premier chapitre classe les établissements pénitentiaires qui sont répartis en:

(a) prisons locales réservées aux détenus soumis à la détention préventive, aux condamnés à de courtes peines et aux contraignables;
(b) maisons centrales destinées aux condamnés à des peines de longue durée;
(c) pénitenciers agricoles, établissements semi-ouverts d'exécution des peines créés au niveau de chaque région;
(d) centres de réforme et d'éducation spécialisés dans la prise en charge des mineurs et des personnes condamnées dont l'âge n'excède pas vingt ans, en vue de leur réinsertion sociale.[3]

Les chapitres suivants sont consacrés:

(a) au greffe judiciaire des établissements pénitentiaires (écrou et détermination de la situation pénale des détenus, renseignements fournis aux autorités, aux détenus et aux personnes leur portant intérêt);
(b) à l'exécution des condamnations (répartition interne, travail des détenus, permissions de sorites exceptionnelle);
(c) à la discipline et à la sécurité des établissements pénitentiaires (police intérieure de l'établissement, mesures disciplinaires, sécurité des établissements);
(d) aux incidents (évasions et du décès d'un détenu);
(e) aux relations des détenus avec l'extérieur (visites, correspondances, doléances des détenus); à la gestion des biens et à l'entretien des détenus (gestion des biens, entretien des détenus, entretien spirituel et intellectuel);[4]
(f) aux services sanitaires (dispositions générales, attributions des médecins des établissements pénitentiaires, hospitalisations, naissance en détention et admission des enfants en bas âge);
(g) aux dispositions relatives à l'entrée en application et à l'abrogation des textes antérieurs.

---

3 Selon le code pénal la majorité pénale est atteinte à seize ans. Toutefois les mineurs de dix huit ans peuvent bénéficier des mesures de protection et de rééducation prévues pour les mineurs. Ces mesures peuvent soit accompagner la peine, soit lui être substituée.
4 Ensemble des règles minima pour le traitement des détenus adoptées par le premier congrès des Nations Unies pour la prévention du crime et le traitement des délinquants tenu à Genève en 1955 et approuvées par le Conseil économique et social dans ses résolutions 663 C (XXIV) du 31 juillet 1957 et 2076 (LXII) du 3 mai 1977.

Cette loi représente un progrès considérable par rapport à la législation antérieure. Ses dispositions respectent les normes internationales admises en matière de droits humains, en particulier l'ensemble des règles minima pour le traitement des détenus.[5] Ainsi la loi prévoit la séparation des détenus (séparation des hommes et des femmes, des détenus en préventions, condamnés et contraints par corps), les visites et les correspondances avec la famille, les règles d'hygiène et les soins médicaux. Les fautes disciplinaires sont énumérées ainsi que les mesures pouvant les sanctionner, avec possibilité du sursis pour tout ou partie de la mesure disciplinaire. Les détenus peuvent présenter leurs doléances au directeur de l'établissement et aux autorités administratives et judiciaires à l'occasion des visites d'inspection.

Reste que ces dispositions sont sans doute en avance sur les possibilités qu'offrent les prisons au Maroc. Malgré un effort de modernisation entrepris par le ministère de la justice, l'état de vétusté de beaucoup d'entre elles ainsi que le nombre trop élevé de détenus par rapport aux places disponibles font qu'un long chemin reste à parcourir pour que cette loi puissent trouver les conditions d'une réelle application.

Enfin on soulignera que l'entrée en vigueur de la loi est soumise à la publication des textes d'application qui n'a toujours pas eu lieu et dont la date n'est pas précisée.

2 DROITS DE LA PERSONNE

Le Maroc n'a pas, comme la France qui a inspiré une partie de sa législation, de code civil. Les différents droits subjectifs sont organisés par des textes divers: dahir formant code des obligations et contrats, code foncier pour les immeubles immatriculés, droit musulman non codifié pour les immeubles non immatriculés, code de statut personnel et successoral (Moudawana) organisant le droit de la famille et des successions.

Les droits de la personnalité (nom, domicile, état civil …) sont, quant à eux, disséminés dans divers textes. Le droit au respect de l'intégrité physique est un des droits fondamentaux de la personne humaine. Le principe d'intangibilité de la personne humaine qui en découle, bien que non affirmé expressément par une disposition législative, peut être considéré comme un principe fondamental du droit. Toute convention portant sur le corps humain serait d'ailleurs nulle comme contraire à l'ordre public, en application de l'article 62 du dahir formant code des obligations et contrats.

Jusqu'à présent, la législation sur les dons d'organes était loin d'assurer le respect de ce principe d'intangibilité du corps humain. Elle était prévue par un dahir du 15 juillet 1952[5] autorisant dans les hôpitaux des prélèvements sur les personnes décédées sans aucune référence à la volonté exprimée ou présumée de ces personnes ou de leur famille.

Une loi n° 16-98 relative au don, au prélèvement et à la transplantation de tissus humains a été promulguée le 25 août 1999, au don promulguée.[6]

---

[5]   Bulletin officiel du 29 août 1952, p. 1197.
[6]   Loi n° 16-98 relative au don, au prélèvement et à la transplantation de tissus

La nouvelle loi comporte quarante-cinq articles regroupés en cinq chapitres. Le premier consacré aux dispositions générales définit l'organe humain comme "l'élément du corps humain, qu'il puisse se régénérer ou non ainsi que les tissus humains à l'exclusion de ceux liés à la reproduction". Il pose le principe de la gratuité du don ou du legs d'organe et du secret de l'identité du donneur et du receveur, ainsi que le but exclusivement thérapeutique des dons, prélèvements et transplantations.

Le don et le legs font l'objet du deuxième chapitre qui traite tout d'abord du prélèvement sur une personne vivante Un tel prélèvement ne peut être effectué que si le don concerne un membre de la famille: ascendant, descendant, frère, sœur, oncle ou tante et leurs enfants. Le donneur doit exprimer son consentement devant le président du tribunal de première instance assisté de deux médecins chargés d'expliquer au donneur la portée de son geste et au magistrat la portée thérapeutique du prélèvement. Aucun prélèvement ne peut avoir lieu sur une personne vivante mineure ou majeure sous tutelle.

Pour le prélèvement sur une personne décédée, la loi prévoit que toute personne peut, de son vivant, faire connaître sa volonté d'autoriser ou interdire le prélèvement d'organes sur sa personne après son décès. Cette déclaration est enregistrée auprès du président du tribunal de première instance, chargé de vérifier, s'il s'agit d'un don, l'intégrité du consentement et la gratuité du don. S'il s'agit d'un refus, la déclaration est adressée aux hôpitaux compétents.

Le prélèvement sur une personne décédée peut être effectué dans les hôpitaux publics agréés dont la liste est dressée par le ministre de la santé. Toute personne rentrant dans un de ces hôpitaux peut faire connaître son refus de tout prélèvement après sa mort, déclaration enregistrée sur un registre spécial prévu par la loi dans chacun des hôpitaux agréés. Si une personne décède sans avoir fait connaître son refus, le prélèvement pourra avoir lieu sauf cas d'opposition du conjoint et à défaut des ascendants et des descendants. En ce qui concerne les mineurs et majeurs sous tutelle, le prélèvement ne peut avoir lieu qu'avec l'autorisation du représentant légal.

Le prélèvement est soumis au constat de mort cérébrale dont la loi fixe les modalités.

Le troisième chapitre est consacré aux transplantations. L'accord du receveur est indispensable. Elles ne peuvent se faire que dans les hôpitaux publics agréés. Toutefois, les greffes de cornée ou d'organes pouvant se régénérer naturellement ou de tissus, peuvent se faire dans des lieux privés agréés par le ministre de la santé publique mais ces lieux ne peuvent effectuer de prélèvements.

Le chapitre 4 prohibe l'importation et l'exportation d'organes humains, sauf autorisation administrative et le chapitre 5 prévoit des sanctions pénales pour:

(a)   la vente ou toute transaction portant sur un organe humain;

---

cont.
      humains, promulguée par dahir n° 1-99-208 du 25 août 1999, Bulletin officiel du 16 septembre 1999, p. 728.

(b)   les prélèvements et transplantations en dehors d'un lieu agréé;
(c)   la violation de l'anonymat du donneur ou du receveur;
(d)   le prélèvement sur une personne vivante dans un but autre que thérapeutique ou scientifique;
(e)   le prélèvement sur une personne vivante majeure sans son consentement;
(f)   le prélèvement sur une personne vivante mineure incapable ou majeure sous tutelle;
(g)   le prélèvement sur une personne décédée lorsque les conditions prévues par la loi ne sont pas respectées;
(h)   les prélèvements sur une personne vivante au profit de personnes non prévues par la loi;
(i)   la conservation d'organes destinés à la transplantation hors des lieux prévus par la loi;
(j)   le prélèvement sur une personne avant que le constat médical de décès ne soit légalement établi;
(k)   l'importation ou l'exportation d'organes humains sans autorisation de l'administration.

Enfin la loi crée un conseil consultatif de transplantation d'organes humains dont les attributions et le fonctionnement seront fixés par voie réglementaire.

3   DROIT DES OBLIGATIONS

Le contrat de bail à usage d'habitation ou professionnel fait l'objet d'une réglementation particulière[7] dérogeant au droit commun des contrats prévu par le dahir formant code des obligations et contrats. Les principales différences portent sur la possibilité de révision des contrats en cours, révision qui peut être obtenue en justice pour le contrat de bail alors que le droit commun interdit la révision des contrats civils, sur les conditions de résiliation du contrat, la sous-location et la cession de bail.

Deux lois sont promulguées en 1999. L'une complète la loi n° 6-79 organisant les rapports contractuels entre les bailleurs et les locataires en introduisant quelques modifications sur les conditions de révisions du loyer.

L'autre est relative au recouvrement des loyers. Il s'agit de la loi n° 64-99 relative au recouvrement des loyers.[8] Cette loi concerne tous les loyers: locaux à usage d'habitation ou à usage professionnel, commercial, industriel ou artisanal.

Le nombre élevé de loyers impayés appelait une intervention législative. En effet, de nombreux propriétaires avaient le plus grand mal à obtenir le

---

[7]   Loi n° 6-79 organisant les rapports contractuels entre les bailleurs et les locataires des locaux d'habitation ou à usage professionnel promulguée par dahir n° 1-80-315 du 25 décembre 1980, Bulletin officiel du 21 janvier 1981, p. 16.
[8]   Promulguée par dahir n° 1-99-211 du 25 août 1999, Bulletin officiel du 7 octobre 1999, p. 800.

paiement d'arriérés de loyers importants, étant donné la longueur des actions et justice et les difficultés d'exécution des décisions judiciaires.

Cette loi prévoit une procédure simplifiée et rapide pour l'obtention du paiement de loyers impayés. La procédure s'applique à condition que la location soit avérée par un acte authentique ou sous seing privé portant la signature légalisée des parties ou par un jugement définitif fixant le montant du loyer. La procédure pour obtenir le paiement du loyer dû est fort simple: le bailleur envoie une mise en demeure de payer autorisée par le président du tribunal de première instance; si cette mise en demeure reste infructueuse, le bailleur peut obtenir du président du tribunal une ordonnance de payer exécutoire sur minute et qui n'est susceptible d'aucune voie de recours ordinaire ou extraordinaire.

Il n'est pas certain que cette procédure règle le problème des loyers impayés. En effet le non-paiement n'est pas toujours le fait de locataire de mauvaise foi mais il est également la conséquence du montant élevé des loyers par rapport aux revenus moyen. En outre, la difficulté à obtenir l'exécution des décisions de justice est un problème récurrent du fonctionnement de la justice au Maroc.

4   DROIT DES AFFAIRES

Jusqu'à ce jour, la protection de la propriété industrielle est assurée par un dahir du 23 juin 1916.[9]

Ce texte s'applique concurremment avec la loi du 4 octobre 1938 relative à la protection de la propriété industrielle dans la zone de Tanger. Son domaine d'application n'a pas été non plus formellement étendu à l'ancienne zone occupé par l'Espagne. Sous le Protectorat français qui a duré de 1912 à 1956 le Maroc était divisé en deux zones: la zone sud sous protectorat français et la zone nord placée sous le contrôle du gouvernement espagnol. Tanger bénéficiait d'un statut spécifique puisque la convention du 18 décembre 1923 en faisait une ville chérifienne internationale. Cette division a conduit à un pluralisme législatif qui a été petit à petit supprimé après l'indépendance par la promulgation de nouveaux textes ou par l'extension des anciens textes applicables en zone française. Cette extension n'a jamais été faite en ce qui concerne le dahir du 23 juin 1916 et la pluralité législative s'est donc maintenue dans ce domaine.

Une nouvelle loi, la loi n° 17-97 relative à la propriété industrielle a été promulguée le 15 février 2000.[10] Elle entrera en vigueur, selon son article 234, six mois après la publication des textes pris pour son application, textes non encore publiés à ce jour.

Outre l'unification indispensable de la législation sur l'ensemble du territoire, l'ancienneté du texte de 1916 appelait également une actualisation.

---

[9]   Dahir du 23 juillet 1916 relatif à la protection de la propriété industrielle, Bulletin officiel du 10 juillet 1916, p. 690.
[10] Promulguée par dahir n° 1-00-19 du 15 février 2000, Bulletin officiel du 16 mars 2000, p. 135.

D'une part ce régime avait peu évolué depuis sa mise en œuvre, d'autre part les accords portant création de l'OMC et plus particulièrement l'accord relatif aux aspects de la propriété industrielle qui concerne le commerce (ADPIC) appelaient une mise à jour de la protection de la propriété industrielle.

Le texte actuel (dahir de 1916) assure la protection de la propriété industrielle qui couvre les brevets d'invention, les marques de fabrique ou de commerce, le nom commercial et les dessins et modèles industriels. Elle confère, pour une durée déterminée, un droit exclusif d'exploitation sur les inventions, marques, dessins et modèles. Elle définit et sanctionne civilement et pénalement les actes susceptibles de porter atteinte aux droits protégés. Sur le plan de la procédure, elle prévoit l'enregistrement des demandes sans examen préalable quant au fond, l'appréciation de la brevetabilité des inventions ou de la disponibilité des marques et de la nouveauté des dessins relevant de la compétence exclusive des tribunaux qui se prononcent en cas de litige.

La nouvelle loi n° 17-97 qui comporte 239 articles se présente selon le plan suivant:

Titre I: Dispositions générales
Titre II: Des brevets d'invention
Titre III: Des schémas de configuration (topographies) de circuits intégrés
Titre IV: Des dessins et modèles industriels
Titre V: Des marques de fabrique, de commerce ou de service
Titre VI: Du nom commercial, des indications de provenance, des appellations d'origine et de la concurrence déloyale
Titre VII: De la protection temporaire aux expositions et récompenses industrielles
Titre VIII: Des actions en justice
Titre IX: Dispositions transitoires

Cette loi améliore les anciennes dispositions notamment par:

(a)   la définition des titres de propriété industrielle: le dahir de 1916 traite des brevets d'invention, marques de fabrique et de commerce, dessins et modèles industriels sans les définir avec précision. La nouvelle loi les définit précisément et introduit, à côté de la marque de fabrique et de commerce, la marque de service qui sert à distinguer non pas les produits mais les services d'une entreprise par rapport à ceux des entreprises concurrentes;

(b)   la rationalisation de la procédure d'enregistrement;

(c)   le raffermissement des droits découlant du dépôt. Dans le dahir de 1916, ce droit s'acquiert par le premier usage, l'enregistrement n'ayant qu'un caractère déclaratif de propriété. La nouvelle loi fait naître le droit exclusif du premier dépôt qui s'acquiert uniquement par l'enregistrement. La durée du droit exclusif d'exploitation sur les inventions, marques, dessins et modèles industriels est ramenée de vingt à dix ans pour les marques (indéfiniment renouvelables) et maintenue à vingt ans pour les brevets. Pour les dessins et modèles industriels, la durée du monopole est de quinze ans (cinq ans renouvelables deux fois) au lieu de cinquante ans actuellement (vint-cinq ans renouvelable une fois). Les droits exclusifs d'exploitation peuvent être cédés, transmis ou faire l'objet de licence contractuelle.

En outre cette loi prévoit de nouvelles dispositions qui concernent:

(a)   la licence obligatoire (articles 60 à 66) qui est une licence d'exploitation pouvant être accordée à une personne, par le tribunal, à certaines conditions, dans l'hypothèse où le titulaire du brevet ne l'exploite pas et a refusé d'accorder une licence d'exploitation à l'amiable;
(b)   la licence d'office (articles 67 à 75) édictée par un acte administratif si les intérêts de la santé publique l'exigent, ou pour les besoins de la défense nationale;
(c)   Les produits pharmaceutiques qui sont désormais protégés (article 21) alors qu'ils étaient exclus de la protection organisée par le texte de 1916;
(d)   les schémas de configuration (topographies) des circuit intégrés (articles 90 à 103). La loi réglemente cette matière en délimitant les droits et obligations des créateurs. La durée de protection est de dix ans à compter de la date du dépôt;
(e)   les inventions de salariés (article 18). La loi n° 17-97 protège les inventions de salariés réalisées au sein d'une entreprise et fixe, à titre supplétif, les règles et procédures que doivent suivre les inventeurs et les employeurs pour faire valoir leurs droits;
(f)   les marques collectives et les marques collectives de certification (articles 166 à 176). La marque est dite collective lorsqu'elle peut être exploitée par toute personne respectant un règlement d'usage établi par le titulaire de l'enregistrement. La marque collective de certification est appliquée au produit ou service qui présente notamment, quant à sa nature, ses propriétés ou ses qualités, des caractères précisés dans son règlement;
(g)   les indications de provenance ou les appellations d'origine (articles 180 à 183) qui sont des dénominations géographiques données à des produits pour les différencier d'autres produits.

Dans le même numéro du Bulletin officiel est publiée une loi n° 13-99[11] portant création de l'office marocain de la propriété industrielle et commerciale.

Cet office est un établissement public doté de la personnalité morale et de l'autonomie financière. Son siège est à Casablanca. Selon l'article 3 de la loi cet office a pour objet:

(a)   la tenue des registres nationaux de propriété industrielle et l'inscription de tous les actes affectant la propriété des titres de propriété industrielle;
(b)   la tenue du registre central du commerce et du fichier alphabétique pour les personnes physiques et morales;

---

[11]   Promulguée par dahir n° 1-00-71 du 15 février 2000, Bulletin officiel du 16 mars 2000, p. 167.

(c)   la conservation des exemplaires des actes afférents au registre du commerce émanant des registres locaux;

(d)   la diffusion auprès du public de toute information nécessaire à la protection des inventions et à l'immatriculation des commerçants au registre du commerce ainsi que l'engagement de toute action de sensibilisation et de formation dans ces domaines.

Cette loi est complétée par un décret d'application fixant les modalités de fonctionnement de l'office.[12]

---

[12]   Décret n° 2-99-71 du 16 mars 2000 pris pour l'application de la loi n° 13-99 portant création de l'office marocain de la propriété industrielle, Bulletin officiel du 16 mars 2000, p. 170.

Tunisia

Afif Gaïgi[*]

L'année 1999 n'a pas connu de grands bouleversements sur le plan législatif. Nous ne pouvons pas révéler de lois ayant introduit des bouleversements notables ou de changements significatifs retenant l'attention. Les lois adoptées au cours de l'année 1999 ont complété et précisé d'anciennes dispositions ou adapté des textes déjà existants aux besoins nouveaux de la société.

Les nouvelles lois à retenir dans notre revue concerne les domaines suivants.

1 DROIT CONSTITUTIONNEL ET ADMINISTRATIF

1.1 Loi 99-18 du 1 mars 1999 modifiant et complétant la loi 93-27 du 22 mars1993 relative à la carte nationale d'identité

Cette loi a pour but de faciliter l'application de la loi du 25 mars 1991 relative au prélèvement et à la greffe d'organes humains. Le législateur autorise désormais de mentionner sur la carte nationale d'identité l'accord de la personne majeure jouissant de ses facultés et de sa capacité de faire don de ces organes après le décès. A cet effet la personne qui désire faire ce don doit faire une déclaration légalisée. La renonciation reste possible et entraînera suppression de la mention de sa carte nationale d'identité.

1.2 Loi 99-27 du 29 mars 1999 complétant la loi 97-48 du 21 juillet 1997 relative au financement public des partis politiques[1]

La présente loi accorde aux partis politiques une nouvelle prime pour subventionner leurs journaux et ce en contribuant aux frais d'impression et de papier et ceci à la condition que la parution de ces journaux soit continue.

---

[*] Avocat à la cour de cassation, enseignant universitaire.
[1] Journal officiel n° 27, p. 470.

363

1.3   Loi 99-28 du 3 avril 1999 modifiant et complétant la loi 85-75 du 5 août 1985 portant statut général des agents des offices, des établissements public à caractère industriel et commercial et des sociétés dont le capital appartient directement à l'état ou aux collectivités publiques locales

La loi nouvelle a introduit des dispositions ayant pour objet de redéfinir d'une part les obligations de l'agent découlant de son travail, de son rang, dans la hiérarchie ou de l'autorité qui lui a été confiée et d'autre part les obligations de l'entreprise vis à vis de son agent. La loi a également redéfini les actes constituant une faute grave. La loi interdit de faire figurer dans le dossier individuel de l'agent toute mention relative à ses opinions politiques, philosophiques, religieuses, ni faire figurer dans ce dossier des indications de son appartenance syndicale. Les nouvelles dispositions de la loi ont apporté des améliorations quant au statut de l'agent relativement aux garanties sur le plan disciplinaire, à la promotion, à l'avancement et à la formation.

1.4   Décret n° 99-824 du 12 avril 1999 portant modification du décret 89-442 du 22 avril 1989 portant réglementation des marchés publics[2]

Le présent texte donne l'avantage jusqu'à la fin de l'année 2003 tient compte de l'entrée en vigueur de la convention qui lie la Tunisie au GATT.

1.5   Décret n° 99-2013 du 13 septembre 1999 modifiant le décret n° 89-442 du 22 avril 1989 portant réglementation des marchés publics[3]

Ce deuxième décret modificatif vise la normalisation des marchés publics. Les dispositions nouvelles imposent aux soumissionnaires de faire une déclaration sur l'honneur affirmant qu'ils n'ont pas fait ou ne feront pas des promesses des dons ou des présents en vue d'influer sur la procédure de conclusion d'un marché. En cas de défaillance à cet engagement le marché peut être résilié.

1.6   Loi constitutionnelle n° 99-52 du 30 juin 1999 portant dispositions dérogatoires au troisième alinéa de l'article 40 de la constitution[4]

La présente loi a eu pour but d'adapter la constitution article 40 aux élections présidentielles de 1999 et ce en permettant à certains candidats de se présenter

---

[2]   Journal officiel n° 33, p. 621.
[3]   Journal officiel n° 77, p. 1732.
[4]   Journal officiel n° 53, p. 1063.

à ces élections. En vertu de la dérogation accordée par la loi exceptionnellement le premier responsable de chaque parti politique peut se porter candidat à la présidence de la république à condition qu'il soit en exercice de ses fonctions le jour du dépôt de sa candidature depuis cinq années consécutives et que le parti ait un député ou plus à la chambre des députés. L'appartenance du député à un parti est celle considérée au moment de sa candidature aux élections législatives.

2   DROIT COMMERCIAL ET FINANCIER

2.1   Loi n° 99-4 du 11 janvier 1999 modifiant et complétant le code d'incitations aux investissements[5]

La nouvelle loi a pour objet d'étendre les bénéfices et avantages accordés par le code d'incitations aux investissements à certains cas lorsque l'investissement réalise une maîtrise ou un développement de la technologie, ou lorsque l'investissement est réalisé dans des zones d'encouragement au titre du développement régional.

La loi accorde certains avantages consistant à mettre à la disposition de certains investisseurs qui réalisent des investissements importants des terrains nécessaires à la réalisation de leurs projets et ce à un prix symbolique et après avis de la commission supérieure d'investissement.

La loi accorde en outre certains avantages fiscaux prévus par le code d'incitation aux investissements aux entreprises rencontrant des difficultés économiques en cas d'acquisition de ces entreprises par d'autres investisseurs que les anciens dirigeants.

La présente loi a été suivie par une deuxième loi en date du 15/7/1999 portant le n°66/99 et qui a apporté quelques modifications supplémentaires quant aux avantages accordés aux entreprises et ce en élargissant les domaines d'activité et les conditions d'action de ces avantages.

2.2   Loi n° 99-8 du 1 février 1999 relatives au fonds National de garantie[7]

La présente loi modifie certaines dispositions des lois de finances pour la gestion 1982 et pour la gestion 1984. La loi nouvelle crée un fonds National de garantie ayant pour objet la garantie du recouvrement de certains crédits octroyés par les institutions de crédits et de certaines participations souscrites par les sociétés d'investissements à capital développement les ressources du fonds et les modalités de son intervention sont fixés par décrets.

---

[5]   Journal officiel n° 5, p.108.
[6]   Publiée au Journal officiel n° 57, p.1179.
[7]   Journal officiel n° 11, p. 191.

2.3   Loi n° 99-9 du 13 février1999 relative à la défense contre les pratiques déloyales à l'importation[8]

La loi n° 99-9 a pour objet de définir les règles applicables aux pratiques déloyales à l'importation et de fixer les conditions dans lesquelles elles sont neutralisées.

La loi vise la défense de produits nationaux contre les pratiques de *dumping* et de subventions. Une enquête visant à déterminer l'existence de *dumping* ou son degré est ouverte par le ministre chargé du commerce suite à une plainte présentée par la branche de production nationale concernée sauf le cas où le ministre est en possession d'éléments de preuves suffisants de l'existence d'un *dumping* ou d'une subvention, d'un dommage et d'un lien de causalité.

Des droits *anti-dumping* ou des droits compensateurs provisoires peuvent être institués par décret pendant le durée de l'enquête à certaines conditions. Les droits *anti-dumping* provisoires ou définitifs peuvent ne pas être institués lorsque l'exportateur s'engage à réviser ses prix de *dumping* volontairement. Normalement les droits *anti-dumping* sont institués pour une période de cinq ans sauf cas de réexamen.

La loi a prévu une procédure de révision judiciaire dans certains cas.

2.4   Loi n° 99-37 du 3 mai 1999 relative à l'organisation de la profession de conseiller en exportation[9]

La loi a défini l'objet de cette activité, les conditions de son exercice, les infractions pouvant être commises à l'occasion de cet exercice et le moyen de les réprimer. On peut relever notamment que l'exercice de cette profession est soumise à l'agrément préalable du ministre chargé du commerce, que les sanctions prévues en cas de non-respect du secret professionnel ou en cas de manquement à ses obligations par le conseiller en exportation peuvent se traduire par le retrait de l'agrément à titre provisoire ou à titre définitif en cas de récidive outre une amende pouvant atteindre 5,000 dinars en cas d'exercice de la profession sans avoir obtenu au préalable l'agrément du ministre chargé du commerce.

2.5   Loi n° 99-41 du 10 mai 1999 modifiant la loi 91-64 du 29 juillet 1991 relative à la concurrence et aux prix[10]

La loi a pour but de prohiber les actions concertées et les ententes expresses ou tacites visant à empêcher, restreindre ou fausser le jeu de la concurrence sur le marché tendant surtout a empêcher la fixation des prix par le libre jeu de l'offre et de la demande, de limiter l'accès au marché à d'autre entreprises

---

8   Journal officiel n° 15, p. 279.
9   Journal officiel n° 37, p. 683.
10   Journal officiel n° 39, p. 703.

ou le libre exercice de la concurrence, de limiter ou de contrôler la production, les débouchés, les investissements ou le progrès technique, de répartir les marchés ou les sources d'approvisionnement.

Les contrats de concession et de représentation commerciale exclusive sont prohibés sauf autorisation exceptionnelle du ministre chargé du commerce. De même qu'est prohibé l'exploitation abusive d'une position dominante sur le marché intérieure. Toute clause, contractuelle ou convention contraire est considérée comme nulle. La loi a institué une commission spéciale dénommée Conseil de la concurrence siégeant à Tunis et a déterminé son objet, sa composition et son fonctionnement. La loi a également interdit certaines pratiques d'offre faites au consommateur de primes à titre gratuit sauf s'il s'agit de marchandises ou services identiques à ceux vendus; est également interdite la pratique des prix illicites (vente d'un produit n'ayant pas fait l'objet d'une décision de fixation de prix, dissimuler des marchandises, ne pas présenter des factures aux agents contrôleurs). Des sanctions pénales ont été prévues par la loi.

2.6 Loi 99-57 du 28 juin 1999 relative aux appellations d'origine contrôlée et aux indications de provenance des produits agricoles[11]

Dans la définition de son objet la loi spécifie qu'elle vise la protection des particularités et des spécificités des produits agricoles et leur valorisation en leur octroyant une appellation d'origine contrôlée et une indication de provenance.

Cette appellation est effectue par arrête du ministre chargé de l'agriculture sur demande des producteurs concernés qui doivent remplir les conditions fixées par un cahier de charge type approuvé par le ministre concerné.

A partir de la date d'acceptation de l'appellation d'origine son usage est interdit par tout produit similaire, de même que l'imitation de cette appellation ou l'usage de tous récipients pour la commercialisation du produit susceptible de créer une confusion quant à son origine.

Un contrôle technique est prévu. Les infractions à la loi sont constatées par des agents désignés à cet effet et des sanctions pénales sont prévues à l'encontre des contrevenants.

2.7 Loi n° 99-63 du 15 juillet 1999 modifiant la loi 95-34 du 17 avril 1995 relative au redressement des entreprises en difficulté économique[12]

Ce texte modificatif a redéfini le domaine d'application de la loi relative au redressement des entreprises en difficulté. Désormais peuvent bénéficier de ce régime de cette loi les personnes physiques ou morales assujetties au

---

[11] Journal officiel n° 54, p. 1088.
[12] Journal officiel n° 57, p.1175.

régime d'imposition réel, exerçant une activité commerciale, industrielle ou artisanale ainsi que les sociétés commerciales, agricoles ou de pêche.

Le nouveau texte a crée une commission pour faire le suivi des entreprises économiques qui centralise les données relatives à l'activité des entreprises en difficulté, les traite dans un réseau informatique en vue de fournir toutes les informations au président du tribunal dans le ressort duquel se trouve la société débitrice. Le président du tribunal est informé des cas des entreprises dont les pertes atteignent le tiers du capital. La commission propose et donne son avis sur les plans de redressement. Elle reçoit toutes informations utiles concernant l'entreprise de l'inspection de travail, de la caisse nationale de sécurité sociale des institutions financières et ceci en particulier lorsque les actes constatés par ces institutions menacent la continuité de l'entreprise notamment en cas de non-paiement des dettes par l'entreprise six mois après leurs échéances. La nouvelle a réglementé la procédure du règlement amiable avant la cessation de paiement de l'entreprise. Le président peut notamment ordonner la suspension des procédures de poursuite et d'exécution d'une dette antérieure à la date d'ouverture du règlement amiable. Ceci inclut surtout l'arrêt du cours des intérêts y compris le leasing, les pénalités de retard, la suspension des délais de déchéance jusqu'au prononcé du jugement.

De nouvelles dispositions dans la loi permettent une grande liberté pour établir un accord de règlement entre l'entreprise et les créanciers représentant les $\frac{2}{3}$ des créances de l'entreprise accord qui sera homologué par le président du tribunal lequel rééchelonnera des autres dettes sur une période ne dépassant pas la durée des l'accord. L'accord sera soumis à une publicité par un dépôt au greffe, un avis au journal officiel et sera communiqué à la commission de suivi. Si un accord n'est pas conclu le président du tribunal ordonne l'ouverture de la procédure de règlement judiciaire. La loi a réglementé la procédure pour se prononcer sur la demande de règlement judiciaire par le tribunal. Sa décision est exécutoire nonobstant tout recours et sera publiée au registre de commerce et publiée au journal officiel. Le tribunal peut décider le maintien de l'entreprise en activité avec application d'un plan de règlement, sinon il décidera la déclaration du débiteur en faillite ou sa liquidation judiciaire selon son régime. Les créanciers reprendront leur poursuite si la liquidation ne couvre pas leurs créances. Le tribunal peut ordonner la radiation du débiteur du registre de commerce en cas de sa cessation d'activité sans disposer de biens suffisants pour couvrir les frais de justice. Un délais est imparti aux créanciers pour inscrire leurs dettes intérieures à la date du jugement d'ouverture à la période d'observation.

La nouvelle loi a concerné les compétences de l'administration judiciaire.

2.8 Loi n° 99-64 du 15 juillet 1999 relative aux taux d'intérêt excessifs[13]

La présente loi a redéfini la réglementation en matière de prêts à des taux usuraires. La nouvelle réglementation a défini le prêt à un taux d'intérêt

---

[13] Journal officiel n°57, p. 1178.

excessif commettant le prêt conventionnel consenti à un taux d'intérêt effectif global qui excède au moment où il est consenti de plus du tiers le taux effectif pratiqué au cours du semestre précédant par les banques et les établissements financiers pour des opérations de même nature.

Les frais, commissions ou rémunérations intervenus dans l'action du prêt entrent en ligne de compte pour le calcul du taux d'intérêt effectif global du prêt.

Le prêteur ayant pratiqué un taux d'intérêt excessif devra restituer les sommes indûment perçus à l'emprunteur majoré d'un intérêt calculé aux taux prévus par le code des obligations et contrats. La loi a prévu des sanctions pénales applicable à tout contrevenant.

2.9 Loi n° 99-92 du 17 août 1999 relative à la relance du marché financier[14]

La loi 99-92 vise à dynamiser le marché financier en cherchant à activer davantage le volume des échanges et des investissements en bourse. Le législateur accorde aux sociétés qui procédant à l'admission de leurs actions ordinaires à la cote de la bourse des avantages fiscaux consistant en une réduction de l'impôt pendant une période déterminée. L'avantage fiscal est retirée en cas de radiation des actions de la cote de la bourse et l'impôt normalement dû devient exigible en sus des pénalités sauf si la radiation n'est pas imputable à la société.

La loi accorde également certains avantages fiscaux aux personnes qui déposent dans des comptes dits "compte épargne en action" servant à acquérir des actions cotées en bourse. Ces sommes ainsi déposées sont déductibles de l'impôt dans la limite de 50 pour cent sans que le montant déductible dépasse 5,000 dinars par an. Pour bénéficier de ces avantages la loi a posé des conditions dont notamment le non retrait des sommes pendant un délai de cinq ans à partir du 1 janvier suivant le dépôt. En cas de retrait l'impôt dû devient exigible en sus des pénalités.

La nouvelle permet désormais aux sociétés admises à la cote d'acheter les actions qu'elle émettent pour réguler leurs cours sur le marché. Ces actions ne donnent droit ni aux dividendes, ni au droit de souscription ni au droit de vote.

3   DROIT DE TRANSPORT

3.1 Loi n° 99-25 du 18 mars 1999 promulguant le code des ports maritimes de commerce[15]

Dans son article premier la présente loi indique qu'elle a pour objet de fixer les règles générales pour assurer la sécurité, la protection et la conservation

---

[14]   Journal officiel n° 67, p. 1463.
[15]   Journal officiel n° 26, p. 430.

du domaine public des ports maritimes de commerce ainsi que les règles et les conditions applicable à l'exploitation et à la gestion dans les ports de commerce.

3.2 Loi n° 99-55 du 28 juin 1999 modifiant le code de la police administrative de la navigation maritime promulguée par la loi n° 76-59 du 11 juin 1976

La loi a modifié la définition de la navigation à la pêche en déterminant les différentes catégories qu'elle inclue.

3.3 Loi n° 99-58 du 29 juin 1999 portant promulgation du code de l'aéronautique civile[16]

La présente loi fixe les règles régissant l'aéronautique civile en ce qui concerne les aéronefs, les aérodromes, le personnel et l'exercice des activités dans ce domaine. Le code comprend plusieurs titres concernant:

(a) les aéronefs dont il réglemente leur immatriculation, les droits les grevant (privilèges-hypothétiques) leurs saisies, leur circulation;
(b) les aérodromes dont la loi traite de leur classification, gestion, des servitudes aéronautiques;
(c) le transport aérien dont le code régit les entreprises qui l'exerce, le contrat y relatif, la location et l'affrètement des aéronefs et enfin la responsabilité du transporteur aérien;
(d) le personnel aéronautique;
(e) les sanctions pénales applicables en cas d'infraction aux dispositions du code commises par le commandant de bord ou exploitant d'aéronef ou usager.

3.4 Loi n° 99-71 du 26 juillet 1999 promulguant le code de la route[17]

Cette loi a eu pour objet la refonte du code de la route régissant les règles du roulage et de la circulation sur les routes et la protection de celle-ci.

La grande innovation de cette loi concerne l'introduction du permis de conduire à points.

4 DROIT PÉNAL ET PROCÉDURE PÉNALE

4.1 Loi n° 99-89 du 2 août 1999 modifiant et complétant certaines dispositions du code pénale[18]

La présente loi redéfini les peines principales en matière pénale et ce en introduisant la peine de travail d'intérêt général. Cette peine peut remplacer

---

16   Journal officiel n° 54, p. 1091.
17   Journal officiel n° 61, p. 1239.
18   Journal officiel n° 63, p.1283.

une peine de prison ferme d'une période ne dépassant pas six mois. La peine de travail d'intérêt général non rémunéré ne peut aller au-delà d'une période ne dépassant pas les 300 heures sur la base de deux heures pour chaque journée de prison. La loi a énuméré limitativement les infractions et les délits sanctionnés par cette peine.

Cette même loi a remplacé l'article 172 du code nouveau et a ajouté de nouveaux articles.

L'article 172 nouveau sanctionne par la prison à vie le fonctionnaire public ou assimilé ou le notaire qui dans l'exercice de ses fonctions commet un faux susceptible de causer un dommage public ou privé dans le cas énuméré par le texte.

L'article 101bis punit d'un emprisonnement de 8 ans le fonctionnaire ou assimilé qui soumet une personne à la torture et ce dans l'exercice de ses fonctions.

L'article 199bis concerne la nouvelle délinquance en matière d'informatique. Le texte prévoit des peines allant de deux mois à cinq ans de prison et des amandes variant de 1,000 à 5,000 dinars pour toute personne:

(a) qui accède ou se maintient dans un système de traitement automatisé de données;
(b) qui cause une altération ou la destruction du fonctionnement des données existantes dans le système même sans l'intention de le faire. La peine est plus lourde lorsqu'il y a intention de causer la destruction ou l'altération;
(c) qui introduit frauduleusement des données dans un système de traitement automatisé de nature à altérer les données que contient le programme ou son mode de traitement ou de transmission. La peine est portée au double au cas où l'acte est commis à l'occasion de l'exercice de l'activité professionnelle.

4.2 Loi n° 99-90 du 2 août 1999 modifiant et complétant certaines dispositions du code de procédure pénale

La dite loi a appuyé les droits des suspects au cours de l'enquête de la police judiciaire même en cas de crimes ou de délits flagrants concernant la durée de la garde à vue, de son renouvellement, de l'information du suspectant à ses droits notamment en réclament un examen médical, les mentions que doit comporter le procès verbal devant être rédigé par l'officier de la police judiciaire.

La loi a également traité de la garde à vue du suspect en cas d'exécution d'une commission rogatoire par le juge d'instruction.

La loi a enfin réglementé le recours au travail d'intérêt général et à la contrainte par corps pour le recouvrement de l'amende et des frais à l'encontre des condamnés.

5 LOIS ET DÉCRETS DIVERS

(a) Décret 99-99 du 11 janvier 1999 portant publication de la convention sur le marquage des explosifs plastiques et en feuilles aux fins de détection conclue à Montréal le 1 mars 1991;[19]

(b) Loi n° 99-8 du 1 février 99 relative au fonds national de garantie ayant pour objet la garantie du recouvrement de certains crédits octroyés par les institutions de crédits et de certaines participations souscrites par les sociétés d'investissement à capital développement. La gestion et l'intervention du fonds sont fixés par décret;[20]

(c) Loi n° 99-19 du 1 mars 1999 portant organisation de la légalisation de la signature et de la certification de conformité des copies à l'original;[21]

(d) Loi n° 99-24 du 9 mars 1999 relative au contrôle sanitaire vétérinaire à l'importation et à l'exportation;[22]

(e) Loi n° 99-29 du 5 avril 1999 portant modification de la loi 73-81 du 31 décembre 1973 portant promulgation du code de la comptabilité publique;[23]

(f) Loi n° 99-30 du 5 avril 1999 relative à l'agriculture biologique;[24] et s'appliquant aux produits portant ou destines à porter des indications se référant au mode de production biologique;

(g) Loi n° 99-32 du 13 avril 1999 relative au système National de la statistique;[25] et définissant les principes fondamentaux de l'activité statistique, la structure du système National de la statistique, sa mission et le rôle de chacune de ses composantes;

(h) Loi n° 99-40 du 10/5/1999 relative à la métrologie légale;[26] ayant pour objet de définir les unités de mesure légales et de fixer les conditions du contrôle métrologique légal, de définir les organismes compétents en matière de métrologie légale et de déterminer les conditions de fabrication, de réparation, d'importation, d'exportation, de vente de détention et d'utilisation d'instruments de mesure soumis au contrôle métrologique légal;

(i) Loi n° 99-59 du 30 juin 1999 relative à la prise en charge de la contribution patronale du régime légal de la sécurité sociale par les entreprises industrielles totalement exportatrices;[27]

(j) Loi n° 99-73 du 26/7/1999 modifiant la loi 85-91 du 22 avril 1985 réglementant la fabrication et l'enregistrement des médicaments destines à la médecine humaine;[28]

---

[19] Journal officiel n° 8, p. 138.
[20] Journal officiel n°11, p. 191.
[21] Journal officiel n° 19, p. 247.
[22] Journal officiel n° 21, p. 368.
[23] Journal officiel n° 28, p. 524.
[24] Journal officiel n° 29, p. 539.
[25] Journal officiel n° 32, p. 591.
[26] Journal officiel n° 39, p. 699.
[27] Journal officiel n° 54, p. 1106.
[28] Journal officiel n° 61, p. 1253.

(k) Loi n° 99-74 du 26/7/1999 modifiant et complétant la loi 94-13 du 31 janvier 94 relative à l'exercice de la pêche;[29]

(l) Loi n° 99-95 du 6 décembre 1999 relatif à la création d'un fonds de garantie de financement des exportations avant expédition;[30] et dont l'objet est de garantir les crédits de financement des exportations avant expédition accordés par les établissements bancaires aux PME réalisant à partir de la Tunisie des exportations assortis par un crédit documentaire confirmé par une banque établi en Tunisie ou couvertes par un contrat d'assurance à l'exportation.

---

[29] *Ibid.*
[30] Journal officiel n° 98, p. 2570.

Pakistan

*Martin Lau**

1 INTRODUCTION

From a legal perspective the year 1999 can only be described as an *annus horribilis*. Fifteen years after martial law dictator and President Zia ul Haq returned the country to democracy, having ruled the country for a period of eight years from 1977 onwards, another *coup d'état* occurred in October 1999. On 12 October 1999 the government of Prime Minister Nawaz Sharif, in power since 1997, was overthrown in a bloodless *coup d'état* by General Musharraf, the Joint Chief of Army Staff. There is little doubt that despite the *prima facie* unconstitutionality of Musharraf's action the population greeted the return to military rule with indifference, and in some quarters with relief. Nawaz Sharif had not managed to fulfil the expectations of Pakistan after his resounding victory in the 1997 elections, which had given him an absolute majority in both the upper and lower house of representatives (the Senate and the National Assembly). Economic stagnation, allegations of corruption, the ill-fated Kargil campaign in Kashmir which had not only led Pakistan to the brink of war with India but had also forced the Pakistani army into a humiliating withdrawal, had all weakened the popularity and authority of the Sharif government.

This year's survey is primarily concerned with the events following the ousting of Nawaz Sharif. Chief Executive General Musharraf's main objective appears to be the eradication of corruption and the stabilization of the country's economy. It is too early to judge Musharraf's success in achieving these aims but following a judgment of the Supreme Court of Pakistan on the validity of his regime Musharraf knows that he has at least three years to turn his policies into reality. However, it is not at all certain that Musharraf will be able to maintain his position for that long: his position in the armed

---

* Barrister and Lecturer in law at the School of Oriental and African Studies, University of London.

374

forces has not remained unchallenged and there are signs that the more conservative Islamic forces in Pakistan both within the army and in society are not wholly supportive of his policies. Musharraf has not made any public commitments to accelerate the process of Islamicization and appears to have little inclination to strengthen Islamic law. The *coup d'état* has been condemned as unconstitutional by the Commonwealth and by the international community and General Musharraf has been urged to return the country to democratic rule.

Apart from the imposition of army rule two other legal developments are noteworthy: first, the Federal Shariat Court invalidated certain sections of the Muslim Laws Ordinance 1961. This has come as a blow for the women's movement in Pakistan which had regarded the Ordinance as an important safeguard against features of Islamic marriage law, especially arbitrary triple *talaq* divorces. There has been no appeal against this decision. Secondly, the Shariat Appellate Bench of the Supreme Court confirmed that all laws providing for the payment of interest are un-Islamic and therefore invalid. The government has been given a certain period of grace to implement this decision but since there can be no appeal the decision itself will have a significant impact on the country's financial institutions. It should be noted that the decision does not affect Pakistan's international financial obligations like IMF loans.

2 THE *COUP D'ÉTAT*

On 12 October 1999 Prime Minister Nawaz Sharif (as he then was) dismissed General Musharraf, the Joint Chief of Army Staff and most senior military officer, and appointed General Ziauddin, the head of the Inter Services Intelligence, as the new Joint Chief of Army Staff. There is no doubt that Nawaz Sharif had, under the provisions of the 1973 Constitution, the power to dismiss General Musharraf as Joint Chief of Army Staff. However, General Musharraf, who happened to be on an official visit to Sri Lanka at that time, did not accept his dismissal but returned to Pakistan on a scheduled commercial flight on the same day. The events surrounding Musharraf's return to Pakistan are currently the subject of criminal proceedings in Pakistan. According to General Musharraf, Nawaz Sharif attempted to prevent his plane from landing at Karachi airport by refusing to give it permission to land. General Musharraf was only able to land at Karachi airport after troops loyal to him had stormed the airport and cleared the runway. The same evening of 12 October 1999, Nawaz Sharif and numerous members of his family and his government were arrested. Martial law was immediately imposed and Musharraf's troops took control of the country by surrounding TV and radio stations and government buildings. Nawaz Sharif and several other government employees were charged with attempted murder and kidnapping and tried by a Special Court for the Suppression of Terrorist Activities. Sharif was found guilty and sentenced to life imprisonment. He is currently appealing against his conviction before the Sindh High Court whereas the government is appealing to have the sentence of life imprisonment enhanced to the death penalty.

A brief summary of the more recent constitutional history of Pakistan seems in order so as to put these dramatic events into perspective. Prior to 12 October 1999 Pakistan was governed under the provisions of the Constitution of Pakistan, 1973. The 1973 Constitution had been held in abeyance between 1977 and 1985 following a military *coup d'état* by General Zia ul Haq, who governed the country as the Chief Martial Law Administrator during this period. In 1985 democracy was restored and elections were held on a non-party basis. The new government of Prime Minister Junejo passed the 8th Amendment to the Constitution immediately after martial law was lifted. The 8th amendment *inter alia* provided Zia ul Haq with immunity from prosecution for treason and made him the President of Pakistan. In 1988 Zia ul Haq dismissed the government of Prime Minister Junejo but shortly afterwards Zia ul Haq died in a plane crash. The dismissal of Prime Minister Junejo was challenged in the Supreme Court of Pakistan. The Supreme Court ruled that the dismissal had been unconstitutional but nevertheless refused to reinstate the old government on the ground that the 1985 elections had been tarnished since they had been held under the shadows of the outgoing martial law administration. Between 1988 and October 1999 Pakistan was a genuine parliamentary democracy: all governments during this period came into power through general elections monitored by the international community. Any change of government took place under the provisions of the 1973 Constitution.

Between 1988 and 1999 several governments ruled Pakistan. After the dismissal of Prime Minister Benazir Bhutto and her cabinet in 1997 new elections were held. Nawaz Sharif and his party the Muslim League emerged as the winners having secured an over-whelming majority in both the lower, i.e. the National Assembly, and the upper house (Senate). The significant majority in the National Assembly enabled Nawaz Sharif to amend the 1973 Constitution. Some features of the 1973 Constitution which had been introduced during martial law were therefore removed from the Constitution. Most notably, Article 58(2)(b) was removed. This article had enabled the President of Pakistan to dissolve the National Assembly and to dismiss the government in the event that the country was in his opinion not any longer governed in accordance with the 1973 Constitution of Pakistan. Both Benazir Bhutto's and Nawaz Sharif's governments had in the past been dismissed by the President under Article 58(2)(b). Despite allegations of corruption and the imposition of a state of emergency on 28 May 1998 Nawaz Sharif's government was both *de jure* and *de facto* the constitutional government of Pakistan until 12 October 1999 when General Pervaiz Musharraf usurped power and imprisoned Nawaz Sharif.

The October 1999 *coup d'état* was preceded by a period of international and domestic instability in Pakistan. In spring 1998 India tested several nuclear warheads. Pakistan followed suit and conducted five nuclear tests. In the aftermath of the Indian nuclear tests Pakistan was placed under a Promulgation of Emergency on 28 May 1998. The Emergency did not affect the fundamental rights chapter of the 1973 Constitution and the validity of the emergency was upheld by the Supreme Court of Pakistan. In the early summer of 1999 the civil war in Kashmir intensified. The Indian government alleged that Pakistan supported and enabled Kashmiri rebels to infiltrate the international Line of Control which separates the Indian state of Jammu Kashmir and the state of Azad Kashmir. The latter is *de facto* controlled by Pakistan and Pakistani troops operate throughout Azad Kashmir despite the state being formally independent. As a result both countries came dangerously close to open hostility and war. In summer 1999 Nawaz Sharif – in response to considerable international pressure – officially withdrew his government's support to the rebels. The situation on the Line of Control has since returned to "normal", i.e. a regular exchange of artillery fire between the two countries but neither making any attempt to invade the other's territory. The *de facto* withdrawal from Jammu Kashmir was regarded as surrender and defeat by extremists political parties and by some sectors of the military: the decision to withdraw from Kashmir brought Nawaz Sharif into direct conflict with the armed forces and intelligence agencies. In response Nawaz Sharif attempted to remove those officers in the army who were threatening his government. Sharif's ill-fated attempt to bring the armed forces under his control must be regarded as the primary reason for the *coup d'état*. By attempting to appoint as the most senior officer of the armed forces the head of the infamous ISI, the Inter Services Intelligence, Sharif also committed a tactical error: General Ziauddin had no troops under his direct control and was therefore not in a position to force his will on to the existing power structures within the armed forces. When he reported to his new post the officer in charge did not accept Ziauddin's letter of appointment but immediately reported to General Musharraf and to his own corps commander. Thus General Ziaddin was never able to assume his new position.

3 MUSHARRAF'S REGIME

Immediately following the *coup d'état* General Musharraf proclaimed an emergency on 14 October 1999. Under the Proclamation of Emergency, which is still in force, the 1973 Constitution is held in abeyance, all elected representative bodies are suspended, both the federal and the provincial governments are dismissed, and the whole of Pakistan has come under the control of the armed forces. The President has remained in power but all other government officials are either army officers or civilians appointed by General Musharraf. General Musharraf selected a number of persons as members of his Security Council but this Council has no power to impose any limits on General Musharraf's rule. On the same day, i.e 14 October 1999, General Musharraf issued the Provisional Constitution Order[1] of 1999. It provided that Pakistan should be governed as nearly as possible in accordance with the provisions of the 1973 Constitution, that all courts were to

---

[1]   *The Dawn*, 26 January 2000.

continue to function subject to the *caveat* that no court was to have the power to make any order against General Musharraf or any person exercising powers under his authority or was to challenge the legal validity of his regime. The order also preserved all laws valid immediately before the Proclamation of Emergency.

General Musharraf proclaimed himself as the "Chief Executive" of Pakistan, a title not known under the 1973 Constitution of Pakistan. In effect, General Musharraf is a military ruler whose only claim to power is based on the fact that he is in charge of the armed forces and that the population has not deposed him by popular protest. There is no legal or constitutional basis to his regime whatsoever. On 25 January 2000 the Oath of Office (Judges) Order, 2000, was proclaimed. Under its provisions all judges who were invited to do so by Chief Executive General Musharraf had to take a new oath. The new oath bound Pakistan's superior judiciary not to the 1973 Constitution but to the Provisional Constitution Order 1999. All judges invited to take the new oath expressly promised not to call into question the validity of the Proclamation of Emergency. The new oath served two purposes: first, General Musharraf was able to remove judges from the superior courts by simply not inviting them to take the new oath. Three judges of the Sindh High Court were not invited to take the new oath. Secondly, the new oath included a stipulation that no judge was to entertain any challenge to the validity of his regime. Four judges of the Supreme Court, including Chief Justice Saeed-uz-Zaman Siddiqui, refused to take the new oath and were therefore removed from office. Currently, Mr Justice Irshad Hassan is the new Chief Justice of Pakistan.[2]

The new oath has effectively cleansed Pakistan's higher judiciary of any meaningful dissent and as a result the independence of Pakistan's judiciary must be viewed with suspicion: judges opposed to Musharraf's regime have either been removed from office or have chosen to resign of their own accord. Further, there is no guarantee that those judges who remained in office are in any way protected against other attacks on their judicial independence: General Musharraf could without any legal sanction change the terms of appointments of judges or the terms of office. The reaction to the new oath was muted partially because it was announced at very short notice: some judges were only summoned to take the new oath with a day's notice, thus leaving no time for a collective response or strategy. Only Sindh High Court Bar Association voiced a strong protest against the new oath.[2]

As a result of the new oath combined with the Provisional Constitution Order 1999 the 1973 Constitution is technically no longer in force. The country is governed in practical terms under some of its provisions but these provisions gain validity under the Provisional Constitution Order. There is no restriction on General Musharraf to amend or to change the present legal order at will.

On 12 May 2000 the Supreme Court of Pakistan ruled on the validity of the military *coup d'état*. The Supreme Court validated martial law for another

---

[2]   *The Dawn*, 27 January 2000.

three years by invoking the doctrine of necessity and expressly empowered Chief Executive Musharraf to amend the constitution as long as this was done for the purposes of restoring order in the country and without violating the salient features of the Constitution. The judgment is based on the judges' acceptance of General Musharraf's submission that Sharif's government had endangered the survival of the country and that the *coup d'état* was justified on the basis of the doctrine of necessity – the time-honoured formula which had also enabled Zia ul Haq to receive the judiciary's approval of his military rule.

So far the Supreme Court has not been moved to review its decision. The Pakistan Bar Council announced that it will file a review petition against this judgment on the grounds that it contained numerous contradictions. For instance, the Pakistan Bar Council has observed that the Supreme Court had held that on the one hand the 1973 Constitution was the supreme law of the land whereas at the same time the judges acknowledged that the 1973 Constitution was held in abeyance under the provisions of the Provisional Constitution Order. However, no specific steps seem to have been taken to ask the Supreme Court to review its decision. This is in any event unlikely since, as already observed, judges are not fully independent. Some were removed in pursuance of the Oath of Judges Ordinance and there is nothing at all to prevent Chief Executive Musharraf from further interfering with the independence of the judiciary. There would be no remedy whatsoever if Chief Executive Musharraf decided to dismiss a judge or if he decided to effect further changes in the legal system of Pakistan. The events surrounding the implementation of the Oath of Office (Judges) Order, 2000, support this view. Not only were a number of judges not invited to take the new oath – among them four judges of the Supreme Court of Pakistan including the Chief Justice of Pakistan – but the residence of the former Chief Justice was surrounded by troops when it emerged that he refused to take the new oath.

4   ANTI-CORRUPTION

General Musharraf's main policy objective appears to be the fight against corruption. For this purpose he proclaimed the Nationality Accountability Bureau Ordinance, 1999, in November 1999. The Nationality Accountability Bureau Ordinance, 1999, provides for the setting up of a National Accountability Bureau (NAB) "so as to eradicate corruption and corrupt practices and hold accountable all those persons accused of such practices and matters ancillary thereto". One of its stated objectives is to facilitate "the recovery of outstanding amounts from those persons who have committed default in the repayment of amounts to Banks, Financial Institutions, Government and other agencies". The ordinance takes effect notwithstanding anything contained in other law. It creates a new criminal offence of "wilful default" which is defined as non-payment or non- return of a loaned amount to the bank on the date that it became due. It should be noted that the offence of "wilful default" has never existed in Pakistan before. Any offence under the ordinance is non-bailable. The only authority which can initiate proceedings against a suspect is the Chairman of the Accountability Bureau. His decision on whether or not to proceed with a case against a suspect is final. Once charged, a suspect becomes liable to immediate and automatic arrest. It is only after an arrest and detention that the Chairman of the National Account-ability Bureau can consider his release. However, any release pending trial is conditional on the accused depositing the amount he is alleged to have obtained or retained illegally with the NAB.

The National Accountability Bureau has to complete its inquiries and investigations within a maximum of seventy-five days. The accused is then tried by the National Accountability Court, which is under a duty to try a suspect within thirty days. In the case of wilful default it is possible for an accused to have his case referred to the Conciliation Committee, which consists of a nominee of the National Accountability Bureau and a representa-tive of the bank. If a repayment schedule can be agreed the agreement itself can be – but does not have to be – accepted by the Chairman of the National Accountability Bureau. If accepted, the accused is released from custody. There is the right to an appeal to a provincial high court but the appeal has to be decided with within thirty days. The maximum punishments are severe: for wilful default it is fourteen years of rigorous imprisonment. Furthermore, there is a lengthy disqualification from being allowed to hold any political office.

Large numbers of defaulters have been arrested under the provisions of the ordinance. On 17 November 1999, one day after the promulgation of the ordinance, twenty-one "loan defaulters" were arrested in Pakistan and 300 defaulters were short-listed for arrest. A number of Pakistanis have also been declared "absconders" and "fugitives" from justice, including Ms Benazir Bhutto, the former Prime Minister of Pakistan. At the end of January 2000 forty-eight people were detained under the ordinance. It appears from newspaper reports that the National Accountability Bureau enjoys wide dis-cretionary powers and is not subject to any effective means of judicial review. Some suspects were arrested without any arrest warrants and held incommuni-cado for a number of days.[3]

One of the most troubling aspects of the NAB is the creation of a new criminal offence, namely wilful default. The retrospective creation of the offence of "wilful default" not only violates Pakistan's Constitution but also appears to violate Article 15 of the United Nations Covenant of Civil Political Rights ("No one shall be held guilty of any criminal offence on account of any act or omission which did not constitute a criminal offence, under national or international law, at the time it was committed"). It is also possible that the new offence of wilful default violates Article 11 of the United Nations Covenant of Civil Political Rights which provides that "No one shall be imprisoned merely on the ground of inability to fulfill a con-tractual obligation."

---

[3]   "Bashir Bilour clears loan, comes out of custody", *The Dawn*, 19 November 1999.

It appears from a very recent newspaper report that the High Court of Sindh has accepted a petition for judicial review of the National Accountability Bureau Ordinance of 1999. The petition claims that the Ordinance is *ultra vires* the 1973 Constitution to the extent that it provides for retrospective punishment and for the initiation of parallel proceedings.[4] However, in a very recent decision of the High Court of Lahore the National Accountability Bureau Ordinance of 1999 was held to be valid.[5] The Lahore High Court held that the offence of "wilful default" was a continuing offence and therefore did not amount to retrospective punishment. The judgement itself has not as yet been reported. There is certainly considerable apprehension and unease in Pakistan about the implementation of the NAB Ordinance of 1999. Official statements on the willingness of the government to pursue loan defaulters at times border on the surreal. On 22 November 1999 *The News International* reported that the regime was considering a proposal under which as a measure of last resort the help of the mafia should be sought by placing head money on suspects residing in the developed world.[6]

5   LOCAL GOVERNMENT REFORM

The second policy goal of Chief Executive Musharraf is equally sweeping and ambitious. On 14 August 2000 the Chief Executive released the Local Government Plan 2000, which promises a radical shake up of the existing system of local government. His attempt to reintroduce democratic institutions at the local level is not new. Both Ayub Khan and Zia ul Haq, two of Musharraf's martial law predecessors, had made a reform of local government one of their policies. Musharraf's plans, at this time still somewhat vague, envisage directly elected local government at the lowest level of administration. The Plan states that:

The Local Government design is based on five fundamentals: devolution of political power, decentralisation of administrative authority, deconcentration of management functions, diffusion of the power–authority nexus, and distribution of resources to the district level. It is designed to ensure that the genuine interests of the people are served and that their rights safeguarded. The new system will create an enabling environment in which the people can start participating in community welfare and be the masters of their own destiny.

The Plan envisages that local governments will be formed at three levels: district, *tehsil* and Union. Whereas there are direct elections at the lowest level, the members of the higher levels of the local government system are elected indirectly. Elections are held on a non-party basis. Law enforcement agencies report directly to the district government.

The Plan is still being discussed and there will no doubt be many changes

---

4   *The News International*, 16 June 2000.
5   *The News International*, 15 June 2000.
6   *The News International*, 22 November 1999.

before it is implemented. However, there is little doubt that the new system will shake up traditional power structures especially in rural areas. Whether the new plan will be able to improve the fate of Pakistan's poor will have to be seen. There is little doubt that the country is facing an unprecedented development crisis. Currently the number of poor people increases by 6 per cent every year, the populations grows by at least 3 per cent and economic growth hovers around 2 per cent. More than 50 per cent of Pakistan's population is below the age of twenty-one. If these trends are allowed to continue Pakistan's present population of 140 million will be matched by 140 million living below the poverty line by the 2020. This is daunting prospect and any attempt to initiate development has to be welcomed. However, it is doubtful whether any meaningful development can take place as long as defence expenditure and debt servicing swallow almost the entire budget.

The local government reform might be a useful tool to free local people from the existing rule of feudal lords but it is nevertheless doubtful that the measures will enjoy long-term success since they are being imposed by an undemocratic government without any meaningful debate or any participation by the main political parties.

6   THE MUSLIM FAMILY ORDINANCE 1961

On 5 January 2000 the Federal Shariat Court (FSC) invalidated important sections of the MFLO 1961 as un-Islamic.[7] The case is significant not only in respect of its effect on the legal position of women and but also because it expands the jurisdiction of the Federal Shariat Court. In 1981, in the decision of *Mst Farishta* (PLD 1981 SC 81) it had been held that Muslim Personal Law was outside the jurisdiction of the Federal Shariat Court and that therefore laws like the MFLO 1961 could not be invalidated by the FSC on the basis of being repugnant to Islam. However, in 1994 the FSC redefined the term Muslim Personal Law holding that only those laws which were peculiar to a particular sect of Islam ought to be regarded as Muslim Personal Law.[8] On the basis of the 1994 judgment, which concerned the Zakat and Ushr Ordinance, the FSC therefore felt entitled to examine the MFLO. Two sections were invalidated: firstly section 4, which had introduced the Shia rule of inheritance that the children of predeceased parents can inherit from their grandparents, and section 7, which made the validity of a divorce dependent on notice of the *talaq* being given by the husband to both his wife and the union council. The divorce only became effective if this notice requirement had been complied with and a period of ninety days had expired without any reconciliation of husband and wife having taken place. However, section 4, which provides for the registration of marriages,

---

7   The case has as yet not been reported.
8   See Art. 203B(c) of the Constitution of Pakistan and *Dr Mahmmod-ur-Rehman Faisal* PLD 1994 SC 607.

and section 5, which imposes criminal punishments on those taking another wife without having obtained the permission of the arbitration council and the first wife, were upheld as being Islamic.

This judgment may have wider repercussions since it is entirely possible that the FSC will now examine other areas of Muslim family law hitherto regarded to be outside its jurisdiction. One possible area is custody and guardianship of children. The "secular" higher judiciary has continued to base custody cases involving minors on the basis of the best interest of the child rather than on the basis of Islamic law. In *Zahoor Ahmed v. Rukhsana Kausar* 2000 SCMR 706 the father of a minor applied to the guardian court for custody. His son was living with his divorced wife. Both the petitioner and his divorced wife had remarried. The guardian court found in favour of the father on the basis of Islamic law but both the district court and the High Court of Lahore disagreed and awarded custody to the mother. In the Supreme Court the father argued that he was financially better off than the mother and that the mother was ill equipped to look after the son due to her re-marriage. The Supreme Court decided in favour of the mother but granted visiting rights to the father. However, unusually and clearly designed to prevent the abduction of the boy by the father, the Supreme Court ordered that "Whenever the petitioner visits his village, and if he so desires, he can approach the learned Guardian Judge for meeting his minor son for an hour or so twice a month in the Court of the learned Guardian Judge whereafter the custody of the minor shall revert to respondents Nos. 2 and 3."[9] The paramount importance of the welfare of the child rather than Islamic law on custody was elevated to a legal principle in the case of *Firdous Iqbal v. Shifaat Ali* 2000 SCMR 838 where the Supreme Court stated that

The welfare of the minor, however, remains the paramount consideration in determining the custody of a minor notwithstanding the right of the father to get the custody after seven years of age of the male minor child. The custody of a minor can, however, be delivered by the Court only in the interest of the welfare of the minor and not the so-called right of the one parent or another.[10]

There is no doubt that these decisions constitute a clear departure from Islamic law and it is most probably only a matter of time before the underlying legislation, namely the Guardians and Wards Act 1891, will be challenged as un-Islamic.

The ordinary higher judiciary, in the meantime, has been unwilling to apply Islamic law as a touchstone for the examination of the constitutionality of statutes. In *Province of Punjab v. National Industrial Cooperative Credit Corporation* 2000 SCMR, a case challenging the constitutionality of the Punjab Undesirable Cooperative Societies (Dissolution) Ordinance of 1992, the Supreme Court reaffirmed the principle laid down in the landmark decision of *Kaniz Fatima v. Wali Muhammad Khan* PLD 1993 SC 901 that the injunctions of Islam cannot be used to challenge the legal validity

---

9   *Ibid.*, at p. 712.
10   *Firdous Iqbal v. Shifaat Ali* 2000 SCMR 838, at p. 843.

of a statutory or constitutional provision. Equally, no attempt was made to test the validity of the imposition of martial law on the basis of Islam.

7   MISCELLANEOUS

The case of *Saleem-ud-Din v. Municipal Committee, Tando Allahyar* 2000 SCMR 460 continues the saga of illegal construction of residential premises in Karachi. The commercial centre of Pakistan has for a long time suffered from an acute housing shortage, sustained population growth through rural–urban migration, and extremely limited services and infrastructure. Builders frequently ignore or circumvent the existing planning regulations by constructing buildings at high speed in the knowledge that once a building has been raised and is perhaps even occupied it is unlikely that a court will make a demolition order. However, the High Court of Sindh has been increasingly assertive and has in some cases ordered the demolition of premises even though the builders had completed the building works and tenants had moved into the illegal structure. In the present case the High Court of Sindh had given a stay order against the builders of a number of shops enjoining them to cease all work on these constructions and to maintain the status quo pending final determination of the legality of the constructions. It was alleged that the builders had violated the stay order. In response the High Court initiated its own inquiries and had sent a court official and an employee of the council to the premises to inspect the illegal structure. The court official, who complained that he had been maltreated by the builders when he carried out his *in situ* investigation, reported to the court that there had been a breach of the stay order. The Sindh High Court sentenced him to six months in civil prison, ordered the demolition of the illegally constructed premises and ordered the builder to pay compensation to the tenants who were already occupying the structures. The builder appealed to the Supreme Court against this decision arguing that the order of the High Court was flawed. Justice Munir Sheikh in a forceful judgment rejected the appeal but showed some leniency: the prison sentence was made suspended under the condition that the illegal structures were demolished within two months from the date of the judgment. The case confounds the often-voiced criticism that courts do not have the power to enforce their decrees: in the present case the builder was ultimately forced to demolish the illegal structures.

The practice of honour crimes was examined in the case of *Abdul Zahir v. The State* 20000 SCMR 406. The Supreme Court of Pakistan held that the defence of grave and sudden provocation was by and large not available in cases of honour crimes, i.e. the murder of women by male relatives on the ground that through their alleged conduct they had dishonoured their families. The concept of *izzat*, i.e. honour, is deeply ingrained in Pakistani society. A daughter, who has tarnished the reputation of herself and her family by marrying outside her sect and without the approval of her family, will be regarded by her own family as having committed a crime against them. It is not at all unusual for male members of a family to track down a female member of the family suspected of immorality and to kill or mutilate her and her partner. Kidnapping of women and their subsequent murder by members of their own families occurs frequently and the societal recognition of this practice means that law enforcement agencies tend to turn a blind eye or, in some cases, if the family is well connected and powerful, even assist in the commission of the "honour crime". There have been reported cases where police officers abducted women in order to return them to their families. The recent report of Amnesty International entitled *Pakistan: Violence against Women in Name of Honour*, ASA 33/1/99 documents a large number of honour killings and the practice has also been the subject of a recent decision of the House of Lords of England and Wales. In *Islam (A.P.) v. Secretary of State for the Home Department Regina v. Immigration Appeal Tribunal and Another ex parte Shah (A.P.)* (Conjoined Appeals), 25 March 1999 it was held that two women who have a well-founded fear of being subjected to honour crimes if they returned to Pakistan, were entitled to be granted political asylum.

The Supreme Court's refusal to condone concepts of honour in the commission of murder is an encouraging sign that Pakistan's elites have taken cognizance of the problem. However, there is still no concerted effort to eradicate the practice. A newly instituted Women's Commission under the chair of Dr Shaheen Sardar Ali, the Health and Social Welfare Minister of the NWFP, is expected to deal with the issue of honour crimes.

8   CONCLUSION

The legal landscape of Pakistan has been shaken deeply. The *coup d'état* has brought to an end fifteen years of democracy. It would be foolish to argue that these fifteen years were a success for democracy in Pakistan: both the governments of Nawaz Sharif and Benazir Bhutto were marred by frequent allegations of corruption, nepotism, abuse of power and incompetence. However, it is doubtful that a sick democracy can be cured by abolishing it completely. Reform of democratic institutions cannot be imposed by martial dicta. General Musharraf's policies, well-intentioned as they may be, do not carry a democratic consensus and are imposed in a political vacuum. Their sustainability is therefore doubtful.

Pakistan's legal institutions have suffered yet another blow. Nawaz Sharif had been able to politicize Pakistan's higher judiciary to a large extent. Best evidence for the unwillingness of the judiciary to challenge Nawaz Sharif is the case concerning the storming of the Supreme Court's premises by Muslim League supporters and politicians in 1997. The events surrounding the contempt proceedings against Nawaz Sharif on 28 November 1997, when supporters of the Pakistan Muslim League stormed the premises of the Supreme Court in order to disrupt the proceedings against the Prime Minister, came up in the context of contempt of court proceedings before the Supreme Court in early 1999.[11] Following the incident the Supreme Court

---

[11]   *State v. Tariq Aziz* 2000 SCMR 751.

prepared an internal report on the incident which identified by name more than fifty persons including members of the provincial and the national assembly who had either been seen to be present when the incident took place or who had been members of the police forces charged with protecting the Supreme Court. However, despite ample documentary evidence in the form of videotapes taken from several closed circuit cameras the Supreme Court declined to find any of the persons named and identified in its own report guilty of contempt of court. Considering the gravity of the incident and the amount of evidence available to the Supreme Court this result is difficult to explain. There is little doubt that to an outside observer the result seems to indicate that the Supreme Court was not willing to pursue the members of the ruling party, especially after the forced resignation of Justice Sajjad Ali Shah as Chief Justice of the Supreme Court. It was Sajjad Ali Shah who had in initiated the contempt of court proceedings against Nawaz Sharif.

The present higher judiciary, purged from all dissenters as a result of the new oath, will have to prove that it is nevertheless willing to provide checks and balances to Musharraf's regime. Musharraf himself indicated that he would abide by decisions of the Supreme Court and there are some encouraging signs indicating that judicial independence has not been completely lost. The first sign that the Supreme Court of Pakistan has not been completely acquiescent in its stance on the legality of the regime of General Pervez Musharraf is the *suo moto* Case No. 1 of 2000 which took judicial notice of a newspaper item reporting that a ban had been imposed on all political rallies and meetings taking place in the open. The Supreme Court stated that this might amount to a violation of the fundamental rights to freedom of movement (Article 15), freedom of assembly (Article 16), freedom of association (Article 17) and freedom of speech (Article 19) and admitted the matter for a full hearing.

However, General Musharraf's willingness to abide by decisions of the Supreme Court has not been taken to a proper test: the validation of his regime for three years entails that the country will have to be returned to democratic rule in two years' time. This will be the ultimate test for General Musharraf's intentions and the Supreme Court of Pakistan's power.

Part III

Selected Documents and Legislation

Resolutions and International Agreements

United Nations–Iraq
Resolutions

RESOLUTION 687 (1991)
ADOPTED BY THE SECURITY COUNCIL AT ITS 2981ST MEETING,
ON 3 APRIL 1991

The Security Council,

Recalling its resolutions 660 (1990) of 2 August 1990, 661 (1990) of 6 August 1990, 662 (1990) of 9 August 1990, 664 (1990) of 18 August 1990, 665 (1990) of 25 August 1990, 666 (1990) of 13 September 1990, 667 (1990) of 16 September 1990, 669 (1990) of 24 September 1990, 670 (1990) of 25 September 1990, 674 (1990) of 29 October 1990, 677 (1990) of 28 November 1990, 678 (1990) of 29 November 1990 and 686 (1991) of 2 March 1991,

Welcoming the restoration to Kuwait of its sovereignty, independence and territorial integrity and the return of its legitimate Government,

Affirming the commitment of all Member States to the sovereignty, territorial integrity and political independence of Kuwait and Iraq, and noting the intention expressed by the Member States cooperating with Kuwait under paragraph 2 of resolution 678 (1990) to bring their military presence in Iraq to an end as soon as possible consistent with paragraph 8 of resolution 686 (1991),

Reaffirming the need to be assured of Iraq's peaceful intentions in the light of its unlawful invasion and occupation of Kuwait,

Taking note of the letter sent by the Minister for Foreign Affairs of Iraq on 27 February 1991 and those sent pursuant to resolution 686 (1991),

Noting that Iraq and Kuwait, as independent sovereign States, signed at Baghdad on 4 October 1963 "Agreed Minutes Between the State of Kuwait and the Republic of Iraq Regarding the Restoration of Friendly Relations, Recognition and Related Matters", thereby recognizing formally the boundary between Iraq and Kuwait and the allocation of islands, which were registered with the United Nations in accordance with Article 102 of the Charter of the United Nations and in which Iraq recognized the independence and complete sovereignty of the State of Kuwait within its borders as specified and accepted in the letter of the Prime Minister of Iraq dated 21 July 1932, and as accepted by the Ruler of Kuwait in his letter dated 10 August 1932,

Conscious of the need for demarcation of the said boundary,

Conscious also of the statements by Iraq threatening to use weapons in violation of its obligations under the Geneva Protocol for the Prohibition of the Use in War of Asphyxiating, Poisonous or Other Gases, and of Bacteriological Methods of Warfare, signed at Geneva on 17 June 1925, and of its prior use of chemical weapons and affirming that grave consequences would follow any further use by Iraq of such weapons,

Recalling that Iraq has subscribed to the Declaration adopted by all States participating in the Conference of States Parties to the 1925 Geneva Protocol and Other Interested States, held in Paris from 7 to 11 January 1989, establishing the objective of universal elimination of chemical and biological weapons,

Recalling also that Iraq has signed the Convention on the Prohibition of the Development, Production and Stockpiling of Bacteriological (Biological) and Toxin Weapons and on Their Destruction, of 10 April 1972,

Noting the importance of Iraq ratifying this Convention,

Noting also the importance of all States adhering to this Convention and encouraging its forthcoming Review Conference to reinforce the authority, efficiency and universal scope of the convention,

Stressing the importance of an early conclusion by the Conference on Disarmament of its work on a Convention on the Universal Prohibition of Chemical Weapons and of universal adherence thereto,

Aware of the use by Iraq of ballistic missiles in unprovoked attacks and therefore of the need to take specific measures in regard to such missiles located in Iraq,

Concerned by the reports in the hands of Member States that Iraq has attempted to acquire materials for a nuclear-weapons programme contrary to its obligations under the Treaty on the Non-Proliferation of Nuclear Weapons of 1 July 1968,

Recalling the objective of the establishment of a nuclear-weapons-free zone in the region of the Middle East,

Conscious of the threat that all weapons of mass destruction pose to peace and security in the area and of the need to work towards the establishment in the Middle East of a zone free of such weapons,

Conscious also of the objective of achieving balanced and comprehensive control of armaments in the region,

Conscious further of the importance of achieving the objectives noted above using all available means, including a dialogue among the States of the region,

Noting that resolution 686 (1991) marked the lifting of the measures imposed by resolution 661 (1990) in so far as they applied to Kuwait,

Noting also that despite the progress being made in fulfilling the obligations of resolution 686 (1991), many Kuwaiti and third country nationals are still not accounted for and property remains unreturned,

Recalling the International Convention against the Taking of Hostages, opened for signature at New York on 18 December 1979, which categorizes all acts of taking hostages as manifestations of international terrorism,

Deploring threats made by Iraq during the recent conflict to make use of terrorism against targets outside Iraq and the taking of hostages by Iraq,

Taking note with grave concern of the reports of the Secretary-General of 20 March 1991 and 28 March 1991, and conscious of the necessity to meet urgently the humanitarian needs in Kuwait and Iraq,

Bearing in mind its objective of restoring international peace and security in the area as set out in recent resolutions of the Security Council,

Conscious of the need to take the following measures acting under Chapter VII of the Charter,

1. Affirms all thirteen resolutions noted above, except as expressly changed below to achieve the goals of this resolution, including a formal cease-fire;

A

2. Demands that Iraq and Kuwait respect the inviolability of the international boundary and the allocation of islands set out in the "Agreed Minutes Between the State of Kuwait and the Republic of Iraq Regarding the Restoration of Friendly Relations, Recognition and Related Matters", signed by them in the exercise of their sovereignty at Baghdad on 4 October 1963 and registered with the United Nations and published by the United Nations in document 7063, United Nations, Treaty Series, 1964;

3. Calls upon the Secretary-General to lend his assistance to make arrangements with Iraq and Kuwait to demarcate the boundary between Iraq and Kuwait, drawing on appropriate material, including the map transmitted by Security Council document S/22412 and to report back to the Security Council within one month;

4. Decides to guarantee the inviolability of the above-mentioned international boundary and to take as appropriate all necessary measures to that end in accordance with the Charter of the United Nations;

B

5. Requests the Secretary-General, after consulting with Iraq and Kuwait, to submit within three days to the Security Council for its approval a plan for the immediate deployment of a United Nations observer unit to monitor the Khor Abdullah and a demilitarized zone, which is hereby established, extending ten kilometres into Iraq and five kilometres into Kuwait from the boundary referred to in the "Agree Minutes Between the State of Kuwait and the Republic of Iraq Regarding the Restoration of Friendly Relations, Recognition and Related Matter" of 4 October 1963; to deter violations of the boundary through its presence in and surveillance of the demilitarized zone; to observe any hostile or potentially hostile action mounted from the territory of one State to the other; and for the Secretary-General to report regularly to the Security Council on the operations of the unit, and immediately if there are serious violations of the zone or potential threats to peace;

6. Notes that as soon as the Secretary-General notifies the Security Council of the completion of the deployment of the United Nations observer unit, the conditions will be established for the Member States cooperating with Kuwait in accordance with resolution 678 (1990) to bring their military presence in Iraq to an end consistent with resolution 686 (1991)

C

7. Invites Iraq to reaffirm unconditionally its obligations under the Geneva Protocol for the Prohibition of the Use in War of Asphyxiating, Poisonous or Other Gases, and of Bacteriological Methods of Warfare, signed at Geneva on 17 June 1925, and to ratify the Convention on the Prohibition of the Development, Production and Stockpiling of Bacteriological (Biological) and Toxin Weapons and on Their Destruction, of 10 April 1972;

8. Decides that Iraq shall unconditionally accept the destruction, removal, or rendering harmless, under international supervision, of:

    (a)   All chemicals and biological weapons and all stocks of agents and all related subsystems and components and all research, development, support and manufacturing facilities;

    (b)   All ballistic missiles with a range greater than 150 kilometres and related major parts, and repair and production facilities;

9.   Decides also for the implementation of paragraph 8 above, the following:

    (a)   Iraq shall submit to the Secretary-General, within fifteen days of the adoption of the present resolution, a declaration of the locations, amounts and types of all items specified in paragraph 8 and agree to urgent, on-site inspections as specified below;

    (b)   The Secretary-General, in consultation with the appropriate Governments and, where appropriate, with the Director-General of the World Health Organization, within forty-five days of the passage of the present resolution, shall develop, and submit to the Council for approval, a plan calling for the completion of the following acts within forty-five days of such approval:

        (i)   The forming of a Special Commission, which shall carry out immediate on-site inspection of Iraq's biological, chemical and missile capabilities, based on Iraq's declarations and the designation of any additional locations by the Special Commission itself;

        (ii)   The yielding by Iraq of possession to the Special Commission for destruction, removal or rendering harmless, taking into account the requirements of public safety, of all items specified under paragraph 8 (a) above, including items at the additional locations designated by the Special Commission under paragraph 9 (b) (i) above and the destruction by Iraq, under the supervision of the Special Commission, of all its missile capabilities, including launchers, as specified under paragraph 8 (b) above;

        (iii)   The provision by the Special Commission of the assistance and cooperation to the Director-General of the International Atomic Energy Agency required in paragraphs 12 and 13 below;

10.   Decides further that Iraq shall unconditionally undertake not to use, develop, construct or acquire any of the items specified in paragraphs 8 and 9 above and requests the Secretary-General, in consultation with the Special Commission, to develop a plan for the future ongoing monitoring and verification of Iraq's compliance with this paragraph, to be submitted to the Security Council for approval within one hundred and twenty days of the passage of this resolution;

11.   Invites Iraq to reaffirm unconditionally its obligations under the Treaty on the Non-Proliferation of Nuclear Weapons of 1 July 1968;

12.   Decides that Iraq shall unconditionally agree not to acquire or develop nuclear weapons or nuclear-weapons-usable material or any subsystems or components or any research, development, support or manufacturing facilities related to the above; to submit to the Secretary-General and the Director-General of the International Atomic Energy Agency within fifteen days of the adoption of the present resolution a declaration of the locations, amounts and types of all items specified above, to place all of its nuclear-weapons-usable materials under the exclusive control, for custody and removal, of the International Atomic Energy Agency, with the assistance and cooperation of the Special Commission as provided for in the plan of the Secretary-General discussed in paragraph 9 (b) above; to accept, in accordance with the arrangements provided for in paragraph 13 below, urgent on-site inspection and the destruction, removal or rendering harmless as appropriate of all items specified above; and to accept the plan discussed in paragraph 13 below for the future ongoing monitoring and verification of its compliance with these undertakings;

13. Requests the Director-General of the International Atomic Energy Agency, through the Secretary-General, with the assistance and cooperation of the Special Commission as provided for in the plan of the Secretary-General in paragraph 9 (b) above, to carry out immediate on-site inspection of Iraq's nuclear capabilities based on Iraq's declarations and the designation of any additional locations by the Special Commission; to develop a plan for submission to the Security Council within forty-five days calling for the destruction, removal, or rendering harmless as appropriate of all items listed in paragraph 12 above; to carry out the plan within forty-five days following approval by the Security Council; and to develop a plan, taking into account the rights and obligations of Iraq under the Treaty on the Non-Proliferation of Nuclear Weapons on 1 July 1968, for the future ongoing monitoring and verification of Iraq's compliance with paragraph 12 above, including an inventory of all nuclear material in Iraq subject to the Agency's verification and inspections to confirm that Agency safeguards cover all relevant nuclear activities in Iraq, to be submitted to the Security Council for approval within one hundred and twenty days of the passage of the present resolution;

14. Notes that the actions to be taken by Iraq in paragraphs 8, 9, 10, 11, 12 and 13 of the present resolution represent steps towards the goal of establishing in the Middle East a zone free from weapons of mass destruction and all missiles for their delivery and the objective of a global ban on chemical weapons;

D

15. Requests the Secretary-General to report to the Security Council on the steps taken to facilitate the return of all Kuwaiti property seized by Iraq, including a list of any property that Kuwait claims has not been returned or which has not been returned intact;

E

16. Reaffirms that Iraq, without prejudice to the debts and obligations of Iraq arising prior to 2 August 1990, which will be addressed through the normal mechanisms, is liable under international law for any direct loss, damage, including environmental damage and the depletion of natural resources, or injury to foreign Governments, nationals and corporations, as a result of Iraq's unlawful invasion and occupation of Kuwait;

17. Decides that all Iraqi statements made since 2 August 1990 repudiating its foreign debt are null and void, and demands that Iraq adhere scrupulously to all of its obligations concerning servicing and repayment of its foreign debt;

18. Decides also to create a fund to pay compensation for claims that fall within paragraph 16 above and to establish a Commission that will administer the fund;

19. Directs the Secretary-General to develop and present to the Security Council for decision, no later than thirty days following the adoption of the present resolution, recommendations for the fund to meet the requirement for the payment of claims established in accordance with paragraph 18 above and for a programme to implement the decisions in paragraphs 16, 17 and 18 above, including administration of the fund; mechanisms for determining the appropriate level of Iraq's contribution to the fund based on a percentage of the value of the exports of petroleum and petroleum products from Iraq not to exceed a figure to be suggested to the Council by the Secretary-General, taking into account the requirements of the people of Iraq, Iraq's payment capacity as assessed in conjunction with the international financial institutions taking into consideration external debt service, and the needs of the Iraqi economy; arrangements for ensuring that payments are made to the fund; the process by

which funds will be allocated and claims paid; appropriate procedures for evaluating losses, listing claims and verifying their validity and resolving disputed claims in respect of Iraq's liability as specified in paragraph 16 above; and the composition of the Commission designated above;

F

20. Decides, effective immediately, that the prohibitions against the sale or supply to Iraq of commodities or products, other than medicine and health supplies, and prohibitions against financial transactions related thereto contained in resolution 661 (1990) shall not apply to foodstuffs notified to the Security Council Committee established by resolution 661 (1990) concerning the situation between Iraq and Kuwait or, with the approval of that Committee, under the simplified and accelerated "no-objection" procedure, to materials and supplies for essential civilian needs as identified in the report of the Secretary-General dated 20 March 1991, and in any further findings of humanitarian need by the Committee;

21. Decides that the Security Council shall review the provisions of paragraph 20 above every sixty days in the light of the policies and practices of the Government of Iraq, including the implementation of all relevant resolutions of the Security Council, for the purpose of determining whether to reduce or lift the prohibitions referred to therein;

22. Decides also that upon the approval by the Security Council of the programme called for in paragraph 19 above and upon Council agreement that Iraq has completed all actions contemplated in paragraphs 8, 9, 10, 11, 12 and 13 above, the prohibitions against the import of commodities and products originating in Iraq and the prohibitions against financial transactions related thereto contained in resolution 661 (1990) shall have no further force or effect;

23. Decides further that, pending action by the Security Council under paragraph 22 above, the Security Council Committee established by resolution 661 (1990) shall be empowered to approve, when required to assure adequate financial resources on the part of Iraq to carry out the activities under paragraph 20 above, exceptions to the prohibition against the import of commodities and products originating in Iraq;

24. Decides that, in accordance with resolution 661 (1990) and subsequent related resolutions and until a further decision is taken by the Security Council, all States shall continue to prevent the sale or supply, or the promotion or facilitation of such sale or supply, to Iraq by their nationals, or from their territories or using their flag vessels or aircraft, of;

 (a) Arms and related material of all types, specifically including the sale or transfer through other means of all forms of conventional military equipment, including for paramilitary forces, and spare parts and components and their means of production, for such equipment;

 (b) Items specified and defined in paragraphs 8 and 12 above not otherwise covered above;

 (c) Technology under licensing or other transfer arrangements used in the production, utilization or stockpiling of items specified in subparagraphs (a) and (b) above;

 (d) Personnel or materials for training or technical support services relating to the design, development, manufacture, use, maintenance or support of items specified in subparagraphs (a) and (b) above;

25. Calls upon all States and international organizations to act strictly in accordance with paragraph 24 above, notwithstanding the existence of any contracts, agreements, licences or any other arrangements;

26. Requests the Secretary-General, in consultation with appropriate Governments, to develop within sixty days, for the approval of the Security Council, guidelines to facilitate full international implementation of paragraphs 24 and 25 above and paragraph 27 below, and to make them available to all States and to establish a procedure for updating these guidelines periodically;

27. Calls upon all States to maintain such national controls and procedures and to take such other actions consistent with the guidelines to be established by the Security Council under paragraph 26 above as may be necessary to ensure compliance with the terms of paragraph 24 above, and calls upon international organizations to take all appropriate steps to assist in ensuring such full compliance;

28. Agrees to review its decisions in paragraphs 22, 23, 24 and 25 above, except for the items specified and defined in paragraphs 8 and 12 above, on a regular basis and in any case one hundred and twenty days following passage of the present resolution, taking into account Iraq's compliance with the resolution and general progress towards the control of armaments in the region;

29. Decides that all States, including Iraq, shall take the necessary measures to ensure that no claim shall lie at the instance of the Government of Iraq, or of any person or body in Iraq, or of any person claiming through or for the benefit of any such person or body, in connection with any contract or other transaction where its performance was affected by reason of the measures taken by the Security Council in resolution 661 (1990) and related resolutions;

G

30. Decides that, in furtherance of its commitment to facilitate the repatriation of all Kuwaiti and third country nationals, Iraq shall extend all necessary cooperation to the International Committee of the Red Cross, providing lists of such persons, facilitating the access of the International Committee of the Red Cross to all such persons wherever located or detained and facilitating the search by the International Committee of the Red Cross for those Kuwaiti and third country nationals still unaccounted for;

31. Invites the International Committee of the Red Cross to keep the Secretary-General apprised as appropriate of all activities undertaken in connection with facilitating the repatriation or return of all Kuwaiti and third country nationals or their remains present in Iraq on or after 2 August 1990;

H

32. Requires Iraq to inform the Security Council that it will not commit or support any act of international terrorism or allow any organization directed towards commission of such acts to operate within its territory and to condemn unequivocally and renounce all acts, methods and practices of terrorism;

I

33. Declares that, upon official notification by Iraq to the Secretary-General and to the Security Council of its acceptance of the provisions above, a formal cease-fire is effective between Iraq and Kuwait and the Member States cooperating with Kuwait in accordance with resolution 678 (1990)

34. Decides to remain seized of the matter and to take such further steps as may be required for the implementation of the present resolution and to secure peace and security in the area.

IMPLEMENTATION OF SECURITY COUNCIL RESOLUTION 986 (1995) AND THE MEMORANDUM OF UNDERSTANDING

Memorandum of Understanding between the Secretariat of the United Nations and the Government of Iraq on the Implementation of Security Council Resolution 986 (1995)

Section 1. General provisions

1. The purpose of this Memorandum of Understanding is to ensure the effective implementation of Security Council resolution 986 (1995) (hereinafter the Resolution).
2. The Distribution Plan referred to in paragraph 8 (a) (ii) of the Resolution, which has to be approved by the Secretary-General of the United Nations, constitutes an important element in the implementation of the Resolution.
3. Nothing in the present Memorandum should be construed as infringing upon the sovereignty or territorial integrity of Iraq.
4. The provisions of the present Memorandum pertain strictly and exclusively to the implementation of the Resolution and, as such, in no way create a precedent. It is also understood that the arrangement provided for in the Memorandum is an exceptional and temporary measure.

Section II. Distribution Plan

5. The Government of Iraq undertakes to effectively guarantee equitable distribution to the Iraqi population throughout the country of medicine, health supplies, foodstuffs and materials and supplies for essential civilian needs (hereinafter humanitarian supplies) purchased with the proceeds of the sale of Iraqi petroleum and petroleum products.
6. To this end, the Government of Iraq shall prepare a Distribution Plan describing in detail the procedures to be followed by the competent Iraqi authorities with a view to ensuring such distribution. The present distribution systems of such supplies, the prevailing needs and humanitarian conditions in the various Governorates of Iraq shall be taken into consideration with due regard to the sovereignty of Iraq and the national unity of its population. The plan shall include a categorized list of the supplies and goods that Iraq intends to purchase and import for this purpose on a six-month basis.
7. The part of the Distribution Plan related to the three northern Governorates of Arbil, Dihouk and Suleimaniyeh shall be prepared in accordance with Annex 1, which constitutes an integral part of this Memorandum.
8. The Distribution Plan shall be submitted to the Secretary-General of the United Nations for approval. If the Secretary-General is satisfied that the plan adequately ensures equitable distribution of humanitarian supplies to the Iraqi population throughout the country, he will so inform the Government of Iraq.
9. It is understood by the Parties to this Memorandum that the Secretary-General will not be in a position to report as required in paragraph 13 of the Resolution unless the plan prepared by the Government of Iraq meets with his approval.
10. Once the Secretary-General approves the plan, he will forward a copy of the categorized list of the supplies and goods, which constitutes a part of the plan, to the Security Council Committee established by resolution 661 (1990) concerning the situation between Iraq and Kuwait (hereinafter the 661 Committee) for information.
11. After the plan becomes operational, each Party to the present Memorandum may suggest to the other for its consideration a modification to the plan if it

believes that such adjustment would improve the equitable distribution of humanitarian supplies and their adequacy.

Section III. Establishment of the escrow account and audit of that account

12. The Secretary-General, after consultations with the Government of Iraq, will select a major international bank and establish there the escrow account described in paragraph 7 of the Resolution, to be known as "the United Nations Iraq Account" (hereinafter the "Iraq Account"). The Secretary-General will negotiate the terms of this account with the bank and will keep the Government of Iraq fully informed of his actions in choosing the bank and opening the account. All transactions and deductions mandated by the Security Council under paragraph 8 of the Resolution shall be made from the "Iraq Account", which will be administered in accordance with the relevant Financial Regulations and Rules of the United Nations.

13. The Iraqi authorities may designate a senior banking official to liaise with the Secretariat of the United Nations on all banking matters relating to the "Iraq Account".

14. In accordance with the United Nations Financial Regulations, the "Iraq Account" will be audited by the Board of Auditors who are external independent public auditors. As provided for in the Regulations, the Board of Auditors will issue periodic reports on the audit of the financial statements relating to the account. Such reports will be submitted by the Board to the Secretary-General who will forward them to the 661 Committee and to the Government of Iraq.

15. Nothing in this Memorandum shall be interpreted to create a liability on the part of the United Nations for any purchase made by the Government of Iraq or any agents acting on its behalf pursuant to the provisions of the Resolution.

Section IV. Sale of petroleum and petroleum products originating in Iraq

16. Petroleum and petroleum products originating in Iraq will be exported via the Kirkuk-Yumurtalik pipeline through Turkey and from the Mina al-Bakr oil terminal. The 661 Committee will monitor the exports through these outlets to ensure that they are consistent with the Resolution. Transportation costs in Turkey will be covered by an additional amount of oil, as foreseen in the Resolution and in accordance with procedures to be established by the 661 Committee. The arrangement between Iraq and Turkey concerning the tariffs and payment modalities for the use of Turkish oil installations has been provided to the 661 Committee.

17. Each export of petroleum and petroleum products originating in Iraq shall be approved by the 661 Committee.

18. Detailed provisions concerning the sale of Iraqi petroleum and petroleum products are contained in Annex II, which constitutes an integral part of this Memorandum.

Section V. Procurement and confirmation procedures

19. The purchase of medicine, health supplies, foodstuffs, and materials and supplies for essential civilian needs of the Iraqi population throughout the country, as referred to in paragraph 20 of resolution 687 (1991), will, subject to paragraph 20 below, be carried out by the Government of Iraq, will follow normal commercial practice and be on the basis of the relevant resolutions of the Security Council and procedures of the 661 committee.

20. The purchase of humanitarian supplies for the three northern Governorates of Arbil, Dihouk and Suleimaniyeh, as provided for in the Distribution Plan, will be carried out in accordance with Annex 1.

21. The Government of Iraq will, except as provided for in paragraph 20, contract directly with suppliers to arrange the purchase of supplies, and will conclude the appropriate contractual arrangements.

22. Each export of goods to Iraq shall be at the request of the Government of Iraq pursuant to paragraph 8 (a) of the Resolution. Accordingly, exporting States will submit all relevant documentation, including contracts, for all goods to be exported under the Resolution to the 661 Committee for appropriate action according to its procedures. It is understood that payment of the supplier from the "Iraq Account" can take place only for items purchased by Iraq that are included in the categorized list referred to in Section II of the present Memorandum. Should exceptional circumstances arise, applications for the export of additional items may be submitted to the 661 Committee for its consideration.

23. As noted above, the 661 Committee will take action on applications for the export of goods to Iraq in accordance with its existing procedures subject to future modifications under paragraph 12 of the Resolution. The 661 Committee will inform the Government of Iraq, requesting States, and the Secretary-General of the actions taken on the requests submitted.

24. After the 661 Committee has taken action on the applications for export in accordance with its procedures, the Central Bank of Iraq will request the bank holding the "Iraq Account" to open irrevocable letters of credit in favour of the beneficiaries. Such requests shall be referred by the bank holding the "Iraq Account" to the United Nations Secretariat for approval of the opening of the letter of credit by the latter bank, allowing payment for the "Iraq Account" upon presentation of credit-conform documents. The letter of credit will require as condition of payment, inter alia, the submission to the bank holding the "Iraq Account" of the documents to be determined by the procedures established by the 661 Committee, including the confirmations by the agents referred to in paragraph 25 below. The United Nations, after consultations with the Government of Iraq, shall determine the clause to be inserted in all purchase orders, contracts and letters of credit regarding payment terms from the "Iraq Account". All charges incurred in Iraq are to be borne by the applicant, whereas all charges outside Iraq are for the account of the beneficiary.

25. The arrival of goods in Iraq purchased under the plan will be confirmed by independent inspection agents to be appointed by the Secretary-General. No payments can be made until the independent inspection agents provide the Secretary-General with authenticated confirmation that the exported goods concerned have arrived in Iraq.

26. The independent inspection agents may be stationed at relevant Iraqi entry points, custom areas or other locations where the functions set out in paragraph 27 of this Section can be performed. The number and location of the stationing points for the agents will be designated by the United Nations after consultations with the Government of Iraq.

27. The independent inspection agents will confirm delivery to Iraq of shipments. They will compare the appropriate documentation, such as bills of lading, other shipping documents or cargo manifests, and the documents issued by the 661 Committee, against goods actually arriving in Iraq. They will also have the authority to perform duties necessary for such confirmation, including: quantity inspection by weight or count, quality inspection including visual inspection, and, when necessary, laboratory testing.

28. The inspection agents will report all irregularities to the Secretary-General and to the 661 Committee. If the problem is related to normal commercial practice (e.g. some shortlanded goods), the 661 Committee and the Government of

Iraq are informed, but normal commercial resolution practices (e.g. claims) go forth. If the matter is of serious concern, the independent inspection agents will hold the shipment in question pending guidance from the 661 Committee.

29. As regards the export to Iraq of parts and equipment which are essential for the safe operation of the Kirkuk-Yumurtalik pipeline system in Iraq, the requests will be submitted to the 661 Committee by the national Government of the supplier. Such requests will be considered for approval by the Committee in accordance with its procedures.

30. If the 661 Committee has approved a request in accordance with paragraph 29, the provisions of paragraph 24 shall apply. However, since the supplier can expect payment against future oil sales, as stated in paragraph 10 of the Resolution, the proceeds of which are to be deposited in the "Iraq Account", the bank holding the "Iraq Account" will issue an irrevocable letter of credit stipulating that payment can only be effected when at the time of drawing the "Iraq Account" has sufficient disposable funds and the United Nations Secretariat approves the payment.

31. The requirement of authenticated confirmation of arrival provided for in this Section shall apply also to the parts and equipment mentioned in paragraph 29.

Section VI. Distribution of humanitarian supplies purchased under the Distribution Plan

32. The distribution of humanitarian supplies shall be undertaken by the Government of Iraq in accordance with the Distribution Plan referred to in Section II of the present Memorandum. The Government of Iraq will keep the United Nations observation personnel informed about the implementation of the plan and the activities that the Government is undertaking.

33. The distribution of humanitarian supplies in the three northern Governorates of Arbil, Dihouk and Suleimaniyeh shall be undertaken by the United Nations Inter-Agency Humanitarian Programme on behalf of the Government of Iraq under the Distribution Plan with due regard to the sovereignty and territorial integrity of Iraq in accordance with Annex 1.

Section VII. Observation of the equitable distribution of humanitarian supplies and determination of their adequacy

General Provisions

34. The United Nations observation process will be conducted by United Nations personnel in Iraq under the overall authority of the Department of Humanitarian Affairs at United Nations Headquarters in New York in accordance with the provisions described below. Such observations shall apply to the distribution of humanitarian supplies financed in accordance with the procedures set out in the Resolution.

35. The objectives of the United Nations observation process shall be:
   (a) to confirm whether the equitable distribution of humanitarian supplies to the Iraqi population throughout the country has been ensured;
   (b) to ensure the effectiveness of the operation and determine the adequacy of the available resources to meet Iraq's humanitarian needs.

Observation Procedures

36. In observing the equitable distribution and its adequacy, United Nations personnel will use, inter alia, the following procedures.

Food items

37. The observation of the equitablity of food distribution will be based on information obtained from local markets throughout Iraq, the Iraqi Ministry of Trade, the information available to the United Nations and its specialized agencies on food imports, and on sample surveys conducted by United Nations personnel. The observation will also include the quantity and prices of food items imported under the Resolution.

38. To provide regular updated observations of the most pressing needs, a survey undertaken by United Nations agencies in cooperation with the appropriate Iraqi ministries will serve as a baseline for the continuing observation of nutritional status of the population of Iraq. This information will take account of public health data generated by the Ministry of Health (MOH) and the relevant United Nations agencies.

Medical supplies and equipment

39. Observation regarding distribution of medical supplies and equipment will focus on the existing distribution and storage system and will involve visits to hospitals, clinics as well as medical and pharmaceutical facilities where such supplies and equipment are stored. Such observation will also be guided by health statistics data from MOH and surveys by relevant United Nations agencies.

Water/sanitation supplies and equipment

40. Observation of distribution of water/sanitation supplies and equipment will focus on the determination that they are used for their intended purposes. Confirmation will be carried out by collecting data on the incidence of water-borne diseases and by water quality control checks by visits to water and sanitation facilities by representatives of relevant United Nations agencies. In this regard the United Nations will rely on all relevant indicators.

Other materials and supplies

41. With reference to materials and supplies which do not fall within the three area indicated above, in particular, those needed for the rehabilitation of infrastructures essential to meet humanitarian needs, observation will focus on confirmation that such materials and supplies are delivered to the predefined destinations in accordance with the Distribution Plan and that they are used for their intended purposes, and on the determination of whether these materials and supplies are adequate or necessary to meet essential needs of the Iraqi population.

Coordination and Cooperation

42. The United Nations observation activities will be coordinated by the Department of Humanitarian Affairs at United Nations Headquarters in New York. Observation will be undertaken by United Nations personnel. The exact number of such personnel will be determined by the United Nations taking into account the practical requirements. The Government of Iraq will be consulted in this regard.

43. The Iraqi authorities will provide to the United Nations personnel the assistance required to facilitate the performance of their functions. United Nations personnel will coordinate with the Iraqi competent authorities.

44. In view of the importance of the functions which United Nations personnel will perform in accordance with the provisions of this Section of the Memorandum, such personnel shall have, in connection with the performance of their functions, unrestricted freedom of movement, access to documentary material

which they find relevant having discussed the matter with the Iraqi authorities concerned, and the possibility to make such contacts as they find essential.

Section VIII. Privileges and Immunities

45. In order to facilitate the successful implementation of the Resolution the following provisions concerning privileges and immunities shall apply:
    (a) officials of the United Nations and of any of the Specialized Agencies performing functions in connection with the implementation of the Resolution shall enjoy the privileges and immunities applicable to them under Articles V and VII of the Convention on the Privileges and Immunities of the United Nations, or Articles VI and VIII of the Convention on the Privileges and Immunities of the Specialized Agencies to which Iraq is a party;
    (b) independent inspection agents, technical experts and other specialists appointed by the Secretary-General of the United Nations or by heads of the Specialized Agencies concerned and performing functions in connection with the implementation of the Resolution, whose names will be communicated to the Government of Iraq, shall enjoy the privileges and immunities accorded to experts on mission for the United Nations or for the Specialized Agency under Article VI of the Convention on the Privileges and Immunities of the United Nations or the relevant Annexes of the Convention on the Privileges and Immunities of the Specialized Agencies respectively;
    (c) persons performing contractual services for the United Nations in connection with the implementation of the Resolution, whose names will be communicated to the Government of Iraq, shall enjoy the privileges and immunities referred to in sub-paragraph (b) above concerning experts on mission appointed by the United Nations.
46. In addition, officials, experts and other personnel referred to in paragraph 45 above shall have the right of unimpeded entry into and exit from Iraq and shall be issued visas by the Iraqi authorities promptly and free of charge.
47. It is further understood that the United Nations and its Specialized Agencies shall enjoy freedom of entry into and exit from Iraq wihout delay or hindrance of supplies, equipment and means of surface transport required for the implementation of the Resolution and that the Government of Iraq agrees to allow them to, temporarily, import such equipment free of customs or other duties.
48. Any issue relating to privileges and immunities, including safety and protection of the United Nations and its personnel, not covered by the provisions of this Section shall be governed by paragraph 16 of the Resolution.

Section IX. Consultations

49. The Secretariat of the United Nations and the Government of Iraq shall, if necessary, hold consultations on how to achieve the most effective implementation of the present Memorandum.

Section X. Final clauses

50. The present Memorandum shall enter into force following signature, on the day when paragraphs 1 and 2 of the Resolution become operational and shall remain in force until the expiration of the 180 day period referred to in paragraph 3 of the Resolution.

51. Pending its entry into force, the Memorandum shall be given by the United Nations and the Government of Iraq provisional effect.

SIGNED this 20th day of May 1996 at New York in two originals in English.

For the United Nations

(Signed) Hans CORELL
Under Secretary-General
The Legal Counsel

For the Government of Iraq

(Signed) Abdul Amir AL-ANBARI
Ambassador Plenipotentiary
Head of the Delegation of Iraq

Annex 1

1. In order to ensure the effective implementation of paragraph 8 (b) of the Resolution, the following arrangements shall apply in respect of the Iraqi Governorates of Arbil, Dihouk and Suleimaniyeh. These arrangements shall be implemented with due regard to the sovereignty and territorial integrity of Iraq, and to the principle of equitable distribution of humanitarian supplies throughout the country.

2. The United Nations Inter-Agency Humanitarian Programme shall collect and analyze pertinent information on humanitarian needs in the three northern Govenorates. On the basis of that information, the Programme will determine the humanitarian requirements of the three northern Governorates for discussion with the Government of Iraq and subsequent incorporation in the Distribution Plan. In preparing estimates of food needs, the Programme will take into consideration all relevant circumstances, both within the three northern Governorates and in the rest of the country, in order to ensure equitable distribution. Specific rehabilitation needs in the three northern Governorates shall receive the necessary attention.

3. Within a week following the approval of the Distribution Plan by the Secretary-General, the Programme and the Government of Iraq will hold discussions to enable the Programme to determine how the procurement of humanitarian supplies for the three northern Governorates can be undertaken most efficiently. These discussions should be guided by the following considerations. The bulk purchase by the Government of Iraq of standard food commodities and medicine may be the most cost-effective means of procurement. Other materials and supplies for essential civilian needs, specifically required for the three northern Governorates, may be more suitably procured through the United Nations system in view of technical aspects related to their proper use.

4. To the extent that purchases and deliveries are made by the Government of Iraq in response to the written communication of the Programme, an amount corresponding to the cost of the delivered goods will be deducted from the amount allocated to the Programme from the "Iraq Account".

5. Humanitarian supplies destined for distribution in the three northern Governorates shall be delivered by the Programme to warehouses located within these Governorates. Such supplies can also be delivered by the Government of Iraq or the Programme, as appropriate, to warehouses in Kirkuk and Mosul. The warehouses shall be managed by the Programme. The Government of Iraq shall ensure the prompt customs and administrative clearances to enable the safe and quick transit of such supplies to the three northern Governorates.

6. The Programme shall be responsible in the three northern Governorates for the storage, handling, internal transportation, distribution and confirmation of equitable distribution of humanitarian supplies. The Programme will keep the Government of Iraq informed on the implementation of distribution.

7. Whenever possible and cost-effective, the Programme shall use appropriate local distribution mechanisms which are comparable to those existing in the rest of Iraq in order to effectively reach the population. Recipients under this arrangement will pay a fee for internal transportation, handling, and distribution as in the rest of the country. The Programme shall ensure that the special needs of internally displaced persons, refugees, hospital in-patients and other vulnerable groups in need of supplementary food are appropriately met, and will keep the Government of Iraq informed.

8. The Programme will observe that humanitarian supplies are used for their intended purposes, through visits to sites and by collecting relevant data. The Programme will report to the Department of Humanitarian Affairs at United Nations Headquarters in New York and the Government of Iraq any violation observed by the Programme.

Annex II

1. The State concerned or, if the 661 Committee so decides, the national petroleum purchaser authorized by the 661 Committee, shall submit to the Committee for handling and approval the application, including the relevant contractual documents covering the sales of such petroleum and petroleum products, for the proposed purchase of Iraqi petroleum and petroleum products, endorsed by the Government of Iraq or the Iraqi State Oil Marketing Organization (hereinafter SOMO) on behalf of the Government. Such endorsement could be done by sending a copy of the contract to the 661 Committee. The application shall include details of the purchase price at fair market value, the export route, opening of a letter of credit payable to the "Iraq Account", and other necessary information required by the Committee. The sales of petroleum and petroleum products shall be covered by contractual documents. A copy of these documents shall be included in the information provided to the 661 Committee together with the application for forwarding to the independent inspection agents described in paragraph 4 of this Annex. The contractual documents should contain the following information: quantity and quality of petroleum and petroleum products, duration of contract, credit and payment terms and pricing mechanism. The pricing mechanism for petroleum should include the following points: marker crude oil and type of quotations to be used, adjustments for transportation and quality, and pricing dates.

2. Irrevocable confirmed letters of credit will be opened by the oil purchaser's bank with the irrevocable undertaking that the proceeds of the letter of credit will be paid directly to the "Iraq Account". For this purpose, the following clauses will have to be inserted in each letter of credit:

   "– Provided all terms and conditions of this letter of credit are complied with, proceeds of this letter of credit will be irrevocably paid into the 'Iraq Account' with ... Bank."

   "– All charges within Iraq are for the beneficiary's account, whereas all charges outside Iraq are to be borne by the purchaser."

3. All such letters of credit will have to be directed by the purchaser's bank to the bank holding the "Iraq Account" with the request that the latter adds its confirmation and forwards it to the Central Bank of Iraq for the purpose of advising SOMO.

4. The sale of petroleum and petroleum products originating in Iraq will be monitored by United Nations independent oil experts appointed by the Secretary-General of the United Nations to assist the 661 Committee. The monitoring of oil exports will be carried out by independent inspection agents at the loading facilities at Ceyhan and Mina al-Bakr and, if the 661 Committee so decides, at the pipeline metering station at the Iraq–Turkey border, and would include quality and quantity verification. They would authorize the loading, after they receive the information from the United Nations oil experts that the relevant contract has been approved, and report to the United Nations.
5. The United Nations will receive monthly reports from SOMO on the actual volume and type of petroleum products exported under the relevant sales contracts.
6. The United Nations Secretariat and SOMO shall maintain continuing contact and in particular United Nations oil experts shall meet routinely with SOMO representatives to review market conditions and oil sales.

Letter dated 20 May 1996 from the Head of delegation of Iraq addressed to the Legal Counsel

In reference to the memorandum of understanding signed today and as I advised you during the discussion that a letter would be sent to you concerning the position of Iraq as to the cost of production and transportation of oil inside Iraq, I state below Iraq's position, which I request that you include in the official record of our discussion:

The Iraqi delegation explained during the discussion that the cost of production and transportation of petroleum excluding expenses in local currency, is currently estimated at US\$ 2.00 per barrel. Such cost had to be deducted from the sale price or recovered through the production and export of extra quantity of petroleum and petroleum products. In either case the amount referred to above would be deposited in the "Iraq account" to be utilized for the import of spare parts and other items necessary for the maintenance and sustaining of production and transportation operations as is the established practice in the oil industry, otherwise production and transportation operations would be hindered and eventually come to a halt.

Nevertheless, and in order to facilitate the conclusion of this memorandum of understanding, the Iraqi delegation agreed not to insist on the acceptance of its position by the United Nations Secretariat delegation at this stage and agreed to have it included in a separate letter addressed to the Head of the delegation of the United Nations Secretariat for consideration in any future discussion.

Although the matter is not discussed, the Iraqi delegation wishes to state that a third outlet for Iraqi petroleum export could be via the Syrian Arab Republic.

(Signed) Ambassador A Amir ANBARI
Head of the delegation of Iraq

S/RES/1280 (1999)
RESOLUTION 1280 (1999)
ADOPTED BY THE SECURITY COUNCIL AT ITS 4077TH MEETING, ON 3 DECEMBER 1999

The Security Council,

Recalling its resolutions 1242 (1999) of 21 May 1999 and 1266 (1999) of 4 October 1999,

Acting under Chapter VII of the Charter of the United Nations,

1. Decides to extend the period referred to in paragraphs 1, 2 and 8 of resolution 1242 (1999) and in paragraph 1 of 1266 (1999) until 11 December 1999;
2. Decides to remain seized of the matter.

RESOLUTION 1281 (1999)
ADOPTED BY THE SECURITY COUNCIL AT ITS 4079TH MEETING, ON 10 DECEMBER 1999

The Security Council,

Recalling its previous relevant resolutions and in particular its resolutions 986 (1995) of 14 April 1995, 1111 (1997) of 4 June 1997, 1129 (1997) of 12 September 1997, 1143 (1997) of 4 December 1997, 1153 (1998) of 20 February 1998, 1175 (1998) of 19 June 1998, 1210 (1998) of 24 November 1998, 1242 (1999) of 21 May 1999, 1266 (1999) of 4 October 1999 and 1275 (1999) of 19 November 1999, and 1280 (1999) of 3 December 1999,

Convinced of the need as a temporary measure to continue to provide for the humanitarian needs of the Iraqi people until the fulfilment by the Government of Iraq of the relevant resolutions, including notably resolution 687 (1991) of 3 April 1991, allows the Council to take further action with regard to the prohibitions referred to in resolution 661 (1990) of 6 August 1990, in accordance with the provisions of those resolutions,

Convinced also of the need for equitable distribution of humanitarian supplies to all segments of the Iraqi population throughout the country,

Determined to improve the humanitarian solution in Iraq,

Reaffirming the commitment of all Member States to the sovereignty and territorial integrity of Iraq,

Acting under Chapter VII of the Charter of the United Nations,

1. Decides that the provisions of resolution 986 (1995), except those contained in paragraphs 4, 11 and 12, shall remain in force for a new period of 180 days beginning at 00.01 hours, Eastern Standard Time, on 12 December 1999;
2. Further decides that paragraph 2 of resolution 1153 (1998) shall remain in force and shall apply to the 180-day period referred to in paragraph 1 above;
3. Requests the Secretary-General to continue to take the actions necessary to ensure the effective and efficient implementation of this resolution, and to continue to enhance as necessary the United Nations observance process in Iraq in such a way as to provide the required assurance to the Council that the goods produced in accordance with this resolution are distributed equitably and that all supplies authorized for procurement, including dual usage items and spare parts, are utilized for the purpose for which they have been authorized;
4. Further decides to conduct a thorough review of all aspects of the implementation of this resolution 90 days after the entry into force of paragraph 1 above and again prior to the end of the 180-day period, on receipt of the reports referred to in paragraphs 5 and 10 below, and expresses its intention, prior to the end of the 180-day period, to consider favourably renewal of the provisions of this resolution as appropriate, provided that the said reports indicate that those provisions are being satisfactorily implemented;
5. Requests the Secretary-General to report to the Council 90 days after the date of entry into force of paragraph 1 above and again prior to the end of the 180-day period, on the basis of observations of United Nations personnel in Iraq, and of consultations with the Government of Iraq, on whether Iraq has

ensured the equitable distribution of medicine, health supplies, foodstuffs, and materials and supplies for essential civilian needs, financed in accordance with paragraph 8(a) of resolution 986 (1995), including in his reports any observations which he may have on the adequacy of the revenues to meet Iraq's humanitarian needs, and on Iraq's capacity to export sufficient quantities of petroleum and petroleum products to produce the sum referred to in paragraph 2 of resolution 1153 (1998);

6. Requests the Secretary-General to report to the Council if Iraq is unable to export petroleum and petroleum products sufficient to produce the total sum provided for in paragraph 2 above and, following consultations with the relevant United Nations agencies and the Iraqi authorities, make recommendations for the expenditure of sums expected to be available, consistent with the priorities established in paragraph 2 of resolution 1153 (1998) and with the distribution plan referred to in paragraph 5 of resolution 1175 (1998);

7. Decides that paragraph 3 of resolution 1210 (1998) shall apply to the new 180-day period referred to in paragraph 1 above;

8. Decides that paragraphs 1, 2, 3 and 4 of resolution 1175 (1998) shall remain in force and shall apply to the new 180-day period referred to in paragraph 1 above;

9. Requests the Secretary-General, in consultation with the Government of Iraq, to submit to the Council no later than 15 January 2000 a detailed list of parts and equipment necessary for the purpose described in paragraph 1 of resolution 1175 (1998);

10. Requests the Committee established by resolution 661 (1990), in close coordination with the Secretary-General, to report to the Council 90 days after the entry into force of paragraph 1 above and again prior to the end of the 180-day period on the implementation of the arrangements in paragraphs 1, 2, 6, 8, 9 and 10 of resolution 986 (1995);

11. Urges all States, and in particular the Government of Iraq, to provide their full cooperation in the effective implementation of this resolution;

12. Appeals to all States to continue to cooperate in the timely submission of applications and the expeditious issue of export licences, facilitating the transit of humanitarian supplies authorized by the Committee established by resolution 661 (1990), and to take all other appropriate measures within their competence in order to ensure that urgently needed humanitarian supplies reach the Iraqi people as rapidly as possible;

13. Stresses the need to continue to ensure respect for the security and safety of all persons directly involved in the implementation of this resolution in Iraq;

14. Decides to keep these arrangements under review including in particular those in paragraph 2 above, to ensure the uninterrupted flow of humanitarian supplies into Iraq, and expresses its determination to act without delay to address the recommendations of the report of the panel established to review humanitarian and other issues in Iraq (S/1999/356) in a further, comprehensive resolution;

15. Decides to remain seized of the matter.

S/RES/1284(1999)
RESOLUTION 1284 (1999)
ADOPTED BY THE SECURITY COUNCIL AT ITS 4084TH MEETING,
ON 17 DECEMBER 1999

The Security Council,

Recalling its previous relevant resolutions, including its resolutions 661 (1990) of 6

August 1990, 687 (1991) of 3 April 1991, 699 (1991) of 17 June 1991, 707 (1991) of 15 August 1991, 715 (1991) of 11 October 1991, 986 (1995) of 14 April 1995, 1051 (1996) of 27 March 1996, 1153 (1998) of 20 February 1998, 1175 (1998) of 19 June 1998, 1242 (1999) of 21 May 1999 and 1266 (1999) of 4 October 1999,

Recalling the approval by the Council in its resolution 715 (1991) of the plans for future ongoing monitoring and verification submitted to the Secretary-General and the Director General of the International Atomic Energy Agency (IAEA) in pursuance of paragraphs 10 and 13 of resolution 687 (1991),

Welcoming the reports of the three panels on Iraq (S/1999/356), and having held a comprehensive consideration of them and the recommendations contained in them,

Stressing the importance of a comprehensive approach to the full implementation of all relevant Security Council resolutions regarding Iraq and the need for Iraqi compliance with these resolutions,

Recalling the goal of establishing in the Middle East a zone free from weapons of mass destruction and all missiles for their delivery and the objective of a global ban on chemical weapons as referred to in paragraph 14 of resolution 687 (1991),

Concerned at the humanitarian situation in Iraq, and determined to improve that situation,

Recalling with concern that the repatriation and return of all Kuwaiti and third country nationals or their remains, present in Iraq on or after 2 August 1990, pursuant to paragraph 2 (c) of resolution 686 (1991) of 2 March 1991 and paragraph 30 of resolution 687 (1991), have not yet been fully carried out by Iraq,

Recalling that in its resolutions 686 (1991) and 687 (1991) the Council demanded that Iraq return in the shortest possible time all Kuwaiti property it had seized, and noting with regret that Iraq has still not complied fully with this demand,

Acknowledging the progress made by Iraq towards compliance with the provisions of resolution 687 (1991), but noting that, as a result of its failure to implement the relevant Council resolutions fully, the conditions do not exist which would enable the Council to take a decision pursuant to resolution 687 (1991) to lift the prohibitions referred to in that resolution,

Reiterating the commitment of all Member States to the sovereignty, territorial integrity and political independence of Kuwait, Iraq and the neighbouring States,

Acting under Chapter VII of the Charter of the United Nations, and taking into account that operative provisions of this resolution relate to previous resolutions adopted under Chapter VII of the Charter,

A

1. Decides to establish, as a subsidiary body of the Council, the United Nations Monitoring, Verification and Inspection Commission (UNMOVIC) which replaces the Special Commission established pursuant to paragraph 9 (b) of resolution 687 (1991);

2. Decides also that UNMOVIC will undertake the responsibilities mandated to the Special Commission by the Council with regard to the verification of compliance by Iraq with its obligations under paragraphs 8, 9 and 10 of resolution 687 (1991) and other related resolutions, that UNMOVIC will establish and operate, as was recommended by the panel on disarmament and current and future ongoing monitoring and verification issues, a reinforced system of ongoing monitoring and verification, which will implement the plan approved by the Council in resolution 715 (1991) and address unresolved

disarmament issues, and that UNMOVIC will identify, as necessary in accordance with its mandate, additional sales in Iraq to be covered by the reinforced system of ongoing monitoring and verification;

3. Reaffirms the provisions of the relevant resolutions with regard to the role of the IAEA in addressing compliance by Iraq with paragraphs 12 and 13 of resolution 687 (1991) and other related resolutions, and requests the Director General of the IAEA to maintain this role with the assistance and cooperation of UNMOVIC;

4. Reaffirms its resolutions 687 (1991), 699 (1991), 707 (1991), 715 (1991), 1051 (1996), 1154 (1998) and all other relevant resolutions and statements of its President, which establish the criteria for Iraqi compliance, affirms that the obligations of Iraq referred to in those resolutions and statements with regard to cooperation with the Special Commission, unrestricted access and provision of information will apply in respect of UNMOVIC, and decides in particular that Iraq shall allow UNMOVIC teams immediate, unconditional and unrestricted access to any and all areas, facilities, equipment, records and means of transport which they wish to inspect in accordance with the mandate of UNMOVIC, as well as to all officials and other persons under the authority of the Iraqi Government whom UNMOVIC wishes to interview so that UNMOVIC may fully discharge its mandate;

5. Requests the Secretary-General, within 30 days of the adoption of this resolution, to appoint, after consultation with and subject to the approval of the Council, an Executive Chairman of UNMOVIC who will take up his mandated tasks as soon as possible, and, in consultation with the Executive Chairman and the Council members, to appoint suitably qualified experts as a College of Commissioners for UNMOVIC which will meet regularly to review the implementation of this and other relevant resolutions and provide professional advice and guidance to the Executive Chairman, including on significant policy decisions and on written reports to be submitted to the Council through the Secretary-General;

6. Requests the Executive Chairman of UNMOVIC, within 45 days of his appointment, to submit to the Council, in consultation with and through the Secretary-General, for its approval an organizational plan for UNMOVIC, including its structure, staffing requirements, management guidelines, recruitment and training procedures, incorporating as appropriate the recommendations of the panel on disarmament and current and future ongoing monitoring and verification issues, and recognizing in particular the need for an effective, cooperative management structure for the new organization, for staffing with suitably qualified and experienced personnel, who would be regarded as international civil servants subject to Article 100 of the Charter of the United Nations, drawn from the broadest possible geographical base, including as he deems necessary from international arms control organizations, and for the provision of high quality technical and cultural training;

7. Decides that UNMOVIC and the IAEA, not later than 60 days after they have both started work in Iraq, will each draw up, for approval by the Council, a work programme for the discharge of their mandates, which will include both the implementation of the reinforcement system of ongoing monitoring and verification, and the key remaining disarmament tasks to be completed by Iraq pursuant to its obligations to comply with the disarmament requirements of resolution 687 (1991) and other related resolutions, which constitute the governing standard of Iraqi compliance, and further decides that what is required of Iraq for the implementation of each task shall be clearly defined and precise;

8. Requests the Executive Chairman on UNMOVIC and the Director General of the IAEA, drawing on the expertise of other international organizations as appropriate, to establish a unit which will have the responsibilities of the joint unit constituted by the Special Commission and the Director General of the IAEA under paragraph 16 of the export/import mechanism approved by resolution 1051 (1996), and also requests the Executive Chairman of UNMOVIC, in consultation with the Director General of the IAEA, to resume the revision and updating of the lists of items and technology to which the mechanism applies;

9. Decides that the Government of Iraq shall be liable for the full costs of UNMOVIC and the IAEA in relation to their work under this and other related resolutions on Iraq;

10. Requests Member States to give full cooperation to UNMOVIC and the IAEA in the discharge of their mandates;

11. Decides that UNMOVIC shall take over all assets, liabilities and archives of the Special Commission, and that it shall assume the Special Commission's part in agreements existing between the Special Commission and Iraq and between the United Nations and Iraq, and affirms that the Executive Chairman, the Commissioners and the personnel serving with UNMOVIC shall have the rights, privileges, facilities and immunities of the Special Commission;

12. Requests the Executive Chairman of UNMOVIC to report, through the Secretary-General, to the Council, following consultation with the Commissioners, every three months on the work of UNMOVIC, pending submission of the first reports referred to in paragraph 33 below, and to report immediately when the reinforced system of ongoing monitoring and verification is fully operational in Iraq;

B

13. Reiterates the obligation of Iraq, in furtherance of its commitment to facilitate the repatriation of all Kuwaiti and third country nationals referred to in paragraph 30 of resolution 687 (1991), to extend all necessary cooperation to the International Committee of the Red Cross, and calls upon the Government of Iraq to resume cooperation with the Tripartite Commission and Technical Subcommittee established to facilitate work on this issue;

14. Requests the Secretary-General to report to the Council every four months on compliance by Iraq with its obligations regarding the repatriation or return of all Kuwaiti and third country nationals or their remains, to report every six months on the return of all Kuwaiti property, including archives, seized by Iraq, and to appoint a high-level coordinator for these issues;

C

15. Authorizes States, notwithstanding the provisions of paragraphs 3 (a), 3 (b) and 4 of resolution 661 (1990) and subsequent relevant resolutions, to permit the import of any volume of petroleum and petroleum products originating in Iraq, including financial and other essential transactions directly relating thereto, as required for the purposes and on the conditions set out in paragraph 1 (a) and (b) and subsequent provisions of resolution 986 (1995) and related resolutions;

16. Underlines, in this context, its intention to take further action, including permitting the use of additional export routes for petroleum and petroleum products, under appropriate conditions otherwise consistent with the purpose and provisions of resolution 986 (1995) and related resolutions;

17. Directs the Committee established by resolution 661 (1990) to approve, on

the basis of proposals from the Secretary-General, lists of humanitarian items, including foodstuffs, pharmaceutical and medical supplies, as well as basic or standard medical and agricultural equipment and basic or standard educational items, decides, notwithstanding paragraph 3 of resolution 661 (1990) and paragraph 20 of resolution 687 (1991), that supplies of these items will not be submitted for approval of that Committee, except for items subject to the provisions of resolution 1051 (1996), and will be notified to the Secretary-General and financed in accordance with the provisions of paragraph 8 (a) and 8 (b) of resolution 986 (1995), and requests the Secretary-General to inform the Committee in a timely manner of all such notifications received and actions taken;

18. Requests the Committee established by resolution 661 (1990) to appoint, in accordance with resolutions 1175 (1998) and 1210 (1998), a group of experts, including independent inspection agents appointed by the Secretary-General in accordance with paragraph 6 of resolution 986 (1995), decides that this group will be mandated to approve speedily contracts for the parts and the equipments necessary to enable Iraq to increase its exports of petroleum and petroleum products, according to lists of parts and equipments approved by the Committee for each individual project, and requests the Secretary-General to continue to provide for the monitoring of these parts and equipments inside Iraq;

19. Encourages Member States and international organizations to provide supplementary humanitarian assistance to Iraq and published material of an educational character to Iraq;

20. Decides to suspend, for an initial period of six months from the date of the adoption of this resolution and subject to review, the implementation of paragraph 8 (g) of resolution 986 (1995);

21. Requests the Secretary-General to take steps to maximize, drawing as necessary on the advice of specialists, including representatives of international humanitarian organizations, the effectiveness of the arrangements set out in resolution 986 (1995) and related resolutions including the humanitarian benefit to Iraqi population in all areas of the country, and further requests the Secretary-General to continue to enhance as necessary the United Nations observation process in Iraq, ensuring that all supplies under the humanitarian programme are utilized as authorized, to bring to the attention of the Council any circumstances preventing or impeding effective and equitable distribution and to keep the Council informed of the steps taken towards the implementation of this paragraph;

22. Requests also the Secretary-General to minimize the cost of the United Nations activities associated with the implementation of resolution 986 (1995) as well as the cost of the independent inspection agents and the certified public accountants appointed by him, in accordance with paragraphs 6 and 7 of resolution 986 (1995);

23. Requests further the Secretary-General to provide Iraq and the Committee established by resolution 661 (1990) with a daily statement of the status of the escrow account established by paragraph 7 of resolution 986 (1995);

24. Requests the Secretary-General to make the necessary arrangements, subject to Security Council approval, to allow funds deposited in the escrow account established by resolution 986 (1995) to be used for the purchase of locally produced goods and to meet the local cost of essential civilian needs which have been funded in accordance with the provisions of resolution 986 (1995) and related resolutions, including, where appropriate, the cost of installation and training services;

25. Directs the Committee established by resolution 661 (1990) to take a decision on all applications in respect of humanitarian and essential civilian needs within a target of two working days of receipt of these applications from the Secretary-General, and to ensure that all approval and notification letters issued by the Committee stipulate delivery within a specified time, according to the nature of the items to be supplied, and requests the Secretary-General to notify the Committee of all applications for humanitarian items which are included in the list to which the export/import mechanism approved by resolution 1051 (1996) applies;

26. Decides that Hajj pilgrimage flights which do not transport cargo into or out of Iraq are exempt from the provisions of paragraph 3 of resolution 661 (1990) and resolution 670 (1990), provided timely notification of each flight is made to the Committee established by resolution 661 (1990), and requests the Secretary-General to make the necessary arrangements, for approval by the Security Council, to provide for reasonable expenses related to the Hajj pilgrimage to be met by funds in the escrow account established by resolution 986 (1995);

27. Calls upon the Government of Iraq:
    (i) to take all steps to ensure the timely and equitable distribution of all humanitarian goods, in particular medical supplies, and to remove and avoid delays at its warehouses;
    (ii) to address effectively the needs of vulnerable groups, including children, pregnant women, the disabled, the elderly and the mentally ill among others, and to allow freer access, without any discrimination, including on the basis of religion or nationality, by United Nations agencies and humanitarian organizations to all areas and sections of the population for evaluation of their nutritional and humanitarian condition;
    (iii) to prioritize applications for humanitarian goods under the arrangements set out in resolution 987 (1995) and related resolutions;
    (iv) to ensure that those involuntarily displaced receive humanitarian assistance without the need to demonstrate that they have resided for six months in their places of temporary residence;
    (v) to extend full cooperation to the United Nations office for Project Services mine-clearance programme in the three northern Governorates of Iraq and to consider the initiation of the demining efforts in other Governorates;

28. Requests the Secretary-General to report on the progress made in meeting the humanitarian needs of the Iraqi people and on the revenues necessary to meet those needs, including recommendations on necessary additions to the current allocation for oil spare parts and equipment, on the basis of a comprehensive survey of the condition of the Iraqi oil production sector, not later than 60 days from the date of the adoption of this resolution and updated thereafter as necessary;

29. Expresses its readiness to authorize additions to the current allocation for oil spare parts and equipment, on the basis of the report and recommendations requested in paragraph 28 above, in order to meet the humanitarian purposes set out in resolution 986 (1995) and related resolutions;

30. Requests the Secretary-General to establish a group of experts, including oil industry experts, to report within 100 days of the date of adoption of this resolution on Iraq's existing petroleum production and export capacity and to make recommendations, to be updated as necessary, on alternatives for increasing Iraq's petroleum production and export capacity in a manner consistent

with the purposes of relevant resolutions, and on the options for involving foreign oil companies in Iraq's oil sector, including investments, subject to appropriate monitoring and controls;

31. Notes that in the event of the Council acting as provided for in paragraph 33 of this resolution to suspend the prohibitions referred to in that paragraph, appropriate arrangements and procedures will need, subject to paragraph 35 below, to be agreed by the Council in good time beforehand, including suspension of provisions of resolution 986 (1995) and related resolutions;

32. Requests the Secretary-General to report to the Council on the implementation of paragraphs 15 to 30 of this resolution within 30 days of the adoption of this resolution;

D

33. Expresses its intention, upon receipt of reports from the Executive Chairman of UNMOVIC and from the Director General of the IAEA that Iraq has cooperated in all respects with UNMOVIC and the IAEA in particular in fulfilling the work programmes in all the aspects referred to in paragraph 7 above, for a period of 120 days after the date on which the Council is in receipt of reports from both UNMOVIC and the IAEA that the reinforced system of ongoing monitoring and verification is fully operational, to suspend with the fundamental objective of improving the humanitarian situation in Iraq and securing the implementation of the Council's resolutions, for a period of 120 days renewable by the Council, and subject to the elaboration of effective financial and other operational measures to ensure that Iraq does not acquire prohibited items, prohibitions against the import of commodities and products originating in Iraq, and prohibitions against the sale, supply and delivery to Iraq of civilian commodities and products other than those referred to in paragraph 24 of resolution 687 (1991) or those to which the mechanism established by resolution 1051 (1996) applies;

34. Decides that in reporting to the Council for the purposes of paragraph 33 above, the Executive Chairman of UNMOVIC will include as a basis for his assessment the progress made in completing the tasks referred to in paragraph 7 above;

35. Decides that if at any time the Executive Chairman of UNMOVIC or the Director General of the IAEA report that Iraq is not cooperating in all respects with UNMOVIC or the IAEA or if Iraq is in the process of acquiring any prohibited items, the suspension of the prohibitions referred to in paragraph 33 above shall terminate on the fifth working day following the report, unless the Council decides to the contrary;

36. Expresses its intention to approve arrangements for effective financial and other operational measures, including on the delivery of and payment for authorized civilian commodities and products to be sold or supplied to Iraq, in order to ensure that Iraq does not acquire prohibited items in the event of suspension of the prohibitions referred to in paragraph 33 above, to begin the elaboration of such measures not later than the date of the receipt of the initial reports referred to in paragraph 33 above, and to approve such arrangements before the Council decision in accordance with that paragraph;

37. Further expresses its intention to take steps, based on the report and recommendations requested in paragraph 30 above, and consistent with the purpose of resolution 986 (1995) and related resolutions, to enable Iraq to increase its petroleum production and export capacity, upon receipt of the reports relating to the cooperation in all respects with UNMOVIC and the IAEA referred to in paragraph 33 above;

38. Reaffirms its intention to act in accordance with the relevant provisions of resolution 687 (1991) on the termination of prohibitions referred to in that resolution;

39. Decides to remain actively seized of the matter and expresses its intention to consider action in accordance with paragraph 33 above no later than 12 months from the date of the adoption of this resolution provided the conditions set out in paragraph 3 above have been satisfied by Iraq.

United Nations–Yemen

UNITED NATIONS COMMISSION ON HUMAN RIGHTS

Decision Relating to Yemen Adopted Without a Vote at the Commission's 22nd (Closed) Meeting on 31 March 2000

The Commission on Human Rights,

Having examined the material relating to the human rights situation in Yemen brought before it under Economic and Social resolution 1503 (XL VIII),

Expressing concern about numerous instances of political violence in the country,

Welcoming the observations, received from the Government of Yemen,

Recalling the establishment in 1998 of the Supreme Committee for Human Rights, and *encouraging* it to develop its full potential as an independent national human rights institution in accordance with the Principles relating to the status of national institutions ('The Paris Principles'),

Commending the Government of Yemen for having hosted the Asia-Pacific Workshop on Strategies for the Realization of Social, Economic and Cultural Rights and the Right to Development from 5 to 7 March 2000,

Taking note with satisfaction of the Memorandum of Intent between the United Nations Office of the High Commissioner for Human Rights and the Government of Yemen on the Mutual Agreement to Co-operate in the Development and Implementation of Comprehensive Programmes for the Promotion and Protection of Human Rights in Yemen signed in Sana'a on 6 February 2000,

Encouraging the Government of Yemen to seek early implementation of the said Memorandum of Intent,

1. *Decides* to discontinue consideration of the human rights situation in Yemen under Economic and Social Council resolution 1503 (XL VIII),

2. *Requests* the Secretary-General to communicate this decision to the Government of Yemen.

Yemen–Saudi Arabia

THE JEDDAH TREATY REGARDING THE SETTLEMENT OF THE
INTERNATIONAL LAND AND MARITIME BOUNDARIES
BETWEEN THE REPUBLIC OF YEMEN AND THE KINGDOM OF
SAUDI ARABIA

Signed in Jeddah, on Monday (12 June 2000)

Article 1

The two Contracting Parties confirm that the Ta'if Treaty, and the Annexes thereto
– including the Borders Reports attached thereto – is mandatory and legitimate; and
also confirm their commitment as regards the Memorandum of Understanding,
signed by the two countries on the 27th day of Ramadhan, 1415 AH.

Article 2

The final and permanent dividing boundary line between the Republic of Yemen and
the Kingdom of Saudi Arabia, is as follows:

(a) Part One: this part begins from the coastal point in the Red Sea [The Exact
Sea pier: Ras Al-Ma'wag Shami Radeef Kurad Outlet], with the co-ordinates
thereof: longitude (8,14,24,16) North – latitude (7,19,46,42) East; and ends
at Jabal Al-Tha'r, with the co-ordinates thereof: (58,21,44) East – (00,26,17)
North. The co-ordinates details are stated in Annex No. 1. The identity of
villages situated on the line of this part of the boundaries is defined according
to what has been stipulated in the Ta'if Treaty and Annexes thereto – including
the tribal affiliation thereof. If any of the co-ordinates is located in a position –
or positions – of a village – or villages – of one of the Parties: the reference for
proving to which Party the village – or villages – belong, shall be their affiliation
to one of the two Parties; and the course of the boundary line – while fixing
the signs – shall be modified, accordingly.

(b) Part Two: concerning that part of the boundary line which has not been
demarcated: the two Contracting Parties have agreed on the demarcation of
this part – amicably. This part begins from Jabal Al-Tha'r, the co-ordinates of
which are defined herein above, and ends at the geographical locality point at
the conjunction of Latitude (19 North) and Longitude (52 East), the
co-ordinates details of which are stated in Annex No. 2.

(c) Part Three: this is the maritime part of the boundaries, which begins at the
land point on the sea coast [The Exact Sea Pier: Ras Al-Ma'wag Shami, Radeef
Kurad Outlet], the co-ordinates of which are stated herein above, and ends

with the end of the maritime boundaries between the two countries, the co-ordinates details of which are stated in Annex No. 3.

Article 3

(1) For the purpose of laying signs [posts] on the boundary line, beginning with the junction point of the boundaries of the two countries with the boundaries of the brotherly Sultanate of Oman – on the geographical locality of the intersection point of latitude (19° North) and longitude (52° East) – and ending at the exact sea pier: Ras Al-Ma'wag Shami Radeef-Kurad Exit, with the co-ordinates thereof stated in Annexe No. 1: the two Contracting Parties shall authorize an international company to undertake a field survey for all the land and maritime boundaries. The executing, specialized company – and the joint team from the two contracting sides – shall strictly adhere to the distances and directions between each point and the point next to it, as well as the rest of the descriptions stated in the Boundaries Reports attached to the Ta'if Treaty, which are provisions binding upon the two Parties.

(2) The international specialized company shall prepare detailed maps, as regards the land boundary line between the two countries. The said maps shall – after being signed by the Representatives of the Republic of Yemen and the Kingdom of Saudi Arabia – be taken to represent official maps illustrating the demarcated boundaries between the two countries, and shall form part and parcel of this Treaty. The two Contracting Parties shall execute an agreement, with regard to covering the costs of the works of the company authorized to construct the signs along the demarcated boundary line between the two countries.

Article 4

The two Contracting Parties hereby confirm their commitment, under Article 5 of the Ta'if Treaty, as regards the evacuation of any military post, the distance of which is less than five kilometres, along the whole boundary line demarcated according to the Boundaries Reports attached to the Ta'if Treaty.

However, the Boundary Line which has not been demarcated, beginning with Jabal Al-Tha'r, up to the meeting point of longitude (19° North) and longitude (52° East), is governed by Annex No. 4 attached to this Treaty.

Article 5

This Treaty shall come into force after the approval thereof shall have been followed, in accordance with the respective appropriate procedures in the two Contracting Countries – as well as the exchange of the approval deeds, by the two countries.

On Behalf of the Republic of Yemen:
Abdul-Kader Abdul-Rehman Ba-Gammal,
Deputy Prime-Minister and Foreign Minister.

On Behalf of the Kingdom of Saudi Arabia:
Su'ood Al-Faisal
Foreign Minister

Jeddah 10/3/1421 AH Corresponding to 10/6/2000 AD

(Signature)	(Signature)
On Behalf of R. Yemen	On Behalf of K.S. Arabia
A.K.Ba-Gammal,	S.Al-Faisal
Deputy Prime Minister	Foreign Minister
and Foreign Minister	

Jeddah 10/3/1421 AH, corresponding to 12/6/2000 AD

Annex No. 1

The Geographical Co-ordinates for the Signs Provided for in the Boundaries Reports –
Attached to the Ta'if Treaty:–
Appendix No. 1: Attached.
Appendix No. 2: Attached.
Appendix No. 3: Attached.
Appendix No. 4: Attached.
[These appendices are not included here.]

Annex No. 2

The Maritime Boundaries Delimitation Line between The Republic of Yemen and
The Kingdom of Saudi Arabia:

1. The line begins from the land point on the exact sea coast: [The Exact Sea Pier:
    Ras Al-Ma'wag Shami, Radeef Kurad Exit], with the following co-ordinates:
    (8,14,24,16/North) – (7,19,46,42/East).
2. The line proceeds in a straight line, parallel to longitudes until it meets latitude
    (00,09,42/East).
3. The line curves, in a north-westerly direction, until it reaches the point with the
    following co-ordinates: (8,14,24,16/North) – (00,09,42/East).
4. From there, the line proceeds in a straight line, parallel to longitudes, in a
    westerly direction, up to the end of maritime boundaries between the two
    countries, at a point with the following co-ordinates:- (24,17,16) – (00,47,41).

Annex No. 3

The Geographical Co-ordinates for the Demarcation of the Second Part of the Land
Boundaries: the Connection Point of latitude (19° North] and longitude [52° East]
– where the Boundaries between Yemen, Saudi Arabia and Oman meet.

Annex No. 4

Of the International Boundaries Treaty between The Kingdom of Saudi Arabia and
The Republic of Yemen, Regarding the Organization of the Rights of Pasture, for
the Saudi Arabian and Yemeni farmers, and of Defining the Positions of the Armed
Forces on the two Sides of the second part of the Boundary Line between the Two
Countries – Referred to in this Treaty – and the Exploitation of the Joint Natural
Wealth Along the Land Boundary Line Separating the Two Countries:

Article 1

(a) The Pasture area on both sides of the second part of the boundary line –
     referred to in this Treaty – shall be defined as twenty kilometres.
(b) Shepherds from both countries have the right to make use of the pasture areas,
     as well as the water resources, on both sides of this part of the boundary line,
     in accordance with the prevailing tribal customs and usage there, over a distance
     not exceeding twenty kilometres.

(c)   The two Contracting Parties shall conduct annual consultations for fixing the crossing points, for the purposes of pasture – in accordance with the prevailing pasture conditions and circumstances.

Article 2

Shepherds – who are nationals of the Kingdom of Saudi Arabia, and nationals of the Republic of Yemen – shall be exempted:

(a)   as regards residency and passport regulations: instead, permit cards shall be given to them, from the respective authorities concerned;
(b)   as regards taxes and duties on the personal belongings, foodstuff and other consumer goods which they carry with them. This does not prohibit either Party from imposing customs duties on the animals and commodities for trading purposes.

Article 3

Either of the Contracting Parties shall be entitled to impose limitations and conditions – which that Party deems appropriate – as regards the number of vehicles accompanying the shepherds back into the territory thereof; as well as the kind and number of firearms which the shepherds are permitted to carry: provided that they have licences to this effect – together with the identity of the holder of the licence – from the respective authorities concerned.

Article 4

In the event of the spread of endemic diseases infecting animal wealth: either Party shall have the right to impose the necessary precautionary measures, and impose restrictions as regards the import and export of the infected animals. The authorities concerned, in the two countries, shall co-operate with a view to preventing – as far as possible – the spread of the disease.

Article 5

Neither of the Contracting Parties shall be entitled to mass its armed forces at a distance less than twenty kilometres – on either side of the second part of the boundary line, which is referred to in this Treaty – and the activities of either Party shall be confined to running security patrols with ordinary weapons.

Article 6

Should joint natural wealth – sufficient for excavation and investment – be discovered along the boundary line between the two countries, commencing with the exact sea point: [Ras Al-Ma'wag Shami Radeef Kurad Outlet], up to the connecting point – longitude (East 19) and latitude (North 52): the two Contracting Parties shall conduct the necessary negotiations on joint exploitation of that wealth.

Article 7

This Annex shall be considered part and parcel of this Treaty, and shall be approved in accordance with the appropriate machinery in the two countries.

Legislation

Yemen

PRIVATIZATION LAW NO. 45/1999

In the Name of the People,

The President of the Republic,

Having perused the Constitution of the Republic of Yemen, and after the consent of the House of Representatives, promulgates the following law:

Part 1: Title, Definitions, Aims, Main Principles and Criteria

Chapter One: Title and Definitions

Section 1: This Law shall be cited as the Privatization Law, and shall regulate the procedures of privatization of the economic enterprises which are owned by the state, provided that they are not inconsistent with the provisions of the Constitution.

Section 2: For the purposes of the application of this law, the following words and expressions shall carry the meanings shown below, unless the context shows otherwise:

Republic: The Republic of Yemen;

Government: The Government of the Republic of Yemen;

Regulations: The Executive Regulations of this Law;

Privatization: The transfer of public property to private property, or the transfer of the operation thereof to third parties;

Economic Enterprise: The economic enterprise provided for in Law No. 35/1991, as amended by Law No. 7/1997, in connection with public corporations, companies or authorities, owned by the state, in whole or in part;

Higher Committee: the Higher Privatization Committee established in accordance with section 6 of this Law;

Technical Bureau: The Technical Bureau of Privatization established in accordance with section 9 of this Law.

Chapter Two: Aims and Objectives

Section 3: The Law defines the aims and objectives of privatization as realizing the following:

419

(a)   to emphasize the state's role in the administration of the economy, in accordance with market theories;

(b)   to reduce the state's burden, by reducing the payments by the state, arising from the state's public ownership of economic enterprises;

(c)   to increase the efficiency of the operation of the economic enterprises according to competitive criteria;

(d)   to encourage private ownership or investment on a competitive basis, and in such a way as not to lead to monopoly, as well as to realize widespread participation through the sale thereof;

(e)   to guarantee the influx of new investments as well as new, modern and advanced technology, which is not dangerous as regards the environment;

(f)   to encourage the establishment of a stock exchange.

Chapter Three: Main Principles and Criteria

Section 4: The main principles and criteria which guide the process of privatization, and which are mandatory upon the Higher Privatization Committee, the Technical Bureau of Privatization and the Ministries concerned with privatization, are the following:

(a)   publicity and transparency: which means that the steps and procedures for the process of privatization shall be according to competitive criteria, where the public at large take part, failing which the process takes the form of bids or direct negotiations: (i) with a list of at least five qualified companies; (ii) terms of reference – public and privatized – for direct negotiations; (iii) all concerned parties participate in the negotiations – including the Audit Organization – with the said companies; (iv) declaration of the results of the negotiations with the said companies, with comparison thereof, and the settlement on the basis of the stated results;

(b)   extension of the foundation of ownership, which means encouragement to make workers, cooperatives, citizens, unions – specialized and professional, or general – owners of all or part of the economic enterprises subject to privatization;

(c)   neutrality of evaluation, which means that the evaluation of the assets of economic enterprises is undertaken by neutral specialized consultants;

(d)   freedom of legitimate competition and prohibition of monopoly, to ensure that the process of privatization does not lead to the creation or existence of monopolies;

(e)   fixing a ceiling on time, which means that the Privatization Technical Bureau and the other government organs concerned shall be under an obligation to implement all steps and procedures in the privatization programmes and plans, efficiently and within the time fixed, in accordance with the Regulations issued under this Law.

Section 5: Under all circumstances, privatization processes and procedures will not commence – within the framework of any of the sectors of the national economy – except after freeing that sector. The Higher Privatization Committee will notify the Standing Committee concerned, in the House of Representatives, of all the privatization processes, and will furnish the afore-mentioned Committee with a complete set of the documents of each privatization process, within one month, with effect from the date of implementation thereof.

The privatization process – in whole or in part – shall be effected through the following methods:

(a) offering shares to the general public, so that the method shall be accorded priority, and with a view to realization of the aims and objectives of this Law;
(b) participation of the workers, through owning all or a defined proportion of the shares of the economic enterprise;
(c) contracts of partnership in the capital and operation;
(d) contracts of management or lease;
(e) sale of the assets owned by the state;
(f) sale of the shares, or the ratio owned by the state, in the mixed sector – so lomg as this is not inconsistent with the Laws in force, and does not lead to a monopoly.

Part II: The Organizations Conferred with the Authority to Implement Privatization

Chapter One: The Higher Committee and Sub-Committees

Section 6: There shall be established by a Republican Resolution a Higher Privatization Committee, consisting of the Prime Minister and the Ministers concerned.
    The responsibilities of the Higher Privatization Committee shall be the following:

(a) approval of the studies and proposals relating to the methodology and means of implementation;
(b) approval of the executive programmes and confirmation of the model proposals of all the transactions and contracts, including transfer of ownership or reserving strategic shares, in accordance with the methods of privatization specified in this Law, and submission thereof to the Cabinet for approval;
(c) appointment of the ad hoc Boards of Management of the economic enterprises, approval for privatization of which, according to the provisions of this Law, shall have been obtained;
(d) preparation of the economic enterprises subject to privatization as regards financial, administrative and legal aspects; and confirmation of the proposals relating to the winding up, merger, amalgamation and splitting up of economic enterprises, branches and divisions thereof, which are necessary, due to the economic and organizational interests, prior to the process of privatization, and submission of recommendations in this connection to the Cabinet for approval;
(e) affirmation of the specifications of the privatization programmes submitted to the Technical Bureau of Privatization right from the initial preparation stage until the final implementation stage, and confirmation of the Regulations and Directions regulating the various stages;
(f) affirmation of the model contracts and documents relating to the privatization transactions, the system of leasing, the issuing of regulations regarding the appropriate working machinery for subscription and negotiability of shares and bonds, and the system of regulation and control of the shares and bonds connected with privatization;
(g) approval of the training and qualifying plans to implement all the transactions connected with the privatization programmes;
(h) naming of the members of the negotiating teams as necessary and in the public interest, in accordance with section 4/a of this Law.

Section 7: The Chairman of the Higher Privatization Committee shall issue the

Standing Orders regulating the work of the Higher Privatization Committee, especially the minutes of the proceedings, in addition to the resolutions and follow-up of the implementation thereof.

Section 8: There shall be established, in the Ministries or economic enterprises under their supervision, ad hoc committees, under the chairmanship of the Minister or anyone authorized by him, and these ad hoc committees shall commence work with effect from the beginning of the process of privatization, and shall cease work when that process shall have come to an end.

The responsibilities of the ad hoc committees shall be the supervision of the privatization activities and follow up with the corporations and authorities under the enterprise. They shall perform their responsibilities, in accordance with the provisions of this Law and the Regulations issued thereunder under the supervision of the Higher Privatization Committee and shall implement the Regulations thereof, in coordination with the Technical Bureau of Privatization. The assignment of the ad hoc committees shall terminate immediately their job comes to a close.

Chapter Two: The Technical Bureau of Privatization

Section 9: There shall be established an advisory technical bureau, called the Technical Bureau of Privatization, which shall at the same time act as the Secretariat of the Higher Privatization Committee.

The Technical Bureau of Privatization shall comprise a group of personnel, who shall be full-time, highly qualified and experienced in the specializations and fields which are required in accordance with the tasks assigned to the Technical Bureau of Privatization.

Section 10: The Director-General of the Technical Bureau of Privatization shall be a full-time appointment, and he shall perform the responsibilities of the Executive-Director of the Technical Bureau of Privatization as well as of administrative and financial affairs, in order to implement the tasks of the Bureau, under the supervision of the Chairman of the Higher Privatization Committee or representatives thereof.

Section 11: The responsibilities of the Technical Bureau of Privatization shall be the following:

(a) Laying down the studies and proposals, and defining the programmes of privatizations, which shall include:
   (i)   the stage for preparation;
   (ii)   the evaluation;
   (iii) submission of proposals with a view to taking decisions;
   (iv)   follow-up of implementation by the Ministries concerned;
   (v)   follow-up of analysis and evaluation of the post-privatization stage;
(b) studying and reviewing the proposals regarding specifying the methods and means of privatization, restructuring and submitting proposals and recommendations relating thereto;
(c) submission of the proposals to the Technical Committees, as well as the sub-committees, to the Higher Privatization Committee regarding the winding up, merger, amalgamation or splitting up of the enterprise owned, or under its control after a review shall have been done, with a view to approval;
(d) preparation of the proposals as regards the Regulations and Procedures of the Technical Committees;
(e) laying down organizational and Directive Regulations for the privatization process relating to every stage, which is provided for in paragraph (o) of this

section, and submission thereof to the Higher Privatization Commission for approval;

(f) preparation of the proposals concerned with the labour force in the economic enterprise under privatization, provided for in section 29, and proposing all kinds of material and moral incentives and assistance, in order to alleviate the consequences of the privatization process and procedures *vis-à-vis* the labour force;

(g) preparation of model contracts for each of the methods of privatization;

(h) participation in the preparation of the relevant documents of the bids, offers and auction procedures, and requirements of the notices thereof for the public;

(i) rendering assistance in submitting opinions and consultations as regards defining the appropriate mechanisms for the purchase and/or sale of the shares and financial documents/papers of the economic enterprises subject to privatization;

(j) ensuring the proper application of the notice method, clarity and neutrality – through publication and advertisement – when implementing the various stages of the privatization process and participation in making public the programmes for the organization and arrangement of seminars and workshops concerned with the privatization process and information media: readable, audible and viewable [or: press, radio and television];

(k) rendering assistance as regards the privatization process;

(l) publication of the results of privatization through the information media;

(m) submission of periodic reports to the Higher Privatization Committee, as regards the privatization process and activities;

(n) keeping the appropriate accounts records, as well as the reports regarding the financial affairs;

(o) submission of proposals for financial and technical assistance requests, as regards privatization strategies from international organizations and other donor countries which support the privatization programmes;

(p) control or supervision of the privatization process, and preparation of periodic reports concerning those economic enterprises which have already been privatized;

(q) carrying out and undertaking all the work and transactions, should that be necessary, with a view to realizing the aims and objectives of this Law.

Section 12: All the present boards of directors of the economic enterprises are under an obligation to provide whatever is requested by the Technical Bureau of Privatization, or the branches thereof, information, data and studies, and shall in particular provide the following:

(a) assessment of their needs, as regards the assistance and technical services required for the application of all works related to the privatization programmes of each Committee;

(b) provision of the necessary facilities for the experts and consultants, authorized by the Technical Bureau of Privatization, with a view to achieving the required works;

(c) adherence to the rules and regulations of works, according to the directives issued by the Technical Bureau of Privatization, as well as punctuality and confidentiality.

Section 13: The Director-General of the Technical Bureau of Privatization may, whenever necessity shall so warrant, take advice from specialized consultants, with a view to accomplishing the tasks assigned to the Technical Bureau of Privatization, in coordination with the Ministries and Central Organs concerned, through:

(a)   secondment for a period limited in accordance with the legislation governing secondment;
(b)   signing of model contracts, to accomplish consultancy tasks, for specialized topics in particular with university cadres, or with specialists engaged by specialized consultancy firms, which operate in accordance with the Laws and Regulations in force; and
(c)   making use of, or resorting to, Arab and foreign experts, specialists in the field of privatization, provided that a local counterpart shall be engaged for the specified period.

Part III: The Guarantees, Conditions and Regulatory Rules

Chapter One: Guarantees and Conditions

Section 14: The Technical Bureau of Privatization shall undertake financial and legal studies and analysis appropriate for every economic enterprise subject to privatization. Should the information and data available be insufficient to undertake the financial and legal studies and analysis, the Higher Privatization Committee may decide to evaluate the economic enterprise by neutral technical consultants, as an exceptional case.

Section 15: All decisions relating to periods and methods appropriate for privatization of the economic enterprise, in whole or in part, are subject to the jurisdiction as well as responsibility of the Cabinet. All decisions shall be taken in the form of executive programmes, acting upon the proposals of the Higher Privatization Committee, in accordance with section 5 of this Law.

Section 16: The state shall guarantee that the new owner – whether an individual or body corporate – shall obtain all the rights of the transfer of title to the property, including areas of land sufficient for the various purposes of the project, in accordance with the contracts of lease or sale, provided that the model contracts shall have been approved by the Higher Privatization Committee, in accordance with the laws in force.

Section 17: The state shall guarantee that the newly entitled owners – whether individuals or bodies corporate – and those operating the economic enterprises, shall be granted all the incentives as well as the facilities granted to all the investors, in accordance with the laws and legislation in force.

Section 18: The Cabinet shall be endowed with the powers to make it mandatory upon the Governor of the Central Bank to reserve the nominal share in the capital of the economic enterprise, provided that such special rights shall be included in the Articles of Association of the share-holding company – established in accordance with section 22 of this Law, enabling the government to reserve the special rights through which they shall become entitled to intervene in whatsoever may effect the supreme public interests. Under all circumstances, and irrespective of the form and substance of privatization, the Cabinet shall guarantee that privatization shall not be repugnant to the supreme public interest.

Section 19: Any person – whether citizen or foreigner – shall be entitled to participate in the processes of privatization which are consistent with the provisions of this Law, or any Regulations issued thereunder.

Section 20: The government shall guarantee the continuation of the activity of the economic enterprise, after the privatization thereof, and shall guarantee the prohibition of utilizing the lands thereof for purposes other than those purposes on the basis of which the economic enterprise has been privatized.

Section 21:

(a) No member/s of the Higher Privatization Committee or the Technical Bureau of Privatization shall communicate to any person/s any special information which may give that person/s – or third parties, in any process, or processes, of privatization an advantage over another person/s. In this event, the member/s, who has/have communicated the information, shall be liable to a maximum imprisonment of two years, or to a minimum fine of YR 500,000, or to whatever greater punishment provided for in any other law in force.

(b) No member/s of the Higher Privatization Committee or the employee/s of the Technical Bureau of Privatization shall – directly or indirectly – have an interest or connection in any of the processes of privatization.

Chapter Two: The Regulatory Rules

Section 22:

(a) The economic enterprise which is owned – in whole or in part by the state, and which is included in privatization programme/s affirmed by the Higher Privatization Committee, and approved by the Cabinet – shall be transferred to a share-holding company or a limited liability company, in accordance with the provisions of this Law and the legislation in force in connection with the commercial companies, and shall be considered a body corporate under the private law, after its assets *in rem* and *in personam*, goodwill and the other investments have been evaluated, and transfer thereof to shares to be deposited under the safe custody of the Governor of the Central Bank, *ex officio*, on behalf of the Republic.

(b) Whenever it shall be evident, for the Higher Privatization Committee, that the establishment of any such company is not viable, the Higher Privatization Committee may decide to wind up the economic enterprise, in accordance with Law No. 35/1991 – as amended by Law No. 7/1997 – in connection with Public Corporations, Authorities and Companies – without necessity to transfer it into a share-holding company or a limited liability company, in accordance with section 5 (f) of this Law.

Section 23: A company established in accordance with section 22 of this Law may retain the name of the privatized economic enterprise, and it may also choose another name commensurate with its purposes. The capital of the company, and the value of each share, shall be fixed in accordance with the provisions of this Law and the other legislation in force, in connection with commercial companies.

Section 24: The company, established in accordance with section 22 of this Law, shall carry out its activities in accordance with the provisions of this Law and the other legislation in force, in connection with commercial companies. All the organs concerned shall be under an obligation to register the company, in accordance with the provisions of this Law and other legislation in force, which shall grant it all the rights and obligations of companies.

Section 25: All the rights and obligations of the privatized economic enterprise shall be transferred to the new companies, established in accordance with section 22 of this Law, with effect from the date of the Cabinet's approval as regards its establishment. The afore-mentioned economic enterprise shall, with effect from the date of the Cabinet's approval, be considered as having been wound up, or dissolved, which shall entail striking it off the special register for the purpose, within a period specified in the resolution of the Cabinet's approval, provided that that period shall not – under any circumstances – exceed thirty days.

Section 26: The workers, regarding the number of whom there has been agreement of their transfer from the economic enterprise – which has been privatized – to the company which has been established, in accordance with section 22 of this Law – shall be transferred on the same previous conditions: as regards salaries; monthly bonus; allowances and other incentives, in accordance with the laws and legislation in force. Their previous periods of service shall be considered as continuous. Should the conditions of service in the new entity be better, the workers shall be treated accordingly.

Section 27: The owner of this new entity shall be under an obligation to retain the workers transferred to it, for a period the minimum of which shall be five years, the exception being anyone who is convicted, by a final judgment passed by a competent court, of an offence punishable by law.

Section 28: In order to ensure the widest possible public purchase, priority shall be accorded those workers – whether or not they have been transferred to the entity which has been privatized – who desire to become shareholders.

Section 29: Each economic enterprise, regarding which a decision has been taken to subject it to privatization – in whole or in part – shall be under an obligation to:

(a) abide by the provisions of this Law and implement the regulations and directions issued by the Higher Privatization Committee and the Technical Bureau of Privatization;

(b) keep registers regarding its work, and records regarding its accounts, where all the data shall be stated;

(c) prepare periodical financial data, and subject it to review, measurement and assessment;

(d) keep a register of the assets *in rem* and compare it with the financial data;

(e) not to do any act, or acts, which lead to the damage of the assets, and not to shoulder any obligations – except those obligations which are essential for carrying out the normal work – without having to obtain prior written approval from the Technical Bureau of Privatization, after the consent of the Higher Privatization Committee shall have been received;

(f) refrain from taking any action, or step, which is likely to cause confusion regarding the work and production.

Section 30: The provisions of section 22 of this Law shall not be applicable as regards those economic enterprises which have been privatized in accordance with the method of management or lease.

Section 31: In the event that the decision shall have been taken to sell the share of the state in the mixed company, the following shall be applied:

(a) adhering to the terms and conditions establishing the mixed company;

(b) negotiating with the partners, with a view to reaching an agreement;

(c) applying the provisions of this Law.

Part IV: The Financial and General Provisions

Chapter One: Financial Provisions

Section 32:

(a) All the proceeds of privatization shall be deposited in a special fund, called

Fund of the Proceeds of Privatization – including the donations and local and foreign finances for the privatization projects. An account shall be opened at the Central Bank, and shall be included in the General Budget – as a special fund – in order to finance the economic and social development projects.

(b) There shall be an independent budget for the Higher Privatization Committee, the Technical Bureau of Privatization thereof and the branches thereof, at the Ministries and the economic enterprises thereunder, approved by the Higher Privatization Committee – the preparation of which, as well as the expenditure for which, shall be in accordance with the Financial Law and the Executive Regulations thereof.

Chapter Two: General Provisions

Section 33: Any chairman of a board of directors, general manager, member/s of boards of directors, any other official, or worker, in the economic enterprise which has been privatized, shall not be immune or exempted or excused from any legal accountability, as a result of having committed an act punishable by Law, prior to the transfer of title *vis-à-vis* all rights and obligations to the company established in accordance with section 22 of this Law.

Section 34: Any provision in any law or legislation, prior to the coming into force of this Law, which is inconsistent with the provisions of this Law, shall be repealed.

Section 35: The Prime Minister shall issue the Regulations, Resolutions and Rules necessary for the application of this Law.

Section 36: This Law shall come into force with effect from the enactment thereof, and shall be published in the Official Gazette.

Enacted at the Republican Presidency – Sana‘a,
on 17th Rajab/1420 AH,
corresponding to 26th October/1999 AD
‘Ali Abdalla Saleh
President of the Republic

Egypt

EXTRACTS FROM LAW NO. 17 OF THE YEAR 1999 PROMULGATING THE COMMERCIAL CODE

The headings of the chapters of this law are as follows:

FIRST: Law No. 17/1999 Promulgating the Commercial Code

---

*   Translated by Kosheri, Rashed & Riad, Legal Consultants & Attorneys at Law,
    16, Maamal El Sokkar St., Garden City, Cairo 11451, Egypt.

Part II, Chapter 1: Transfer of Technology

Article 72

1. The provisions of this Chapter shall apply to each contract for transfer of technology to be used in the Arab Republic of Egypt, whether such transfer is international lying across the regional borders of Egypt, or inland, without taking into consideration in both cases the nationality of the parties to the agreement or their places of residence.
2. The provisions of this Chapter shall also apply to each agreement for transfer of technology that is concluded by virtue of a separate contract or within another contract.

Article 73

The transfer of technology contract is an agreement according to which the (supplier of technology) undertakes to transfer, against payment, technical information to the (importer of technology) to use it in a special technical way, for the production or development of a specific commodity or for the installation or operation of machines or equipment, or for the provision of services. The mere sale, purchase, lease, or rental of commodities shall not be considered a transfer of technology. Nor shall sale of trade marks or commercial names, or licensing their use, unless this is set forth as part of, or is concerned with the transfer of technology contract.

Article 74

1. The Technology Transfer Contract has to be concluded in writing, otherwise it shall be null and void.
2. The Contract has to comprise a statement of the know-how elements and ancilliaries that are to be transferred to the importer of the technology. Mention of this statement may be accompanied by feasibility studies, instructions, designs, engineering drawings, charts, pictures, computer software and other know-how defining documents, in appendices that are attached to and considered an inseparable part of the contract.

Article 75

Any condition prescribed in the Technology Transfer Contract, which restricts the freedom of the importer in its use, development, acquaintance of the product or its advertisement, may be invalidated. This shall apply in particular to the conditions binding the importer with one of the following requirements:

(a) accepting the improvements introduced by the supplier of the technology, and paying their value;
(b) prohibiting the introduction of improvements or modifications to the technology to suit the local conditions or the conditions of the importer's establishment, as well as prohibiting the acquisition of another technology similar to or competing with the technology subject of the contract;

(c)   use of specific trademarks to distinguish the commodities for which the technology was used in their production;

(d)   limiting the volume of production, its price, the method of its distribution or its export;

(e)   participation of the supplier in running the establishment of the importer or his interference in choosing its permanent employees;

(f)   purchase of the raw materials, equipment, machines, apparatuses, or spare parts for operating the technology, from the supplier alone, or from the establishments exclusively specified by him;

(g)   restricting the sale of the production, or the delegation for its sale exclusively to the supplier or the persons which he defines.

The foregoing shall apply unless any of these conditions is prescribed in the technology transfer contract, with the aim of protecting the consumers of the producer, or to safeguard a serious and legal interest of the technology supplier.

Article 76

The supplier of technology has to disclose the following to the importer, in the contract, or during the negotiations preceding its conclusion:

(a)   the risks that might occur from using the technology, and in particular those connected with the environment, public health, or the safety of lives or property. He shall also inform him about the methods he knows of to avoid these risks;

(b)   the judiciary actions and other obstructions that might impede the use of technology-related rights, and in particular those connected with patents;

(c)   the provisions of the local law concerning the authorization to export the technology.

Article 77

1.   The supplier has to submit to the importer the information, data and other technical documents that are necessary for assimilation of the technology, and also the necessary technical services requested by the importer for operation of the technology, and in particular the expertise and training.

2.   The supplier also has to inform the importer of the improvements that he might introduce to the technology during the validity period of the contract, and he has to transfer these improvements to the importer if the latter requests him to do so.

Article 78

The supplier, during the period of validity of the contract, has to provide to the importer, upon the latter's request, the spare parts he produces and which are required for the machines or equipment used in operating his establishments, and if the supplier does not produce these parts in his own establishments, he shall advise the importer of the sources where they are available.

Article 79

The importer, in operating the technology, has to employ workers with a measure of technical skill, and to have recourse to technical experts whenever necessary, providing the selection of these workers or experts shall be among Egyptians residing in Egypt or abroad, whenever this is feasible.

Article 80

The importer shall inform the supplier of the provisions of the national legislation connected with the import of technology.

Article 81

The importer may not assign the technology he has obtained, to a third party, except with the approval of its supplier.

Article 82

1. The importer shall pay the charges for the technology and for the improvements introduced to it, at the time and place agreed upon.
2. The charges may be a lump sum payable in one or in several instalments. They may also be a share in the capital invested in operating the technology or in a portion of the yield of this operation.
3. The charges may as well be in the form of a certain quantity of the commodity, which the technology is used for its production, or raw material that is produced by the importer and which he undertakes to export to the supplier.

Article 83

1. The importer has to maintain the confidentiality of the technology he obtains and of the improvements introduced to it. He shall be accountable for the damages occurring from divulging this confidentiality whether it takes place during the stage of negotiating for the conclusion of the contract or later.
2. The supplier shall also maintain the confidentiality of the improvements introduced by the importer and transferred thereby to the supplier by virtue of a condition prescribed in the contract, and the supplier shall be liable for compensating the harm caused from divulging this confidentiality.

Article 84

Agreement may be reached that the importer of technology shall alone have the right of using it and trading in the production, providing that this right shall be limited to a specified geographical area, and to a determined period to be agreed upon by the two parties.

Article 85

1. The supplier shall guarantee the conformity of the technology and the documents attached to it, to the conditions prescribed in the contract. He shall also guarantee production of the commodity, or performance of the services agreed upon, according to the specifications prescribed in the contract, unless otherwise agreed upon in writing.
2. Each of the supplier and the importer shall separately and not jointly be liable for the harm caused to the persons, and property from using the technology or the commodity produced by applying that technology.

Article 86

Either party to the technology transfer contract may, after the lapse of five years from the date of its conclusion, request its termination or reconsideration of its terms by amending them to suit the general existing economic conditions. Submitting this request may be repeated whenever five years have elapsed unless another period is agreed upon.

Article 87

1. The Egyptian Courts shall have the jurisdiction to decide on the disputes arising from the technology transfer contract referred to in Article 72 of this Law. Agreement may be reached in settling the dispute amicably or via arbitration to be held in Egypt according to the provisions of the Egyptian Law.

2. In all cases, deciding the subject of the dispute shall be according to the provisions of the Egyptian Law, and any agreement to the contrary shall be null and void.

Chapter 5. Commercial Agency

First Section: General Provisions

Article 148

The provisions of commercial agency shall apply, if the agent's profession is to perform trading transactions for the account of third parties.

Article 149

1. If grant of the commercial agency is absolute, it shall only apply to commercial transactions.
2. If the commercial agency is granted specifically for a specified commercial transaction, the agent may perform all operations necessary for carrying out this transaction without need for permission from the principal.

Article 150

1. The Commercial Agency is granted against payment.
2. The pay shall be due to the commercial agent as soon as the transaction he is charged with is concluded. The pay shall also be due to him if he establishes that non conclusion of the transaction is due to a reason attributed to the principal.
3. In other than the two cases referred to in the previous paragraph, no pay but only a compensation shall be due to the agent for the effort he exerted, in accordance to commercial custom.
4. Not withstanding the provisions of the second paragraph of Article 709 of the Civil Code, if agreement is reached on the pay of the commercial agent, this pay shall not be subject to the estimation of the judge.

Article 151

1. The agent shall follow the instructions of the principal. If he contravenes them without acceptable justification, the principal may refuse the deal.
2. If no instructions are given by the principal concerning the deal, the agent shall delay its conclusion and ask for the instructions from the principal, unless delaying the deal will cause harm to the principal, or if the agent was delegated to work without instructions from the principal.

Article 152

If the goods or objects held by the agent for the account of the principal are threatened with quick deterioration or drop in value, while the agent has received no instructions from the agent in their respect at a suitable time, the agent may request from the concerned judge at the court within the circuit of which lies the agent's business center, to issue a court writ on a petition to sell them in a manner to be determined by the judge.

Article 153

The agent shall have the right to refrain from carrying out the work entrusted to him if performing that work will require unusual expenses and the principal has not sent these expenses to him, unless it was agreed that, or the previous dealings between the two parties demonstrated that the principal pays these expenses.

Article 154

If the agent refuses to carry out the deal entrusted to him, he shall have to notify the principal thereof immediately. In this case, the agent shall preserve the goods and other objects he holds for account of the principal until he receives instructions in their respect. If the instructions are not received at a suitable date, the agent may request from the concerned judge at the court within the circuit of which lies the centre of the agent's business to issue a court writ on a petition to deposit the goods or objects with a trustee to be appointed by the judge.

Article 155

1. The agent shall be accountable for the destruction or deterioration of the goods or objects he holds for account of the principal unless this results from causes the agent or his subordinates have nothing to do with, or from an inherent defect in the goods or the object.
2. The agent shall not be obliged to insure the objects he holds for account of the principal unless the principal asks him to do so, or if insuring the objects is an exigency of trade practices or is necessitated by the nature of the object.

Article 156

1. The agent may not designate himself as a second party to the deal he is charged to conclude, except in the following cases:

   (a) if he is so permitted by the principal;
   (b) if the instructions of the principal regarding the deal are explicit and specific and the agent carries them out precisely as instructed;
   (c) if the deal is connected with a commodity having a fixed price in the market and the agent bought it or sold it at that price.

2. The agent, in the cases mentioned in the previous section, shall not receive any pay in return for the agency.

Article 157

The third party who deals with the agent may request to be shown the agency deed, the correspondence and other documents proving or restricting the power of the agent. The restrictions imposed on the power of the agent may not be invoked *vis-à-vis* third parties unless it is established that the third party was aware of them at the time of signing the contract.

Article 158

1. The agent has to notify the principal of the deals he concludes for his account.
2. The agent has also to submit to the principal, at the time agreed upon between them or according to trade practices or previous dealings between them, an account of the works he concludes for his account. This account has to be correct. If it comprises premeditatedly incorrect data, the principal may refuse the deals connected with these data, in addition to his right to claim compensation, and the agent shall not recieve any pay for these transactions.

Article 159

1. In addition to his right to withhold the goods, the agent shall have a lien on the goods and other objects sent to him, or deposited with or delivered to him by the principal.
2. The lien shall guarantee the agent's pay, as well as the expenses and amounts he pays for or lends to the principal, and other amounts due to the agent because

of the agency, whether they are spent before delivery of the goods or objects or during their existence in the possession of the agent.

3. The lien shall be determined regardless of whether the debt arose from works connected with the goods or objects that are still in the agent's possession or with other goods or objects that were previously sent to, deposited with, or delivered to him.

Article 160

1. The agent shall not have the lien referred to in the previous article unless he is in possession of goods or objects for that account of the principal. This possession shall be realized in the following cases:

   (a) if the agent has actually received the goods or objects;
   (b) if they were placed at his disposal in the customs or in a general or special warehouse;
   (c) if he was a possessor of the goods or objects before their arrival by virtue of a bill of lading or any other transport instrument;
   (d) if he had exported them and is still possessor thereof by virtue of a bill of lading or any other transport instrument.

2. If the goods or objects subject of the lien are sold and delivered to the buyer, the agent's lien shall be transferred to the price.

Article 161

The trade agent's lien shall have precedence over all other liens, except the judiciary expenses and the taxes and duties owed to the state.

Article 162

1. The procedures of levying execution on the commercially mortgaged object shall apply to the execution on the goods and objects existing in the commercial agent's possession.

2. However, if the agent is charged to sell the goods or objects in his possession, he may levy execution on them by selling them without need to follow the procedures referred to in the previous section unless it is impossible for him to execute the instructions of the principal concerning the sale.

Article 163

Either party to the commercial agency contract may terminate the contract at all times. The compensation shall not be due unless termination of the contract occurs without prior notice or at an unsuitable time. If the contract is for a definite period, its termination has to be based upon a serious and acceptable reason, otherwise compensation shall be due.

Article 164

If the principal does not have a known domicile in Egypt, his agent's domicile shall be considered a domicile for the principal, and he may be sued and the official judiciary papers may be served to him at that domicile in connection with the works carried out by the agent for the account of his principal.

Article 165

With regard to the organization of work in the commercial agency business in Egypt, the laws and decrees related thereto shall be applicable.

Second Section: Certain Types of Commercial Agency

1. Commission Agency

Article 166

1. A commission agency is a contract by virtue of which the agent undertakes to effect in his name a legal transaction for the account of the principal.
2. In addition to the general provisions on commercial agency, the provisions prescribed in the following articles shall apply to the commission agency.

Article 167

1. If the commission agent sells at less than, or buys at higher than the price determined by the principal, the principal shall, if he desires to refuse the deal, notify the agent of his decision at the nearest time from learning of it, otherwise he shall be considered as accepting the price.
2. The principal may not refuse the deal if the commission agent accepts to bear the price difference.

Article 168

1. If the commission agent buys for account of the principal goods differing from the kind or type required by the principal, he shall not be committed to accepting them.
2. If the agent buys goods conforming to the required goods, but in a larger quantity, the principal shall only be bound to accept the quantity he required. But, if the quantity is less, then the principal shall have the choice of either accepting or refusing it.

Article 169

If the commission agent concludes a contract with better terms than those determined by the principal, the benefit shall devolve to the principal and the agent has to submit his account on the true basis upon which the deal was concluded.

Article 170

1. If the commission agent mandated to sell, grants the buyer a period to settle the price, or allows him to settle by instalments, without the principal's permission, the principal may require the agent to settle the whole price immediately, and in this case the commission agent may retain the price difference if the deal has been concluded at a higher price.
2. However, the commission agent may grant a time for settlement or allow settlement of the price by instalments without the principal's permission, if trade practices in the area where the sale was concluded provide for that, unless the principal's explicit instructions oblige him to sell with advance payment.

Article 171

If the principal's instructions provide for sale with deferred price, and the commission agent sells with advance payment, the principal may not require him to pay the price except at the maturity date determined by him, and in this case, the commission agent shall have to pay the price on the basis of deferred sale.

Article 172

1. The commission agent may not change the trademarks placed on the goods he receives from the principal or for his account unless this takes place within the limits of the law and by express authorization to do so.

2. If the commission agent holds a quantity of goods of the same type, which are sent to him from different principals, he shall have to place on each item a statement characterizing it.

Article 173

1. The commission agent may mention the name of the principle whom he deals for unless the principal instructs him not to disclose his name. Such disclosure of the principal's name shall not alter the nature of the agency as long as the agent concludes the contract in his name.
2. The commission agent shall have to disclose to the principal the name of the third party who concluded the contract with him, if the principal requires him to do so and if the commission agent refrains from disclosing the name of the third party, without acceptable justification, he may then be considered a guarantor for execution of the deal.

Article 174

1. The commission agent shall be directly responsible *vis-à-vis* the third party with whom he contracted. The third party shall also be directly responsible *vis-à-vis* the commission agent.
2. The third party who contracted with the commission agent shall not have the right of recourse against the principal, nor may the principal have recourse against the third party by lodging a direct court action unless otherwise provided by law.

Article 175

1. If the commission agent who is charged to sell becomes bankrupt before receiving the price from the buyer, the principal may directly claim from the buyer to settle the price to him.
2. If the commission agent who is charged to buy becomes bankrupt before receiving the sold goods, the principal may directly claim from the seller to deliver the sold goods to him.

Article 176

1. The commission agent shall not guarantee the settlement of obligations of the third party with whom he contracted unless he expressly pledges to guarantee him, or if it is prescribed in law or provided for in trade practices of the area wherein he exercises his activities.
2. Special pay shall be due to the guarantor commission agent, which shall be determined by the court if no agreement or trade practices exist in respect thereof.

2. Contracts Agency

Article 177

The contracts agency is a contract under which a person undertakes on a permanent basis, and in a specific area of activity to promote, negotiate and conclude transactions in the name and for the account of the principal in return for pay. His assignment may also comprise their execution in the name and for the account of the principal.

Article 178

The contract agent shall assume the exercise of his agency works and the management of his commercial activity in respect thereof, on an independent basis. He shall alone bear the expenses necessary for managing his activities.

Article 179

The principal shall not have recourse to more than one contract agent in the same area and for the same branch of activity. Nor shall the contract agent be an agent for more than one establishment exercising the same activity in the same area unless otherwise agreed upon explicitly by the two parties.

Article 180

The contract agency deed has to be recorded in writing. In it shall particularly be indicated the limits of the agency, the pay of the agent, the area of his activity, and the duration of the contract if it is for a limited period.

Article 181

If it is stipulated in the contract that the contract agent shall erect buildings for display, stores for commodities, or repair or maintenance establishments, the term of the contract shall not be for less than five years.

Article 182

1. The contract agent may not receive the rights of the principal, unless the principal grants him this right and in this case the agent shall not grant a reduction or a term without a special authorization.
2. The contract agent may receive the orders related to execution of contracts concluded through him. He shall be considered a representative of his principal in the legal actions connected with these contracts, which are brought by or against him in the area of the agent's business.

Article 183

1. The principal has to settle the agreed upon pay to the agent.
2. This pay may be a percentage of the value of the transaction and this percentage may be calculted on the basis of the selling price to customers unless otherwise agreed upon.

Article 184

If the contract agency is confined to one agent in a defined area, the contract agent shall receive his pay for the transactions concluded by the principal directly or via third parties in this area, even if these transactions have not been concluded through the endeavours of this agent, unless otherwise explicitly agreed upon between the two parties.

Article 185

The principal has to provide the agent with all data and information necessary for execution of the agency, and supply him, in particular, with the specifications of the commodities, models, drawings, trademarks and other data that assist him in promoting the sale of the commodities subject of the agency as well as their marketing.

Article 186

The contract agent has to preserve the rights of the principal. He shall have the right to take all protective measures that are necessary to preserve these rights and he shall have to provide his principal with the data and information concerning the status of the market in the area of his activities.

Article 187

The contract agent may not disclose the secrets of the principal to which he has access on the occasion of executing the agency, even after termination of the contractual relationship.

Article 188

1. The contract agency contract shall be concluded in the common interest of the two parties. If the contract is for an indefinite period, the principal may not terminate it without commission of a fault by the agent, otherwise he shall be obliged to compensate him for the damage caused to him as a result of his dismissal and any agreement to the contrary shall be null and void.
2. The agent shall also compensate the principal for the damage caused to him if he relinquishes the agency at an unsuitable time and without an acceptable excuse.

Article 189

1. If the contract is for a definite period, and the principle decides not to renew it at the expiry of its period, the agent shall have the right to receive a compensation to be determined by the judge, even if there is an agreement to the contrary.
2. The conditions for entitlement to this compensation are the following:

    (a) that the agent shall not have committed a fault or negligence in the course of executing the contract;
    (b) that the activity of the agent shall have led to evident success in promoting the sales of the commodity or increasing the number of customers.

3. In estimating the compensation, due consideration shall be given to the damage caused to the agent and the degree of benefit accruing to the principal from the agent's efforts in promoting the sales of the commodity and increasing the number of customers.

Article 190

1. The legal action for compensation referred to in the previous article shall lapse after ninety days from termination of the contract.
2. All other actions resulting from the contracts agency contract shall lapse after two years from termination of the contractual relationship.

Article 191

Notwithstanding the rules of jurisdiction prescribed in the Code of Procedures, the court, within the circuit of which lies the place of execution of the contract shall view all disputes arising from the Contracts Agency Contract.

Document

Roundtable on Strategies to Address "Crimes of Honour": A Summary Report

A Roundtable on Strategies to Address "Honour Crimes" was held in London from 12–13 November 1999. It was jointly organized by the Centre for Islamic and Middle Eastern Law (CIMEL) at the School of Oriental and African Studies at London University and by INTERIGHTS, the International Centre for the Legal Protection of Human Rights, under the auspices of the CIMEL/INTERIGHTS "Honour Crimes" Project.[1] Participants included some twenty scholars, lawyers, journalists and human rights advocates, working domestically in the UK and countries of South Asia and the Middle East, and/or internationally.[2] This report was compiled

---

[1] The project is jointly coordinated by Lynn Welchman, Director of CIMEL and Sara Hossain, Legal Officer (South Asia) at INTERIGHTS, in consultation with Professor Abdullahi An Na'im of the Emory School of Law, and with research assistance from Samia Bano, PhD Candidate, Warwick University. Administrative support for the meeting was provided by Lisa Finch, Programme Assistant, INTERIGHTS, and by Fouzia Khan and Keetha Singham, volunteers at INTERIGHTS. The project is funded by the Ford Foundation.

[2] Participants included: Abdullahi An-Na'im (Emory University School of Law); Samia Bano (CIMEL; Warwick University); Stephanie Farrior (at the time, Director of the Legal Office, Amnesty International, London); Leyla Gulcur (Senior Programme Officer, International Women's Health Coalition, New York); Sara Hossain (INTERIGHTS); Shamshad Hussain (Manningham Housing Association, Bradford); Rana Husseini (*Jordan Times* journalist, Amman); Isis Nusair (Human Rights Watch/Women's Rights Division, Washington DC); Gulsah Seral (Women for Women's Human Rights, Istanbul); Asma Jahangir (Advocate, Supreme Court of Pakistan, and UN Special Rapporteur on extrajudicial, summary or arbitrary executions); Pragna Patel (Southall Black Sisters, London); Angelika Pathak (Amnesty International); Emma Playfair (INTERIGHTS); Asad Rehman (Amnesty International UK); Purna Sen (Director, CHANGE, and Visiting Research Fellow, LSE); Nafisa Shah (journalist and researcher, Wolfson College, Oxford); Nadera Shalhoub-Kevorkian (Women's Centre for Legal Aid and Counselling, Jerusalem; and Hebrew University); Hannana Siddiqui (Coordinator, Southall Black Sisters, London); Aida Touma Sliman (Women Against Violence, Nazareth); Sohail Warraich (Shirket Gah, Lahore); Lynn Welchman (CIMEL). As the discussions at the meeting were expected to be preliminary and exploratory in nature, no attempt was made to involve participants representing the full range of those working on combating "honour crimes" or able to comment comprehensively on the range of

on the basis of discussions at the Roundtable and edited for publication by Lynn Welchman. Particular thanks for contributions to the editing process are due to Sara Hossain, and to Samia Bano, Vanessa Gosselin and Emma Playfair. Thanks are also due to the following participants for helpful comments and feedback: Stephanie Farrior, Leyla Gulcur, Nadera Kevorkian, Purna Sen and Gulsah Seral, and to the participants as a group for agreeing to the publication of this summary report based on their contributions at the meeting.

BACKGROUND TO THE CIMEL/INTERIGHTS PROJECT ON STRATEGIES OF RESPONSE TO "CRIMES OF HONOUR"

The project was initiated in response to the reports of the murders of Samia Sarwar in Pakistan and Rukhsana Naz in the UK in early 1999 and the explicit articulation of an "honour"-based defence by the alleged perpetrators in each case.[3] The Project is premised on a loose definition of "honour crimes" as patterns of conduct cutting across communities, cultures, religions and nations and manifested in a range of forms of violence directed, in the majority of cases, against women, including murder ("honour killings") and forced marriage. When the meeting was held, the following activities were also being undertaken as part of the project:

(a) preparation of an annotated bibliography on "crimes of honour", comprising materials (mostly in English) drawn from different regions including books, articles, and cases;[4]
(b) preparation of a list of statutory provisions relevant to crimes of "honour" in the penal codes of certain states in the Middle East and North Africa;
(c) preparation of a list of relevant international human rights law provisions;
(d) identification of the scope and manifestations of "crimes of honour" and of the range of initiatives to address these globally; and
(e) commissioning of a study from Southall Black Sisters, UK, documenting and analysing their casework on forced marriage as a "crime of honour".[5]

Over the course of the months preceding the meeting, several other initiatives had been taken nationally, regionally and internationally to address "honour crimes". These included:

---

cont.

    manifestations. Observers at the meeting included staff from the Office of the United Nations High Commissioner for Human Rights.

[3] In April 1999, Samia Sarwar was shot and murdered by a man accompanying her mother in the chambers of her lawyer, Hina Jilani, in Lahore, where she had gone to meet with her mother and uncle at their request. Samia's decision to obtain a divorce and to marry a man of her choice was not accepted by her family. See "LHRLA condemns killing of woman in HRCP office", *The Dawn* (staff reporter) 8 May 1999; and pages 19–22 in the Amnesty International Report on Pakistan cited below (note 7). In May 1999, Rukhsana Naz's mother and brother were convicted of her murder in Nottingham, after arguing in their defence that their honour had been violated by her decision to refuse a forced abortion following her relationship with a man against their will. S. Hall, "Life for 'honour': killing of pregnant teenager by mother and brother", *The Guardian*, 26 May 1999.

[4] The Bibliography has been made available on the Internet by the International Women's Health Coalition, at http://www.iwhc.org/bibliointro.html.

[5] A preliminary paper, "Forced Marriage: A Crime of Honour", was produced in July 2000 by Hannana Siddiqui of SBS.

(a) the launch of the Jordanian National Campaign against "honour killings";
(b) the establishment by the British Home Office of a Working Party on Forced Marriages and increased attention to the issue of forced marriage in the UK press;[6]
(c) the publication of Amnesty International's report on "honour killings" in Pakistan;[7]
(d) the publication of Human Rights Watch's report[8] on violence against women in Pakistan, including "crimes of honour" and the organization's advocacy in support of the Jordanian national campaign;
(e) the broadcast of the documentary *Murder in Purdah/In the Name of Honour* on "honour crimes" and violence against women in Pakistan, on BBC/BBC World and ABC Nightline in the USA respectively;
(f) the launch of the International Network For the Rights of Female Victims of Violence in Pakistan (INRFVVP), initiated by Dr Riffat Hassan, from Louisville, Kentucky, USA;
(g) the coordination by the International Women's Human Rights Clinic at Georgetown University, USA, of a submission on "honour killings" as a violation of women's human rights for the United Nations' Special Rapporteur on Violence Against Women; and
(h) the undertaking by CHANGE, UK, of a Research Programme on Non-Consensual Sex in Marriage which seeks to map, *inter alia*, the practices of forced marriage and early marriage, in all UN member states.

The substantial increase in media coverage of the issue – in particular in the Western and international press – was a matter of specific concern to participants in the meeting. Many felt that further consideration of the promises and perils of the surge of international interest in the subject of "honour crimes" was needed. They were also concerned that such attention – including international solidarity work – should contribute to the success of initiatives to address "honour crimes", rather than posing additional complications to internal work within communities by rendering potential interlocutors more obdurate and thus jeopardizing the possibility of access to and dialogue with those affected.

OBJECTIVES OF THE MEETING

The Roundtable aimed to provide an opportunity for activists working on the issue of "honour crimes" in different regions to share information regarding their incidence, their varying manifestations and initiatives to address the phenomenon. It also aimed to provide a forum for discussion of strategies to address "honour crimes", including the potential for using international and comparative human rights law to this end in national, regional and international fora.

---

6   *A Choice By Right*, the report of the working group on forced marriage, was published in June 2000 by the UK Home Office Communications Directorate.
7   Amnesty International, *Pakistan: Violence against Women in the Name of Honour*, 22 September 1999, AI Index: ASA 33/17/99.
8   Human Rights Watch, *Crime or Custom? Violence Against Women in Pakistan*, New York: Human Rights Watch, August 1999. The Women's Rights Division of Human Rights Watch, which prepared this report, had previously investigated the "honour defence" to wife-murder in Brazilian law and practice (*Criminal Injustice: Violence Against Women in Brazil*, Women's Rights Project and Americas Watch, October 1991, pp. 18–29) and forced virginity tests in Turkey

More specifically, the meeting aimed to contribute to the following objectives:

(a)   examine the "crime against family honour" and the diversity of its manifestations including the "hidden incidence" of such crimes;
(b)   reach a consensual definition of a "crime of honour";
(c)   assess the incidence of "crimes of honour" in different countries of the world, and identify the range of ongoing initiatives by practitioners to address such crimes within diverse legal, political, religious and cultural contexts;
(d)   identify commonalities in incidence, practice and law that might assist activists and lawyers in developing strategies to challenge the phenomenon of "honour crimes"; and
(e)   build, in coordination with those active on and concerned with this issue, a consensus on developing supporting strategies to combat "honour crimes" against women and girls wherever they occur, through the collection of reliable data and provision of technical assistance, support and information exchange.

OVERVIEW OF SELECTED INITIATIVES ADDRESSING "CRIMES OF HONOUR"

Participants from Jordan, Pakistan, Palestine/Israel, Turkey and the United Kingdom discussed specific manifestations of and responses to "honour crimes" within their respective contexts.[9]

Jordan

In Jordan,[10] the honour-based defence is often explicitly invoked by men who kill their female relatives. The law provides for the murderer to be either exempted from liability or to receive a much-reduced sentence, depending upon circumstances. In many cases, the task of killing may be assigned to a minor boy to ensure that the sentence is lenient, and that even if convicted, he will be placed in a juvenile centre rather than a gaol. The killers are frequently assured of strong family support for their action and particular assistance on leaving gaol, including financial help. Families in which the murderer and the victim are of the same blood do not, as a rule, support prosecution of the murderer, waiving their legally recognized personal interest (*al-haqq al-shakhsi*) in the prosecution and penalization of the murderer.

However, in many cases of murder where honour is invoked by the killer as a defence, honour itself does not seem to be a prime consideration or motive. In such cases, the real motivation may be economic or based on family enmity and linked to attempts to prevent women from claiming their inheritance rights or from exposing allegations of incest or sexual abuse.

---

cont.
   (*Human Rights Watch Global Report on Women's Human Rights*, August 1995, pp. 418–444).
9 This section is a summary of the presentations by Rana Husseini, Asma Jahangir, Aida Touma-Sliman, Nadera Shalhoub-Kevorkian, Gulsah Seral and Hannana Siddiqui.
10 The British Council has facilitated a Family Protection Project in Jordan, which addresses, among other issues, child abuse, domestic violence and so-called "honour crimes". The project focuses on policy development and practice and involves both governments and NGOs.

In February 1999, a national campaign that attracted the support of the palace[11] was initiated in Jordan to end "honour crimes". By November 1999, 13,000 signatures had been collected on a petition calling for the repeal of the Penal Code provisions permitting exemption and mitigation in the event of a proven defence on grounds of honour. In response, the government drafted a bill to repeal Article 340 of the Penal Code, which was duly presented to Parliament at the end of 1999 but failed to pass.[12] In fact, most alleged perpetrators in cases of "honour killings" rely on Article 98, which allows mitigation and a reduction in sentence (to one year in prison in the case of murder) if the perpetrator establishes he/she was overcome by a "fit of fury" in response to an "unrightful" act by the victim. Nevertheless, Article 340, as an article that explicitly exonerates the killers of women in certain circumstances, is clearly and legitimately a target for the efforts of the national movement against "honour crimes" and indeed for those supporting them internationally. It is also worth noting that although some prominent Jordanian figures have accused the movement of seeking to impose Western values,[13] religious leaders have also made public statements asserting that "honour killings" have no basis in religion.[14]

Pakistan

In Pakistan, under the *Qisas* and *Diyat* Ordinance,[15] the heirs of a victim of murder are entitled to pardon the murderer. Thus, in cases where a woman is murdered by her father, *qisas* (the maximum penalty of the death sentences as "talion") cannot be imposed, nor can a death sentence be given under Tazir criminal laws. The legal penalty is *diyat* ("blood money" or financial compensation); in addition, the court is empowered to impose a prison sentence of up to fourteen years, but in practice a prison sentence is rarely given in such cases. Although the Court may convict the accused in such circumstances, no sentence will be imposed. Women's organizations have called for an amendment of this law. Activists and lawyers in Pakistan have been working on the issue of "honour crimes", in particular "honour killings", for over

---

11   See, for example, Alan Philips, "Princes oppose murder of unfaithful wives", *Daily Telegraph*, 16 February 2000. The piece was reporting the participation of Prince Ali in a march through Amman demanding the repeal of Article 340 of the Penal Code, and more generally the Palace's support for the amendment of the law.
12   Although the Upper House (Senate) endorsed the proposed amendment, the Lower House (Chamber of Deputies) rejected it twice.
13   Nadia Shamroukh of the Jordanian Women's Union reported that in the November parliamentary debate on the bill to repeal Article 340 of the Penal Code, certain deputies charged that the recent national campaign and efforts to get the article repealed were attempts by the West to infiltrate Jordanian society and demoralize women. Rana Husseini, "Women activists pledge to continue struggle against 'crimes of honour' despite Parliament decision", *Jordan Times*, 23 November 1999.
14   Shaykh al-Tamimi's paper to a meeting on "crimes of honour", convened by the NGO Terre des Hommes in Amman in July 1999, took the view that "honour killings" were not supported by Islamic law because of the warnings in the Qur'an against acting on the bases of unproven doubt and suspicions (Chambers v.12; 4.264; and 2.232).
15   First promulgated as an ordinance in 1990 and subsequently re-issued on a number of occasions until passed by Parliament in 1997: see Amnesty International, *Pakistan*, p. 44.

ten years. A nationwide debate on the justification or condemnation of "honour killings" was recently prompted by specific cases in which women were killed or threatened with death by their families for seeking to marry of their own free will. In several cases (in contrast to the situation in Jordan and Palestine), the women concerned were from influential families, and this triggered more intense media attention than in other cases.

The experience of lawyers and activists on women's human rights has proved that in Pakistan, as elsewhere, purely legal strategies are unsuccessful when combating "honour crimes". It was reiterated that human rights and women's rights organizations must work together and at a grassroots level to raise awareness of the issue among human rights workers in the field. Only after building up a consensus on the issue on the ground will it be possible to link up with the media, which in turn will affect influential sectors of society such as the judiciary.

After Samia Sarwar's killing, the media followed the case relentlessly with reports appearing in both the Urdu and English language press on an almost daily basis. Of course, such media campaigns backfired on occasion, and in some cases newspapers started to publish not only hostile reports on those women's organizations which run shelter homes, but also personal attacks on the activists and lawyers concerned. Part of this backlash was to accuse the organizations working on the issue of "honour killings" of being Western oriented. In such cases it may sometimes be more effective if those working on the issue speak from within the community.

Nationally, the debate has become starkly polarized between parliamentary members and tribal leaders on the one hand, and human rights and women's rights organizations, lawyers, the left, trade unions and youth groups on the other. In August 1999, the overwhelming majority of members of the upper House of Parliament refused to support a proposed resolution to condemn "honour crimes".[16] On the other hand, important statements were made by Islamic scholars and religious groups recognizing that "honour crimes" have no basis in religion. Another potentially important initiative is the proposed declaration by the Council of Islamic Ideology that "honour killings" are not a part of Islamic tradition.

Palestine and the Palestinian community in Israel

In the Palestinian West Bank, there has been no sustained attention to the issue either by organizations or by the press. The research project carried out by the Women's Centre for Legal Aid and Counselling's (WCLAC) on femicide stands to make a real contribution in this regard.[17] This research relates to the following categories:

---

[16] See, for example, Javed Jaidl, "Rumpus in Senate on Samia resolution", *The Dawn*, 3 August 1999. In January 2000 the UN Special Rapporteur on extrajudicial, summary or arbitrary executions, Asma Jahangir, noted that "the Government of Pakistan has further refused to condemn 'honour killings' despite public protests throughout the country against the decision of the Senate" (UN Doc.E/CN.4/2000/3, para. 81). Later in 2000, after he seized power in Pakistan, General Musharraf appeared to indicate an intention to move more firmly against the perpetrators of "honour crimes": "Pakistan announces steps to improve human rights", *The International News*, 2000; and see Riffat Hassan, "Extremism on the rise again", *The Dawn*, 28 June 2000, on the context of Musharraf's statement.

[17] WCLAC's report, *Mapping and Analyzing the Landscape of Femicide in Palestinian Society*, was completed in the summer of 2000. The project was

(a) women who are perceived (by themselves or by a therapist) to be under threat of femicide;
(b) women who are subjected to verbal or non-verbal attacks;
(c) women who are subjected to threatened attack of femicide; and
(d) women who are victims of "honour crimes" or femicide.

WCLAC's work indicates that the definition of honour is flexible, and that often women's misbehaviour is seen as sufficient violation of accepted codes of honour. It further appears that gossip or rumours about a woman may often be enough to invoke a "fit of fury" by men and to result in an "honour killing". WCLAC is trying, through its work, to analyse the concept of honour and to find alternative definitions. In documenting cases of femicide, WCLAC draws on various sources of data, both formal and informal. Formal sources include the records maintained by the Palestinian Bureau of Statistics. However, these records do not identify the gender of the victims, and appear to underestimate the actual incidence of cases. For example, in 1999, the police recorded five cases of femicide in the West Bank and thirteen in the Gaza Strip. Other formal sources include post mortem reports, many of which record women's deaths as being due to natural causes such as diabetes, high blood pressure, etc. They also include records from the Attorney General's office: in these records for 1996–1998, WCLAC found 234 cases of women having died, of which 177 files were closed, the cause of death being ascribed to "fate". As the records are not gender specific, the numbers of women killed can only be identified by checking against the names entered in the records. In some cases, corroboration is sought by searching the records of the Ministry of Health. Other important sources of information include the questions put by judges during trials and the data received by the "hotline".

Informal sources of data on femicide include interviews with police officers, prosecutors, forensic experts, politicians, tribal leaders, the District Attorney, judges and village heads (*mukhtars*).[18] Information is also collected about the role of doctors of forensic medicine indicating that in certain cases, forensic experts may be unduly influenced by the women's families to change the reports. Where possible, the court records of femicide cases are also examined. The research has shown that, as a whole, the judicial system conspires against victims, and that patriarchy, masculinity, and control measures critically affect court decisions in these matters. In addition, there is a pattern of tribal heads excluding women by institutionalizing them or forcing them into marriage.

Inside Israel, Women against Violence provides legal and social assistance to women survivors of violence within the Palestinian community. It provides clinical therapy and operates a shelter. It is also engaged in campaigning and advocacy for policy and law reform on the issue of violence against women and runs educational workshops to raise public awareness. The organization is part of Al-Badeel (The Alternative), the Coalition against the "Crime of Family Honour". The Coalition's work includes the publication of a newsletter that documents the names and histories of women who have been murdered in "honour killings" and the holding of commemorative events.

Although there are some progressive Israeli laws on violence against women, there have been cultural complications for the minority Palestinian community in appealing to those laws and shortcomings in the remedies they have provided. Furthermore,

---

cont.
    directed by Nadera Shalhoub-Kevorkian. See also UNIFEM, *Violence Against Women Campaign: Western Asia Report 1999*, p. 24.
18 Jordanian law empowers the *mukhtar* to furnish a death certificate.

the Israeli authorities have sought political benefit through the selective support of different communities. For example, the political authorities have at times underpinned the tribal system to secure votes. The campaign against "honour crimes" was itself sparked off by mobilization against a local authority mayor who supported a man in court who had killed a woman in an "honour crime".

Turkey

The majority of cases of "honour crimes" in Turkey occur in the east and south-east of the country. In a recent survey conducted in eastern Turkey regarding the threat of such crimes, 66 per cent of the respondents stated that they were afraid that they could become victims of "honour killings".[19]

In Turkey, the penalty for premeditated murder is twenty-four years in prison. A crime within the family is considered to involve an exacerbating circumstance and the punishment for murders within the family is accordingly augmented to life imprisonment. However, provocation can be a mitigating justification. The definition of provocation depends on the courts, but it is based on society's understanding of the concept. There are two articles in the Turkish Penal Code on provocation, differentiating the general article on provocation from severe provocation. In the case of an "honour killing", severe provocation is cited as a mitigating circumstance. Severe provocation can reduce a life term to fifteen years. Subsequent processes used to reduce the sentence have meant that in practice, killers may be able to go free after six years. In practice, the sentence may be further reduced on the grounds of the perpetrator's age, since in many cases families arrange for minor boys to carry out the killings, in the knowledge that their age will be a mitigating factor in the sentencing process.

In most cases of "honour killings", both those responsible for representing the victim's interests, that is her family, and the perpetrator, often a legal minor, are in collusion, and no party presses for the woman victim's rights. As a result, many women lawyers and women's groups have been lobbying the government for an amendment to the penal code that would allow interested parties to represent the women killed in the name of honour. Women for Women's Human Rights (WWHR), together with the Equality Watch Committee and the Purple Roof Women's Shelter Foundation, has been active in campaigning for this amendment in legislation. It was especially vocal on the issue of "honour killings" in the NGO Shadow Report presented at the 1997 session of the UN Committee on the Elimination of All Forms of Discrimination against Women. WWHR is also active on the Legal Committee of the government's General Directorate on the Status and Problems of Women and is engaged in a campaign to abolish the Penal Code provision in regard to severe provocation where the sentences may be reduced to one-eighth of the original sentence. Within the framework of this campaign, WWHR also works with the media and sends out urgent action alerts in specific cases of "honour killings". The Human Rights and Legal Literacy Training Programme for Women, conducted by the WWHR at grassroots level across sixteen provinces in Turkey, includes discussion of such killings as a violation of women's human rights, specifically the right to life.

---

[19]   See Pinar Ilkkaracan and Women for Women's Human Rights, "Exploring the Context of Women's Sexuality in Eastern Turkey", *Reproductive Health Matters*, November 1998, vol. 6, no. 12, pp. 66–75.

United Kingdom

Southall Black Sisters (SBS) is a frontline women's advice centre, which focuses on providing support to women on a range of issues, including violence against women and matrimonial matters. SBS also campaigns for change within the criminal justice system and calls for scrutiny of social policy which, in many cases involving Asian women, tends to adopt a non-interventionist approach to women and violence. It also examines developments within the immigration field as well as related developments and connections internationally. For example, it was involved in monitoring the outcome of the important recent decision of the House of Lords in *Shah and Islam*[20] which is of great strategic importance to women in situations of violence, in particular those under threat of "honour killings".

SBS receives over 1,000 cases and inquiries every year, many of which concern allegations of domestic violence. These include cases of assault, murder, forced marriage, the abduction of girls and women, female genital mutilation, acid attacks and violence following demands for dowry. About 25 per cent of all domestic homicides concern the killing of women: in many such cases (as in many matrimonial and custody cases) men invoke a cultural defence. Campaigning to end domestic violence has meant that SBS has addressed the issue both within the community and outside it. It has raised issues regarding domestic violence and the role of community leaders to prevent or punish such violence. It has also taken a leaf from the Indian women's movement in adopting the strategy of turning the notions of honour and shame on their heads. Thus, it has held demonstrations outside the alleged perpetrator's home, denouncing the men who have acted shamefully and brought dishonour on their family's head by killing women. SBS is also examining the reasons why some women feel driven to kill violent partners; here, women's inability to escape situations of extreme violence appears to be linked to their own notions of honour. Women may themselves be so inculcated with the notion that breaking up a marriage is a violation of the community's honour that they see their only route to escape from violence as lying in the killing of the violent partner.

SBS works with school students and also conducts training programmes with practitioners and professionals on domestic violence. Its work often differs from that of other women's groups, in particular those based on religion or those with a particularly conservative orientation. Such groups have begun to call for alternatives to the use of the criminal justice system in cases of domestic violence, and the possibility of mediation, followed by reconciliation within the family, rather than challenging the customs and abuse that force women to remain there. As a result of its work, SBS has often been accused by anti-racist organizations of washing the community's dirty linen in public and of risking a racist backlash against ethnic minority communities.

SBS was represented on the Home Office's Working Party on Forced Marriage, and has been one of the few voices critical of the state's role in relation to forced marriages. SBS is particularly concerned about the failure of service providers to address the needs of women and girls at risk of forced marriages. Such service providers may cite cultural grounds for such failure, on the assumption that minority communities are self-policing, and that they are, therefore, not required to intervene on behalf of women within these communities. SBS believes that there is a need for the government to issue proper guidelines regarding the response of the state and

---

[20] *Islam (AP) v. Secretary of State for the Home Department; R v. Immigration Appeal Tribunal ex Parte Shah (AP)* [1999] 2 WLR 1015, [1999] 2 All ER 545.

law enforcing agencies to forced marriage cases and to focus more closely on the question of enforcement.

Some forced marriage cases carry an international element, for example in cases of abduction, immigration or asylum. In the last category, there is a real tension between the need to demonstrate that the woman concerned is at risk of severe abuse if forced to return to her country of origin and the need to avoid reinforcing negative stereotypes of that country. In many cases of abduction and forced marriage of dual nationals, the Foreign and Commonwealth Office (FCO) refuses to intervene formally; a culturally relativist notion of multiculturalism appears to underpin this decision. SBS is currently considering the scope for civil and criminal actions relating to the FCO's lack of formal intervention in such cases.

RELEVANCE OF A HUMAN RIGHTS PERSPECTIVE TO "CRIMES OF HONOUR": WHAT IS AN "HONOUR CRIME"?

In seeking to define "honour crimes", participants focused on attempts to:

(a)   conceptualize the notion of and to discuss the contexts in which honour is seen to be embodied or encapsulated;
(b)   identify the constituent elements of a "crime of honour", whether for the perpetrators, the victims, the authorities, or activists;
(c)   differentiate between "crimes of honour" and "crimes of passion";
(d)   consider the role of the state in the perpetuation of "crimes of honour", in particular through examining whether the values of those affirming the legitimacy of such crimes find resonance in the law and in state institutions.

The discussion was prefaced by an introduction summarizing the varying forms of "honour crimes" documented in the background material for the meeting, their apparent cause, and the reflection and embodiment of the notion of honour in various legal codes.[21] The following summary outlines thematically the main points raised during this discussion.

"Crimes of honour" take diverse forms, including but not confined to "honour killings", forced marriages, coerced marriage to an alleged rapist, and unlawful confinement/restrictions on movement. The incidents that appear to trigger off an "honour crime" range from women exercising their right to choose a spouse, seek a divorce, or engage in any behaviour which breaches family or community norms, in particular sexual conduct, but also, for example, merely being absent from the family house. In the last case, the notion of honour is invoked through asserting suspicion of the woman having been engaged in sexual assignations during her absence. The tight control of the movement of unaccompanied women in some communities can thus also be an expression of control over their sexuality. The perception of loss of such control may be articulated as a justification for an honour-based crime. Whether this is all about sexual control and patriarchy, or whether it is all about property and patriarchy, or whether it can be and is part of all those elements and so a moving target, in that sense, for advocates and activists, are issues that differ in place and time. However, where the various constituent elements can be teased out, whether in individual cases or as patterns, they can help to contextualize the problem, identify groups "at risk" and indicate possible measures of response.

One of the elements that may need to be distinguished, where this is possible, is

---

[21]   The introduction was presented by Lynn Welchman.

between a "crime of passion" and a "crime of honour". Some have voiced concern that "only Muslims" – or, for example inside Israel, "only Arabs" – are seen as having the latter in their culture while murders of women in other cultures are "dignified"[22] by the term "crime of passion", a concept recognized in French and certain south European jurisprudence. This is complicated by the fact that the crime of passion defence is only available to a man who is or has been sexually involved with the woman he has killed, and thus can claim that he is defending the "conjugal honour" or his individual masculine honour. The term "crime of honour" appears to be wider, and in such cases, the perpetrators may include the victim's closest blood relatives – none of whom, at least by law, may be or have been in a sexual relationship of any kind with her.[23] The honour being defined here is not asserted as a personal or conjugal honour. On the other hand, the honour defence is asserted by husbands as well as by family members, and in some laws the murderer's distinct relationship in this regard to the victim is collapsed in the legitimation of the honour defence. In the Amnesty International report on "honour crimes" in Pakistan, figures from Sindh illustrate the substantial proportion of cases (in *karo-kari* killings) where husbands are the murderers.[24] In Jordan, information provided by the Amman District police department indicated a lower proportion of husbands implicated in what the police classified as "honour killings".[25]

Research into "honour murders"/"crimes of passion" in some Latin American countries indicates a close identification of the two concepts and the tendency of laws to accommodate social norms permitting a man to kill his allegedly adulterous wife on the grounds of damage to his honour. A Human Rights Watch report on violence against women in Brazil describes the evolution of this defence. The explicit defence available in Portuguese colonial law to a man who kills his wife and her lover on catching them in the act of adultery was repealed by Brazilian law and replaced by the crime of passion defence. This in turn has further developed into the ambiguity existing in the courts in the 1990s. Thus, the "legitimate self-defence" develops into the crime of passion defence. According to Human Rights Watch, "in essence, the honour defence equates a wife's adulterous act (or allegedly adulterous act) with a physical act of aggression by the accused".[26]

---

22 In the same sense that for those sympathetic to the concept, "crimes of honour" are dignified by that description. See Ian Leader-Elliott, "Passion and insurrection in the law of provocation", in N. Naffisen and R.J. Owens (eds.), *Sexing the Subject of the Law*, Sydney, Sweet & Maxwell, 1997, on a "passion which expresses the virtues of the ordinary man … The ordinary man is a sanguine man, a hot man, whose blood boils when his most vital interests are threatened" (at p. 162) – compared to the generally reviled "cold-blooded killer".

23 See further Lama Abu Odeh, "Crimes of Honour and the Construct of Gender in Arab Societies", in Mai Yamani (ed.), *Feminism and Islam*, Ithaca Press, 1996, pages 141–194.

24 Where data of known cases revealed the relationship of the perpetrator and victim and the woman was killed alone as *kari* during 1998 in Sindh, forty of the eighty-one murdered women were killed by their husbands: see Amnesty International's Pakistan report, at p. 6.

25 The information provided for the three years from 1995 to 1997 identified fifty-six perpetrators in what the unit classified as "honour killings", including the victim's brother as her killer in 80 per cent of the cases, her father in 14.5 per cent and her husband in 5.5 per cent. Working paper of the Family Protection Unit in the Amman District Police Department, 1999.

26 Human Rights Watch's report on Brazil, at p. 21. Argentina saw similar tensions between law and social norms and has a reduced penalty for murder "in a state of violent emotion" in circumstances that "make it excusable", while Venezuelan

A recent article traces the development over time of the English and Australian law on sexual provocation, a defence in cases where women are killed from jealousy or possessiveness. It argues that "sexual provocation is a cultural defence which transcends religion or ethnic origin, and claims for itself a constituency almost exclusively masculine".[27] It also argues that the abolition of the offence of adultery (originally based on the perception of women as chattel and adultery as a crime against property, in English law) has been accompanied by the "progressive enlargement" of the partial excuse for murdering women provided through the defence of provocation. In Pakistan, the *Qisas* and *Diyat* Ordinance contains no reference to grave and sudden provocation, but the courts continue to invoke this concept in mitigating charges of murder, including in caes of "honour killings", whether the murderer is the partner or a male relative. In the UK, debates on the defence of provocation have been catalysed by those defences presented by women who killed a violent partner. Until recently, the courts appeared to find the use of such a defence by women less acceptable than by men. One question on legal strategy which has implications for the crime of passion concept is whether the concept of provocation and passion should be linked, or whether the definition of provocation should be redefined so as to make it more easily available to women.[28]

In Pakistan, the *Qisas* and *Diyat* Ordinance, which governs murder, contains no reference to grave and sudden provocation, but the courts continue to invoke this concept in mitigating charges of murder, including in cases of "honour killings", whether the murderer is the partner or a male relative.

In Jordan, "honour killings" are most frequently mitigated through a defence based on the killer having been "in a state of great anger/a fit of fury resulting from a wrongful and dangerous act on the part of the victim".[29] Perceived or suspected breaches of the "honour code" may be considered by the court to constitute "a wrongful and dangerous act on the part of the victim" towards the honour of her killer, whether this person be her husband or a close male relative. Similar provisions exist and are used in defence in, *inter alia*, Syria and Lebanon. There may be some comparison to be made here with the tendencies in Brazilian cases noted above. The penal codes in certain Middle Eastern states (e.g. in Syria) have also recognized a partial defence based on an honourable motive for a crime. The concepts of crimes of passion and "crimes of honour" are collapsed in codified laws that provide an

---

cont.

    law maintains a maximum three-year sentence for a man who kills his wife and/or her lover on finding them in the act of adultery. See papers by A. Segura for the Georgetown International Women's Human Rights Clinic. By contrast, the story of the "honour killing" set by Gabriel Garcia Marquez in a Colombian village, and given "legal-sociological interpretation" by Teubner ("Regulatory Law: Chronicle of a Death Foretold", *Social and Legal Studies*, 1992, vol. 1, no. 4) is of the (reluctant) murder by two brothers of the seducer of their sister.

[27] Leader-Elliott, "Passion and insurrection", at p. 153.
[28] Leader-Elliott argues that defences based on claims of self-defence by women who kill their violent partners have been subjected to "unspoken limits" in North American, English and Australian law, "preserved by a steadily widening conception of provocation". In regard to whether sexual provocation should reduce murder to manslaughter he concludes (at p. 169) that "given the disparity between the sexes in the matter of who kills whom, women may be far more likely than men to conclude that this particular claim to compassion is an anachronism".
[29] Article 98, Penal Code: see further Abu Odeh, "Crimes of honour", pp. 158–161 and note 37 p. 192.

exemption or a mitigation to the man who kills his wife or a close female relative whom he catches in an adulterous encounter.

There are real and obvious problems in defining an "honour crime" based on the claims made by the perpetrators, who seek to "legitimize/dignify", in their respective cultural context, the murder of a woman – or another violation of her rights – on the basis of honour and thereby obtain a reduced penalty. Accepting that such a crime has occurred as claimed may obscure – as may be the intention – the "real motivation" for the crime or attempted crime. These two problems converge in the question of definition and strategies.

The concept of honour appears to be intrinsic to many tribal laws. A view from the Arab world saw honour as linking the notion of revenge exclusively to the murder of men, and the concept of shame only to a woman and her natal family. Thus, if a woman's husband divorces her, and then her family murders her, there is no one left to avenge her death. This value structure may explain why, in "honour killing" cases, the woman's (alleged) paramour is not killed. By comparison, in Sindh, Pakistan, honour appears both to exist in its "original" or purist version, and also to have been re-invented through modernity.[30] Honour emblematizes an alternate moral value system. The perpetrators often feel that by committing an "honour killing", they have saved face and can stand up in society again. In this context, honour also requires revenge (or *badlo*) killings. Honour is seen as exclusively masculine and shame as exclusively feminine. From this perspective, if a man's honour is seen as damaged, he is shamed and has to reinvent his masculinity by undertaking a killing. Given that feuding is also intrinsic to tribal culture and is part of how notions of honour may be played out, a marriage conflict may be constructed into a feud. This may be conducted through the generations and undergo transformations down the years, with an "honour killing" perhaps eventually transmogrifying into a land dispute. "Honour crimes" have also been transformed in certain aspects by the entry of market forces. Now, it is possible to demand compensation to avenge an "honour killing" either in the form of monetary payment or the transfer of another woman. That is, where a family kills a woman for reasons of its honour, it may claim compensation or the transfer of another woman in compensation for the woman of whom it has been deprived through the murder. The terminology of honour may shift from a rural to urban context and an "honour crime" may take different forms depending on whether the perpetrator is outside the woman's family or within it. The notion of honour is linked to the perception of control by and economic advantage of males. So, for example, in Pakistan, it is considered honourable for women in tribal courts to forgo inheritance and for men to sell women. And, a father may be dishonoured by his daughter marrying against his will, but not by his alleging that she is an adulteress (as happened in the *Saima Waheed* case in Pakistan).[31]

In the informal or customary legal system that condones "honour crimes", there is a reversal of the relationship between the victim and violator on the one hand, and the consequent expectations of retribution as it exists within the state or formal system of justice on the other. There is a valorizing of the right to kill. Thus, a

---

30 Nafisa Shah presented the analysis of honour in Sindh summarized in this section. Her many writings on the subject include "*Faislo*: The Informal Settlement System and Crimes Against Women in Sindh", in Farida Shaheed *et al.* (eds.), *Shaping Women's Lives: Laws, Practices and Strategies in Pakistan*, Lahore, Shirkat Gah, 1998, pp. 227–252; "Honour Killings: Code of Dishonour", *The Review*, 19–25 November 1998, p. 8; and *A Story in Black: Karo Kari Killings in Upper Sindh*, Reuter Foundation Paper 100, Oxford 1998.

31 *Waheed v. Jahangir & Anor*, PLD 1997 Lahore 301.

woman who is killed may be seen as the guilty party, as happened with Samia Sarwar. Similarly, Asma Jahangir and Hina Jilani, Samia's lawyers, who continue to be targeted by those supporting Samia's family, are seen as responsible for her death, and those accused of the murder are seen as victims. Thinking through the issue of "honour crimes" from within a very different worldview poses real difficulties to those outside that worldview.

The concept of honour is elastic, changing according to time and place and forms of articulation and expression in society. In cases of "honour crimes", the dominant view of honour held by the perpetrators, most often shared by (or at least not challenged by) their immediate community, is one that some activists are seeking to challenge by asserting a different meaning of honour. For example, in Pakistan, activists have named the killers of women as dishonourable. The dominant view of honour is linked to the assumption that honour attaches only to a good woman. Thus, in the UK for example, activists argued that Zoora Shah was considered by the Court of Appeal to have no honour left to transgress.[32] By raising the notion of honour, a woman's sexual history may be used to deny her justice. The same approach is found in court decisions in the West Bank. The notion of honour is used by women to show how they are constrained from escaping violence, and by men to excuse the violence, which they perpetrate upon women. One strategy might indeed be to work on recovering the notion of honour, identifying how women of all kinds have an honour that attaches to them. However, other participants responded to this suggestion by noting the dangers of using the notion of honour. They suggested that such cases might be more effectively defended through the argument that a woman's failure to speak out about her situation of abuse was due to her fear for her children, and possible repercussions on them, rather than because she was not willing to compromise her honour by describing the degradations she had suffered.

The connection of honour with the control of the exercise of female sexuality permits the description of "honour crimes" as violations of women's rights to sexual autonomy. However, it was pointed out that this may not be appropriate in certain contexts where victims of "honour crimes" may be children, who as a group have a particular need and right to protection, and who remain vulnerable to sexual abuse (including "honour crimes"). Making the connection to women's sexuality also raises issues of violence against women that appear to fall outside the "crimes of honour" category – or at least, outside the "crimes of family honour" category. Such examples include acid attacks against women in Bangladesh, often by men whose sexual advances have been rejected, and the killing of women by militias in Algeria on the basis of the imposition of dress codes or lifestyle/conduct codes, by persons unconnected with the women concerned. Some felt that caution needed to be exercised in not collapsing too many forms of violence against women into the definition of "honour crimes".

Similarly, "honour crimes" against women are clearly located within the broad spectrum of crimes of violence against women, making it possible to address them within a rights-based approach, which imposes upon the state an obligation to provide protection to women. It would be strategically important to identify the value and advantage of, on the one hand, "separating out" a "crime of honour" as a particular phenomenon or form of violence against women, and, on the other, campaigning

---

[32] Zoora Shah, a Muslim woman in Bradford, UK who killed her partner, allegedly after years of physical, sexual and economic abuse, was sentenced to twenty years in prison. Southall Black Sisters led a campaign on her behalf. See Susan Edwards, "Beyond belief: the case of Zoora Shah", *New Law Journal*, 8 May 1998, pp. 667–668. In January 2000 her tariff was considerably reduced on appeal.

on "crimes of honour" solely within the broader spectrum of violence against women. Any attempt to address "honour crimes" separately would have to be handled very carefully, given the risks of a racist backlash and cultural stereotyping; lessons might be learned in this regard from the complex dynamics that marked the international campaigning effort on female genital mutilation. It is essential that the issue not be sensationalized (this issue was also discussed in relation to the role of the media: see below).

THE HUMAN RIGHTS AND THE INTERNAL CULTURAL DIALOGUE APPROACHES

Participants considered the human rights approach to "crimes of honour", including the use of the law, legal mechanisms and international human rights mechanisms. They also considered challenges for advocacy and dialogue with and within different communities asserting the legitimacy of "crimes of honour" or tolerating their perpetration. The following seeks to summarize the points made and discussed during the session.[33]

Violations such as "honour crimes" press us to reflect on the limitations of "standard" (international human rights law-based) human rights activism as an approach to addressing them. The human rights approach needs to supplement rather than undermine other approaches and to recognize the need for (and the validity of) complementary approaches. A critical re-examination of existing approaches would mean, at the very least, recognizing that certain principles, such as rights to sexual autonomy or the choice of a partner or lifestyle, may be new to many of the societies in which activists work. Denying such social realities could undermine the potential effectiveness of both human rights and women's organizations. One difficult question that needs to be asked is whether the kind of human rights approach currently deployed forces women to face untenable choices between the community and the self, or between a social death and a physical death. Will women forced to confront such dilemmas be able to lead a normal life? A successful strategy would involve persuasion, rather than compulsion, to bring a community to accept a particular position.

The problematic aspects of a human rights approach are due in part to the reality of a situation of human rights dependency. This involves human rights in the South being protected by human rights organizations in the North who create pressure on the governments of the North to, in turn, exert pressure on the governments in the South to address human rights violations.[34] This dependency reflects real economic dependencies (contrast for example the treatment of human rights violations in Saudi Arabia and Pakistan). Some might consider that this approach is exemplified in the recent reports on "honour killings" in Pakistan by Amnesty International and Human Rights Watch, neither of which address the role of civil society in Pakistan in addressing "honour crimes", and which might appear to assume that civil society is a mere beneficiary rather than an agent of any process of social change. By contrast, a useful and effective human rights approach is one which diminishes dependency and takes civil society seriously, including its concerns regarding sexuality, patriarchy and sexual autonomy.

---

[33] Initial presentations were made by Abdullahi An-Na'im and Asma Jahangir.
[34] For a more detailed exposition of this concept see Abdullahi An-Na'im, "Problems of Dependency: Human Rights Organizations in the Arab World", *Middle East Report*, Spring 2000.

In response to the points summarized above, it was observed that the dichotomy set up between religious and secular, or a rights-based and a community-based approach, may reflect the state's response, rather than women's experience. Although many women may identify with religious principles, they also make their own choices, sometimes in defiance of social norms. In doing so, they choose to exercise their individual human rights. Culturally relativist arguments in defence of "honour crimes", particularly those which claim that the articulation of the right to choose whether and whom to marry is an imposition of liberal values on certain societies, fail to address the fact that such societies have embraced liberal values in respect of their economic policies, educational systems and infrastructure. Why do "liberal values" falter only when it comes to state policies on women, and particularly in this case, women in the family? It was also pointed out that in developing a rights-based strategy, many campaigners have, in fact, been careful to begin work at a local level, and to move to the international plane at a later stage.

In developing a rights-based approach, there is a need to challenge another false dichotomy between the community and women, which somehow places women outside the community. The actions of women's and human rights organizations in challenging "honour crimes" have resulted in the beginnings of a redefinition of notions of community, citizenship and the individual. With regard to women being able to lead a "normal" life, the very notion of "normal" needs to be questioned. Women *can* and *do* create their own communities, and alternative spaces, such as shelters. A sound human rights approach thus includes within itself the vision and the capacity for imagination of such alternative communities.

The question of possible alternatives to a human rights approach was raised. Are there other ways of mainstreaming the position of marginal groups in our societies? Is it useful, effective, or even possible for rights activists to engage with developing strategies to address "honour crimes" together with those who perpetrate, sanction or condone "honour killings" within particular communities?

Particular challenges are posed by the conflation and entanglement of male control of female sexuality and the toleration of "crimes of honour" as culturally "authentic" and part of a strategy of resistance to Western colonization by certain non-state Islamist groupings.

State responsibility under international human rights law entails both enacting legislation and implementing it, and also the duty to transform culture. For example, the International Convention on the Elimination of All Forms of Racial Discrimination requires states to take steps in relation to culture, education and the media in order to change the prejudices which lead to racial discrimination.[35] The Women's Convention requires states to modify the social and cultural patterns of men and women in order to eliminate discrimination against women.[36] How, when addressing

---

[35]   Article 7 of the Convention: States Parties undertake to adopt immediate and
       effective measures, particularly in the fields of teaching, education, culture and
       information, with a view to combating prejudices which lead to racial
       discrimination and to promoting understanding, tolerance and friendship among
       nations and racial or ethnical groups, as well as to propagating the purposes and
       principles of the Charter of the United Nations, the Universal Declaration of
       Human Rights, the United Nations Declaration on the Elimination of All Forms
       of Racial Discrimination, and this Convention.
[36]   See article 5(a) of the Convention on the Elimination of All Forms of
       Discrimination against Women, which states that States Parties shall take all
       appropriate measures, including legislation, "to modify the social and cultural
       patterns of conduct of men and women, with a view to achieving the elimination
       of prejudices and customary and all other practices which are based on the idea of

the issue of state responsibility, is it possible to take adequate account of – and confront – the realities of the uneven reach and commitment of the state, and the fact that many state institutions are themselves infused with tribal ideology?

IDENTIFYING SPECIFIC STRATEGIES TO ADDRESS "CRIMES OF HONOUR"

Research and documentation

Participants discussed particular efforts to document the incidence of "crimes of honour" and to research the response to such crimes by relevant actors (for example, the state, including the judiciary, community or religious leaders and institutions, NGOs and the media). The following is a summary of the points raised and discussed.[37]

In conducting research on the issue of "honour crimes", we need to be very sensitive to the context in which we work and to differentiate between long-term and short-term strategies. One of the first questions to decide in conducting such research relates to identifying the best sources of information. These may include, depending on where the research is being conducted: victims themselves or their families; the police; the legal community (lawyers, bar associations, court officers, Advocate/Attorney General's office); the medical profession (doctors, hospitals); local government institutions; and the media. In Palestine, WCLAC's methodology for compiling data on "honour killings" has included the use of victim surveys and the collection of data from tribal sources. Particular difficulties in undertaking such research include the lack of statistics, in particular gender-disaggregated data, the under-reporting of incidents of "honour crimes" and killings, due in part to collusion between state officials and the victims' families in a conspiracy of silence and the lack of access to public records, including judgments and sentences, combined with inadequate case reporting. On the positive side, it is clear that such research is more effective where it is action-oriented. Interviewees are far more responsive if they know that the research will have an outcome – for example, in Palestine, the police have begun to refer cases of "honour killings" to WCLAC after having become aware of the organization's ongoing efforts to conduct research on this issue.

In documenting the issue of "honour crimes", as in the case of other human rights documentation and research, it is important to be conscious of the constraints of undertaking such research without alienating the local community. It is also important to work out how international organizations can best work with local or national organizations to share information and to bring the results of their research to a wider audience. Amnesty International, for example, receives considerable cooperation from local lawyers and activists in preparing its reports, which are, in turn, aimed at enabling its membership to act at different levels.

Regarding specific research methodologies, some participants expressed reservations on the use of victim surveys as a method of checking prevalence rates for violence. A research project on domestic violence in Morocco, co-funded by UNICEF, UNIFEM and UNDP, was suggested as a possible model for research methodologies. It was suggested that it might often be more useful to present specific

---

cont.
　　the inferiority or the superiority of either of the sexes or on stereotyped roles for
　　men and women.".
[37] 　The discussion was prefaced by presentations by Nadera Shalhoub-Kevorkian and
　　Angelika Pathak.

stories, rather than confining the presentation of research to statistical data and analysis, and that advocacy could be built into research methods as they were developed.

Law-related strategies

In this session, participants were requested to consider the potential and limitations of litigating or presenting cases of "honour crimes" before domestic courts or human rights institutions (and, if relevant, before regional and international courts, tribunals and mechanisms) and the local or community impact of such strategies. They were also asked to consider the response of the judiciary, and other state institutions, such as law enforcement agencies, in particular the police, and the need for availability of support services that enable survivors of "honour crimes" to access the law, including shelters and counselling services. Finally, they were requested to consider the relevance and interplay of human rights law and criminal or civil remedies and the international dimension of certain cases, including the scope for submitting communications to relevant international human rights mechanisms. A specific issue for discussion was the possibility of submitting information to the UN Special Rapporteurs on extrajudicial, summary or arbitrary executions and on violence against women, its causes and consequences, with a view to enabling them to address the issue of "honour crimes" more fully in their reports. A summary of the points raised and discussed follows below.[38]

The scope for legal action at the national level was illustrated through a review of experiences in the UK. Here, women's rights organizations have pinpointed the issue of the state's responsibility to prevent and to protect women from violence, particularly from domestic violence and rape. They have challenged the state to recognize domestic violence, and now "honour crimes", as crimes rather than customary practices to be condoned and/or tolerated. Asian and black women's organizations have confronted particular difficulties as minorities seeking to negotiate with an oppressive and racist state and have challenged the police's failure to underpin an understanding of diversity with notions of equality. Specifically, this has meant challenging the police's failure to intervene in cases of domestic violence, and more recently, in cases of forced marriage, where attempts are made to justify such non-intervention on culturally relativist grounds.

Experience with such cases has revealed the extent to which survivors are themselves criminalized by the state or the community, the relative impotence of available remedies and the failure of existing mechanisms to hold the police accountable. All of this reinforces women's complaints about their lack of effective citizenship. In their experience, the state and community often conspire to undermine and prevent the protection of women against violence. This situation is exacerbated by the assumption that minority communities should be self-policing. There is a risk of further deterioration if demands for the recognition of greater autonomy for minority communities, and for families within them, are met by the state.

Women's rights organizations in the UK have adopted different legal strategies, including both civil actions against the police, as well as human rights law-based challenges (the latter will become possible in the national courts in the UK after the Human Rights Act comes into force in 2000). The decision of the European Court

---

[38]   The discussions were introduced by presentations from Asma Jahangir, Aida Touma Sliman and Pragna Patel.

of Human Rights in *Osman v. UK*[39] is a valuable addition to the relevant jurisprudence in this regard.

In many cases of "crimes of family honour" in the Palestinian community in Israel, the victims are themselves revictimized and face sanctions from their own families. One strategy developed in such cases is to enable women to build alternative communities and support structures for themselves, in particular through the provision of shelters. For example, the first shelter for Palestinian women was set up in Israel in 1993. There was considerable resistance to it at first from within the community, but it was found that where women were forced to choose between the community and themselves, they did indeed choose themselves and opted for the shelter. The shelter is currently funded by the state. This is not ideal, as it imposes controls and invokes the paternalism inherent in the relationship of those who give and those who take. This paternalism is reinforced in this particular situation where those who operate and use the shelter are from a minority community. At the same time, the proposal to privatize shelters, due to start in Israel from 2000, is also of great concern. The real challenge is in securing autonomy and adequate funding for such shelters, which could assist in the design and implementation of context-specific interventions. Even where there is no state-run shelter, the state is responsible for the protection of those in existing shelters. The importance of framing guidelines regarding state responsibility in this regard is an issue that could be taken up by the two Special Rapporteurs mentioned above.

There is a continuum between the various strategies to be used at the national and international levels. At the national level, given the need for legal remedies, the judiciary provides the primary avenue for redress. Thus, the sensitization of the judiciary is an important task. The exposure of judges to human rights principles, through, for example, participation in INTERIGHTS Judicial Colloquia on the Domestic Application of International Human Rights, may yield real results.

Internationally, of the various UN human rights bodies, "honour crimes" were explicitly addressed by three UN Special Rapporteurs in 1999: the Special Rapporteurs on extrajudicial, summary or arbitrary executions, on violence against women, its causes and consequences, and on the independence of judges and lawyers.[40] Particular concern was voiced at the impunity or mitigation provided by some states to the perpetrators of such crimes, whether through legislative or judicial recognition of the defence of honour, or by non-intervention of police to protect victims. The Special Rapporteurs are cooperating in their efforts to address the issues.[41] The reports of

---

[39] *Osman v. The United Kingdom*, ECHR (87/1997/871/1083).

[40] Respectively, UN Docs.E/CN.4/1999/39, E/CN.4/1999/68; and E/CN/4/1999/60.

[41] All three Special Rapporteurs addressed the issue explicitly and in some cases in greater length in their reports of 2000. Asma Jahangir, the Special Rapporteur on extrajudicial, summary or arbitrary executions, recorded receiving reports of "honour killings" from Bangladesh, Turkey, Jordan, Israel, India, Italy, Sweden, the United Kingdom, Pakistan, Brazil, Ecuador, Uganda and Morocco, went into some detail on the various legislative provisions in different countries and noted certain efforts at reform; in her concluding remarks, she stated that "The Special Rapporteur further feels a personal commitment and responsibility to address the unacceptable practice of so-called 'honour killings', which she concludes may constitute violations of the right to life when condoned or ignored by the authorities." See UN Doc.E/CN.4/2000/3. See also reports by the Special Rapporteur on violence against women, E/CN.4/2000/68 and by the Special Rapporteur on the independence of judges and lawyers, E/CN.4/2000/61.

the Special Rapporteurs were to be submitted on 15 December 1999, and a request for material to be submitted was made to the meeting.

In addition to making submissions to these Special Rapporteurs, it is important strategically to try to mainstream gender issues before all international bodies, and to raise the issue of "honour crimes" as a human rights violation before as many UN human rights bodies as possible. Strategically, it may also be useful to raise the issue of shelters in the context of any discussion on "honour crimes", so that it can also be raised in relation to the broader issue of domestic violence. In particular, it is important to submit communications and shadow reports to the UN human rights treaty bodies. These include the Human Rights Committee, the Committee on the Elimination of Racial Discrimination, the Committee on Economic, Social and Cultural Rights, the Committee Against Torture and the Committee on the Rights of the Child. Communications could be submitted to other mechanisms, such as the Working Group on Arbitrary Detention, as well as to the Special Rapporteur on Torture. Another suggestion that might be followed up was a review of the definition of genocide, to examine whether any provision could be made to define a gender-specific form of genocide.

Cross-cultural and internal cultural dialogue

Participants were asked to consider the scope and process for conducting dialogue across and within communities on the issue of "honour crimes". A summary of the discussion is set out below.[42]

For many human rights activists, there are tensions in developing a religious discourse because of the sense of legitimizing a paradigm in which they are neither comfortable nor competent. However, involvement in such a discourse is part of a long-term investment in social transformation.[43] In many contexts, for example, it will be necessary to clarify that Islam does not condone "honour killings" in order to obtain the political support of ordinary Muslims on the street and to mobilize them against the practice. Where there is a constituency which believes and trusts in religious leaders, and listens to them, it is necessary to engage with that leadership. This engagement requires a sound methodology and cannot be based simply on picking out elements that appear to support the desired position.

The risks of engaging with religious arguments also need to be recognized. Such engagements may provoke certain figures into taking oppositional statements to the purposes or persons involved in campaigns to end "crimes of honour". Various forms of this problem have already occurred in some places, with such engagements provoking those asserting a "religious" status outside a formal religious hierarchy, whether or not allied with particular political (for example, Islamist) tendencies or parties, to take hostile positions to increase their own standing in the constituency of religious conservatism.

Different approaches will be needed in different contexts regarding the possibility and nature of cultural dialogue. There is a need to engage directly with the issue of culture-based support for "crimes of honour", as compared to – or as well as –

---

[42]   The discussion was introduced by comments from Abdullahi An-Na'im.
[43]   See some of An-Na'im's writings on this in for example: "The Dichotomy Between Religious and Secular Discourse in Islamic Societies", in Mahnaz Afkhami (ed.), *Faith and Freedom: Women's Human Rights in the Muslim World*, London, I.B.Tauris 1995, pp. 51–60.

religion-based support, and to explore the resonance of a secular discourse grounded in culture to oppose the practices. In Pakistan, for example, there is a certain space available within which intra-community dialogue can be fostered. It could be useful to open up a dialogue with tribal *sardars* or *pirs* who give shelter to women threatened by "honour killings". For many women the state-run shelter is very much the last resort, after these more traditional and familiar avenues of refuge have been exhausted. A number of tribal *sardars* recently gave a statement saying they would not use women as a form of compensation for murder, another example of space opening for dialogue on these issues.

Furthermore, as the state tends to be responsive to the voices of community leaders, it is important to explore the extent to which those voices can be enlisted in the struggle against "crimes of honour". It may be that this dialogue has to employ the vocabulary of humanity and compassion, rather than sexual autonomy. It is important to remember, however, that the kinds of dialogue required within minority communities are likely to be very different from those where the community in question which condones or sanctions "honour crimes" is part of a majority population, whether religious or ethnic. Other questions for consideration include how a methodology of dialogue could address conflicts and tensions within communities over the incidence of "honour killings", and even conflicts among the perpetrators, some of whom may commit such crimes under coercion (real or anticipated) from others within their families and/or communities.

In its work on femicide, WCLAC (led by project director Nadera Shalhoub-Kevorkian) has developed two intervention programmes designed specifically to respond to contextual sensitivities. The first, the "dialogue tent", aims to help women to dialogue their positions and status in society after centuries of silence; the second, termed "My Life on Trial", follows up the first and seeks methods of activating resources to prevent women from being excluded.

Advocacy and media strategies

Participants discussed their experiences of advocacy on "honour crimes", including working with the media, focusing on both negative and positive interactions. The following is a summary of the points raised and discussed.[44]

Media strategies and responses need to be developed in relation to different types of media (press and broadcast; international and national), and in light of the limitations of the media. Considerable caution is needed when working with the media on the issue of "honour crimes", which can easily be sensationalized, and where careless reporting can result in placing informants in serious danger. It was felt that those working on the issue could not avoid giving information to the national or local media, given that they are able to locate the information they need even without the help of women's or human rights groups. Also, involvement of these groups reduces the chances of a negative spin being put on the information. A particular concern is with sensationalization of the issue in the press. The combination of sex and violence involved in "honour crimes" lends itself readily to lurid images and, in the case of the Western media, cultural stereotyping, which can result in a backlash on the issue at a national level.

In Pakistan, advocacy on the issue of "honour crimes" has been conducted

---

[44] The discussion was prefaced by presentations Aida Touma Sliman, Nafisa Shah and Sohail Warraich.

through domestic, regional and international networks and support mechanisms, usually around specific issues and incidents. With the print media, there is a greater possibility in directing the nature of information that is put out, through press releases or rejoinders or clarifications to misleading reports. Given the sensitivity of the issue, there is a need to be very careful about identification of organizations that provide such information. Frequently, alerts and statements are issued that are not actually the work of the named originator. Sensationalizing of the issue has been a problem; the publication of photographs of men and women murdered in "honour killings" almost entails a pornography of violence.

In the UK, the media coverage of Rukhsana Naz's murder and the trial and conviction of her killers contributed to catalysing the establishment of the Home Office's Working Party on Forced Marriage. The media coverage was overwhelmingly positive, providing a space for women to speak out on the issue, and to put forward alternative constructions of her case. In this case, it gave voice to the voiceless. A high degree of vigilance is needed to ensure quality coverage and to challenge the essentializing and stereotyping of minority communities – and the explicit cultural relativist arguments that deny women protection – which may be in evidence when the report is presented for public debate.

In Palestine, activists have felt a need to monitor newspaper reports on the issue, since both overexposure and negative reporting – particularly the type of reporting that identifies the work as being "westernized" etc. – can be damaging. There is also a risk that reports of such cases in the media may provoke copycat attacks.

In Turkey, the media – particularly journalists with whom links have previously been built up, or who are broadly supportive of the issues involved in women's rights – are a useful conduit to information about pending legislation and parliamentary proceedings. Such links enable information to flow in two directions, and also help activists, through their contacts with journalists, to track developments of relevance to work on violence against women.

Particular challenges are involved in working with the Western and/or international media on the subject of "honour crimes". Sensationalist images and analysis are in frequent use in this media, as are generalized or simplified explanations of the phenomenon. The views of activists – those who purvey or convey the information and analysis regarding "honour crimes" – will rarely tally with the views of journalists – those responsible for their wider dissemination in the media – and much is lost in the process of transference. When such material is broadcast or reported in the Western media, there is a real risk of backlash from the government or the communities involved when such material is broadcast or reported.

The media often want to interview the women concerned and organizations have to think carefully about how to deal with requests for contacts. One obvious rule is only to identify women as interviewees where they have stated their willingness to speak publicly about their experiences. Whether or not a survivor chooses to interact with the media may depend on her stage of recovery; some may find it an empowering experience. Some may give media interviews in order to acknowledge publicly the organizations that have supported them or provided them with legal help or shelter. Support groups cannot prevent women being interviewed by the media; but they need to be sure that women are not agreeing to do this only out of a feeling of indebtedness to the organization.

On issues such as "honour crimes", it is crucial to frame the context and the background for discussion of the phenomenon. Amnesty International has found it useful to organize training for journalists on human rights, to ensure they are aware of the complexity and context of particular issues. Building up connections with journalists can prove very useful. It is possible and arguably necessary for activist organizations to engage both with the state and the media, while maintaining at all times their institutional independence and autonomy.

The meeting concluded with a consensus on the need for greater communication and interchange between lawyers, activists and academics working to address "honour crimes". Participants made specific recommendations relating to the development of activities undertaken by the CIMEL/INTERIGHTS project and also proposed initiating or building upon existing proposals for action-research and advocacy on "honour crimes" at the various national levels.

Part IV

Selected Cases

Arbitral Award

In the Second Stage of the Proceedings in the Matter of the Arbitration Between Eritrea and Yemen (Maritime Delimitation)*

INTRODUCTION – PROCEEDINGS IN THE DELIMITATION STAGE OF THE ARBITRATION

1. This Award in the Second Stage of the Arbitration is rendered pursuant to an Arbitration Agreement dated 3 October 1996 (the "Arbitration Agreement"), between the Government of the State of Eritrea ("Eritrea") and the Government of the Republic of Yemen ("Yemen") (hereinafter "the Parties").

2. The Arbitration Agreement, which appears as Annex 1 on page 51, was preceded by an "Agreement on Principles" done at Paris on 21 May 1996, which was signed by Eritrea and Yemen and witnessed by the Governments of the French Republic, the Federal Democratic Republic of Ethiopia and the Arab Republic of Egypt. The Agreement on Principles provided that the Tribunal should decide questions of territorial sovereignty and to that end the Tribunal rendered an Award in the First Stage finding the sovereignty of the disputed islands in the Red Sea to belong either to Eritrea or to Yemen. (See Award in the First Stage, Chapter XI, Dispositif, paragraphs 527–528.)

3. In a correspondence concerning the Written Pleadings for the Second Stage, and including requests for an extension of the time allowed, a question was raised by Eritrea relating to the Traditional Fishing Regime and how it might be pleaded and argued in the Second Stage of the Arbitration. The President's reply was: "the Tribunal is of the view that it is for Eritrea itself to determine the contents of its written pleadings for that stage". This is referred to in Chapter IV below.

4. Pursuant to the time table set forth in the Arbitration Agreement, the Parties filed written Memorials in the Second Stage on 9 March 1999 and Counter-Memorials on 9 June 1999. On 25 May 1999, Mr Tjaco van den Hout, Secretary-General of the Permanent Court of Arbitration, succeeded as Registrar Mr Hans Jonkman, who had retired. Pursuant to Article 7(2) of the Arbitration Agreement, Ms Phyllis Pieper Hamilton, First Secretary of the Permanent Court of Arbitration, served as Secretary to the Tribunal.

---

* Extracts from the First Stage of the Arbitration appeared in this *Yearbook*, vol. 5 (1998–1999), pp. 513–542.

5. Prior to the Hearings in the Second Stage of the Arbitration, after consultation with the Parties, the Tribunal as contemplated by Article 7(4) of the Arbitration Agreement sought assistance with the calculations of the maritime boundaries and the technical preparation of the corresponding chart. On 8 July 1999, pursuant to Article 7(4) the Tribunal communicated an Order to the Parties designation Ms Ieltje Anna Elema, a geodetic engineer, Head of the Geodesy and Tides Department of the Hydrographic Service of the Royal Netherlands Navy, as its expert in geodesy.

6. Article 2 of the Arbitration Agreement provides that:

    1. The Tribunal is requested to provide rulings in accordance with international law, in two stages.
    2. The first stage shall result in an award on territorial sovereignty and on the definition of the scope of the dispute between Eritrea and Yemen ...
    3. The second stage shall result in an award delimiting maritime boundaries. The Tribunal shall decide taking into account the opinion that it will have formed on questions of territorial sovereignty, the United Nations Convention on the Law of the Sea, and any other pertinent factor.

7. Pursuant to the time table set forth in the Arbitration Agreement for the various stages of the Arbitration, and with the consent of the Parties regarding venue, the Oral Proceedings in the second stage of the Arbitration were held 5–16 July 1999 in the Great Hall of Justice in the Peace Palace in the Hague. By Agreement between the Parties, Yemen began the Oral Proceedings.

8. The Tribunal's task was greatly facilitated by the excellence of the oral presentations on both sides.

9. During the Oral Arguments, pursuant to the Article 8(3) of the Arbitration Agreement authorizing the Tribunal to request the Parties' written views on the elucidation of any aspect of the matters before the Tribunal, counsel were asked to respond to various questions. On 13 August 1999 the Parties submitted written responses to questions put to them by the Tribunal on 13 and 16 July. The Tribunal's questions and the answers provided by the Parties are set out in Annex 2 on page 61.

CHAPTER I

The Arguments of the Parties

Introduction

10. The purpose of the present Chapter is to summarise what the Tribunal understands to have been the main arguments of the Parties. For the Tribunal's reasons for acceptance or rejection or modification of those arguments, it may be necessary to turn to later Chapters. In this Chapter describing the arguments of the Parties, it will be convenient in general to follow the order agreed by them for the Oral Presentations and so put first the arguments of Yemen followed by arguments of Eritrea.

11. It may be said at once that both Parties claimed a form of median international boundary line, although their respective claimed median lines follow very different courses and do not coincide. They do, however, follow similar courses in the narrow waters of the southernmost portion of the line. Eritrea's median line is equidistant between the mainland coasts, but its historic median line takes into account Eritrea's islands (but not the Yemen mid-sea islands); the

Yemen line is equidistant between the Eritrean coast (including certain selected points on the Dahlak islands) and the coast of all the Yemen islands. The Yemen line was plotted with WGS 84 coordinates of the turning points; the Eritrean line was not, although, in answer to a question from the Tribunal, the coordinates of the base points were provided. The rival claimed lines are reproduced on the Charts (Eritrea's Maps 3 and 7 and Yemen's Map 12.1) to be found in the map pocket at the back [not included].

Yemen's Proposed Boundary Line

12. The Yemen claimed line was described in three sectors divided by lines of latitude: 16°N;14°25′N; and 13°20′N. So there was (i) a northern sector between the Yemen islands of Jabal al-Tayr and the Jabal al-Zubayr group on the one hand, and the Eritrean Dahlak islands on the other; (ii) a central sector between the Zuqar-Hanish group of Yemen and the opposite mainland coast of Eritrea together with the Mohabbakahs, the Haycocks and the South West Rock; and (iii) a southern sector between the respective mainland coast of Yemen and Eritrea south of the Zuqar-Hanish group. These sectors were fixed by the latitude of the controlling base points of the Yemen line. Thus, for instance, 14°25′N was the point on the line where the controlling base points changed from the points on the islet Centre Peak in the Zubayr group to the base points on the coast of Zuqar.

13. Yemen began its argument with the general understanding, as endorsed by the International Court of Justice in the North Sea Continental Shelf cases,[1] that a median line normally produced an equitable result when applied between opposite coasts. Therefore, argued Yemen, a major preliminary task for the Tribunal was to decide which were the coasts to be used a baselines.

14. In the northern sector, the proposed Yemen line assumed that the Dahlak islands, a closely knit group of some 350 islands and islets, the largest of them having a considerable population, should be recognised as being part of the Eritrean mainland coast and the waters within them as internal waters. It followed that the easternmost islets of that group might be used as base points of the median line. Yemen used the high water line as baseline on these islands.

15. Yemen proposed that the eastern base points of the line should be found on the low-water line of the western coast of the lone mid-sea island of Jabal al-Tayr and on the western coats of the mid-sea group of Jabal al-Zubayr. Yemen argued that these islands should be used as base points because they were as important, or even more important, than the very small uninhabited outer islets of the Dahlak group. In this way, said Yemen, there would be a "balance" in the treatment of island base points on the west and the east coasts, arguing that in this northern area "each Party possesses islands of comparable size, producing similar coastal facades lying at similar distances from their respective mainlands".

16. In the central sector the Yemen claimed line proceeded through the narrow waters between the Hanish group of islands and the Eritrean mainland coast. (This part of the boundary line area was called the "central" one by Yemen but sometimes called the "southern" one by Eritrea.) The Yemen line was a line of equidistance between the high-water line on the Eritrean mainland coast

---

[1] ICJ Reports 1969, p.36, para. 57.

and the low-water line on the westernmost coasts of Yemen's Hanish Island group.

17. Yemen suggested that the "small Eritrean islets in between" the Eritrean mainland coast and the large Yemen islands were inappropriate for a delimitation role. Thus, the computing and the drawing of Yemen's boundary line ignored both the South West Rocks and the three Haycocks (which had been found in the Award on Sovereignty to belong to Eritrea) as being no more than small rocks whose only importance was that they were navigational hazards. The Eritrean sovereignty over these islets was, however, recognised by placing them in limited enclaves.

18. In Yemen's "southern sector", the line entered a narrow sea which had few islets and was relatively free from complicating mid-sea islands or islets, and the line became a simple median between the opposite mainland coasts. By using the islands of Fatuma, Derchos and Ras Mukwar as base points it did, however, recognise that the Bay of Assab was an area of Eritrean internal waters. Yemen added the comment that:

This method of delimitation has been selected in order to accord the islands in the Southern Sector the same treatment as the islands in the Northern Islands Sector.

19. Summing up the three sectors, Yemen observed that, in accordance with the applicable legal principles, the appropriate delimitation would be achieved by a median line between the relevant coasts. There was no justification for any adjustment of this line on the basis of equitable principles. This median line delimitation between the relevant coasts was the only equitable solution compatible with the purpose of this arbitration.

20. Yemen also addressed other relevant factors. There was the factor of proportionality and this, together with Eritrea's argument under the same heading, is dealt with below. There was also discussion of certain "non-geographical relevant circumstances", the first one being "dependency of the fishing communities in Yemen upon Red Sea fishing". This is a matter upon which both Parties held strong and differing views, which are described and considered in Chapter II below.

21. The other of these relevant circumstances maintained by Yemen was "the element of security of the coastal State". This, according to Yemen, "connotes nothing more exciting than non-encroachment". It was chiefly in the narrow waters between the Hanish group of islands and the Eritrean coast that the question of security or non-encroachment arose. According to Yemen, this concern is automatically addressed by the application of the principle of equidistance which was intended to effect equality of treatment.

Eritrea's Proposed Boundary Line

22. Eritrea asserted that there was a legal flaw in the Yemen argument for its claimed line. This criticism illuminated some of the basic ideas underlying Eritrea's own claimed line.

23. Eritrea pointed with some insistence to what it regarded as a fundamental contradiction in the Yemen argument. In the northern part of the line, where the question of the influence upon it of the northern mid-sea islands arose, the maritime boundary was between the respective continental shelves and exclusive economic zones (hereinafter EEZ). These two boundaries, of continental shelf and of EEZ, are governed by Articles 74 and 83 of the United Nations

Convention on the Law of the Sea. In neither of these two articles is there even a mention of equidistance; there is, however, a clear requirement that a delimitation of these areas should "achieve an equitable solution". Nevertheless, for these very areas, Yemen insisted upon an equidistance line having included as base points for it the coasts of its small northern mid-sea islets.

24. In contrast, Eritrea contended in oral argument that, in the narrow seas between the Hanish group of islands and the Eritrean mainland coast, there was an area involving distances less than 24 miles[2] and which was therefore all territorial sea to which Article 15 of the Convention "is going to be most directly applicable in the more southern reaches of the delimitation area in question, the area round the Zuqar and Hanish Islands. The reason for that, of course, is that the distances there are smaller. What that means is that in the area around the Zuqar and Hanish islands there is a basic rule of equidistance."

25. This would favour a median line that takes full account of South West Rocks and the Haycocks, which in the Award on Sovereignty were found to belong to Eritrea. Applying Article 15, moreover, there could be no question of enclaves of these islands.

26. Eritrea also objected that Yemen's proposed enclaves would in practice mean that there was no access corridor for Eritrea through the surrounding Yemen territorial sea. Thus, both the Eritrean South West Rocks and the Haycocks would be "completely isolated". Eritrea objected to the enclave solution because Eritrea claimed this would have put the western main shipping channel, "between the Haycock Island and South West Rocks", into Yemen territorial waters while the eastern main channel, which goes east of Zuqar, was already in undisputed Yemen territorial waters. Thus, Yemen's proposal would result in "inclusion of both the main shipping channels within what would be Yemen's territorial waters if Yemen's proposed delimitation were accepted".

27. Eritrea's own proposed solution of the delimitation problem was in two parts. There was the proposed international boundary, and there was the proposal for certain delimited "boxes" of the mid-sea islands, the purpose of which was to delimit the area which Eritrea claimed to be "joint resource areas". This delimitation of "the shared maritime zones around the islands" was distinguished from recognition of "the exclusive waters of Yemen, to the east, and the exclusive waters of Eritrea, to the west". These ideas represented Eritrea's understanding of what in its view was meant by the reservation in the Award of Sovereignty of the traditional fishing regime, and what was needed to ensure the fulfilment of that regime. Of this Eritrea said, "if this regime is to be perpetuated, the Parties must know what it is and where it holds sway in a technically precise manner".

28. It is to be noted that the "exclusive" Eritrean waters on the west included not merely the territorial sea but also all the waters west of the mid-sea islands and west of the historic median line. These two Eritrean proposals – the two versions of the median line and the joint resource area boxes – belonged together because they were both essential parts of the Eritrean proposal as a whole. Thus, Eritrea's "historic median line" was – although with some variations to be noted later – one drawn as a median between the mainland coasts and ignoring the existence of the mid-sea islands of Yemen, but taking into account the islands of Eritrea. (There are precedents for this kind of boundary line in the petroleum agreements discussed in Chapter III.) Eritrea's "resource box

---

[2]   Throughout this Award the use of "miles" refers to nautical miles.

system" provided the essential elements of a complex solution for the problem of these islands. The boxes were offered in a variety of shapes and sizes (see Eritrea's Maps 4 and 7 [not included]). These "joint resources boxes" seem to have been advanced by Eritrea as a flexible set of suggestions. Its main concern was the reasonable one that it wanted to be able to tell its fishermen precisely where they might fish.

29. The coupling in the Eritrean pleadings of the two questions – the nature of the traditional fishing regime and the delimitation of the international boundary – is in contradistinction to Yemen's arguments. Yemen had expressed the view that "the traditional fishing regime should not have any impact on the delimitation of the maritime boundaries between the two Parties in the Second Stage". Yemen, in answer to a question from the Tribunal, also expressed the view that "Article 13, paragraph 3 of the Arbitration Agreement (see Annex 1) and the framework created by the 1994 and 1998 Agreements obviated any need further to take into account the traditional fishing regime in the delimitation of the maritime boundary". (The two Agreements of 1994 and 1998 are reproduced in Annex 3 to this Award.)

30. Eritrea replied to this letter from Yemen on 24 August saying that:

> Yemen's submission conveys the impression that the two States have conducted discussions since October 1998 which have resulted in arrangements for the implementation of Eritrea's traditional rights. No such discussions have taken place on this subject and no arrangements have been made to protect or preserve Eritrea's traditional rights in the waters around the mid-sea islands.

Arguments about Historic Rights and Sovereignty

31. Sovereignty over the disputed islands was the subject of the First Stage of this Arbitration. The Arbitration Agreement enjoins the Tribunal in this Second Stage to take into account "the opinion it will have formed on questions of territorial sovereignty". It is not surprising, therefore, that both Parties raised some interested questions in this Second Stage about the nature of sovereignty and its relation to the question of delimitation and, not least, to the question of the traditional fishing regime.

32. Eritrea was moved to return to the history of the formerly disputed islands and especially to the period of Italian influence and presence. From these and some other considerations was precipitated the view urged upon the Tribunal that Yemen's "recently acquired" sovereignty over islands made them of less importance as factors to be taken into consideration for the purposes of the delimitation. This approach was expressed in these words:

> Eritrea also considers that the [mid-sea] islands come within the category of small uninhabited islands of recently acquired sovereignty and near the median line that should be recognised by the Tribunal to possess diminished maritime zones.

33. The Eritrean Prayer for Relief took this idea even further when it said in Article 4 that:

> The outer borders of the maritime zones of the islands in which these shared rights exist shall be defined as extending:
>
> A. on the western side of the Red Sea, to the median line drawn between the two coasts, which shall include the islands historically owned by either State prior to the decade preceding commencement of this arbitration in accordance with Article 121 of the United Nations Convention on the Law of the Sea; and

        B. on the eastern side of the Red Sea, as far as the twelve mile limit of Yemen's territorial sea.

34. Continuing the same theme Article 5 of the Prayer for Relief provided:

      5. The waters beyond the shared area of the mid-sea islands shall be divided in accordance with a median line drawn between the two coasts, which shall include the islands historically owned by either State prior to the decade preceding commencement of this Arbitration in accordance with Article 121 of the United Nations Convention on the Law of the Sea.

35. Eritrea felt, therefore, able to urge that "Eritrea possesses historic title to all waters to the west of the historic median line, drawn by reference to the historically owned islands". This idea, it will be noted, yielded a rather different historic median line from the one drawn between the mainland coasts.

36. Yemen's reply was that Yemen's title to the formerly disputed islands was not created by the adjudication in the Award on Sovereignty, but that the adjudication was rather a confirmation of an already existing title; and, that "in arbitrations the issue of title is determined both prospectively and retroactively". These considerations led to some discussion of the effect of a critical date.

37. Yemen was also concerned that Eritrea's proposed joint resource zones were founded upon a supposition that the sovereignty awarded to Yemen in the First Stage was a sovereignty "only limited or conditional". This seems to be partly a war of words. All sovereignty is "limited" by international law. Eritrea can hardly be suggesting that Yemen's sovereignty over the islands is "conditional" in the legal sense according to which failure to observe the condition might act as a cesser of the sovereignty.

38. Eritrea, however, responded by pointing to paragraph 126 of the Award on Sovereignty which speaks of the traditional fishing regime as having, by historical consolidation, established rights for both Parties "as a sort of '*servitude internationale*' falling short of territorial sovereignty". Other aspects of these arguments are discussed in Chapter IV below.

Proportionality

39. This factor was argued strenuously and ingeniously by both Parties. Both relied upon the statement in the North Sea cases that a delimitation should take into account "a reasonable degree of proportionality, which a delimitation carried out in accordance with equitable principles ought to bring about between the extent of the continental shelf areas appertaining to the coastal State and the length of its coast measured in the general direction of the coastline".[3] Both were in agreement with the warning in the Anglo-French Arbitration case[4] that this is a test of equitableness and not a method of delimitation, and that what had to be avoided was a manifest disproportionality resulting from the line selected. So there was little between the Parties as to principle but there was strong disagreement about the measurement of the length of their respective coasts and the significance of that measurement when it was made. The measurement is a matter on which several views are possible when Eritrea's coast extends also to be opposite to Yemen's neighbouring State, the Kingdom of Saudi Arabia; with which the maritime boundary remains undelimited.

---

3   ICJ Reports 1969, p. 57, para. 101.
4   18 ILM 60; 54 ILR 6.

40. The Yemen position was that proportionality is a factor to be taken into account in testing the equitableness of a delimitation already effected by other means. In relation in particular to the line to be drawn in the central sector, Yemen suggested that the relative lengths of the coasts overall were not significant because (i) in the restricted seas between the Yemen islands and the Eritrean coast any modifications of the median line would involve the principle of non-encroachment; (ii) further, in the central sector, given the general configuration of the coasts, equal division alone guarantees an equitable result; (iii) equal division is reinforced by the principle of non-encroachment; (iv) the relevant coasts for this delimitation are the Eritrean coast and the Yemen islands; (v) State practice supported the median line; and (vi) proportionality cannot be applied in the context of overlapping territorial sea.

41. The Eritrean reply to this was to question whether the Yemen claimed line in the central sector really was the median line envisaged in Article 15 of the Convention; and Eritrea suggested that it was not so, because it ignored the low-water line base points of the Eritrean islands of South West Rocks and the Haycocks.

42. It is not possible here to describe the many variations to be found in the pleadings on the theme of the method of measurements to be employed, or the discussions of the ambiguities of "oppositeness", although the Tribunal has examined them all. Suffice it to say that whereas Yemen calculated that its own claimed line nearly divided the sea areas into almost equal areas, which according to Yemen's measurements of the length of the coasts were the correct proportion, Eritrea found, in a final choice of one of its several different methods of calculations, that its own historic median line between the mainland coasts would produce respective areas favouring Eritrea by a proportion of 3 to 2, which again was said to reflect accurately the proportion of the lengths of coast according to Eritrea's method of measuring them.

43. It should be mentioned that Eritrea was particularly concerned that, in calculating the areas resulting from the delimitation, account should not be taken of the internal waters within the Dahlaks or the bays along its coasts, including the Bay of Assab.

The Northern and Southern Extremities of the Boundary Line

44. There also arose a question about where to stop the boundary at its northern and southern ends, considering that in these areas it might prejudice other boundary disputes with neighbouring countries. The Kingdom of Saudi Arabia indeed had written to the Registrar of the Tribunal on 31 August 1997 pointing out that its boundaries with Yemen were disputed, reserving its position, and suggesting that the Tribunal should restrict its decisions to areas "that do not extend north of the latitude of the most northern point on Jabal al-Tayr island". Yemen for its part wished that determination to extend to the latitude of 16°N, which is the limit of its so-called northern sector. Eritrea on the other hand stated that it had "no objection" to the Saudi Arabian proposal.

45. At the southern end, the third States concerned have not made representations to the Tribunal, but the matter will nevertheless have to be determined. Eritrea was most concerned here about the arrow with which Yemen terminated its claimed line, as this arrow, according to Eritrea, pointed in such a direction as to "slash" the main shipping channel and cause it to be in Yemen territorial

waters. Yemen had also used an arrow to terminate the northern end of its line and there was some discussion and debate from both sides about the propriety or otherwise of these arrows.

46. At the southern end of the line, as it approached the Bab-al-Mandab, there is the complication of the possible effect upon the course of the boundary line of the Island of Perim. This question might clearly involve the views of Djibouti. It follows that the Tribunal's line should stop short of the place where any influence upon it of Perim Island would begin to take effect. The Tribunal has taken into consideration these positions variously expressed and has reached its own conclusions, as more fully detailed in Chapter V below.

* * *

The submissions of Yemen and the Prayer for Relief of Eritrea appear below.

Submissions of Yemen

On the basis of the facts and legal considerations presented in Yemen's pleadings; and Rejecting all contrary submissions presented in Eritrea's "Prayer for Relief", and In view of the provisions of Article 2(3) of the Arbitrations Agreement; The Republic of Yemen, respectfully requests the Tribunal to adjudge and declare:

1. That the maritime boundary between the Parties is a median line, every point of which is equidistance from the relevant base points on the coast of the Parties as identified in Chapters 8 through 10 of Yemen's Memorial, appropriate account being taken to the islets and rocks comprising South West Rocks, the Haycocks and the Mohabbakahs;
2. That the course of the delimitation, including the coordinates of the turning points on the boundary line established on the basis of the World Geodetic System 1984 (WGS 84), are those that appear in Chapter 12 to Yemen's Memorial.

Eritrea's Prayer for Relief

(Paragraph 274, Memorial of the State of Eritrea)

Article 2, paragraph 3, of the Arbitration Agreement requires the Tribunal to issue an award delimiting the maritime boundaries between the Parties in a technically precise manner. In order that such precision shall be achieved, the State of Eritrea respectfully requests the Tribunal to render an award providing as follows:

1. The Eritrean people's historic use of resources in the mid-sea islands includes fishing, trading, shell and pearl diving, guano and mineral extraction, and all associated activities on land including drying fish, drawing water, religious and burial practices, and building and occupying shelters for sleep and refuge;
2. The right to such usage, to be shared with the Republic of Yemen, extends to all of the land areas and maritime zones of the mid-sea islands;
3. The right to such usage shall be preserved intact in perpetuity, as it has existed in the past, without interference through the imposition of new regulations, burdens, curtailments or any other infringements or limitations of any kind whatsoever, except those agreed upon by Eritrea and Yemen as expressed in a written agreement between them;

4. The outer borders of the maritime zones of the islands in which these shared rights exist shall be defined as extending:
   A. on the western side of the Red Sea, to the median line drawn between the two coasts, which shall include the islands historically owned by either State prior to the decade preceding commencement of this arbitration in accordance with Article 121 of the United Nations Convention on the Law of the Sea: and
   B. on the eastern side of the Red Sea, as far as the twelve mile limit of Yemen's territorial sea.
5. The waters beyond the shared area of the mid-sea islands shall be divided in accordance with a median line drawn between two coasts, which shall include the islands historically owned by either State prior to the decade preceding commencement of this Arbitration in accordance with Article 121 of the United Nations Convention on the Law of the Sea;
6. The two Parties are directed to negotiate the modalities for shared usage of the mid-sea islands and their waters in accordance with the following terms:
   A. Immediately following the Tribunal's rendering of an award in the second Phase, the Parties shall commence negotiations, in good faith, with a view toward concluding an agreement describing the ways in which nationals of both Parties may use the resources of the mid-sea islands and their maritime zones, as those zones are described in the Award of the Tribunal, and detailing a mechanism of binding dispute resolution to settle any and all disputes out of the interpretation or application of the agreement;
   B. The Parties shall submit this agreement to the Tribunal for its review and approval no later than six months after the date the Tribunal renders its award in the second Phase;
   C. The Tribunal shall determine whether the agreement is in accord with its award in the second Phase, and in particular whether it faithfully preserves the traditional rights of the two Parties to usage of the resources of the mid-sea islands.
   D. If the Tribunal determines that the agreement is not satisfactory according to the criteria described in the preceding paragraph, or if the Parties fail to submit an agreement, the Tribunal shall issue an award that either describes such modalities or else appoints the water between the two Parties equally. The Tribunal may request submissions from the Parties on this point.
   E. If the Tribunal finds that the agreement (or a revised agreement) is satisfactory, according to the criteria set forth above, it shall communicate its approval to the Parties, endorse the agreement as its own award and further direct the Parties to execute the agreement in the form of a binding treaty to be deposited with the Secretary-General of the United Nations.
7. The Tribunal shall remain seized of the dispute between the Parties until such time as the agreement regarding shared usage of the mid-sea islands has been received for deposit by the Secretary-General of the United Nations.

CHAPTER II

The General Question of Fishing in the Red Sea

47. This chapter will first deal with the evidence and argument advanced by the Parties concerning the general question of fishing in the Red Sea. It will then set forth the Tribunal's conclusions on these arguments and evidence.

The Evidence and Arguments of the Parties

48. Each Party made much of fishing, including both the past history and the present situation, and as related not only to its own nationals but also the practices of the nationals of the other Party. The evidence advanced by the Parties and the arguments made by them can essentially be broken down into five subjects. These are: (1) fishing in general; (2) the location of fishing areas; (3) the economic dependency of the Parties on fishing; (4) consumption of fish by the populations of the Parties; and (5) the effect of fishing practices on the lines of delimitation proposed by the Parties.

49. The arguments of each Party were advanced essentially in order to demonstrate that the delimitation line proposed by that Party would not alter the existing situation and historical practices, that it would not have a catastrophic effect on local fishermen or on the local or national economy of the other Party or a negative effect on the regional diet of the population of the other Party and, conversely, that the delimitation line proposed by the other Party would alter the existing situation and historical practice, would have a catastrophic or at least a severely adverse effect on the local fishermen or on the first Party's regional economy, and would also have a negative effect on the diet of the population of the first Party.

50. These elements were introduced directly and indirectly by each side against the general background of the "catastrophic" and "long usage" tests originated in the Anglo-Norwegian Fisheries Case of 1951 – and as brought forward in the provisions *inter alia* of Article 7, paragraph 5 of the 1982 United Nations Convention on the Law of the Sea.

51. They also found an echo in the "equitable solution" called for by paragraph 1 of Articles 74 and 83 of the Convention, it being assumed that no "solution" could be equitable which would be inconsistent with long usage, which would present a clear and present danger of a catastrophic result on the local economy of one of the Parties, or which would fail to take into account the need to minimise detrimental effects on fishing communities, and the economic dislocation, of States whose nationals have habitually fished in the relevant area.

Fishing in General

52. The position taken by Eritrea was as follows. The historical record demonstrated that the Eritrean fishing industry was substantial before the civil war in Ethiopia and had been, second only to Egypt, the most important regional fishing economy. Since the end of the civil war and independence, serious efforts were underway to reestablish the Eritrean fishing economy. It was, therefore, a mistake to consider that the Eritrean fisheries were – as Yemen argued – to a large extend dependent on Eritrean freshwater fisheries; in fact these have had no importance. On the other hand, the Yemen fishing industry was substantially based on its Indian Ocean fisheries and did not rely significantly on the Red Sea. Although Yemen's fishing industry in the Red Sea is much less significant than Yemen has claimed, it is nonetheless well established and in no event dependent for protection on the particular delimitation line proposed by Yemen.

53. Yemen argued that Yemeni nationals have long dominated fishing activities in the Red Sea; the Yemen traditional fishing activities – conducted in small boats, whether sambouks or houris – had been of much greater significance in the past than those of Eritrea, whose fishing activities had largely been concentrated

on fishing close inshore along the Eritrean coastline and in and among the Dahlaks. Moreover, Hodeidah in Yemen was the most active market for fisheries production from Eritrean and Yemeni fishermen alike.

Economic Dependency on Fishing

54. The position of Eritrea was that considerable efforts had been made since the close of the war to reorganise and build up the Eritrean fishing industry – including efforts sponsored by the UNDP and FAO – and that the prospects for significant future development of the Eritrean fisheries were both promising and important. Although Eritrea did not claim present economic dependency on fishing, it did make the point that the existing fisheries practices of its nationals should not be restricted or curtailed by the delimitation to be decided by the Tribunal. As to Yemen, Eritrea asserted not only that the Yemen's Red Sea fisheries presence was far less important than Yemen had claimed, but also that most fish landed in Hodeidah were brought there by Eritrean fishermen.

55. On the other hand, Yemen argued that its fishermen have always depended on the Red Sea fisheries as their fishing grounds and that this fishing activity had long constituted an important part of Yemen's overall national economy and been a dominant part of the regional economy of the Tihama region along the Red Sea coast. Yemen claimed that Eritrea had no basis for arguing that it possessed any substantial dependency on fishing, fisheries, fish or fish consumption, and that most of Eritrea's concerns as manifested by documentary evidence submitted to the Tribunal in both Stages of the Arbitration had concerned proposals and projects for the development of future fishing activity and fisheries resources of Eritrea that did not now exist or were not now utilised.

Location of Fishing Areas

56. The arguments of Eritrea were to the following effect: at present, fishing in the Red Sea was by and large dominated by Eritrean artisanal fishermen who caught their fish around the Dahlaks, along the Eritrean coast, around the Mohabbakahs, the Haycocks, and South West Rocks, and in the waters around the Zuqar-Hanish group of "mid-sea islands". (As noted above, Eritrea denied that any part of its fish catch depended on inland Eritrean fisheries such as in lakes and reservoirs.) As to Yemen, Eritrea claimed that Yemeni fishermen had hardly, if at all, relied on the deep-water fishing grounds to the west of the mid-sea islands and around the Mohabbakahs, the Haycocks, and South West Rocks; there was little evidence of any Yemeni nationals' activity west of the Zuqar-Hanish group; and Yemen had failed to prove that a single gram of fish consumed in Yemen was taken from those waters.

57. For its part, Yemen argued that its artisanal and traditional fishermen had long fished in the waters around Jabal al-Tayr and the Zubayr group, in the waters around the Zuqar-Hanish group, and in the deep waters west of Greater Hanish and around the Mohabbakahs, the Haycocks, and South West Rocks. Supporting these assertions was evidence produced in the form of witness statements in the First Stage of the Arbitration in which individual fishermen indicated that they had fished in the waters in question for a long time. As to the other Party, Yemen again asserted that Eritrea's fishing activities were confined to waters of the Dahlak archipelago and the inshore waters along the Eritrean

coast and did not to any substantial extent impinge on waters surrounding the
islands at issue in the First Stage of the Arbitration – including the deep waters
west of Greater Hanish and around the Mohabbakahs, the Haycocks, and South
West Rocks.

Consumption of Fish by the Population

58. Eritrea argued that the Eritrean coastal population consumed far more fish than
Yemen claimed and that, in addition, efforts were taking place to increase the
popularity and availability of fresh fish for human consumption by its general
population. It further asserted that the Yemeni population's dependence on
fresh fish from the Red Sea as a food source had been greatly exaggerated by
Yemen's pleadings, and that the Yemeni population of the Tihama – and *a
fortiori* the population of Yemen as a whole – did not rely to any significant
extent on fresh fish as a food. For its part, Yemen maintained that its population,
particularly in the coastal areas such as the Tihama, consumed substantial
quantities of fish and that – by contrast – Eritrean fish consumption was
negligible.

Effect on Lines of Delimitation Proposed by the Parties

59. The Eritrean position was that the Tribunal's indication of a line of delimitation
such as the "historic median line" suggested by Eritrea would respect the
historic practice of the Parties, would not displace or adversely affect Yemen's
fishing activity, and would be an equitable result for both Parties. In Eritrea's
view, however, the Yemen proposed "median line" would deprive Eritrean
fishermen of valuable fishery areas east of the mid-sea islands, and would award
to Yemen areas to the west of the mid-sea islands and around the Mohabbakahs,
the Haycocks, and the South West Rocks – where Eritrean fishermen had long
been plying their trade and where Yemeni nationals had never engaged in
substantial fisheries activity. To that extent Eritrea argued that the proposed
Yemen delimitation line would be inequitable and would deprive Eritrean
fishermen of an important resource.
60. On the other side, Yemen maintained that the median line proposed by it
would correctly reflect historical practices, would not give Yemen anything it
did not have before, would respect existing rights, would not "penalise" existing
or past Eritrean fishing activity, and would constitute an equitable result. As far
as the Eritrean proposed "historic median line" was concerned, it would
encroach on Yemen's traditional fishing grounds without justification, would
deprive Yemeni fishermen of deep water fisheries west of the mid-sea islands,and
would give a corresponding windfall to Eritrea.

* * *

The Tribunal's Conclusions on the Evidence

61. The purposes of the arguments and evidence of the Parties were several, but
were essentially directed to establishing that the delimitation advanced by each
Party would respect existing historical practices, would not have a catastrophic

effect on local fishermen or population, would not have a generally negative effect on the economy (or future plans) of the other Party, and would not have a deleterious effect on the diet and health of the population of the other Party. By the same token, each Party asserted or implied that the line of delimitation advanced by the other would have precisely the converse effect. The evidence advanced by the Parties has to a very large extent been contradictory and confusing.

On the basis on the arguments and evidence advanced before it the Tribunal reaches the following conclusions.

As to Fishing in General

62. Fishing in general is an important activity for both sides of the Red Sea coast. This was recognised in the Award on sovereignty of the Tribunal. It is not necessary and probably misleading to seek to determine the precise extent of its importance at any particular time, but the plain fact appears to be that – as the Tribunal stated in paragraph 526 of its Award in Sovereignty – "the traditional fishing regime in the region … has operated, as the evidence presented to the Tribunal amply testifies, around the Hanish and Zuqar Island and the islands of Jabal al-Tayr and the Zubayr group".

63. Moreover, the whole point of the Tribunal's holding in paragraph vi of its Dispositif in the Award on Sovereignty – that this traditional fishing regime shall be perpetuated so as to include "free access and enjoyment for the fishermen of both Eritrea and Yemen" – is that such traditional fishing activity has already been adjudged by the Tribunal to be important to each Party and to their nationals on both sides of the Red Sea. It thus suffices to say that fishing, fishermen, and fisheries are, and remain, of importance to each Party in the present case. Precisely because of this significance of paragraph 526 of the Award of Sovereignty and paragraph vi of its Dispositif, the fishing practices of the Parties from time to time are not germane to the task of arriving at a line of delimitation.

As to Economic Dependency on Fishing

64. It is not possible or necessary for the Tribunal to reach a conclusion that either Eritrea or Yemen is economically dependent on fishing to such an extent as to suggest any particular line of delimitation. The evidence before the Tribunal suggests that fishing activity and income appear to form an important part of Yemen's economic activity – particularly of the Tihama region – and that revitalisation and development of the Eritrean fishing industry is a priority objective of the Government of Eritrea and has received significant attention since Eritrean independence.

As to Location of Fishing Areas

65. The evidence advanced in both Stages of the Arbitration included evidence that many fishermen from Eritrea tended largely to fish in and around the Dahlak archipelago and on inshore waters along the Eritrean coastline, but it also

appears that some Eritrean fishermen used the waters in and around the Hanish and Zuqar Islands as well as the deep waters to the west of the mid-sea islands and around the Mohabbakahs, the Haycocks, and South West Rocks. This conclusion was adumbrated by the Tribunal's concern for maintenance of the traditional fishing regime "in the region" as a whole, "including free access and enjoyment for the fishermen of both Eritrea and Yemen" (Award on Sovereignty, Dispositif, paragraph 527, subparagraph vi).

66. There is abundant historical data indicating that fishermen from both the eastern and western coasts of the Red Sea freely undertook activities, including fishing and selling their catch on the local markets, regardless of their national political affiliation of their place of habitual domicile.[5]

67. This information concerning the social and economic conditions affecting the lives of the people on both sides of the Red Sea also reflects deeply-rooted and common social and legal traditions that had prevailed for centuries among these populations, each of which was under the direct or indirect rule of the Ottoman Empire until the latter part of the XIXth Century.

68. The evidence before the Tribunal further appears to establish that over the years Yemeni fishermen have operated as far north as the Dahlak archipelago and Jabal al-Tayr and the Zubayr group, and as far west as the Mohabbakahs, the Haycocks, and South West Rocks. Again, this conclusion is implicit in the Tribunal's concern for maintenance of the traditional fishing regime "in the region" as a whole.

69. On a subject not unrelated to fishing areas, it should be noted that the evidence is quite clear that Eritrean fishermen as well as Yemeni also appear to have enjoyed free and open access to the major fish market at Hodeidah on the Yemen side of the Red Sea without impediment by reason of their nationality. (This element was again taken into account by the Tribunal in its Award on Sovereignty, Dispositif, paragraph 527, subparagraph vi.)

As to Consumption of Fish by the Population

70. The evidence concerning fish consumption advanced by each Party was presumably aimed at establishing that the Tribunal's adoption of the line of delimitation proposed by the other Party would constitute a serious dietary or health threat to the population of the first Party. However, the evidence on this matter is conflicting and uncertain. It is difficult if not impossible to draw any generalised conclusions from the welter of alleged facts advanced by the Parties in this connection.

71. The Tribunal can readily conclude, without having to weigh intangible and elusive points of proof or without having to indulge in nice calculations of nutritional theory, that fish as a present and future potential resource is important for the general and local populations of each Party on each side of the Red Sea. The Tribunal can also conclude, as a matter of common sense and judicial notice, that interest in and development of fish as a food source is an important and meritorious objective. Based on these two conclusions, however, the Tribunal can find no significant reason on these grounds for accepting – or rejecting – the arguments of either Party as to the line of delimitation proposed by itself or by the other Party.

---

5   See footnotes 9 and 11 to paragraphs 121 and 128 respectively of the Award on Sovereignty.

Concerning the Effect on Lines of Delimitation Proposed by the Parties

72.   Based on the foregoing, the Tribunal finds no significant reason on any other
        grounds concerning fishing – whether related to the historical practice of fishing
        in general, to matters of asserted economic dependency on fishing, to the
        location of fishing grounds, or to the patterns of fish consumption by the
        populations – for accepting, or rejecting, the arguments of either Party on the
        line of delimitation proposed by itself or by the other Party. Neither Party has
        succeeded in demonstrating that the line of delimitation proposed by the other
        would produce a catastrophic or inequitable effect on the fishing activity of its
        nationals or detrimental effects on fishing communities and economic disloca-
        tion of its nationals.[6]
73.   For these reasons, it is not possible for the Tribunal to accept or reject the line
        of delimitation proposed by either Party on fisheries grounds. Nor can the
        Tribunal find any relevant effect on the legal reasons supporting its own selection
        of a delimitation line arising from its consideration of the general past fishing
        practice of either Party or the potential deprivation of fishing areas or access to
        fishing resources, or arising from nutritional or other grounds.
74.   For the above reasons, the evidence and arguments advanced by the Parties in
        the matter of fishing and fisheries could have no significant effect on the
        Tribunal's determination of the delimitation that would be appropriate under
        international law in order to produce an equitable solution between the Parties.

CHAPTER III
Petroleum Agreements and Median Lines

75.   In the matter of the pertinence and probative force for this Stage of the
        proceedings of petroleum contracts and concessions entered into by Yemen and
        by Ethiopia or Eritrea the Parties exhibited a reversal of roles.
76.   In the First Stage, Yemen laid great weight on oil contracts and concessions
        concluded by it. It introduced into evidence a number of such oil agreements
        and maps illustrating them, many of which were prepared by Petroconsultants
        SA of Geneva. Since some of these arrangements embodied western boundaries
        to the east of which lay some of the islands in dispute, Yemen argued that these
        arrangements demonstrated that both Yemen and the contracting oil companies
        were of the view that Yemen enjoyed sovereignty over those disputed islands.
        It contended that, where a State enters into a concession covering a specified
        area, it holds itself out as having sovereignty over that area; and that, where a
        foreign oil company enters into that concession, and expends resources in
        pursuance of it, it does not because it accepts and acts in reliance upon the

---

[6]   Cf. Article 70, paragraph 5 of the United Nations Convention on the Law of the
        Sea: "Developed geographically disadvantaged States shall, under the provisions
        of this article, be entitled to participate in the exploitation of living resources only
        in the exclusive economic zones of developed coastal States of the same sub-
        region or region having regard to the extent to which the coastal State, in giving
        access to other States to the living resources of its exclusive economic zone, has
        taken into account the need to minimize detrimental effects on fishing
        communities and economic dislocation in States whose nationals have habitually
        fished in the zone.".

sovereignty of that State. Yemen emphasised that not only were some of its petroleum contracts of a geographical extent that encompassed the disputed islands; it was also significant, it claimed, that none of the oil contracts and concessions concluded by Ethiopia or Eritrea did so. As the Award on Sovereignty summarised: "Yemen contended that the pattern of Yemen's offshore concessions, unprotested by Ethiopia and Eritrea, taken together with the pattern of Ethiopian concession, confirmed Yemen's sovereign claims to the disputed Islands, acceptance of and investment on the basis of that sovereignty by oil companies, and acquiescence by Ethiopia and Eritrea" (paragraph 390).

77. In the First Stage, Eritrea in contrast argued that conclusion by a State of an oil contract or concession with a foreign oil company was not evidence of title but, at most, a mere claim. Such arrangements lacked probative force unless activities in pursuance of them took place. Nevertheless Eritrea countered Yemen's argument by introducing evidence of a concession concluded by Ethiopia which covered part of all of Great and Lesser Hanish Islands. Neither Eritrea nor Yemen attached importance to the fact that a number of the petroleum arrangements concluded by Yemen and Ethiopia or Eritrea extended to a median line between their respective coastlines.

78. In its Award on Sovereignty, the Tribunal concluded:

> 437. The offshore petroleum contracts entered into by Yemen, and by Ethiopia and Eritrea, fail to establish or significantly strengthen the claims of either party to sovereignty over the disputed islands.
> 438. Those contacts however lend a measure of support to a median line between the opposite coasts of Eritrea and Yemen, drawn without regard to the islands, dividing the respective jurisdiction of the Parties.

79. In the Second Stage of these Proceedings, Eritrea placed great emphasis upon paragraph 438, and other passages of the Award, that found that various petroleum arrangement indicate limits drawn along a median line, and contended that the Tribunal's Award provided support for the "historic median line" which it now advanced as the maritime boundary line between Eritrea and Yemen. Eritrea stressed that, in several petroleum contracts concluded by Yemen, the contractual area extended from the mainland coast of Yemen in the east to the median line of the Red Sea, drawn without regard to base points on the disputed islands. It observed that a contract concluded by it, and another concluded by Yemen, ran through Greater Hanish along a median line. It pointed out that one of Yemen's concession contracts contains a median line, marked "Ethiopia" to the west and "Yemen" to the east. It maintained that maps prepared by Petroconsultants, introduced along a median line between the coasts of Yemen and Eritrea, cannot now be discounted by Yemen because it introduced them for another purpose. Eritrea acknowledged that contracts and conduct of Yemen and of Ethiopia and Eritrea are not tantamount to mutual acceptance of a median maritime boundary or even of a *modus vivendi* line. But it contended that they nevertheless provide a persuasive basis for taking an "historic median line" to divide the waters of the Red Sea, to be drawn without according the "mid-sea" disputed islands influence on the course of that line.

80. Yemen for its part contended that, while it introduced the Petroconsultants maps as evidence of Yemen's sovereignty over the disputed islands, it did so not to show maritime boundaries; that the Petroconsultants maps contain "mistakes"; and that these and other maps introduced in the First Stage contain disclaimers about lines affecting or prejudicing the contracting government's sovereign rights. Yemen emphasised the Tribunal's holding that the concessions

were "issued with commercial considerations in mind and without particular regard to the existence of the islands" (Award on Sovereignty, paragraph 412).

81. It should be noted that, in the course of making its holdings sovereignty over the disputed islands, the Tribunal held that the petroleum contacts do "lend a measure of support to a median line between the opposite coasts of Eritrea and Yemen, drawn without regard to the islands, dividing the respective jurisdiction of the Parties".

82. At this juncture, however, the Tribunal acts in the light of the dispositive provisions of paragraph 527 of its Award. Which islands are subject to the territorial sovereignty of Eritrea, and which are subject to the territorial sovereignty of Yemen, has been determined. In delimiting the maritime boundaries of the Parties, the Tribunal is required in this Second Stage of the proceedings to take into accounts, *inter alia*, the opinion that it formed on the question of territorial sovereignty.

83. As is set out in other passages of this Award, the Tribunal has taken as its starting point, as its fundamental point of departure, that, as between opposite coasts, a median line obtains. The Award on Sovereignty's examination of petroleum arrangements does show, as just indicated, repeated reference to a median line between the coasts of Yemen and Eritrea. To that extent, Eritrea's position in this Stage of the proceedings is sustained by those references. But that it not the same as saying that the maritime boundary now to be drawn should be drawn throughout its length entirely without regard to the islands whose sovereignty has been determined; nor is it to say that that boundary should track Eritrea's claimed "historic median line". The concession lines were drawn without regard to uninhabited, volcanic islands when their sovereignty was indeterminate. Those lines can hardly be taken as governing once that sovereignty has been determined. While initial weight is to be given to the mainland coasts and their island fringes, some weight is to be or may be accorded to the islands, certainly in respect of their territorial waters. What weight, and why and how, are questions addressed below.

84. In respect of petroleum arrangements and a maritime boundary between the Parties in the Red Sea, the Tribunal recalls conclusion of the International Court of Justice in its Judgement in the *North Sea Continental Shelf* cases,[7] that delimitation of States' areas of continental shelf may lead to "an overlapping of the areas appertaining to them. The Court considers that such a situation must be accepted as a given fact and resolved either by an agreed, or failing that by an equal division of the overlapping areas, or by agreements for joint exploitation, that latter solution appearing particularly appropriate when it is a question of preserving the unity of a deposit." Judge Jessup in his separate opinion in that case referred to a seminal article by William T. Onorato[8] and cited examples of such cooperation; and in the last thirty years there has grown up a significant body of cooperative State practice in the exploitation of resources that straddle maritime boundaries. The papers in a volume published by The British Institute of International and Comparative Law summarise and analyse this practice,[9] as does a more recent study by Masahiro Miyoshi, *The Joint*

---

[7] ICJ Reports 1969, p. 52.

[8] Apportionment of an International Petroleum Deposit, 17 ICLQ 85 (1958).

[9] Edited by Hazel Fox, Joint Development of Offshore Oil and Gas (1990) by R.R. Churchill, Kamal Hossein, Isa Huneidi, Masahiro Miyoshi, Ian Townsend-Gault, Anastasia Strati, H. Burmester, Clive R. Symmons, Thomas H. Walde, Brenda Barrett, P. Birnie and A.D. Read.

Development of Offshore Oil and Gas in Relation to the Maritime Boundary Delimitations, International Boundaries Research Unit, 1999.[10]

85.   That practice has particular pertinence in the current case. The Red Sea is not to be compared to the great oceans. Yemen and Eritrea face one another across a relatively narrow compass. Their peoples have had a long and largely beneficent history of intermingling, a history not limited to the free movement of fishermen but embracing a wider trade, and a common rule as well as a common religion. These relations long antedate the relatively modern, European-derived, concept of exclusionary sovereignty. While oil and gas in commercial quantities have not to date been found beneath the waters of the Red Sea that lie between ,Eritrea and Yemen, it is possible that either or both may be.

86.   In paragraph 1 of its Prayer for Relief, Eritrea requests the Tribunal to determine that "The Eritrean people's historic use of resources in the mid-sea islands includes ... mineral extraction". For reasons explained in paragraph 104 of this Award, the Tribunal is not in a position to accede to this request. However, it is of the view that, having regard to the maritime boundary established by this Award, the Parties are bound to inform one another and to consult one another on any oil and gas and other mineral resources that may be discovered that straddle the single maritime boundary between them or that lie in its immediate vicinity. Moreover, the historical connections between the peoples concerned, and the friendly relations of the Parties that have been restored since the Tribunal's rendering of its Award on Sovereignty, together with the body of State practice in the exploitation of resources that straddle maritime boundaries, import that Eritrea and Yemen should give every consideration to the shared or joint or unitised exploitation of any such resources.

CHAPTER IV

The Traditional Fishing Regime

87.   In paragraph 526 of its Award on Territorial Sovereignty and Scope of the Dispute the Tribunal found:

> In finding that the Parties each have sovereignty over various of the Islands the Tribunal stresses to them that such sovereignty is not inimical to, but rather entails, the perpetuation of the traditional fishing regime in the region. This existing regime has operated, as the evidence presented to the Tribunal amply testifies, around the Hanish and Zuqar Islands and the islands of Jabal al-Tayr and the Zubayr group. In the exercise of its sovereignty over these islands, Yemen shall ensure that the traditional fishing regime of free access and enjoyment for the fishermen of both Eritrea and Yemen shall be preserved for the benefit of the lives and livelihoods of this poor and industrious order of men.

88.   Immediately after, in paragraph vi of its Dispositif, The Tribunal determined that:

> the sovereignty found to lie within Yemen entails the perpetuation of the traditional fishing regime in the region, including free access and enjoyment for the fishermen of both Eritrea and Yemen.

---

[10]   See also, I.F.I. Shihata and W.T. Onorato, Joint Development of International Petroleum Resources in Undefined and Disputed Areas, International conference of the LAWASIA Energy Centre, Kuala Lumpur, 1992.

89.   Eritrea has taken the view that these findings entail the establishment of joint resource zones, which the Tribunal should delimit in its Award in the Second Stage. Eritrea, in its Prayer for Relief, also urged the Tribunal to direct the Parties to negotiate so as to achieve certain results it regards as required by paragraph 527(vi) of the Dispositif in the Award on Sovereignty, and to take certain other powers in relation thereto. To fail to do so, contended Eritrea, would be *infra petita*. Eritrea further contended that the final paragraph of the latter of 9 November 1998 from the President of the Tribunal to the counsel and co-agent for Eritrea left Eritrea full liberty so to submit during this Stage of the Arbitration. Some of the elements contained in Eritrea's Prayer for Relief were not pursued in oral argument; there the main plea was that the Court specify with precision what was entailed by its finding as to the traditional fishing regime and where that regime lay within the Red Sea. However, the Prayer for Relief, unamended, was said by Eritrea to represent its final submissions.

90.   Yemen took the view that it was clear from paragraph 526 of the Award on Sovereignty that it was for it, Yemen, in the exercise of its sovereignty, to ensure the preservation of that traditional fishing regime; that, while the 1994 and 1998 Agreements might prove to be useful vehicles for that exercise in sovereignty, there was no question of Yemen's sovereignty having been made conditional and thus no agreement with Eritrea was necessary for the administrative measures that might relate to this regime; that the Tribunal had not made any finding that there should be joint or common resource zones; that the Tribunal's finding that Yemen's sovereignty entailed the perpetuation of the traditional fishing regime was a finding in favour of the fishermen of Eritrea and Yemen, not of the State of Eritrea; that Article 3(1) of the Agreement on Principles and Article 2(3) of the Arbitration Agreement meant that it would be ultra vires for the Tribunal to respond favourable to Eritrea's Prayer for Relief; and that the President's letter of 9 November 1998 indeed showed that the Prayer for Relief was irregular. Further, Yemen contended that there had traditionally been no significant Eritrean fishing in the vicinity of the islands.

91.   The details of the positions taken by Eritrea and Yemen is recalled above at paragraphs 48–60.

92.   The Tribunal recalls that it based this aspect of its Award on Sovereignty on a respect for regional legal traditions. The abundant literature on the historical realities which characterised the lives of the populations on both the eastern and western coasts was noted in the award of the Arbitral Tribunal in the First Stage of the Proceedings, paragraph 121, footnote 9 and paragraph 128, footnote 11. This well-established factual situation reflected deeply rooted common legal traditions which prevailed during several centuries among the populations of both coasts of the Red Sea, which were until the latter part of the nineteenth century under the direct or indirect rule of the Ottoman Empire. The basic Islamic concept by virtue of which all humans are "stewards of God" on earth, with an inherent right to sustain their nutritional needs through fishing from coast to coast with free access to fish on either side and to trade the surplus, remained vivid in the collective mind of Dankhalis and Yemenites alike.

93.   Although the immediate beneficiaries of this legal concept were and are the fishermen themselves, it applies equally to States in their mutual relations. As a leading scholar has observed: "Islam is not merely a religion but also a political community (*umma*) endowed with a system of law designed both to protect

the collective interest of its subjects and to regulate their relations with the outside world".[11]

94. The sovereignty that the Tribunal has awarded to Yemen over Jabal al-Tayr, the Zubayr group and the Zuqar-Hanish group is not of course a "conditional" sovereignty, but a sovereignty nevertheless that respects and embraces and is subject to the Islamic legal concepts of the region. As it has been aptly put, "in today's world, it remains true that the fundamental moralistic general principles of the Quran and the Sunna may validly be invoked for the consolidation and support of positive international law rules in their progressive development towards the goal of achieving justice and promoting the human dignity of all mankind".[12]

95. The Tribunal's Award on Sovereignty was not based on any assessment of volume, absolute or relative, of Yemeni or Eritrean fishing in the region of the islands. What was relevant was that fishermen from both of these nations had, from time immemorial, used these islands for fishing and activities related thereto. Further, the finding on the traditional fishing regime was made in the context of the Award on Sovereignty precisely because classical western territorial sovereignty would have been understood as allowing the power in the sovereign state to exclude fishermen of a different nationality from its waters. Title over Jabal al-Tayr and the Zubayr group and over the Zuqar-Hanish group was found by the Tribunal to be indeterminate until recently. Moreover, these islands lay at some distance from the mainland coasts of the Parties. Their location meant that they were put to a special use by the fishermen as way stations and as places of shelter, and not just, or perhaps even mainly, as fishing grounds. These special factors constituted a local tradition entitled to the respect and protection of the law.

96. It is clear that the Arbitration Agreement does not authorise the Tribunal to respond affirmatively to paragraphs 6 and 7 of Eritrea's Prayer for Relief. Nor, indeed, would it have been able so to do even if the arbitration had been conducted within the framework of a single stage or phase, as originally envisaged by Article 3(1) of the Agreement on Principles.

97. However, Eritrea is entitled to submit to the Tribunal that its findings as to the traditional fishing regime has implications for the delimiting of maritime boundaries in the Second Stage; and the Tribunal is at liberty to respond to such submissions.

98. Indeed, it is bound to do so, because it is not otherwise in a position to respond to the submissions made by Yemen as well as by Eritrea in this Second Stage. It cannot be the case that the division of the Arbitration into two stages meant that the Parties may continue to debate whether the substantive content of the Tribunal's findings on the traditional fishing regime has any relevance to the task of delimitation, but that the Tribunal must remain silent. Such formalism was never the object of the agreement of both Parties to divide the Arbitration into two Stages.

99. Of course, in making its Award on Sovereignty the Tribunal did not "prefigure" or anticipate the maritime delimitation that it is now called upon to make in the Second Stage, after full pleadings by the Parties. Beyond that the Tribunal is not to be artificially constrained in what it may respond to be the procedural structures agreed for the Arbitration. The two-stage mechanism is not to be read either as forbidding Parties to make the arguments they wish,

---

[11] Khadduri, *Encyclopedia of Public International Law*, vol. 6, p. 227.
[12] *Ibid.*, vol. 7, page 229.

when they wish; nor as limiting their entitlement to seek to protect what they perceive as their substantive rights.

100. Article 15 of the Arbitration Agreement (the meaning of which is otherwise not readily intelligible) lends support to this view. Paragraph 2 speaks of the Arbitration Agreement as "implementing the procedural aspects" of the Agreement on Principles. And Paragraph 1 provides that:

Nothing in this Arbitration Agreement can be interpreted as being detrimental to the legal positions or to the rights of each Party with respect to the questions submitted to the Tribunal, nor can affect or prejudice the decision of the Arbitral Tribunal or the considerations and grounds on which those decisions are based.

101. As the Tribunal has indicated in its Award on Sovereignty, the traditional fishing regime around the Hanish and Zuqar Islands and the islands of Jabal al-Tayr and the Zubayr group is one of free access and enjoyment for the fishermen of both Eritrea and Yemen. It is to be preserved for their benefit. This does not mean, however, that Eritrea may not act on behalf of its nations, whether through diplomatic contacts with Yemen or through submissions to this Tribunal. There is no reason to import into the Red Sea the western legal fiction – which is in any event losing its importance – whereby all legal rights, even those in reality held by individuals, were deemed to be those of the State. That legal fiction served the purpose of allowing diplomatic representation (where the representing State so chose) in a world in which individuals had no opportunities to advance their own rights. It was never meant to be the case however that, were a right to be held by an individual, neither the individual not his State should have access to international redress.

102. The Tribunal accordingly now responds to the diverse submissions advanced in this Stage by the Parties, both as to the substantive content of the traditional fishing regime referred to in paragraphs 526 and 527(vi) of its Award on Sovereignty and as to any implications for its task in this stage of the Arbitration. The correct answer is indeed to be gleaned from the pages of that Award itself. Attention may in particular by drawn to paragraphs 102, 126–128, 340, 353–357 and 526.

103. The traditional fishing regime is not an entitlement in common to resources nor is it a shared right in them. Rather, it entitles both Eritrean and Yemeni fishermen to engage in artisanal fishing around the islands which, in its Award on Sovereignty, the Tribunal attributed to Yemen. This is understood as including diving, carried out by artisanal means, for shells and pearls. Equally, these fishermen remain entitled freely to use these islands for those purposed traditionally associated with such artisanal fishing – the use of the islands for drying fish, for way stations, for the provision of temporary shelter, and for the effecting of repairs.

104. In paragraph 1 of the Prayer for Relief, Eritrea asks the Tribunal to determine that "The Eritrean people's historic use of resources in the mid-sea islands includes guano and mineral extraction ...". In the pleadings before the Tribunal Eritrea referred specifically in this context to guano extraction which has been licensed by Italy. Guano extraction is not be assimilated to mineral extraction more generally. Further, as the Award on Sovereignty made clear, Eritrea's rights today are not derived from a claimed continuity from rights once held in Italy. The traditional fishing regime covers those entitlements that all the fishermen have exercised continuously through the ages. The Tribunal has received no evidence that the extraction of guano, or mineral extraction more generally, forms part of the traditional fishing regime that has existed and continues to exists today.

105. The FAO Fisheries Infrastructure Development Project Report of 1995 was a report on fishing in Eritrean waters. However, its findings on artisanal fishing would be of general application in this region. The 1995 Report makes clear that both the artisanal vessels and their gear are simple. The vessels are usually canoes fitted with small outboard engines, slightly larger vessels (9–12 m) filled with 40–75 hp engines, or fishing sambuks with inboard engines. Dugout canoes and small rafts (ramas) are also in use.[13] Hand lines, gill nets and long lines are used. In its Report on Fishing in Eritrean waters, the FAO study states that this artisanal fishing gear, which varies according to the boat and the fish, is "simple and efficient".[14]

106. However, the term "artisanal" is not to be understood as applying in the future only to a certain type of fishing exactly as it is practised today. "Artisanal fishing" is used in contrast to "industrial fishing". It does not exclude improvements in powering the small boats, in the techniques of navigation, communication or in the techniques of fishing; but the traditional regime of fishing does not extend to large-scale commercial or industrial fishing nor to fishing by nationals of third States in the Red Sea, whether small-scale or industrial.

107. In order that the entitlements be real and not merely theoretical, the traditional regime has also recognised certain associated rights. There must be free access to and from the islands concerned – including unimpeded passage through waters in which, by virtue of its sovereignty over the islands, Yemen is entitled to exclude all third Parties or subject their presence to licence, just as it may do in respect of Eritrean industrial fishing. This free passage for artisanal fishermen has traditionally existed not only between Eritrea and the islands, but also between the islands and the Yemen coast. The entitlement to enter the relevant ports, and to sell and market the fish there, is an integral element of the traditional regime. The 1994 Memorandum of Understanding between the State of Eritrea and the Republic of Yemen for Cooperation in the Areas of Maritime Fishing, Trade, Investment, and Transportation usefully identifies the centres of fish marketing on each coast. Eritrean artisanal fisherman fishing around the islands awarded to Yemen have had free access to Maydi, Khoba, Hodeidah, Khokha and Mocha on the Yemen coast, just as Yemeni artisanal fishermen fishing around the islands have had an entitlement to unimpeded transit to and access to Assab, Tio, Dahlak and Massawa on the Eritrean coast. Nationals of the one country have an entitlement to sell on equal terms and without any discrimination in the ports of the other. Within the fishing markets themselves, the traditional non-discriminatory treatment – so far as cleaning, storing and marketing is concerned – is to be continued. The traditional recourse by artisanal fisherman to the acquil system to resolve their disputes *inter se* is to be also maintained and preserved.

108. Yemen and Eritrea are, of course, free to make mutually agreed regulations for the protection of this traditional fishing regime. Insofar as environmental considerations may in the future require regulation, any administrative measures impacting upon these traditional rights shall be taken by Yemen only with the agreement of Eritrea and, so far as access through Eritrean waters to Eritrean ports in concerned, vice versa.

109. The traditional fishing regime is not limited to the territorial waters of specified islands; nor are its limits to be drawn by reference to claimed past patterns of

---

[13] FAO 24/95 ADB-ERI.4, 27 February 1995, at paras. 2.19 and 3.44.
[14] *Ibid.*, para. 2.20.

fishing. It is, as Yemen itself observes in its Answers to the Tribunal's Questions, Annex 2, page 64, a "regime that has existed for the benefit of the fishermen of both countries throughout the region". By its very nature it is not qualified by the maritime zones specified under the United Nations Convention on the Law of the Sea, the law chosen by the Parties to be applicable to this task in this Second Stage of the Arbitration. The traditional fishing regime operates throughout those waters beyond the territorial waters of each of the Parties, and also in their territorial waters and ports, to the extent and in the manner specified in paragraph 107 above.

110.   Accordingly, it does not depend, either for its existence or for its protection, upon the drawing of an international boundary by this Tribunal. This much was indeed acknowledged by Yemen in its Answers to the Tribunal's Questions, when it observed that "the holdings of the Tribunal in the first award with respect to the traditional fishing regime constitute res judicata without prejudice to the maritime boundary that the Tribunal decides on in the second stage of the proceedings" (Annex 2, page 63). Yemen informed the Tribunal that it was "fully committed to apply and implement the Award in all its aspects, including with respect to the perpetuation of the traditional fishing regime for the fishermen of both Eritrea and Yemen". Nor is the drawing of the maritime boundary conditioned by the findings, in the Award on Sovereignty, of such a regime.

111.   As the Tribunal has explained above, no further joint agreement is legally necessary for the perpetuation of a regime based on mutual freedoms and an absence of unilaterally imposed conditions. However, should Eritrea and Yemen decide that the intended cooperation exemplified by the 1994 Memorandum of Understanding and the 1998 Agreement can usefully underpin the traditional regime, they may choose to use some of the possibilities within these instruments. The subject matter of the 1994 instrument has a particular pertinence. (Moreover, it is the understanding of the Tribunal that the Parties did not jointly intend to deprive fishermen of their rights under this traditional regime if they failed to submit a fishing licence to the other Party within three months from the date of the signing of the Memorandum of Understanding.)

112.   The Tribunal has responded to the pleadings that both Parties have made, as they were entitled to do, in this phase of the proceedings. Its answer indicates how its Award on Sovereignty is to be understood in relation to the matters that the Parties have now raised before it.

CHAPTER V

The Delimitation of the International Boundary

The Tribunal's Comments on the Arguments of the Parties

113.   Since, as it will appear below, the international maritime boundary line decided upon by the Tribunal differs in some respects from both the one claimed by Yemen and the one, or the ones, claimed by Eritrea, it is right first to explain briefly where and why the boundaries claimed by the Parties have not been endorsed in this Award. This will now be done taking generally first the Yemen claim and then the Eritrean claim, as this was the order in which the Parties agreed to argue in the Oral Proceedings of this Second Stage of this Arbitration.

114.   Yemen claimed one single international boundary line for all purposes. The single line it claimed was described as a "median line", because Yemen treated the westward-facing coasts of all of its islands as relevant coast for purposes of the delimitation. For the Eritrean coast, Yemen used base points on the mainland coast of Eritrea and thus ignored the Eritrean mid-sea islands for the purpose of delimitation of the boundary. Yemen also claimed that its line can properly be described as a coastal median line. For Yemen the relevant coasts included not only the islands over which it has been awarded sovereignty, but also of certain among the Dahlak islands; thus Yemen, like Eritrea, was prepared to treat the Dahlaks as being part of the Eritrean coast, and so used base points on the islets forming the outer fringe of the group. When on the other hand Eritrea spoke of what it called "the coastal medial line", it meant that median line between what in the Eritrean view represented the mainland coasts of both Parties. At the same time Eritrea claimed a historic median line using only its own islands as base points, and thus ignoring those of Yemen. These variations produced different claimed median lines. See Eritrea's Maps 3 and 7, and Yemen's Map 12.1. See also Charts 1 and 2 showing the base points as provided by Eritrea [not included].

115.   It is in what Yemen called the northern sector of the boundary line where this difference caused the greatest divergence, actually of several nautical miles, between the lines claimed by the Parties because of the question of how much "effect" on the line should be given to the Yemen northern islands, namely the small sole mid-sea island of Jabal al-Tayr and the mid-sea groups of islands and islets called Zubayr. Yemen allowed them full effect on the line; Eritrea's line allowed them none.

116.   In considering this marked divergence of view it is well to recollect that the boundary line in its northern stretch – including indeed both the opposing claimed lines – are boundaries between the Yemen and the Eritrean continental shelves and EEZ; and are therefore governed by Articles 74 and 83 of the 1982 Convention. In any event there has to be room for differences of opinion about the interpretation of articles which, in a last minute endeavour at the Third United Nations Conference on the Law of the Sea to get agreement on a very controversial matter, were consciously designed to decide as little as possible. It is clear, however, that both Articles envisage an equitable result.

117.   This requirement of an equitable result directly raises the question of the effect to be allowed to mid-sea islands which, by virtue of their mid-sea position, and if allowed full effect, can obviously produce a disproportionate effect – or indeed a reasonable and proportionate effect – all depending on their size, importance and like considerations in the general geographical context.

118.   Yemen understood this problem very clearly. Its argument was that, although these mid-sea islands and islets are small and uninhabitable (these questions figured prominently in the First Stage of this Arbitration), those considerations were nicely matched, or "balanced", by the complementary smallness and lack of importance of the outer islets of the Dahlak group which were the base points on the Eritrean side of the boundary. However, the situation of these Dahlak islets is very different from that of the mid-sea islands. The Dahlak outer islets are part of a much larger group of islands which both Parties were agreed are an integral part of the Eritrean mainland coats. Consequently, between these islets and the mainland, the sea is Eritrean internal waters. The Tribunal had therefore, as will be seen below, no difficulty in rejecting this "balancing" argument of Yemen, as it does not compare like with like.

119.   In its assessment of the equities of the "effect" to be given to these northern

islands and islets, the Tribunal decided not to accept the Yemen plea that they be allowed a full, or at least some, effect on the median line. This decision was confirmed by the result that, in any event, these mid-sea islands would enjoy an entire territorial sea of the normal 12 miles – even on their western side.

120. One practical result of the Yemen balancing argument regarding the northern mid-sea islands is that Yemen did not argue in the alternative about possible base points on the islands fringing the Yemen mainland coast – which islands could much more cogently be said to balance the Dahlaks.

121. The Eritrean argument concerning this northern stretch of the line was relatively simple: it argued strongly against the Yemen balancing suggestions, and here asked for the mainland coastal median line. At first, it was not clear what were the base points used by Eritrea. However, in answer to a question from the Tribunal, Eritrea did produce two complete sets of base points for the Eritrean coast and also a set for the Yemen coast. (See Charts 1 and 2 [not included].)

122. The latitude of 14°25N – where the Yemen northern sector becomes the Yemen central sector – results from another factor on which the Parties differ. This line of latitude is not chosen at random by Yemen. It is the point at which the Yemen median line is no longer controlled by Zubayr as a base point but enters under the control of the north-western point of the island of Zuqar. The Eritrean lines, for indeed there are two of them, continue southwards, ignoring the possible effect of the Zuqar-Hanish group. The "historic" median line (Map 3 [not included]) cuts through Zuqar, and the coastal median line cuts through Zuqar, and the coast median line cuts through the island of Greater Hanish (Map 7 [not included]).

123. The Tribunal did not find it easy to resolve this divergence of method, but finally the Tribunal decided to continue its line as a mainland coastal line until the presence of Yemen's Zuqar-Hanish group compels a diversion westwards. (The Tribunal's line, as will appear below, is neither the Yemen line nor yet the Eritrean line.)

124. In support of its enclave solution for certain of the Eritrean islands, Yemen entered upon an assessment of the relative size and importance of the Eritrean islands generally, as if they were islands whose influence on the boundary line falls to be assessed, not as being possibly in an area of overlapping territorial sea, but as if they were to be assessed solely by reference to Articles 74 and 83 of the Convention. This approach enabled Yemen to argue that these Eritrean "navigational hazards" were insignificant even when compared with the Yemen Zuqar-Hanish group; and that accordingly the South West Rocks and the Haycocks ought to be enclaved and the boundary line taken onto the Eritrean side of them, thus leaving the two enclaves isolated on the Yemen side of the boundary line.

125. The Tribunal, as will appear below, has had little difficulty in preferring the Eritrean argument, which brings into play Article 15. This solution has the advantage of avoiding the need for awkward enclaves in the vicinity of a major international shipping route.

126. The Yemen "southern sector" began at the line of latitude 13°20'N. Again, this is not an arbitrary choice. It was the point at which Yemen's median line, which had hitherto been controlled by Suyul Hanish, first came under the control of the nearest point on the mainland coast of Yemen. The Yemen line then continued throughout the southern sector as a coastal median line.

127. In the main part of this southern sector, therefore, there were only differences

of detail between the Yemen and Eritrean lines because there was no mid-sea islands to complicate the problem. There was indeed the large complication of the Bay of Assab and of its off-lying islands, but here Yemen rightly assumed that this bay is integral to the Eritrean coast and its internal waters, and that the controlling base points would therefore be on the low-water line of the outer coastal islands.

128. In the course of its passage from the overlapping territorial seas areas to the relatively simple stretch between parallel coasts of the southern sector, the Yemen line was again a median line controlled by the Yemen islands as well as by the Eritrean mainland coast. However, the line preferred by the Tribunal, mindful of the simplicity desirable in the neighbourhood of a main shipping lane, is one that would mark this passage directly and independently of the Yemen and Eritrean islands. It is not easy to trace the Eritrean median line in this area because of the complication of its box system for the traditional fishing areas. Indeed, this review of the Parties' arguments and the Tribunal's view of them does somewhat scant justice to the complicated and carefully researched Eritrean scheme for delimitation of the traditional fishing areas, but this matter has been dealt with in Chapter IV.

This chapter will now turn to describe the boundary line determined by the Tribunal.

The Boundary Line Determined by the Tribunal

129. The task of the Tribunal in the present Stage of this Arbitration is defined by Article 2 of the Arbitration Agreement, and is to "result in an award delimiting the maritime boundaries". The term "boundaries" is here used, it is reasonable to assume, in its normal and ordinary meaning of denoting an international maritime boundary between the two State Parties to the Arbitration; and not in the sense of what is usually called a maritime "limit", such as the outer limit of a territorial sea or a contiguous zone; although there might be places where these limits happen to coincide with or be modified by the international boundary.

130. Article 2 also provides that, in determining the maritime boundaries, the Tribunal is to take "into account the opinion it will have formed on questions of territorial sovereignty, the United Nations Convention on the Law of the Sea, and any other pertinent factor". The reasons for taking account of the Award on Sovereignty are clear enough and both Parties have agreed in their pleadings that, in the Second Stage, there can be no question of attempting to reopen the decisions made in the First Award. The requirement to take into account the United Nations Convention on the Law of the Sea of 1982 is important because Eritrea has not become a party to that Convention but has in the Arbitration Agreement thus accepted the application of provisions of the Convention that are found to be relevant to the present stage. There is no reference in the Arbitration Agreement to the customary law of the sea, but many of the relevant elements of customary law are incorporated in the provisions of the Convention. "Any other pertinent factors" is a broad concept, and doubtless includes various factors that are generally recognised as being relevant to the process of delimitation such as proportionality, non-encroachment, the presence of islands, and any other factors that might affect the equalities of the particular situation.

131. It is a generally accepted view, as is evidenced in both the writings of commentators and in the jurisprudence, that between coasts that are opposite to each

other the median or equidistance line normally provides an equitable boundary in accordance with the requirements of the Convention, and in particular those of its Articles 74 and 83 which respectively provide for the equitable delimitation of the EEZ and of the continental shelf between States with opposite or adjacent coasts. Indeed both Parties to the present case have claimed a boundary constructed on the equidistance method, although based on different points of departure and resulting in very different lines.

132.   The Tribunal has decided, after careful consideration of all the cogent and skilful arguments put before them by both Parties, that the international boundary shall be a single all-purpose boundary which is a median line and that it should, as far as practicable, be a median line between the opposite mainland coastlines. This solution is not only in accord with practice and precedent in the like situations but is also one that is already familiar to both Parties. As the Tribunal had occasion to observe in its Award on Sovereignty (paragraph 438), the offshore petroleum contracts entered into by Yemen, and by Ethiopia and by Eritrea, "lend a measure of support to a median line between the opposite coasts of Eritrea and Yemen, drawn without regard to the islands, dividing the respective jurisdiction of the Parties". In the present stage the Tribunal has to determine a boundary not merely for the purposes of petroleum concessions and agreements, but a single international boundary for all purposes. For such a boundary the presence of islands requires careful consideration of their possible effect upon the boundary line; and this is done in the explanation which follows. Even so it will be found that the final solution is that the international maritime boundary line remains for the greater part a median line between the mainland coasts of the Parties.

133.   The median line is in any event some sort of coastal line by its very definition, for it is defined as a line "every point of which is equidistant from the nearest points on the baselines from which the breadth of the territorial seas of the two States is measured" (Article 15 of the Convention), although the same definition will be found in many maritime boundary treaties and also in expert writings. The "normal" baseline of the territorial sea as stated in Article 5 of the Convention – and this again accords with long practice and with the well established customary rule of the law of the sea – is "the low-water line along the coast as marked on large scale charts officially recognised by the coastal State". There do arise some questions about what is to be regarded as the "coast" for these purposes, especially where islands are involved; and these questions, on which the Parties differ markedly, require decisions by the Tribunal.

134.   First, it is necessary to deal with a complication that arises in the present case concerning this general rule of measuring from the low-water line. The domestic legislative definition of the territorial sea of Eritrea is still the 1953 enactment by Ethiopia which fixed Ethiopia's territorial waters as "extending from the extremity of the seaboard at maximum annual high tide". This was done even though an Ethiopian customs enactment of 1952 had provided for a customs zone measured from the "the mean low-water mark at neap tides". The Yemen claim was that, in view of this 1953 legislation, the Tribunal should measure the median line boundary from the high-water line instead of the low-water line along the Eritrean coast (and indeed Yemen's median line does).

135.   In this matter the Tribunal prefers the Eritrean argument that the use of the low-water line is laid down by a general international rule in the Convention's Article 5, and that both Parties have agreed that the Tribunal is to take into

account the provisions of the Convention in deciding the present case. The median line boundary will, therefore, be measured from the low-water line, shown on the officially recognised charts for both Eritrea and Yemen, in accordance with the provision in Article 5 of the Convention. The officially recognised charts used by the Tribunal are BA (British Admiralty) Charts; those Charts used as a Chart Datum approximately the level of the Lowest Astronomical Tide. These Charts were among those relied on by the Parties in the present Stage of the Proceedings.

Northern and Southern Extremities of the Boundary Line

136. There is also a problem relating to both the northern and the southern extremities of the international boundary line. The Tribunal has the competence and the authority according to the Arbitration Agreement to decide the maritime boundary between the two Parties. But it has neither competence nor authority to decide on any of the boundaries between either of the two Parties and neighbouring States. It will therefore be necessary to terminate either end of the boundary line in such a way as to avoid trespassing upon an area where other claims might fall to be considered. It is, however, clearly necessary to consider the choices of the base points controlling the median line first, and then to look at the cautionary termination matter when the line to be thus terminated at its northern and southern ends has been produced.

137. The construction of the international single boundary decided upon by the Tribunal, working generally from the north to the south, will now be described.

The Northernmost Stretch of the Boundary Line

138. In this stretch, where the two lines claimed respectively by Eritrea and Yemen differed so markedly in their courses, there were three main problems: what to do about the Dahlak islands on the Eritrean side; what to do about the lone mid-sea island of Jabal al-Tayr and the mid-sea island group of Jabal al-Zubayr; and what to do about the cluster of islands and rocks off the northern coast of Yemen. These three questions will now be considered in that order.

The Dahlaks

139. This tightly knit group of islands and islets, or "carpet" of islands and islets as Eritrea preferred to call it, of which the larger islands have a considerable population, is a typical example of a group of islands that forms an integral part of the general coastal configuration. It seems in practice always to have been treated as such. It follows that the waters inside the island system will be internal or national waters and that the baseline of the territorial sea will be found somewhere at the external fringe of the island system.

140. A problem that arises here, however, is that the Dahlak fringe of coastal islands is also suitable for the application not of the "normal baseline" of the territorial sea, but of the "straight baselines" described in Article 7 of the Convention (as there distinguished from the "normal" baseline described in Article 5). The straight baseline system is there described as "the method of straight

baselines joining appropriate points". Yemen appears to have little difficulty in agreeing that the Dahlaks form an appropriate situation for the establishment of a straight baseline system.

141. Eritrea for its part claimed that it has such a system already established. In answer to a question from the Tribunal, Eritrea did give the coordinates for the base points on the Eritrea side for both versions of its claimed "median line". But these base points in the region of the Dahlaks appear to have been located on a line touching two or perhaps three of the outer islands and the Negileh rock (for which see below paragraphs 146–147) and then continuing in a more or less straight line out to sea in a south-easterly direction. This scheme is probably part of the "quadrilateral" straight baseline system to which Eritrea referred in argument.

142. The reality or validity or definition of this somewhat unusual straight baseline system said to be existing for the Dahlaks is hardly a matter that the Tribunal is called upon to decide. The Tribunal does however have to decide on the base points which are to control the course of the international boundary line. In plotting its own claimed median line boundary, Yemen has employed as its western base points the high-water line of the small outer islets of Segala, Dahret Segala, Zauber and Aucan. These islets could reasonable be included in a straight baseline system of the ordinary and familiar kind.

143. Eritrea, however, has in particular suggested a feature called the "Negileh Rock" which lies further out than these larger but still small and uninhabited islets. Yemen objected to the use of this feature by reason of the fact that on the BA Chart 171 this feature is shown to be a reef and moreover one which appears not to be above water at any state of the tide. A reef that is not also a low-tide elevation appears to be out of the question as a base point, because Article 6 of the Convention (which is headed "Reefs") provides:

> In the case of islands situated on atolls or of islands having fringing reefs, the baseline for measuring the breadth of the territorial sea is the seaward low-water line of the reef, as shown by the appropriate symbol on charts officially recognized by the coastal State.

144. This difficulty about the Negileh Rock is reinforced if there is indeed a straight baseline system in existence for the Dahlaks, for paragraph 4 or Article 7 provides:

> 4. Straight baselines shall not be drawn to and from low-tide elevations, unless lighthouses of similar installations which are permanently above sea level have been built on them or in instances where the drawing of straight baselines to and from such elevation has received general international recognition.

145. Although Eritrea is not a party to the Convention; nevertheless it has agreed to its application in the present case; and since Eritrea claims the existence of a straight baseline system, that claim seems to foreclose any right to employ a reef that is not proud of the water at low-tide as a baseline of the territorial sea.

146. As will appear more particularly below, the Tribunal has decided that the western base points to be employed on this part of the Eritrean coast shall be on the low-water line of certain of the outer Dahlak islets, Mojeidi and an unnamed islet east of Dahret Segala.

* * *

Next, it is necessary to decide on the treatment of the mid-sea islands of al-Tayr and Zubayr, for on this decision depends the question of whether it will be necessary to consider base points on the coast of Yemen.

Jabal al-Tayr and the Zubayr Group

147. Yemen employed both the small single island of al-Tayr and the group of islands called al-Zubayr as controlling base points, so that the Yemen-claimed median line boundary is "median" only in the area of sea west of these islands. These islands do not constitute a part of Yemen's mainland coast. Moreover, their barren and inhospitable nature and their position well out to sea, which have already been described in the Award on Sovereignty, mean that they should not be taken into consideration in computing the boundary line between Yemen and Eritrea.

148. For these reasons, the Tribunal has decided that both the single island of al-Tayr and the island group of al-Zubayr should have no effect upon the median line international boundary.

* * *

Base Points on the Coast of Yemen

149. Since Jabal al-Tayr and the Zubayr group are not to influence the drawing of the median line boundary, it is necessary to decide upon the base points to be used for this part of the coast of Yemen. For here again there is, if not a carpet, at least a considerable scattering of islands and islets which are the beginning of a large area of coastal islands and reefs which, extending northward, ultimately form part of a large island cluster or system off the coast of Saudi Arabia.

150. There is also the relatively large, inhabited and important island of Kamaran off this part of the Yemen coast. This island, together with the large promontory of the mainland to the south of it, forms an important bay and there can be no doubt that these features are integral to the coast of Yemen and part of it and should therefore control the median line. One significant controlling base point is therefore on the westernmost extremity of Kamaran. It seems reasonable also to use as base points the very small islands immediately south of Kamaran and west of the promontory headland mentioned above.

151. The question remains as to the islands to the north of Kamaran. The relatively large islet of Tiqfash, and the smaller islands of Kutama and Uqban further west, all appear to be part of an intricate system of islands, islets and reefs which guard this part of the coast. This is indeed, in the view of the Tribunal, a "fringe system" of the kind contemplated by Article 7 of the Convention, even though Yemen does not appear to have claimed it as such. Indeed the Tribunal does not have the advantage of any views of Yemen about this part of the coast because it chose to deploy its arguments differently. It is however the view of the Tribunal that it is right to use as median line base points not only Kamaran and its satellite islets which appear in the Yemen Map 12.1, but also the islets to the northwest named Uqban and Kutama.

152. The above decisions having been made, it is now possible to compute and plot the northern stretch of the boundary line between turning points 1 and 13 (the list of the coordinates of the turning points is given below; see also the illustrative Charts 3 and 4 [not included]). For this entire part of the line, the boundary should be a mainland-coastal median, or equidistance, line.

153. At the turning point number 13, however, a simple mainland/coastal median line approaches the area of possible influence of the islands of Zuqar-Hanish

group, and clearly some decisions have to be made as to how to deal with this situation.

The Middle Stretch of the Boundary Line

154. It will be convenient for obvious reasons if the Tribunal first decides the question of the boundary in the narrow seas between the south-west extremity of the Hanish group on the one hand and the Eritrean island of the Mohabba-kahs, High Island, the Haycocks and the South West Rocks on the other. In this part of the boundary there is added to the boundary problem of delimiting continental shelves and EEZ the question of delimiting an area of overlapping territorial seas. This comes about because Zuqar and Hanish, attributed to the sovereignty of Yemen, both generate territorial seas which overlap with those generated by the Haycocks and South West Rocks, attributed to the sovereignty of Eritrea. It would appear from Yemen Map 12.1 that Yemen assumed that Eritrea is entitled only to a strictly 12 mile territorial sea extending from the Eritrean base points chosen by Yemen along the high-water line on the Eritrean coast; that outcome would be, according to Yemen, that the Haycocks and South West Rocks are thus left isolated outside and beyond the Eritrean territorial sea proper.

155. This proposition is questionable, quite apart from the obvious impracticality of establishing limited enclaves around islands and navigational hazards in the immediate neighbourhood of a main international shipping lane. There is no doubt that an island, however small, and even rocks provided they are indeed islands proud of the water at high-tide, are capable of generating a territorial sea of up to 12 miles (Article 121.2 of the Convention). It follows that a chain of islands which are less than 24 miles apart can generate a continuous band of territorial sea. This is the situation of the Eritrean islands out to, and including, the South West Rocks.

156. The point that the Yemen suggestion omits to take into account is that the effect of what has been referred to as "leap-frogging" the Eritrean islands and islets in this area is to extend the mainland coast territorial sea beyond the limit of 12 miles from the mainland coast. According to Article 3 of the Convention, the territorial sea extends "up to a limit not exceeding 12 nautical miles, measured from the baselines determined in accordance with this Convention". This is permissible because each island, however small or unimport-ant of itself, creates a further low-water baseline from which the coastal territorial sea is to be measured. This "leap-frogging" point was invoked strongly in support of Eritrea's claims to sovereignty. This reasoning was not accepted by the Tribunal in its Award on Sovereignty, it nonetheless has relevance in the present context.

157. If any further reason were needed to reject the Yemen suggestion of enclaving the Eritrean islands in this area beyond a limit of 12 miles from the high-water line of the mainland coast, it may be found in the principle of non-encroachment which was described by Judge Lachs in the Guinea/Guinea-Bissau Award[15] in the following terms:

As stated in the award, our principal concern has been to avoid, by one means or another, one of the Parties finding itself faced with the exercise of rights, opposite to

---

[15] 25 ILM 251.

and in the immediate vicinity of its coast, which might interfere with its right to development or put its security at risk.

158. It will be seen that the international boundary line must therefore lie somewhere in a belt of sea no more than four or five miles wide. Once it is established that there is an area of Eritrean mainland coast territorial sea, potentially extending beyond the South West Rocks and the Haycock group of islands on the one hand and overlapping the territorial sea generated by the Yemen islands of the Hanish group on the other, the situation suggests a median line boundary. Under Article 15 of the Convention the normal methods for drawing an equidistant median line could be varied if reason of historic title or other special circumstance were to indicate otherwise. However, the Tribunal has considered these reasons and circumstances and finds no variance necessary.

159. Further bearing in mind its overall task of delimitation, the Tribunal also finds this line to be an entirely equitable one. The decision of the Tribunal is therefore that the median line is the international boundary line where it cuts through the area of overlap of the respective territorial seas of the Parties.

There remains, however, the part of the boundary line which is to connect the mainland coastal median line and the line delimiting the overlapping territorial seas. To the description of this line the Award now turns.

The Boundary Line Which Connects Turning Point 13 and Turning Point 15

160. If the mainland coastal median were continued south of turning point 13, it would cut first the territorial sea of Zuqar and then the territorial sea of Hanish, and then cut through the land territory of the island of Hanish. It must therefore divert to the west round the Zuqar-Hanish group, also respecting the territorial seas of these islands if they are to be regarded as generating a territorial sea. That they ought be regarded as having a territorial sea seems reasonable.

161. Various possibilities were considered by the Tribunal. If therefore the international boundary is, after turning point 13 where it meets a 12-mile territorial sea extending from the island of Zuqar territorial sea boundary until it has to turn southward again in order to join the Article 15 boundary. The Tribunal has decided, however, that it would be better that the line here should be a geodetic line joining point 13 with point 14, making the necessary southwestwards excursion to join the territorial sea median line described above. Moreover, the Tribunal's task is, as mentioned above, to determine the maritime boundary; this does not include setting the limits of the territorial seas.

162. From turning point 14, again with a simple line in view, the southward excursion of the international boundary is a geodetic line joining points 14 and 15 where it becomes the Article 15 median. This boundary decided upon by the Tribunal between turning points 14 and 15 is also very near to the putative boundary of a Yemen territorial sea in this area, but makes for a neater and more convenient international boundary.

The Southern Part of the International Boundary Line

163. From turning point 20, which is the southernmost turning point on the overlapping territorial seas median line, the boundary needs to turn generally

south-eastwards to rejoin the mainland coast median line. This it does through a geodetic line which connects turning point 20 and point 21, the latter being the intersection of the extended overlapping territorial seas median line and the coastal median line. Thence the international boundary line resumes as a median line controlled by the two mainland coasts. The Bay of Assab is internal waters, so the controlling base points of the boundary line are seaward of this bay.

The Northern and Southern End Points of the Boundary Line

164.   Reference has been made above to the need not to extend the boundary to areas that might involve third parties. The points where the decision of the Tribunal halts the progress of the boundary line are, for the northern end, turning point 1 and, for the southern end, point 29. The effect can, of course, also be seen on the illustrative Charts 3 and 4 in the map pockets of the Award. The Tribunal believes that these terminal points are well short of where the boundary line might be disputed by any third State.

The Test of Proportionality

165.   The principle of proportionality was described by the International Court of Justice in the North Sea Continental Shelf cases as "the element of a reasonable degree of proportionality, which a delimitation in accordance with equitable principles ought to bring about between the extent of the continental shelf areas appertaining to the coastal State and the length of the coast measured in the general direction of the coastline, account being taken for this purpose of the effects, actual or prospective, of any other continental shelf delimitations between adjacent States in the same region". This was also described as one of the "factors" to be taken into account in delimitations.[16] It is not an independent mode or principle of delimitation, but rather a test of the equitableness of a delimitation arrived at by some other means.[17] So, as the Award stated in the Anglo-French Channel case, "it is disproportion rather than any general principle of proportionality which is the relevant criterion or factor".[18]

166.   The Parties in the present case have disagreed strongly in their arguments of this matter, not so much about the meaning of "proportionality" as over the respective lengths of their coasts for the purposes of this calculation. There is in the Tribunal's view no doubt that the "general direction" of the coast means that the calculation of the Eritrean coastal length should follow the outer circumference of the Dahlak group of islands, although Eritrea was more inclined to have it follow the line of the mainland coast.

167.   A much debated point was: how far north the Eritrean coast should go. Eritrea wished to include in the proportionality calculation the whole of its mainland coast up to the latitudinal line of 16°N; and indeed, this line was used by Yemen to define what it called its northern sector of the area in question. The Tribunal however doubts that appropriateness of employing a horizontal line

---

[16]   ICJ Reports 1969, p. 54.
[17]   See ICJ Reports 1981, p. 58, the *Libya/Malta* case.
[18]   18 ILM 60.

of latitude to divide, for the purposed of the proportionality test, waters of the Red Sea which lie at an angle of roughly 45°. The Tribunal has therefore considered the relevant proportion of the Eritrean coast, which can be said to be "opposite" that of Yemen, as ceasing where the general direction of that coast meets a line drawn from what seems to be the northern terminus of the Yemen land frontier at right angles with the general direction of the Yemen coast. In the same say the Tribunal determined the southern end point to be considered for the computation of the length of the Yemen coast.

168.   The Tribunal through its expert in geodesy has calculated the ratio of the lengths of the coasts concerned, measured by reference to their general direction, and the ratio between the water areas it has attributed to the Parties. The first ratio, of coastal lengths, Yemen: Eritrea, is 387,026 metres to 507,110 metres, or 1:1.31. The second ratio of water areas, including the territorial seas, Yemen: Eritrea, is 25,535 kilometres² to 27,944 kilometres², or 1:1.09. The Tribunal believes that the line of delimitation it has decided upon results in no disproportion.

CHAPTER VI

Dispositif

Accordingly, THE TRIBUNAL, taking into account the foregoing considerations and reasons,

UNANIMOUSLY FINDS IN THE PRESENT CASE THAT

The International Maritime Boundary between Eritrea and Yemen is a series of geodetic lines joining, in the order specified, the following points. The points are defined in degrees, minutes and seconds of the geographic latitude and longitude, based on the World Geodetic System 1984 (WGS 84). The line and the numbers of the turning points are shown for purpose of illustration only in Charts 3 and 4 in the map pocket of this Award [not included].

Turning point	Latitude	Longitude
1	15°43′10″N	41°34′06″E
2	15°38′58″N	41°34′05″E
3	15°15′10″N	41°37′31″E
4	15°04′00″N	41°46′43″E
5	15°00′12″N	41°50′42″E
6	14°46′06″N	41°58′47″E
7	14°43′30″N	42°00′42″E
8	14°36′05″N	42°10′02″E
9	14°35′14″N	42°11′35″E
10	14°27′16″N	42°16′54″E
11	14°21′11″N	42°22′04″E
12	14°15′23″N	42°26′09″E
13	14°08′39″N	42°31′33″E
14	14°03′39″N	42°28′39″E
15	13°39′30″N	42°37′39″E
16	13°36′13″N	42°38′30″E
17	13°35′51″N	42°38′14″E
18	13°33′38″N	42°39′37″E

Turning point	Latitude	Longitude
19	13°27′28″N	42°43′25″E
20	13°26′39″N	42°48′21″E
21	13°24′01″N	42°52′47″E
22	13°14′23″N	42°59′47″E
23	13°10′54″N	43°03′03″E
24	13°06′57″N	43°05′21″E
25	13°06′08″N	43°06′06″E
26	13°04′05″N	43°08′42″E
27	13°00′27″N	43°10′54″E
28	12°58′10″N	43°12′45″E
29	12°54′23″N	43°13′58″E

Done at London this 17th day of December 1999

The President of the Tribunal
Professor Sir Robert Y. Jennings

The Registrar
Tjaco van den Hout

Extracts from the first stage of the proceedings of the Arbitral Award appeared in vol. 5 of this *Yearbook* (1998–1999), p. 513.

Part V

Book Reviews

Book Reviews

The Ordinances of Government (Al-Ahkam al-Sultaniyya), translated by Wafaa H. Wahba, Garnet Publishing, first paperback edition, 2000, 312 pp, £15.00

This paperback edition of *The Ordinances of Government* by the famous *qadi* Abu Al-Hasan al-Mawardi, translated into English by W. H. Wahba, is the recent work in the Great Books of Islamic Civilization project established by the Centre for the Muslim Contribution to Civilization in Qatar. Those in the field of Islamic studies will be familiar with the name of Al-Mawardi and this book, which has established itself as a classic reference source in Islamic history. It is perhaps the major literary contribution of a man wishing to remain faithful to the ideals of his faith while at the same time recognizing the changing political realities of the period in which he lived.

As with other works in this series, the book comes with adequate notes about the series itself, the members of the board, the translator's introduction and a useful glossary at the end. The translation, like the original Arabic, has been divided into twenty chapters, with the author's own preface at the beginning explaining that he is fundamentally obeying caliphal authority in writing such a book. His hope is that by doing so the Muslim leader will familiarize himself with the views of various scholars regarding the duties of government and the principles of holding public office. The book's primary aim is therefore to serve as a manual for the leader of the Islamic community.

Thus, in Chapter 1 al-Mawardi established the legitimacy of the Muslim ruler – the imam. Despite writing at a time when Abbasid caliphal authority was in effect largely subdued by the military rule of the Shi'ite military Buyids, al-Mawardi's approach to the imamate is not that of the Shi'ite institution of the imam based on hereditary succession or divine appointment. The argument is stated touching briefly on philosophical rationales, but relying mainly on select Qur'anic verses and Prophetic *hadith* for the justification of such an office and the obligation on the believer to obey the imam. The Qur'anic citation is kept brief and used fundamentally to substantiate al-Mawardi's own viewpoint rather than being a source of debate. For example, al-Mawardi justifies the rule of leadership in the community thus: "O ye who believe! Obey Allah, the messenger and those of you who are in authority" (4:39). He has thus made it obligatory for us to obey those in authority, namely "the sovereigns with power over us" (p. 3). Al-Mawardi's focus is not so much on whether the imam is necessary for the believing community but rather on the election of the imam and the actual duties which accompany his office. There are various stories illustrating this point and references are made frequently to the early caliphal period when the question of electing a leader was a fundamental concern of people like 'Umar. Al-Mawardi's style is to combine the *hadith* anecdotes with his own juristic arguments to draw upon all the diverse areas of the office and its necessary responsibilities and qualifications. Interspersed throughout his fairly concise arguments are extracts of poetry and also well-known maxims and other traditions. It should be pointed out that the translator has also used the words "sovereign" and "supreme ruler" to denote imam and the words imam and caliph are used interchangeably throughout the Arabic and likewise in the English translation.

The Arabic of the *Ahkam* is often quite dense but the translation runs very smoothly for the most part. The sixth chapter on the "Appointment of Judges" (*wilayat al-qada*) is an example that contains several interesting arguments on the prerequisites of holding the office of a judge and in which al-Mawardi displays a competent ability to draw upon the relevant thinking of the other Sunni schools of law. In particular, he compares the Hanafi position with the Shafi'i – the *madhab* to which he belonged himself. In addition, he does not hesitate to reject those opinions which he regards as straying fundamentally from the intended meaning of the Qur'an. For example, the question of whether women can hold the office of *qadi*, al-Mawardi's own view is quiet clearly that this position can only be held by a man. The opposing view of al-Tabari who believes women eligible to hold judgeships under all circumstances is met with the argument "There is no strength in a view that meets with unanimous rejection, in addition to God's own words, 'Men are in charge of women, for God has preferred one of them in bounty over the other' (4:34) that is, in mind and judgment, so that is improper for them to take precedence over men" (p. 72).

In Chapter 19, al-Mawardi examines the legal arguments concerning crimes and punishments. One finds here the usual array of issues frequently arising in the legal texts. He discusses the *hadd* penalties for drinking, fornication, theft, etc., and displays once again an ability to cite various authorities to present the *ikhtilaf,* while at the same time keeping the arguments concise. Al-Mawardi often puts forward his own viewpoint by ending a discussion sharply with a relevant *hadith.* The reference to a single *hadith* with very little background detail is often the basis for his stance on the law. For example, in the case of whether an unbeliever may be punished for fornication, Abu Hanifa says the unbeliever is exempt, but al-Mawardi refutes this by claiming that the Prophet flogged two Jews who admitted fornication (p. 243). These arguments do not contain the fluidity and diversity of opinion of traditional *fiqh* texts of the classical period. They are meant to guide and instruct rather than serve as sources for further exploration and hair-splitting debate between scholars.

Al-Mawardi attempts to show through the course of the whole book all the varying duties that ultimately lie with the caliph or leader, albeit he may appoint ministers, governors, officials and aides to help him with the efficient running of the state. The chapters are divided largely into diverse areas such as prayer leaders, war commanders, alms administrators, tax collectors, those who decide upon the spoils of war, rules of chancery, etc. The aim is to show that a good and able leadership is not a symbolic institution, but the only means whereby a Muslim state can realize the rules and ideals of the sacred law, the *shari'a.* In al-Mawardi's view, therefore, the *shari'a* justifies the caliphate and the caliphate in return must realize the accepted norms of the *shari'a.*

The *Ordinances of Government* is an extremely useful translation of a classic in Islamic scholarship. Wahba has demonstrated considerable care and determination in providing a competent translation of an enjoyable and scholarly book.

Mona Siddiqui

Democracy, the Rule of Law and Islam, edited by Eugene Cotran and Adel Omar Sherif, Kluwer Law International, 1999, 578 pp

In his foreword to this work, Lord Woolf, Master of the Rolls, counsels that this book "deserves to be read by a very wide audience". One hopes that advice from such an eminent authority will be readily heeded if only to stimulate a greater desire to know more, from authentic sources rather than the media, about the concerns of Islam and Muslim jurisprudence for the rule of law and human rights. As noted by one of the contributors, Alexei Vassiliev, writing on "Islam in Russia: Cooperation and Contradictions of Two Civilizations, of Two Legal Systems", "[p]reconceived and distorted ideas about Islam dominate [Russian society, including the media and state institutions] which are not conducive to good interreligious relations, to smooth-ening and find [sic] solutions for interethnic conflicts" (p. 428). Domination of "preconceived and distorted ideas about Islam" is not limited to Russian society, but is rather widespread in Western societies, the media and institutions. The contributions in this book, written by persons eminent in their fields, will help to put those interested on the right path of investigation and may dispel some of those preconceived and distorted ideas.

The present volume is a sequel to an earlier volume of this CIMEL Book Series, *Human Rights and Democracy: The Role of the Supreme Constitutional Court of Egypt*, with emphasis on the attitude of the *shari'a*, in its classical sources, and modern practice of a leading modern Islamic judicial authority, the Egyptian Supreme Constitutional Court, to questions of human rights as set out in modern international instruments.

Professor Abdel Haleem, in his paper on "Human Rights in Islam and the United Nations Instruments", demonstrates that, from its early days, Islam was concerned about and provided for the protection of individual human rights both in the Qur'an (the Muslim Holy Book) and the Sunna (the sayings and practice of the Prophet of Islam). Neither of these two sources was in the form of modern codes, but the provisions are there in clear terms and can easily be reduced to codification. Abdel Haleem refers to a basic point in the consideration of rights: by reason of the historical background of the United Nations instruments on the subject, the emphasis is on individual rights; the rights of society are largely ignored. In Islam, the rights of society are also given prominence. Society has also to be protected. Most of the problems now faced in the exercise of human rights arise from the lack of consideration in these instruments to the rights of society.

In Muslim countries, the pressing question is the enforcement of human rights, rather than the recognition of the *shari'a* of these rights. For example, Islam has recognized rights of women from its earlier days, but, as is shown by a contribution from Mai Yamani ("Muslim Women and Human Rights: The New Generation in Saudi Arabia") women are still struggling in a number of Muslim countries for many of the rights explicitly recognized by the *shari'a*.

Nathan Brown of George Washington University ("Islamic Constitutionalism in Theory and in Practice") rightly points out that Islamic jurisprudence has paid little attention to the question of procedure, concentrating, in the main, on substantive rules, and this tendency seems to prevail even today. This has left enforcement of human rights, and indeed constitutional rights in general, dependent upon the piety of the ruler and judge and the general respect for the *shari'a*. In constitutional matters, some modern Muslim states have tried to remedy the situation. As in many other fields, Egypt has led the way through the creation of the Supreme Constitutional Court. The first President of this Court, Awad Mohammed Al-Morr, surveys some of the recent decisions of this Court on human rights questions in a paper entitled

"Recent Landmark Decisions of the Supreme Constitutional Court of Egypt". Clearly, the Court has shown no reluctance in invalidating measures violative of human rights, and the judgments of the Court are an important contribution to the general jurisprudence on the subject. However, the Court has been rightly reminded that its decisions on human rights are rarely based on the *shari‘a*. It is hoped that this aspect will receive the attention of the Court in order to enrich further Muslim concepts of human rights and put them on the agenda for general consideration.

Apart from the direct issues of Islam and democracy, this volume has provided an opportunity for the contributors to look more closely at definitions and concepts. This is amply illustrated by the penetrating discussion of freedom of religion by three of the contributors in a special section devoted to this question. The complexities of dealing with this question in international humanitarian law deserve particular mention by reason of the rising religious intolerance and extremism in many countries. Kevin Boyle, Wolfgang Bock and Alexei Vassiliev, the three contributors on the subject, have highlighted these complexities and the urgent need to clarify the concepts involved and above all the need for better understanding.

The volume is divided into two main parts. Part 1 is on "The International, Regional and Egyptian Context" and Part II on "Freedom of Religion and Islam". Part I is divided into four main sections: (i) Judicial Independence, Judicial Review and Other Remedies, (ii) Human Rights, Democracy and the Rule of Law, (iii) Judicial Experiments from Egypt and (iv) Democracy and Development. Part II consists of three main sections: (i) Freedom of Religion, (ii) Human Rights and Islam and (iii) Constitutionalism and Islam as a Source of Legislation. Each section is divided into chapters totalling in all twenty-nine chapters with twenty-nine contributors. The editors have provided a good service to the reader through the inclusion of a short note on each of the contributors and by giving a short summary of each contribution as an introduction to the part to follow.

A book review of a volume containing so many contributions by eminent scholars can never do justice to each contribution. It is certainly a work that should be read not only by those interested to know about Islam and human rights, but also by those interested in human rights in general to whom most of Part 1 is particularly addressed while forming a necessary introduction to the main purpose of the work.

Anis Al-Qasem

Gender and Human Rights in Islam and International law: Equal before Allah, Unequal Before Man? by Shaheen Sardar Ali, Kluwer Law International, 2000, 35 pp including bibliography, index and annexes, £69.00

The most immediate impression this book makes is of the ambitious nature of the project attempted by Shaheen Sardar Ali. Divided into three parts, the chapters range from a conceptual analysis of human rights and women's human rights in Islamic law and international law in Part I, continuing in Part II with a detailed examination of women's "equality" rights in Pakistani law and practice, along with a consideration of customary practices in the North West Frontier Province. In Part III the author presents an overview of the development of the international norm of non-discrimination on the basis of sex in international law, and a consideration of reservations made to the Women's Convention[1] by Muslim states, before concluding the study on the theme of the convergence between international and Islamic schemes of women's human rights. The work comes as a welcome addition to the burgeoning literature on women's rights in Islamic law, with a solidly legal and comparative focus on international human rights law and law in society.

The book underlines a number of important themes familiar to the literature on gender, women's rights and Islam, including the inherent diversity and plurality of the Islamic legal tradition, subversion of this by patriarchy and patriarchal custom combined with political expediency, and the need to revive "the more egalitarian aspect of Islam" and the dynamism of the tradition:[2]

By deconstructing the position of women in Islam as enunciated in diverse legal systems of Islamic countries, and rebuilding a core of human rights for women in Islam on the basis of the primary sources of Islamic law, one hopes to retrieve, to a certain extent, the egalitarian spirit of Islam with particular reference to the position of women.[3]

In an interesting development of the focus on the gap between law and practice in regard to women's rights, Professor Ali also draws out the functioning of what she terms an "operative Islamic law", which "is not entirely in keeping with traditional Islamic law principles nor completely irreconcilable with current international human rights instruments".[4] This concept is a valuable articulation of developing forms and functions of "Islamic law" in the world today, and one can see it entering the discourse as a model for comparison. However, just as it is important to distance the reader from any remaining perception of the monolithic nature of "traditional Islamic law principles" (or "traditional Islamic law"), as Ali herself insists, so it is advisable to avoid generalization of the nature of this "operative Islamic law", particularly as between different Muslim (and, indeed, non-Muslim) jurisdictions. For example, Ali makes a valuable point about the non-utilization of the Qanoon-i-Shahadat Order, 1984 in Pakistan ("no court has led evidence in accordance with the new 'Islamic' provision") indicating the "operative" Islamic law principle according equal value to the testimony of men and women; but this cannot be taken as indicative of jurisdictions outside Pakistan or of a more generally accepted "operative Islamic law".[5]

---

1   Convention on the Elimination of All Forms of Discrimination Against Women.
2   At p. 3.
3   At pp. 5–6.
4   At p. 90.
5   At p. 282. Similarly, in her overview of rights in "the Islamic tradition", Ali appears to move between Quranic verses and later rulings of *fiqh*, and in her treatment of judicial *khul'* she appears to present Pakistani case law as standard "Islamic law". See p. 39: "Islamic law also accords the Muslim male a unilateral right to dissolve the marriage tie without assigning any cause and without the

In examining ways forward in the struggle for women's rights, Professor Ali highlights the difficulties in translating the international norm of non-discrimination on the basis of sex, which exists on the books in human rights law, into a universally accepted norm. Her own position comes across as incremental and strategic, with a very interesting focus for example on the Convention on the Rights of the Child as "a common denominator between international human rights affecting women, and women's human rights in the Islamic tradition".[6] Similarly, having examined the categorization of rights as between the international and Islamic traditions, she concludes that:

It might be strategically opportune to seek a rigorous implementation of all the protective/corrective category of rights before embarking upon the "equality" and non-discrimination path. By applying the Islamic paradigm of equality of human dignity and worth, and requiring "those in authority" i.e. men and the state to accept responsibility for fulfilling the material needs of women, children and other disadvantaged sections of society in their charge, and provide them access and control over resources, a move towards substantive as opposed to mere formal equality for all may be possible.[7]

This argument and other parts of the contents of this book will be familiar to readers of this *Yearbook*, having been published in previous volumes as articles,[8] and the book as a whole tends to give the impression of a collection of papers, partly accounted for by the broad range of topics that it seeks to cover. Despite the overall need it displays for a further edit (to remove, for example, repetition of footnotes and text as well as to eliminate inconsistencies between chapters), it certainly works as a book, and Professor Ali is to be congratulated for tackling a wide area of the women's rights debate currently generating intense interest in various parts of the Muslim world.

There are, however, pitfalls in seeking to cover so broad a range of aspects of the debate, and some of them are illustrated in the first part of the book, where gaps in the literature arguably constrain representation of the field. Thus Professor Ali's treatment of the early development of Islamic law appears to depend heavily on English language scholarship of the 1950s and 1960s, and includes the kind of unqualified statement about the closing of the "gate of *ijtihad*"[9] that is rarely seen nowadays following the extensive writings of such scholars as Wael Hallaq.[10] This

---

cont.

interference of the court. On the other hand it confers on a woman the right to seek dissolution of the marriage tie by forgoing her dower, with the difference that the woman has to convince the court of her fixed aversion and irretrievable breakdown of the marriage (khula)" (at p. 39 and see also p. 60 note 64). See Carroll, "Qur'an 2:229: A Charter Granted to the Wife? Judicial Khul' in Pakistan", *Islamic Law and Society*, 1996, 3,1, pp. 91–126. The recent (and widely debated) incorporation of judicial *khul'* in Egyptian legislation (Law No. 1/2000) could on the other hand be invoked as evidence for the current development of this as a wider norm of "operative Islamic law".

6   At p. 278.
7   At p. 88.
8   "Women's Human Rights in Islam: Towards a Theoretical Framework", in vol. 4 of this *Yearbook* (1997–1998), pp. 117–152; and "Is an Adult Muslim Woman *Sui Juris?* Some Reflections on the Concept of 'Consent in Marriage' without a Wali (with Particular Reference to the *Saima Waheed* Case)", in vol. 3 of this *Yearbook* (1996), pp. 156–174. In the reviewed volume, Chapter 2, pp. 42–91 and Chapter 4, pp. 150–172.
9   At p. 23, p. 84 note 160; and p. 247.
10   Notably, of course, "Was the Gate of Ijtihad Closed?" IJMES 16, 1984,

more recent scholarship does not figure in the bibliography, but the final part of Hallaq's *History of Islamic Legal Theories* would arguably have also substantially enriched Ali's consideration in her second chapter of current arguments about the interpretation of Quranic verses on such issues as inheritance portions and polygamy.[11] To this end, Ali includes comparative references to the jurisprudential positions of such scholars as Mahmud Taha, Abdullahi an-Naim, Fazlur Rahman, Fatima Mernissi and Riffat Hassan. However, there is no reference to the contemporary work of the Syrian Muhammad Shahrur, described by Hallaq as "a unique contribution to the reinterpretation of the Quran and Sunna in particular, and to law as a comprehensive system in general" offering "both depth and range, virtually unparalleled in modern writings on the subject".[12] His radical approach to the verses on inheritance portions and on polygamy are summarized by Hallaq, although not it is true within a specific framework of women's rights.[13] Another regrettable gap is the contemporary work of a group of Iranian clerics in Qom, reported and analysed by Ziba Mir-Hosseini as arguing "for gender equality on all fronts and seek[ing] a novel interpretation of the *shari'a* provisions".[14] Although Ali's overview is clearly not intended to be exhaustive, it could have been useful to point readers also to contemporary scholars not writing in nor yet translated into the English language. Unnecessarily confining reference in this regard may run the risk of suggesting to the wider reading public an erroneous conclusion as to the range of those involved in "rethinking" issues of gender and women's rights in Islamic law. This criticism might be made of the book as a whole, in fact, since the select bibliography – in and of itself an extremely useful resource – includes only English-language material.

In Part II, Ali presents a case study of Pakistan, the content and context of which clearly frame the book as a whole. These are a set of three fascinating and compelling chapters that cover a huge amount of ground looking at law and practice in Pakistan affecting women's human rights, and which are complemented in Part III by a detailed review of the process of Pakistan's ratification of the Women's Convention. Part III also includes a very useful summary of the development of the international norm of non-discrimination on the basis of sex, and a consideration of the concept of "complementarity" of gendered rights advanced by some Muslim thinkers (and states) in response to the "equality" or non-discrimination argument. After considering very briefly the views of Mawdudi and Tabandeh on women's human rights, Professor Ali moves on to trace the development of women's rights in a number of documents presented as articulating an "Islamic model of human rights".[15] Part of the discussion here is framed by Ali's responses to the criticisms of Ann Elizabeth

cont.
    pp. 3–41, and the development of this work in his *History of Islamic Legal Theories*, Cambridge, CUP, 1997.
11 In Chapter 2. Similarly, omission of consideration of Fadel's article from the section on the evidentiary value of women's testimony is a pity (Fadel, "Two Women, One Man: Knowledge, Power and Gender in Medieval Sunni Legal Thought", IJMES 29, 1997, pp. 185–204.
12 Hallaq, *History*, p. 246, commenting on Shahrur's *al-Kitab wa'l-Qur'an: Qira'a Mu'asira*, Cairo and Damascus, Sina lil-Nashr, 1992. Hallaq also examines Fazlur Rahman's thinking in the same chapter.
13 *Ibid.*, pp. 249–253.
14 Mir-Hosseini, "Rethinking Gender: Discussions with Ulama in Iran", *Critique*, Fall 1998, pp. 45–59, at p. 50. See in more detail her *Islam and Gender: The Religious Debate in Contemporary Iran*, London, I.B. Tauris, 1999.
15 At p. 222.

Mayer.[16] The examination concentrates on relevant provisions of Universal Islamic Declaration of Human Rights, the Cairo Declaration on Human Rights in Islam, the Tehran Declaration on the Role of Women in the Development of Islamic Society and the Islamabad Declaration on the Role of Muslim Women Parliamentarians in the Promotion of Peace, Progress and Developments of Islamic Societies. All four documents are usefully appended to the text.

In the final chapter (barring the conclusion) Professor Ali moves to the much-covered ground of reservations to the Women's Convention by Muslim states,[17] with a focus on reservations to Articles 2, 9, 15 and 16. Inevitably, the examination suffers somewhat from lack of space to go in any detail into the implications of the nuances in the reservations cited. For example, in the Middle East and North Africa – at least among women's movements – the fact and the content of Algeria's reservations is a matter of great interest, particularly given their timing, entered as they were on Algeria's relatively late accession to the Convention in 1996 (notably, post-Beijing Conference); for her part, Mayer cites them as an example of "a new phenomenon, one that might be labelled as disappearing Islamic reservations".[18] It is also unfortunate that Professor Ali gets the chronology of the Libyan reservations the wrong way round, thereby possibly missing the resonance between these later types of reservations.[19]

Parts of this last section underline the impression that the book really should have gone through a further edit, which would surely have caught mistakes such as the statement that polygamy is "legally and officially abolished" in Algeria.[20] Earlier on in the text, a further edit would have presumably also reworked the phrasing in an extraordinarily unfortunate footnote which, as it currently stands, suggests that the action of Nimeiri's government in hanging Mahmud Taha in 1985 can be taken as some kind of evidence that the ideas he and others of the Republican Brotherhood (including Abdullahi An-Na'im) put forward "are far from acceptable to the large majority of Muslims".[21] It should be immediately noted that the text in no way condones Nimeiri's action, but the statement stands in real need of correction.

---

[16] In Mayer's *Islam and Human Rights: Tradition and Politics*, Boulder, Westview Press, 1995.

[17] Ali indicates some of the literature on this subject in footnotes and in the bibliography (e.g. p. 239 note 6, p. 27 note 72), although it is surprising that she omits the two articles on this subject by Mayer, whose work is criticized in the previous chapter. See Mayer, "Rhetorical Strategies and Official Policies on Women's Rights: The Merits and Drawbacks of the New World Hypocrisy", in Mahnaz Afkhami (ed.) *Faith and Freedom: Women's Human Rights in the Muslim World*, London, I.B.Tauris 1995, and "Islamic Reservations to Human Rights Convention: A Critical Assessment", 15 *Recht van de Islam* 1998, 25–45.

[18] Mayer, *Islam and human* Rights, p. 33.

[19] At pp. 253–254. The original reservation stated that "such accession cannot conflict with the laws on personal status derived from the Islamic *shari'a*," while the later (1995) replacements are more specific and of a different tone, against providing interesting material against which to assess developments in the wording of reservations before and after the Beijing Fourth World Conference on Women. See Mayer's view on this in 1998, p. 31.

[20] At p. 261.

[21] At p. 21 note 44: "Taha and A.A. An-Naim subscribe to this view [i.e. that 'it would be legitimate to base a rule of law upon a repealed verse if doing so advanced the interests of justice.'] Taha was the founder-leader of the Republican Brotherhood in the Sudan, who had little electoral success but under the leadership of Taha emphasized the need for Islamic reform and liberation. That their ideas are far from acceptable to the large majority of Muslims can be

To end, the final paragraph of Professor Ali's conclusion gives some indication of the breadth of the subjects covered in this work, as well as pointing forwards to the work that has yet to be done, insisting on the responsibility of humans in realizing the justice inherent in Islam:

Islam, in common with other world religions, had as its primary mission, access to justice, equity, and equality for all, irrespective of distinctions. The effectiveness to implement these principles, however, has always been limited either by their misuse at the hands of groups who have taken upon themselves to act as the sole interpreters of the religious text in Islam, or by the weaknesses inherent in traditional cultural systems. The true impact of the Islamic teachings on the emancipation of human beings can only be evaluated in the light of the many cultures that modify, refine, diffuse and apply these norms.[22]

Lynn Welchman

---

cont.

ascertained from the fact that Ustad [*sic*] Taha was hanged by the Sudanese government of Jafar Numairy in 1985 as an apostate from Islam." See Abdullahi An-Na'im, "The Islamic law of apostasy and its modern applicability: a case from the Sudan", *Religion* 16, 1986, pp. 197–224.

[22] At p. 285.

The Justice of Islam, by Lawrence Rosen, Oxford University Press, 2000, 234 pp

This book is a welcome addition to the sparse literature on the subject matter of Islamic law. Although the title suggests a developed consideration of the many facets of the notion of justice in Islam, it is not in fact a book that follows a single line or lines of argument from a beginning to a definable conclusion (unlike Khadduri's *The Islamic Conception of Justice* or Gerber's *Islamic Law and Culture*, which does exactly that); rather it is a collection of essays which seek to elucidate the difficulty subject of what justice in Islam entails with specific reference to the practice of Islamic courts in modern day Morocco. The subtitle of the book is "Comparative Perspectives on Islamic Law and Society" and is thus a pertinent indicator of what is described in the text.

The book contains twelve chapters split into three parts. Part 1 deals with "The Socio-Logic of Islamic Legal Reasoning"; Part 2 is entitled "In and Out of Court" and Part 3 "Justice Past and Present". Some of the chapters have been previously published, although the author indicates in the introduction that before inclusion in this work they have been significantly revised. These admitted origins of the book account for its slightly unusual structure and particularly for the lack of an over-arching theoretical framework with which to introduce it and a defining conclusion to end it which could have brought together the various strands of argument that the author deals with.

The author is a distinguished legal anthropologist whose research over the last thirty years has been in the Islamic Courts of Morocco and particularly those of a small town named Sefrou. The fruits of this important and continuing research have been presented in a number of articles and an interesting monograph, entitled *The Anthropology of Justice in Islam* which put forward his now famous but controversial thesis about how to understand the practice of contemporary Islamic law through contextualizing it within its locality and populace. The present work follows this same thesis and develops some aspects of it by considering Islamic law in an historical setting, in contemporary practice and by considering possible future developments.

Professor Rosen's research work was mainly done in the 1960s and early 1970s. He describes in this book in some detail his research in the courts of Sefrou and indicates that in his early work he chose to spend time going through all the case records in one particular year (1965) to give him an overview and insight into the way the courts operated. This was followed up by further research in the town, the latest of which was in the early 1990s when he spent a little time investigating the creation of a new set of small claims courts. As the title of his previous monograph shows, Professor Rosen's approach is mainly anthropological. The language of his research is anthropological and his insights are more those of an anthropologist than a mere lawyer.

The area Professor Rosen deals with is one of burgeoning interest for the scholar of Islamic law. One of the biggest gaps in the Western literature on Islamic law is the area of the practical application of Islamic law by courts in the Islamic world be they Islamic (*shari'a*) courts or secular courts (headed by a *qadi*) applying Islamic or quasi-Islamic legal norms. Some research has been done on the little documented historical material, but much less has been done on contemporary practice. The consideration by Professor Rosen of first hand research in the courts of Morocco is therefore extremely useful and interesting for shedding light on the way these Islamic courts operate. One of the best aspects of the book is the frequent reference to cases either from the court record or from personal experience of the author which are used to support various arguments throughout the book. If anything, however, the book would have benefited from further use of such material some of which is used repetitively.

From his experience of the practice of Islamic law in the courts in Morocco, Professor Rosen puts forward a thesis about the way Islamic law works in practice which was first propounded by him in his earlier work *Anthropology of Justice in Islam*. Basically his thesis is that Islamic law in a *qadi*'s court cannot be understood without looking at the culture and context in which the *qadi* operates, which is unexceptionable as far as it goes. However, in doing that Professor Rosen puts forward the thesis that the *qadi* does not make judgments by applying defined legal rules to ascertained facts; rather he looks at the social positions of the parties to the litigation; considers the consequences of any remedy he may apply and produces a remedy which most suits the social and cultural situation of the parties. Professor Rosen holds that there is a delicate balance of obligations between people within the Islamic community which has to be harmonized by the *qadi*'s judgment. Professor Rosen labels this process "bargaining" by the parties, the negotiating of which is the *qadi*'s main domain.

Professor Rosen further considers the sources of law which the *qadis* in Morocco use in coming to their decisions. He is particularly good at discussing the unique characteristic of the Moroccan *qadis* which has been to use books of precedent known as the *'amal* literature. He also considers the importance of custom as a source and finds that, contrary to traditional notions of Islamic law, the Moroccan *qadi* openly uses local custom as an important source of law and goes so far as to say that the *qadi* considers the application of custom to be an application of Islamic law itself. Finally, although these arguments originate out of research taken in the courts of Morocco, Professor Rosen indicates that in his view the thesis is one which he considers to be true of the rest of the Islamic world. Furthermore in this volume, in a new chapter entitled "Mohammed's sociological jurisprudence", he speculates that this view may have historical roots in the jurisprudence developed by the Prophet Mohammed himself.

The problem with this thesis of Professor Rosen's is that he restricts himself to a consideration of what is really a very small amount of research material. His main material is gleaned from the courts of a small town in Morocco over a period of years but mainly from court records and experience that seems in the main to be over thirty years old. The majority of the cases referred to by Professor Rosen in the book all date back to the 1960s and 1970s except for a small discussion of the experiment on the small claims courts in the 1990s. He admits that the majority of his research was at one stage dealing with looking at the Court record for one particular year. Although he provides statistical evidence for change he does not indicate whether or not he has been able to consider cases in these later periods. In fact, he develops his thesis in the earlier chapters based entirely upon his research in the 1960s and 1970s while indicating in a later chapter that many changes have occurred which have caused a negation of some of the trends that he had outlined in the earlier cases. Thus the material he refers to is of a limited nature within only a small town in a country which cannot by any means be accepted as providing a model for the rest of the Arab world or the Middle East region.

Professor Rosen's central thesis is of the negotiating/bargaining position of the individuals involved and of the attempt by the *qadi* to produce a judicial remedy by considering the position of the litigants within their social and cultural milieu. This method of action by the *qadi* is certainly unknown to me in my experience from other Middle Eastern countries such as Egypt and the Gulf states and I find it difficult to accept that this is the case even in Morocco. The cases which Professor Rosen puts forward in support of this do not seem to be ones which clearly indicate that his thesis is followed by the courts. At pages 17 to 20 he deals with a case from 1961 in which he says this occurred. This is on the basis that the *qadi* in his final decision indicated that he knew that the plaintiff wife had lived as a good woman. There is no indication as to how the *qadi* knew this and Professor Rosen merely states that the *qadi* consulted "notables". Furthermore, there is no indication in the judgment that the *qadi* in fact used this consultation as the basis for his decision. Although Professor Rosen says that the *qadi* "violated the strict letter of the law" in giving the wife a divorce which was irrevocable, he does not indicate why this should be the case, particularly as Article 66 of the Moroccan Law of Personal Status says that all judicial divorces are irrevocable except in the cases of *'ila* and failure to maintain. Moreover, it is perfectly possible for the *qadi* to have used Article 57 on absence or Article 56 on harm (*darar*) although he did not specifically indicate that this was what he was doing. This case in my view therefore does not support the overall thesis and nor do any of the other case references that are put forward. In fact, statements of the thesis occur throughout the work with very little supporting material to the extent that they are eventually put forward as self-evident truths. This is an over-generalization at best.

Professor Rosen also underestimates in my view the difference between the way a *qadi* operated in historical terms (that is to say up to the end of the Ottoman Empire) and the way a *qadi* in modern day Arab society (and particularly a country like Morocco where the *qadi* is integrated into a modern judicial system) operates who is called upon more often than not to apply a codified or partially codified system of Islamic law rules. This has had the inevitable result that *qadis* in the modern day have assimilated much of their procedure, and the way in which they consider their judicial role, to the role of the judge in a secular court. Of course in a large number of substantive areas of law the *qadi* will still tackle issues of law from an Islamic perspective. This is particularly true of areas of family law and liability including the payment of blood money; but it cannot be said without more that the roles of the *qadi* historically and those of present day *qadis* are easily comparable.

It is this reviewer's view that a *qadi* outside Morocco does not behave in the way that Professor Rosen suggests a *qadi* behaves in Morocco. And even in Morocco it is difficult to see how a *qadi* hearing twenty cases in two hours can spend much time considering the cultural and social position of the parties.

The position of the *qadi* – even in a secularised role – is, however, very different from that of an ordinary judge. A *qadi* traditionally has an obligation to encourage the litigants to settle the differences between themselves (by mutual agreement or *sulh*) rather than make a judgment or decision on the facts. This is still very much the way *qadis* act today in most Arab countries. This is why there are frequent adjournments to give the parties the opportunity to discuss their differences. A *qadi* does this in different ways. A *qadi* may indicate which of two parties he thinks has a stronger argument and suggest that they go away and think about what he has said. A *qadi* may involve himself directly in the affairs of the litigant but this again is only to obtain a better understanding of the facts in order to suggest to the parties what would be the best way forward for them. For example, a very common case in family law in a state where polygamy is permitted is whether or not a wife is properly housed (i.e whether she is given a *shari'* lodging). A *qadi* will frequently insist on visiting such lodging to see for himself what is offered. This may have the effect of shaming the husband into producing something better or it will be the basis for the *qadi* giving an indication as to which party he considers to be in the wrong. He may indicate his feelings about the property without having to come to a judgment. In my view this is not the same as considering the persons and the cultural context of the persons or their bargaining position to be more important than the facts. It is merely an aspect of the particular and unusual role of the *qadi* as a mediator as well as someone who can make binding decisions upon found facts. This aspect of a *qadi*'s role is not referred to by Professor Rosen at all.

It may be that the *qadi* in Morocco because of the unusual nature of the *'amal* literature and the role of custom sees himself as having a more particular role to play balancing obligations and harmonising relationships within a community. But in my view this is a localized phenomenon which cannot be extrapolated to the rest of the Arab world.

Professor Rosen's book will attract much interest. Unfortunately the generality of the title belies the specialist nature of the material in the text. One non-Muslim, non-specialist reviewer has already praised the book as being "extensively researched, closely argued and highly informative". He says it serves the purpose of explaining how Islamic law is adjudicated on a daily basis and is "an eye opener to the intricacies of Islamic law in action." He concludes that the book "will serve as a necessary tool to understanding one fifth of humanity". Unfortunately this sort of gushing uncritical praise (which is partly based upon a broadly based introduction of Professor Rosen) indicates the dangers inherent in a specialist work of this sort attempting to portray the complex, varied and multifaceted subject of Islamic law in too simplistic a way.

Ian Edge

Essays and Addresses on Arab Laws, by W.M. Ballantyne, Curzon Press, 2000, 278 pp, £50.00

No reviewer of *Essays and Addresses on Arab Laws* can do justice to this momentous book unless the author's background is also outlined, for the book contents span over fifteen years out of a fascinating half century of professional life. I have had the good fortune to know William (Bill) Ballantyne for many years, to have worked with him on court and arbitration cases and to have had the privilege of his friendship.

Had he followed a conventional career at the Bar in the UK he would have most probably ended up with domestic honours and the usual collection of court anecdotes that every lawyer is prone to gather during a professional life.

Instead, after five years as an RAF pilot during World War II, he studied law at Cambridge, worked as a solicitor of the Supreme Court for a mere two years, and then opened law offices in Bahrain, Kuwait and the Emirates. That was before the oil boom transformed a sedate way of life into a hectic consumer society; he had also witnessed the transition.

When in 1986 he closed his remaining Bahrain office, his experience and knowledge of Arab law did not stop there. In 1977 and he had established chambers in London specializing in the commercial laws of the Arab Middle East and he then started teaching the subject at SOAS as well as writing books and articles. In keeping contact with the practical world, he was, and still is, much in demand for delivering expert opinions and for sitting as an arbitrator.

As its title indicates, the book is a collection of *Essays and Addresses* written and delivered by Professor Ballantyne throughout one and a half decades. The occasional repetitions, inevitable and acknowledged by the author, do actually serve to drive home a message intended for both East and West, and which I believe to be of great significance not only for the author but also for all broad-minded people.

The author is well qualified to be the messenger – here justification for outlining his career becomes obvious – and the message would have been in danger of being rejected outright had it been carried by someone else.

If I am not mistaken the message which emanates from the whole work is otherwise explicitly defined in the following passage:

[T]he West must stop dismissing the Shari'a as something unknown, to be feared, and thus resisted; while the Arabs must stop regarding the Shari'a as a holy subject, with any incursion by the West resented. In that way only could a way perhaps be found of reconciling two systems which appear, at first assessment, to be wholly irreconcilable. (p. 189)

Professor Ballantyne is far from preaching the abandonment of, or the tampering with the *shari'a*'s immutable provisions derived from the Qur'an and the Sunna. The distinction he made – and I fully concur with it – is between these immutable provisions and the provisions which stem from the *fiqh* and which have acquired a reverential status which may have no foundation "unless the door of ijithad is reckoned to be closed – the majority opinion would appear to be that it is *not*, that it is open" (p. 206).

What is implied is that the charge against the *shari'a* of being an irremovable object would become largely irrelevant if and when the provisions derived from *fiqh* come under the fresh scrutiny of present-day scholars.

I cannot resist quoting another passage from the book which leaves no doubt that Professor Ballantyne is fully aware of the difficult task of putting in effect the implications of his message; hence when he risked – as he modestly said – indulging in some generalizations concerning the differences between the *shari'a* and the occidental systems, he wrote, "I dare to say this: occidental laws assume a fair degree of immorality and try to counteract it, the Shari'a, *par excellence*, having its roots in religion, assumes a fair degree of religious rectitude, and legislates accordingly."

Besides a message, the work contains a warning as well, mainly for the benefit of the West, about the danger of ignoring the role of the *shari'a* in the law of contract, particularly at a time when reassertion of the *shari'a* is on the increase. The warning could have been deemed offensive by those it is directed against, but not when Professor Ballantyne makes it. His warning stems from a real empathy with the Arab world and is expounded with such elegance and subtlety that many Muslims would be able to accept it as their own. That is a real *tour de force* which was achieved for the simple reason that the author is known for his intellectual probity and not as someone engaged in scoring points against a foreign system of law rooted in a religion not his own.

Eighteen papers are published under the title of the book: *Essays and Addresses on Arab Laws*. All are not of the same importance but all are of interest; a number I consider to be outstanding.

"A short introduction to the Shari'a" (paper III) may be short but is none the less illuminating as a sweeping overview of what the *shari'a* means within its historical context.

Paper IX is a review of the new Civil Code of the United Arab Emirates. It contains an original and contributory study of the principle of the abuse of rights as stipulated in the new Code and as in the *fiqh* (Article 106). The author had perceived the close relationship between abuse of right and the principle of good faith in contracting (Article 246 of the new Code) which, as he emphasized, is a fundamental principle of the continental system, the *shari'a* and common law which calls it estoppel.

Professor Ballantyne is one of the very few lawyers who have been exposed to three legal systems: common law, Arab law and continental law. This, added to his lucid observation and objective judgment, gives enormous value to his writings.

"Back to the Shari'a" (paper XI) makes enthralling and lively reading about a subject which is not easily accessible. It complements paper III. Here again I cannot resist quoting from the paper the following: "Moral and religious values swept under the rug of material prosperity are apt to surface in a welter of guilt." Is there a better description of the quick adoption by the Gulf states of Western concepts of law which seemed justified by the bonanza of the early oil years and which, once the windfall has ended, is called into question?

"Secular Law and the Shari'a: *Pacta Sunt Servanda* and the *Theory of Imprévision*" is the title of paper XV which contains a comparative study of *imprévision* in the Arab codes, the *shari'a* and in the rulings of French, common law and German courts.

Anyone who is intent on acquiring a fair-minded view of the commercial laws of the Gulf Arab states, on learning how pitfalls and costly mistakes could be avoided when dealing with those states, or simply on reading about an outstanding professional experience written in a beautiful and simple language, should go over *Essays and Addresses on Arab Laws*.

Nabil Saleh

As Professor Ballantyne remarks in his acknowledgment, he has been in professional practice for over fifty years; what he does not mention is that for much of that period he has been one of the foremost authorities on commercial law in the Arab Gulf states. During the latter part of that period he has written much. However, these pieces are widely dispersed, and they are gathered here together for the first time. This collation serves two additional purposes: the first is to be, if not a revision of his well-known and much used *Commercial Law in the Arab Middle East: The Gulf States*, a follow on or alternative to that volume; the second is to serve as a textbook for the Arab Comparative Commercial Law course at SOAS.

Professor Ballantyne's subject is, as one would expect, the commercial law of the Arab Gulf States. Within this framework, the collection of eighteen "essays and addresses" in this book reflects the breadth and depth of Professor's Ballantyne's experience and expertise, with a range of subjects, going from the quite general (and constantly recurring) theme of the role of the *shari'a* in commercial law throughout the region and its growing, if variable, importance, passing through still quite general, if more jurisdiction-specific topics such as the Civil Code of the UAE and the Commercial Code of Bahrain, to more technical matters, such as the efficacy of international arbitration, agency, syndicated loans and construction contracts in the countries of the region (although even here, the *shari'a* is never far away). There are several "sports" which fit into neither category, such as the discussion of the Arab Monetary Fund case and the English conflict of law rules relating to (Arab) international corporations, and the chapter on the background to Islamic banking.

On the more general theme of the *shari'a*, the author gives lucid expositions not only of its rules and the way in which it is technically significant as a result of the constitutional law of the states under study, but more importantly a "feel" for the way in which it developed, its character, the reasons for its influence in those states (he stresses here the role of Islam and of the Arabic language) and the reasons why, in the author's opinion, it is incompatible with modern, Western-inspired commerce. Speaking from this reviewer's experience of the difficulties encountered by students unfamiliar with the region and its particularities, and the difficulties encountered by their teachers in communicating the nature of the laws of the region to such students, this aspect of the work is very useful indeed.

The more specific pieces show another side to Professor Ballantyne's expertise. They are models of detailed legal analysis, and set the standard for work of this nature. Those articles which deal with the comparative law of contract are of particular interest, given the relative paucity of writing in this area. For example, the piece entitled simply "The Shari'a" (Chapter VI), comparing the different attitudes of civilian, common law and *shari'a* towards changing circumstances in contract, is, as one would expect, of great use for anyone dealing with contracts in the Arab world, but is also a very valuable general comparative article.

This said, one cannot ignore the problems which arise from the very nature of the book. The most serious is the age of many of the pieces. The most recent dated piece is the short concluding chapter, a speech given in 1995; the oldest goes back to 1981. True, the already published chapters are interspersed with hitherto unpublished, and more up to date, lectures given on the SOAS LLM course, but this does not make up for the fact that a fairly large proportion of the content to the book is quite severely out of date. One of the most striking examples is that regarding the UAE Commercial Code: in Chapter XIII ("A Reassertion of the Shari'a: The Jurisprudence of the Gulf States") it is stated that there is "as yet, no commercial code in the UAE. (p. 216). This is very misleading for anyone not familiar with the region, despite the fact that there is a very learned discussion of the relationship of the Civil Code and the Commercial Code in Chapter IX ("The New Civil Code of the UAE:

a Further Reassertion of the Shari'a"). None of the pieces has been brought up to date, or even cross-referenced in any way to avoid the confusion which will inevitably arise in the minds of some readers. The lack of an index (which the author categorizes as a "nuisance" in a work of this sort), exacerbates the problem.

The disparate and unedited nature of the papers causes other difficulties. One such is the fairly large amount of repetition. It is true, as Professor Ballantyne states, that repetition has much value as a teaching tool, but it can be overdone, and there is a definite risk of tedium for the student who reads the book from beginning to end (it should in fairness be said, however, that such readers will be rare). Another difficulty is the lack of detail in some areas, a result of the circumstances for which many of the chapters were prepared – conferences where the time available to the author was limited. The chapter on construction contracts is a good example. It is a very useful and interesting introduction to the subject, but the references to the detail of construction contracts are few, as the author had tailored the contents to his audience, which consisted of lawyers with very little knowledge of the *shari'a*.

Typographically the book is of a high standard, with rare exceptions, one of which (the "cannon" law of Islam (p. 259)) is mentioned here only for its amusement value.

This book, then, is not perfect. It needs to be read with care, particularly by the neophyte. However, given the other calls upon Professor Ballantyne's time, we can be grateful that we have something (with many outstanding virtues), rather than nothing.

N.H.D. Foster

Arbitral Awards of the Cairo Regional Centre for International Commercial Arbitration, compiled, translated and annotated by Mohie Eldin I. Alam Eldin, Kluwer Law International, 2000, 258 pp, £71.00

The publication of a collection of court judgments or arbitral awards is always welcomed by lawyers practising in the related jurisdiction, eager as they are to acquire a better knowledge of how the law responds to real situations. The book under review has more than one reason to be well received by lawyers interested in the Arab Middle East for it presents two additional advantages: the author and others who lent him their assistance undertook the painstaking task of translating into the English language large parts of awards written in Arabic, and furthermore the work allows the reader to follow the development of the Cairo Regional Centre for International Commercial Arbitration (CRCICA) from the first award given under its aegis, in 1984, up to a recent one given in 1996.

The overall impression one gets after going through the book is that Egypt's new Arbitration Act of 1994 and new Commercial Code of 1999 have removed serious legal impediments which had in the past made the foreign party unenthusiastic about referring disputes to the CRCICA.

According to the new Arbitration Act parties to a dispute may choose any foreign law to settle that dispute, as well as the method of selecting arbitrators, the place and the language of the arbitration. Arbitrators may be given the power to order conservative or interim measures without precluding the court's right to order the same.

Although the new Arbitration Act is silent on the matter of interest, the 1948 Civil Code provided for an interest of 4 per cent in civil matters and 5 per cent in commercial matters, which would be deemed extremely low compared to actual bank rates. The new Commercial Code of 1999 has remedied the situation for it provides for higher rates of interest equivalent to, or less than, the rates declared periodically by the Central Bank of Egypt.

This is an undeniable effort from the Egyptian legislators to pave the way for Cairo becoming a widely acceptable place for the settlement of disputes through arbitration.

With these changes in Egypt's laws there is a good prospect of the CRCICA becoming a very attractive centre for overseeing arbitrations either between Arab parties or between Arab and non-Arab ones. That could well be the case provided arbitrators are selected for their integrity and knowledge and not because they are part of an inner circle of cronies or for whatever other reason. The danger is real, even though the parties to a dispute referred to arbitration under the CRCICA Rules may agree on an appointing authority other than the Centre, nevertheless there are times when the appointment has to be made by that Centre.

Assuming that the selection of arbitrators is dealt with in a proper manner, it would be only justice that Egypt took a vanguard position in the field of arbitration, for other Arab countries owe much to its legislators and lawyers. One has only to recall the role played by the great Abdul Razzak Sanhouri in shaping the laws of most Arab countries after independence to acknowledge a debt of gratitude to his country of birth.

Arbitral Awards of the Cairo Regional Centre for International Commercial Arbitration reviews 32 arbitration cases out of over 130 to the credit of the CRCICA. One has to assume that the cases which were selected are the most interesting.

A preface by Dr M.I.M. Aboul-Enein, director of CRCICA, is followed by a summary of the cases listed under nine categories. Come next useful annexes, namely the CRCICA Rules, the Egyptian Arbitration Act 27/94 and articles of Egypt's Civil Code regarding contracts.

The nine categories are (1) supply and services cases, (2) work and material contracts, (3) construction contracts, (4) maritime contracts, (5) rates of exchange, (6) joint ventures, (7) interpretation of contracts, (8) management contracts, and (9) commercial agency contracts.

The author has followed the same pattern for each case: first a summary of the decision, then the facts, the award and a commentary.

The commentaries are most interesting but with one possible drawback. The commentator has often stated what is the rule of the Islamic *shari'a* relevant to the case and compared it to the rule which was relied on in the published award. The two rules may not lead to the same conclusion and hence create confusion, for the commentary may convey the wrong message that the *shari'a* plays a major role in the Egyptian law of contract, which it does not. This wrong impression might frighten an unaware foreign party by making him believe that a religious law will censor a secular act, which is not the case as evidenced by several awards. Hence an award on damages include lost profit and loss suffered (case no. 2) which is not strict *shari'a* and another awards interest (case no. 28), which is not allowed by the strict interpretation of the religious law, etc.

It is a fact that Egypt's law of contract prior to the 1948 Civil Code had been deeply French inspired for about a century, and that the chief architect of the 1948 Civil Code, Abdul Razzak Sanhouri, was himself a law student of Paris universities. Hence he was most comfortable in his attempted blending operation between principles of the *shari'a* and those French inspired, when it came to the requirement of good faith in the performance of contracts (Article 148 of Egypt's Civil Code).

Indeed, this principle, which is condoned by the *shari'a*, is also to be found in French law and in most continental systems of law but not in common law. A common law lawyer would not depart from the four corners of a contract and would not investigate what was in the mind of the contracting parties, whether to construe a contract or to assess how it was implemented.

Therefore it came as no surprise that a number of the cases published in the book under review touch on the concept of good faith in the performance of contract (case nos. 4, 7, 16).

The author of the work under review is to be thanked for the difficult but useful task he has undertaken and discharged very honourably. His reward will be to be counted among the authors who succeed in conveying to the reader how the law works in practice. That category of author is much needed and much in demand in the Arab world which has long suffered (less in the case of Egypt, Lebanon and a few other Arab countries) from the difficulty of finding out what the applicable law is. That vexed question is no more and the time has come for law writers to tell us not only what is the law but also how the judiciary applies and interprets it.

Nabil Saleh

The Middle East in the New Millennium: Economic Development and Business Law,
by Gil Feiler, Kluwer Law International, 2000, 461 pp

This book is said to be an "in depth portrait of investment opportunity in the Middle
East as it stands today". It deals with sixteen countries in the Middle East. Each
chapter conforms to the same structure which is to briefly look at recent political
developments; consider in some detail the recent economic developments in the
country; to consider the business environment and finally to provide a legal review
of the business laws. The material is based upon databases of Middle East information
provided by the author's research consultancy which is available on the Internet. The
political developments are said to be updated to December 1999 and the economic
developments up to February 2000.

The material in this book is of a particularly general nature. Most of each chapter
is spent considering economic development and the business environment. This
material is probably available in other formats such as the *Middle East Economic
Digest* and the Middle East Executive Reports. In this sense it does not add much
to present information and necessarily is out of date as soon as it is printed and in
this case is already almost a year out of date. The legal review in each chapter is
necessarily cursory. In some cases it is wrong, particularly in areas relating to the
court system and the way the law operates in certain countries. It is better on the
provisions of business laws and tax laws but again is insufficiently detailed to give
anything more than a cursory understanding of what is often a complicated area of law.

The "Note to the Reader" at the front of the book indicates that it is intended
to provide an "overview" of the region but "does not purport to be a comprehensive
review or treatment of the subjects contained in it ... and should not be relied upon
when making specific business decisions." This caveat is most importantly provided
in this reviewer's opinion. It is difficult to see exactly whom the book is aimed at:
for the lawyer it is extremely cursory in its dealings with the legal aspects; for the
businessman its information is out of date and better provided in the various commercial journals that deal with the Middle East on a weekly or a monthly basis.

Ian Edge

The Palestine Exodus 1948–1998, edited by Ghada Karmi and Eugene Cotran, Ithaca Press, 1999, London

In his introduction, Ian Gilmour depicts the Zionist scheme in Palestine as being a unique attempt at colonization based on the "conversion" of Arab land into Jewish land, or its "transfer", and the substitution of a Jewish population in place of the indigenous Arab inhabitants. In Moshe Dayan's words "we came here to this country which was settled by Arabs, and we are building a Jewish state". Since Palestine was not a deserted country, the Zionists had to force the Arabs to desert their lands. The "transfer" of the Arab population was therefore the very essence of the Zionist scheme, which began with the expulsions of 1948–1949 and continued thereafter in the 1950s and once again in the aftermath of the 1967 occupation of the remainder of mandate Palestine – expulsions which continue to this day. Effectively, as Karmi points out, this is equivalent to "ethnic cleansing", employing different guises and implemented through a variety of means. Sometimes expulsions are implemented through brute force; at other times they are implemented through sophisticated and administrative measures, as in the present policy of gradual evacuation of the Arab population from the city of Jerusalem.

The book is a collection of papers presented at a conference organized jointly in May 1997 by the International Campaign for Jerusalem (ICJ) and the Centre of Islamic and Middle Eastern Law at the School of Oriental and African Studies (SOAS), University of London. The papers deal with various aspects of the unceasing exodus of Palestinian refugees from their land. Nur Masalah examines the causes of the 1967 exodus in the light of new historical evidence. Both John Quigley and Anis Al-Qasem deal with legal aspects of the right of Palestinian refugees to return to their homes. Salman Abu Sitta returns to his familiar ground of refuting the Israeli argument on the "impossibility" of the return of Palestinian refugees. He argues that 80 per cent of Israeli Jews actually occupy less than 15 per cent of Israeli 1948 borders, mainly in the coastal areas around Tel-Aviv.

Both Rashid Al-Khalidi and Ghada Karmi present ideas on future settlements for the refugee issue. Khalidi in his search for truth, justice and reconciliation, outlines four elements for the solution of the refugee problem. They are a formal recognition of Israel's primary responsibility for the creation of the Palestinian refugee problem; that Palestinian refugees and their descendants must have the right to return to their homes *in principle*; the provision of compensation or reparations for all those who choose not to return, or are not allowed to do so under the final negotiated settlement; the right to live in the newly independent Palestinian state and to become its citizens; and a special arrangement to be negotiated between a Palestinian state and host countries for those refugees who live in these countries.

Karmi discussed the question of compensation, making an analogy with the compensation of Jewsih victims of Nazism. She criticizes the double standards of Western countries, which become evident when the case of Balkan refugees and the international pressure exerted for them to return is compared to the case of Palestinian refugees who have been left in limbo for the past sixty years.

The papers offer, as Judge Cotran points out, an insight into the issues involved in the Palestinian refugee problem and delineate the necessary ingredients for a solution to the Israeli-Palestinian conflict and for a just and lasting peace.

Abbas Shiblak

The Status of Palestinian Refugees in International Law, by Lex Takkenberg, Clarendon Press, Oxford, 1998, 411 pp

Whether one agrees or not with the analysis or views expressed in this work, there is no doubt in my mind that all those concerned about peace and respect for human rights will be grateful to the author for providing for the first time a comprehensive study of this question. Dr Takkenberg is especially qualified for the task: in addition to being a distinguished lawyer, he has direct knowledge and personal experience of the question. In 1983 he worked for a while as a legal officer with the Dutch Refugee Council. Thereafter, he joined UNRWA (the United Nations Relief and Works Agency for Palestine Refugees in the Near East). For some time he was troubled by the question as to why Palestinian refugees "constituted the only category [of refugees] kept outside the general international refugee regime and what consequences this had for their position". This book, first submitted as a doctoral thesis, is the answer to the question.

The book is divided into ten chapters. The first is an introduction comprising a historical background, the number of refugees and their geographic distribution, the United Nations and the Palestinian refugees, the "Madrid" process and its relevance, and scope of the study. The second chapter is entitled "Palestinian refugees" and has four subdivisions: general remarks on the notion of "Palestinian refugee", Palestinian refugees as distinguished from other refugees, the UNRWA definition of a Palestinian refugee, and defining Palestinian refugees in the context of Peace Negotiations. The third chapter is on the 1951 Convention relating to the status of refugees comprising a detailed analysis of Article 1D in particular and Article 1 in general. The fourth chapter is on the status of Palestinian refugees in the Arab world.

With Chapter V, the author begins the second part of the book on other areas of international law. Chapter V is on the law relating to stateless persons and raises the question as to whether Palestinian refugees can be treated as stateless persons. Chapter VI deals with humanitarian law and considers the following aspects: rules of humanitarian law concerning the protection of civilians and their relevance for Palestinian refugees, the position of Palestinian refugees in the territories occupied by Israel, and the relevance of the PLO–Israeli Declaration of Principles. Chapter VII is the last chapter in Part Two and deals with human rights law: the right of return and compensation, the right to self-determination and family reunification and the principle of unity of family.

In Part Three, the author deals with international protection and the search for a durable solution. Chapter VIII, the first chapter of this part, deals with international protection: the role of UNRWA in protection of refugees in the Near East, protection of the refugees outside UNRWA's area of operations – the role of the UNHCR, ICRC and the protection of Palestinian refugees, and other attempts at providing international protection. Chapter IX deals with the search for durable solution. In this chapter the author considers durable solutions to refugee problems in general – voluntary repatriation, local integration, and resettlement in third countries. Within this context he looks at relevant principles of international law, and raises the question of a durable solution to the Palestinian refugee problem. In the same chapter, he considers possible scenarios for the permanent status of the Palestinian territories occupied in 1967: autonomy without full sovereignty, establishment of a Palestinian state, and Jordanian–Palestinian federation or confederation. Finally he deals with the permanent status negotiations on the refugee issue. The final chapter X is a summary and conclusions.

Three annexes are included: selected United Nations resolutions of concern to Palestinian refugees, UNRWA instructions concerning registration and eligibility (excerpts), and League of Arab States instruments on Palestinian refugees. The book concludes with a bibliography and an index.

From this presentation of the topics considered by the author, it should be clear that some parts, such as the proposed durable solution, might not receive total acceptance. However, even in this most controversial issue, the objectivity of the author on a sensitive subject is to be admired. One is inclined to agree with the author that no ultimate solution could be seriously attempted before final solution of the underlying conflict over Palestine. In his opinion, the resolution of this basic conflict "can only be seriously approached once the parties have mutually accepted the present reality, i.e. that the former Mandate Palestine is the home of two nations, two faiths, two tongues and two historic experiences" (p. 377). The author further thinks that "only if the *intentions* of the refugees are seriously taken into consideration, will the solution be ultimately satisfactory, thereby contributing to a first and lasting peace in the Middle East" (p. 327).

The author has done a great service by drawing attention to a matter, which seems to have been neglected by the international community: protection of the Palestinian refugees. The arrangements which removed the Palestinian refugees temporarily from the jurisdiction of the United Nations High Commissioner for Refugees, left the Palestinian refugees without protection. They were massacred and relentlessly bombed in their camps and the culprits have not been tried or punished. Had these refugees been under the protection of the UNHCR at least a voice would have been raised asking for accountability. This situation has not changed, and Palestinian refugees remain vulnerable. It is hoped that the author's call will be heeded.

In conclusion, this is a timely work worth serious study by all those interested in refugee problems in general and in particular by those concerned about solving the problem of Palestinian refugees.

Anis Al-Qasem

Islamic Law of Inheritance, by Hamid Khan, Pakistan Law House, Platinium Publishing Limited, second edition, 1999

There is a saying among Muslims that to know the law of inheritance is to be possessed of half the knowledge of the world. The law of succession on death is, without doubt, the greatest achievement of the *shari'a*. It is a highly complex structure which follows its own inexorable logic. It is also the area of the law in which there is the greatest diversity between the different schools and sects of Islam.

N.J. Coulson's *Succession in the Muslim Family* was the first text to make a comparative study of the Islamic law of inheritance, both traditional and contemporary. When this book went out of print, there was a sad lacuna in the material available for the study of this important area of Islamic law, which is still applied with only very few changes to Muslims living within the jurisdiction of the Muslim world. Thus, the second edition of Hamid Khan's *Islamic Law of Inheritance* is to be greatly welcomed, for his book, unlike other texts emanating from the Indian subcontinent, adopts Coulson's comparative approach and examines the law of all four schools of Sunni Islam and of the Ithna Ashari sect of the Shi'a, as well as changes which have been effected in both the law of the Middle East and of the Indian subcontinent.

The first thirty pages of the book are devoted to setting the scene by explaining the nature of Islamic law, its sources and its diversity, and will be of help, particularly, to readers who have no prior knowledge of Islamic law. The remaining chapters of the book deal with the substantive law of both testate and intestate succession on death in a clear and concise fashion.

Understanding the Islamic law of inheritance will never be an easy task, but this book will be an excellent guide for anyone seeking to explore its complexities and to acquire some knowledge of this difficult subject. Of particular use in such a quest is the table of sharers, which sets out the shares of the twelve Quranic and quasi-Quranic sharers recognized by Sunni Islam, the conditions in which the shares will be inherited and when special circumstances will affect them.

A criticism of the book is that perhaps too much space, in what is a comparatively small volume, is devoted to the distant kindred, that is, the heirs recognized by Sunni law who are neither Quranic sharers nor residuaries. Obviously, in a text which aims to be of both a practical and academic nature, no aspects of the law can be ignored. Indeed, the law relating to distant kindred is, perhaps, one of the most intellectually challenging areas of Islamic law as a whole. It is, however, from a practical point of view, of little significance as the chance of any member of this class's heirs inheriting is extremely remote.

The book contains a few typographical errors, which will no doubt be expunged in its next edition. A particularly glaring example occurs on page 66, where it is stated that the father will receive his one-sixth Quranic share unless there is a surviving son of the deceased present. Obviously the opposite is intended, but these are minor criticisms of a text which will prove to be of great interest to anyone having a practical or academic interest in the Islamic law of succession on death.

Doreen Hinchcliffe

Index

NOTE: Page numbers followed by n indicate relevant information is to be found in a footnote.

527